A COURSE IN URDU

This edition has been made possible
by generous assistance from the
Pakistan-American Foundation and
the Institute of Islamic Studies
at McGill University

A COURSE IN
URDU

ابتدائی اُردُو

MUHAMMAD ABD-AL-RAHMAN BARKER

and

HASAN JAHANGIR HAMDANI

KHWAJA MUHAMMAD SHAFI DIHLAVI

SHAFIQUR RAHMAN

VOLUME ONE

Spoken Language Services, Inc.

Library of Congress Cataloging in Publication Data

Main entry under title:

A Course in Urdu =   ابتدائی اردو

   (Spoken language series)
   Reprint of the 1967 ed. published by the Institute of Islamic Studies, McGill University, Montreal.
   1. Urdu language--Conversation and phrase books.
I. Barker, Muhammad Abd-al-Rahman.
PK1975.C64 1975   491.4'39'82421   75-15183
ISBN 0-87590-340-8

Spoken Language Services, Inc.
P. O. Box 783
Ithaca, New York 14851

To Ambereen

یہ اُردو زباں کامل و پُر اثر

زبانوں کی سُورج، ادب کی قمر

فصاحت میں پایہ ہے اِس کا بلند

سراپا بلاغت، دَہن پُر گُہر

قلمروئے اقلیمِ مشرق کے بعد

بڑھی سُوئے مغرب بفتح و ظفر

کنیڈا میں اُردو کا پہلا نصاب

مرتب ہُوا ہے بعد کرّہ و فر

ہوئی فکرِ تاریخ کی جب مجھے

صدا دی یہ ہاتف نے مت فکر کر

جہانگیر تاریخ کردے رقم

مرقّعِ ادب دلبر و خوب تر

─────────

۱۹۶۷ء

The Badshahi Mosque, Lahore. Built by the Mughal Emperor Aurangzeb in 1674, it is one of the largest mosques in the world.

PREFACE

Work on this course was begun in 1960 at the Language Unit, Oriental College, the University of the Panjab, Lahore, West Pakistan, under the auspices of a project sponsored jointly by the British Council, the Ford Foundation, and the University of the Panjab. During 1960-62, basic research was carried out, and Units I through V and VII were written by Dr. Barker and Mr. K. M. Shafi. The Language Unit was terminated in 1962, and Dr. Barker continued the work at the Institute of Islamic Studies, McGill University, Montreal, Quebec, Canada. Mr. Shafi was brought to Canada in 1962 but had to return to Pakistan after only one year. New support was obtained for the project from the United States Office of Education, Department of Health, Education, and Welfare, in 1963, and Prof. Iqtida Hasan and Mr. H. J. Hamdani joined the staff of the project in that year. Mr. Hamdani had already worked on another portion of the Urdu project with Dr. Barker in Lahore. Prof. Hasan had to return to his permanent post at the University of Naples in 1964, and Mr. Shafiqur Rahman joined the project in that year. The work of the latter part of the project, thus, was done mainly in collaboration with Messrs. Hamdani and Rahman. Mr. Shafi also continued to serve as research consultant in Lahore and supervised the writing of the Urdu script portions of the course.

Mrs. Ambereen Barker served from the inception of the project as secretary-typist, proofreader, and administrative assistant.

The Urdu script portions of the course were written in Lahore by a professional calligrapher, Mr. Muhammad Ashraf Rahat.

A number of part-time assistants were also employed as proofreaders, copyists, "voices" for the recorded dialogues, etc. The author and his colleagues wish to thank Messrs. M. H. Alavi, A. H. Siddiqi, L. A. Hanafi, H. A. Naqvi, Mushir-ul-Haq, and Mrs. Abida Ahmad and Miss Rehana Khan for their assistance. Thanks also go to the staff of the Language Laboratory, McGill University, for their help in preparing the tape recordings which should accompany this course.

Aside from the great debt of gratitude owed to those sponsoring bodies mentioned in the first paragraph of this preface who made the publication of this course possible, the author and his colleagues would also like to express their appreciation to the Principal and staff of Oriental College and also to the Director and staff of the Institute of Islamic Studies. Both of these institutions provided the members of this project with a most congenial atmosphere in which to work.

Muhammad Abd-al-Rahman Barker

TABLE OF CONTENTS

UNIT ELEVEN

UNIT TWELVE

UNIT THIRTEEN

UNIT FOURTEEN

UNIT FIFTEEN

INTRODUCTION

0. 001.   The Language.

"Urdu, " "Hindi," and "Hindustani" are all names for what is essentially the same
language, spoken by more than one hundred and sixty million persons in West Pakistan and
northern India.   Urdu-Hindi-Hindustani also serves as an important second language for
many more millions of people in these two countries, and, in its simplest form, it is used
as a lingua franca almost throughout the whole of the Subcontinent.   It is also spoken in
various other areas by large groups of Indo-Pakistani emigrants.

"Urdu" is the name generally given to that variety of this language written in the Arabic
script.   Earlier authors also called this form "Hindustani, " but this has fallen into disuse.
Urdu draws a very large percentage of its literary and technical vocabulary (and also some
features of its grammatical apparatus) from Arabic and Persian, two languages which
play an important part in the religious and cultural heritage of the Muslim community.
Urdu is now one of the three official languages of the Republic of Pakistan (the two others
being Bengali and English).   It is also the major language of some fifty to sixty million
Muslims living in the Republic of India and is one of the fourteen "Regional Languages"
recognised under the Indian constitution.

Modern Urdu is a fairly homogeneous language (-- an older southern form, Deccani
Urdu, is now obsolete).   Two varieties must be mentioned, however: the Urdu of Delhi
and the Urdu of Lucknow.   These two varieties are really almost identical, differing only
in certain minor points, such as the genders of a few nouns, some verb forms, and various
matters of usage and idiom.   Both of these varieties are considered "Standard Urdu, " and
the student should thus be prepared to find some minor divergences.   The author has also
noted recent "Panjabi-ising" tendencies in some Urdu works produced in Pakistan -- and
analogous "Hindi-ising" tendencies in some materials written in India.

"Hindi" usually denotes that variety of this language which is written in the Deva Nagari
script (essentially the same script as that employed for Sanskrit).   Literary Hindi relies
heavily upon Sanskrit (and terms coined from Sanskrit) for its stock of erudite and technical
terminology.   In this form, literary Hindi is a rather recent development.   It is now
recognised as the national language of the Republic of India.

The term "Hindi" is also used as an inclusive name for a great many regional dialects,
some of which are quite distinct from the literary language: e. g.   Braj, Avadhi, Magadhi,
etc.   Although some of these forms are as different from literary Hindi as Cockney is from
rural Alabaman English, they still share the same basic phonological and grammatical
structures and must be included within "Urdu-Hindi-Hindustani. "

Some modern Indian writers use the term "Hindustani" to refer to the common "core"
language -- the lingua franca of the marketplace and of everyday speech -- reserving
"Urdu" and "Hindi" for the two great literary traditions.   Pakistani authors would, of course

consider the "core" language also a form of "Urdu." These terms are really only names for varieties of one and the same basic linguistic structure, but each carries its own connotations: Urdu is thought of mainly as that form of the language developed under the patronage of the Muslim rulers of Delhi, Lucknow, etc. and connected with the Muslims of the Subcontinent. Hindi is similarly linked with the North Indian Hindu community. Closer inspection will show that this division is really a superficial one: many Hindus are numbered among the "greats" of Urdu literature, and similarly there are Muslim contributors to Hindi. Real differences between these varieties are often somewhat blurred (ignoring the matter of script for the moment), since one must consider not only the Hindu-Muslim communal dichotomy but also such factors as regional variation, class and caste stratification, individual circumstances, etc. The partition of the Subcontinent in 1947 and the creation of the separate states of India and Pakistan have served to crystallise and intensify differences between literary Urdu and literary Hindi, so that now -- again apart from the matter of script -- vocabulary differences alone have become so great as to make these two traditions almost mutually unintelligible.

Linguistic and literary history will be discussed again in Unit XXIV.

0.002. This Course.

These lessons constitute an introduction to spoken and written Urdu. Although much of the basic material presented here can also be employed for a study of Hindi, the moment one leaves the sphere of everyday speech -- "Hindustani" -- one must acquire either the Perso-Arabicised constructions and lexicon of literary Urdu or the Sanskritised formations of literary Hindi. For pedagogical reasons, the author feels that these two traditions really deserve separate treatment, and he has thus followed his own personal inclinations in choosing to describe Urdu -- an enthusiasm which he hopes the students of this course will come to share. The writing of an exhaustive course and reference grammar for literary Hindi is still an important desideratum.

So far as Urdu itself is concerned, the course is based upon a literate (but not pedantic) variety of Dihlavi (i. e. of Delhi) Urdu as employed today in India and Pakistan. An attempt has been made to steer a course between the overly-erudite pronunciation and usage of the traditional Urdu scholar on the one hand and the colloquial spoken language of the streets on the other. In many cases a note has been added to indicate other usages: e. g. "literary ...," "common ...," etc.

The choice of the Dihlavi dialect over that used in Lucknow does not imply primacy or superiority. This choice is simply due to the fact that the author's chief collaborators, Mr. K. M. Shafi and Mr. H. J. Hamdani, are both speakers of the Dihlavi dialect. Forms from the Lucknow dialect have been supplied in those cases where a difference was noted.

A language, moreover, does not exist in a vacuum. Real understanding cannot be attained until one has some knowledge of the socio-cultural milieu in which the language is spoken. Thus, along with the primary objective of this course -- language learning -- brief sketches of some facets of Indo-Pakistani life have been added. These materials are oriented towards the Muslim community of the Subcontinent in general and towards present-day West Pakistan in particular. Although a large part of this information is thus also applicable to northern India as well, much of it is strictly "Pakistani" in content. This orientation is partially due to personal reasons -- the course was first conceived at Oriental College in Lahore, West Pakistan, and the author's colleagues are mostly Pakistanis -- but is also partly based on the fact that, although a certain amount of modern India-oriented teaching materials exists for "Urdu-Hindi-Hindustani, " the author has seen almost nothing in print which might equip a student for life in modern Pakistan. The author and his colleagues do not necessarily agree with all of the opinions and attitudes expressed (e. g. by characters in the Conversation Sections), but have tried instead to present a "Pakistani" point of view appropriate to the context.

Most of the photographs which appear in this book were taken during the author's stay in Pakistan in 1959-62 (or during a more recent visit to the Subcontinent in 1966). Pressure of work kept the author mainly in Lahore and its environs, and thus pictures of other parts of India and Pakistan are unfortunately few.

Urdu speakers may feel that some of the materials of the course are a trifle stilted or artificial, especially in earlier Units. This is due, of course, to the method, which requires that all new material be completely explained within the Unit (or already given in some previous Unit), and that there be no anticipation of vocabulary or constructions from some later Unit, no matter how appropriate and felicitous they may seem.

Similarly, the English translations of Urdu materials may appear unnatural or un-idiomatic. The author and his colleagues believe that a semi-literal translation is of more assistance to the student than a smoother and more fluent free rendition.

Much of the Urdu material of the course is given in an English-like transcription, rather than in the traditional Urdu variety of the Arabic script. It has been found that reading and writing are more easily acquired once the basic sound structure, sentence patterns, grammatical apparatus, and basic vocabulary of a language have been internalised. The transcription employed here is "phonemic" (i. e. each unit of sound is represented by one letter), and classroom testing has shown that it can be mastered within a very short time. The Arabic script used for Urdu, however, is complex and not completely phonemic. Once one has learned some basic spoken Urdu, thus, one can more quickly assimilate the script and then read in terms of words and known patterns of words, rather than in the older and more laborious letter-by-letter and word-by-word method. It is not the intention of this book to ignore reading and writing, however; the Arabic script is gradually introduced beginning with Unit VI, and its use is increased stage by stage until all essay and drill materials are given in this script alone.

Although the phonemic transcription used here contains symbols for all of the consonants and vowels and also "punctuation" to indicate major sentence and phrase intonation, the finer details of the pitch-stress-intonation system are not marked. The author feels that superscript numerals, lines, or arrows tend to clutter up a beginner's text, and students usually ignore them anyhow. It is assumed that an Indo-Pakistani tutor and a set of recorded tapes will normally be employed with this course, and the burden of acquiring a proper intonation for Urdu is thus laid upon these and upon the student's ability to mimic.

0.003. The Method.

This is intended to be an intensive course. Ideally, at least ten classroom hours per week are needed, together with several more hours of language laboratory practice with tape recordings. It is possible, however, to make do with considerably less teaching time, and the course has even been used in situations where only three classroom hours per week were available. This requires considerable outside work and diligence on the part of the student, however, since it entails (a) complete omission of such "extras" as discussions of Sections given only for reference, (b) condensation of phonological and grammatical expositions, (c) assigning Sections dealing with minor matters of usage and cultural background information to be read entirely as homework with little or no commentary in class, (d) complete omission of some drills and partial omission of many others, gauging class progress upon the students' rate of assimilation, and (e) relegation of much drill material to outside work with a tape recorder. It is possible, however, to use this course without significant omissions in a programme which permits five classroom hours per week, plus some language laboratory time.

This course is not really a "teach-yourself" book (although an intelligent student using it alone can certainly gain something from it). It is meant to be taught by a person familiar with at least the rudiments of modern linguistic science and with recent developments in language teaching methodology. If the instructor himself is not a native speaker of Urdu, an Urdu-speaking "informant" or tutor may be employed. In the author's experience, most educated Indo-Pakistanis can master the phonemic transcription of this book almost without conscious effort, and he or she can then be asked to do most of the classroom drills, with the English-speaking instructor providing explanations and assistance. A set of tapes has been prepared to accompany the course, but there is nothing to match such a "live performance" in the classroom for efficacy.

It may be found that the tutor's pronunciation differs in some particulars from that given in the course, and there may also be some disparity in matters of usage and idiom. This is to be expected in almost any language. In such cases, the student should follow the tutor.

0.004. Arrangement of Materials.

Units of this course follow four different patterns. These differ only in minor matters of content and arrangement.

(1) Units I through V and VII, IX, and XI are constructed as follows:
(a) The ".000" Section in each Unit contains a conversation in which all new constructions and vocabulary for the Unit are introduced. These dialogues are not just "grammarian's sentences" but are intended to be real conversations.

In early Units these Conversation Sections present materials the student can use in adjusting to life in Pakistan: greetings and introductions, a visit to someone's home, a dinner party, shopping, a railway trip and staying in a hotel, sightseeing, etc. These Sections should first be assigned for home study, then practised in the language laboratory, then analysed and drilled in class, and finally read as real dialogues with various students taking the different parts. All of these conversations have been recorded twice: the first time quite slowly with pauses for repetition between the various items, and the second time by a group of speakers in actual conversational style.

(b) The ".100" Section is called "Word Study." It serves two purposes: firstly to discuss the meanings and usage of individual words, presenting further semantic and idiomatic material and examples, and secondly as a place for cultural background information about topics introduced in the Conversation Section. Within each Word Study Section items are arranged serially according to their occurrence in the Conversation Section. These materials are mainly to be studied as homework and will require only occasional comment in class.

(c) The ".200" Section of each Unit deals with phonology. The entire phonological system and the phonemic transcription are briefly introduced in Sec. 1.200 ff. Subsequent Phonetics Sections then take up individual sets of phenomena, particularly those which are difficult for English speakers. The Urdu data are contrasted with English structures, and sets of examples are given. These examples and subsequent drill Sections have been recorded and should be practiced in the language laboratory. Occasional classroom drills may also be helpful.

(d) The ".300" Section of each Unit is called "Analysis." It contains an explanation of all new grammatical and syntactic material and should be discussed in connection with examples occurring in the Conversation Section. Since these Sections are often quite detailed and occasionally contain materials to be used for reference only, the instructor should lay special stress upon basic patterns in his classroom presentation.

(e) The ".400" Section is that of the Supplementary Vocabulary. In most cases this is very brief, containing only a few items which complete sets of forms described in the Analysis Section or which somehow "fit in" with other items given in the Conversation Section. Since the numerals from one to one hundred are "irregular" (although the discerning student will soon perceive certain patterns), this Section will also present an average of five new numerals per Unit until all have been given. Each Supplementary Vocabulary Section also contains a few brief exercises in order to introduce these new items in a suitable context.

(f) The ".500" Section of each Unit is called "Vocabulary and Grammar Drill." Various types of exercises employed in these Sections are discussed in detail in Sec. 1.500. These should be done in class with the tutor employing both group and individual practice until fluency has been achieved. The next

xix

to the last drill in each of these Sections consists of another conversation which carries on the dialogue begun in the Conversation Section of the Unit. These have been tape recorded as real conversations using several speakers and should be practiced in the language laboratory until easy auditory comprehension is attained.

(g) The ".600" Section of each Unit is a final vocabulary of all new items. These are alphabetised according to the phonemic transcription (which is, however, approximately in English order); for a statement of this alphabetical order, see the Appendices, Sec. A.202.

(2) Units VI, VIII, X, and XII belong to the second group of lessons. They introduce the Arabic script employed for Urdu and are constructed as follows:

(a) Introductory Sections contain an exposition of a number of letter groups, together with a discussion of the correspondence of these written symbols with the spoken language. The alphabet itself is completed in Unit X, and Unit XII is devoted to the writing of numerals, prices, punctuation, special signs, etc.

(b) The second part of each Script Unit contains lists of special "spellings," reading exercises to be done in class, and writing exercises to be assigned as homework.

(3) Units XIII through XX comprise the third group of Units. They differ in only a few particulars from those described above under (1).

(a) All but one of the Conversation Sections now deal more with matters connected with Pakistani life and culture, rather than with materials oriented toward a foreign visitor: e.g. village problems, the Islamic religion, marriage customs, the governmental system of Pakistan, etc. Further information about these facets of the society is presented in the Word Study Sections.

(b) The ".200" Section is now called "Script," and the Phonetics Section is discontinued. Each Script Section contains lists of special "spellings," reading drills (one of which is always a portion -- or the whole -- of the Conversation Section of the Unit), and writing exercises, including translations from English to (written) Urdu, etc.

(c) The Analysis Sections of these Units contain considerable "reference material" -- i.e. information which is not to be learned at once but which should be read and then referred to from time to time). For example, the Analysis Section of Unit XVII contains an exposition of Arabic grammatical constructions employed in Urdu. Unit XVIII similarly discusses Persian formations, and Unit XIX has an analysis of Hindi affixes and compounds used in Urdu (although this discussion is by no means sufficient for literary Hindi).

(d) Other Sections of these Units are as described above under (1).

(4) Units XXI through XXV are also similar to those above but contain the following new materials:

(a) Instead of an introductory conversation, these latter Units begin with an essay, written in the Arabic script. Topics include such things as the ancient and mediaeval history of the Subcontinent, the creation of Pakistan, the development of the Urdu language and Urdu poetry, and the history of Urdu prose, journalism, and drama. These Essay Sections have been tape recorded in "radio speech" style. They should be practiced for auditory comprehension in the language laboratory and then read in class.

(b) The ".100" Section of each of these Units is now occupied by a "Serial Vocabulary" in which all new items are listed in order of their occurrence in the essay. These are given both in the Arabic script and in phonemic transcription. The Word Study Section is now Sec. .200 ff.

(c) Reading and writing exercises are no longer separate but are included in the Vocabulary and Grammar Drill Section of each Unit. The use of the Arabic script is gradually increased until almost all materials in these Sections are written in it rather than in transcription.

(d) Other Sections of these Units are much as has been described above under (1) and (2).

The course also includes five appendices. The first contains a brief list of abbreviations and conventions; the second is an Urdu-English vocabulary of all items introduced to be learned; the third is an English-Urdu finder list for the preceding vocabulary; the fourth appendix is a brief supplementary Urdu-English vocabulary of useful items mentioned in the course which were not given to be learned; and the fifth appendix is an English-Urdu finder list for the foregoing. There is also a final index. These sections are self-explanatory.

The student is strongly advised to make flash cards for the vocabulary of the course. These should be small pieces of light card stock (two by three inches is a handy size) and should have the phonemic transcription (and later the Arabic script) for each item on one side and the English meaning and information about gender, etc. on the other.

As a final note, it may be mentioned that this course is intended to serve as the first part of a connected series of Urdu teaching materials. Other items in preparation include a reader of Urdu newspaper prose, a reader of modern Urdu poetry, and a wordcount of newspaper Urdu (to be used as a reference work).

The Mall, a major commercial street in Lahore.

1.000. CONVERSATION

Mr. Smith, an American professor teaching in Pakistan, meets Dr. Rəhim at a party.

greetings!	adab ərz
sir	jənab
S: Hello, sir!	adab ərz, jənab.
disposition	myzaj
noble	šərif
R: How are you?	myzaj šərif?
kindness	myhrbani
S: Thank you.	myhrbani.
you [honorific]	ap
American	əmrikən
are	hǝ̄y
R: Are you an American?	ap əmrikən hǝ̄y?
term of respectful address	ji
yes	hā
S: Yes.	ji hā.
what? [Also introduces a question requiring a yes or no answer]	kya
Urdu	wrdu
pleasing	pəsənd
is	həy
R: Do you like Urdu? [What, is Urdu pleasing?]	kya, wrdu pəsənd həy?
much, very	bəhwt
S: Yes, I like it very much.	ji hā, bəhwt pəsənd həy.
of	ka
name, noun	ysm
name [honorific]	ysme šərif
R: What is your name?	ap ka ysme šərif kya həy.
my	mera
name	nam
Smith	ysmyth [or /symyth/ or /səmyth/]
S: My name is Smith.	mera nam ysmyth həy.
work, job	kam
Pakistan	pakystan
in	mē
R: What is your job in Pakistan?	ap ka kam pakystan mē kya həy.
I	mə̄y

1

English	Urdu
university	yunyvərsyTi [or /yunyvərsTi/]
professor	profesər
am	hū
S: I'm a professor in the University.	mə̄y yunyvərsyTi mē profesər hū.
also, too	bhi
S: Are you also in the University?	kya, ap bhi yunyvərsyTi mē hə̄y?
no, not	nəhĩ
R: No, I'm not in the University.	ji nəhĩ, mə̄y yunyvərsyTi mē nəhĩ hū.
hospital	həspətal
doctor	DakTər
R: I'm a doctor in the [or: in a] hospital.	mə̄y həspətal mē DakTər hū.
when?	kəb
from, with, by	se
R: How long [lit. from when?] have you been [lit. are] in Pakistan?	ap pakystan mē kəb se hə̄y.
one, a, an	ek
year	sal
here	yəhā
S: I've been here for [lit. from] one year.	mə̄y ek sal se yəhā hū.
house, home	ghər
America	əmrika
where?	kəhā
R: Where is your home in America?	ap ka ghər əmrika mē kəhā həy.
New York	niw yark [or /niw yəwrk/]
S: My home is in New York.	mera ghər niw yark mē həy.
Lahore (a city in West Pakistan)	lahəwr
R: Where is your home here in Lahore?	ap ka ghər yəhā lahəwr mē kəhā həy.
Lawrence Road	larəns roD
on	pər
S: [It] is on Lawrence Road.	larəns roD pər həy.
number	nəmbər
R: What is the number of the house?	ghər ka nəmbər kya həy.
two	do
S: [It] is number two.	do nəmbər həy.
that [he, she, it, they, those]	vw [slow speech /vwh/]
far, distant, distance	dur
R: Is it [lit. that] far from here?	kya, vw yəhā se dur həy?
near	nəzdik
S: No, it is very near.	ji nəhĩ, bəhwt nəzdik həy.

1.100. WORD STUDY

1.101. /adab ərz/ is used both for "hello" and "goodbye." Alone, /adab/ means "etiquette, polite forms of address, salutations"; /ərz/ means "petition, request," but neither of these words will be of immediate use to the student, and the phrase should therefore be learned as a unit. Although this form of greeting is employed mainly in areas influenced by Muslim culture, it is not restricted to Muslims alone. To another Muslim, a Muslim would employ the Arabic greeting /səlam ələykwm/, to which the answer would be /va ələykwm səlam/. In Hindu society the greeting /nəməste/ (to which the answer also is /nəməste/) is in general use. The student is advised to employ the polite (but religiously colourless) form /adab ərz/ in urban society in North India and Pakistan.

1.102. /jənab/ "sir" may also be used in addressing women, even though as an independent noun its reference is masculine.

1.103. /myzaj šərif/ "How are you?" may be treated as a unit for the present, although both words are used independently elsewhere. /šərif/ as an adjective means "noble" or "gentle."

1.104. /myhrbani/ "kindness" is used in situations where English speakers employ set phrases like "thank you," "you're welcome," and also "please." Another common expression for "thank you" is /šwkria/.

1.105. /ji hā/ and /ji nəhī/ are the common, polite ways of saying "yes" and "no." /ji./ alone with a falling intonation is often heard in reply to a yes or no question (meaning "yes") and also as a sign of acceptance of an order. With a rising intonation, /ji?/ means "What did you say?" In Hindu society this word is added as a respectful title to proper names: e.g. /ysmyth ji/ "Mr. Smith," /gādhi ji/ "Gandhi." This is not done in Muslim culture, however.

1.106. The /e/ in /ysme šərif/ "name [polite]" represents a Persian construction which will be explained in a later Unit. Used independently, /ysm/ does not mean "name" in modern Urdu but only "noun." It is also correct to say /ap ka nam kya həy./ "What is your name?" but this does not carry the polite connotations of /ysme šərif/.

1.107. English words are very common in spoken Urdu. Each has its own local pronunciation, and the student should learn and use this rather than his own. There may also be variant pronunciations, depending upon the degree of assimilation into Urdu, the speaker's regional dialect, the speaker's knowledge of English, etc. One thus hears /DakTər/ for "doctor," but also /DɔwkTər/ (with an attempt at the vowel of the Southern British English pronunciation); similarly, /gəwrnmənT/ or /gəvərnmənT/ for "government," /yunyvərsyTi/ or /yunyvərsTi/ for "university," etc. Since Urdu has no /sm/ at the beginning of a word, "Smith" becomes /ysmyth/ in Eastern and Central Urdu (as far west as Delhi), and /səmyth/ or /symyth/ in the Panjab. Similarly, /yskul/, /səkul/, or /sykul/ for "school," /ysTešən/, /səTešən/ or /syTešən/ for "station," etc. Less assimilated words and names may admit of several alternate pronunciations.

1.108. /ghər/ means both "house" (i.e. a residential building) and "home" (one's personal residence). There is another word, /məkan/, which means "house" only: a building used as a residence. Neither /ghər/ nor /məkan/ can be employed in the sense of "building," as in "factory building," "school building," etc. /məkan/ will be introduced in the Supplementary Vocabulary section of this Unit.

1.109. /do nəmbər/ "number two" may vary freely with the more Anglicised order /nəmbər do/. Both are common.

1.200. PHONETICS

The following description of the Urdu phonetic-phonemic inventory will serve to introduce the student to the transcription employed in this book. Further details and drills will be given in succeeding Units.

1.201. /a/.

A low central unrounded vowel, quite close to the standard midwestern American pronunciation of the vowel a in father (not to the vowel of the southern British pronunciation of this word). E.g.

/ap/   you [honorific]
/nam/   name
/xwda/   God

1.202. /ə/.

A lower-mid central unrounded vowel, similar to English u in but or a in above. Examples:

/ərz/   request
/jənab/   sir

/ə/ and /a/ have the same pronunciation wo rd-finally, except for one or two monosyllabic words in which the contrast is maintained. /a/ is arbitrarily chosen as the symbol for word-final vowels of this quality, except in /nə/ "not," and a few other items.

In the environment /əhCV/ (i.e. before /h/ followed by another consonant and a vowel), /ə/ has another quality entirely: it is lowered and fronted to a position between the e of set and the a of cat (i.e. between [æ] and [ɛ]). The same applies to /əh/ at the end of a monosyllabic word. When /əhC/ occurs at the end of a word or before some further consonant (i.e. /əhCC/), however, a brief, lenis "echo vowel" of the same quality (i.e. [æ] or [ɛ]) occurs after /h/. This phenomenon is quite predictable: if a vowel-initial suffix is added to /əhC/, there is no echo vowel; if /əhC/ occurs at the end of the word or before a consonant-initial suffix, then the echo vowel occurs. Examples:

/rəhta/   staying (phon. [ræhta] or [rɛhta]: /əhCV/)
/bəhnẽ/   sisters (phon. [bæhnẽ] or [bɛhnẽ]: /əhCV/). Cf.
/bəhn/   sister (phon. [bæhᵋn]: /əhC#/
/šəhr/   city (phon. [šæhᵋr]: /əhC#/)
/kəh rəha həy/   is saying (phon. [kæh]: /#Cəh#/)

In the sequence /əhV/, however, /ə/ does not have this fronted and lowered variety. Instead, it is like the u in but, as described above. E.g.

/rəha/ msc. sg. stayed (phon. [rəha]; cf. /rəhta/ above)

/ə/ is also fronted and lowered in the sequence /əy/: before a consonant, phonetically [æⁱ] or [ɛⁱ]; at the end of a word with a lower offglide, almost equivalent to a lenis [e]: [æᵉ] or [ɛᵉ]. This diphthong is not found in English and must be carefully learned. (In

5

the South, however, /əy/ is pronounced like the ie of tie, but this does not occur in the North.) In the sequence /əyV/, /ə/ again has the sound of u in but (e.g. /gəya/ "msc. sg. went"). E.g.

/pəyda/　born, produced (phon. [pæⁱda] or even [pæda])

/həy/　is (phon. [hæ^e] or [hɛ^e])

In the sequences /əwC/ or /əw#/ (i.e. before /w/ before a following consonant or at the end of a word), /ə/ ranges back toward the aw of law (phonetically [ɔ]). In some pronunciations, words like /məwt/ "death" and /lahəwr/ "Lahore" sound like [mɔt] and [lahɔr]. E.g.

/səw/　hundred (phon. [sɔ^u] or [sɔ])

/səwt/　voice, sound (phon. [sɔ^ut] or [sɔt])

The sequences /əhw/ and /əhw̃/ in most pronunciations sound like [ɔhɔ] and [ɔ̃hɔ̃]. In rapid speech these may be heard as [ɔh] and [ɔ̃h]. E.g.

/bəhwt/　many, much, very (phon. [bɔhᵓt] or [bɔht])

/pəhw̃cta/　arriving (phon. [pɔ̃hᵓ̃cta] or [pɔ̃hcta])

1.203.　/b/.

A voiced bilabial stop, like the b in big, rib. E.g.

/bəhwt/　much, many, very

/abdar/　shiny

/jənab/　sir

1.204.　/c/.

A voiceless alveopalatal affricate: the ch of cheese or church but with a somewhat less aspirated release. E.g.

/ciz/　thing

/nocta/　scratching

/səc/　true

1.205.　/d/.

A voiced post-dental stop: the French or Spanish "soft d" (or "dental d"). Although English does have a sound similar to /d/ in a few environments (e.g. the d of width), the student must beware of pronouncing /d/ as the "ordinary English d" (i.e. the d of dog, etc.) since this will be interpreted by Urdu speakers as /D/. E.g.

/dyl/　heart

/wrdu/　Urdu

/pəsənd/　pleasing

1.206.　/D/.

A voiced alveolar or post-alveolar retroflex stop. The tip of the tongue is turned slightly back to touch the alveolar ridge at a point somewhat behind that used by English speakers for English d̲. It is this turning back of the tongue tip that is important rather than the backed point of articulation. Urdu speakers hear English d as their /D/, but this is phonetically inaccurate, although speakers of midwestern American English do have a similar sound in the d of words like hard or order. E. g.

> /Dalna/ to pour
> /DakTər/ doctor
> /ənDa/ egg
> /DənDa/ stick, club

1.207. /e/.

A tense mid front unrounded vowel: similar to a in fate but without the "y-like" diphthongal offglide of the English word. Urdu /e/ is a "pure vowel," similar to Spanish e in me, French é in été (though longer than the French vowels), or German ee in See. If English say is compared with Urdu /se/, the "y-like" offglide of the former will be clearly audible.

A shorter, lower, and more lenis sound, similar to the e in met, is found in a few environments but is only contrastive in some pronunciations of a borrowed word like /cek/ (phonetically [cɛk]). This vowel also contrasts with /e/ (phonetic [e]) in poetry, for reasons of metre. In view of its limited distribution, it will not be written with a separate symbol in this book. E. g.

> /ek/ one, a, an
> /seb/ apple
> /se/ from, with, by
> /cek/ cheque

1.208. /f/.

A voiceless labiodental fricative: the f of fish, fog, etc. Some dialects produce this sound bilabially rather than labiodentally, but educated urban speakers use the labiodental pronunciation. E. g.

> /fəta/ victory
> /həfta/ week; Saturday
> /šərif/ noble

1.209. /g/.

A voiced velar stop: the g of go. NEVER the g of gym or gist! E. g.

> /gae/ cow
> /jwgnu/ firefly
> /log/ people

7

1.210. /ɣ/.

A voiced velar fricative: the "ghayn" of Arabic. Some German speakers have a similar sound in the g of Wagen, and Parisian French has a closely similar sound in the r of Paris. E.g.

/ɣərib/   poor
/mwɣəl/   Mughal
/faryɣ/   free, at leisure

1.211. /h/.

A voiceless faucal fricative at the beginning of words: the English h in hat, hurt, etc. Between vowels and after a vowel before a consonant, /h/ is at least partially voiced. E.g.

/həy/   is
/bahər/   outside

Word final /h/ presents a problem: the majority of Urdu speakers tend to have a final /h/ in slow, deliberate speech (as when pronouncing a word for a foreign beginner), but this almost invariably disappears in normal speed speech. Only a few monosyllabic words consistently retain a final /h/ in normal speed utterances (e.g. /kəh/ "say," /rəh/ "stay," etc.). Other words have two forms: a slow-speech form with /h/ and a normal-speed form without it: /gwnah/ "sin" and /gwna/, /badšah/ "king" and /badša/, etc. If some further suffix is added, however, the /h/ will always occur: /gwnahõ/ "sins," /badšahõ/ "kings." Slow-speech words ending in /əh/ may have normal speech forms ending in /a/ or sometimes /ha/: /swbəh/ "morning" occurs as /swba/ and sometimes /swbha/. The problem is complicated by the spelling system, which often writes final h for final /a/ (this h never appears in plural forms, etc.); Urdu speakers may thus tend to feel that a word "ends in h," when this is phonetically never the case.

/gwnah/   sin (Or /gwna/)
/swbəh/   morning (/swba/ or /swbha/)
/vw/   that (Only rarely /vwh/)
/ky/   that [conj.] (Almost never /kyh/ but written as such)

After consonants before a vowel or a consonant, /h/ occurs as aspiration (a puff of breath). After voiceless stops (/p, t, T, c, k/) the aspiration is voiceless; after voiced stops and resonants (/b, d, D, j, g, l, m, n, R/), the aspiration is voiced. Initial voiceless stops are aspirated in English (i.e. p in pin is phonetically [pʰ], t in tin phonetically [tʰ], and k in kin phonetically [kʰ]); in Urdu, aspirated stops (/ph/, like the p of pin) contrast with unaspirated stops (/p/ like the p of spin). There are no counterparts in English or other European languages for the voiced aspirates (/bh, dh, Dh/, etc.), and these must be learned by practice with the instructor and with a tape recorder. The student may test the degree of aspiration of a consonant by holding a slip of paper in front of his mouth; if the paper flutters as he pronounces the word, then aspiration is present. E.g.

/phəl/   fruit (Compare:)

/pəl/   moment
/thal/   large circular metal tray (Compare:)
/tal/   rhythm
/bat/   matter, thing (Compare:)
/bhat/   cooked rice

After a vowel and before a consonant, /h/ is followed by a slight "echo vowel" which approximates the quality of the preceding vowel but is more lenis and shorter in duration. See above, Sec. 1.202. E. g.

/myhrbani/   kindness (phon. [mIh^{I}rbani])

1.212. /i/.

A high front unrounded vowel: similar to the i in machine but without the "y-like" diphthongal offglide. This is the "pure vowel" of Spanish or French (e. g. Spanish pide, French vive). In order to provide a contrast, the instructor may compare Urdu /si/ with English see. E. g.

/iman/   faith
/šərif/   noble
/ji/   term of respect

1.213. /j/.

A voiced alveopalatal affricate: the j of Jim, judge, etc. E. g.

/jənab/   sir
/byjli/   lightning, electricity
/myzaj/   disposition

1.214. /k/.

A voiceless velar stop: the k of skin (NOT of kin, which is closer to Urdu /kh/; see above under Sec. 1.211). E. g.

/kam/   work, job
/nwkta/   dot, point
/nak/   nose

1.215. /l/.

A post-dental lateral continuant: the "light l" of Spanish or French, never the "dark l" of English ball. Many English dialects have a "light l" at the beginning of words and a "dark l" (i. e. a velarised alveolar l) before consonants and word-finally. Have the instructor compare Urdu /məl/ with English mull, /syl/ with sill, etc. E. g.

/lahəwr/   Lahore
/jəldi/   quickly, soon, speed

/sal/   year

1.216. /m/.

A voiced bilabial nasal continuant: the m of man, dim, etc. E.g.
>/mē/   in
>/nəmbər/   number
>/kam/   work

1.217. /n/.

A voiced post-dental nasal continuant: the n of Spanish or French, made with the tongue tip at the juncture of the upper teeth and the gums, rather than the alveolar n of English, which is made further back on the alveolar ridge. E.g.
>/nəhĩ/   no, not
>/janta/   knowing
>/jan/   life

/n/ contrasts with vowel + nasalisation in most environments. /n/ following a vowel is clearly pronounced and has a duration of its own: i.e. /Vn/ is of two mora length, while /Ṽ/ is of one mora duration only. This will be discussed again below. E.g.
>/tynka/   straw (Compare:)
>/tə̃g/   tight, narrow
>/ynqylab/   revolution

Before /T/ and /D/, /n/ is articulated slightly further back on the alveolar ridge. Here it is similar to the n of under. E.g.
>/ənDa/   egg

1.218. /o/.

A mid-back rounded vowel: the "pure vowel" of Spanish or French (e.g. Spanish loco, French côte). It lacks the "w-like" diphthongal offglide of English o in go, oa in boat, etc. Compare Urdu /lo/ with English low. E.g.
>/os/   dew
>/profesər/   professor
>/do/   two

1.219. /p/.

A voiceless bilabial stop: the p of spin (NOT the p of pin, which is closer to Urdu /ph/; see above under Sec. 1.211). E.g.
>/pani/   water
>/əpna/   one's own
>/ap/   you [honorific]

1.220. /q/.

A voiceless back-velar stop: similar to /k/ but pronounced further back on the velum. This is the qaf of Classical Arabic. Although not all dialects have /q/ (e.g. Panjabi-ised dialects which have /k/ only), the most prestigeful forms of Urdu do have it, and the student should strive to imitate these. E.g.

/qərib/ near
/myqdar/ amount, quantity
/šəwq/ fondness, pleasure

1.221. /r/.

A voiced post-dental flap: the Spanish r of pero. The American voiced retroflex continuant (the r of peril) is not acceptable. Speakers of southern British dialects and southeastern American dialects of English must be careful to pronounce this sound before consonants and at the end of words. E.g.

/rat/ night
/mera/ my
/kərta/ doing
/dur/ far, distance

1.222. /R/.

A voiced alveolar or post-alveolar retroflex flap. To produce this sound, one draws the body of the tongue back in the mouth and turns the tongue tip up (as though about to touch the roof of the mouth with the tongue tip). The tongue is then brought forward, and the underside of the tongue tip is flapped forward and down against the back of the alveolar ridge. This is perhaps the most difficult sound in Urdu for foreign learners, and it must be practised assiduously.

It may be noted that /R/ and /D/ do not seem to have always contrasted: /R/ occurs between vowels, before consonants, and word-finally; /D/ is found at the beginning of words and after /n/. This pattern has been disrupted, however, by the introduction of words like /soDa/ "soda." E.g.

/bəRa/ big
/ləRka/ boy
/bheR/ sheep

/R/ may also occur with aspiration. E.g.

/pəRhta/ reading, studying
/gəRh/ fort

1.223. /s/.

A voiceless post-dental grooved fricative: similar to the s in sin but slightly further

11

forward on the alveolar ridge. E. g.

      /sal/   year
      /ysm/   name
      /pas/   near

1.224. /š/.

A voiceless alveopalatal grooved fricative: similar to the <u>sh</u> in <u>shin</u> but made slightly further forward on the alveolar ridge. E. g.

      /šərif/   noble
      /hošyar/   intelligent, clever
      /košyš/   effort, try

1.225. /t/.

A voiceless post-dental stop: the <u>t</u> of Spanish or French (e. g. Spanish <u>tu</u>, French <u>té</u>). Most English speakers will have this sound in a word like <u>eighth</u> (phonetically [eᶦtƟ]). /t/ is unaspirated (like the <u>t</u> of <u>sting,</u> but post-dental instead of alveolar); it contrasts with /th/ (see Sec. 1.211). E. g.

      /tin/   three
      /ytna/   this many, this much
      /bat/   thing, matter

1.226. /T/.

A voiceless alveolar or post-alveolar retroflex stop. The tip of the tongue is turned back to touch the alveolar ridge at a point somewhat behind that employed by English speakers for English <u>t</u>. It is this turning back of the tongue that is distinctive, rather than the backed point of articulation. Although Urdu speakers tend to hear English t as their /T/, in actuality only Americans have a sound approximating /T/ in words like <u>heart, barter.</u> /T/ is unaspirated (like the <u>t</u> of <u>sting,</u> but retroflex rather than alveolar); it contrasts with /Th/ (see Sec. 1.211). E. g.

      /Tāg/   leg
      /TəTTu/   pony
      /kaT/   cut

1.227. /u/.

A high-back rounded vowel: the "pure vowel" of Spanish or French (e. g. Spanish <u>puro</u>, French <u>blouse</u>). Like /o/, it also lacks the "w-like" diphthongal offglide of the <u>oe</u> in <u>shoe</u>, the <u>oo</u> in <u>boot</u>, etc. E. g.

      /upər/   above, up
      /pura/   whole

/tu/   thou

1.228. /v/.

A voiced labiodental fricative: similar to the v of vine but not identical, since the friction is weaker, and the lips tend to be more rounded. It thus sometimes sounds like the v in vine and at other times like the w in wine -- there is no contrast in Urdu. E. g.

/vw/   that; he, she, it, they
/vəhā/   there
/həva/   wind, air

1.229. /w/.

A lower-high-back rounded vowel: similar to the u in put or the oo in book, took. E. g.

/wrdu/   Urdu
/twm/   you [nonhonorific]

The sequence /əw/ is in some dialects pronounced almost like the aw of law, but with a slight offglide toward [ᵘ] (i. e. phonetically [ɔ] or [ɔᵘ]). See Sec. 1.202. E. g.

/məwt/   death (phon. [mɔt] or [mɔᵘt])

In the environment of /h/, /w/ tends to be lower, tending toward a lenis [o] position or even to [ɔ]. If /wh/ is followed by a consonant, a lenis "echo vowel" occurs after the /h/: e. g. /mwhr/ "seal" (phon. [mUhᵁr]). See Sec. 1.211. E. g.

/bəhwt/   many, much, very (phon. [bɔhᵓt] or [bɔht])

1.230. /x/.

A voiceless velar fricative: similar to the German ch in ach or the Scottish ch in loch. /x/ is the voiceless counterpart of /γ/. E. g.

/xwda/   God
/səxt/   hard, stern, difficult
/šax/   branch, bough

1.231. /y/.

This symbol is used for both consonantal [y] (a voiced alveopalatal continuant: the y of yes, you) and for a lower-high-front unrounded vowel (the i of pin, sit). These sounds do not contrast in Urdu: before and after vowels /y/ is consonantal; elsewhere this symbol denotes the vowel. E. g.

/yəhā/   here (Consonantal)
/nəya/   new (Consonantal)
/kya/   what? (Consonantal)
/ysm/   noun, name (Vowel)

13

/kytna/ how much, how many? (Vowel)

/yy/ this; he, she, it, they (The first /y/ is consonantal; the second is a vowel: phonetically [yI])

1.232. /z/.

A voiced post-dental grooved fricative: similar to z in zoo but slightly further forward on the alveolar ridge. In rural dialects and in some regional pronunciations, this sound does not occur, being replaced by /j/. E. g.

/zəban/ tongue, language
/myzaj/ disposition
/saz/ instrumental accompaniment

1.233. /ž/.

A voiced alveopalatal grooved fricative: similar to z in azure or s in pleasure. This sound is quite rare in Urdu, occurring mostly in Persian loanwords. E. g.

/žala/ hoar, frost
/əždəha/ serpent, dragon
/pəžmwrda/ withered

1.234. /ʔ/.

The glottal stop, /ʔ/ (the t of Cockney bottle), is not really a phoneme in the dialect of Urdu most useful to the student. It occurs only in very literary pronunciations of Arabic loanwords written with the letters hamza or ayn (and particularly the latter). The great majority of Urdu speakers have no single phonetic-phonemic representation for these two letters at all, either omitting them entirely or replacing them with vowel clusters. Since most Urdu speakers find the glottal stop pronunciation affected and over-learned, the student is advised to avoid it. The phonetic-phonemic form of words written with hamza and ayn will be discussed in those Units dealing with the Arabic script as used in Urdu. A few examples may be added here, however:

/təʔarwf/ introduction [of someone] (Commonly /təarwf/ or even /tarwf/)
/jəmaʔət/ class, group (Commonly /jəmaat/ or /jəmat/)
/mwʔəssər/ having effect (Commonly /mwəssər/)
/məvaqyʔ/ occasions, opportunities (Commonly /məvaqe/, /məvaqy/, or even /məvaqeʔ/)

1.235. Long and Short Vowels.

The vowels /i, e, a, u, o/ differ in duration as well as in quality from the other vowels, being approximately twice as long (i.e. taking about twice as much time to say). These vowels (+ the two diphthongal sequences /əy/ and /əw/) may thus be classed as "long," and /y, ə, w/ may be termed "short." Compare the vowels of /bin/ "snake

14

charmer's flute" and /byn/ "without"; compare these also with English bean and bin. The difference lies not only in the quality of these vowels but in their duration as well. E.g.

/cwl/ itch (Compare:)
/cul/ tenon, pivot
/myl/ meet, get! (Compare:)
/mil/ mile

Word-finally, there is very little contrast between long and short vowels. In words of more than one syllable, only long final vowels occur (except for some pronunciations of Arabic loanwords ending in ayn: see Sec. 1.234 and those Units dealing with script). Word-final vowels tend to be of somewhat lesser duration than non-final vowels. E.g.

/se/ from, with, by (Compare:)
/seb/ apple

There is, however, a contrast between long and short final vowels in a few monosyllabic words of common occurrence:

/nə/ not (Compare:)
/ka/ of [nom. msc. sg.]
/ky/ that [conj.] (Compare:)
/ki/ of [fem.]

1.236. Nasalised Vowels.

All of the vowels described above are oral vowels: all of the air used in their production passes out through the mouth, and none is allowed to escape through the nose. All of these vowels may also occur with a component of nasalisation: i.e. with some of the air passing out through the nasal passages. The symbol for nasalisation is /~/. Nasalised vowels are found in French: e.g. bon (cf. Urdu /kytabõ/ "books").

As was stated above in Sec. 1.217, nasalised vowels contrast with /Vn/. A nasalised vowel followed by /g/ or /k/ is phonetically quite similar to English ng (as in finger, not singer) and nk: phonetically [ŋg] and [ŋk]. E.g.

/jəhã/ where (Compare:)
/jəhan/ world
/hə̃s/ laugh! (Compare:)
/həns/ goose

1.237. Double (or Long) Consonants.

Most Urdu consonants may occur doubled (or "long" or "geminated"). This means, in effect, that the consonant is "held" for the duration of two single consonants. This phenomenon is rare in English: the author's dialect has only holy and wholly. E.g.

/gəla/ throat (Compare:)
/gəlla/ flock
/bəTa/ distributed (Compare:)
/bəTTa/ upper grinding stone

A doubled consonant may also be followed by aspiration: e.g.

/bəcca/   child (Compare:)
/əccha/   good, well

1.238. Phonetic Drill: Long Versus Short Vowels.

Various difficulties are usually encountered by the English speaking student in the acquisition of the correct pronunciation of the Urdu vowels. These include:

1. English speakers may differentiate the long and short vowels by giving them different qualities only, ignoring their difference in length.

2. Even very advanced students tend to retain their "y-like" and "w-like" offglides in pronouncing /i, e/ and /u, o/: i.e. they may produce /iy, ey, uw, ow/ as they would do in speaking English.

3. Since English lacks sounds of the exact quality of Urdu /əy/ and /əw/, many learners will at first pronounce these like the i in kite and the ou of house. The /əy/ sequence should begin with a vowel almost as low and fronted as the a of rat, followed by an offglide somewhat like the e of set (or even a little higher, like the a of fate). The /əw/ begins like the aw of law followed by a little "u-like" lip rounding.

4. Many Americans, especially those from the Midwest, tend to nasalise vowels in English. Since nasal and oral vowels contrast in Urdu, this must be carefully controlled. If one holds the nose closed while prolonging a vowel, a feeling of pressure and a muffled nasal quality will identify a nasal vowel.

5. British speakers of the "Standard Received Pronunciation" tend to diphthongise /o/, making it sound as though it were "eo". Another common problem is a tendency to insert a "y" after /t, T, d, D/ before /u/, as in British English tune or tube. British speakers may also find difficulty with their pronunciation of /a/; this should not be the British a of father but rather the American pronunciation of the same word.

The following drill should be repeated over and over after the instructor or after a tape recording. The meanings of the words used here are unimportant and do not necessarily form part of the vocabulary of the course; correct, fluent pronunciation is the goal.

/kyl [gəya]/ became nailed	/kil/ nail
/kər/ do!	/kar/ work
/cwl/ itch	/cul/ tenon, pivot
/nər/ male	/nar/ fire [Arabic]
/cyl/ dry cold	/cil/ kite [bird, sp.]
/ələm/ sorrow	/aləm/ universe
/nykəlna/ to go out	/nykalna/ to take out
/dhwl [gəya]/ was washed	/dhul/ dust
/cər/ eat [fodder]!	/car/ four
/pyl/ attack, rush against!	/pil/ elephant
/əməd/ intention	/aməd/ advent, coming
/bhwna/ became grilled	/bhuna/ grilled [trans.]

16

/myl/ meet, get!   /mil/ mile

/myl/ meet, get!	/mil/ mile
/Dər/ fear	/Dar/ flock, herd in a line
/sykh/ Sikh	/sikh/ learn!
/pwr/ full	/pur/ city [Hindi]
/syl/ lower grinding stone	/sil/ moisture, damp
/kəTna/ to be cut	/kaTna/ to cut
/əndhi/ blind	/ādhi/ windstorm
/swkh/ rest, comfort	/sukh/ dry!
/mər/ die!	/mar/ beat, hit!
/ser/ a measure of weight [2 lbs.]	/səyr/ walk, stroll
/bir/ brother [Hindi]	/ber/ a fruit
	/bəyr/ enmity
/myl/ meet, get!	/mel/ affinity, friendship
/mil/ mile	/məyl/ body dirt, filth
/swr/ note, tone	/sur/ trumpet
/səwr/ Taurus	/šor/ noise, uproar
/mwl/ wine	/mul/ capital
/mol/ purchasing	/məwlsri/ sp. tree
/ju/ rivulet	/jəw/ barley
	/jo/ who [rel. pron.]
/tyr [gəya]/ passed across, got across	/ter/ pass [time]!
/tir/ arrow	/təyr/ swim

1.239. Phonetic Drill.

The instructor will dictate the following series of drill items for auditory recognition.
The student may write each dictated item down or point to its written form on the blackboard. Each student should then read each series aloud for the instructor to correct. The
series given below are only samples; the instructor may construct others from the drill
material as the need arises.

1. syl   mil   cil   bir   myl   ser   bəyr   ber   təyr

2. ələm   kəTna   Dar   cər   mar   nər   aməd   kar   əndhi   əməd

3. dhul   pwr   cwl   mol   jəw   sukh   jo   bhuna   məwlsri   ju

4. ādhi   pil   ser   əndhi   kər   təyr   nykalna   aməd   cwl

5. swr   ter   səyr   bhwna   mər   ber   nar   Dar   sikh   aləm   sykh

1.300. ANALYSIS

1.301. Sentence Patterns.

The basic pattern for declarative sentences is:

SUBJECT	PREDICATE (VERB)	
mǝy	hū.	I am.
vw	hǝy.	That is [it].

This pattern is also used to express English "there is," "there are":

ek ǝmrikǝn	hǝy.	There is an American.

When "there" means "in that place," however, Urdu has a locative adverb equivalent.

Equivalential or copulative sentences are expressed by a similar pattern. The predicate complement precedes the verb. The pattern is the same whether the complement is a noun (e.g. "doctor" in "He is a doctor.") or an adjective (e.g. "pleasing" in "Urdu is pleasing."):

SUBJECT	PREDICATE		
	COMPLEMENT	VERB	
vw	DakTǝr	hǝy.	He is a doctor.
mera nam	ysmyth	hǝy.	My name is Smith.
wrdu	pǝsǝnd	hǝy.	Urdu is pleasing.

The negative form of the simple Subject-Verb sentence is:

SUBJECT	NEGATIVE	VERB	
vw	nǝhī	hǝy*	That is not [it].

*The verb is optionally omitted.

The negative form of the Subject-Complement-Verb sentence is:

SUBJECT	COMPLEMENT	NEGATIVE	
mera nam	ysmyth	nǝhī.	My name is not Smith.
vw	pǝsǝnd	nǝhī.	That is not pleasing.

Some form of the verb "to be" (/hǝy/, /hǝy/, etc.) may indeed be added after the negative, but this gives a somewhat emphatic connotation. /nǝhī/ alone is generally sufficient for "is not."

Optional temporal and locative elements are rather free in order of occurrence. A very frequent sequence is as follows:

SUBJECT	(TEMPORAL)	(LOCATIVE)	(COMPLEMENT)	VERB
vw	ek sal se	hǝspǝtal mē	DakTǝr	hǝy.

He has been [lit. is] a doctor in the hospital for one year.

The negative form requires /nǝhī/ after the Complement and (generally) omits the verb:

mera ghǝr	yǝhā se	dur	nǝhī.

My house is not far from here.

The order of words for questions is THE SAME as for declarative sentences. There are two main types of question pattern:

(1) A statement pattern with a final rising intonation contour. This may be sub-

divided into:

    (1a) A statement pattern with only a final rising intonation to mark it as a question:

        /ap əmrikən hə̄y?/   Are you an American?

        /vw DakTər hə̄y?/ Is he a doctor?

    (1b) A statement pattern preceded by /kya/ "what?" and ending with a final rising intonation:

        /kya, wrdu pəsənd həy?/ Is Urdu pleasing?

        /kya, ap bhi yunyvərsyTi mē hə̄y?/ Are you also in the University?

  (2) A statement pattern containing some interrogative word or phrase. In a normal (i.e. not emphatic, sarcastic, etc.) question of this type, there is no final rising intonation (cf. English "What is that?" which has the same pitch pattern as "I did that."). The interrogative word or phrase usually precedes the verb.

        /ap ka nam kya həy./ What is your name?

        /ap pakystan mē kəb se hə̄y./ How long have you been in Pakistan?

If the interrogative word is an adjective, however, it precedes the noun or noun phrase which it modifies. /kya/ "what?" may be both an adjective and an independent interrogative, and thus the following order is also found.

        /ap ka kya nam həy./ What is your name? [Exactly the same in meaning as /ap ka nam kya həy./]

Examples containing an interrogative word or phrase end in /./ rather than /?/ although they are semantically questions. /./ marks a falling and fading final intonation contour, while /?/ shows a final pitch rise. These symbols are thus not "just punctuation" but indicate something important about the pronunciation of the sentence. Intonation patterns cannot be fully illustrated by such symbols, however, and the student should carefully copy the instructor's speech and spend as much time as possible with the tape recorder.

As a final note, it should be pointed out that Urdu--like all languages--abounds in "partial sentences": single words, phrases, groups of phrases, or whole clauses which do not make "complete grammatical sentences" but which are proper and idiomatic within the context. It is only necessary to learn which fragments can occur as "partial sentences" in Urdu and which cannot. For example, when an English speaker asks "Who knows John?" he may hear "I do." as the response, in which both "John" and "know" are understood from context. In Urdu, such a response is not possible--at least the subject and the verb must be present (i.e. "I know."). Urdu, however, permits the omission of a subject previously mentioned in the context. Sentences like the following are common:

        /hā, bəhwt pəsənd həy./ Yes, [it] is very pleasing.

        /DakTər həy./ [He] is a doctor.

        /nəhī̆ həy./ [It] is not.

1.302. Word Order Within the Noun Phrase.

Adjectives precede their nouns:

        /ek əmrikən/ an American [or: one American]

Possessive adjectives or phrases precede the noun and also precede any adjective:

/mera nam/   my name

/ap ka ghər/   your house

/ap ka ek məkan/   one house of yours [lit. your one house]

1.303. Postpositions.

Where English employs "prepositions" which precede the noun, Urdu has "post-positions" which follow it. The last two examples in 1.302 contain the postposition /ka/ "of" (or "'s", as in "house's"). Others are:

/pakystan mẽ/   in Pakistan

/larəns roD pər/   on Lawrence Road

/kəb se/   from when? Or:

/kəhã se/   from where?

1.304. Pronouns and the Verb "to be."

So far, the student has been introduced to the following:

PRONOUN	VERB	
mẽy	hũ	I am
ap	hɛ̃y	you [honorific] are [sg. or pl.]
vw	həy	that [he, she, it] is
vw	hɛ̃y	those [they] are

Plural pronouns and verbs are often used in Urdu to refer to a single person as a mark of respect. /vw hɛ̃y/ may thus also mean "he [she] is." /ap hɛ̃y/ "you are" may be similarly employed for the singular or the plural. The following sentence is grammatically ambiguous but would be clear from the context:

/vw DakTər hɛ̃y./   He [she, they] is [are] doctor[s].

The singular form should never be employed when speaking about someone who is present and whose status commands respect within the society. To say /vw DakTər həy./ about a person who is present is quite impolite. This form may indeed be used when speaking about someone who is absent, but even then the plural is considered better.

The most honorific and polite way of speaking of a third person who is present is to employ /ap/ as a special sort of third person pronoun. Thus:

/ap DakTər hɛ̃y./   He [she] is a doctor.

The reference of /ap/ must thus be made clear from the context.

Other pronouns, not yet introduced, include:

PRONOUN	VERB	
tu	həy	thou art
twm	ho	you [nonhonorific] are
həm	hɛ̃y	we are

/tu/ is almost obsolete, like English "thou." It is now used only when addressing God, small children, people of very low status (e.g. sweepers), one's beloved, or persons one wishes to insult. The student should avoid this form.

/twm/ is used to servants, persons of lower status, children, close family members of inferior age or status, etc. It also need not be memorised as yet.

Possessive pronouns are grammatically a type of adjective. Some have a special form (e. g. /mera/ "my" but /məy/ "I"); others have a special "oblique" form followed by /ka/ "of" (see Units II and III); and one has no special form but occurs directly before /ka/: /ap ka/ "your [honorific]. "

1.305. Demonstratives and the Article.

Urdu has no exact equivalent of the English articles "the" and "a." Definiteness and indefiniteness are specified either by a demonstrative (a type of adjective) or by a numeral (also an adjective):

/vw əmrikən/ that [the] American
/ek əmrikən/ one [an] American

/vw/ and /ek/ emphasise the definiteness or indefiniteness of the noun. Many Urdu sentences seem to contain an ambiguity which is not really there, since the meaning is almost always clear from context. E. g.

/vw DakTər həy. / He [she] is a doctor.

He [she] is the doctor.

They are doctors.

They are the doctors.

1.400. SUPPLEMENTARY VOCABULARY

1.401. Supplementary Vocabulary.

This section will be used to present further vocabulary items which can be fitted into the grammatical patterns of the Unit without difficulty. Further members of grammatical sets, numerals, nouns and adjectives semantically related to items presented elsewhere in the Unit, etc. will be introduced here. Since these items will be used freely in the exercises of the Unit in which they are introduced (and also in following Units), they should be treated as an integral part of the student's vocabulary.

ə̄grez	Englishman
car	four
dəftər	office
məkan	house, residential building
pakystani	Pakistani [noun or adj.]
pāc	five
tin	three

1.402. Supplementary Exercise I.

The form of this exercise is discussed in the introduction to Sec. 1.500.

1. mera məkan larəns roD pər   nəmbər do həy
                                  number one
                                  number three
                                  number five
                                  number four

2. kya, ap əmrikən hə̄y?
            Englishman
            Pakistani

3. mə̄y ek sal se   pakystan mē   hū.
        from three years[1] in the university
        from five years   in the office
        from four years   in America

[1]Translate "from three years," etc. as "from three year."

22

1.500. VOCABULARY AND GRAMMAR DRILL

Exercises are based upon the sentence patterns and grammatical constructions introduced in the Units. The vocabulary of the exercises will include items from the Conversation and Supplementary Vocabulary sections (plus items from these sections of preceding Units). Words used in the Phonetics section or employed casually in examples in the Analysis section will not be included.

Nine basic types of exercise will be employed (plus reading and writing drills in those Units dealing with the Urdu script), although all of the types will not be used in any single Unit by any means.

1. Substitution. The instructor will slowly read the pattern sentence two or three times and then say it again at normal speed with the proper intonation pattern. Each student will then in turn take one of the sets of English substitutions, translate it into Urdu, and repeat the pattern sentence with the new item in place of the original underlined portion. The sentence should then be drilled for fluency. The main object of this type of exercise is vocabulary practice.

2. Transformation. The instructor explains the grammatical or syntactic change desired, works one example on the blackboard, and then pronounces a pattern sentence. The student repeats the pattern sentence and then repeats it again with the desired alteration(s). Mastery of the grammatical apparatus is the object of this type of exercise.

3. Fill the Blanks. This type will be occasionally employed as a means of checking on the student's command of such grammatical points as adjective-noun agreement, subject-verb agreement, etc.

4. Multiple Choice. The instructor will read the pattern sentence to the student and then read the various choices at normal speed. The student should insert the proper choice and repeat the sentence. When a choice of Urdu statements is given as possible responses to a given context, the student should repeat the correct one (i. e. not just reply, "The second one is correct. ").

5. Variation. Each set of sentences consists of model sentences followed by variations using different vocabulary and varying expansions of one or more of the tactic blocks. Later on, this type of exercise will also include pattern sentences showing variations in usage, idiom, etc. The goals of this type of exercise include easy recognition of expansions of basic "tactic blocks," vocabulary drill, and practice with the semantic range of individual items. Each model and its variations should be drilled for fluency and verbally translated into idiomatic English.

6. Translation. This may consist of (a) sets of English sentences to be translated into Urdu, (b) sets of Urdu sentences to be rendered into English, or (c) sets of difficult Urdu sentences with a following English translation. The student should attempt to translate this latter type from English to Urdu and from Urdu to English verbally, after having once understood the grammatical and semantic difficulties of the sentence.

7. Response. The instructor asks the question at normal speed, and the student

should reply with a full Urdu sentence. Although answers to the questions may be prepared at home, the student should not read these from a written script. The instructor may, however, wish to assign the writing of answers to these questions as homework.

8. Conversation Practice. This type consists of one or more dialogues in Urdu using the materials given in the Conversation and Supplementary Vocabulary sections (plus those of any preceding Units) as a basis. The student should listen to these on a tape recorder, going through them several times with the prepared script and then trying to listen for comprehension alone without the text. The instructor should check on comprehension by asking questions (at first in English and later in Urdu) about the content of these dialogues.

9. Conversation Stimulus. The student should prepare his own brief conversations based on the material of the Unit and preceding Units. Later on, the student may be asked to prepare and memorise short dialogues (two or three students to a group) and present them to the class as a sort of play for the other students' comprehension practice. The instructor may also ask two or more students in class to use the material in the exercise as the basis for an impromptu dialogue.

1.501. Substitution.

1. kya, ap əmrikən hə̃y?
         doctor
         professor
         Englishman

2. kya, wrdu pəsənd həy?
         Pakistan
         America
         your work
         that hospital
         my house

3. ap ka kam pakystan mẽ kya həy.
             on Lawrence Road
             in America
             in [the] hospital
             in [the] university

4. ap pakystan mẽ kəb se hə̃y.
    in Lahore
    here
    in America
    on Lawrence Road
    in [the] house

5. mə̃y ek sal se yəhã hū.
    from two year[s]
    from three year[s]

24

6. mera məkan   yəhã se   nəzdik   həy.

the university	from here	very near
your house	from [the] hospital	far
America	from Pakistan	very far
that house	from Lawrence Road	near

7. ap ka kam   pakystan mẽ   kya   həy.

your house	in Lahore	where?
he	in America	from when?

8. wrdu   bəhwt pəsənd   həy.

America	[is] not
[the] university	is
that house	[is] not
my work	is

9. ap ka ghər   yəhã lahəwr mẽ   kəhã həy.

your office	in New York
[the] university	on Lawrence Road
your hospital	in Lahore

10. vw məkan   dur   nəhĩ.

my office	very near
your hospital	very far
New York	pleasing

1.502. Transformation.

Make the subject and the verb agree in number:

1. mə̃y   əmrikən   hũ.

he	is
you [honorific]	are

2. vw profesər ek sal se yəhã   hə̃y.

I	am
you [honorific] also	are
that doctor	is
he [she, it]	is
they	are

1.503. Response.

1. ap pakystan mẽ kəb se hə̃y.
2. ap ka ysme šərif kya həy.
3. kya, ap ka ghər nəzdik həy?
4. ap ka kam yəhã kya həy.
5. kya, ap ə̃grez hə̃y?

6. kya, ap do sal se lahəwr mẽ hə̄y?
7. vw həspətal dəftər se dur həy?
8. kya, pakystan pəsənd həy?
9. ap ka məkan əmrika mẽ kəhā həy.
10. kya, ap bhi dəftər mẽ hə̄y?

1.504. Conversation Practice.

Dr. Rəhim meets Mr. Smith.

R: adab ərz, jənab. ap ka ysme šərif kya həy.
S: mera nam ysmyth həy. kya, ap bhi yunyvərsyTi mẽ hə̄y?
R: ji nəhī̃. mə̄y əmrikən həspətal mẽ DakTər hū̃. kya, ap profesər hə̄y?
S: ji hā. mə̄y ek sal se lahəwr mẽ hū̃.
R: kya, lahəwr pəsənd həy?
S: ji hā.

Mr. Smith stops a passerby on the road.

S: adab ərz, jənab. əmrikən həspətal kəhā həy.
P: əmrikən həspətal bəhwt nəzdik həy. yunyvərsyTi se nəzdik həy.
S: myhrbani, jənab.
P: kya, wrdu pəsənd həy?
S: ji hā.
P: ap ka ghər yəhā kəhā həy.
S: vw larəns roD pər həy. yəhā se bəhwt dur nəhī̃.

1.505. Conversation Stimulus.

1. Mr. Smith meets Dr. Rəhim. He greets him and asks how he is. Dr. Rəhim thanks him and asks how Mr. Smith is. Mr. Smith replies, "Thank you." Dr. Rəhim then asks what Mr. Smith's work in Pakistan is. Mr. Smith replies that he is a professor in the university. Mr. Smith then asks Dr. Rəhim how long he has lived in Lahore. He replies that he has been here for three years.

2. Mr. əziz meets Mr. Smith. He greets him and asks how he is. Mr. Smith replies with thanks. Mr. əziz asks where Mr. Smith's house is. Mr. Smith replies that it is number two. It is on Lawrence Road. It is not far from the university. Mr. əziz replies, "Thank you."

1.600. VOCABULARY

This section includes only those items given in the Conversation section and the Supplementary Vocabulary section (i.e. omitting words given as examples in the Phonetics section or in the Analysis section).

,adab ərz	greetings
ap	you [honorific]
əmrika	America
əmrikən	American
ə̃grez	Englishman
bəhwt	much, many, very
bhi	also, too, even
car	four
dəftər	office
do	two
dur	far, distant, distance
DakTər	doctor
ek	one, a, an
ghər	house, home
hā	yes
həspətal	hospital
həy	is
hə̃y	are
hū	am
jənab	sir
ji	term of respect [and also interrogation]
ka	of, -'s
kam	work, job, task
kəb	when?
kəhā	where?
kya	what? [Also question-introducing particle]
lahəwr	ʟahore (a city in West Pakistan)
larəns roD	Lawrence Road
məkan	house, residential building
mə̃y	I
mera	my
mē	in
myhrbani	kindness [thank you; please]
myzaj	disposition
nam	name
nəhī̃	no, not, [is] not
nəmbər	number

27

nəzdik	near
niw yark [or /niw yəwrk/]	New York
pakystan	Pakistan
pakystani	Pakistani [both noun and adj.]
pāc	five
pər	on, at
pəsənd	pleasing
profesər	professor
sal	year
se	from, with, by
šərif	noble, honourable, gentle
tin	three
vw [slow speech /vwh/]	that, those; he, she, it, they
wrdu	Urdu [both noun and adj.]
yəhā	here
ysm	noun, name [used as "name" in /ysme šərif/ "name [honorific]"]
yunyvərsyTi [or /yunyvərsTi/]	university

Three proper names have also been introduced: /əziz/, /rəhim/, and /ysmyth/. Even though the first two may occur as meaningful words ("beloved, friend" and "compassionate"), they will not be counted as vocabulary items.

A modern commercial building on the Mall, Lahore.

UNIT TWO

2.000. CONVERSATION

Mr. Smith asks the way to Dr. Rəhim's house from a passerby.

    sir, gentleman   sahəb

    [you, he, we, they] know[s]   jante hə̃y

S: Do you know Mr. Rəhim's house?   kya, ap rəhim sahəb ka ghər jante hə̃y?

    in front, opposite   [ke] samne

P: Yes, it is in front.   ji hã. vw samne həy.

    few, little (in quantity)   kəm

    [I] understand   səməjhta hū

S: I understand [only a] little Urdu.   mə̃y wrdu kəm səməjhta hū.

    there   vəhã

    that, he, she, it [OS]   ws

    big [MOS, MNP, MOP]   bəRe

    blue [MOS, MNP, MOP]   nile

    of, -'s [MOS, MNP, MOP]   ke

    ahead, in front   [ke] age

P: It is there. It is ahead of that big blue   vəhã həy. vw ws bəRe nile məkan ke age
house.   həy.

    good, well [MNS]   əccha

S: Very good. Thanks.   bəhwt əccha. myhrbani.

Mr. Smith knocks on Dr. Rəhim's door, and a servant answers.

    this, he, she, it [OS]   ys

    [you, he, we, they] live[s]   rəhte həy

S: Does Mr. Rəhim live in this house?   kya, rəhim sahəb ys ghər mẽ rəhte həy?

    inside   [ke] əndər

Sr: Yes, he's inside.   ji hã, vw əndər həy.

    who? [NS, NP]   kəwn

R: [from inside] Who is it?   kəwn sahəb həy.

    to meet, get, meeting [+ /se/ = with]   mylna

    [you, they, we, he] want[s]   cahte həy

Sr: A gentleman wants to see you. [Lit.   ek sahəb ap se mylna cahte həy.
wants to meet with you]

    his, her, their, of that, of those [NS]   wn ka

R: What is his name?   wn ka nam kya həy.

S: Sir, I am [Mr.] Smith. I'd like to see   jənab, mə̃y ysmyth hū. ap se mylna həy.
you. [Lit. It is to meet with you.]

    just now   əbhi

    [I] come   ata hū

R: All right, I'm coming. [Lit. I just now   əccha, mə̃y əbhi ata hū.
come.]

In the sitting room with Dr. Rəhim's three sons.

this, these, he, she, it, they [N] yy[h]

my [MOS, MNP, MOP] mere

boys [MNP] ləRke

all səb

big, large [MNS] bəRa

boy [MNS] ləRka

R: These are my three boys. This is the biggest boy. [Lit. This from all big boy is.] yy mere tin ləRke hɛ̃y. yy səb se bəRa ləRka həy.

[he] does kərta həy

S: What does he do? yy kya kərta həy.

college kalyj

[he] reads, studies pəRhta həy

R: He studies in [a] college. yy kalyj mɛ̃ pəRhta həy.

who, which? [OS] kys

Government College gəwrnmənT kalyj

S: In which college does he study? Does he study in Government College? yy kys kalyj mɛ̃ pəRhta həy. kya, gəwrnmənT kalyj mɛ̃ pəRhta həy?

Islamia College yslamia kalyj

R: No, he doesn't study in Government College. He studies in Islamia College. ji nəhĩ, yy gəwrnmənT kalyj mɛ̃ nəhĩ pəRhta. yy yslamia kalyj mɛ̃ pəRhta həy.

every hər

day roz

morning swba [or /swbəh/ or /swbha/]

[I] go jata hũ

and əwr

evening šam

to [object marker; idiomatically: /šam ko/ "to evening" = "in the evening"] ko

brother bhai

[I] do, make kərta hũ

Eldest Son: I go to college every morning, and in the evening also [I] work in [my] brother's office. mɛ̃y hər roz swba kalyj jata hũ, əwr šam ko bhi bhai ke dəftər mɛ̃ kam kərta hũ.

second, other [MNS] dusra

[he] goes jata həy

first [MOS, MNP, MOP] pəhle

boy [MOS] ləRke

clever, intelligent hošyar

but məgər

R: This is my second [eldest] boy. He goes [to] the office. [He] is more intelligent than the first boy, but [he] doesn't study. [Lit. From the first boy [he] is intelligent ...] yy mera dusra ləRka həy. yy dəftər jata həy. pəhle ləRke se hošyar həy, məgər pəRhta nəhĩ.

small, little [in size] [MNS] choTa

third [MNS] tisra

32

school

R: This is my youngest [lit. than all small] and third boy. He goes to school.

his, her, its, their, of this, of these [NS]

S: Where is his school?

nearby, next to, at, having

behind, in back

Chartered Bank

R: [It] is near my office. [It] is behind the big hospital and in front of the Chartered Bank.

now

to go, going

[I] want

S: Now I'd like to go.

tomorrow, yesterday

dinner, food; to eat [MOS]

R: I want to invite you to dinner tomorrow. [Lit. I want to meet with you on dinner tomorrow.]

dinner, food; to eat [MNS]

time

S: What time is the dinner?

eight

o'clock [lit. struck]

R: Dinner is [at] eight o'clock.

God

protector, keeper, guardian [/xwda hafyz/ "God [be your] protector" = "Goodbye"]

S: Very well, sir. Goodbye.

R: Goodbye.

---

yskul

yy mera səb se choTa əwr tisra ləRka həy. yy yskul jata həy.

yn ka

yn ka yskul kəhã hey.

[ke] pas

[ke] piche

carTərD bə̃yk

mere dəftər ke pas həy. bəRe həspətal ke piche əwr carTərD bə̃yk ke samne həy.

əb

jana

cahta hū

əb mə̃y jana cahta hū.

kəl

khane

mə̃y kəl ap se khane pər mylna cahta hū.

khana

vəqt

khana kys vəqt həy.

aTh

bəje

khana aTh bəje həy.

xwda

hafyz

bəhwt əccha, jənab. xwda hafyz.

xwda hafyz.

2.100. WORD STUDY

2.101. /sahəb/ "sir, gentleman" has several uses: (1) as a term of address similar to /jənab/; (2) after proper names with a meaning something like "Mister": e.g.

/rəhim sahəb/ Mr. Rəhim

/ysmyth sahəb/ Mr. Smith

(3) in a similar construction after certain titles (some of which denote females): e.g.

/DakTər sahəb/ doctor

/raja sahəb/ king

/mem sahəb/ Mrs., lady [From English "Madame"; used only to or about married European women]

/mys sahəb/ Miss, lady [From English "Miss"; used only to or about unmarried European women, usually by servants or lower class people customarily having dealings with Europeans]

/begəm sahəb/ Madame, lady [Used mostly for non-European ladies of high status]

The terms /mem sahəb/ and /mys sahəb/ have a certain connotation of the servant quarters or of the old British-Indian order of society about them, and the term /mwhtəryma/ is used in the educated Urdu-speaking classes for any woman with whom one is on formal terms.

(4) /sahəb/ is also used as a noun meaning "gentleman": e.g.

/ek sahəb yəhā h͞əy./ There is a gentleman here.

2.102. Where one says "I meet him, " "I meet them, " etc., in Urdu one must say "I meet <u>with</u> him, " etc. "With" here is expressed by /se/. /mylna/ has several other important uses, including "to get, obtain, be mixed, be joined"; these will be discussed later.

2.103. /əbhi/ "just now" may be analysed as originally /əb/ "now" + an emphatic particle /hi/. The uses of the latter will be described in a later Unit.

2.104. /gəwrnmənT/ "government" is occasionally used as a common noun synonymous with the more generally employed Urdu word /hwkumət/. Some English-speaking educated speakers use /gəwrnmənT/ to refer to "The Government" (i.e. of Pakistan) and use /hwkumət/ to refer to "government" generally.

2.105. /hər roz swba/ "every morning" slightly emphasises "every"; just /roz swba/ would be enough for "daily each morning. " Many time words occur with no postposition (e.g. /swba/ "morning" or "in the morning"; /roz/ "day" or "daily"). Others idiomatically require a postposition (e.g. /šam ko/ "in the evening" --lit. "to evening"). Combinations of time words are very common. The student should be able to recognise the following:

/kəl šam ko/ tomorrow evening [Or "yesterday evening"]

/kəl swba/ tomorrow morning [Or "yesterday morning"]

/kəl aTh bəje/ tomorrow at eight o'clock [Or "yesterday at eight o'clock"]

/hər roz šam ko/ every evening

/hər sal/ every year

2.106. /əwr/ "and" connects two like elements (i.e. two words, two phrases, two clauses, etc.): e.g.

> /mɜ̃y əwr ap/ I and you [The first person comes first in Urdu; */ap əwr mɜ̃y/ "you and I" is not idiomatic]
>
> /bəRa məkan əwr choTa dəftər/ a big house and a small office.
>
> /mɜ̃y yskul jata hū, əwr vw bhi jata həy./ I go to school, and he also goes.

/əwr/ is also used as an adjective: it occurs before nouns with the meaning "another, other, a different" and sometimes "a further, another"; it is also found after nouns (still within the noun phrase) meaning "another, a further, one more." E.g.

> /ek əwr ləRka yəhā̃ həy./ There is another [a different] boy here.
>
> /ek ləRka əwr yəhā̃ həy./ There is another [a further] boy here.
>
> /ek əwr sal həy./ It's another year. [I.e. it is not the year you are talking about but another one]
>
> /mɜ̃y ek sal əwr rəhna cahta hū./ I want to stay one more year.

/əwr/ may also occur alone meaning "another" or "more," and in this usage it is also found with a plural suffix (/əwrõ/; see Unit IV): e.g.

> /mɜ̃y ap ko əwr deta hū./ I give you another. [Or: I give you more. The meaning will be clear from context.]

It also is used as a modifier before an adjective meaning something like "even...er": e.g.

> /əwr əccha/ even better

/əwr/ is also found in many combinations: e.g. /kwch əwr/ (or /əwr kwch/) "something else," /ek əwr/ "one more, another," /əwr kya/ "what else?" etc. E.g.

> /ek əwr jana cahta həy./ One more wants to go.

2.107. /kəl/ means "tomorrow" or "yesterday" depending upon the context and the tense of the accompanying verb. There are a few other time words which similarly have past or future reference: e.g. /pərsõ/ "day after tomorrow, day before yesterday," /ətərsõ/ "the third day past or to come," and /nərsõ/ "the fourth day past or to come."

2.108. /xwda hafyz/ "goodbye" may be used to persons of any religious community. /xwda/ "God" occurs alone and may be used to refer to either the Christian or Muslim concept of the Deity (it is not normally employed for a Hindu deity, however). /hafyz/ also occurs alone, but its main use is as a designation for someone who has committed the whole of the Holy Qwran to memory. The phrase /xwda hafyz/ should thus be considered a unit by the beginner.

2.200. PHONETICS

2.201. Nasalised Versus Oral Vowels.

As stated in Sec. 1.236, Urdu distinguishes between a set of vowels pronounced with the velic closed (the oral vowels) and a set of vowels pronounced with the velic open and with some of the air from the lungs passing out through the nose (the nasalised vowels). French contains a set of nasalised vowels (but not quite the same ones as Urdu): e. g. bon "good, " pain "bread, " un "one, " and banc "bench. " The contrast between nasalised and oral vowels is often a very difficult one for the English-speaking beginner to learn and maintain, since some dialects of English have no nasalised vowels at all, and other dialects tend to nasalise all of the vowels in various environments.

The following drill should be repeated over and over after the instructor or after a tape recording, as described in Sec. 1.238.

/kəhā/ said [msc. sg.]	/kəhā̃/ where?
/həy/ is	/hə̃y/ are
/ae/ might come [sg.]	/aẽ/ might come [pl.]
/ho/ [you nonhonorific] are	/hõ/ [you honorific] may be
/kəhi/ said [fem. sg.]	/kəhī̃/ somewhere, anywhere
/tanta/ draws, pulls [msc. sg.]	/tãta/ in series
/gae/ cow	/gaẽ/ cows
/ai/ came [fem. sg.]	/aī̃/ came [fem. pl.]
/həns/ goose	/hə̃s/ laugh!
/nac/ dance	/ãc/ feeling of heat
/thi/ was [fem. sg.]	/thī̃/ were [fem. pl.]
/gao/ sing!	/gaõ/ village
/doa/ prayer	/dhũā̃/ smoke
/cəlau/ common, ordinary	/cəlaũ/ I may cause to go
/jəhan/ world	/jəhā̃/ where
/ain/ law	/aī̃/ came [fem. pl.]
/xasa/ passable, good	/khā̃sa/ coughed [msc. sg.]
/kũara/ bachelor [common: /kũāra/]	/kũā̃/ well
/bəhwt/ much, many, very	/pəhw̃c/ arrive!
/vwhi/ that very one	/vəhī̃/ right there
/mə̃hga/ expensive	/mẽ/ in
	/mẽh/ rain
/səw/ one hundred	/gə̃w/ advantage, want, need
/ru/ face	/hũ̃/ am
/bhora/ crumb	/bhə̃wra/ sp. of insect
/jhoTa/ bull	/jhõTa/ swing

2.202. Phonetic Drill: Auditory Dictation.

Instructions are as given above in Sec. 1.239. Note that this drill contains a few further items besides those given in Sec. 2.201. The student should easily be able to distinguish these.

1. gao cəlau gaõ kūā səw ru gə̃w hū cəlao ho bhə̃wra

2. xasa kəha vəhā hə̃s kuara kūā tāta khãsa jəhan

3. ai aẽ aī ao aū aõ gə̃w gaõ gae gaī ain jhõTa

4. mə̃hga āc bəhwt hə̃s kəha həns pəhwc tanta mẽh

5. mẽ aẽ thi aī kəhī thī həy ae vwhi hə̃y vəhī

2.203. Vowel Clusters.

Urdu contains both diphthongs and vowel clusters: the former consist of a vowel + an offglide and are of the same duration as a single vowel (diphthongs include only /əy/ and /əw/); in a vowel cluster, on the other hand, each segment is given the same prominence as a full syllable. Clusters of two vowels are very common, and clusters of three or even four vowels are not unknown. Once the student has mastered the long-short and oral-nasal distinctions, no difficulty should be encountered with vowel clusters.

/ao/ come!

/cəlao/ cause to go!

/gao/ sing!

/ləkhnəu/ Lucknow

/chua/ touched [msc. sg.]

/ae/ may come [sg.]

/soe/ slept [msc. pl.]

/sia/ sewed [msc. sg.]
/aie/ please come

/bhai/ brother
/rai/ mustard
/bhaiõ/ brothers [obl.]

/ae/ may come [sg.]
/aẽ/ may come [pl.]

/cəlau/ common, ordinary
/cəlaū/ I may cause to go

/gaõ/ village
/gaū/ I may sing

/cəlau/ common, ordinary
/rəw/ tempo

/dhūā/ smoke
/kūā/ well

/aī/ came [fem. pl.]
/ain/ law

/soi/ slept [fem. sg.]
/soū/ I may sleep

/cīā/ tamarind seed
/soie/ please sleep
/chuie/ please touch

/rae/ opinion
/bhae/ liked, suited [msc. pl.]
/jhaRuõ/ brooms [obl.]

2.204. Phonetic Drill: Auditory Dictation.

1. soi   aie   cī̄a   aī̄   dhū̃ã   soe   aē̃   ain   rai   rae

2. ləkhnəu   gə̄w   gaõ   gaū   cəlao   cəlaū   bhaiõ   jhaRuõ

3. sia   chuie   soe   aē̃   ao   ae   chua   bhae   kū̃ã   gaõ

4. gao   soū   aē̃   rae   gə̄w   cī̄a   cəlaū   bhai   bhae

5. chua   chuie   ao   aī̄   ae   soe   soi   soū   gao   gaū

2.205. Auditory Dictation of Secs. 2.202 and 2.204.

1. ain   gao   bhaiõ   hə̄s   rəw   chua   tanta   jəhã   hū   ho

2. kəhi   thī̆   soe   tãta   hə̃y   kū̃ã   aē̃   gaõ   mə̃hga   gə̄w   jhoTa

3. kəhã   hə̄s   həns   khãsa   kuara   pəhw̃c   mẽ   cī̄a   rae

2.301. Sentence Patterns (Continued).

As was seen in Sec. 1.301, the Urdu sentence contains two major "building blocks": the subject and the predicate, usually in this order. Verbal sentences are also of this pattern:

SUBJECT	PREDICATE	
məy	jata hū.	I go.
vw	pəRhta həy.	He reads, studies.

The subject will consist of a pronoun or a noun phrase (or two or more pronouns or noun phrases connected by a conjunction such as /əwr/ "and"). Aside from the verb or verb phrase, the predicate may contain an adverb, a negative, and--in its expanded form-- an object, an indirect object, an object and an indirect object, two objects, etc.

Aside from these most basic "blocks," the sentence may also include temporal and locational words or phrases. The order of these elements within the sentence is rather free, but perhaps the commonest sequence is:

SUBJECT	TEMPORAL	LOCATIONAL	VERB
məy	hər roz	kalyj	jata hū.
I go to college every day.			
vw	šam ko	yskul mẽ	pəRhta həy.
He studies in school in the evening.			

(The object and the indirect object will be discussed in a later Unit.)

The above order may be modified somewhat, due to various factors of style, emphasis, etc. The position of the verbal phrase at the end of the sentence is almost invariable, and the subject usually occurs in first position in a normal, declarative sentence. Temporals and locatives are, however, rather more free. Two considerations may be mentioned here:

(1) A slightly stronger degree of emphasis is obtained by bringing a given tactic block closer to the verb: e.g.

/šam ko yəhā məy kam kərta hū./ I work here in the evening. [/məy/ will also carry slightly more stress.]

/məy yəhā šam ko kam kərta hū./ I work here in the evening. [Slight emphasis on "evening"]

(2) A tactic block which refers to some previously mentioned or queried context may be brought to the beginning of the sentence as a kind of "bridge": e.g. the reply to "What do you do here in the evening?" might be:

/šam ko məy yəhā kam kərta hū./ In the evening I work here. [The speaker establishes a connection with the question by placing /šam ko/ first.]

Similarly, in reply to "What do you do here?":

/yəhā məy šam ko kam kərta hū./ Here I work in the evening.

A negative is usually placed directly before the verb. If the affirmative form of the verb contains some present tense form of the auxiliary "to be" (/həy/, etc.), the auxiliary normally WILL NOT occur in the corresponding negative: e.g. /jata həy/ "[he] goes" but /nəhī jata/ "[he] does not go." Further examples:

/vw hər roz yskul nəhĩ jata./ He doesn't go [to] school every day.
[/nəhĩ jata həy/ is unidiomatic.]

/mə̄y šam ko yəhã kam nəhĩ kərta./ I don't work here in the evening.

A slight degree of emphasis (usually contrasting the negative sentence with some accompanying affirmative one) is obtained by placing the negative word after the verb. This is rather commonly found with a negative clause after /məgər/ "but" and various other conjunctions which call for a contrast. E.g.

/vw hošyar həy, məgər pəRhta nəhĩ./ He is intelligent, but [he] doesn't study.

/vw jata nəhĩ!/ He doesn't go! [In spite of your insistence that he does]

2.302. Interrogative Order.

If an interrogative word or phrase occurs, it is usually placed just before the verb or verb phrase. The order, however, is rather free. As a rough generalisation, one may say that an interrogative usually follows a temporal element, almost always follows the subject, precedes or follows locational or object elements, and always precedes the verb. Where a noun object is closely bound to the verb (the "complex verb" construction, to be more thoroughly discussed in a later Unit), the interrogative always precedes this object: e.g.

/ap roz kəb yskul jate hə̄y./ When do you go to school each day? [Or:]

/ap roz yskul kəb jate hə̄y./ [Same meaning. No other word order combinations are possible with this sentence.]

/ap šam ko kəhã kam kərte hə̄y./ Where do you work in the evening?
[/kam kərna/ "to work"--lit. "to do work"--is an example of a complex verb formation: a noun or adjective element closely bound to a following verb, which serves to "verbalise" the idea contained in the substantive: i.e. instead of having two separate words "to rely" and "reliance," as English does, Urdu has only "reliance" and a complex verb formation "to make [do] reliance."]

It must be remembered that, if the interrogative word is an adjective, however, it precedes the noun which it modifies. See Sec. 1.301. E.g.

/ap kys yskul mē pəRhte hə̄y./ In which school do you study? [No other word order possible]

/ap šam ko kya kam kərte hə̄y./ What work do you do in the evening?
[/kya/ "what?" here is an adjective.]

If the sentence is negative, an interrogative will usually occur directly before the negative word:

/vw ləRka hər roz kəhã nəhĩ jata!/ Where doesn't that boy go every day? [Ironic]

When the verbal phrase contains an infinitive, an interrogative will occur before it. If the infinitive is the verbal portion of a complex verb formation, however, the interrogative will normally precede the accompanying noun or adjective element.

/vw ghər kəb jana cahta həy./ When does he want to go home?

/ap se kəhã mylna həy./ Where is [it] [necessary] to meet you. [= Where should [I] meet you?]

/vw kəhã kam kərna cahta həy./ Where does he want to work? [/kam kərna/ is a complex verb and is treated as a unit.]

40

2.303. Order Within the Noun Phrase.

The noun phrase has the following order:

POSSESSIVE	DEMONSTRATIVE INTERROGATIVE NUMERAL	ADJECTIVE	NOUN
mere bhai ka	vw	hošyar	ləRka
that intelligent boy of my brother's			
ws ka	kəwnsa	əmrikən	profesər
which American professor of his?			
mere bhai ka	ek	bəRa	ləRka
one big boy of my brother's			
mere profesər ke	do	choTe	ləRke
my professor's two small boys			

2.304. The Comparative and Superlative

There is no Urdu equivalent of English "-er" in "smarter" or "-est" in "smartest."
Instead, the Urdu speaker says "X is smart from Y" and "X is from all smart" (or "X is from all Y's smart"). E.g.

/yy ləRka ws ləRke se hošyar həy./ This boy is smarter than that boy.
[Lit. This boy from that boy is intelligent.]

/yy ləRka səb se hošyar həy./ This boy is the smartest. [Lit. This boy is from all intelligent.]

/mera məkan wn ke məkan se choTa həy./ My house is smaller than their house.

/mera məkan səb se choTa həy./ My house is the smallest.

/ap ka kalyj mere kalyj se dur həy./ Your college is farther than my college.

/ap ka kalyj səb se dur həy./ Your college is the furthest.

2.305. Masculine Nouns.

Two types of noun have been introduced.
Type I:
/ek ghər həy./ There is a [one] house.
/ek ghər se/ from a [one] house
/do ghər hə̃y./ There are two house[s]
Type II:
/ek ləRka həy./ There is a [one] boy.
/ek ləRke se/ from a [one] boy
/do ləRke hə̃y./ There are two boys.

Both /ghər/ "house" and /ləRka/ "boy" are masculine nouns. They are examples of the two major masculine noun classes.

As in some European languages, there are two grammatical genders in Urdu:

41

masculine and feminine. This division has a partial basis in reality, since male persons and animals are masculine, and female persons and animals are feminine. The vast majority of nouns, however, refer to objects which have no real sex gender, and these are arbitrarily classed as masculine or feminine also. Some nouns may be treated either as masculine or feminine, depending upon the sex of the referent: e.g. /DakTər/ "doctor" may be treated as a masculine noun when it refers to a male doctor and as a feminine when used for a female doctor. There are also many nouns having disputed genders, differing in usage from dialect to dialect, region to region, social class to social class, or even from person to person: e.g. /qələm/ "pen," which is masculine in one area and feminine in others.

There are two numbers: singular and plural. Most nouns may occur both as singular and plural, but various abstract nouns, collective nouns, etc. are only found in singular form. In some cases the plural is marked by a suffix (and the singular either by another suffix or by no suffix), and in those cases where there is no overt plural marker (see Type I above), an agreeing adjective (or the verb, where the noun is the subject governing the verb) will often show both gender and number.

There are three cases, called "nominative," "oblique," and "vocative." The last of these is of comparatively little importance. These are not true "cases" in the Latin sense, showing the use of the noun in the sentence (e.g. the "nominative" case used for a subject, the "accusative" case for an object, the "dative" for an indirect object, etc.); instead, to be quite brief, the Urdu "oblique case" is used for any noun which is followed by a postposition (e.g. /ek ghər se/ "from a house," /ek ləRke se/ from a boy"), and the "nominative case" is employed wherever the noun is NOT followed by a postposition (e.g. /ek ləRka həy/ "There is a boy," /do ghər hɛ̄y./ "There are two houses."). Some apparent exceptions to this simple rule will be discussed below.

Some abbreviations may prove useful at this point:

"M" = "masculine"
"F" = "feminine"
"N" = "nominative"
"O" = "oblique"
"V" = "vocative"
"S" = "singular"
"P" = "plural"

The total pattern for the Urdu masculine noun class is thus:

MNS   MNP
MOS   MOP
[MVS   MVP]

Reverting to the examples of Type I and Type II masculine nouns given at the beginning of this Section, it can be seen that some of the forms are at least outwardly "the same." The actual pattern is: ["∅" = "no suffix"]

	TYPE I			TYPE II	
MNS	∅	/ghər/	MNS	a	/ləRka/
MOS	∅	/ghər/	MOS	e	/ləRke/
MNP	∅	/ghər/	MNP	e	/ləRke/
MOP	given later		MOP	given later	

Type I nouns may end in any sound, including all consonants and vowels. Type II nouns, however, end only in /a/ or /ā/ in the MNS. In other words, the stem of a Type I noun may occur alone without any further suffix as a word, while the stem of a Type II noun is obligatorily followed by one of the gender-case-number suffixes given above.

Type I masculine nouns will be indicated in the vocabulary as "M1"; Type II masculine nouns will be denoted by "M2." A similar class division will be seen in Unit III for feminine nouns.

2.306. Masculine Adjectives.

Adjectives follow a pattern very similar to that of the nouns. Again, there are two types:

	TYPE I			TYPE II	
MNS	∅	/hošyar/	MNS	a	/bəRa/
MOS	∅	/hošyar/	MOS	e	/bəRe/
MNP	∅	/hošyar/	MNP	e	/bəRe/
MOP	∅	/hošyar/	MOP	e	/bəRe/

Like the nouns, adjectives of Type I may end in any sound, but Type II adjectives must end in one of the above suffixes (or in /ā/ - /ē/). In the vocabulary "A1" will stand for "Type I adjective" and "A2" for "Type II adjective." Some examples should make the agreement of adjectives and nouns clear:

> /mera pəhla ləRka hošyar həy./ My first [i.e. firstborn] boy is intelligent. [/mera/ and /pəhla/ are A2, agreeing with /ləRka/, which is M2. /hošyar/, however, is A1 and shows no agreement. Compare:]

> /mera pəhla ləRka choTa həy./ My first boy is small. [Here /choTa/ is A2 and agrees with /ləRka/.]

> /mere pəhle ləRke choTe hɛ̃y./ My first boys are small. [/ləRke/ is MNP, and the adjectives agree.]

> /mere pəhle ləRke se/ from my first boy [/ləRke/ is MOS here because of the postposition /se/; the adjectives are thus also MOS.]

> /mere hošyar ləRke se/ from my intelligent boy [/hošyar/ is A1 and does not show agreement, although /mere/ does.]

> /mere ghər se/ from my house [/ghər/ is M1 and thus has no overt marker to show that it is MOS; /mere/, however, is A2 and thus indicates gender-case-number.]

2.307. The Postposition /ka/ "of."

The postposition /ka/ is the commonest means of indicating possession. It functions exactly like a Type II adjective (see above), ending in /a/ if the following noun is nominative and in /e/ if the noun is oblique or plural. It also has a feminine form (see Unit III). Since /ka/ is a postposition, any noun or noun phrase preceding it will be oblique. E. g.

> /mere ləRke ka dəftər həy. / [It] is the office of my boy. [Here /ka/ is MNS because it agrees with /dəftər/; /mere ləRke/, however, is MOS because it is followed by a postposition.]

If /dəftər/ in the preceding example were itself to be followed by a postposition, then /ləRka ka/ would have to become MOS: /ləRke ke/. E. g.

> /vw mere ləRke ke dəftər mē hǎy. / He is in my boy's office.

> /vw mere ləRke ke dəftər se jata həy. / He goes from my boy's office.

The succession of adjectives and adjectival possessive phrases may be expanded almost at will:

> /mere ləRke ke bəRe dəftər ka nila məkan yəhā həy. / The blue building of my boy's office is here. [/mere ləRke/ is MOS because it is followed by a postposition; /ke/ is MOS because it modifies a MOS noun; /bəRe dəftər/ is MOS because it is followed by a postposition; /ka/ is MNS because it modifies a MNS noun.]

> /vw mere ləRke ke bəRe dəftər ke nile məkan se jata həy. / He goes from the blue building of my boy's big office. [Here the second /ke/ is MOS because it modifies a MOS noun; /nile məkan/ is MOS because it is followed by a postposition.]

/ka/ is used with all nouns, demonstratives, interrogatives, etc. and also with some pronouns. A few possessive pronouns have special forms, however, as was seen in Unit I. These are: /mera/ A2 "my," /tera/ A2 "thy," /həmara/ A2 "our," and /twmhara/ A2 "your [nonhonorific]."

2.308. Compound Postpositions.

Nouns (etc.) + /ka/ and the possessive pronouns occur also before a class of items called compound postpositions. In fact, these are simply a sort of locative substantive which must be "possessed" by the noun or pronoun. Instead of "behind me," therefore, the Urdu speaker is in effect saying "my behind[ness]." E. g.

> /nile məkan ke age/ ahead of the blue building.

> /mere dəftər ke pas/ near my office

> /bəRe həspətal ke piche/ behind the big hospital

> /ghər ke əndər/ inside the house

> /ghər ke nəzdik/ near the house [much the same as /ghər ke pas/]

> /ghər ke samne/ opposite to, facing, in front of the house

Examples of the possessive pronouns with compound postposition:

> /mere age/ in front of, ahead of me

> /ap ke əndər/ inside of you [honorific]

> /həmare nəzdik/ near us

> /twmhare piche/ behind you [nonhonorific]

> /mere pas/ near me [Also used to express "I have."]

> /həmare samne/ facing, opposite to, in front of us

Note that the compound postpositions are always treated as if they were OBLIQUE nouns, and they are thus preceded by the oblique form of the possessive pronoun or by /ke/

(rather than /ka/). One cannot say */mera age/ or */ləRke ka samne/.

Elements included in the compound postposition group are of morphologically heteroge-
neous origins. Some are oblique nouns: e.g. /samna/ M2 is used as a noun meaning
"confrontation"; /picha/ M2 means "following, pursuit, rear, " etc. Others are adjectives:
e.g. /nəzdik/ A1 "near. " Still others are locative adverbs: e.g. /əndər/ Adv "inside";
several items are found only in the compound postposition construction: e.g. /lie/ "for. "

The difference between compound and simple postpositions must be carefully noted: the
form of a noun or pronoun occurring before the former is always oblique possessive; the
form occurring before a simple postposition, on the other hand, is oblique only. Contrast:

/ləRke ke piche/ behind the boy

/ləRke se/ from the boy [Never */ləRke ke se/!]

Many of the compound postpositions may be employed in sentences translatable with an
English locative adverb or with a predicate adjective:

/vw ghər age həy./ That house is ahead.

/vw ləRka əndər həy./ That boy is inside.

/vw ghər nəzdik həy./ That house is nearby.

/vw ghər pas həy./ That house is nearby. [Same as the last but somewhat less common.]

/vw ghər piche həy./ That house is behind.

/vw ghər samne həy./ That house is in front.

2.309. The Demonstratives.

English distinguishes a series of third person pronouns ("he, " "she, " "it, " and "they")
and a set of demonstratives ("this, " "that, " "these, " and "those"). In Urdu, the two
demonstratives, /yy(h)/ and /vw(h)/, serve both functions. Paradigms are:

/yy(h)/ "this"		/vw(h)/ "that"	
MNS	yy(h)	MNS	vw(h)
MOS	ys	MOS	ws
MNP	yy(h)	MNP	vw(h)
MOP	yn	MOP	wn

A comparison of these paradigms will reveal that "nearness" is indicated by a /y-/
base, and "distance" by a /v-/ or /w-/ base. This is borne out by /yəhā/ "here" and /vəhā/
"there, " and later on the student will be introduced to several more such sets.

Note that, in the nominative form, these demonstratives do not distinguish gender or
number: /yy(h)/ may thus mean "he, " "she, " "it, " "they, " "this, " or "these. " Similarly,
/vw(h)/ denotes "he, " "she, " "it, " "they, " "that, " or "those. " The oblique forms distinguish number (i.e. /ys/ can mean "he, " "she, " "it, " or "this" but never "they" or "these")
but not gender.

These forms may stand alone as demonstrative pronouns, or they may be used as demonstrative adjectives modifying a following noun. /yy(h)/ is employed when the person or
object referred to is nearby, present, or most recently mentioned. /vw(h)/ is used when
the referent is distant, absent, or less recently mentioned (in comparison with something
more recent). E.g.

/yy mera ləRka həy. /　This [he] is my boy.

/yy mere ləRke hə̄y. /　These [they] are my boys.

/vw məkan yəhā̃ nəhī̃. /　That house is not here.

/yy ləRka hošyar həy. /　This boy is intelligent.

/ys se/　from him [her, it, this]

/ws pər/　on him [her, that, it]

/yn mē/　in them [these]

/wn ke age/　ahead of them [those]

/ys ke nəzdik/　near him [her, it, this]

/ys məkan mē/　in this building

/ws məkan mē/　in that building

It must also be remembered that plural forms are often used for a singular person to show respect. Thus:

/wn ka məkan/　his [her, their, that one's, those persons'] house

2.310. /kəwn/ "who? which?"

The interrogative /kəwn/ "who? which?" has a paradigm quite similar to those of /yy(h)/ and /vw(h)/:

MNS	kəwn
MOS	kys
MNP	kəwn
MOP	kyn

The nominative form, /kəwn/ means only "who?" Before postpositions, /kys/ and /kyn/ may denote either "who?" or "which?" but before a noun (i.e. as interrogative adjectives), they mean only "which?" E.g.

/vw kəwn sahəb hə̄y. /　Who is that gentleman? [Lit. That who gentleman are?]

/vw DakTər kəwn həy. /　Who is that doctor? [Lit. That doctor is who?]

/yy kys ka məkan həy. /　Whose house is it? [Lit. This whose house is?]

/vw kys mē həy. /　In which [whom] is it?

/yy kyn ke dəftər hə̄y. /　Whose [pl.] offices are these?

/vw kys məkan mē kam kərta həy. /　In which building does he work?

Note the difference between the following:

/kys ke məkan mē/　in whose building?

/kys məkan mē/　in which building?

2.311. Oblique Locatives and Temporals With No Postposition.

Nouns denoting places are often found in the oblique form with no following postposition when used as the goal of a verb of motion. Thus, instead of saying "go to the office, " the Urdu speaker says "go the office, " a construction similar to English "go home. " E.g.

/vw dəftər jata həy. /　He goes [to] the office.

/vw yskul jata həy. /　He goes [to] school.

46

/vw ghər jata həy./ He goes home.

/dəftər/, /yskul/, and /ghər/ are all Type I nouns, and since their MNS and MOS
forms are identical, the fact that they are grammatically oblique cannot be seen from these
examples. This will become clear, however, if a Type II noun be substituted:

/vw Dakxane jata həy./ He goes to the postoffice. [/Dakxana/ M2
"postoffice"; MOS /Dakxane/, cf. /Dakxane mẽ/ "in the postoffice,"
/Dakxane se/ "from the postoffice," etc.]

Similarly, there are a great many temporal expressions which contain oblique forms
followed by no postposition: e.g.

/khana kys vəqt həy./ What time is dinner? [/kys/ is OS here, although
the noun it modifies, /vəqt/, is not followed by a postposition.]

/khana aTh bəje həy./ Dinner is at eight o'clock. [/bəje/ is the MOS
form of /bəja/, the past participle of /bəjna/ "to ring, strike, play."]

These formations are, however, somewhat dependent upon usage and idiom; there
are also locative expressions which require a postposition and also temporal words and
phrases which cannot occur without one (e.g. /šam ko/ "in the evening, at evening"). Each
of these will be discussed as it is introduced.

2.312. The Verb: the <PreP + /həy/> Construction.

Before proceeding to a discussion of the verb forms given in this Unit, it will be useful to present a brief, general introduction to the Urdu verb system.

Every verb form consists of a single "stem," which carries the main semantic content
of the verb, ± one or more suffixes, and ± one or more auxiliary verbs. A "stem" may be
composed either of a single verbal "root" or of a "root" + one of two causative suffixes.
Since there are no active verbal prefixes in Urdu, the "root" may be defined as the first
morpheme after juncture (i.e. treating the word as a linear sequence and beginning with
that portion which is spoken first, the root will be the first meaningful piece which can be
cut off, and this piece will be found to carry the "main meaning" of the verb. The
difference between a "root" and a "stem" can best be illustrated with some examples:

/pəRh/ [thou] read!

/pəRhta/ reading [present participle, MNS]

/pəRha/ read [past participle, MNS]

/pəRho/ [you nonhonorific] read!

/pəRhie/ please read!

/pəRhũ/ if [I] read, [I] may read

/pəRhũga/ [I] will read

/pəRhna/ to read, the reading [MNS]

/pəRhata/ causing to read, teaching [present participle, MNS]

/pəRhao/ [you nonhonorific] cause to read, teach!

/pəRhaũga/ [I] will cause to read, teach

/pəRhana/ to cause to read, teach, the teaching [MNS]

The first eight examples contain a stem, /pəRh/ "read," which consists only of a
root, /pəRh/. The last four examples contain a stem, /pəRha/ "cause to read," which
consists of the root /pəRh/ + a causative suffix /a/. Both stems may be found in the same

47

distributions: i.e. both /pəRh/ and /pəRha/ may occur with the same inflectional suffixes and auxiliaries.

All Urdu verbal constructions are built upon one of the following patterns:

(a) A single word, consisting of a stem alone: e.g. the "thou" form of the imperative singular, now mostly obsolete:

/pəRh/ [thou] read!

(b) A single word, consisting of a stem + imperative, polite imperative, conditional, or future suffixes:

/pəRho/ [you nonhonorific] read!
/pəRhie/ please read!
/pəRhū̃/ if [I] read, [I] may read
/pəRhū̃ga/ [I] will read

(c) A single word, consisting of (a) the "present participle" or (b) the "past participle":

/pəRhta/ reading [MNS]
/pəRha/ read [MNS]

(d) A single word, consisting of a stem + the "infinitive" suffix /n/ + one of the Type II noun-adjective suffixes:

/pəRhna/ to read, the reading

(e) Two or more words, consisting of a stem + an auxiliary verb or + /kər/ "having ...":

/pəRh səkūga/ [I] will be able to read
/pəRh rəha hū̃/ [I] am reading
/pəRh kər/ having read

(f) Two or more words, consisting of the present or past participle + an auxiliary verb:

/pəRhta həy/ reads
/pəRha həy/ has read

(g) Two or more words, consisting of the "infinitive" + an auxiliary verb:

/pəRhna həy/ must read, is to be read
/pəRhne ləga/ began to read

In discussing these formations the following abbreviations will be employed: "R" = "root," "S" = "stem," "I" = "infinitive," "PreP" = "present participle," "PasP" = "past participle," Formulae for constructions will be enclosed in < ... >

In this Unit the <PreP + /həy/> construction has been introduced. As the formula indicates, this is composed of a present participle + one of the present tense forms of the auxiliary /həy/ (here /hū̃/, /hə̃y/, /ho/, etc. are subsumed under /həy/ for the purposes of the formula). The present participle is composed of a verb stem + the suffix /t/ + the Type II noun-adjective suffixes: e.g.

/ja-t-a/ going [MNS]
/ja-t-e/ going [MNP]
/pəRh-t-a/ reading [MNS]
/a-t-e/ coming [MNP]

48

The full paradigm of the <PreP + /həy/> formation is as follows:

PRONOUN	VERB	
mə̄y	pəRhta hū	I [M] read
[tu	pəRhta həy	thou [M] readest]
vw	pəRhta həy	he [it, M] reads
[həm	pəRhte hə̄y	we [M] read]
[twm	pəRhte ho	you [nonhonorific, M] read]
ap	pəRhte hə̄y	you [honorific, M] read
vw	pəRhte hə̄y	they [he, M] read[s]

Note that both the present participle and the auxiliary agree, so far as possible, with the number-gender of the subject.

This construction denotes action which generally takes place or which occurs during an unspecified general present: e.g. "I go to school every day," "I live in Lahore," "I understand Urdu," etc. It may also have an immediate future sense (usually with certain time words): e.g.

/mə̄y əbhi ata hū./ I am just coming. [I have not begun the action of coming yet, but I am just about to start.]

Note that this construction does NOT denote an actual or continuative present: e.g. "I am reading this book," "I am washing this dish now," etc.

The negative form of this construction consists of /nəhī̃/"no, not" followed by the present participle. The auxiliary verb is almost always omitted in the negative form. E.g.

/mə̄y nəhī̃ pəRhta./ I don't read.

/vw nəhī̃ ata./ He does not come.

/həm nəhī̃ jante./ We do not know.

2.313. The Verb: the <I + /həy/> Construction.

The "infinitive" or verbal noun is used in a great many ways. It is composed of a stem + /n/ + the Type II noun-adjective suffixes: e.g.

/ja-n-a/ to go, the going [MNS]

/ja-n-e/ to go, the going [MOS]

/pəRh-n-a/ to read, the reading [MNS]

/a-n-e/ to come, the coming [MOS]

There are, however, no plural forms.

The infinitive is basically a kind of noun, and it may occur as the subject of a sentence, as an object, etc. E.g.

/jana əccha həy./ The going is good. [= It is good to go.]

/rəhna bəhwt pəsənd həy./ Staying is very pleasant.

/jane se/ from going

/ws ke jane pər/ on his going

/mere jane mē̃/ in my going

If the infinitive has a semantic subject which is an animate, rational being, the subject possesses the infinitive (as in the last two examples). If the subject of the infinitive is not animate and rational, it may possess the infinitive but more often occurs in the

49

nominative form: e.g.

/ādhi [ke] ane pər/   on the coming of the storm. [/ādhi/ F2 "duststorm, storm"]

The <I + /həy/> construction is usually translatable as "must," "has to," "is necessary to," etc. The degree of obligation expressed, however, is not great, and it connotes general necessity rather than real compulsion. E.g.

/ap se mylna həy./   [I] have to meet you.

/əb lahəwr jana həy./   Now [I] must go to Lahore.

/yəhā rəhna həy./   [I] must remain here.

/ap se nəhī̃ mylna./   [I] must not meet you.

/kam kərna həy./   [I] have to work.

The student cannot yet express the semantic subject of this construction (the "I" in brackets in the above examples), since it is always marked by the postposition /ko/ "object marker, 'accusative'" or its equivalent. In Urdu one thus literally says: "To me is [the] going [to] Lahore," "To me is [the] remaining here," etc.

2.314. The Verb: the <I + /cahta həy/> Construction.

The infinitive also occurs with /cahna/ "to wish, want, like, love" with the meaning "want to ..." E.g.

/mə̃y ghər jana cahta hū̃./   I want to go home.

/mə̃y ap se mylna cahta hū̃./   I want to meet you.

/vw lahəwr ana cahta həy./   He wants to come to Lahore.

/mə̃y ghər jana nəhī̃ cahta./   I don't want to go home. [Or: /mə̃y ghər nəhī̃ jana cahta./   There is some freedom of order.]

/vw ghər kəb jana cahte həy./   When does he [they] want to go home? [The interrogative word is usually inserted directly before the infinitive. Again, there is some freedom of order: cf.]

/vw kəhā kam kərna cahta həy./   Where does he want to work? [The alternate order, /vw kam kəhā kərna cahta həy./   would also be possible.]

2.400. SUPPLEMENTARY VOCABULARY

2.401. Supplementary Vocabulary.

Numerals are all of the Type I adjective paradigm. Even those ending in /a/ do not change for gender or case.

chəy [or /che/]	six	bara	twelve
sat	seven	tera	thirteen
nəw	nine	cəwda	fourteen
dəs	ten	pəndra	fifteen
gyara	eleven		

Some speakers give the numerals from eleven to eighteen a "spelling pronunciation" with /h/: /gyarha/, /barha/, /terha/, /cəwdha/, /pəndhra/.

Further colour terms are:

kala A2	black
lal Al	red
səfəyd [or /səfed/] Al	white

2.402. Supplementary Exercise 1.

1. mə̃y ek sal se lahəwr mẽ hū.
       from six years
       from fourteen years
       from seven years
       from twelve years
       from eleven years

2. <u>pəndra ləRke</u> mere kalyj mẽ hə̃y.
   nine Americans
   thirteen Pakistanis
   seven Englishmen and eleven Americans
   his two brothers
   my three boys

3. mera məkan wn ke məkan se <u>nila</u> həy.
                        white
                        red
                        large
                        black

4. <u>do</u> ləRke roz swba yskul jate hə̃y.
   all
   fifteen
   nine
   ten
   fourteen

2.501. Substitution.

1. khana   <u>aTh bəje</u> həy.
        seven o'clock
        tomorrow
        tomorrow evening
        two o'clock
        nine o'clock

2. kya, rəhim sahəb   <u>ys dəftər mẽ</u> kam kərte hẽy?
                        in that college
                        in the university
                        on Lawrence Road
                        in the big school
                        in the Chartered Bank

3. ek sahəb <u>ap se</u> mylna cahte hẽy.
        with him [polite]
        with this [one] [polite]
        with that [one] [polite]
        with that American
        with this professor

4. ap kəhã   <u>rəhte hẽy</u>.
        do work
        read
        go
        want to go
        want to live

5. yy mera səb se <u>choTa əwr tisra ləRka</u> həy.
            big house
            intelligent boy
            first office
            good work

6. vw gəwrnmənT kalyj mẽ <u>nəhĩ pəRhta</u>.
                doesn't live
                doesn't go
                doesn't want to study
                doesn't want to live

7. <u>yy ləRka</u>   <u>pəhle ləRke se</u>   <u>hošyar</u> həy.
    the Chartered Bank   from that blue building   nearby
    this house   from that house   big
    my school   from your college   small
    my first boy   from your second boy   big

                    this Pakistani   from that American   small

8. wn ka yskul <u>mere dəftər ke pas</u> həy.
                    behind your college
                    opposite their house
                    ahead of the big building
                    near the big hospital
                    inside the university

9. vw <u>dəftər</u> jata həy.
        home
        school
        college
        hospital
        Pakistan

10. <u>ap se mylna</u> həy.
        staying in Lahore[1]
        going [to] Pakistan
        studying in college
        doing work
        doing much work in Pakistan

[1] The infinitive has been rendered by English "-ing" forms in these examples.

2.502. Transformation.

1. Change the following to negative sentences.
    a. mə̃y roz dəftər jata hū̃.
    b. mə̃y wrdu səməjhta hū̃.
    c. rəhim sahəb ys ghər mẽ rəhte hə̃y.
    d. ap se mylna həy.
    e. vw lahəwr jana cahte hə̃y.
    f. vw kalyj mẽ pəRhta həy.
    g. yy mera dusra ləRka həy.
    h. khana aTh bəje həy.
    i. mə̃y yəhā̃ kam kərta hū̃.
    j. vw əbhi ate hə̃y.

2. Change the following sentences to a first person singular subject and make the
    verb agree. Then change the subject to "you [honorific]" and then to "he," etc.
    a. vw ləRke gəwrnmənT kalyj mẽ pəRhte hə̃y.
    b. yy səb se bəRa həy.
    c. mere ləRke ys yskul mẽ nəhĩ pəRhte.
    d. vw kəl ap se khane pər mylna cahte hə̃y.
    e. rəhim sahəb ys ghər mẽ rəhte hə̃y.
    f. ek sahəb ap se mylna cahte hə̃y.
    g. vw bəhwt kəm wrdu səməjhta həy.

53

h. ap rəhim sahəb ka ghər jante hə̄y.

i. vw roz swba kalyj jate hə̄y.

j. vw yəhā̃ kam kərta həy.

3. Change the subject of each sentence (together with any agreeing adjectives) to the plural and make the verb agree.

a. vw bəRa ləRka ys kalyj mē̃ pəRhta həy.

b. mera dəftər yəhā̃ se nəzdik həy.

c. vw sahəb larəns roD pər rəhte hə̄y.

d. vw bəRa nila məkan yəhā̃ həy.

e. əb vw jana cahta həy.

f. vw gəwrnmənT kalyj mē̃ nəhī̃ pəRhta.

g. vw ləRka əbhi ata həy.

h. yy ləRka roz yskul jata həy, məgər pəRhta nəhī̃.

i. ap ka nila məkan bəhwt əccha həy.

j. vw əccha ləRka ap se mylna cahta həy.

4. Change the following sentences to questions by inserting the question word given at the end in brackets into its proper place.

a. vw pakystan mē̃ hə̄y.   [from when?]

b. rəhim sahəb lahəwr mē̃ rəhte hə̄y.   [where?]

c. ap ate hə̄y.   [from where?]

d. vw kalyj mē̃ pəRhta həy.   [which?]

e. khana kəl həy.   [at what time?]

f. vw ə̄grez kam kərte hə̄y.   [what?]

g. ap roz yskul jate hə̄y.   [when?]

h. vw həy.   [who?]

i. yy tin ləRke hə̄y.   [who?]

j. wn ka nam həy.   [what?]

5. Change the locational phrases in the following sentences to each of the following possibilities (wherever semantically suitable): /ke age/, /ke pas/, /ke əndər/, /ke nəzdik/, /ke samne/, /ke piche/.

a. vw ws bəRe məkan ke piche rəhte hə̄y.

b. yy ləRka mere məkan ke pas rəhta həy.

c. vw profesər mere ghər ke samne rəhte hə̄y.

d. yy yskul mere dəftər ke nəzdik həy.

e. wn ka ghər yskul ke age həy.

2.503. Fill the Blanks.

1. Fill the blanks in the following sentences with /a/ or /e/.

a. mə̄y ws bəR _ nil _ məkan k_ samne rəhta hū̃.

b. yy mer_ səb se choT_ əwr tisr_ ləRk_ həy.

c. mer_ do ləRk_ yəhā̃ nəhī̃ pəRht_.

54

d. ap k_ bhai k_ dəftər bəhwt bəR_ həy.

e. ap kys k_ məkan mẽ rəhte hə̃y.

f. ek choT_ məkan əwr do bəR_ yskul samne hə̃y.

g. ap k_ tisr_ ləRk_ mer_ dusr_ ləRk_ se hošyar həy.

h. yy kam ws pəhl_ kam se əcch_ həy.

i. mer_ profesər ws nil_ məkan mẽ rəhte hə̃y.

j. kya, ap k_ khan_ kəl aTh bəj_ həy?

2. Fill the blanks in the verb forms:

a. mə̃y ws DakTər se mylna caht_ h_.

b. ap kys ke məkan mẽ rəht_ h_.

c. mere do ləRke yskul jat_ h_, məgər pəRht_ nəhĩ.

d. kya, ap wrdu jant_ h_?

e. vw əgrez wrdu nəhĩ səməjht_.[1]

f. vw sahəb kya kam kərt_ h_.

g. mə̃y hər roz yəhã at_ h_.

h. mere profesər hər sal lahəwr jat_ h_.

i. kya, ap yəhã rəhna caht_ h_?

j. pãc ləRke ys dəftər mẽ kam kərt_ h_.

[1]Two possible answers.

2.504. Response.

1. kya, ap roz yəhã ate hə̃y?

2. ap kys kalyj mẽ pəRhte hə̃y.

3. kya, ap wrdu səməjhte hə̃y?

4. kya, ap hər sal niw yəwrk jate hə̃y?

5. ap ys kalyj mẽ kəb se pəRhte hə̃y.

6. kya, ap pakystan jana cahte hə̃y?

7. ap šam ko kya kam kərte hə̃y.

8. ap kys se mylna cahte hə̃y.

9. kya, ap ka məkan yunyvərsyTi ke nəzdik həy?

10. ap ka khana kys vəqt həy.

2.505. Conversation Practice.

Mr. Smith is on his way to see Dr. Rəhim. He asks the way from a passerby.

S: adab ərz, jənab. kya, ap rəhim sahəb ka məkan jante hə̃y?

P: ji nəhĩ, mə̃y nəhĩ janta, məgər ek məkan samne həy. ek sahəb ws mẽ rəhte hə̃y.

S: rəhim sahəb ek choTe nile məkan mẽ rəhte hə̃y. vw həspətal mẽ DakTər hə̃y.

P: ji hã. vw məkan age həy.

Mr. Smith arrives at the home of Dr. Rəhim. A servant answers the door.

S: kya, rəhim sahəb hə̄y?

Sr: ji hā, jənab. əndər hə̄y. ap kəwn hə̄y.

S: mera nam ysmyth həy. rəhim sahəb se mylna cahta hū.

Sr: bəhwt əccha jənab. vw əbhi ate hə̄y.

R [coming into the room]: ysmyth sahəb, adab ərz! kya, ap əb yunyvərsyTi se ate hə̄y?

S: ji hā. ap se mylna həy.

    Dr. Rəhim's three sons arrive home.

R: ysmyth sahəb, yy mere tin ləRke hə̄y. mera səb se bəRa ləRka yunyvərsyTi ke nəzdik kam kərta həy. ys ka dəftər yunyvərsyTi ke samne həy.

Eldest Boy: kya, ap mera dəftər jante hə̄y?

S: ji hā. do məkan vəhā hə̄y. ek bəRa həy, əwr ek choTa həy. ap ka dəftər kys məkan mē həy.

Eldest Boy: mera dəftər bəRe məkan mē həy.

R: yy mera dusra ləRka həy. yy kalyj mē pəRhta həy.

Second Boy: mə̄y gəwrnmənT kalyj mē pəRhta hū. mə̄y roz swba kalyj jata hū, əwr šam ko ghər mē kam kərta hū.

S: ap kya kam kərte hə̄y.

Second Boy: mə̄y pəRhta hū, əwr kalyj ka kam kərta hū.

S: kya, ek əmrikən profesər ap ke kalyj mē hə̄y?

Second Boy: ji hā. pāc əmrikən hə̄y, əwr sat ə̄grez hə̄y. dəs pakystani profesər bhi hə̄y.

R: yy mera tisra ləRka həy. yy bəhwt choTa həy, məgər roz yskul jata həy.

S: yy kys yskul mē pəRhte hə̄y.

R: yy yslamia yskul mē pəRhta həy.

S: əb vəqt kya həy.

R: əb chəy bəje hə̄y. kya, ap jana cahte hə̄y?

S: ji hā. əb jana həy.

R: mə̄y kəl ap se khane pər mylna cahta hū.

S: bəhwt əccha. khana kys vəqt həy.

R: khana sat bəje həy.

S: bəhwt əccha. myhrbani.

R: əccha. xwda hafyz.

S: xwda hafyz, jənab.

    2.506. Conversation Stimulus.

    1. Mr. Smith greets Dr. Rəhim. He asks him what time it is. Dr. Rəhim replies that he does not know. Mr. Smith then asks Mr. əziz, who replies that it is three o'clock. Mr. əziz asks Mr. Smith whether he is an American. Mr. Smith replies that he is, and also that he is a professor in the university. Mr. əziz says that he is studying in the university.

    2. Mr. Smith is chatting with Dr. Rəhim. He tells Dr. Rəhim that he has been in Pakistan two years. Dr. Rəhim inquires where Mr. Smith's office is. Mr. Smith replies

that it is in the Chartered Bank [building]. He states that the Chartered Bank is just past [ahead of] the university. He says that three Americans work in his office, and also that one Pakistani works there. Mr. Smith says that the name of the Pakistani is əziz. Dr. Rəhim says that he knows Mr. əziz. He asks whether Mr. əziz does good work, and Mr. Smith replies that he does very good work.

2.600. VOCABULARY

Items are not necessarily listed here in just that form given in the Conversation and Supplementary Vocabulary sections. Instead, each vocabulary item will be subsumed under an arbitrarily chosen "basic form." The following conventions will be observed.

(1) All nouns and adjectives are listed under their NS forms.

(2) Nouns are followed by their gender ("M" or "F" or "M/F") and by their declension type: "Type I" nouns (e. g. /ghər/ "house") are indicated by "1" and "Type II" nouns (e. g. /ləRka/ "boy") by "2" immediately following the gender symbol: "M1," "M2," etc.

(3) "Type I" and "Type II" adjectives (e. g. /hošyar/ "intelligent" and /əccha/ "good") will be symbolised by "A1" and "A2" respectively.

(4) At first other grammatical form classes will be indicated only where confusion might arise. As the student becomes more familiar with Urdu grammar, however, more and more grammatical information will be given.

(5) Irregular possessive, oblique, etc. forms of pronouns, demonstratives, interrogatives, etc. will be separately alphabetised.

(6) All verb forms will be subsumed under the "infinitive" (the form ending in /na/) unless they are irregular.

[ke] age	in front of, ahead of
ana	to come
aTh A1	eight
əb	now
əbhi	just now
əccha A2	good, well
[ke] əndər	inside
əwr A1 Conj Adv	and; other, another, a further, more
bara A1	twelve
bəje	o'clock
bəRa A2	big, large, elder
bhai M1	brother
cahna	to wish, want, desire, love, like
carTərD bɛ̃yk M1	Chartered Bank
cəwda A1	fourteen
chəy [or /che/] A1	six
choTa A2	small, little, young
dəs A1	ten
dusra A2	second, other, another, next
gəwrnmənT F1	government
gyara A1	eleven
hafyz M/F1	guardian, protector; one who has memorised the Holy Qwran [/xwda hafyz/ "goodbye. "]
hər A1	every, each
hošyar A1	intelligent, clever

jana	to go
janna	to know
kala A2	black
kalyj M1	college
kəl	tomorrow; yesterday
kəm A1 Adv	few, little (in amount); rarely
kərna	to do, make
kəwn NS, NP	who?
khana M2	food, dinner
ko	to [marker of the object]
kys OS	who? which?
lal A1	red
ləRka M2	boy
nəgər	but
mylna	to meet, get, obtain, join, mix
nəw A1	nine
nila A2	blue
[ke] pas	near, at, having
pəhla A2	first
pəndra A1	fifteen
pəRhna	to read, study
[ke] piche	behind, in back
rəhna	to live, stay, remain
roz M1	day, daily
sahəb [also /sahyb/] M1	sir, gentleman
[ke] samne	in front, opposite, facing
sat A1	seven
səb A1	all
səfəyd [or /səfed/] A1	white
səməjhna	to understand
swba [or /swbəh/ or /swbha/] F1	morning
šam F1	evening [/šam ko/ "in the evening"]
tera A1	thirteen
tisra A2	third
vəhã	there
vəqt M1	time
wn OP	those; he, she, it, they
ws OS	that; he, she, it
xwda M1	God [/xwda hafyz/ "goodbye"]
yn OP	these; he, she, it, they
ys OS	this; he, she, it
yskul M1	school
yslamia A1	Islamia (used mostly in proper names of organisations, institutions, etc.)

yy [slow speech /yyh/] NS, NP   this, these; he, she, it, they

The gender and declension class of each of the nouns given in Unit I are as follows:

əmrika M1	America
əmrikən M1 A1	American
ə̃grez M1 A1	Englishman, English
dəftər M1	office
dur F1 A1	far, distant, distance
DakTər M/F1	doctor
ghər M1	house, home
həspətal M1	hospital
kam M1	work, job, task
Lahəwr M1	Lahore
larəns roD F1	Lawrence Road [/roD/ is F1 on the analogy of /səRək/ F1 "road, street."]
məkan M1	house, residential building
myhrbani F2	kindness
myzaj M1	disposition
nam M1	name
nəmbər M1	number
niw yark [or /niw yəwrk/] M1	New York
pakystan M1	Pakistan
pakystani M/F1 A1	Pakistani
profesər M/F1	professor
sal M1	year
wrdu F1	Urdu
ysm M1	noun, name
yunyvərsyTi [or /yunyvərsTi/] F2	university

The declension types of adjectives given in Unit I may also be recapitulated here: [Adjectives which also occur as nouns are listed above and need not be repeated.]

bəhwt A1	much, many, very
car A1	four
do A1	two
ek A1	one, a, an
kya A1 [and also other uses]	what?
mera A2	my
nəzdik A1	near [/[ke] nəzdik/ functions as a compound postposition also.]
pãc A1	five
šərif A1	noble, honourable, gentle
tin A1	three

A dinner party in traditional style.

UNIT THREE

3.000. CONVERSATION

Mr. Smith, his wife, and his three daughters have been invited to Dr. Rəhim's house for dinner.

R: Hello!   adab ərz!

S: Hello! How are you?   adab ərz! myzaj šərif?

    thanks, gratitude; thank you M2   šwkria

    dignity, honour FNS, FOS   təšrif

    please put, place, keep [/təšrif rəkhie/   rəkhie
    please sit down]

R: Thanks. Please sit down.   šwkria. təšrif rəkhie.

    my FNS, FOS, FNP, FOP   meri

    wife FNS, FOS   bivi

    girls FNP   ləRkiã

S: This is my wife, and these are my three girls.   yy meri bivi hɘy, əwr yy meri tin ləRkiã hɘy.

    please meet   mylie

R: Please meet my wife.   meri bivi se mylie.

    of, -'s FNS, FOS, FNP, FOP   ki

    only Al Adv   syrf

MR [to Mrs. Smith]: Do you have only three girls?   ap ki syrf tin ləRkiã hɘy?

MS: No, I have three girls and also two boys.   ji nəhĩ, meri tin ləRkiã hɘy, əwr do ləRke bhi hɘy.

MR: Where are the boys?   ləRke kəhã hɘy.

    father M1   vʌlyd

MS: [They] are with my father in New York.   mere vʌlyd ke pas niw yəwrk mẽ hɘy.

    day M1 [/dyn ko/ during the day]   dyn

    service, employment, job FNS, FOS   nəwkri

    night FNS, FOS [/rat ko/ at night]   rat

MS: One works in [an] office during the day, and at night [he] works in the university.   ek dyn ko dəftər mẽ nəwkri kərta həy, əwr rat ko yunyvərsyTi mẽ kam kərta həy.

    third FNS, FOS, FNP, FOP   tisri

    class FNS, FOS   kylas

MS: The other [lit. second] is very small and studies in the third class [i. e. the third grade].   dusra bəhwt choTa həy, əwr tisri kylas mẽ pəRhta həy.

MS: Do you have only three boys?   kya, ap ke syrf tin ləRke hɘy?

MR: No, I also have two girls.   ji nəhĩ, meri do ləRkiã bhi hɘy.

    mother FNS, FOS   valda

MR: [They] are with my mother.   meri valda ke pas hɘy.

    ages FNP   wmrẽ

MS: What are their ages?   wn ki kya wmrẽ hɘy.

age FNS, FOS

twenty Al

MR: One is twenty years old. [Lit. One's age is twenty years.]

second, other, next FNS, FOS, FNP, FOP

eighteen Al

MR: The other's age is eighteen.

big, large, elder FNS, FOS, FNP, FOP

girl FNS, FOS

for, in order to

to send

[I F] want, wish, desire

MR: I want to send the eldest girl to America to study.

ready Al

R [to MR]: Is dinner ready?

known PA1

servant M1

[I F] ask

MR: [I] don't know. I [will] ask the servant.

table FNS, FOS

MR [to the servant]: Is dinner on the table?

madame FNS, FOS

Sr: Yes, Madame, it's ready.

room M2

please bring [/təšrif laie/ please come]

MR: Please come into the dining room [lit. food's room].

hand M1

to wash

R: Do you want to wash [your] hand[s]?

clean Al

S: No, thanks. My hands are clean.

we NP, OP

people M1

[table]knife FNS, FOṢ

fork M2 [lit. thorn]

[you, he, we, they] eat

therefore [lit. for this]

necessary Al

R: We [lit. we people] don't eat with knife [and] fork. Therefore, washing the hands is necessary.

wmr

bis

ek ki wmr bis sal həy.

dusri

əTThara

dusri ki wmr əTThara sal həy.

bəRi

ləRki

[ke] lie

bhejna

cahti hū

mย̄y bəRi ləRki ko pəRhne ke lie əmrika bhejna cahti hū.

təyyar

kya, khana təyyar həy?

malum

nəwkər

puchti hū

malum nəhī. nəwkər se puchti hū.

mez

kya, khana mez pər həy?

begəm

ji hā̃, begəm sahəb, təyyar həy.

kəmra

laie

khane ke kəmre mē̃ təšrif laie.

hath

dhona

kya, ap hath dhona cahte hə̄y?

saf

ji nəhī, šwkria. mere hath saf hə̄y.

həm

log

chwri

kāTa

khate hə̄y

ys lie

zəruri

həm log chwri kāTe se nəhī khate hə̄y. ys lie, hath dhona zəruri həy.

The group sits down at the dinner table.

meat curry Ml salən

please take lijie

R [to MS]: Please take [some] curry. salən lijie.

[I F] take leti hū.

MS: All right, I'll take [some]. What is in bəhwt əccha, mēy leti hū. ys mē kya həy.
this?

goat FNS, FOS bəkri

meat Ml gošt

clarified butter Ml ghi

pepper FNS, FOS myrc

salt Ml nəmək

plate FNS, FOS pyleT [or /pəleT/]

cow FNS, FOS gae

some Al kwch

vegetable[s] FNS, FOS səbzi

R: In it are goat's meat, clarified butter, ys mē, bəkri ka gošt, ghi, myrc, əwr
pepper, and salt, and in that plate are nəmək həy, əwr ws pyleT mē gae ka gošt
beef [lit. cow's meat] and some əwr kwch səbzi həy.
vegetable[s].

peppers FNP myrcē

more, much, too much, too many Al zyada

MS: The curry is very good, but [there] are salən bəhwt əccha həy, məgər mere lie
too many peppers for me. myrcē zyada hēy.

little [in amount] A2 thoRa

water Ml pani

please drink pijie

Mrs. mysəz [or /mysyz/]

glass Ml gylas

empty Al xali

please give dijie

R: Please drink a little water. [To MR] Mrs. thoRa pani pijie. -- mysəz ysmyth ka
Smith's glass is empty. Please give her gylas xali həy. wn ko pani dijie.
[some] water.

[I F] give deti hū

MR: I'll just give her [some]. əbhi deti hū.

chicken, hen FNS, FOS mwrɣi

egg M2 ənDa

R [to MS]: Please take [some] chicken and mwrɣi əwr ənDe lijie.
eggs.

MS: No, thanks. ji nəhī̆, šwkria.

nothing [lit. some not] kwch nəhī

[you, she, we, they F] do[es] [not] eat khatī̆

rice Ml cavəl

R [to S]: Mrs. Smith doesn't eat anything. mysəz ysmyth kwch nəhī̆ khatī̆ -- ap cavəl
[To MS] Please take [some] rice. lijie.

bread FNS, FOS	roTi
I have [lit. with me, by me]	mere pas
MS: No, I still [lit. just now] have [some] bread.	ji nəhĩ, roTi əbhi mere pas həy.

When dinner is finished, the group goes into the sitting room.

coffee FNS, FOS	kəwfi [or /kafi/]
R: Mrs. Smith, please take [a cup of] coffee.	mysəz ysmyth, ap kəwfi lijie.
cup FNS, FOS	pyali
tea FNS, FOS	cae
[I F] drink	piti hũ
MS: No, thanks. At night I drink only one cup [of] tea.	ji nəhĩ, šwkria. məy rat ko syrf ek pyali cae piti hũ.
how much, how many? A2	kytna
milk M1	dudh
how much, how many? FNS, FOS, FNP, FOP	kytni
is needed, needs	cahie
sugar FNS, FOS	cini
R: How much milk and how much sugar do you need?	ap ko kytna dudh əwr kytni cini cahie.
spoon M2	cəmca
not	nə
MS: One spoon [of] sugar. Please don't give [me any] milk.	ek cəmca cini. dudh nə dijie.
permission FNS, FOS	yjazət
S: It is time we were going now. [Lit. Please give us permission now.]	əb həm ko yjazət dijie.
Monday M1 [/pir ko/ on Monday]	pir
our A2	həmara
with, in the company of, accompanying	[ke] sath
market, "bazaar" M1	bazar
please go, please move	cəlie
S: Please go to the market with us on Monday.	ap log pir ko həmare sath bazar cəlie.
busy A1	məsruf
Tuesday M1	mə̃gəl
all right, fine, well, good	Thik
R: I'm busy on Monday. Tuesday is all right.	pir ko məy məsruf hũ. mə̃gəl Thik həy.
S: Very well. Goodbye.	bəhwt əccha. xwda hafyz.

3.100. WORD STUDY

3.101. /təšrif/ Fl has been loosely translated as "dignity." In fact, it is primarily employed in certain honorific constructions with specialised meaning: e.g. /təšrif lana/ "to come" (lit. to bring [one's] dignity), /təšrif rəkhna/ "to sit down" (lit. to place [one's] dignity), etc. Although /ana/ "to come" is just as "correct" as /təšrif lana/, the latter is more appropriate when addressing non-familiar equals and superiors. /ana/ is more idiomatic when speaking to familiar equals and inferiors.

3.102. /valyd/ Ml "father" and /valda/ Fl "mother" are also "polite language." The more familiar terms, /bap/ Ml "father" and /mā/ Fl "mother," are also quite acceptable but are less frequently employed in formal discourse. /valyd/ and /valda/ are Arabic loanwords, and they are examples of a type of masculine-feminine formation much employed in that language and sometimes borrowed into Urdu. The Arabic form of /valda/ is /valyda/, but most Urdu speakers omit the /y/ in pronunciation.

3.103. /dyn/ Ml "day" is somewhat commoner and more colloquial than /roz/ Ml "day." There are many places where either of these items might be employed, and there are also numerous idiomatic usages: e.g. /roz/ (or /hər roz/) can occur as an adverb meaning "daily"; /dyn/ cannot. /dyn/ is used with /ko/ to mean "during the day," whereas */roz ko/ is not possible. E.g.

/vw tin dyn se yəhā̃ həy./ He has been here for three days. [/tin roz se/ is also possible.]

/mə̃y [hər] roz yskul jata hū̃./ I go to school daily. [/dyn/ cannot be employed here.]

/vw dyn ko kam kərta həy./ He works during the day. [/roz/ cannot occur here.]

3.104. /[ke] pas/ "near, at, having" is translatable as "with" in a sentence like /ləRke mere valyd ke pas hə̃y./ "The boys are with my father." This means that the boys are at my father's (home, place). Compare /ləRke mere valyd ke sath hə̃y./ "The boys are in the company of my father."

3.105. /nəwkər/ Ml "servant" and /nəwkri/ F2 "service, job, employment" are an example of the abstract noun forming suffix /i/. All nouns ending in this suffix are F2. This construction will be more fully analysed in a later Unit.

3.106. /[ke] lie/ "for" may be rendered "to" or "in order to" after the OS form of the infinitive: e.g.

/vw jane ke lie təyyar həy./ He is ready to go.

/vw khane ke lie ghər jata həy./ He goes home to eat.

/ys lie/ "therefore" is an exception to the rule that compound postpositions must follow a possessive phrase or a possessive pronoun (as, e.g., /ləRke ke lie/ "for the boy," /mere lie/ "for me"). Note the contrast between the idiomatic phrase /ys lie/ "therefore" and /ys ke lie/ "for this [one], him, her, it." Similarly, /kys lie/ means "why?" while /kys ke lie/ denotes "for whom?"

3.107. /janna/ "to know" denotes the knowledge of a general fact, of a subject (e.g. mathematics), of a person, etc. /malum/ "known" denotes the knowledge of a single fact or a group of ascertainable facts: e.g. the time of day, the price of something, the where-abouts of a person or object, etc. /janna/, however, overlaps much of the distribution of /malum/: i.e. it can be used in most of the situations in which /malum/ would also be appropriate. The converse is not true, however: /malum/ is not appropriate in a great many situations in which /janna/ can be employed.

It may be noted that /malum/ is not a verb like /janna/; neither is it an adjective like /bəRa/, /hošyar/, etc. since it can never stand before a noun as a modifier. Instead, it occurs only as a "predicate complement" with /hona/ and /kərna/ in a "complex verb formation" (briefly discussed in 2.302). When the accompanying verb is /hona/ "to be," the logical subject is marked by /ko/, and one literally says "To him X is known." E.g.

/rəhim sahəb ko yy malum həy./ Mr. Rəhim knows this.

/kya, ap ko vəqt malum həy?/ Do you know the time?

/ys ləRke ko kwcłf malum nəhī./ This boy knows nothing. [Lit. To this boy something is not known.]

/vw wrdu janta həy./ He knows Urdu. [One cannot say */ws ko wrdu malum həy./ since Urdu is a subject and not a single fact.]

/vw rəhim sahəb ko janta həy./ He knows Mr. Rəhim. [*/ws ko rəhim sahəb malum həy./ is not possible since Mr. Rəhim is a person.]

3.108. In English, "to ask" may take two objects: the thing asked (e.g. a question), and the source asked (e.g. John): I asked John a question. In Urdu, the thing asked takes the direct object form, but the source asked is expressed with /se/ "from, with, by": e.g.

/məy nəwkər se puchti hū./ I[F] [will] ask the servant [a question].

/məy ap se yy puchna cahta hū./ I want to ask you [lit. from you] this.

3.109. /log/ M1 "people" is added to plural pronouns referring to people (and also to some nouns) to emphasise plurality. Since /log/ is M1, the resulting pronoun or noun phrase is masculine even if the referent be feminine. Compare the "you-all" of some southern American dialects or the "you folks" of various western American dialects. Pronouns to which /log/ may be added include:

/həm log/ we [people]

/ap log/ you [honorific] [people]

[/twm log/ you [nonhonorific] [people]

/yy log/ they [people] [lit. these people]

/vw log/ they [people] [lit. those people]

3.110. /chwri kāTa/ "knife [and] fork" is an example of a special type of noun compound consisting of two semantically allied nouns with no intervening conjunction. Both /chwri/ F2 "knife" and /kāTa/ M2 "fork" may be used alone.

3.111.   /khana/ M2 "food, dinner" is homophonous with (or identical with?) the
infinitive form of the stem /kha/ "eat. " /khana əccha nəhĩ. / may thus mean either "The
food is not good" or "Eating is not good. " Only a few Urdu verbs have this type of verbal
noun formation, however.

3.112.   The basic meaning of /salən/ M1 is "any stew-like dish eaten with rice or
bread. " The basic criterion is that the dish must contain liquid; i. e. /salən/ must have
sauce or gravy. It is commonly understood, moreover, that /salən/ will contain meat,
although this is not strictly necessary. There are, of course, a great many varieties of
/salən/, and each of these has its individual name.

3.113.   /kəm/ A1 and /thoRa/ A2 both mean "little, a small quantity. " /kəm/,
however, has the sense of "too little (for a stated purpose), " while /thoRa/ indicates only
"a small amount, a small number. " E. g.
        /kəm pani həy. /   There is too little water. [I. e. too little for the
            purpose.]
        /thoRa pani həy. /   There is a little [i. e. a small amount of] water.
/kəm/ also means "few [in number], " and as an adverb it denotes "rarely" or "seldom. "
E. g.
        /bəhwt kəm log vəhã jate hə̃y. /   Very few people go there.
        /vw bəhwt kəm jata həy. /   He goes very seldom.
   Both /kəm/ and /thoRa/ must be carefully distinguished from /choTa/ A2 "small,
little [in size], young. "

3.114.   /roTi/ F2 "bread" usually refers to flat circular patties of unleavened wheat
bread (of which the commonest type is termed /cəpati/ F2). /roTi/ may also be employed
as a generic term for many varieties of special breadstuffs, all of which have individual
names as well.   /roTi/ is also used as a general term for food;
        /vw roTi khane ke lie jata həy. /   He goes to eat [his] food [lit. bread].
           [I. e. he goes to eat lunch, dinner, etc.]
   The bread with which Westerners are familiar is called /Dəbəl roTi/ "double bread"
(from English "double").

3.115.   /əb həm ko yjazət dijie. /   "Please give us permission [to depart] now. " is
again "polite language. " Similarly, one may say /əb həm yjazət cahte hə̃y. /   "Now we
would like permission [to leave]. " etc. etc. Among more intimate acquaintances less
formal phrases would also be appropriate; e. g. /əb jana həy. /   "Now [we] have to go. "
/əb jana cahie. /   "Now [we] must go. " /əb həm jana cahte hə̃y. /   "Now we would like to
go. "

3.200. PHONETICS

3.201. Aspirated and Unaspirated Voiceless Stops.

In a normal English pronunciation, the p, t, ch, and k of such words as pin, tin, chin, and kin are usually released with a noticeable puff of breath ("aspiration"). This can easily be demonstrated by holding a slip of paper in front of one's mouth and pronouncing these words. The aspiration will cause the slip to flutter sharply. (This may be less noticeable in the case of chin since the affrication of the ch tends to diffuse the sharpness of the aspirated release, at least in the author's pronunciation.) If, on the other hand, one attempts the same experiment with spin, stint, and skin (there being no *sch in English in word initial position), the paper will not flutter as much, if at all. As a rule, thus, it may be said that word-initial /p, t, c, k/ before a vowel are aspirated in English, whereas after /s/ before a vowel they are not. The English speaker has learned to vary the degree of aspiration automatically, and this very unconscious mastery of his own phonology may become a serious obstacle to learning to speak a language like Urdu, for in this latter language it is ABSOLUTELY NECESSARY to differentiate between aspirated and unaspirated stops EVERYWHERE, since these sounds are in contrast (i.e. they may make the difference between two separate words). Just as an example of how one's unconscious speech habits may cause confusion, once when the author was travelling in one of the remoter areas of North Central India, he stopped at a small village to rest. When the village headman appeared, the author asked for water (/pani/). The old gentleman looked somewhat puzzled, but he called a young man and explained something to him in the local dialect. The young man went off on his errand, and the author sat on a cot with the headman, the centre of all eyes. Time passed, and the author grew thirstier and thirstier. At long last the young villager returned bearing handfuls of a species of grass -- /phani/ in their dialect.

The aspirated stops (/ph, th, Th, ch, kh/) are somewhat more fortis (more strongly aspirated) than the aspiration of English pin, etc. The student should try saying bookhouse, gatehouse, etc., for a start, trying to isolate the kh, t[e]h. For /p, t, T, c, k/, try to pronounce spin, stint, skin (and such artificial items as *schin, and sTin) first with the /s/ and then without it.

/pəl/ moment	/phəl/ fruit
/Təlua/ owner of a store of wood	/Thəlua/ jobless, idle person
/cuna/ lime	/chuna/ to touch
/kəTTa/ young buffalo	/khəTTa/ sour
/tal/ rhythm	/thal/ big circular metal tray
/cal/ gait	/chal/ bark [of a tree]
/kal/ famine	/khal/ skin
/pəkna/ to ripen, become cooked	/phūkna/ to blow
/bəcca/ [male] child	/əccha/ good
/TaT/ mat	/ThaTh/ dignity, pomp
/cəl/ go, move!	/chəl/ dodge, deceit
/kāsi/ bronze	/khāsi/ cough

/kwnD/ spring, pool
/məcan/ platform
/Tykana/ to put, place [for awhile]
/təkna/ to gaze, stare
/jəpna/ to recite the name of God on a rosary
/ləT/ lock of hair
/nak/ nose
/cola/ cloak, garment
/tan/ tune, keynote

/cor/ thief
/kaj/ buttonhole
/səc/ truth, true
/cwkna/ to be finished, settled

/sat/ seven

/kona/ corner

/puc/ (or /pūc/) tail
/paR/ scaffold

/kari/ penetrating

/tyhi/ empty
/pəhn/ wear, put on!
/pəla/ raised, brought up [msc. sg.]

/khənD/ portion, part, piece
/kəchar/ alluvial land; tiger's lair
/Thykana/ place, residence, whereabouts
/thəkna/ to be fatigued
/jəphna/ = /jəpna/; different dialect
/ləTh/ big bamboo stick
/lakh/ one hundred thousand
/chola/ sp. of gram
/than/ place; stall for cattle; bale of cloth
/chor/ border, limit, end
/khaj/ itching
/kwch/ some
/cəkhna/ to taste, relish
/chəkna/ to be satiated
/sath/ with
/saTh/ sixty
/khona/ to lose
/kwhna/ old
/puch/ ask!
/phaR/ tear!
/pəhaR/ mountain
/khari/ saline water
/kəhari/ a servant caste
/thi/ [she, it] was
/phən/ cobra's hood
/phəla/ fruitful
/pəhla/ first

3.202. Phonetic Drill: Auditory Dictation.

1. səc   bəcca   chal   puch   chor   məcan   əccha   cəl   cuna   cwkna   cor
   chəkna   cal   chuna   chola

2. Təlua   ThaTh   saTh   ləT   Thəlua   Thykana   ləTh   Tykana   kəTTa
   TaT

3. pəkna   pəl   phəla   phaR   phūkna   puc   jəphna   pəhn   phəl   paR   pəhaR

4. tyhi   thəkna   tal   tan   sath   thi   thal   təkna   than   sat

5. kāsi   kəTTa   khal   khaj   kona   cəkhna   nak   təkna   kari   kwhna
   khāsi   lakh   cwkna   kəhari   kaj

6. TaT   cal   pəhla   cola   ləT   jəpna   məcan   kaj   tyhi   təkna   pəhn
   kal   bəcca   Təlua   kəTTa   kwnD

7. khāsi   chuna   puch   phaR   ləTh   kəchar   Thykana   chor   than
   chola   kwch   phən   khənD   cəkhna   thi

8. phəla   ləT   chor   nak   jəphna   əccha   chəl   cal   pəl   khal   ThaTh
   sat   təkna   chəkna   kona

9. cəl   chuna   kal   khona   Tykana   Thəlua   səc   puch   tan   thi   pəla
   phəla   nak   lakh

10. kari   kəhari   khari   sat   sath   saTh   phəla   pəla   pəhla   paR   pəhaR
    cwkna   cəkhna   chəkna

3.300. ANALYSIS

3.301. Sentence Patterns (Continued): the Indirect Object.

An indirect object (e.g. "to him" in "I give water to him." or "I show the house to him.") is marked by /ko/ "to" or its equivalent. In normal sentence order, an indirect object usually precedes the direct object.

SUBJECT	INDIRECT OBJECT	DIRECT OBJECT	VERB
mə̄y	mysəz ysmyth ko	khana	deta hū.

I give food to Mrs. Smith. [Or: "I will just ..."]

rəhim sahəb	nəwkər ko	khana	bhejte hə̄y.

Mr. Rəhim sends food to the servant.

This order may be varied for emphasis. When temporal or locational elements occur in the sentence, there are several possible orders, some of which lay slight emphasis on one or another "tactic building block" (i.e. on the subject, on a temporal word or phrase, on a locational element, on an indirect object, on an object, etc.). A common, non-emphatic order is:

SUBJECT	INDIRECT OBJECT	TEMPORAL	LOCATIVE	DIRECT OBJECT	VERB
mə̄y	ws ko	roz	vəhā	khana	bhejta hū.

I send food to him there daily.

3.302. Adverbs Modifying Adjectives.

Adjectives may be preceded by a modifier:

/syrf tin ləRke/ only three boys
/bəhwt əccha go**š**t/ very good meat
/zyada bəRi bəkri/ an especially big goat, too big a goat

Note that /bəRa/ A2 "big, large" may also be used in this way. It has the same meaning as /bəhwt/, but the latter is somewhat more common.

/bəRa əccha kam/ very good job
/bəRi əcchi ləRki/ very good girl

3.303. Feminine Nouns.

Two types of feminine noun have now been introduced:

Type I:
/ek mez həy./ There is a [one] table.
/ek mez pər/ on a [one] table
/do mezē̃ hə̄y./ There are two tables.

Type II:
/ek ləRki həy./ There is a [one] girl.
/ek ləRki se/ from a [one] girl

/do ləRkiã hɛ̄y./ There are two girls.

Feminine Type I nouns may have a FNS form ending in any sound except /i/. Feminine Type II nouns have a FNS form ending in /i/. The pattern is: ["∅" = "no suffix"]

	TYPE I			TYPE II	
FNS	∅	/mez/	FNS	i	/ləRki/
FOS	∅	/mez/	FOS	i	/ləRki/
FNP	ē	/mezē/	FNP	iã	/ləRkiã/
FOP	given later		FOP	given later	

Thus, the stem of a Type I noun may occur alone as a word, while the stem of a Type II noun is obligatorily followed by one of the gender-case-number suffixes given above.

Although the /i/ "feminine" and /a/ "masculine" distinction provides a valuable clue to the gender of a new word, it can never be taken as infallible. For example, /valda/ F1 "mother" is feminine in spite of its /a/ ending. /ghi/ M1 "clarified butter" and /pani/ M1 "water" are masculine, although they end in /i/.

Many nouns having a MNS form ending in /a/ have a corresponding FNS form ending in /i/ indicating a sex distinction or a size distinction (the MNS form indicates a large object, while the FNS form denotes a smaller variety of the same object). Thus, for example: /ləRka/ "boy" and /ləRki/ "girl," /beTa/ "son" and /beTi/ "daughter," etc.

Type I feminine nouns will be indicated in the vocabulary by "F1"; Type II feminine nouns will be marked by "F2."

3.304. Mass Nouns.

Nouns which denote an indefinite quantity or number of a substance and which are not normally specified in terms of individual units are called mass nouns. In English, words like "water," "wheat," "rice," etc. are grammatically singular. They cannot be particularised: i.e. one cannot say "a rice" or "rices" (unless one speaks of plural species of rice). The situation in Urdu is similar: most mass nouns are treated as singulars: e.g. /pani/ M1 "water," /cini/ F2 "sugar," /dudh/ M1 "milk," etc.

/bəhwt cini hɛ̄y./ There is a lot of sugar. [Not /hɛ̄y/.]

/thoRa pani həy./ There is a little water.

/kwch səbzi həy./ There are some vegetable[s]. [/kwch səbziã hɛ̄y./ would denote plural kinds of vegetables.]

These nouns remain singular (and require a singular verb!) even when a plural measure is employed:

/mysəz ysmyth ko do cəmce cini cahie./ Mrs. Smith needs two spoons of sugar. [/cahie/ is singular because /cini/ is a singular mass noun.]

/ap ko kytna pani cahie./ How much water do you need? [/kytna/ is MNS, and /cahie/ is singular.]

/nəwkər ko do pyali cae cahie./ The servant needs two cups of tea.

The word /cavəl/ M1 "rice" requires comment: in the Western part of the Urdu-speaking area, this word is commonly treated as plural, especially in the sense of "cooked rice." In the meaning of "uncooked rice," however, it may be used as a singular. East of Lucknow this word is usually singular·

/ap ko kytne cavəl cahiẽ. /   How much rice do you need? [Western usage:
always for cooked rice and possibly for uncooked rice. Eastern
dialects would have /cahie/.]

/əbhi mere pas bəhwt cavəl həy. /   As yet I have a lot of rice [Eastern for
both cooked and uncooked. Western for uncooked rice only.]

3.305. Nouns Used as Measures.

A noun denoting a measure usually precedes that denoting the thing measured directly
(i. e. without any intervening /ka/ "of"). The Urdu speaker thus says "one cup tea"
instead of "one cup of tea. " A construction with /ka/ would not be "wrong, " but it is not
as idiomatic.

/ek pyleT gošt/ a plate of meat. [Instead of /gošt ki ek pyleT/]

/do gylas pani/ two glass[es] of water. [Instead of /pani ke do gylas/]

/ek pyali kəwfi/ one cup of coffee. [Instead of /kəwfi ki ek pyali/]

/do cəmce cini/ two spoons of sugar. [Instead of /cini ke do cəmce/]

Note that masculine Type II nouns used as measures always mark the plural: e. g.
/do cəmce cini/ "two spoons of sugar. " Feminine nouns used as measures, however, are
most often singular: e. g. /do pyali cae/ "two cups of tea, " rather than /do pyaliã cae/.
Although the latter is not "wrong, " it is less idiomatic than the singular form.

3.306. Series of Nouns.

In English, a series of nouns joined by "and" requires a plural verb: e. g. "In this
are goat's meat, ghi, pepper, and salt. " In Urdu, the number of the verb depends upon
the type of noun in the series: if the joined nouns are inanimate, irrational objects, then
the number of the verb depends upon the number of the last object in the series: if the last
noun is singular, the verb will be singular, and if it is plural, then the verb will be plural.

/ys mẽ bəkri ka gošt, ghi, myrc, əwr nəmək həy, əwr ws pyleT mẽ gae
ka gošt əwr kwch səbzi həy. / In this are goat's meat, clarified
butter, pepper, and salt, and in that plate are cow's meat and some
vegetable[s]. [The first /həy/ is singular because /nəmək/ is
singular, and the second /həy/ is singular in agreement with /səbzi/.]

If the nouns in the series denote animate, rational beings, then the verb will be plural.

/ysmyth sahəb, mysəz ysmyth, əwr DakTər rəhim məsruf hɛ̃y. /   Mr.
Smith, Mrs. Smith, and Dr. Rəhim are busy.

With regard to the gender of the verb, when the series contains only inanimate,
irrational nouns, the verb will agree in gender with the last item in the series. When the
series contains only masculine animate, rational nouns, the verb will be masculine;
similarly, if the nouns are all feminine animate, rational beings, then the verb will be
feminine. If the series contains both masculine and feminine animate, rational nouns,
then the verb is usually masculine.

/ysmyth sahəb, mysəz ysmyth, əwr wn ke ləRke aTh bəje khana khate hɛ̃y./ Mr. Smith, Mrs. Smith, and their children eat at eight o'clock.

/mysəz ysmyth, wn ki valda, əwr wn ki ləRkiã roz bazar jati hɛ̃y./ Mrs. Smith, her mother, and her daughters go to the market daily.

3.307. Feminine Adjectives.

Type I and Type II adjectives both have only one form before feminine nouns, no matter what the number or case of the noun may be. Type I adjectives may end in any sound, but Type II adjectives must end in /i/ (or /í/ in some cases). The pattern is:

	TYPE I			TYPE II		
FNS	∅	/hošyar/	FNS	i	/bəRi/
FOS	∅	/hošyar/	FOS	i	/bəRi/
FNP	∅	/hošyar/	FNP	i	/bəRi/
FOP	∅	/hošyar/	FOP	i	/bəRi/

Examples:

/meri bəRi ləRki hošyar hɛ̃y./ My eldest girl is intelligent.

/ap ki do nili mezẽ choTi hɛ̃y./ Your two blue tables are small.

/ap ki tin ləRkiã lahəwr mẽ rəhti hɛ̃y./ Your three girls live in Lahore.

/yy səfəyd pyali ws kali pyali se zyada pəsənd həy./ This white cup is more pleasing than that black cup.

3.308. Adjectives Used as Nouns.

Some adjectives may be used as nouns. It is difficult to establish a set rule for this phenomenon, since it depends upon semantic usage. Thus, /bəRe ko/ "to the big [M one]" is idiomatic and meaningful, whereas /nile ko/ "to the blue [M one]" sounds somewhat strange, although it could occur in a context. The student must depend upon observation and experience.

/mɛ̃y bəRi ko əmrika bhejna cahta hũ./ I want to send the big [F one] to America.

/mɛ̃y bəRe ko əmrika bhejna cahta hũ./ I want to send the big [M one] to America.

/ek ki wmr bis sal həy./ The age of one is twenty years. [Since /ek/ is A1, the gender of its referent is ambiguous without context.]

3.309. /həm/ "we."

The first person plural pronoun /həm/ has now been introduced. Its oblique form is also /həm/, and its possessive form is /həmara/, a Type II adjective like /mera/. See also Sec. 3.109.

/həm roz yskul jate hɛ̃y./ We go to school every day.

/həm se nə puchie./ Please don't ask us!

/vw həmare ghər mẽ rəhta həy./ He lives in our house.

76

3.310. /ko/ "to."

Several uses of the postposition /ko/ have now been introduced:

(1) /ko/ is used with various temporal words. It may mean "in," "at," "on," "during," etc., depending upon the English idiom. E.g.

    /dyn ko/   during the day

    /rat ko/   at night

    /pir ko/   on Monday. [And similarly with the other days of the week]

(2) /ko/ marks the direct object of a transitive verb:

  (a) When the object is a proper name or a definitely specified person. When the object is an indefinite person, /ko/ is not used.

    /mɜ̄y bɜRi lɜRki ko ɜmrika bhejna cahta hū̃. /   I want to send the eldest girl to America.

    /mɜ̄y ap ke pas ek nɜwkɜr bhejna cahti hū̃. /   I [F] want to send a servant to you. [/ek nɜwkɜr/ is indefinite, and /ko/ thus does not occur.]

    /mɜ̄y rɜhim sahɜb ko janta hū̃. /   I know Mr. Rɜhim.

  (b) /ko/ is also optionally used when the object is inanimate and irrational, but only when one wishes to emphasise its object status. Inanimate, irrational direct objects more commonly occur without /ko/. Again, when the direct object is indefinite, /ko/ does not occur.

    /ek mez bhejie. /   Please send a [one] table.

    /vw mez bhejie. /   Please send that table.

    /ws mez ko bhejie. /   Please send that table.

(3) When a verb takes two objects (e.g. "to make") or an indirect object and a direct object (e.g. "to give," "to show"), one of the objects or, in the second case, the indirect object will be marked by /ko/.

    /mysɜz ysmyth ko salɜn dijie. /   Please give Mrs. Smith [some] curry.

    /mɜ̄y ysmyth sahɜb ko khana bhejna cahta hū̃. /   I want to send Mr. Smith [some] food.

(4) Certain adjectives and predicate adjectives have an "object" marked by /ko/. This is often translatable in English as the subject of the sentence.

    /kya, ap ko yy malum hɜy? / Do you know this? [Lit. What, to you is this known?]

    /rɜhim sahɜb ko gošt pɜsɜnd hɜy. / Mr. Rɜhim likes meat. [Lit. To Mr. Rɜhim meat is pleasing.]

(5) Similarly, /ko/ marks the object of /cahie/ "is needed, needs. " Again, this is translatable as the subject of the sentence.

    /ap ko kytna dudh ɜwr kytni cini cahie. /   How much milk and how much sugar do you need? [Lit. To you ... is needed?]

    /ysmyth sahɜb ko roTi cahie. /   Mr. Smith needs bread. [Lit. To Mr. Smith bread is needed.]

(6) /ko/ also marks the object of the <I + /hɜy/> construction (see Sec. 2.313). This is also translatable as the subject in English.

    /rɜhim sahɜb ko jana hɜy. /   Mr. Rɜhim has to go. [Lit. To Mr. Rɜhim going is.]

    /ap ko yɜhā̃ rɜhna hɜy. /   You have to stay here. [Lit. To you here staying is.]

(7) /ko/ marks the possessor of an abstract noun: e.g. "I have trouble," "I have pleasure," etc. See Sec. 3.311.

(8) A pronoun or a demonstrative used as an object or an indirect object must be marked by /ko/ (or its equivalent; see below): e.g. /ap ko/ "to you [honorific]," /ys ko/ "to him, her, it," /həm ko/ "to us," /kys ko/ "to whom?" etc. There are, however, special alternate object forms for all of the pronouns and demonstratives with the single exception of /ap ko/, and these special forms are generally considered to be more "elegant," "smooth," and "idiomatic" in modern Urdu. Thus, although /həm ko/ "to us" occurs and is correct, many educated speakers would consider it inelegant. The special object forms will be introduced in Unit V.

3.311. "To Have."

There are three ways of expressing "to have":

(1) The possessive construction is used when the possessed object is material and tangible but the ownership is intangible: i.e. legal ownership, kinship relationship, the possession of an inseparable body part, etc.

> /mere tiṅ ləRke hə̃y./ I have three boys. [Lit. "My three boys are.]
> /mere tin məkan hə̃y./ I have three houses. [Lit. My three houses are. Legal ownership.]
> /ap ki do ləRkiã hə̃y./ You have two girls.
> /ws kä syrf ek hath həy./ He has only one hand. [Inalienable possession of a body part]

(2) /[ke] pas/ "at, near" is used for "to have" when the object is material and when the ownership is physical possession.

> /əbhi mere pas roTi həy./ I still have bread. [Lit. Now by me bread is.]
> /wn ke pas ek bəkri həy./ They [he, she] has a goat. [Lit. By them one goat is.]
> /kya, ap ke pas ek chwri həy?/ Do you have a knife?
> /mere pas bəhwt kam həy./ I have a lot of work. [I.e. physical objects to work on, as files piled up on one's desk]

(3) When the thing possessed is abstract, an object form (i.e. a noun or pronoun + /ko/ or its equivalent) is used: "To me is trouble." = "I have trouble."

> /ap ko bəhwt kam həy./ You have a lot of work. [I.e. abstract work, many duties, much to do, etc.]

3.312. The Verb: Feminine Forms of the <Prep + /həy/> Construction.

In affirmative sentences, a present participle agreeing with a feminine subject ends in /i/, exactly like a feminine Type II adjective.

PRONOUN	VERB	
mə̃y	pəRhti hũ	I [F] read
[tu	pəRhti həy	thou [F] readest]

PRONOUN	VERB	
vw	pəRhti həy	she [it, F] reads
həm	pəRhti hə̄y	we [F] read
[twm	pəRhti ho	you [nonhonorific, F] read]
ap	pəRhti hə̄y	you [honorific, F] read
vw	pəRhti hə̄y	they [she, F] read[s]

Women often use the masculine form, /həm pəRhte hə̄y/, for the first person plural instead of the expected /həm pəRhti hə̄y/. Other verb forms must always agree with the gender of the grammatical subject.

The negative form of this construction normally consists of /nəhī̃/ "no, not" followed by the present participle without any auxiliary. When this is the case, the plural forms of the feminine present participle end in /ī/ instead of /i/. If the auxiliary occurs, however, the plural forms end in /i/, as in the paradigm given above. E.g.

/həm nəhī̃ jatī̃./ We [F] do not go.
/vw nəhī̃ pəRhtī̃./ They [she, F] do[es] not read
/ap nəhī̃ pəRhtī̃./ You [honorific, FS or FP] do not read
/ap nəhī̃ pəRhti hə̄y./ You [honorific, FS or FP] do not read.

When /log/ Mpl "people" is added to emphasise plurality, an agreeing verb form will always be masculine plural, even though the sex of the subject may be feminine.

/həm log pəRhte hə̄y./ We people [M or F] read.
/vw log jate hə̄y./ Those people [M or F] go.

3.313. The Verb: the <S + /ie/> Construction.

The polite imperative consists of a verb stem + /ie/. There is no distinction for number or gender. This form may be translated by "please ...!" E.g.

/mylie/ please meet! [Stem /myl/]
/pəRhie/ please read! [Stem /pəRh/]
/rəhie/ please stay! [Stem /rəh/]
/aie/ please come! [Stem /a,/]
/jaie/ please go! [Stem /ja/]

Four common verbs have a special stem alternant before the polite imperative suffix. The suffix also has a special form, being /jie/ instead of /ie/.

/dijie/ please give! [Stem /de/; stem alternant /di/]
/kijie/ please do! [Stem /kər/; stem alternant /ki/]
/lijie/ please take! [Stem /le/; stem alternant /li/]
[/hwjie/ please become! [Stem /ho/; stem alternant /hw/] [This form is somewhat rare in modern Urdu.]

One verb stem ending in /i/ occurs with /jie/ instead of /ie/:

/pijie/ please drink! [Stem /pi/]. [Compare: /siie/ "please sew!" Stem /si/]

There are no other irregular polite imperative forms in Urdu.

The negative employed with the polite imperative is usually /nə/:

/əb nə jaie!/ Please don't go now!

/yy nə pijie!/   Please don't drink this!

/nəhī/ "no, not" may occasionally be found with this form, but then it usually follows the verb and has the force of a polite and urgent request.

/yəhā̃ rəhie nəhī!/   Please don't stay here!

3.314.   /cahie/.

/cahie/ "is needed, is necessary, must" is historically the polite imperative of /cah/ "wish, want, desire, love." It is now used almost exclusively as an impersonal, gender-less semi-verb. Its grammatical subject is the thing needed, and the person or object requiring is marked by /ko/ "to" or its equivalent. E.g.

/kya, ap ko pani cahie?/   Do you need water?

/mysəz ysmyth ko roTi cahie./   Mrs. Smith needs bread.

/ysmyth sahəb ko kya cahie./   What does Mr. Smith need?

/ap ko ek nəwkər cahie./   You need a servant.

The negative form of this construction is made with /nəhī/, inserted just before /cahie/:

/mysəz ysmyth ko roTi nəhī cahie./   Mrs. Smith does not need bread.

An infinitive may also occur as the grammatical subject of /cahie/. Again, the person or object requiring the action is marked by /ko/ or its equivalent. This construction is perhaps best translated by "must ...," etc.

/ap ko cəlna cahie./   You must go.

/ws ləRke ko pəRhna cahie./   That boy ought to study.

/rəhim sahəb ko rəhna cahie./   Mr. Rəhim should stay.

When the infinitive preceding /cahie/ has an object of its own, then two cases arise: in most eastern dialects of Urdu, the infinitive will always be masculine singular in form; in western dialects, the infinitive AGREES in number-gender with the OBJECT like a Type II adjective. The number-gender of the logical subject (marked by /ko/) does not influence the number-gender of the infinitive at all. In these western dialects, there is only one exception to this mandatory agreement of object and infinitive: if the object is followed by /ko/, then this "cuts off" any agreement with the infinitive, and the latter will be masculine singular in form. In this course, the western usage will be followed. E.g.

/ap ko wrdu pəRhni cahie./   You ought to study Urdu. [/wrdu/ is F1; hence /pəRhni/ instead of /pəRhna/. In the East, this would be /ap ko wrdu pəRhna cahie./]

/ap ko yy gylas dhona cahie./   You ought to wash this glass. [/gylas/ is M1, hence the MNS form of the infinitive.]

/ap ko yy səb gylas dhone cahiẽ./   You ought to wash all these glasses. [See below for /cahiẽ/.]

/ap ko yy pyali dhoni cahie./   You ought to wash this cup. [/pyali/ is F2.]

/ap ko yy pyaliã̃ dhoni cahiẽ./   You ought to wash these cups. [Compare:]

/ap ko ys pyali ko dhona cahie./   You ought to wash this cup. [Here /ko/ "cuts off" the object from the verb, and the latter thus occurs in an "impersonal" MNS form.]

80

/ap ko kəwfi nə pini cahie. /   You should not drink coffee.   [Object-verb agreement holds good also in a negative sentence.]

The /cahie/ construction differs grammatically from the polite imperative form in that the former has a plural form, /cahiẽ/, when its subject (the object required) is plural.

/ysmyth sahəb ko tin nəwkər cahiẽ. /   Mr. Smith needs three servants.

/mysəz ysmyth ko do pyaliã cahiẽ. /   Mrs. Smith needs two cups.

/ys salən ke lie pãc ənDe cahiẽ. /   Five eggs are required for [i. e.   to make] this curry.

3.400. SUPPLEMENTARY VOCABULARY

3.401. Supplementary Vocabulary.

The following numerals are all Type I adjectives. See also Sec. 2.401.

sola	sixteen
sətra	seventeen
wnnys	nineteen

The number nineteen also has a "writing pronunciation": /wnnis/.

Other days of the week are:

bwdh M1	Wednesday
jwmerat F1	Thursday
jwma M2	Friday
həfta M2	Saturday [Also "week"]
ytvar M1	Sunday

3.402. Supplementary Exercise I.

1. meri bivi <u>ek sal se</u> lahəwr mē rəhti hɔ̃y.
   from two weeks
   from seventeen days
   from thirteen years
   from sixteen weeks
   from twenty days

2. <u>həfte ko</u> mɔ̃y məsruf hũ. <u>pir ko</u> aie.
   on Thursday   on Sunday
   [in the] morning   at night
   on Wednesday   on Friday
   during the day   in the evening
   tomorrow   on Tuesday

3. həmari kylas mē <u>gyara</u> ləRkiā hɔ̃y.
   fourteen
   nineteen
   twelve
   ten
   seventeen boys and five

4. vw <u>pãc</u> ləRkiā <u>həfte ko</u> kylas mē nəhĩ atĩ.
   seven   on every Friday
   seventeen   on every Wednesday
   sixteen little daily
   twenty   in the evening
   fifteen   on every Tuesday

82

3.500. VOCABULARY AND GRAMMAR DRILL

3.501. Substitution.

1. | meri | syrf tin ləRkiā | hə̄y. [1] |
    |---|---|---|
    | our | four houses | |
    | my | five boys | |
    | your | six servants | |
    | Mr. Smith's | seven girls | |
    | Mrs. Smith's | only two brothers | |

    [1] These sentences will be idiomatically translated with "have" in English.

2. | mere pas [1] | roTi | həy. |
    |---|---|---|
    | near you | much meat | |
    | near Mr. Rəhim | one small cup | |
    | near us | a little rice | |
    | near him | too little sugar | |
    | near them | a black chicken | |

    [1] /[ke] pas/ has been rendered as "near" in these examples. These sentences should be translated with "have" in English, however.

3. | thoRa pani | pijie. |
    |---|---|
    | a cup of coffee | |
    | a cup of tea | |
    | some milk | |
    | a glass of water | |
    | two spoons of milk | |

4. | mere ləRke | mere valyd ke pas niw yəwrk mẽ | hə̄y. |
    |---|---|---|
    | the seventeen girls | with our professor in school | |
    | Mr. Smith's servants | with my brother in the office | |
    | Mr. Rəhim's wife | with our doctor in the hospital | |
    | my goats | with my boy in the market | |
    | my wife | with Mrs. Smith in Lahore | |

5. | ap log pir ko | həmare sath | bazar | cəlie. |
    |---|---|---|---|
    | in the evening | with Mr. Smith | college | |
    | on Tuesday | with me | office | |
    | on Saturday | with my wife | home | |
    | on Friday | with my boy | hospital | |
    | tomorrow | with them | Lahore | |

6. | khana | təyyar | həy. |
    |---|---|---|
    | rice | good | |
    | Monday | all right | |
    | permission | necessary | |
    | fork | small | |
    | water | too little | |
    | pepper | pleasing | |

ghi	good
salt	too much
the glass	empty
my little girl	busy

7. **mysəz ysmyth ko**   **pani**   dijie.

to Mr. Smith	chicken
to my boy	cow's meat
to his girl	curry and rice
to my wife	a plate of rice
to the Pakistani professor	food

8. **nəwkər se**   puchti hū.

from this girl
from the eldest [lit. big] boy
from that doctor
from that Englishman
from his father

9. **mysəz ysmyth**   **kwch**   nəhĩ   **khatĩ.**

Urdu	understands
too much water	drinks
hands	washes
peppers	takes
tea	drinks

10. **khane ke kəmre mē**   təʃrif laie.

in my house
tomorrow for dinner
one day to me [lit. near me]
on Thursday in class
[at] three o'clock in my room

11. **ap ko**   **kytna dudh əwr kytni cini**   cahie.

to Mr. Smith	how much vegetable
to your father	how much tea
to that little boy	how much meat
to your wife	how much bread
to your mother	how much salt

12. **mə̄y** **rat ko**   **syrf ek pyali cae**   piti hū.

during the day	two cups of coffee
in the evening	a glass of water
every day	too much coffee
[in the] morning	too little milk
every night	a little milk

13. **meri bivi se**   mylie.

with Mr. Smith's little girl
with our eldest [lit. big] boy

with my professor

with Mr. Rəhim's eldest [lit. big] brother

with Mr. əziz' wife

14. mə̃y   bəRi ləRki ko   pəRhne ke lie   əmrika   bhejna cahti hū.

    your big boy   for staying   Lahore

    the other [lit.   for asking   market
    second] servant

    his wife   for bringing tea   home

    the little girl   for giving food   office

    your brother   for taking permission Lawrence Road

15. əb   yjazət dijie.

    please sit down

    please send food

    please ask [from] the servant

    please take vegetable[s]

    please wash [your] hands

16. dudh   nə dijie.

    too much pepper   please don't take

    water   please don't drink

    home   please don't go

    in this house   please don't stay

    that curry   please don't eat

    food   please don't send

    this plate   please don't wash

    from that boy   please don't ask

    tomorrow   please don't come

    here   please don't read

3.502. Transformation.

1. Change the underlined verbs of the following sentences to the corresponding
    feminine forms.

    a. mə̃y bazar jana cahta hū.

    b. vw yəhā nəhī̃ rəhta.

    c. həm ws nəwkər ko roz khana bhejte hə̃y.

    d. kya, ap hər šam ko bazar jate hə̃y?

    e. vw swba hath dhote hə̃y.

    f. vw log yskul jate hə̃y, məgər pəRhte nəhī̃.

    g. mə̃y wrdu nəhī̃ səməjhta.

    h. vw salən nəhī̃ khate.

    i. ap bəhwt khana khate hə̃y.

    j. vw hər roz šam ko mere sath cae pita həy.

2. Replace the underlined nouns by the Urdu translation of the words or phrases in
    brackets. Make adjectives and verbs agree in number-gender, where necessary.

a. mere <u>hath</u> saf hə̄y.   [cups]

b. thoRa <u>pani</u> pijie.   [coffee]

c. ap ko kytna <u>dudh</u> cahie.   [tea]

d. vw ws bəRe <u>kalyj</u> mē pəRhte hə̄y, məgər mə̄y ys choTe <u>yskul</u> mē pəRhta hū.
   [university] [class]

e. mere do <u>ləRke</u> ap ki <u>kylas</u> mē pəRhte hə̄y.   [girls] [room]

f. ys bəRi <u>mez</u> pər thoRa <u>khana</u> cahie.   [bread] [clarified butter]

g. vw kala <u>cəmca</u> ws bəRe <u>cəmce</u> se zyada əccha həy.   [goat] [cow]

h. mere <u>valyd</u> roz <u>dəftər</u> jate hə̄y.   [mother] [university]

i. <u>jwma</u> əccha nəhī̃. <u>mə̄gəl</u> Thik həy.   [Thursday] [Wednesday]

j. <u>mysəz ysmyth</u> ko thoRa <u>pani</u> dijie.   [my wife] [coffee]

3. Change the underlined verbs to the polite imperative form.

a. ap lahəwr mē <u>rəhte hə̄y.</u>

b. ap kwch khana <u>bhejti hə̄y.</u>

c. ap log yəhā̃ təšrif <u>rəkhte hə̄y.</u>

d. ap yəhā̃ hath <u>dhote hə̄y.</u>

e. ap wn ke sath bazar <u>jate hə̄y.</u>

f. ap syrf ek pyali cae <u>piti hə̄y.</u>

g. ap log swba <u>ate hə̄y.</u>

h. ap mere kalyj mē <u>pəRhte hə̄y.</u>

i. wn ke nəwkər se <u>puchte hə̄y.</u>

j. ap salən <u>khate hə̄y.</u>

4. Change the following to negative sentences.

a. meri ləRki ys yskul mē pəRhti həy.

b. mysəz ysmyth hath dhona cahti hə̄y.

c. kya, ap ko mwrɣi cahie?

d. vw ləRkiā̃ kwch kam kərti hə̄y.

e. meri bivi roz ghər mē khati hə̄y.

f. həmari valda wrdu səməjhti hə̄y.

g. həm hər bwdh ko ap ke pas ate hə̄y.

h. mə̄y rəhim sahəb ko janti hū.

i. meri bivi mere valyd ke pas hə̄y.

j. vw yunyvərsyTi mē rəhti hə̄y.

3.503. Multiple Choice.

Only one of Mr. Smith's three responses to Dr. Rəhim's sentence is the proper one.
Repeat it to the instructor as if you were answering Dr. Rəhim.

1. R: əb kya vəqt həy, jənab.
   S: (a) ənDe əcche nəhī̃.
      (b) həmari valda nəwkri nəhī̃ kərtī̃.
      (c) əb sat bəje hə̄y.

2. R: salən lijie, sahəb.
   S: (a) šwkria. yy bəhwt əccha həy.
   (b) ws kale məkan ke piche həy.
   (c) mere dəftər se bəhwt dur nəhĩ.
3. R: kya, ap hath dhona cahte hə̃y?
   S: (a) mə̃y ap ki valda se puchta hũ.
   (b) ji hã. mə̃y hath se khata hũ.
   (c) ji nəhĩ. bwdh ko mə̃y məsruf hũ.
4. R: ap kys kalyj mẽ pəRhte hə̃y.
   S: (a) mə̃y yunyvərsyTi mẽ rəhta hũ.
   (b) mə̃y chwri kāTe se nəhĩ khata.
   (c) mə̃y yslamia kalyj mẽ pəRhta hũ.
5. R: ap ki kytni ləRkiã hə̃y.
   S: (a) həm car bhai hə̃y.
   (b) meri tin ləRkiã hə̃y.
   (c) mera syrf ek məkan həy.
6. R: kya, ap əziz sahəb ka məkan jante hə̃y?
   S: (a) ji nəhĩ. mə̃y nəhĩ janta.
   (b) ji hã. vw dəftər ys məkan ke age həy.
   (c) ji nəhĩ. meri syrf ek ləRki həy.
7. R: ap ka tisra ləRka kya kərta həy.
   S: (a) vw hath se nəhĩ khatĩ.
   (b) vw mere bhai ke pas niw yəwrk mẽ həy.
   (c) yy bəhwt əccha həy, məgər ys mẽ myrcẽ zyada hə̃y.
8. R: kya, ap ys lal məkan mẽ rəhte hə̃y?
   S: (a) ji hã. həmari kylas mẽ sola ləRke hə̃y, əwr wnnys ləRkiã bhi hə̃y.
   (b) ji nəhĩ. mə̃y ws səfəyd məkan mẽ rəhta hũ.
   (c) ji hã. ytvar ko mə̃y xali hũ. kya, bazar jana cahte hə̃y?
9. R: ys kam ke lie ek chwri zəruri həy.
   S: (a) bəhwt əccha, mə̃y əbhi leta hũ.
   (b) vw ws nəwkər ko khana bhejta həy.
   (c) Thik həy. mə̃y əbhi deta hũ.
10. R: kya, ap syrf ek gylas pani pina cahte hə̃y?
    S: (a) ji hã. əbhi cəlna cahie.
    (b) šwkria. əbhi ys gylas mẽ pani həy.
    (c) ji hã. bəkriã bəhwt pəsənd hə̃y.

3.504. Response.

1. ap ke kytne bhai hə̃y.
2. kya, ap ke valyd əwr valda yəhã hə̃y?
3. kya, ap həmare sath ytvar ko bazar cəlna cahte hə̃y?
4. ap ke valyd kəhã nəwkri kərte hə̃y.

5. ap kys ke məkan mẽ rəhte hə̃y.

6. kya, ap ke pas ek nəwkər həy?

7. kya, ap ko salən pəsənd həy?

8. kya, ap bwdh ko məsruf hə̃y?

9. ap swba kya pina cahte hə̃y.

10. kya, əmrika jane ke lie yjazət cahie?

11. khane ki mez pər kya həy.

12. ap cae ke sath kytni cini lete hə̃y.

13. kya, ap hath se khana cahte hə̃y?

14. ap kys vəqt khana khate hə̃y.

15. kya, ap mere ghər təšrif lana cahte hə̃y?

3.505. Conversation Practice.

Mr. Smith and Dr. Rəhim are seated in a restaurant.

R: ap kya khana cahte hə̃y.

S: mə̃y bəkri ka gošt əwr kwch səbzi khana cahta hũ.

R [to the servant]: ysmyth sahəb ke lie ek pyleT bəkri ka gošt əwr ek pyleT səbzi laie.
    yy əmrikən hə̃y, əwr əmrikən log myrcē zyada nəhĩ khate.

Sr: bəhwt əccha. [To Dr. Rəhim]: ap ko kya cahie.

R: mere lie mwrγi əwr gae ka gošt laie. ys ke sath kwch cavəl bhi laie.

They begin to eat.

S: salən bəhwt əccha həy, məgər myrcē kwch zyada hə̃y.

R: ji hã, pakystani log myrcē bəhwt khate hə̃y. -- ap ko cae cahie?

S: ji nəhĩ. kəwfi Thik həy.

R [to the servant]: kya, kəwfi təyyar həy?

Sr: ji hã. əbhi lata hũ.

Mr. əziz arrives.

R: əziz sahəb, adab ərz! təšrif laie!

ə: adab ərz!

R: myzaj šərif?

ə: šwkria.

R: təšrif rəkhie. ysmyth sahəb se mylie.

ə: myzaj šərif?

S: myhrbani.

R [to the servant]: yy mez choTi həy. kya, dusri bəRi mez xali nəhĩ həy?

Sr: ji hã. vw samne həy. vəhã təšrif laie.

The party moves to the bigger table.

R [to Mr. əziz]: ap kya khana cahte hə̃y.

ə: mə̃y kəwfi pini cahta hũ.

R [to the servant]: ek xali pyali laie, əwr ek gylas pani bhi cahie.

Sr: mə̃y əbhi lata hū.

ə [to Mr. Smith]: kya, ap əmrikən hə̃y?

S: ji hā, mə̃y əmrikən hū. mə̃y yunyvərsyTi mē profesər hū. ap kya kam kərte hə̃y.

ə: mə̃y carTərD bə̃yk mē kam kərta hū.

S: ap ke valyd kya kam kərte hə̃y.

ə: vw ek dəftər mē kam kərte hə̃y.

S: kya, ap ke əwr bhai hə̃y?

ə: ji hā. mere tin bhai hə̃y.

S: wn ki kya wmrē hə̃y.

ə: pəhle ki wmr wnnys sal, dusre ki wmr sətra sal, əwr tisre ki wmr sola sal həy.

R [to Mr. Smith]: ysmyth sahəb, yy cavəl lijie. bəhwt əccha həy.

S: šwkria. əbhi mere pas salən əwr roTi həy.

ə: ap kāTe əwr chwri se khate hə̃y. həm log hath se khate hə̃y.

S: ji hā. həm cavəl bhi kāTe əwr chwri se khate hə̃y.

ə [to Dr. Rəhim]: meri cae ki pyali mē cini kəm həy. ek cəmca cini əwr dijie.

R: yy lijie.

ə [to Mr. Smith]: ap pakystan mē kəb se hə̃y.

S: mə̃y do sal se pakystan mē hū.

ə: kya, pakystan pəsənd həy?

S: ji hā, bəhwt pəsənd həy.

ə: əccha, əb yjazət cahta hū.

R: kya, kwch zəruri kam həy?

ə: ji hā. meri ləRkiā mere sath bazar jana cahti hə̃y. wn ke sath jana həy. [To Mr. Smith:]
mə̃y ap se mə̃gəl ko mylna cahta hū.

S: mə̃gəl ko mə̃y kylas leta hū. ap log həfte ko mere sath khana khaie.

ə: bəhwt əccha. xwda hafyz.

S and R [together]: xwda hafyz.

S: mə̃y bhi əb cəlna cahta hū. ap həfte ko khane pər təšrif laie.

R: bəhwt əccha, jənab. xwda hafyz.

3.506. Conversation Stimulus.

1. Mr. Smith and Dr. Rəhim are eating. Mr. Smith asks Dr. Rəhim for eggs,
vegetable[s] and salt. Dr. Rəhim replies that the eggs are not good; he does ask Mr.
Smith to take the vegetables and salt. Mr. Smith asks Dr. Rəhim what he would like to
drink. Dr. Rəhim replies that he takes only one cup of tea daily, and he only wants to
drink a glass of water. Mr. Smith remarks that he himself drinks too much coffee. Dr.
Rəhim says that Mr. Smith is an American, and American people drink a lot of coffee. Mr.
Smith replies that people in Pakistan drink a lot of tea. They drink tea with [/ke sath/]
milk and sugar. Some American people only drink tea.

2. Mrs. Smith is chatting with Mrs. Rəhim. Mrs. Rəhim asks Mrs. Smith whether
she has any sons ["boys"]. Mrs. Smith replies that she does not have any sons, but she
has three daughters. They are studying in New York. They are living with Mrs. Smith's

89

mother. The eldest ["big"] one wants to come to Pakistan. The second wants to study in college in New York. The third does nothing now. Mrs. Rəhim says that she has two sons. Does Mrs. Smith know the elder one? He is a doctor in the American hospital. Mrs. Smith replies that she knows him. Mrs. Rəhim says that her other son is working in the office. He works in her brother's office. Mrs. Smith says that she does not know him.

3.600. VOCABULARY

Further abbreviations include:

(1) Feminine Type I and Type II nouns are indicated by "F1" and "F2" respectively.

(2) Nouns which occur only in the plural are marked by a "p" inserted immediately after the letter denoting their gender: "Mp1" "masculine plural Type I," "Fp2" "feminine plural Type II," etc.

(3) Nouns having no plural are indicated by "np" in brackets after their gender-type symbols.

(4) "PA" stands for "predicate adjective." Essentially, this is an adjective-like element which occurs only in complex formations with verbs and never as a modifier before a noun. The predicate adjective also displays the Type I - Type II dichotomy seen for adjectives. It will be discussed in detail in a later Unit.

ənDa M2	egg
əTThara A1	eighteen
bazar M1	market, bazaar
bəkri F2	(female) goat
begəm F1	madame, lady
bhejna	to send
bis A1	twenty
bivi F2	wife
bwdh M1 [pl. rare]	Wednesday
cae F1 [mass noun: pl. rare]	tea
cahie	is needed, necessary, must, ought, should
caval M1 [mass noun: pl. rare]	rice
cəlna	to move, go
cəmca M2	spoon
chwri F2	knife, tableknife
cini F2 [mass noun: pl. rare]	sugar
dena	to give
dhona	to wash
dudh M1 [mass noun: pl. rare]	milk
dyn M1	day
gae F1	cow
ghi M1 [mass noun: pl. rare]	clarified butter, "ghee"
gošt M1	meat
gylas M1	drinking glass
hath M1	hand
həfta M2	Saturday; week
həm	we
həmara A2	our
jwma M2 [pl. rare]	Friday

jwmerat F1 [pl. rare]	Thursday
kāTa M2	thorn; fork
kəmra M2	room
kəwfi F2 [mass noun: pl. rare]	coffee
khana	to eat
kwch A1	some, any, something, anything, somewhat
kylas F1	class
kytna A2	how much? how many?
lana	to bring
ləRki F2	girl
lena	to take
[ke] lie	for, in order to
log Mpl	people
malum PA1	known
məsruf A1	busy, engaged
mə̄gəl M1 [pl. rare]	Tuesday
mez F1	table
mwrɣi F2	hen, chicken
myrc F1	pepper
mysəz [or /mysyz/] F1 [np]	Mrs.
nə	no, not
nəmək M1 [mass noun: pl. rare]	salt
nəwkər M1	servant
nəwkri F2	service, employment, job
pani M1 [mass noun: pl. rare]	water
pina	to drink
pir M1 [in eastern dialects; F1 in the west] [pl. rare]	Monday
puchna	to ask (a question)
pyali F2	cup
pyleT [or /pəleT/] F1	plate
rat F1	night
rəkhna	to put, place, set down, keep
roTi F2	bread, a slice of bread [idiomatically: "food, a meal"]
saf A1	clean
salən M1	meat curry
[ke] sath	with, accompanying
səbzi F2	vegetable
sətra A1	seventeen
sola A1	sixteen
syrf A1 Adv	only
šwkria M2	thanks, gratitude, thank you
təšrif F1 [np]	honour, dignity

92

təyyar A1	ready
thoRa A2	a little (in amount), a small quantity of
Thik A1	all right, fine, well, good
valyd M1	father
valda F1	mother
wmr F1	age (of a person), lifespan
wnnys [or /wnnis/] A1	nineteen
xali A1	empty
yjazət F1	permission
ys lie	therefore
ytvar M1 [pl. rare]	Sunday
zəruri A1	necessary
zyada A1	more, much, too much, too many

Anarkali, a bustling commercial centre in Lahore.

UNIT FOUR

4.000. CONVERSATION

Mrs. Smith and Mrs. Rəhim are on their way to the market to do some shopping.

people MOP — logõ

"tonga," a type of horse carriage M2 — tāga

"tonga" driver M2 — tāgevala

[you, he, we, they] will ask — puchẽge

MR: We need a tonga. We'll ask this tonga driver. — həm logõ ko ek tāga cahie. ys tāgevale se puchẽge.

place F1 — jəga [or /jəgəh/ or /jəgha/]

TD: Where do you want to go? [Lit. Which place is to go?] — kys jəga jana həy.

Delhi F2 [np] — dyhli

money M2 — pəysa

you [nonhonorific, M] will take — ləge

MR: [We] have to go to Delhi Bazaar. How much money will you take? — dyhli bazar jana həy. kytne pəyse ləge.

two and a half A1 — Dhai

rupee M2 [MOS and MNP: /rupəe/] — rupəya

[I M] will take — lũga

TD: I'll take two and a half rupees. — mõy Dhai rupəe lũga.

this much, this many, so much, so many A2 — ytna

[you, he, we, they] will give — dẽge

one and a half A1 — DeRh

MR: This is too much. We won't give so much. We'll give one and a half rupees. — yy zyada həy. ytna nəhĩ dẽge. həm DeRh rupəya dẽge.

[I M] will go — jaũga

a quarter more than ... A1 — səva

TD: No, this is very little. I won't go. Give [me] two and a quarter rupees. — nəhĩ, yy bəhwt kəm həy. mõy nəhĩ jaũga. səva do rupəe dijie.

MR: No, we'll give two rupees. We won't give more than this [lit. from this more]. — nəhĩ, həm do rupəe dẽge. ys se zyada nəhĩ dẽge.

please sit — bəyThie

which? A2 — kəwnsa

shop, store F1 — dwkan

TD: All right, please sit down. Which shop are you going to in Delhi Bazaar? [Lit. In Delhi Bazaar on which shop is [it] to go?] — əccha, bəyThie. dyhli bazar mẽ kəwnsi dwkan pər jana həy.

[I F] will tell — bətaũgi

today — aj

[you, she, we, they] will buy — xəridẽgi

MR: I'll just tell [you]. [To Mrs. Smith:] What do you want to buy today? — əbhi bətaũgi. -- ap aj kya xəridẽgi.

95

me OS	mwjh
[one's] own A2	əpna
cloth, clothing M2	kəpRa
MS: I need some cloth for myself.	mwjh ko əpne lie kwch kəpRa cahie.
cloth merchant M2	kəpRevala
MR: Let's go to my cloth merchant's shop.	mére kəpRevale ki dwkan pər cəlie.
you [nonhonorific]	twm
shoes MOP	jutõ
MR: Do you know that big shoe shop [lit. that big shoes' shop]? In front of it there is a cloth merchant's shop.	kya, twm ko jutõ ki vw bəRi dwkan malum həy? ws ke samne ek kəpRevale ki dwkan həy.
street F1	səRək
left A2 [MOS and MNP: /bãē/]	bãyã
direction, side F1	tərəf
TD: Yes, it is on the left side of the street.	ji hã, vw səRək ke bãē tərəf həy.

As they ride along in the tonga.

right A2 [MOS and MNP: /dãē/]	dãyã
books FOP	kytabõ
utensils, vessels MOP	bərtənõ
carpet merchant M2	qalinvala
fruit merchant M2	phəlvala
MR: To the right of this shop there are bookstores. Utensil shops are opposite. On ahead are carpet merchants, and this way are fruit merchants.	ys dwkan ke dãē tərəf kytabõ ki dwkanē hõy. bərtənõ ki dwkanē samne hõy. age qalinvale hõy, əwr ys tərəf phəlvale hõy.
TD: This is your cloth merchant's shop.	yy ap ke kəpRevale ki dwkan həy.
wait [nonhonorific]!	Thəyro
speed; rapidly, quickly F2 Adv	jəldi
back, again	vapəs
[you, he, we, they] will come	aēge
MR: All right, wait! We'll return quickly.	əccha, Thəyro! həm jəldi vapəs aēge.

The two ladies enter the cloth merchant's shop.

please show	dykhaie
price F1	qimət
MS: Please show [me] that cloth. What is its price?	vw kəpRa dykhaie. ws ki kya qimət həy.
three quarters, a quarter less than ... A2	pəwna
yard M1	gəz
CM: This is two and three quarters [lit. a quarter less than three] rupees a yard.	yy pəwne tin rupəe gəz həy.
expensive A2	mə̃hga
cheap A2	səsta
or	ya

MS: This is [too] expensive. Please show [us some] cheap cloth, or make the price of this less.

    yy mə̃hga həy. səsta kəpRa dykhaie, ya ys ki qimət kəm kijie.

[I M] sell   bᵉcta hū

opinion M1   xyal [or /xəyal/]

that Conj   ky

pretty, beautiful A1   xubsurət

CM: I won't [lit. don't] sell this for less than two and a half rupees a yard. It's my opinion that you take this. It's very pretty.

    mə̃y Dhai rupəe gəz se kəm nəhī̃ bᵉcta hū. mera xyal həy, ky ap yy lijie. bəhwt xubsurət həy.

please cut   kaTie

MS: All right. Please cut four yards [for me].   əccha. car gəz kaTie.

[you, she, we, they] will see   dekhē̃gi

CM: Won't you see [some] more cloth?   kya, ap əwr kəpRa nəhī̃ dekhē̃gi?

enough! Interjection   bəs

enough A1   kafi

MS: Enough, [that] is sufficient.   bəs, kafi həy.

The ladies return to the tonga.

go, move [nonhonorific]!   cəlo

hour M2   ghənTa

fare, rent M2   kyraya

you [nonhonorific, M] take   lete ho

MR [to the driver]: Go to a fruit merchant's shop. What fare do you take for one hour?

    phəlvale ki dwkan pər cəlo. twm ek ghənTe ka kya kyraya lete ho.

"anna," a coin worth one sixteenth of a rupee M2   ana

after   [ke] bad

TD: The first hour's fare is one rupee four annas. After this, one rupee.

    pəhle ghənTe ka kyraya ek rupəya car ane həy. ys ke bad ek rupəya.

The ladies enter a fruit shop.

your [nonhonorific] A2   twmhara

fruit M1   phəl

MR: What fruits do you have?   twmhare pas kya phəl hə̃y.

apple M1   seb

banana M2   kela

mango M1   am

FM: Apples, bananas, mangoes -- What do you need?   seb, kele, am -- ap ko kya cahie.

how A2   kəysa

MS: How are the apples?   seb kəyse hə̃y.

these days, nowadays   ajkəl

FM: Nowadays apples are not good. Take mangoes.   ajkəl seb əcche nəhī̃. am lijie.

mangoes MOP   amõ

price, rate M1   bhao

MR: What is the price of mangoes?   amõ ka kya bhao həy.

--- and a half A1   saRhe

"seer," a measure of weight: approximately   ser
two pounds M1

FM: Five and a half rupees a seer.   saRhe pãc rupəe ser.

give [nonhonorific]!   do

MS: Give [me] two seers of mangoes.   do ser am do.

The ladies return to the tonga.

you [nonhonorific, M] know   jante ho

MR [to the driver]: Do you know the   kya, twm yunyvərsyTi jante ho?
University?

TD: Yes.   ji hã.

why?   kyõ [or /kyũ/]

MS: Why are you going there?   ap vəhã kyõ jati hãy.

friend M/F1   dost

sisters FOP   bəhnõ

MR: [I] have to meet the sisters of a friend   rəhim sahəb ke dost ki bəhnõ se mylna
of Rəhim Sahəb's.   həy.

MS: All right, I'll go along too.   əccha, mãy bhi sath cəlti hũ.

4.100. WORD STUDY

4.101. A /tāga/ M2 "tonga" is a small, two-wheeled horse carriage. It is still the commonest means of passenger transport in many northern Indian and Pakistani cities, although it is being replaced by motor rickshas and taxis in larger centres. The common European spelling, "tonga," implies a pronunciation something like the vowel + nasal of a word like "tong." The correct vowel is like that of the American pronunciation of "father," except that it is nasalised.

4.102. /pəysa/ M2 has two meanings: "money" and "a coin, worth one fourth of an anna (i. e. one sixty-fourth of a rupee)." Under the old system, a rupee consisted of sixteen annas or sixty-four /pəyse/. The decimal system has recently been introduced both in India and Pakistan, and the rupee is now divided into one hundred /nəe pəyse/ (/nəya/ A2 "new"). In larger cities, many shops have completely changed over to the decimal system, but smaller merchants and villagers still employ /ane/ and /pəyse/ (and even /pai/ F2 "pie": each /pəysa/ was divided into three /pai/, but this unit is almost obsolete).

Note that /pəysa/ is used in the singular for "money" in a general sense. When the plural is used, it often means money in a physical sense: "cash, bills, coins." E.g.

/mere pas bəhwt pəysa həy./   I have a lot of money. [I. e. I am wealthy.]

/mere pas bəhwt pəyse hə̃y./   I have a lot of money. [I. e. I have a lot of cash, bills, coins.]

4.103. "More than ..." and "less than ..." are expressed by /... se zyada/ and /... se kəm/ respectively. This construction is similar to the comparative and super-lative formations discussed in Sec. 2.304. E.g.

/ys se zyada nəhĩ dẽge./   [We] won't give more than this.

/mə̃y Dhai rupəe gəz se kəm nəhĩ becta hũ./   I won't [lit. don't] sell [this] for less than two and a half rupees a yard.

/ek ghənTe se zyada yəhã nəhĩ Thəyrna cahie./   [You] should not stay here more than one hour.

4.104. Urdu has two words for "which?":

(1) The oblique forms of /kəwn/ "who?": singular /kys/ and plural /kyn/, discussed in Sec. 2.310. /kys/ and /kyn/ occur before postpositions meaning either "whom?" or "which?"; they occur before oblique nouns only with the meaning "which?".

(2) /kəwnsa/ A2 means only "which?"; it may occur before both nominative and oblique nouns. This form actually consists of /kəwn/ + an enclitic /sa/ A2, which will be introduced later.

There is a slight semantic difference between /kys/ - /kyn/ (meaning "which?") and /kəwnsa/: before postpositions and oblique nouns, the former may denote either "which one of a number of objects" or "which type of a number of types" or "which abstract of a number of abstracts": the latter, on the other hand, signifies only "which one of a number of objects." The matter is complicated by the fact that /kys/ and /kyn/ cannot occur before

99

nominative nouns, however, and there /kəwnsa/ must serve both functions. E. g.

/ap ko kəwnsa məkan pəsənd həy. /   Which house do you like?

/yy kəwnsi kytab həy. /   Which book is this?

/ap kys dwkan pər jana cahte hə̄y. /   To which shop do you wish to go?
[Either "which type of shop" or "which out of all these shops. "
Compare:]

/ap kəwnsi dwkan pər jana cahte hə̄y. /   To which shop do you wish to go?
["Which out of all these shops" only]

/ap kys tərəf jaēge. /   Which direction will you go? [/tərəf/ Fl "way,
direction" is an abstract. /kəwnsi tərəf/ is not idiomatic.]

4.105. In Urdu, one must say "on the shop" where an English speaker would say "to
the shop" or "at the shop. " This usage is idiomatic and thus unpredictable. If one wishes
to specify "inside, " /mē/ or /[ke] əndər/ are used. If "in the neighbourhood" or "in the
vicinity" are meant, /[ke] pas/ will be employed. /[ke] pas/ is also used for going "to"
a person. Many nouns denoting places are used with no postposition at all (see Sec. 2.311).

/yunyvərsyTi cəlo. /   Go to the university.

/yunyvərsyTi mē cəlo. /   Go inside the university. [I. e. inside the gates,
inside the grounds.]

/yunyvərsyTi ke pas cəlo. /   Go to the university. [I. e. close by, in the
vicinity.]

/DakTər ke pas cəlo. /   Go to the doctor. [No other postposition can be
employed here.]

/dwkan pər cəlo. /   Go to the shop. [/pər/ occurs idiomatically here.]

4.106. In the singular, /kəpRa/ M2 is a mass noun denoting "cloth. " In the plural,
it may denote either different varieties of cloth or "clothes, clothing. " E. g.

/yy mera kəpRa həy. /   This is my cloth.

/yy mere kəpRe hə̄y. /   These are my clothes.

4.107. Although /cəlna/ has a great many idiomatic usages, it has been introduced
so far only in its basic meaning: "to go, move. " It is important to note that it has the
sense of "to go with the person spoken to, " whereas /jana/ simply means "to go. " Thus,
Mrs. Smith says, /əccha, mə̄y bhi sath cəlti hū. /   "All right, I'll go along too. " If she
were going alone or with someone other than the person to whom she is speaking, she
would have used /jati hū. /. Similarly, /jaie/ means "please go! " with the connotation of
going alone or with some third person, while /cəlie/ means "please go [with me]! " or just
"let's go! "

4.108. Although /tərəf/ "way, direction, side" is clearly feminine, many Urdu
speakers treat it as masculine when it occurs as a sort of compound postposition: /ke ...
tərəf/ "on, to, at the ... side. " E. g.

/dwkan ke dāē tərəf/   on the right side of the shop. [Instead of the
expected /ki dāī tərəf/, which is also heard]

/səRək ke bāē tərəf/   on the left side of the street. [Instead of /ki bāī
tərəf/, which is also correct but less common]

4.109. /qimət/ F1 "price" is used for the price of an item sold in individual units; it is also employed for the price of commodities sold by measurement or weight, but somewhat less commonly. /bhao/ M1, on the other hand is used only for the price or rate of items sold by measurement or weight.

4.110. /bəs/ "enough!" is used mainly as an interjection. It also has an idiomatic usage as a Type I noun meaning "capability, ability." The Type II adjective /kafi/, on the other hand, signifies "enough [for a purpose]" and also, colloquially, "lots of, a large amount of." E.g.

> /yy mere bəs mē nəhī ati./ This doesn't come within my capability. [I.e. This is beyond my powers.]
>
> /rəhim sahəb ke pas kafi pəysa həy./ Mr. Rəhim has enough money [for some previously mentioned purpose]. [Or:] Mr. Rəhim has plenty of money.

4.111. /kəysa/ is used as a Type II adjective meaning "how?" and also "what kind of ... ?" or "what sort of ... ?" It is also employed in a predicate containing a verb as an adverb meaning "how?" and in this latter usage it is always in the MOS form: /kəyse/. E.g.

> /ap ki kəwfi kəysi həy./ How is your coffee? [/kəysi/ is a predicate adjective in this sentence, agreeing with /kəwfi/ F2.]
>
> /ap ka ləRka kəysa həy./ How is your boy? [/kəysa/ agrees with /ləRka/ M2.]
>
> /yy kele kəyse hэ̄y./ How are these bananas? [/kəyse/ agrees with /kele/ M2, MNP.]
>
> /yy kəysi ləRki həy./ What sort of girl is she?
>
> /ap ka ləRka yskul kəyse jata həy./ How does your boy go to school? [/kəyse/ is an adverb here and does not agree with the subject.]
>
> /ap ki ləRki yskul kəysɛ jati həy./ How does your girl go to school?

The adverbial form, /kəyse/, is also employed to ask the price or rate of commodities sold by weight, by measurement, or by dozens (e.g. plates, cups, knives, etc.). Compare:

> /yy cini kəysi həy./ How is this sugar? [I.e. Is this sugar good or bad?]
>
> /yy cini kəyse həy./ How [much] is this sugar? [I.e. What is its price?]
>
> /seb kəyse hэ̄y./ How are the apples? [Or:] How much are the apples?

4.112. /ajkəl/ "these days, nowadays" is a compound of /aj/ "today" and /kəl/ "tomorrow, yesterday."

4.113. A /ser/ M1 is a measure containing slightly more than two pounds. The English transliteration "seer" is misleading, since one would expect a pronunciation something like */sir/. A /ser/ is divided into four /pao/ M1; a /pao/ contains four /chəTāk/ M1; a /chəTāk/ is divided into five /tola/ M2. A /ser/ thus contains eighty /tole/. The next largest unit above a /ser/ is the /mən/, containing forty /ser/ (roughly eighty pounds).

4.201. Aspirated and Unaspirated Voiced Stops.

The voiced aspirated stops (/bh, dh, Dh, jh, gh/) have no counterpart in English or in other European languages. They consist of a voiced stop component (/b, d, D, j, g/) + a voiced aspirate release. They are thus not really like such English sequences as the bh in clubhouse, the dh in madhouse, the gh in doghouse, etc., since the English voiced stop tends to become somewhat devoiced before the voiceless /h/.

In the author's experience, the very differentness of these sounds renders them more distinctive and more of a challenge, and thus easier to master. The student should practise sequences like /əb hi/, /ad ha/, /bwj hao/, /bəg har/, etc., attempting to bring the stop and the aspiration closer each time until they form one sound: i.e. until the /b/, /d/, /D/, /j/, or /g/ is released into the /h/. It must be pointed out also that a sequence like /bh/ may contrast with /b h/; in the latter sequence the /b/ is completely released before the /h/ is begun, and the /h/ also tends to be voiceless.

/bəla/ calamity; evil spirit	/bhəla/ good
/do/ two	/dhoo/ wash!
/Dol/ bucket	/Dhol/ drum
/jəR/ root	/jhəR/ rain shower
/gwl/ rose	/ghwl/ dissolve, melt!
/bəjao/ ring, strike, play!	/bwjhao/ extinguish!
/bap/ father	/bhap/ steam
/dəmək/ glitter, flash	/dhəmək/ thumping sound
/gwn/ quality	/ghwn/ weevil, termite
/bat/ word, matter, thing	/bhat/ cooked rice
/dud/ smoke	/dudh/ · milk
/gyn/ count!	/ghyn/ nauseous disgust
/jal/ net	/jhal/ soldered patch
/bag/ reins	/bagh/ tiger
/bədna/ to wager	/bədhna/ type of clay pot with a spout
/dar/ scaffold	/dhar/ edge
/Dalna/ to pour	/Dhalna/ to cast, mold
/bura/ raw sugar	/bhura/ brown
/pujta həy/ worships	/bujhta həy/ solves [an enigma]
/gat/ woman's torso, figure	/ghat/ ambush
/gəda/ beggar	/gədha/ donkey
/jina/ to live	/jhina/ to lay a fire well
/duni/ double	/dhuni/ incense
/Dak/ mail, post	/Dhak/ sp. tree
/gol/ round	/ghol/ dissolve, melt! [Transitive]
/DeRh/ one and a half	/DheR/ menial caste in the Deccan
/swmba/ tool used to break stones	/swmbha/ [same as /swmba/; alternate pronunciation]

/dwnya/ world   /dhwnya/ one who gins cotton
/ag/ fire   /magh/ name of a month in the Hindu
                                              calendar
/səmaj/ assembly, society   /səməjh/ understanding
/adi/ habituated   /adhi/ half [F]
/gənna/ sugar-cane   /gəhna/ ornaments, jewellery
                                      /ghəna/ close, thick [as jungle, hair]
/jəRən/ setting stones in jewellery   /jhəRən/ crumbs
/gəRa/ penetrated, fixed   /ghəRa/ water pitcher
                                      /gəRha/ pit, hole
/bai/ mistress; wind   /bhai/ brother
                                      /bəhai/ "Bahai," a member of the Bahai
                                              sect
/ber/ fruit, berry   /bheR/ sheep
                                      /bəheRh/ a medicinal herb
/bari/ turn, time   /bhari/ heavy
                                      /byhari/ a person from Bihar
/gəhn/ eclipse   /ghən/ anvil
/dəhk/ burning, blazing   /dhək/ shock, sudden fright

4.202. Phonetic Drill: Auditory Dictation.

1. bəjao   bwjhao   jal   bujhta   jhəR   jhəRən   jina   jhal   pujta   səmaj

2. gəRa   gat   ghol   gəhn   ghyn   bagh   magh   gwn   bhag   ghəRa

3. dud   dhəmək   bədna   adhi   dhar   dəhk   dhwnya   dhək   gəda   dudh

4. bari   bhura   swmbha   bhat   bhag   bhəla   bəla   bəjao   bhai   bhari

5. Dol   Dak   DheR   Dhalna   Dhol   Dalna   DeRh   Dhak

6. ghən   ghəna   ghwn   ghwl   ghat   bheR   bhat   bhag   bhura   bhai

7. dhəmək   dhoo   bədhna   gədha   dhuni   DheR   Dhol   Dhalna   Dhak

8. jhina   jhal   bujhta   səməjh   jhəR

9. dəhk   dhək   gəhn   ghən   bəhai   bhai   gənna   ghəna   bheR   bəheRh

10. bwjhao   dudh   bujhta   bagh   swmbha   magh   səməjh   bədhna   adhi
     gədha

4.203. Aspirated Stops in Contrast with a Stop + /h/.

Certain aspirated stops (/bh/, /dh/, /kh/, and /th/) and the affricate /jh/ are also
found in contrast with a syllable-final /b/, /d/, /k/, /t/, or /j/ followed by a syllable-
initial /h/. The /dh/ of /wdhəm/ M1 [np] "noise, turmoil" is thus seen to be different
from the /d/ + /h/ of /ədhəm/ M1 "black-coloured horse." Etymologically speaking,
words containing aspirated stops and affricates are of Indo-Aryan origin, while those having

a stop followed by syllable-initial /h/ are loanwords or compounds borrowed from Arabic and Persian. These latter words are almost all of a literary nature, and many are quite rare.

There are two possible solutions: (1) A "juncture" (written /-/) can be inserted into the Perso-Arabic loanwords -- useful enough, perhaps, in a compound (e.g. /bəd-hal/ Al "wretched, miserable," where /bəd/ and /hal/ are both separable elements) but rather incongruous when inserted into a single word (e.g. /tət-hir/ Fl [np] "sanctity, purity"). (2) An alternative solution is to consider all aspirated stops as single units and then treat a stop followed by syllable-initial /h/ as a consonant cluster. This requires some sort of separate notation: perhaps a raised "^{h}" for an aspirated consonant and an "h" on the line to denote the separate phoneme /h/. The words mentioned above can thus be unambiguously rewritten: /wd^{h}əm/, /ədhəm/, /bədhal/, and /təthir/.

In view of the rarity of this contrast (and also for typographical reasons), the author has made no attempt to indicate this phenomenon in the alphabet employed in this book. Only one item containing a stop followed by a syllable-initial /h/ occurs in the entire Course, and the majority of speakers pronounce it too with an aspirated /j^h/ unless they are speaking quite carefully: /rwjhan/ Ml "inclination, trend, desire" (introduced in Unit XXIV). Except for this word (and the compound /bədhal/, which is mentioned as an example but is not introduced), occurrences of a stop followed by /h/ in this book are assumed to be aspirated consonants.

Some examples of this contrast may be of interest, however. For illustration purposes, the second solution presented above is employed.

/mwbhəm/ ambiguous, vague

/məbhut/ amazed, astonished

/ybham/ ambiguity, doubt

/ədhəm/ black-coloured horse

/mədhoš/ intoxicated, out of one's senses

/məkhul/ having collyrium on the eyes

/təthir/ sanctity, purity

/ythar/ sanctification, purification

/məjhul/ unknown, passive (grammatical term)

/rwjhan/ trend, inclination, desire

/wb^{h}ar/ raising, swelling

/kəb^{h}i/ sometime, anytime

/wd^{h}əm/ noise, turmoil

/wd^{h}ar/ debt

/məd^{h}wr/ sweet (as music)

/mək^{h}ana/ sp. of seed

/nyt^{h}arna/ to filter a liquid, allow a liquid to settle

/ət^{h}ah/ bottomless, deep

/məj^{h}ola/ middle

/ryj^{h}ana/ to make happy

4.300. ANALYSIS

4.301. The Oblique Plural of Nouns.

Oblique plural nouns are marked by the suffix /ō/. In the case of Type I nouns (both
masculine and feminine) and also Type II masculine nouns, this suffix is found immediately
after the noun stem; in the case of Type II feminine nouns, it occurs after the feminine
suffix /i/. Full paradigms are:

MASCULINE

	TYPE I				TYPE II	
MNS	∅	/ghər/		MNS	a	/ləRka/
MOS	∅	/ghər/		MOS	e	/ləRke/
MNP	∅	/ghər/		MNP	e	/ləRke/
MOP	ō	/ghərō/		MOP	ō	/ləRkō/

FEMININE

	TYPE I				TYPE II	
FNS	∅	/mez/		FNS	i	/ləRki/
FOS	∅	/mez/		FOS	i	/ləRki/
FNP	ē	/mezē/		FNP	iā	/ləRkiā/
FOP	ō	/mezō/		FOP	iō	/ləRkiō/

4.302. The Oblique Plural of Adjectives.

There are no number-case distinctions for Type I (masculine or feminine) or Type II
feminine adjectives. Type II masculine adjectives, however, display a special MNS form.
Paradigms are:

MASCULINE

	TYPE I				TYPE II	
MNS	∅	/hošyar/		MNS	a	/bəRa/
MOS	∅	/hošyar/		MOS	e	/bəRe/
MNP	∅	/hošyar/		MNP	e	/bəRe/
MOP	∅	/hošyar/		MOP	e	/bəRe/

FEMININE

	TYPE I				TYPE II	
FNS	∅	/hošyar/		FNS	i	/bəRi/
FOS	∅	/hošyar/		FOS	i	/bəRi/
FNP	∅	/hošyar/		FNP	i	/bəRi/
FOP	∅	/hošyar/		FOP	i	/bəRi/

Many adjectives may be employed as nouns, however, and when this is the case the
various plural suffixes may occur with the adjective stem. E. g.

/bəRõ ko bətana cahie. / [You] ought to tell the elders. [Lit. "big-
[one]-s. " /bəRõ/ here may mean "adults, " "elders, " "important
persons"; in other contexts it may refer to "large ones" (e. g. as
large fruit).]

4.303. Nouns and Adjectives Ending in /aya/, /āya/, /āyā/, /əya/.

Type II nouns and adjectives ending in /aya/, /āya/, /āyā/, /əya/, etc. in the MNS
have MOS and MNP forms without the /y/. The /y/ is normally retained in the MOP forms,
but there are various exceptions (e. g. /rupõ/ as the MOP form of /rupəya/ M2 "rupee" --
as well as the expected form /rupəyõ/ in certain dialects; similarly the MOS MNP form
is either /rupəe/ or /rupəy/). The feminine forms of Type II adjectives of this sort also
have no /y/. Sample paradigms are:

MNS	[y]a	/rupəya/	MNS	[y]a	/kyraya/
MOS	e	/rupəe/	MOS	e	/kyrae/
MNP	e	/rupəe/	MNP	e	/kyrae/
MOP	[y]õ[1]	/rupəyõ/	MOP	[y]õ	/kyrayõ/

[1]Or; more commonly perhaps, /rupõ/.

/dāyā/ A2 "right, dexter" may be taken as a sample of an adjective of this pattern:

MNS	[y]ā	/dāyā/	FNS	r̄	/dār̄/
MOS	ē	/dāē/	FOS	r̄	/dār̄/
MNP	ē	/dāē/	FNP	r̄	/dār̄/
MOP	ē	/dāē/	FOP	r̄	/dār̄/

4.304. Order Within the Noun Phrase (Continued).

Although the basic structure of the Urdu noun phrase was described in Sec. 2.303,
further details still remain to be discussed. At certain points Urdu structure is so different
from English as to require considerable elucidation. There are also innumerable differences
of idiom: for example, some English compound nouns are expressed by a possessive phrase
in Urdu:

/kytabõ ki dwkan/ bookstore. [Lit. books' store.]
/jutõ ki dwkan/ shoestore. [Lit. shoes' store.]
/khane ka kəmra/ dining room. [Lit. food's room.]

When one wishes to express "that bookstore, " a subtle semantic distinction can be made
by placing the demonstrative in different positions:

/vw kytabõ ki dwkan/ that bookstore
/kytabõ ki vw dwkan/ that bookstore

The former order lays no special stress either on "books" or on "store"; the latter
order slightly stresses "store":

/kytabõ ki vw dwkan age həy. / THAT bookSTORE is on ahead.

Note that if the demonstrative had modified "books, " it would have had to be OP in order
to agree with its noun:

/yn kytabõ ki dwkan/ these books' store. [I. e. the store where these specific books may be found]

In English, a phrase like "that fruitseller's shop" is ambiguous: does the "that" refer to the shop or to the fruitseller? In Urdu, there are four possibilities, each with its own slight semantic emphasis:

/vw phəlvale ki dwkan/   that fruitseller's shop. [No special emphasis]

/phəlvale ki vw dwkan/   that shop of the fruitseller. [Slight emphasis on "shop" -- perhaps he has more than one]

/ws phəlvale ki dwkan/   that fruitseller's shop. [That specific fruitseller]

/ws phəlvale ki vw dwkan/   that shop of that fruitseller. [A specific shop (out of several) belonging to a specific fruitseller]

In such phrases, an adjective will usually occur just before the noun it modifies:

/kytabõ ki bəRi dwkan/   big bookstore. [Lit. books' big store]

/jutõ ki vw bəRi dwkan/   that big shoestore. [Lit. shoes' that big store]

4.305. Possessive Modifiers of a Phrase.

At times, two separate possessive modifiers may precede a noun; the first, however, really modifies an "encapsulated" unit composed of the second possessive + the noun. This may be symbolised as [N ka] [N ka N]. E.g.

/mere tāge ka ek ghənTe ka kyraya/   my tonga's one hour's fare

Here, two possessive modifiers occur before /kyraya/. Both end in the MNS postposition /ka/. /mere tāge ka/ does not modify just /kyraya/, however; it really modifies a phrase composed of another possessive modifier (/ek ghənTe ka/) + the noun /kyraya/: i.e. [my tonga's] [one hour's fare]. Compare:

/mere ləRke ke dost ka məkan/   my boy's friend's house

Here, /mere ləRke ke/ is a satellite of /dost ka/, and both together are employed as a satellite of /məkan/. This may be symbolised as [[N ke] N ka] [N].

4.306. Phrases Specifying Quantity or Price.

Words denoting a price, an amount, or a measure occur directly before the noun denoting the measure. The latter may then be followed by the noun denoting the substance measured or priced. No postposition is necessary. E.g.

/tin rupəe gəz/   three rupees [a] yard

/tin rupəe roz/   three rupees [per] day

/tin ser am/   three seer[s] [of] mango[es]

After a noun denoting a measure, the noun denoting the substance measured will be (a) SINGULAR if the substance is a single piece, an aggregate of tiny objects too numerous to be counted, or a liquid: e.g. meat, cloth, a single fruit (from which one wishes to measure off a piece), rice, sugar, milk, water, etc.; and (b) PLURAL if the substance is divisible into countable units: e.g. fruits, wood (when divisible into sticks), coal, etc. There are, of course, many borderline cases in which either a singular or a plural form may be employed. Usage also differs from speaker to speaker. Many persons lean toward the singular form, especially when the substance measured is Type II feminine: e. g.

/tin mən ləkRi/ three "maunds" of wood. [Rather than /tin mən ləkRiā/, which is less common although also correct.]

Other examples:

/tin gəz kəpRa/ three yards of cloth. [Cloth is treated as a single piece and hence is singular.]

/tin ser kele/ three seers of bananas. [Bananas are countable and therefore plural here.]

/tin ser cini/ three seers of sugar. [Sugar is an aggregate of tiny grains and is therefore singular.]

/tin ser dudh/ three seers of milk. [Milk is a liquid and therefore is singular.]

In English, a verb agreeing with a plural measure is always itself plural: e. g. "three pound_s of meat _are in this package" "five yard_s of cloth _are enough, " etc. In Urdu, the situation is rather different: a very rough rule similar to that just given above must be formulated: (a) if the substance measured is indivisible (i. e. a single piece, a liquid, etc.), any agreeing verb will be SINGULAR; if the substance is divisible into units (e. g. fruits, wood, coal, etc.), the verb will be PLURAL.

There are many exceptions to this "rule," however: (a) some grains and grain-like substances are treated as plural, while others are idiomatically singular: e. g.

/tin ser cavəl hə̄y. / There _are three seers of rice.

/tin ser gehū̃ hə̄y. / There _are three seers of wheat. [But note:]

/tin ser cini həy. / There _is three seers of sugar. [And:]

/tin ser aTa həy. / There _is three seers of flour. [And:]

/tin ser məkəi həy. / There _is three seers of maize.

(b) Some substances may be treated as singular or plural depending upon whether a single variety is being considered or several varieties:

/tin ser dal həy. / There _is three seers of pulse. [One variety only. Compare:]

/tin ser dalē̃ hə̄y. / There _are three seers of [various varieties of] pulse.

(c) A few items idiomatically belong to one category or the other with no apparent semantic "reason":

/tin ser pyaz həy. / There _is three seers of onion[s]. [Onions are logically div̄isible into un̄its like mangoes, bananas, etc. and should be treated as a plural. They are idiomatically singular, however.]

Usage will be indicated in the Exercises wherever necessary.

When made definite by a preceding numeral, nouns denoting measures, units of time, units of money, etc. are OBLIQUE SINGULAR before a postposition where one might expect the OBLIQUE PLURAL. When the measure is indefinite, however, such nouns occur before the postposition in their expected oblique plural form. E. g.

/tin rupəe mē̃/ in three rupees. [Instead of */tin rupõ mē̃/. Compare /tin məkanõ mē̃/ "in three houses".]

/tin ghənTe mē̃/ in three hours. [Not */tin ghənTõ mē̃/.]

/do ser mē̃/ in two seers. [Not */do serõ mē̃/.]

/car dyn ke bad/ after four days. [Not */car dynõ ke bad/. Compare:]

/kwch dynõ ke bad/ after some days. [/kwch/ Al "some" is _indefinite; the oblique plural form /dynõ/ must thus occur.]

4.307. Fraction Words.

Various common fractions are expressed by single words. Fractions up to and including one and three quarters are treated as singular (i.e. modify singular nouns and
agree with singular verbs); fractions above one and three quarters are treated as plural.
Fraction words include:

(1) /DeRh/ A1 "one and a half." This word may be used just as one would use any
other numeral adjective. E.g.

/DeRh bəja həy./ It is 1:30. [Note that this is treated as singular,
since the fraction is less than two.]

/kyraya DeRh rupəya həy./ The fare is one and a half rupees.

/DeRh ser am dijie!/ Please give [me] one and a half seers of mangoes!

(2) /Dhai/ A1 "two and a half" is used like /DeRh/, except that it is treated as a
plural. E.g.

/Dhai bəje hə̄y./ It is 2:30.

/vw Dhai ghənTe mẽ aẽge./ They'll come in two and a half hours. [For
/ghənTe/ instead of */ghənTõ/ here, see the last paragraph of Sec.
4.306.]

/Dhai ser am dijie!/ Please give [me] two and a half seers of mangoes!

(3) /adha/ A2 and /adh/ A1 both denote "half." /adh/ is used only before recognised
units of measurement: e.g. /ser/ M1 "seer," /ghənTa/ M2 "hour," /mən/ M1 "maund,"
/mil/ M1 "mile," etc. /adha/ is used elsewhere. Modern usage, however, tends to
employ /adha/ freely in all situations: one may thus say either /adha mil/ or /adh mil/.
Note that neither /adha/ nor /adh/ may enter into any time phrases with /bəja/ or /bəje/
"o'clock." E.g.

/vw adh ghənTe mẽ aẽge./ They'll come in half an hour. [/adhe ghənTe
mẽ/ is also correct.]

/syrf adhi pyali kəwfi dijie!/ Please give me only half a cup of coffee!
[*/adh pyali/ cannot occur since /pyali/ F2 "cup" is not a recognised
measurement.]

/ysmyth sahəb ko adha gylas pani cahie./ Mr. Smith needs half a glass
of water.

/adh ser seb dijie!/ Please give me half a seer of apples! [/adha ser/
is also possible.]

(4) /səva/ A1 "a quarter more than" may occur directly before a noun and also as a
modifier before a numeral. It may be idiomatically employed with numerals from "one"
through "nineteen" and also with units denoting hundreds, thousands, etc. (see below);
although it is grammatically "correct" with numerals from "twenty" through "ninety-nine,"
it is not idiomatic. The following examples will clarify its usage and meaning:

/səva bəja həy./ It is 1:15. [This is treated as singular because the
fraction is less than two.]

/səva ek bəja həy./ It is 1:15. [Same as the last.]

/səva car bəje hə̄y./ It is 4:15. [This is plural because the fraction is
more than two.]

/vw səva ghənTe mẽ aẽge./ He'll come in an hour and a quarter.

/səva do ser am dijie!/ Please give [me] two and a quarter seers of
mangoes.

(5) /pəwna/ A2, /pəwne/ A1, and /pəwn/ A1 "three quarters, a quarter less than"
are used as adjectives and also as modifiers of a following numeral. /pəwna/ occurs before
nouns (and also before /bəja/ "o'clock") meaning "three quarters of a ..." /pəwne/ occurs
before numerals over "one" and under "twenty" meaning "a quarter less than ..."; like
/səva/, this form is correct but not idiomatic with numerals between "twenty" and "ninety-
nine." /pəwn/ occurs before some -- but not all -- nouns denoting recognised units of
measurement (see (3) above). E.g.

> /pəwn bəja həy./ It is 12:45. [This is singular because the fraction is
> less than two. /pəwna bəja həy./ is also found but is considered less
> correct.]

> /pəwna ek bəja həy./ It is 12:45. [Same as the last.]

> /pəwne tin ghənTe mẽ aẽge./ [They] will come in two and three quarters
> hours. [I.e. a quarter less than three.]

> /pəwne do ser am dijie!/ Please give [me] one and three quarters seers
> of mangoes. [I.e. a quarter less than two.]

> /vw pəwn ghənTe mẽ aẽge./ They'll come in three quarters of an hour.
> [Compare the third example above.]

> /pəwn gəz kəpRa dijie!/ Please give [me] three quarters of a yard of
> cloth. [Compare the fourth example above.]

(6) /saRhe/ "... and a half" is not truly an adjective; it does not occur before nouns
but only before some following numeral. Note that /saRhe/ can never be used before a
noun meaning "half of a ..."; see /adha/ under (3) above. Nor can /saRhe/ be used with
/ek/ A1 "one" or /do/ A1 "two," since these amounts are expressed by /DeRh/ and /Dhai/
respectively (see nos. (1) and (2) above). E.g.

> /saRhe tin bəje hẽy./ It is 3:30.

> /vw saRhe pãc ghənTe mẽ aẽge./ They'll come in five and a half hours.

> /saRhe bara gəz kaTie!/ Please cut twelve and a half yards.

Before larger numeral units (e.g. /səw/ A1 "hundred," /həzar/ A1 "thousand," /lakh/
A1 "hundred thousand," /kəroR/ A1 "ten million," etc.), /DeRh/, /Dhai/, and /səva/ may
occur directly. /pəwne/ and /saRhe/ may be used only as modifiers of a numeral followed
by one of these larger units. Neither /adha/ nor /adh/ commonly occur before these units,
although one may occasionally hear an instance (e.g. /adh lakh/ "half a lakh" -- it is
considered better to say /pəcas həzar/ "fifty thousand"). E.g.

> /Dhai səw/ two hundred and fifty. [Lit. two and a half hundred.]

> /DeRh həzar/ one thousand five hundred. [Lit. one and a half thousand.]

> /səva lakh/ one hundred and twenty-five thousand. [Lit. one and a
> quarter lakh.]

When /səva/, /pəwne/, and /saRhe/ occur as modifiers of a numeral preceding one
of these larger units, they refer to a fraction of the larger unit and NOT to a fraction of
the intervening numeral: e.g.

> /səva do səw/ two and a quarter hundred = 225. [/səva/ here expresses
> a quarter more of a hundred and not a quarter more of two.]

> /pəwne tin lakh/ two and three quarters lakhs = 275,000. [Lit. a
> quarter less than three lakhs. /pəwne/ denotes three quarters of a
> lakh here, rather than three quarters of three.]

> /saRhe sat həzar/ seven thousand five hundred = 7,500. [The "half"
> applies to "thousand" and not to "seven."]

Again, these fractions are commonly used only before numerals from "one" through "nineteen" (and with the restrictions on /pəwne/ and /saRhe/ noted above). E. g.

/pəwne nəw həzar/   eight and three quarters thousand = 8, 750.
/səva pəndra səw/   fifteen and a quarter hundred = 1, 525.
/saRhe əTThara həzar/   eighteen and a half thousand = 18, 500.

4. 308.   The Suffix /val/.

This affix has several uses, only one of which is introduced here: added to a noun and followed by the Type II number-gender suffixes, it denotes the seller, doer, user, agent, etc. of the noun. The noun to which /val/ is added will be in the oblique singular form (or, less commonly, in the oblique plural). E. g.

/tāgevala/   tonga driver. [/tāga/ M2 "tonga"]
/kəpRevala/   cloth merchant. [/kəpRa/ M2 "cloth"]
/jutevala/   shoe merchant. [/juta/ M2 "shoe"]
/qālinvala/   carpet merchant. [/qalin/ M1 "carpet"]
/phəlvala/   fruit merchant. [/phəl/ M1 "fruit"]

Feminine forms would be:

/kəpRevali/   [fem.] cloth merchant. [Etc.]

4. 309.   The Oblique Form of /mə̄y/ "I."

The oblique form of /mə̄y/ "I" is /mwjh/. This is found before the simple postpositions: /mwjh se/ "from me," /mwjh pər/ "on me," /mwjh ko/ "me, to me" (but note that /mwjh ko/ is considered somewhat less elegant than the special object form to be introduced in Unit V; see Sec. 3. 310). It must be remembered that the possessive form, /mera/ A2 "my," occurs before the "compound postpositions" rather than /mwjh/.

4. 310.   /twm/   "you [nonhonorific]. "

The pronoun /twm/ "you [nonhonorific]" has now been introduced. The oblique form is also /twm/: e.g. /twm se/ "from you [nonhonorific]," /twm pər/ "on you [non-honorific]," etc. The possessive form is /twmhara/ A2 (compare /həmara/ A2 "our"). Present tense forms of verbs agreeing with /twm/ end in /-te ho/ for the masculine and /-ti ho/ for the feminine: e. g. /twm jate ho/ "you [nonhonorific masculine] go, " /twm jati ho/ "you [nonhonorific feminine] go, " etc.   /twm/ may refer either to singular or plural, although -- like /ap/, /həm/, /vw/, etc. -- plurality may be emphatically indicated by the addition of /log/ Mpl "people": e. g. /twm log/ "you people [nonhonorific], " /twm logō se/ "from you people [nonhonorific], " etc. Note, however, that the possessive pronoun /twmhara/ cannot be "pluralised" by /log/.

It is also important to note that the term "nonhonorific" does not mean "impolite. " There is just none of the courteous, honorific connotation which accompanies /ap/. Forms of /twm/ may be used between familiars of equal status (although nowadays /ap/ is

increasingly employed even among close friends and to one's children) and also by a
superior to an inferior, an elder to a younger person, etc.: e.g. to children, to servants,
to younger kinship relations, to lower class people, etc. This situation seems to be
constantly changing, however, in favour of a levelling and equalising use of /ap/. It is
thus not "wrong" to use /ap/ to inferiors, but it is definitely impolite to employ /twm/ with
a non-familiar equal or with a superior. The student should use /ap/ while exploring the
cultural limitations on the use of /twm/ forms.

4.311. /əpna/ "one's own."

The possessive adjective /əpna/ A2 "one's own" is required wherever the possessor
of a noun is the same as the subject of the sentence. In English, one says "I meet my
friend daily," "Will you work in your office today?" "We send our boy to school," etc.
In Urdu, "my," "your," and "our" in such sentences MUST be expressed by a form of
/əpna/: e.g.

/mẽy roz əpne dost se mylta hũ. / I meet [my] own friend daily.

/kya, ap əpne dəftər mẽ kam kərẽge?/ Will you work in [your] own
office?

/həm əpne ləRke ko yskul bhejte hẽy. / We send [our] own boy to school.

When the verb of the sentence is /cahie/ (Sec. 3.314) or the <I + /həy/> construction,
/əpna/ is required if the logical subject (marked with /ko/ in these constructions) is the
same as the possessor of some noun in the sentence. E.g.

/ysmyth sahəb ko əpne dost se mylna həy. / Mr. Smith has to meet [his]
own friend. [Although the logical subject /ysmyth sahəb/ is here
grammatically marked as an object by /ko/, /əpna/ must occur.]

/ap ko əpni kytab cahie. / You need [your] own book.

A third person subject and a third person possessor (of the same gender and number)
are ambiguous in English but not in Urdu. In sentences like "He meets his friend," "She
meets her friend," or "They meet their friend," the referent of "his," "her," and "their"
is ambiguous: whose friend -- the subject's or some other third person's? Compare the
following Urdu sentences:

/vw əpne dost se mylta həy. / He meets [his] own friend. [Compare:]

/vw ws ke dost se mylta həy. / He meets his friend. [Someone else's
friend]

/vw əpni kytab pəRhti həy. / She reads [her] own book. [Compare:]

/vw ws ki kytab pəRhti həy. / She reads her book. [Someone else's
book. Since /ws/ does not show gender, this could also be "his
book. "]

/əpna/ also occurs after a possessive noun phrase or a possessive pronominal
adjective with the meaning "one's very own." This construction places strong emphasis
on the possessor and is used only in a situation in which the ownership of the item is being
contested. E.g.

/yy ws ka əpna məkan həy. / This is his [or her] very own house. [And
no one else's!]

/yy mere dost ki əpni kytab həy. / This is my friend's very own book.
[And no one else's!]

112

4.312. Further Oblique Locatives With No Postposition.

/kys jəga/ "which place?" and /ys tərəf/ "this way, direction" are two more examples of oblique locative constructions without a postposition. See Sec. 2.311. Similarly, one may encounter /ys jəga/ "this place here," /ws jəga/ "that place there," /kys tərəf/ "which way?" /ws tərəf/ "that way," etc. /tərəf/ Fl "way direction" is also used as a compound postposition: e.g.

/vw meri tərəf dekhta həy./   He looks toward me, in my direction.
/bāē tərəf jaie./   Please go to the left. [See Sec. 4.108.]

4.313. The Verb: the <S + /ega/> Construction.

Future tense forms are composed of (a) a verb stem, (b) the person-number affixes /ū/, /e/, /ē/, and /o/, (c) the suffix /g/, and (d) suffixes like those of the Type II adjective: /a/, /e/, and /i/.

The paradigm of the future tense is as follows:

PRONOUN	VERB: MASCULINE	FEMININE	
mə̄y	pəRhūga	pəRhūgi	I will read
[tu	pəRhega	pəRhegi	thou wilt read]
vw	pəRhega	pəRhegi	he, she, it will read
həm	pəRhēge	pəRhēgi	we will read
twm	pəRhoge	pəRhogi	you [nonhonorific] will read
ap	pəRhēge	pəRhēgi	you [honorific] will read
vw	pəRhēge	pəRhēgi	they will read

The "conditional," a form consisting of just the verb stem + the person-number affixes (e.g. /jaū/ "may I go," /pəRhē/ "may we (etc.) read"), will be introduced in Unit VI.

The "we [F]" form ending in /i/ is rather uncommon. Women usually employ the masculine form: /pəRhēge/ "[we [M or F]] will read." See Sec. 3.312.

The negative employed with the future tense is /nəhī̆/: e.g.

/mə̄y nəhī̆ jaūga/   I will not go
/vw nəhī̆ pəRhega/   he will not read

Two common verbs have different stem forms before the future tense suffixes: /dena/ "to give" has a stem alternant /d/, and /lena/ "to take" has /l/. See also Sec. 3.313. Paradigms are:

PRONOUN	VERB: MASCULINE	FEMININE	
mə̄y	dūga	dūgi	I will give
[tu	dega	degi	thou wilt give]
vw	dega	degi	he, she, it will give
həm	dēge	dēgi	we will give
twm	doge	dogi	you [nonhonorific] will give
ap	dēge	dēgi	you [honorific] will give

113

PRONOUN	VERB: MASCULINE	FEMININE	
vw	dḗge	dḗgi	they will give
mə̄y	lūga	lūgi	I will take
[tu	lega	legi	thou wilt take]
vw	lega	legi	he, she, it will take
həm	lḗge	lḗgi	we will take
twm	loge	logi	you [nonhonorific] will take
ap	lḗge	lḗgi	you [honorific] will take
vw	lḗge	lḗgi	they will take

4.314. The Verb: the <S + /o/> Construction.

The nonhonorific imperative form consists of a verb stem + /o/. It is employed in those cultural contexts described above for /twm/ "you [nonhonorific]"; see Sec. 4.310. There is no differentiation for singular and plural. E.g.

/twm pəRho!/ You [nonhonorific] read!

/twm age cəlo!/ You [nonhonorific] go on ahead!

/twm log yəhā Thəyro!/ You [nonhonorific] people wait here!

The negative employed with this form is commonly /mət/ or, with a somewhat politer connotation, /nə/. E.g.

/yy kam mət kəro!/ [You nonhonorific] don't do this work!

/yy kam nə kəro!/ [You nonhonorific] don't do this work!

Again, /dena/ "to give" and /lena/ "to take" have the stem alternants /d/ and /l/ respectively. E.g.

/ytne pəyse lo!/ Take this much money!

/do ser am do!/ Give two seers of mangoes! [/do/ Al "two" is homophonous with /do/ "[you nonhonorific] give!"]

/ysmyth sahəb ko myrc mət do!/ Don't give pepper to Mr. Smith!

4.315. Stem Alternants ± /ə/.

Many stems have two alternant forms: one ending in VCəC[h] before a consonant or before juncture (i.e. the end of the word), and another ending in VCC[h] before a vowel. [Here, "V" means "any vowel," and "C" denotes "any consonant."] E.g.

/səRək/ Fl road, street. [Here /ə/ occurs between /R/ and /k/ because /-əRək/ is of the pattern VCəC and occurs before juncture (i.e. /əRək/ is the end of the word).]

/səməjh/ Fl understanding. [Here the pattern is VCəC[h] before juncture.]

/səməjhta həy/ [he] understands. [Here the pattern is VCəCh before a following consonant.]

Compare:

/səRkḗ/ FNP roads, streets. [Here a vowel follows /k/, and the pattern is thus /VCC/ with no /ə/.]

/səRkõ/ FOP roads, streets, [Same as above.]

/səmjhūga/ [I M] will understand. [The vowel /ū/ follows the stem, and the pattern is thus VCCh.]

/qimtē/ FNP prices.

It must be noted that the /ə/ in /səRək/, /qimət/, /səməjh/, etc. is not just an "echo vowel," like that heard after the /h/ in a word like /bəhn/ F1 "sister." There is a contrast in standard Urdu between a final VCəC and VCC: e.g. /nəzər/ F1 "sight, vision" versus /nəzr/ F1 "offering." [This contrast disappears, however, in lower class dialects.]

It must also be emphasised that this phenomenon occurs only when the stem ends in VCəC[h]; VCCəC[h], for example, retains the /ə/ everywhere. E.g.

/bərtən/ M1 vessel, utensil

/bərtənõ/ MOP vessels, utensils. [The /ə/ occurs even though the stem is followed by a vowel.]

In literary Urdu, there are also many words ending in VCəC which retain the /ə/ before a following vowel suffix.

4.400. SUPPLEMENTARY VOCABULARY

4.401. Supplementary Vocabulary.

The following numerals are all Type I adjectives. See Sec. 2.401.

ykkys	twenty-one
bays	twenty-two
teys	twenty-three
cəwbys	twenty-four
pəccys	twenty-five

All of the above have a "writing pronunciation" ending in /is/ instead of /ys/: e.g. /ykkis/, /pəccis/. This is not common in speech.

Other items are:

adha A2 [or /adh/ A1]	half [See Sec. 4.307]
dwkandar M1	shopkeeper
jutevala M2	shoe merchant
mət Adv	no, not [Used only with nonhonorific imperative; see Sec. 4.314]
qalin M1 [F1 according to some]	carpet

4.402. Supplementary Exercise I.

1. yn <u>bərtənõ</u> ki qimət <u>teys rupəe</u> həy.

shoes	twenty-two rupees
carpets	twenty-five rupees, eight annas
books	eight annas
plates	twenty-four rupees, seven annas
cups	twenty-one rupees, twelve annas

2. mere nəwkər ko <u>saRhe tin ser cini</u>   dijie.

half a seer of milk
half a cup of tea
half a plate of meat
half a yard of cloth
twenty-one seers of rice

3. <u>vw qalinvala</u>   <u>dəs dyn ke bad</u>   vapəs aega.

my friend	after half an hour
the shopkeeper	after three hours and a half
the shoe merchant	after two and a half hours
that tonga driver	after some days
that cloth merchant	after twenty-three days

4.500. VOCABULARY AND GRAMMAR DRILL

4.501. Substitution.

1. mə̃y <u>Dhai rupəe</u> lūga.
   three seers of mangoes
   two and three quarters yards of cloth
   five and a half cups of sugar
   half a seer of meat
   seven and a quarter rupees

2. <u>ys</u> se zyada nəhĭ dẽge.
   five rupees
   two seers
   ten and a quarter annas
   this much ghi
   this price

3. kya, <u>twm ko</u>   <u>jutõ ki vw bəRi dwkan</u>   malum həy?
       to him   that carpet merchant's shop
       to you   that street
       [honorific]
       to them   that fruit seller's little shop
       to your wife   number five Lawrence Road
       to this servant   that utensil shop

4. vw <u>səRək ke bãẽ tərəf</u> həy.
   on the right side of this shop
   on the left side of my house
   on my right hand
   behind the shoestore
   in front of [opposite to] the University

5. həm <u>jəldi</u>   vapəs <u>aẽge</u>.
       tomorrow   will go
       in three hours your book   will send
       after two days this sugar   will give
       after two weeks your boy   will bring
       in the evening this table   will take

6. <u>meri bəhn ko</u>   <u>kəpRa</u>   dykhaie.
   to Mrs. Smith   [a] cheap carpet
   to my friend   that blue plate
   to the shopkeeper   this fruit
   to this girl   that black cup
   to my mother   these red books

7. <u>ys</u> ki qimət kəm kijie.
   these bananas
   that white plate

117

these eggs

that knife

that blue cloth

8. mə̃y <u>Dhai rupəe gəz</u>   se kəm nəhĩ <u>becta hũ.</u>

      three and a quarter rupees   will take [F]

      six and a half seers   will give [M]

      eleven rupees a seer   will sell [M]

      twenty carpets   will buy [F]

      seventeen yards of cloth   will sell [F]

9. kya, ap əwr <u>kəpRa</u>   nəhĩ <u>dekhẽgi?</u>

      shoes   will take

      carpets   will show

      vessels   will buy

      spoons   will give

      rupees   will send

10. twm <u>ek ghənTe</u> ka kya kyraya lete ho.

      two days

      three weeks

      five years

      this room

      [your] own shop

11. <u>seb</u>   <u>kəyse</u> hə̃y.

      your sister   how?

      your little girls   how?

      his father   how?

      your mother   how?

      those boys   how?

12. ap vəhã kyõ <u>jati hə̃y.</u>

          stay [F]

          study [F]

          sit [M]

          eat [F]

          work [F] [Lit. do work]

13. aj <u>rəhim sahəb ke dost ki bəhnõ</u> se mylna həy.

      [my] own brother's boys

      their wives

      the doctor's girls

      [my] own friends' professors

      the shopkeeper's mother

14. <u>phəlvale ki dwkan pər</u>   cəlo![1]   [3, 4]

      to the hospital   [1, 3, 4]

      to Mr. Rəhim's office   [1, 3, 4]

      to my office   [1, 3, 4]

| to the bookstore | [2, 3, 4] |
| to Islamia College | [1, 3, 4] |

[1]As stated in Sec. 4.105, there are four possible directive locatives in Urdu: (1) a general locative with no postposition; (2) /pər/ "on, at, at the door of"; (3) /mẽ/"in, into, inside"; and (4) /[ke] pas/ "near, in the vicinity of." The numerals in brackets indicate which of these four translations is possible for each of the above sentences.

15. mera xyal həy, ky ap <u>yy</u>   lijie. [1]

         this table

         these chickens

         those spoons

         those carpets

         these black shoes

[1]Each of the above has two possible translations: (1) a nominative object with no postposition: e.g. /mera xyal həy, ky ap <u>yy</u> lijie./; (2) an oblique object marked by /ko/: e.g. /mera xyal həy, ky ap <u>ys ko</u> lijie./ See Sec. 3.310. Give both translations for each of the above.

4.502. Transformation.

1. Change the verb forms of the following sentences to the corresponding future forms.

   a.   ap ke dost vəhã kyõ <u>jate həy</u>.

   b.   mə̃y pakystan mẽ <u>rəhta hũ</u>.

   c.   vw ys kəpRe ko <u>xəridti həy</u>.

   d.   ap ke valyd nəwkərõ ko pəyse <u>dete həy</u>.

   e.   vw phəlvala əcche phəl <u>lata həy</u>.

   f.   kya, twm wrdu <u>pəRhte ho</u>?

   g.   mə̃y roz ap se <u>mylti hũ</u>.

   h.   yy tãgevala kya kyraya <u>leta həy</u>.

   i.   kya, ap bhi sath <u>cəlte hə̃y</u>?

   j.   vw log nəhĩ <u>səməjhte</u>.

   k.   vw roz <u>ata həy</u>.

   l.   vw ləRkiã mere ghər nəhĩ <u>atĩ</u>.

   m.   vw log meri tərəf <u>dekhte hə̃y</u>.

   n.   həm dãẽ hath se <u>khate hə̃y</u>.

   o.   twm kys jəga <u>jati ho</u>.

2. Change the underlined OS nouns in the following sentences to OP forms. Change any agreeing adjectives where necessary.

   a.   əpni <u>ləRki</u> ko əmrika bhejũgi.

   b.   ys <u>mez</u> pər khana nə rəkhie.

   c.   ws <u>məkan</u> ka kya kyraya həy.

   d.   mera ghər ys <u>səRək</u> se dur nəhĩ.

   e.   vw mere <u>dost</u> ko dəs rupəe dega.

   f.   mere <u>profesər</u> ki <u>bivi</u> se puchie.

g. mə̃y əpne nəwkər ko tin ser am dũga.

h. yy ləRki əpni bəhn se xubsurət həy.

i. kwch log qalin pər bəyThẽge.

j. yy qimət ws qimət se kəm həy.

k. vw cəmce se nəhĩ khaẽge.

l. ws bəkri ko kaTo!

m. vw log ys bəRi dwkan mẽ kam kərte hə̃y.

n. ys xali gylas ko dhoie!

o. vw ys choTe kāTe əwr ys bəRi chwri ko xəridẽge.

3. Change the verb forms in the following sentences from the honorific imperative to the nonhonorific imperative. Change the subject pronoun where necessary. Note: the negative employed with the nonhonorific forms may be either /nə/ or /mət/, as described in Sec. 4.314.

a. ysmyth sahəb ko pani dijie!

b. yəhã nə bəyThie!

c. age cəlie!

d. ws dwkandar ko khana bhejie!

e. səva car rupəe lijie!

f. ap yəhã Thəyrie!

g. mere pas aie!

h. əccha kəpRa dykhaie!

i. ap log khana khaie!

j. mere nəwkər sʒ puchie!

k. ytna dudh nə pijie!

l. yy kam jəldi kijie!

m. ws dwkan mẽ dekhie!

n. ek pyleT gošt laie!

o. ys jəga nə rəhie!

4.503. Variation.

1. kys jəga jana həy.
   ap ko kys jəga jana həy.
   aj ap ko kys jəga jana həy.
   aj rəhim sahəb ko kys jəga jana həy.
   aj rəhim sahəb ko kys vəqt jana həy.
   kəl rəhim sahəb ko kys kalyj jana həy.

2. həm do rupəe dẽge.
   həm syrf do rupəe dẽge.
   həm ys nəwkər ko syrf do rupəe dẽge.
   vw tãgevale ko syrf DeRh rupəya dega.
   vw ap ko Dhai rupəe nəhĩ degi.
   vw log ytne kəpRe ke lie ys kəpRevale ko do rupəe nəhĩ dẽge.

120

3. əbhi bətaũgi.
    əbhi ap ko bətaũgi.
    əbhi ap ko yn ka nam bətaũgi.
    mə̃y ysmyth sahəb ko ys kəpRe ki qimət bətaũgi.
    mə̃y kəl ap logõ ko ys phəl ka nam bətaũgi.
    mə̃y do dyn ke bad ap ko ys məkan ka kyraya bətaũgi.
4. ap aj kya xəridẽge.
    ap kəl kytna kəpRa xəridẽge.
    ap yəhã kəwnsa phəl xəridẽge.
    ap log ys kytab ko kyõ xəridẽge.
    ap log kəyse bərtən xəridẽge.
    ap log kys dwkan se jute xəridẽgi.
5. ws ke samne ek kəpRevale ki dwkan həy.
    ys phəlvale ke samne do kəpRevalõ ki dwkanẽ hə̃y.
    ys phəlvale ki dwkan ke piche meri dwkan həy.
    yn dwkanõ ke piche ek əwr dwkan həy.
    yn dwkanõ ke age mere bhai ki dwkan həy.
    yn qalinvalõ ke bãẽ tərəf ek əwr khane ki dwkan həy.
6. həm jəldi vapəs aẽge.
    həm ap ke pas jəldi vapəs aẽge.
    həm ap ke valyd sahəb ke pas jəldi vapəs aẽge.
    həm log car ghənTe ke bad ys dwkan pər vapəs aẽge.
    həm log tin həfte ke bad vapəs aẽge.
    həm log do sal ke bad vapəs aẽge.
7. mere dost ko kəpRa dykhaie.
    həm logõ ko əccha əwr səsta kəpRa dykhaie.
    həm logõ ko ys se əccha əwr səsta kəpRa dykhaie.
    həm logõ ko ek nila qalin dykhaie.
    əpne dost ko yy pyaliã dykhaie.
    meri bivi ko səfəyd jute dykhaie.
8. mera xyal həy, ky ap yy lijie.
    mera xyal həy, ky ap aj nə jaie.
    həmara xyal həy, ky twm yəhã bəyTho.
    yn ka xyal həy, ky ap vw phəl xəridie.
    wn ka xyal həy, ky ap ke dost lahəwr nəhĩ jaẽge.
    ws ka xyal həy, ky ap nə jaie.
9. əccha, car gəz kaTie!
    əccha jənab, ys mwrγi ko kaTie!
    əccha sahəb, mere lie ys phəl ko kaTie!
    əccha, ys chwri se ys seb ko kaTie!
    əccha, ys gae ke gošt ko jəldi kaTie!
    əccha, mə̃gəl ko ys gae ko kaTie!
10. pəhle ghənTe ka kyraya ek rupəya car ane həy.

121

dusre ghənTe ka kyraya syrf gyara ane həy.
tisre dyn ka kyraya pəwne pãc rupəe həy.
ek həfte ka kyraya pəccys rupəe pəndra ane həy.
ys tãge ka ek dyn ka kyraya tera rupəe tin ane həy.
mere məkan ka ek həfte ka kyraya bis rupəe chəy ane həy.
11. bəs, kafi həy.
    bəs, yy mere lie kafi həy.
    bəs, yy pani kafi həy.
    bəs, ys pyali mẽ kafi pani həy.
    bəs, ytna dudh mere lie kafi həy.
    bəs, yn ke lie ytni kəwfi kafi həy.
12. amõ ka kya bhao həy.
    ys phəl ka kya bhao həy.
    ajkəl sebõ ka kya bhao həy.
    ap ki dwkan mẽ kelõ ka kya bhao həy.
    ys phəlvale ki dwkan mẽ amõ ka bhao kya həy.
    kya, ys phəlvale ki dwkan mẽ amõ ka bhao kəm həy?
13. ap vəhã kyõ jate hə̃y.
    ap ghər kyõ jaẽge.
    twm ys tãge mẽ kyõ jate ho.
    vw əpne dost ke sath kyõ jaega.
    vw log ws ki dwkan pər kyõ jaẽge.
    vw ləRkiã gəwrnmənT həspətal kyõ jaẽgi.
14. mə̃y bhi sath cəlti hũ.
    mə̃y bhi ap ke sath cəlti hũ.
    mə̃y bhi ap ke sath dyhli bazar cəlna cahti hũ.
    mə̃y əwr ap ki bəhn dyhli bazar nəhĩ jaẽge.
    mə̃y əpni valda ke sath jati hũ.
    mə̃y əpne bhai ke pas rəhti hũ.

4.504. Translation.

1. Covering section (b) of this exercise, translate the following sentences into English. Then uncover section (b) and check your results. Cover section (a) and translate the sentences in section (b) into Urdu.

   a: 1. mysəz ysmyth bətati hə̃y, ky vw do sal se pakystan mẽ nəwkri kərti hə̃y.
      2. pakystan mẽ səb log dãẽ hath se khate hə̃y. bãẽ hath se nəhĩ khate.
      3. kwch əmrikənõ ko pakystani khana pəsənd nəhĩ.
      4. yy phəlvala dusre phəlvalõ se zyada qimət leta həy.
      5. mə̃y ap ki dwkan ko dekhna cahta hũ, məgər ys ytvar ko mə̃y bəhwt məsruf hũ.
      6. yy qalin ytne kəm pəyse mẽ kəwn becega!
      7. ap ko səb se səste əwr əcche bərtən dykhaũga.

122

8. mɛ̃y wn ki wrdu nəhĩ səməjhta.

9. vw kys gylas se pani piega.

10. ap kys dəftər mɛ̃ kam kərɛ̃ge.

11. vw kəwnsi ləRki həy. mera xyal həy, ky mɛ̃y ws ko janta hū.

12. ap pir ko mere kalyj aɛ̃ge, ya nəhĩ.

13. ek nəwkər ko ytna pəysa nəhĩ dena cahie.

14. aj jute kəwnsi dwkan se xəridɛ̃ge.

15. meri bivi ko ytna nəmək əwr myrc pəsənd nəhĩ.

b: 1. Mrs. Smith says that she has been working in Pakistan for the last two years.

2. In Pakistan everybody eats with the right hand. [They] don't eat with the left hand.

3. Some Americans don't like Pakistani food.

4. This fruitseller charges more [lit. takes more price] than other fruit-sellers.

5. I want to see your shop, but this Sunday I'm very busy.

6. Who would sell this carpet for so little money! [Lit. This carpet in this-much little money who will sell!]

7. I'll show you the cheapest and best utensils.

8. I don't understand their Urdu.

9. From which glass will he drink water?

10. In which office will you work?

11. Which girl is she? I think that I know her.

12. Will you come to my college on Monday or not?

13. [One] should not give so much money to a servant.

14. From which shop shall [we] buy shoes today? [If the subject is not expressed, as in the sentence in section (a), it could also be "you [honorific]" or "they." The choice will depend upon the context.]

15. My wife doesn't like so much salt and pepper.

2. The following time expressions can all be employed in the frames /... bəja həy./ or /... bəje hɛ̃y./ "It is ... o'clock." Practice this drill until fluency is achieved.

12:45[1]	1:45	2:45	3:45	4:45	5:45	6:45
1:00	2:00	3:00	4:00	5:00	6:00	7:00
1:15	2:15	3:15	4:15	5:15	6:15	7:15
1:30	2:30	3:30	4:30	5:30	6:30	7:30

7:45	8:45	9:45	10:45	11:45
8:00	9:00	10:00	11:00	12:00
8:15	9:15	10:15	11:15	12:15
8:30	9:30	10:30	11:30	12:30

[1]"12:45" = "3/4 of one"

3. Wherever possible, the student should put the following prices into two frames: (a) /... rupəe ... ane/, and (b) a frame employing one of the fraction words

(/saRhe/, /pəwne/, /səva/, etc.). According to the old notation, prices are
abbreviated as follows: Rs. 3/12/9 = three rupees, twelve annas, nine /pai/;
Rs. 3/-/6 = three rupees, no annas, six /pai/. /pai/ are not used in this exercise.

Rs. 4/8/-	Rs. 10/14/-	Rs. 25/12/-	Rs. 13/12/-
Rs. 23/11/-	Rs. 1/8/-	Rs. 6/4/-	Rs. 9/8/-
Rs. 19/4/-	Rs. -/8/-	Rs. 21/8/-	Rs. 2/12/-
Rs. -/4/-	Rs. 22/5/-	Rs. 15/10/-	Rs. 24/3/-
Rs. 2/8/-	Rs. 18/4/-	Rs. 24/11/-	Rs. 9/15/-

4. The following prices are given in the new decimal notation. The student should
employ the frame /... rupəe ... [nəe] pəyse/.

Rs. 2.12	Rs. 4.02	Rs. 1.01
Rs. 17.25	Rs. 16.08	Rs. 22.13
Rs. 5.15	Rs. 9.10	Rs. 17.06
Rs. 20.06	Rs. 11.21	Rs. 19.09
Rs. 1.24	Rs. 7.18	Rs. 2.07

4.505. Response.

1. ap ys kylas ke bad kəhā jaēge.
2. ap ko seb pəsənd hōy, ya kele.
3. kya, ap ko malum həy, ky pakystan mē əmrikən kəpRa becte hōy, ya nəhī.
4. kya, əmrika mē ap ke valyd sahəb ka əpna məkan həy?
5. ap ki bivi pakystan kəb aēgi.
6. ap yəhā se kyō jaēge.
7. mysəz ysmyth əwr mysəz rəhim bazar kəyse jati hōy.
8. kya, aj ap əpni wrdu ki kytab pəRhēge?
9. ek rupəe mē kytne ane hōy.
10. ajkəl bazar mē kəwnse phəl əcche hōy.
11. ap əpne kəmre ka kya kyraya dete hōy.
12. ap pakystan mē kya dekhna cahte hōy.
13. aj šam ko kwch dost ap ke pas aēge, ya nəhī.
14. kya, ap ki bivi ap ke sath pakystan jaēgi?
15. ap ke kytne bhai əwr kytni bəhnē hōy.

4.506. Conversation Practice.

Mrs. Smith and Mrs. Rəhim are shopping together in the bazaar.

MR: mōy aj mwrγi əwr ənDe xəridūgi. ap kya xəridēgi.

MS: mera xyal həy, ky aj kwch phəl xəridūgi, əwr thoRa bəkri ka gošt. kwch myrcē əwr
nəmək bhi cahie.

MR: yy mwrγi əwr ənDe ki dwkan həy. mōy yəhā se xəridti hū.

They enter the shop, and Mrs. Rəhim points to a hen.

124

MR [to the shopkeeper]: ys mwrɣi ki kya qimət həy.

Sh: səva tin rupəe.

MR: yy bəhwt mə̃hgi həy. səsti dijie.

Sh: yy lijie. ys ki qimət kəm həy. syrf Dhai rupəe həy.

MR: yy bəhwt choTi həy. bəRi ki qimət kəm kijie, ya əwr dykhaie. vw mwrɣi kəysi həy.

Sh: vw bəhwt bəRi həy. ap yy səfəyd mwrɣi lijie. ys ki qimət syrf do rupəe chəy ane həy.

MR: ys ki qimət do rupəe loge?

Sh: bəhwt əccha. əwr kya cahie.

MR: bara ənDe bhi dijie. wn ki qimət kya həy.

Sh: səva do rupəe.

MR: əccha, həmare lie bara ənDe kafi hə̃y.

The two ladies enter a fruit shop.

MR: mera xyal həy, ky ajkəl phəl əcche nəhĩ, məgər ys phəlvale se puchẽge. [To the fruit-seller:] twmhare pas kəwnse phəl əcche hə̃y.

FS: syrf am əwr kele hə̃y. əb əcche seb nəhĩ ate, məgər kwch dynõ ke bad aẽge.

MR: am dykhao. ek am ko kaTo. mə̃y dekhũgi.

FS: bəhwt əccha, yy dekhie. yy yəhã ke am nəhĩ hə̃y. dyhli ke am hə̃y.

MS: yn ka kya bhao həy.

FS: saRhe car rupəe ser. yy dur se ate hə̃y. ys lie mə̃hge hə̃y.

MS: bəhwt əccha. Dhai ser do. [To Mrs. Rəhim:] aj šam ko kwch dost khane pər aẽge. wn ko am pəsənd hə̃y. ysmyth sahəb ko bhi bəhwt pəsənd hə̃y. ek dyn mẽ vw dəs am khate hə̃y.

MR: yy kwch nəhĩ! rəhim sahəb ek dyn mẽ pãc ser khate həy!

The two ladies come out of the shop.

MR: kya, ap aj kwch kəpRa dekhna cahti hə̃y? ek kəpRevale ki dwkan ys dwkan ke bāē tərəf həy.

MS: aj kəpRa nəhĩ dekhũgi. meri ləRkiã ek ghənTe ke bad yskul se aẽgi, əwr wn ka khana təyyar nəhĩ. ys lie ghər jəldi jana həy.

On their way, they pass a shop selling kitchen utensils.

MS: Thəyrie. mə̃y ys dwkan mẽ bərtən dekhũgi. həmare pas pyleTẽ kəm hə̃y.

Sh: ap log kya dekhna cahti hə̃y.

MS: wn nili pyleTõ ki kya qimət həy.

Sh: bara ki qimət səva cəwda rupəe həy.

MS: wn ke dāē tərəf vw lal pyleTẽ hə̃y. vw kəyse hə̃y.

Sh: vw səsti hə̃y. bara pyleTõ ki qimət syrf saRhe dəs rupəe həy.

MS: kwch cəmce, kāTe, əwr chwriã bhi dykhaie.

Sh: mere pas bəhwt xubsurət əmrikən cəmce hə̃y. bara ki qimət syrf pəwne pəndra rupəe həy.

MS: bəhwt mə̃hge hə̃y! pakystani cəmce əcche hə̃y, əwr səste bhi hə̃y. vw dykhaie.

Sh: yn ki qimət səva nəw rupəe həy. yy kāTe dekhie. yn ki qimət sat rupəe aTh ane həy. yn chwriõ ki qimət nəw rupəe cəwda ane həy.

125

MS [to Mrs. Rəhim]: ap ka kya xyal həy.

MR: mera xyal həy, ky yy əcche həy. ap yy cəmce, chwriã, əwr kāTe lijie.

MS: bəhwt əccha, chəy cəmce, chəy chwriã, əwr chəy kāTe dijie. səb ki qimət kya həy.

Sh: tera rupəe pāc ane.

MS: mere pas ytne pəyse nəhī̃ həy.

MR: mwjh se lijie.

MS: kəl vapəs dūgi.

The two ladies leave the shop and approach a tonga driver.

TD: tāga cahie? kys jəga jana həy.

MR: gəwrnmənT həspətal jante ho? ws ke nəzdik jana həy.

TD: ji hā. məy Dhai rupəe lūga.

MR: yy bəhwt zyada həy. kyraya kəm kəro!

TD: ji nəhī̃. kafi dur həy, əwr ap ki dost əmrikən həy. əmrikən logō ke pas bəhwt pəyse həy.

MR: ajkəl səb tāgevale əmrikənō se zyada pəyse lete həy. vw jante hə̃y, ky wn ko yəhā ki qimtē əwr kyrae malum nəhī̃, əwr vw ys lie zyada dete həy.

MS: məy syrf thoRe dynō se pakystan mē hū̃, əwr məy bhi kyrae əwr qimtē nəhī̃ janti. məy kya kərūgi.

MR: mwjh se ya dusri pakystani dostō se puchie. vw ap ko səb kwch bətaē̃gi. [To the tonga driver:] kəm kəro, ya həm dusra tāga lēge!

TD: məy do rupəe lūga. ys se kəm nəhī̃ lūga.

MR: bəs, jao! həm dusre tāge mē bəyThēge!

TD: nəhī̃, nəhī̃, Thəyrie! məy DeRh rupəya lūga!

MR: Thik həy. cəlo.

4.507. Conversation Stimulus.

1. Mr. Smith is in a cloth shop. He asks the shopkeeper what the price of that red cloth is. The shopkeeper replies that it is three and a half rupees a yard. Mr. Smith says that this is too much and asks the shopkeeper to please show him something else [/əwr/]. The shopkeeper asks him to look at this white cloth. Mr. Smith replies that he doesn't like it and that he will look in [/pər/] other [/əwr/ or /dusri/] shops.

2. Dr. Rəhim asks Mr. Smith where he will go today. Mr. Smith replies that he wants to go to the bazaar. He needs some meat and some milk. Dr. Rəhim says that he wants to go with him. He also wants to buy some meat. He says that there is a very good shop in Delhi Bazaar. He suggests that they go there. Mr. Smith agrees and asks whether they will go in a tonga. Mr. Smith says that there is a tonga there. Dr. Rəhim replies that they will go in a tonga.

3. Mr. Smith asks Dr. Rəhim's servant if Dr. Rəhim is at home. The servant replies that he is not, but that he will come back soon. He asks Mr. Smith to please sit down. Mr. Smith thanks him but says that he will not sit down. A friend will come from Delhi today, and he wants to tell this to Dr. Rəhim. The servant says, "Very well, I'll tell him."

4. Mrs. Smith is in a fruit shop. She asks the shopkeeper which fruits are good these days. He replies that the bananas are very good. Mangoes are also good. He asks her what she wants ["needs"]. She replies that she likes the bananas. She asks him to please give her six bananas. She then asks the price of mangoes. He says that it is three and three quarters rupees per seer. She asks him to give her two seers. She then asks if there is a vegetable shop near [/ke nəzdik/] this shop. She wants ["needs"] vegetables. He replies that, yes, there is a vegetable shop to the left ["on the left side of"] of his shop.

adha A2 [or /adh/ A1]	half
aj Adv	today
ajkəl Adv	these days, nowadays
am M1	mango
ana M2	"anna," a coin worth 1/16 of a rupee
əpna A2	[one's] own
[ke] bad	after
bays [or /bais/] A1	twenty-two
bãyã A2	left (hand)
bəhn F1	sister
bərtən M1	vessel, utensil
bəs Inter M1	enough!; capability, capacity
bətana	to tell, inform
bəyThna	to sit
becna	to sell
bhao M1	rate, price
cəwbys [or /cəwbis/] A1	twenty-four
dãyã A2	right (hand)
dekhna	to see
dost M/F1	friend
dwkan F1	shop, store
dwkandar M/F1	shopkeeper
dyhli F2 [np]	Delhi
dykhana	to show
DeRh A1	one and a half
Dhai A1	two and a half
gəz M1	yard (measure)
ghənTa M2	hour
jəga [or /jəgəh/ or /jəgha/] F1	place
jəldi F2 Adv	speed; quickly
juta M2	shoe
jutevala M2	shoe merchant
kafi A1	enough; sufficient, a lot of
kaTna	to cut
kəpRa M2	cloth [The plural, /kəpRe/, denotes "clothing."]
kəpRevala M2	cloth merchant
kəwnsa A2	which (of pl.)?
kəysa A2 Adv	how; what sort of?
kela M2	banana
ky Conj	that (conj.)
kyõ [or /kyũ/] Adv	why?

kyraya M2	rent, fare
kytab Fl	book
mət Adv	no, not [Used only with nonhonorific imperative; see Sec. 4.314]
məhga A2	expensive, costly
mwjh OS	me
pəccys [or /pəccis/] Al	twenty-five
pəwna A2 [or /pəwn/ Al]	three quarters; a quarter less than
pəysa M2	money; a coin worth 1/4 of an anna. In the new decimal system, a coin worth 1/100 of a rupee
phəl Ml	fruit
phəlvala M2	fruitseller
qalin Ml [or Fl]	carpet
qalinvala M2	carpet merchant
qimət Fl	price
rupəya M2 [MOP either /rupõ/ or /rupəyõ/]	rupee
saRhe	... and a half; half of the following numeral
səRək Fl	road, street, highway
səsta A2	cheap, inexpensive
səva Al	a quarter more than
seb Ml	apple
ser Ml	"seer," a measure weighing approx. two pounds
tãga M2	"tonga," a type of two-wheeled horse carriage
tãgevala M2	tonga driver
tərəf Fl	direction, way, side
teys [or /teis/] Al	twenty-three
twm NS, NP, OS, OP	you [nonhonorific]
twmhara A2	your [nonhonorific]
Thəyrna	to wait, stop for awhile, tarry
vapəs Adv	back, again
xəridna	to buy
xubsurət Al	pretty, beautiful
xyal [or /xəyal/] Ml	opinion, thought, idea
ya Conj	or
ykkys [or /ykkis/] Al	twenty-one
ytna A2	this much, so much, this many, so many

The State Bank of Pakistan, Karachi.

UNIT FIVE

5.000. CONVERSATION

Mr. Smith approaches the ticket window in the railway station.

forgiven PA1

Rawalpindi (a city in West Pakistan) F2 [np]

car, vehicle, train F2

S [to the clerk]: Excuse me, at which times do the Rawalpindi trains go?

having rung, struck [/bəjna/ "to ring, strike, play"]

twenty-nine A1

minute M1

early afternoon F1

C: The first [is] at 7:29 A.M. [lit. [in the] morning on seven having struck, twenty-nine minutes]. The second [is] in the afternoon at 1:55 [lit. to the afternoon, on five minutes in the striking [of] two].

S: How far is Rawalpindi?

anybody, somebody; any, some; approximately, about A1 NS NP

hundred A1

mile M1

to arrive

C: [It] is about two hundred miles. The train arrives in seven hours.

ticket, stamp M1

is able to be obtained MS

S: Where can [one] get a ticket?

right here Adv

class, degree, level M2

C: [It] is [lit. will be] available right here. For [lit. of] which class do you require a ticket?

to be, become

S: What is [meant by] "class?"

country M1

railway, train F1

better A1

C: There are four classes in the railways of our country. In my opinion the second class will be better for you.

having said, done [/fərmana/ "to command, grant, say, do [honorific]"]

maf [literary: /mwaf/]

ravəlpynDi

gaRi

maf kijie, ravəlpynDi ki gaRiã kys kys vəqt jati həy.

bəj kər

wnəttys [or /wnəttis/; also /wntys/ or /wntis/]

mynəT

dopəhr

pəhli, swba sat bəj kər wnəttys mynəT pər. dusri, dopəhr ko do bəjne mẽ pāc mynəT pər.

ravəlpynDi kytni dur həy.

koi

səw

mil

pəhwcna

koi do səw mil həy. gaRi sat ghənTe mẽ pəhw̃cti həy.

TykəT

myl səkta həy

TykəT kəhã se myl səkta həy.

yəhĩ

dərja

yəhĩ se mylega. ap ko kys dərje ka TykəT cahie.

hona

dərja kya hota həy.

mwlk

rel

byhtər

həmarɛ mwlk ki relõ mẽ car dərje hote hãy. mere xyal mẽ, ap ke lie dusra dərja byhtər hoga.

fərma kər

131

[I M] can catch [/pəkəRna/ "to catch, grasp, seize"]	pəkəR səkta hū
S: Now it's twenty minutes to two. [Lit. now there are twenty minutes in the striking of two]. Please [lit. having done kindness] give [me] a ticket quickly. I can still [lit. just now] catch this train.	əb do bəjne mẽ bis mynəT hɜ̃y. myhrbani fərma kər, jəldi TykəT dijie. mɜ̃y əbhi yy gaRi pəkəR səkta hū.
me, to me OS	mwjhe
coolie, porter Ml	qwli
S [to Mr. Hamyd, who is standing on the platform]: Excuse me. Can I get a porter?	maf kijie. kya, mwjhe koi qwli myl səkta həy?
to call	bwlana
H: Yes, I'll just call a coolie [for you].	ji hã, mɜ̃y əbhi qwli ko bwlata hū.
trouble, pain, difficulty Fl	təklif
S: Please don't trouble yourself! [Lit. please don't do trouble!]	təklif nə fərmaie!
thing, matter, word, talk Fl	bat
concern, worry Fl	fykr
arrangement[s], management Ml	yntyzam
this very OS	ysi
[I M] am going [continuative]	ja rəha hū
baggage, article[s], things Ml	saman
H: No matter. Don't worry. I'll just make all the arrangements. I too am going by this same train. Where is your baggage?	koi bat nəhĭ. ap fykr nə kijie. mɜ̃y əbhi səb yntyzam kərta hū. mɜ̃y bhi ysi gaRi se ja rəha hū. ap ka saman kəhã həy.
taxi F2	Təyksi
cook Ml	xansamã
right there Adv	vəhĭ
S: It's in the taxi. My cook is right there too.	Təyksi mẽ həy. mera xansamã bhi vəhĭ həy.
to cause to alight, take down, take off, unload	wtarna
box, compartment M2	Dybba
H [to a coolie]: Look, ·unload the gentleman's baggage from the taxi, and put it into the Rawalpindi compartment!	dekho, sahəb ka saman Təyksi se wtaro, əwr ravəlpynDi ke Dybbe mẽ rəkho!
cigarette Ml	sygreT
S: Thanks. [He offers Mr. Hamyd a cigarette.] Do you smoke [lit. drink] cigarette[s]?	šwkria. -- kya, ap sygreT pite həy?
H: Yes. Thanks.	ji hã. myhrbani.
sp. of orange (similar to a tangerine but larger) M2	səntra [literary: /sɜ̃gtəra/]
newspaper Ml	əxbar
S: I want to buy some oranges and [a] newspaper.	mɜ̃y kwch səntre əwr əxbar xəridna cahta hū.
station Ml	ysTešən
closed, shut Al	bənd
pomegranate Ml	ənar
grape[s] Ml	ɜ̃gur

suitcase M1   suTkes

H: The fruit shop [lit. fruits' shop] of this station is closed, but I have oranges, pomegranates, and grapes with me. There is a newspaper in my suitcase too. Now please sit down [in the compartment] quickly. There is little time.

ys ysTešən ki phəlõ ki dwkan bənd həy, məgər mere sath səntre, ənar, əwr ãgur hõy. əxbar bhi mere suTkes mẽ həy. əb jəldi bəyThie. vəqt kəm həy.

They arrive at their destination and enter a hotel.

hotel (also "restaurant") M1	hoTəl
us, to us OP	həmẽ
are able to be obtained MP	myl səkte hõy

S: Can we get two rooms in this hotel?

kya, ys hoTəl mẽ həmẽ do kəmre myl səkte hõy?

to take out, remove	nykalna
sixth A2	chəTa
seventh A2	satvã

C: Yes. [To a bearer:] Take the gentlemen's luggage out of the taxi, and look here -- put it in rooms number six and seven [lit. in the rooms of the sixth and seventh number]!

ji hã. -- sahəb ka saman Təyksi se nykalo, əwr dekho -- chəTe əwr satvẽ nəmbər ke kəmrõ mẽ rəkho!

Bearer: Very well.   bəhwt əccha.

register M1	ryjysTər
address M2	pəta
to write	lykhna
key F2	cabi

C [to Mr. Smith]: Please write your name and address on the register. Here are your keys.

ryjysTər pər əpna nam əwr pəta lykhie. yy ap ki cabiã hõy.

Mr. Smith enters his hotel room.

window F2	khyRki
to open	kholna
door M2	dərvaza
bathroom M2	ɣwslxana
cold A2	ThənDa
hot A1	gərm
bath M1	ɣwsl
having done, made	kər ke
city M1	šəhr
towel M2 [also F1]	təwlia
soap M1	sabwn [or /sabən/]

S [to the bearer]: Open the window and close the door! I'm going to Mr. Hamyd's room to talk [lit. for making talk]. You put cold and hot water in the bathroom! Having bathed [lit. having made a bath], I have to go quickly to the city. -- Look, [I] need a towel and soap too.

khyRki kholo, əwr dərvaza bənd kəro! mẽy hamyd sahəb ke kəmre mẽ bat kərne ke lie ja rəha hũ. twm ɣwslxane mẽ ThənDa əwr gərm pani rəkho! ɣwsl kər ke, mwjhe jəldi šəhr jana həy. -- dekho, təwlia əwr sabwn bhi cahie.

thing, object F1	ciz
[I M] am bringing	la rəha hū
bedsheet F1	cadər
[I M] am changing [/bədəlna/ "to change"]	bədəl rəha hū
anybody, somebody; any, some A1, OS	kysi
need, necessity F1	zərurət

B: I'm just bringing everything. I'm also just going to change the sheet. Do you need anything else [lit. to you is there any other thing's need?]? — mə̃y əbhi səb cizẽ la rəha hū. cadər bhi bədəl rəha hū. ap ko kysi əwr ciz ki zərurət həy?

having picked up [/wThana/ "to raise, lift, pick up"]	wTha kər
chair F2	kwrsi

S: Yes, pick up my suitcase and put it on the chair. What time is dinner? — hã, mera suTkes wTha kər, kwrsi pər rəkho! khana kys vəqt hota həy.

up to, until	tək

B: From 7:30 until 9:00. — saRhe sat bəje se nəw bəje tək.

[I M] am coming	a rəha hū.
telephone M1	Telifun

S: All right, you fix up [lit. make good] all the baggage. I'm just coming from Mr. Hamyd's room. -- Yes, look, I have to use [lit. do] the telephone. — əccha, twm səb saman Thik kəro. mə̃y hamyd sahəb ke kəmre se əbhi a rəha hū. -- hã, dekho, mwjhe Telifun kərna həy.

to say, tell	kəhna

S: Tell my cook that I don't need him anymore [tonight]. [Lit. Say with my cook that now his necessity is not.] — mere xansamã se kəho, ky əb ws ki zərurət nəhī̃.

B: All right, I'll just tell him. — bəhwt əccha, mə̃y əbhi ws se kəhta hū.

5.100. WORD STUDY

5.101. /gaRi/ F2 is a generic term for "car, cart, vehicle." In the proper contexts it may be heard either for "automobile (including car, bus, or truck)" or for "railway train." It also is common as the second member of loose noun compounds: e.g.

> /bəyl gaRi/ F2 oxcart. [/bəyl/ M1 "ox"]
>
> /ghoRa gaRi/ F2 horse-cart. [/ghoRa/ M2 "horse"]
>
> /moTər gaRi/ F2 automobile. [/moTər/ F1 is often heard alone for "automobile" also.]
>
> /rel gaRi/ F2 railway train. [/rel/ F1 may also occur alone for "train" as well.]
>
> /ūT gaRi/ F2 camel-cart. [/ūT/ M1 "camel"]

5.102. Historically, the day was divided into eight "watches" of three hours each, called /pəhr/ F1. These were distinguished by a preceding Persian numeral: "the one-watch," "the two-watch," etc. Only two of these terms have survived into modern Urdu: /dopəhr/ F1 "early afternoon (from noon until 3:00 P.M.)" and /syhpəhr/ F1 "late afternoon (from 3:00 P.M. until about 6:00 P.M.)." /do/ (or /du/) and /syh/ are the Persian numerals for "two" and "three" respectively. /syhpəhr/ is rather less common than /dopəhr/.

5.103. /dur/ A1 F1 "far, distant, distance" is employed both as an adjective and as a noun. In a sentence like /ravəlpynDi kytni dur həy./ "How far is Rawalpindi?" /kytni/ is feminine not because of /ravəlpynDi/ F2 [np], but because of /dur/. Such sentences might be literally translated as "Rawalpindi, how much is the distance?" Compare:

> /lahəwr kytni dur həy./ How far is Lahore? [/kytni/ cannot agree with /lahəwr/ here, since the latter is M1 [np].]
>
> /ravəlpynDi bəRi dur həy./ Rawalpindi is very far.
>
> /lahəwr thoRi dur həy./ Lahore is not far away [lit. a little far].

5.104. /mylna/ was introduced in Unit II in the meaning of "to meet" (+ /se/). It also means "to get, obtain, acquire." The object obtained is the grammatical subject of the sentence, and the person who obtains it stands as an object and is marked by /ko/ or its equivalent. One thus says, "To me rice is gotten" instead of "I get rice." E.g.

> /ap ko ek kəmra mylega./ You'll get a room. [Lit. To you a room will be gotten.]
>
> /ajkəl əcche seb myl səkte hə̄y./ [One] can get good apples these days. [Lit. These days good apples can be gotten.]
>
> /yy pəysa kysi ko nəhī́ mylega./ No one will get this money. [Lit. This money to someone will not be gotten.]

5.105. Both Indian and Pakistani railways have four classes. These are, in descending order of fare, facilities, and comfort: /fərsT/ "first," /səykənD/ "second," /ynTər/ or /ynTərkylas/ "interclass," and /thərD/ "third." /kylas/ F1 "class" is also common instead of /dərja/ M2.

135

5.106. /byhtər/ Al "better" is a Persian loanword, although it is similar in form and meaning to English "better." / ... se byhtər/ is exactly equivalent to / ... se əccha/, although the former is a trifle more literary.

5.107. The basic meaning of /fərmana/ is "to order, command." It is commonly employed in Urdu, however, as "polite language" for "to say, tell" (in place of the less-honorific /kəhna/) It is also used honorifically in place of /kərna/ "to make, do" in complex verbal constructions: e.g.

/əta fərmana/ "to give. [/əta/ Fl "gift. "]

/ynayət fərmana/ to give, grant. [/ynayət/ Fl "gift, grant, favour, benefit. "]

/ɣəwr fərmana/ to inspect carefully. [/ɣəwr/ Ml "concentration, reflection, deliberation. "]

/myhrbani fərmana/ to be kind. [/myhrbani/ F2 "kindness. "]

/təšrif fərmana/ to sit down. [/təšrif/ Fl "honour, dignity. "]

/šəwq fərmana/ to begin, taste (as a dish), enjoy. [/šəwq/ Ml "desire, enthusiasm, taste, predilection. "]

5.108. /qwli/ Ml "porter, manual labourer" is the source of the English word "coolie." The exact origins of this word are disputed.

5.109. /bat/ Fl is used for "thing, matter" in the non-physical sense, while /ciz/ Fl denotes "thing" in the material sense of "an object." E.g.

/yy kya bat həy. / What is this thing? [I. e. What is the matter?]

/yy kya ciz həy. / What is this thing? [I. e. What is this object?]

Note also:

/mə̃y ws se bat kərni cahta hū. / I want to talk to him. [/bat kərna/ is a complex verb formation meaning "to talk, converse. "]

/koi bat nəhī̃. / No matter. [Also: "You're welcome. "]

5.110. /saman/ Ml has a wider range of meaning than just "baggage, luggage." It is also used for "articles, things, paraphernalia," for "household effects," and for "raw materials" (e.g. the /saman/ brought for the building of a house, the raw vegetables, spices, and other ingredients brought from the market to cook dinner, etc.). It also occurs as the second member of the compound /xansamā/ Ml "cook": lit. "master [of] the supplies. "

5.111. /wtarna/ not only means "to unload, take off (objects from a vehicle, off a table, etc.), to cause to alight," but also "to take off clothing": e.g.

/mə̃y kəpRe wtarna cahta hū. / I want to take off [my] clothing.

5.112. /Dybba/ M2 is used for "box" (though not for luggage cases) and also for "compartment." A very small box, such as a cigarette packet or a matchbox, is called by the diminutive form, /Dybya/ Fl.

5.113. /dekho!/ "see!" is used much as "look!" or "look here!" in English; i.e.
as a means of drawing the hearer's attention. In an honorific context, /dekhie!/ "please
see!" would be employed.

5.114. In Urdu one does not "smoke" a cigarette, pipe, cigar, or waterpipe; /pina/
"to drink" is used instead. E. g.

/mɚy sygreT nəhĩ pita./ I don't smoke cigarette[s].

/kya, ap hwqqa pite hɚy?/ Do you smoke the waterpipe? /hwqqa/ M2
"waterpipe"]

/mwjhe payp pina zyada pəsənd nəhĩ./ I don't like pipe smoking very
much. [/payp/ M1 "pipe"]

5.115. In this Unit Mr. Smith is depicted as staying at a rather old-fashioned hotel.
In many of the older and cheaper hotels, the "bearer" (/bəyra/ M2) brings a bucket full of
cold water and another of hot water to the bathroom; he also places a bottle of cooled
drinking water on the table and performs various small services, such as laying out the
traveller's things, running errands, etc. More modern hotels in all the major cities of
India and Pakistan, however, now have running water (often including hot water, though not
always).

Note that /hoTəl/ M1 means "restaurant" as well as "hotel." In a restaurant, the
/bəyra/ performs the duties of a "waiter."

5.116. /zərurət/ F1 "necessity, need" is a noun derived from the same Arabic root
as /zəruri/ A1 "necessary," introduced in Unit III. Another derivative, the adverb /zərur/
"certainly," will be introduced in Unit XI. E. g.

/əb jana zəruri həy./ Now [I] have to go. [Lit. Now going is necessary.]

/əb mwjhe pani ki zərurət həy./ Now I need water. [Lit. Now to me
the necessity of water is. This is equivalent to /əb mwjhe pani
cahie./]

/mwjhe bəhwt zəruri kam həy./ I have some very necessary work. [Lit.
To me very necessary work is.]

/əb ap zərur jaie!/ Now you [should] certainly go!

5.117. "To tell [to] someone" is expressed by / ... se ... kəhna/ in modern Urdu,
not by / ... ko ... kəhna/. The latter means "to call someone something (e. g. a bad
name)." E. g.

/vw mwjh se kəhega./ He will tell me.

/hamyd sahəb se kəhie, ky mɚy nəhĩ a səkūga./ Please tell Mr. Hamyd
that I will not be able to come.

/vw ws se kya kəh rəha həy./ What is he saying to him?

Compare:

/vw mwjhe wllu kəhta həy./ He calls me a fool. [Lit. owl; /wllu/ M1
"owl. "]

5.201. Retroflex and Dental Stops.

English has only two alveolar stop consonants: a voiceless t and a voiced d. Urdu, on the other hand, has eight contrasting types of stop consonant made in the same general articulatory area. These are:

	Dental	Retroflex
Unaspirate voiceless	t	T
Unaspirate voiced	d	D
Aspirate voiceless	th	Th
Aspirate voiced	dh	Dh

This set of contrasts is one of the most important in Urdu, and it is one of the most difficult for English speakers to master. English t and d range from dental (e.g. as in width) almost to retroflex (as in the American pronunciation of hard or heart), depending upon surrounding consonants. The Urdu dental series, on the other hand, is always pronounced with the tip of the tongue just touching the back of the upper teeth. The actual point of articulation for the retroflex series varies slightly; some speakers pronounce these sounds almost in the same way an American speaker makes his t and d, while others touch the tongue tip somewhat farther back on the alveolar ridge. The retroflexed series is, however, always distinguished by the slight curling back of the tongue tip. It is this "curling back" rather than the actual point of articulation which makes the difference between Urdu /T, D/ and English t and d. See Sec. 4.201 for the articulation of the aspirated stops /Th, Dh/.

/thən/ udder
/tən/ body
/sat/ seven

/tāt/ string of gut
/dāt/ tooth
/dar/ scaffold
/dər/ door
/dhək/ baby louse
/tər/ moist, damp

/dal/ pulses

/dəb/ sink (in the earth), depress!

/dha/ wet nurse
/dhak/ reknown, awe

/Thən/ sound of a gong
/Tən/ ton; sound of a gong
/saTh/ sixty
/sath/ with

/TāT/ skull [colloq.]
/DāT/ rebuke
/Dar/ flock, herd in a line
/Dər/ fear
/Dhək/ cover!
/Tər/ fair held on the 2nd day of "Id" festival
/Thər/ habit
/Dal/ pour!
/Dhal/ shield
/Dəb/ a type of hidden pocket
/Dhəb/ manner, way
/Dha/ pull down!
/Dak/ mail, post
/Dhak/ sp. of tree

138

/dət/ a Hindu name

/lət/ bad habit

/thali/ tray
/tut/ mulberry
/dəs/ ten
/gənda/ dirty
/ghat/ ambush
/bat/ matter, thing, talk, word
/pəta/ address
/pətta/ leaf

/bəyt/ verse
/bit/ befall [vb. root]
/leta hū̃/ I take
/tota/ parrot

/gwdda/ thick tree bough
/bwddha/ Buddha
/mwnd/ be closed!

/bādh/ tie!
/dhənda/ occupation
/twk/ sense; rhyme

/dhət/ addiction
/DəT/ be fixed!
/ləT/ lock of hair
/ləTh/ big bamboo staff
/Thali/ free, at leisure [colloq.]
/TuT/ break!
/Dəs/ bite, sting (snake, scorpion, bee)
/gənDa/ bullet-shaped talisman
/ghaT/ bathing place
/baT/ weight used on a pair of scales
/pəTa/ game played with sticks
/pəTTa/ dog collar
/pəTTha/ young of an animal; sinew
/bəyTh/ sit!
/biT/ bird dung
/leTa hū̃/ I am lying down
/thotha/ hollow inside
/ToTa/ loss
/gwDDa/ male doll
/bwDDha/ old
/mwnD/ be shaved!
/mwnDh/ ringleader
/bhãD/ type of minstrel
/DənDa/ staff, stick
/Twk/ just now
/Thwk/ be hammered!

5.202. Phonetic Drill: Auditory Dictation.

1. tən Tər tāt baT pəta pəTa ləT tər twk TuT

2. dāt Dər mwnd DənDa dəs Dal gənda Dar dəb DāT Dəs

3. saTh Thər thali ləTh sath thən Thwk Thən bəyTh pəTTha

4. dhənda bādh mwnDh dhət Dhak dhək Dhal dha Dhək bwDDha Dhəb

5. gwDDa TāT leTa pətta bwddha leta ləTh gwdda bhãD Dhək

6. tota pətta gənDa leta thotha dhənda gənDa thali pəTTa gwDDa

7. dət bat lət biT dət Dar dal tut bit twk

8. mwnDh DəT dəb dhət mwnD bəyTh pəTa Dər tər mwnd

9. Twk Thali dar tən leTa dhənda dəs dhək dāt bādh

10. bit thotha ghaT saTh Tən bwDDha Dhəb pəTTha ghat sat Thər

139

5.301. Substantive Composition: Compounds with /xana/.

Urdu compound nouns are derived from several sources, the two commonest being Perso-Arabic and Hindi. /xana/ M2 "room of, place of, place where, house of" is a very common second element in such compounds. This item is also found alone as a separate word meaning "section, pigeon-hole" as well as in a few "frozen" idiomatic usages. The following examples are all compounds similar in construction to /ɣwslxana/ M2 "bathroom." It may be noted that the first element may be of either Perso-Arabic or Hindi origin.

/Dakxana/ M2 postoffice. [/Dak/ Fl "post, mail" is of Hindi origin.]

/karxana/ M2 factory. [/kar/ Ml "work" is Persian and does not occur except in compounds in Urdu.]

/kwtwbxana/ M2 library. [/kwtwb/ Fpl is the Arabic plural of /kytab/ Fl "book." /kwtwb/ is occasionally seen in more literary Urdu as a substitute for /kytabẽ/ or /kytabõ/.]

/qəydxana/ M2 jail, prison. [/qəyd/ Fl "imprisonment" is of Perso-Arabic origin.]

5.302. Repetition of Substantives.

The repetition of a word has two quite separate functions in Urdu: (1) the repetition of an adjective of quality usually denotes the intensification of that quality; generally speaking, only adjectives of common daily use are thus repeated (e.g. "hot," "big," "small," etc.) and not adjectives of a more literary nature. (2) Interrogatives, numerals, and indefinite elements are often repeated to suggest difference, variety, distributiveness, etc. E.g.

/meri bəhn ke ləRke səb choTe choTe hə̃y./ My sister's boys are all very young [lit. small]. [This has much the same meaning as / ... bəhwt choTe hə̃y./.]

/mwjhe gərm gərm cae dijie!/ Please give me very hot tea!

/ap kya kya cizẽ xəridẽge./ What [different, various] things will you buy?

/gaRiã kys kys vəqt jati hə̃y./ At which [various] times do the trains [lit. cars] go?

/əmrika mẽ ap kəhã kəhã jaẽge./ In America where [to which various places] will you go?

/yy am car car ane hə̃y./ These mangoes are four annas [each].

/həm əpne əpne ghər jaẽge./ We'll [each] go to [our] own homes.

The repeated form of /kəwnsa/ A2 "which?" is /kəwn kəwnsa/ rather than */kəwnsa kəwnsa/. Here /sa/ is not felt to be part of the same word as the /kəwn/ but rather an enclitic (i.e. a stressless particle closely bound to a preceding word). E.g.

/ap ko kəwn kəwnse phəl pəsənd hə̃y./ Which [various] fruits do you like?

5.303. Special Object Forms.

Object forms of the pronouns and demonstratives may be expressed in two ways: (1) the oblique form + /ko/, and (2) the oblique form + a suffix variously realised as /e/, /ē/, or /hē/. The only major difference between these two formations is perhaps best stated as stylistic: modern, literary style tends to have the special object forms (/mwjhe/, /həmē/, /ynhē/, etc.) rather than the /ko/ forms (e.g. /mwjh ko/, /həm ko/, /yn ko/). The author has noticed that this is especially true when the object referred to is a person; if the object is a nonrational object or animal, either form may be found. Various informants also stated that there was a connotation of "Sahib's Urdu" (i.e. foreignness) about forms like /mwjh ko/, /həm ko/, etc.

Special object forms for the pronouns and demonstratives are:

/mwjhe/ me, to me. [= /mwjh ko/]
[/twjhe/ thee, to thee. [= /twjh ko/]]
/yse/ him, her, it; to him, to her, to it. [= /ys ko/]
/wse/ him, her, it; to him, to her, to it. [= /ws ko/]
/həmē/ us, to us. [= /həm ko/]
/twmhē/ you, to you [nonhonorific]. [= /twm ko/]
/ynhē/ them, these; to them, to these; him, her; to him, to her.
    [= /yn ko/]
/wnhē/ them, those; to them, to those; him, her; to him, to her.
    [= /wn ko/]

Only /ap/ "you [honorific]" lacks a special object form. It is found only with /ko/: /ap ko/ "you, to you [honorific]."

The interrogative /kəwn/ "who?" also has special object forms closely paralleling those given above:

/kyse/ to whom, whom? [= /kys ko/]
/kynhē/ to whom, whom [pl.]? [= /kyn ko/]

The relative pronoun /jo/ "who, which" also has special object forms like those of /kəwn/: /jyse/ and /jynhē/. /jo/ will be introduced in Unit IX.

It may also be noted that the /e/ form of the object suffix occurs with forms denoting a singular, while /hē/ and /ē/ follow those denoting a plural.

5.304. /koi/ "Anybody, Somebody; Approximately."

The oblique form of /koi/ A1 "anybody, somebody; approximately" is /kysi/. Like most indefinites, /koi/ may occur as a modifier before a noun and also alone. E.g.

/koi tāgevala ap ko bəta səkega./   Any tonga driver will be able to tell
    you.
/kya, koi ghər mē hēy?/   Is there anybody at home? [In the nominative
    form, /koi/ may be treated as singular or plural; when there is no
    honorific sense it is usually singular.]
/koi nəhī aega./   Nobody will come. [When the verb is negative, /koi/
    may be translated as "no one, nobody."]
/kysi nəwkər se puchie!/   Please ask any servant!
/kysi əwr phəlvale ke pas jana cahie./   [We] ought to go to some other
    fruit seller.

141

The oblique form of /koi/ is always treated as singular. /kysi/ must be carefully distinguished from /kys/ "whom, to whom, who?" the OS form of /kəwn/ "who?" E.g.

/kysi ko/ to someone, anyone

/kys ko/ whom, to whom? [OS]

/koi/ also has a special usage before numeral adjectives: there it means "approximately, about." Note that in this construction it has no oblique form /kysi/, even when the noun modified by the numeral is oblique and followed by a postposition. E.g.

/koi do səw mil həy. / [It] is about two hundred miles.

/yy səRək koi do səw mil tək jati həy. / This road goes about two hundred miles [lit. up to about two hundred miles].

/khane pər koi pəccys ləRke aẽge. / About twenty-five boys will come to [lit. on] dinner.

5.305. Ordinal Numeral Adjectives.

It has been seen that all cardinal numerals are Type I adjectives; the opposite is the case with ordinals: these are always Type II in form. Except for five items made irregularly, all ordinal numerals consist of the cardinal numeral stem + /vā/ - /vẽ/ - /vī/. E.g.

/satvā/ seventh [MNS]

/satvẽ/ seventh [MOS, MNP, MOP]

/satvī/ seventh [FNS, FOS, FNP, FOP]

The five irregular ordinals are:

/pəhla/ A2 first. [Cf. /ek/ A1 "one, a"]

/dusra/ A2 second, other. [Cf. /do/ A1 "two"]

/tisra/ A2 third. [Cf. /tin/ A1 "three"]

/cəwtha/ A2 fourth. [Cf. /car/ A1 "four"]

/chəTa/ A2 sixth. [Cf. /chəy/ A1 "six"]

Ordinals from eleven to eighteen display some slightly irregular stem forms, however, and there is also a good deal of difference of opinion among informants as to their pronunciation. These are:

/gyarhvā/ or /gyarəvā/ A2 eleventh

/barhvā/ or /barəvā/ A2 twelfth

/terhvā/ or /terəvā/ A2 thirteenth

/cəwdhvā/ or /cəwdəvā/ A2 fourteenth

/pəndhərvā/ or /pəndhrəvā/ or /pəndrəvā/ A2 fifteenth

/solhvā/ or /soləvā/ A2 sixteenth

/sətərhvā/ or /səthərvā/ or /sətərəvā/ or /sətərvā/ A2 seventeenth

/əTTharhvā/ or /əTTharəvā/ A2 eighteenth

Ordinal forms of the decades (e.g. "fortieth," "thirtieth," etc.) are occasionally seen, but other ordinals above twenty are somewhat uncommon.

5.306. The Enclitic /hi/ "Emphasis."

In an English sentence, a word may be emphasised by means of special intonation patterns (louder stress, higher pitch) and various changes in word order, etc. While Urdu also employs these devices, it also has a special "enclitic" (a word having little or no stress of its own which is closely attached to some preceding word) denoting "emphasis." This element, /hi/, may occur after nouns, pronouns, and other types of substantives, and also after the first element in various verb formations which are composed of more than one word. The word preceding /hi/ may also be further stressed by special intonational devices: e.g. louder stress, higher pitch. Some examples should clarify the usage of /hi/:

/mɑ̄y hi bazar nəhī̆ ja səkta./ I cannot go to the market. [I.e. I am the only one who cannot go; everyone else may go.]

/mɑ̄y bazar hi nəhī̆ ja səkta./ I cannot go to the market. [I.e. I can go everywhere but to the market.]

/mɑ̄y bazar ja hi nəhī̆ səkta./ I can't go to the market at all. [I.e. Going is simply out of the question. Note the change of word order: /hi/ follows the verb stem, which in turn is followed by the negative and by the remaining element.]

/əb həmɛ̄ bazar jana hi cahie./ Now we must go to the market. [It has become urgent that we go now.]

/mɑ̄y pani pi hi rəha hū./ I am drinking water. [Why do you keep telling me to drink -- I am drinking!]

/hi/ also occurs in various forms as a suffix. The student has already met with /əbhi/ Adv "just now" (cf. /əb hi/ "only now"). /hi/ occurs as /i/ in the following constructions:

/mwjhi/ just me [OS]. [Note that the NS form occurs as /mɑ̄y hi/ and never */mɑ̄yhi/, etc.]

/twjhi/ just thee [OS]. [Very rare.]

/yyhi/ this very, these very, just he, etc. [NS, NP]

/vwhi/ that very, those very, just he, etc. [NS, NP]

/ysi/ this very, him, etc. [OS]

/wsi/ that very, him, etc. [OS]

In other forms /hi/ occurs as /ī/ or /hī̆/:

/həmī̆/ just we, us. [NP, OP]

/twmhī̆/ just you [nonhonorific] [NS, OS, NP, OP]

/ynhī̆/ these very, them, etc. [OP]. [Also /ynhi/]

/wnhī̆/ those very, them, etc. [OP]. [Also /wnhi/]

/yəhī̆/ right here. [/yəhā̄/ + /hi/]

/vəhī̆/ right there. [/vəhā̄/ + /hi/]

/kəhī̆/ somewhere, anywhere. [/kəhā̄/ + /hi/. Note the semantic change: /kəhī̆/ is not used as an interrogative but as an indefinite locative adverb.]

5.307. Complex Verbal Formations.

A great many verbal ideas are expressed in Urdu not by a single verb stem but rather by a complex formation made with a noun, adjective, or predicate adjective + some auxiliary verb. Thus, "to arrange" is literally "to make arrangement"; "to bathe" is "to make bath"; "to talk" is "to make word"; etc. The commonest auxiliary verbs found in such formations are /kərna/ "to do, make" which provides a transitive sense, and /hona/ "to be, become," which denotes an intransitive, medio-passive action. E.g.

/yntyzam kərna/ to make arrangement[s], to arrange

/yntyzam hona/ to be arranged, to become arranged. [The action occurs of itself.]

Adjectives and nouns occurring in complex formations require separate discussion. The former must also be divided into two classes: "true adjectives" and "predicate adjectives."

(1) The "true adjective" is defined as a word which may occur before (and thus "modify") a following noun. Adjectives of various sub-types also occur alone (and then function syntactically as nouns); certain adjectives are also found as syntactic adverbs, etc. Many adjectives occur in "complex verbal formations" also. E.g.

/yy Thik bat həy./ This is correct. [Lit. This is a right word. /Thik/ occurs before /bat/ and modifies it. /Thik/ is thus an adjective.]

/ap ki bat Thik həy./ What you say is correct. [Lit. Your word is right. Here /Thik/ functions as a predicate adjective.]

/ap Thik kəhte hə̄y./ What you say is correct. [Lit. You say correct[ly]. /Thik/ is employed as an adverb here.]

/mə̄y ys ko Thik kərū̃ga./ I'll fix this. [Lit. I will make this right. [/Thik/ is employed here as a predicate adjective with the "verbaliser" /kərna/ "to make, do."]

(2) The "predicate adjective," on the other hand, does not occur as a modifier before a noun. Members of this class are usually found only in complex verbal formations. E.g.

/mwjhe yy bat malum həy./ I know this. [Lit. To me this word is known. /malum/ here is a predicate adjective.]

/mə̄y ap ke lie malum kər səkta hū̃./ I can find out for you. [Lit. I can make known for you. Again /malum/ occurs in a complex verbal formation as a predicate adjective.]

*/ek malum jəga mē̃/ in a known place. [This phrase is not correct, since a predicate adjective never can modify a noun. Here lies the main difference between a "true adjective," such as /Thik/ above, and a predicate adjective.]

/mwjhe maf kijie!/ Please forgive me! [/maf kərna/ "to forgive" is again a complex verbal formation composed of the predicate adjective /maf/ and the "verbaliser" /kərna/ "to make, do."]

*/vw ek maf ləRka həy./ He is a forgiven boy. [Since /maf/ is a predicate adjective only, this sentence cannot occur.]

Both adjectives and predicate adjectives occur with /kərna/ "to make, do" and with /hona/ "to be, become." When /kərna/ is used, the object of the transitive action is usually marked by /ko/ (or its equivalent; see Sec. 3.310). There is, however, a smaller class of predicate adjectives which mark the logical object with /ka/ "of"; e.g.

/dərvaza bənd kəro!/ Shut the door! [/bənd kərna/ "to close, shut" consists of the adjective /bənd/ A1 "closed, shut" (here used as a predicate adjective) + /kərna/. Since /dərvaza/ M2 "door" is in-animate, it does not require /ko/ as an object marker; see Sec. 3.310.]

/mə̄y ys ko pəsənd kərta hū̃./ I like this. [/pəsənd kərna/ "to like" consists of /pəsənd/ "pleasing, liked" + /kərna/. /pəsənd/ is a predicate adjective because it never occurs as a modifier before a noun: i.e. */pəsənd jəga/, */pəsənd bat/, etc. cannot occur.]

/twm ys kəmre ko saf kəro!/ Clean this room! [/saf kərna/ "to clean" consists of the adjective /saf/ A1 "clean" + /kərna/. /saf/ is an adjective because it can occur in phrases like /saf jəga/, /saf kəpRe/, etc.]

/əb yy saf həy./ Now this is clean. [/saf hona/ "to be clean"]

/mə̃y ys ka pabənd hū./ I adhere to this. [/pabənd/ PA1 "restricted, bound to, following, adhering, observing" belongs to that class of predicate adjectives which marks a kind of object with /ka/ "of." See under predicate nouns below.]

If an adjective or predicate adjective belongs to the Type II declension, it will (a) agree with the <u>object</u> in number-gender if the object is not marked by /ko/ or its equivalent (i. e. a special object form of a pronoun, etc.); (b) if the object is marked by /ko/ (etc.), then the adjective or predicate adjective in a complex verbal formation will invariably be MNS.

/mə̃y yy dərvaza bəRa kər səkta hū./ I can enlarge this door. [/bəRa/ is MNS here, agreeing with /dərvaza/ M2 "door."]

/mə̃y yy təsvir bəRi kərūga./ I'll enlarge this picture. [/bəRi/ is FNS here, agreeing with /təsvir/ F1 "picture."]

/mə̃y ys dərvaze ko bəRa kər səkta hū./ I can enlarge this door. [/bəRa/ is MNS because the object is marked by /ko/.]

/mə̃y ys təsvir ko bəRa kərūga./ I'll enlarge this picture. [Here /bəRa/ is MNS in form because the agreement with /təsvir/ is "cut off," as it were, by /ko/.]

A great many nouns also occur in complex verbal formations. The majority of these employ /kərna/ as a transitive "verbaliser" and /hona/ as its intransitive counterpart. This group must again be subdivided into (a) those which mark the logical object by /ko/ (or its equivalent), and (b) those which mark the logical object by /ka/ "of." E. g.

/mə̃y wse Telifun kərna cahta hū./ I want to telephone him. [/Telifun kərna/ marks the object with /ko/ (etc.).]

/mə̃y ys ka yntyzam kərūga./ I'll arrange this. [Lit. I will make its arrangement. The object of /yntyzam kərna/ is marked by /ka/, possessing /yntyzam/.]

/mə̃y ap ki fykr nəhĩ kərūga./ I won't worry about you. [Lit. I will not do your worry. /ki/ is used because /fykr/ "worry" is F1.]

/vw meri tarif kərta həy./ He praises me. [/tarif/ F1 "praise" has not yet been introduced. Here the logical object is the possessive pronominal adjective /meri/ "my"; it is FNS because /tarif/ is F1.]

Still another large group of nouns occur in complex verbal formations with /dena/, /lena/, and /mylna/, rather than with /kərna/ and /hona/. E. g.

/mə̃y ap ko ys ki yjazət nəhĩ de səkta./ I can't give you permission for this. [The person permitted is marked by /ko/, and the thing permitted possesses /yjazət/ F1 "permission" with /ki/.]

/mə̃y ap se ys ki yjazət lūga./ I'll take permission from you for this. [The person permitting is marked with /se/, and the thing permitted possesses /yjazət/.]

/mwjhe ys ki yjazət mylegi./ I'll get permission for this. /yjazət mylna/ "to get permission, to be permitted" marks the person permitted with /ko/ (etc.) and the thing permitted with /ki/ (etc.).]

Various other verbs may also be employed as "verbalisers": /rəhna/ "to live, stay, dwell" imparts a sense of permanency to the quality denoted by a predicate adjective or noun, while /rəkhna/ "to keep" indicates that the quality or action is consciously retained or maintained by the actor. E. g.

/ws ki dwkan bənd rəhti həy./ His shop [always] stays closed.

/ap ys ko saf rəkhie!/ Please keep this clean!

Some useful complex verbal formations possible with the student's present vocabulary are:

/[... se] bat kərna/ to talk [with]

/[... ko] bənd kərna/ to close, shut

/[... ki] fykr kərna/ to worry [about]

/ɣwsl kərna/ to bathe

/kam kərna/ to work

/[... ko] maf kərna/ to forgive

/nəwkri kərna/ to work, serve as an employee

/[... ko] pəsənd kərna/ to like, enjoy

/qwli kərna/ to employ a coolie.

/[... ko] saf kərna/ to clean

/[... ke lie] təklif kərna/ to take trouble [for]

/[... ko] Telifun kərna/ to telephone [to]

/[... ko] Thik kərna/ to fix, repair, make well

/[... ka] xyal kərna/ to think about, remember, watch out for, care for

/[... ka] yntyzam kərna/ to arrange [for]

In an honorific context /kərna/ can be replaced by /fərmana/ in many of the above formations: e.g. /maf fərmana/ "to forgive."

It must be understood, of course, that the system described here is only a general outline; there are a great many irregularities and special usages. Some items, for example, occur with /kərna/ but have no intransitive form with /hona/; with others the converse is true. There are many words which belong to more than one of the above classes: i.e. which occur both with /kərna/ - /hona/ and with /dena/ - /lena/ - /mylna/: e.g. /təklif kərna/ "to take trouble" and also /[... ko] təklif dena/ "to trouble, cause trouble [for]." It is clearly impossible to describe all of these peculiarities in such a way that the student can assimilate them, and therefore only the most common complex verbal formations will be listed in a special section under Word Study in each Unit.

5.308. The Verb: the <S + /kər/ or /ke/> Construction.

The "conjunctive participle" is formed by adding the enclitic /kər/ or /ke/ to any verb stem. Generally, this construction denotes an action preceding that of the main verb of the sentence. /kər/ and /ke/ are completely interchangeable except for one instance: /kər ke/ "having done" is the only possible form of this construction with /kərna/ "to make, do"; */kər kər/ does not exist. It is important to note that this construction does not inflect for person, number, or gender.

Constructions with /kər/ and /ke/ may usually be translated literally as "having ... ed": e.g. "Having picked up the suitcase, put it on the table"; "Having arrived home, I will eat dinner." A more idiomatic translation -- but one which does render the Urdu exactly -- would be: "Pick up the suitcase and put it on the table"; "I'll go home and eat dinner"; etc. In various special contexts this construction may be translated by an adverb (e.g. /soc ke/ "thoughtfully" -- lit. "having thought" from /socna/ "to think, consider") or even as "in spite of" (e.g. /ho ke/ "having been, become" in certain idiomatic usages). E.g.

/vw khana kha kər pani piega./ He'll eat and [then] drink water. [A /,/ may also occur after /kər/.]

/ghər ja kər kam kərna cahie./ [You] ought to go home and work. [Lit. Having gone home, [one] ought to do work.]

/mera ləRka khana kha kər pəRh rəha həy./ My son has finished eating and is reading. [Lit. My son having eaten food is reading.]

/rupəe nykal kər, wse dijie!/ Take out the money and give it to him! [Lit. Having taken out the rupees, please give [it] to him.]

/ravəlpynDi pəhw̃c kər, mə̃y ap ke pas aūga./ On arriving at Rawalpindi, I'll come to you. [Lit. Having arrived at Rawalpindi, I will come to you.]

This construction is employed to indicate minutes after the hour, using /bəj kər/ "having struck." One thus says "Ten having struck, twenty-three minutes are"; "Five having struck, twelve minutes are"; etc. (The quarter hour, the half hour, and the three-quarters hour are usually expressed by the fraction words introduced in Sec. 4.307, however.) It may be noted here that after the half hour, it is usual to count back from the coming hour rather than forward from the past hour. Thus, instead of "Ten having struck, thirty-eight minutes are," one says "In the striking of eleven, twenty-two minutes are." E.g.

/əb car bəj kər wnnys mynəT hə̃y./ It is now 4:19.

/yy gaRi gyara bəj kər cəwda mynəT pər jati həy./ This train goes at 11:14.

/pãc bəjne mẽ bis mynəT hə̃y./ It is 4:40 [lit. in the striking of five, twenty minutes.]

/lahəwr ki rel gaRi dəs bəjne mẽ dəs mynəT pər pəhw̃cti həy./ The Lahore train arrives at 9:50. [Lit. in the striking of ten, ten minutes.]

5.309. The Verb: /hona/ "to Be, Become."

There is an important semantic difference between the following sentences:

/khana kys vəqt həy./ What time is dinner?

/khana kys vəqt hota həy./ What time is dinner?

The former asks for the time of a particular dinner; the second example asks about dinner generally -- what is the usual time of dinner? Wherever the idea is one of a general nature, extending over a general, undefined period, then the /hota həy/ construction is used. E.g.

/ys bat se mwjhe təklif hoti həy./ I am hurt by this matter. [I.e. this matter causes me pain over a general, undefined period; it is not a matter of a single specific occasion.]

/ajkəl mə̃y bəhwt məsruf hota hū./ These days I am very busy [as a rule].

/pakystan mẽ khana əccha hota həy./ In Pakistan food is [generally] good.

/dyhli ke am bəhwt mə̃hge hote hə̃y./ Delhi mangoes are [generally] very expensive.

/hona/ has a slightly irregular future paradigm:

PRONOUN	VERB: MASCULINE	FEMININE	
mə̃y	hūga	hūgi	I will be, become

147

PRONOUN	VERB: MASCULINE	FEMININE	
[tu	hoga	hogi	thou wilt be, become]
vw	hoga	hogi	he, she, it will be, become
həm	hõge	hõgi	we will be, become
twm	hõge	hõgi	you [nonhonorific] will be, become
ap	hõge	hõgi	you [honorific] will be, become
vw	hõge	hõgi	they will be, become

Future forms of /hona/ denote simple future time. They may also indicate supposition on the part of the speaker: "must be, ought to be, should be. " E. g.

> /vw ghər pər hõge. /   He will be [ought to be, must be, should be] at home.
>
> /əb vw əmrika mẽ hoga. /   Now he will be [must be, etc.] in America.
>
> /ys salən mẽ, bəhwt myrcẽ hõgi. / There will be [must be, probably will be] many peppers in this curry.

Future forms of /hona/ may also be employed in place of /həy/ (etc.) in the <S + /rəha həy/> construction, the <PreP + /həy/> construction, etc. Here again, the connotation is one of supposition and probability. E. g.

> /Thəyrie, vw əbhi ata hoga. /   Please wait, he must be coming just now.
>
> /vw ghər mẽ pəRh rəha hoga. /   He must be reading at home.
>
> /ajkəl vw bəhwt jəldi jata hoga. / These days he must go very early [lit. quickly].

5.310. The Verb: the <S + /səkna/> Construction.

/səkna/ "to be able" occurs only following a verb stem. Unlike English "can, " /səkna/ cannot occur by itself as an independent verb: i. e. one cannot say */mãy səkta hũ/ as one can say "I can. " The preceding verb stem must always be retained, even when one is replying to a question: e. g.

> /kya, ap ja səkte hãy. /   Can you go? [The reply would be:]
>
> /ji hã, mãy ja səkta hũ. /   Yes, I can go. [Never */ji hã, mãy səkta hũ. /]
>
> /ap yy kam kər səkẽge. /   You will be able to do this work.
>
> /twm yəhã nəhĩ Thəyr səkte ho. /   You cannot remain here.
>
> /mãy əwr nəhĩ kha səkta. /   I can't eat any more.

5.311. The Verb: the <S + /rəha həy/> Construction.

The "continuative" construction consists of the verb stem followed by what may be termed the past participle of /rəhna/ "to live, stay, dwell. " This will be followed in turn by some form of /hona/ "to be, become. "

The pattern is:

148

PRONOUN	VERB: MASCULINE	FEMININE	
mə̄y	kha rəha hū	kha rəhi hū	I am eating
[tu	kha rəha həy	kha rəhi həy	thou art eating]
vw	kha rəha həy	kha rəhi həy	he, she, it is eating
həm	kha rəhe hə̄y	kha rəhi hə̄y	we are eating
twm	kha rəhe ho	kha rəhi ho	you [nonhonorific] are eating
ap	kha rəhe hə̄y	kha rəhi hə̄y	you [honorific] are eating
vw	kha rəhe hə̄y	kha rəhi hə̄y	they are eating

As previously noted, women usually employ the masculine plural form for "we":
/həm kha rəhe hə̄y/ instead of /həm kha rəhi hə̄y/.

The negative employed with this construction is /nəhī́/, and any present tense auxiliary
(/həy/, etc.) is usually dropped. Future tense forms of /hona/ are not dropped, however.
As with other constructions, the omission of the auxiliary in the negative feminine plural
forms requires the nasalisation of the participle: e.g. /nəhī̃ kha rəhī́/, etc.

/vw nəhī̃ ja rəha./ He is not going.

/aj vw nəhī̃ pəRh rəha hoga./ He will [probably] not be studying today.

/meri ləRkiã nəhī̃ pəRh rəhī́./ My girls are not studying.

The present continuative contrasts with the general present (i.e. the <PreP + /həy/>
construction) in that the former denotes continuation of an action over a period of time;
the latter denotes only the general occurrence of an action. Both constructions may,
however, be employed to denote immediate future time: e.g.

/mə̄y əbhi pani la rəha hū./ I'm just bringing water. [Or:]

/mə̄y əbhi pani lata hū./ I'm just bringing water.

If there is any difference at all here, it is very slight: while both forms may denote
the immediate future, the continuative form may indicate a slightly more distant future
than the general present: i.e. /lata hū/ carries some degree of immediacy, while /la rəha
hū/ might refer to a somewhat more distant completion of the action.

5.400. SUPPLEMENTARY VOCABULARY

5.401. Supplementary Vocabulary.

The following numerals are all Type I adjectives. See Sec. 2.401.

chəbbys	twenty-six
səttays	twenty-seven
əTThays	twenty-eight
tis	thirty
həzar	thousand

The first three of the above have a "writing pronunciation" ending in /is/ instead of /ys/: e.g. /chəbbis/. This is not common in speech.

The only remaining irregular ordinal not yet introduced is:

cəwtha A2	fourth

Other items:

hi enclitic particle	emphatic

5.402. Supplementary Exercise I: Substitution.

1. ys bazar mē koi <u>bis</u>   dwkanē hǝy.

  twenty-eight
  twenty-six
  thousand
  twenty-seven
  thirty

5.403. Supplementary Exercise II: Fill the Blanks.

1. Fill the blanks with the ordinal form of the cardinal numerals given in brackets.

   a. meri lǝRki ____ kylas mē pǝRh rǝhi hǝy.   [car, dǝs, nǝw]
   b. sahǝb ka saman ____ kǝmre mē rǝkho!   [bays, pǝccys, aTh]
   c. ____ mǝkan hǝmara hǝy.   [pāc, bara, bis]
   d. vw ____ Dybbe mē hõge.   [sat, aTh, chǝy]
   e. ____ kǝmre mē rǝhta hū̃.   [tera, chǝbbys, pǝndra]

150

5.500. VOCABULARY AND GRAMMAR DRILL

5.501. Substitution.

1. vw sahəb <u>bat</u> kər rəhe hǝ̄y.
   bath
   work
   telephone
   arrangement
   worry

2. myhrbani fərma kər, <u>mwjhe</u>   <u>dəsvā</u>   kəmra dijie.
   to him   ninth
   to us   sixth
   to my wife   fourteenth
   to them   first
   to my   fourth
   friend

3. vw <u>qwli ko</u> bwla rəhe hǝ̄y.
   [his] own cook
   that very servant
   whom [sg. or pl.]?
   that very cloth-seller
   him[1]
   [1]Four forms are possible.

4. kya, mwjhe yəhā <u>ek bəRa suTkes</u> myl səkta həy?
   some hot water
   cold milk
   a room
   a towel
   yesterday's newspaper

5. mera suTkes <u>vəhǐ</u> rəkho!
   on that small table
   inside this
   behind that
   right here
   with my baggage

6. meri valda lahəwr mē <u>pāc dyn tək</u> Thəyr səkti hǝ̄y.
   up to two years
   up to seven weeks
   up to tomorrow
   up to [this] afternoon

7. <u>ravəlpynDi</u> <u>lahəwr</u> se <u>do səw mil</u>   dur həy.
   my house your house   two miles

the hotel	the market	one and a half miles
my room	your room	a little
the city	there	about three miles
the bath-room	this room	very

8. <u>həmẽ</u>   <u>Təyksi</u>   ki zərurət həy.

    to these bath

    to me   this very thing

    to him two tickets for Lahore[1]

    to those your address

    to my some blue cloth
    wife

      [1]Lit. Lahore's two tickets

9. sahəb, <u>hoTəl ka Telifun</u>   <u>xərab</u> həy.

           your tea   hot

           that door   closed

           that other cook[1] busy

           this chair   better

           your cup   empty

      [1]Lit. that second cook

10. mẽy əbhi <u>səb cizẽ</u> la rəha hũ.

           today's newspaper

           two towels and four sheets

           a taxi and a coolie

           the gentleman's baggage

           some grapes and oranges

5.502. Transformation.

1. Change the verb forms underlined in the following sentences to:
      (1) the future; e.g. /jata hũ/ to /jaũga/
      (2) the present continuative; e.g. /jata hũ/ to /ja rəha hũ/
      (3) the "can" form using /səkna/; e.g. /jata hũ/ to /ja səkta hũ/

  a. yy xansamã yn logõ ka kam <u>kərta həy</u>.

  b. hamyd sahəb aTh bəj kər pəccys mynəT pər <u>pəhw̃cte h̃əy</u>.

  c. vw dəftər se <u>ate h̃əy</u>.

  d. mẽy ek qwli ko <u>bwlata hũ</u>.

  e. ap ke mwlk mẽ kya <u>hota həy</u>.

  f. vw nəwkər Təyksi se saman <u>wtarta həy</u>.

  g. twm hoTəl mẽ kya kam <u>kərte ho</u>.

  h. həm wn se bat kərne ke lie <u>jate h̃əy</u>.

  i. meri ləRki ap ke lie səb cizẽ <u>lati h̃əy</u>.

  j. meri bivi lahəwr ati <u>h̃əy</u>.

2. Change the underlined object pronoun + /ko/ to the corresponding special object form: e.g. /mwjh ko/ to /mwjhe/.

   a. həm ko ek gylas pani dijie.
   b. yn ko kys ciz ki zərurət həy.
   c. mwjh ko bətaie.
   d. mɔ̃y ys ko pəkəRna cahta hũ.
   e. mɔ̃y twm ko cabi dũga.
   f. lahəwr a kər, mɔ̃y wn ko səb batẽ bəta səkũga.
   g. mɔ̃y ws ko kalyj bhejna cahta hũ.
   h. ap kys ko dekhne ke lie jaẽge.
   i. kya, ap həm ko jante hɔ̃y?
   j. vw əpna pəysa kyn ko dẽge.

3. Change the verb forms underlined in the following sentences to:
   (1) the present general occurrence form: e.g. /həy/ to /hota həy/
   (2) the future-suppositional form: e.g. /həy/ to /hoga/

   a. ys mwlk ke log bəhwt xərab hɔ̃y.
   b. mera xansamã vəhĩ həy.
   c. ys hoTəl ki cae əcchi həy.
   d. lahəwr mẽ kəpRa bəhwt səsta həy.
   e. ajkəl vw məsruf hɔ̃y.
   f. tãge ke kyrae bəhwt zyada hɔ̃y.
   g. yn hoTlõ mẽ γwslxane nəhĩ. [1]
   h. pakystan ke qalin bəhwt xubsurət hɔ̃y.
   i. ws ke pas bəhwt kəm pəysa həy.
   j. ys šəhr ki səRkẽ saf nəhĩ. [1]

   [1]The present tense verb has been dropped because the sentence is negative. The present general occurrence form and the future form do not drop the verb: e.g. /nəhĩ hota/ "is not [generally]" and /nəhĩ hoga/ "will not [must not] be."

4. Change the underlined pronouns and demonstratives to the emphatic form: e.g. /mwjh pər/ to /mwjhi pər/.

   a. mwjh se puchie!
   b. mera xyal həy, ky ap ys ko xəridie.
   c. mɔ̃y twm se bat kərũga.
   d. vw ws kəmre mẽ rəhte hɔ̃y.
   e. yy səb khana həm khaẽge.
   f. vw mere profesər hɔ̃y.
   g. yy wn ko nə dijie!
   h. yy mwjhe pəsənd həy.
   i. ap aẽge. hamyd sahəb nəhĩ aẽge.
   j. yn logõ se lijie!

5. Change the first sentence of the following pairs into a conjunctive clause ending in /kər/ or /ke/: e.g. /hoTəl jaũga. mɔ̃y khana khaũga./ to /hoTəl ja kər, mɔ̃y

153

khana khaūga. /

a. bazar jaie! kəpRa xəridie!

b. kəmre mē jaegi. cadər bədlegi.

c. səbzi kaTūga. pani mē dhoūga.

d. saman wtaro! ysi mez pər rəkho!

e. myhrbani fərmaie! ysmyth sahəb ka pəta bətaie!

f. myrcē khaūga. pani pina cahie.

g. Telifun kərūga. ap ko bətaūga.

h. pakystan jaūga. vəhā ek sal tək rəhūga.

i. phəl xəridēge. ysmyth sahəb ke pas cəlēge.

j. ys tāge mē bəyTho! DakTər ke pas jəldi jana cahie.

5.503. Fill the Blanks.

1. Fill the blanks with the proper form of the word or words in brackets.

a. ____ka kam həy. [koi, kəwn [sg.], kəwn [pl.]]

b. ap ____se bat kərēge. [koi, kəwn [sg.], kəwn [pl.]]

c. ____ke lie yntyzam kərna həy. [koi, kəwn [sg.], kəwn [pl.]]

d. ____əwr nəwkər se puchna cahie. [koi]

e. ____tin səw gylasõ mē, ek xərab hoga. [koi]

f. kya, ____ghər mē həy? [koi]

g. ap ____ko de səkte hõy. [koi, kəwn [sg.], kəwn [pl.]]

h. lahəwr yəhā se ____do səw mil dur həy. [koi]

i. mera saman ____Dybbe mē həy. [koi, kəwn [sg.]]

j. ____khyRki ko kholie. [koi]

2. The following time expressions can all be put into the frames / ... bəj kər, ... mynəT pər/ or / ... bəjne mē, ... mynəT pər/. In some cases one of the fraction words discussed in Sec. 4.307 may also be substituted. As an exercise, all of these possibilities should be employed in the frame sentence /mere dost ki gaRi____ pəhw̄cegi. /

1:15	2:30	10:22	7:02
12:07	3:17	8:29	12:09
7:47 [13 to 8]	4:40 [20 to 5]	9:39 [21 to 10]	11:45 [15 to 12]
9:55 [5 to 10]	6:45 [15 to 7]	11:28	4:27

5.504. Variation.

1. maf kijie, ravəlpynDi ki gaRiā kys kys vəqt jati hõy.

maf kijie, ap ke profesər kys kys vəqt kylasē lete hõy.

maf kijie, ap ki dwkan kys kys dyn bənd hoti həy.

maf kijie, ap pakystan mē kys kys šəhr jaēge.

maf kijie, ap kəwn kəwnsi cizē dekhēge.

maf kijie, ap kəhā kəhā jaēge.

2. gaRi sat ghənTe mē pəhw̄cegi.

   gaRi do dyn ke bad pəhw̄cegi.

   ravəlpynDi ki rel gaRi aj aTh bəje pəhw̄cegi.

   mera ləRka tin dyn mē lahəwr pəhw̄c rəha həy.

   mera ləRka aj nəhĩ pəhw̄c səkta.

   ap aj lahəwr nəhĩ pəhw̄c səkēge.

3. ap ko kys dərje ka TykəT cahie.

   ap ko kəwnsa nəwkər cahie.

   yn ko kəwnse nəwkər se puchna cahie.

   ws ko kys gaRi se jana cahie.

   kysi se yy nəhĩ kəhna cahie.

   kysi ko mera pəta nəhĩ bətana cahie.

4. mere mwlk mē relõ mē car dərje hote hə̃y.

   əmrika mē bəhwt əcche phəl hote hə̃y.

   ys mwlk mē səb logõ ko təklif hoti həy.

   ys ryjysTər mē hər nəwkər ka nam hota həy.

   ys bazar mē Təyksiã bəhwt hoti hə̃y.

   ys šəhr mē tãge bəhwt kəm hote hə̃y.

5. mere xyal mē ap ke lie dusra dərja byhtər hoga.

   mere xyal mē yn ke lie yy suTkes byhtər hoga.

   mere xyal mē ləRkõ ke lie yəhã ke yskul byhtər hõge.

   mere xyal mē ys šəhr mē səRkē əcchi nəhĩ hõgi.

   mere xyal mē ys vəqt yəhã koi Təyksi nəhĩ hogi.

   mere xyal mē ys hoTəl mē rəhne ka yntyzam əccha nəhĩ hoga.

6. maf kijie. kya, mwjhe koi qwli myl səkta həy?

   maf kijie. kya, mwjhe yəhã ek gylas pani myl səkta həy?

   maf kijie. kya, ys hoTəl mē do kəmre myl səkte hə̃y?

   maf kijie. kya, həmē ys hoTəl mē khana myl səkta həy?

   maf kijie. kya, həm logõ ko koi gaRi myl səkti həy?

   maf kijie. kya, ynhē ys dwkan se aj ka əxbar myl səkta həy?

7. dekho, sahəb ka saman Təyksi se wtaro!

   dekho, mera suTkes ws gaRi se wtaro!

   dekho, yy phəl saf pani se dhoo!

   dekho, ek TykəT ws dəftər se xərido!

   dekho, mera gylas ws Dybbe se nykalo!

   dekho, ek əxbar bazar se xərid kər lao!

8. əb jəldi bəyThie! vəqt kəm həy.

   əb jəldi cəlie! vəqt nəhĩ həy.

   əb cae pijie! vəqt bəhwt kəm həy.

   əb vapəs jaie! vəqt thoRa həy.

   əb ek ghənTa yəhã Thəyrie! vəqt kafi həy.

   əb saman jəldi wtaro! vəqt nəhĩ.

9. mə̃y hamyd sahəb ke kəmre mē bat kərne ke lie ja rəha hũ.

155

mɛ̃y lahəwr kəpRa xəridne ke lie ja rəha hū̃.

mɛ̃y aj šəhr dekhne ke lie ja rəha hū̃.

mɛ̃y DakTər ke pas əpni ləRki ko dykhane ke lie ja rəha hū̃.

mɛ̃y dəftər Telifun kərne ke lie ja rəha hū̃.

mɛ̃y əbhi ap ke lie yntyzam kərne ke lie ja rəha hū̃.

10. mɛ̃y əbhi səb cizē la rəha hū̃.

vw əbhi ap ke lie kwch sygreT la rəha həy.

həm əbhi ap ko ek ser am bhej rəhe hɛ̃y.

vw nəwkər əbhi ap ke lie səb yntyzam kər rəha həy.

vw nəwkər dəftər se yjazət le rəha həy.

vw nəwkər həmari cae kyõ nəhĩ bhej rəha.

11. kya, ap ko kysi əwr ciz ki zərurət həy?

kya, ap ko kysi nəwkər ki zərurət həy?

kya, həmē vəhā̃ jane ki zərurət həy?

kya, twm ko kwch kam ki zərurət həy?

kya, yy bat bətane ki koi zərurət həy?

kya, ap ko ek Təyksi ki zərurət həy?

12. ap ko ys kytab ki kya zərurət həy.

ap ko meri wmr bətane ki kya zərurət həy?

ap ko kam kərne ki kya zərurət həy.

ap ko ravəlpynDi jane ki kya zərurət həy.

ap ko yəhā̃ bəyThne ki kya zərurət həy.

ap ko yy ciz xəridne ki kya zərurət həy.

13. mere xansamā se kəho, ky əb ws ki zərurət nəhĩ.

mere nəwkər se kəho, ky əb ws ke lie kwch kam nəhĩ.

mere profesər se kəho, ky mɛ̃y wrdu nəhĩpəRh səkta.

mere dost se kəho, ky mɛ̃y aj nəhĩja səkūga.

meri bivi se kəho, ky mɛ̃y car bəje tək nəhĩ pəhw̃c səkta.

DakTər se kəho, ky wnhē aj həspətal nəhĩ jana həy.

14. mɛ̃y əbhi ws se kəhta hū̃.

mɛ̃y aj wn se səb kwch kəhūga.

vw əpne xansamā se kəhēge.

ap wrdu mē ys ko kya kəhēge.

mɛ̃y wrdu mē ys ko "dərvaza" kəhūga.

mɛ̃y ap se yy bat pir ko kəhūga.

15. sahəb, hoTəl ka Telifun əbhi xərab həy.

sahəb, yy nəmbər əbhi xərab həy. [1]

sahəb, meri gaRi əbhi xərab həy.

sahəb, mere dost ka myzaj əbhi kwch xərab həy.

sahəb, ys šəhr ka pani ajkəl bəhwt xərab həy.

sahəb, ys hoTəl ka khana xərab nəhĩ.

[1] I. e. this telephone is out of order.

16. əbhi bara bəj rəhe hɛ̃y.

əbhi saRhe bara bəj rəhe hə̄y.

əbhi pəwne pāc bəj rəhe hə̄y.

əbhi səva chəy bəj rəhe hə̄y.

əbhi Dhai bəj rəhe hə̄y.

əbhi DeRh bəj rəha həy.

5.505. Translation.

The following sets of sentences illustrate some of the uses of /hi/"emphatic" and /bhi/ "also, too." Note that /bhi/ does not occur in as many positions in the sentence as /hi/. The instructor may also take other sentences from the text and exercises and ask the students to insert /hi/ and /bhi/ wherever possible and explain their use.

1. hamyd sahəb ys sal pakystan aḗge.
   a. hamyd sahəb hi ys sal pakystan aḗge. [Out of several persons mentioned, only Mr. Hamyd will be coming.]
   b. hamyd sahəb ysi sal pakystan aḗge. [This very year]
   c. hamyd sahəb ys sal hi pakystan aḗge. [Only this year -- somewhat stronger than the last above]
   d. hamyd sahəb ys sal pakystan hi aḗge. [He will only be coming to Pakistan, not to other places mentioned.]
   e. hamyd sahəb bhi ys sal pakystan aḗge. [Mr. Hamyd will be coming, as well as others mentioned.]
   f. hamyd sahəb ys sal bhi pakystan aḗge. [He's also coming this year. He came last year too.]
   g. hamyd sahəb ys sal pakystan bhi aḗge. [He will be coming to other places as well.]

2. mə̄y ys qwli ko dəs ane dūga.
   a. mə̄y hi ys qwli ko dəs ane dūga. [I alone will give him ten annas. My companions will give him different amounts.]
   b. mə̄y ysi qwli ko dəs ane dūga. [I will give ten annas only to this coolie.]
   c. mə̄y ys qwli ko hi dəs ane dūga. [I'll give this very coolie ten annas. This is stronger than the last above. /ys qwli hi ko/ is also correct.]
   d. mə̄y ys qwli ko dəs hi ane dūga. [I will give him only ten annas -- not eleven or twelve, etc.]
   e. mə̄y ys qwli ko dəs ane hi dūga. [I'll give him only ten annas -- not a rupee or more.]
   f. mə̄y bhi ys qwli ko dəs ane dūga. [I too will give him money.]
   g. mə̄y ys qwli ko bhi dəs ane dūga. [I'll pay this coolie, as well as the others.]
   h. mə̄y ys qwli ko dəs ane bhi dūga. [I'll give him ten annas, as well as something else previously mentioned.]

3. vw ys gaRi se ravəlpynDi ja səkte hə̄y.
   a. vwhi ys gaRi se ravəlpynDi ja səkte hə̄y. [He alone can go.]

157

b. vw ysi gaRi se ravəlpynDi ja səkte hɔ̄y. [He can go by this very train.]

c. vw ys gaRi se hi ravəlpynDi ja səkte hɔ̄y. [He can go only by this very train. Stronger than the last above. /ys gaRi hi se/ is also possible.]

d. vw ys gaRi se ravəlpynDi hi ja səkte hɔ̄y. [He can only get to Rawalpindi by this train -- nowhere else.]

e. vw ys gaRi se ravəlpynDi ja hi nəhī̃ səkta. [He can't get to Rawalpindi at all by this train. Or: it is absolutely impossible for him to take this train to Rawalpindi. Note that /hi/ cannot occur in the affirmative form of this sentence.]

f. vw bhi ys gaRi se ravəlpynDi ja səkte hɔ̄y. [He too can go.]

g. vw ys gaRi se bhi ravəlpynDi ja səkte hɔ̄y. [He can go by this train too, as well as by others.]

h. vw ys gaRi se ravəlpynDi bhi ja səkte hɔ̄y. [He can also go to Rawalpindi by this train, as well as to other places.]

i. vw ys gaRi se ravəlpynDi ja bhi səkte hɔ̄y ... [This is somewhat incomplete, since a correlative clause like / ... əwr vapəs bhi a səkte hɔ̄y. / is understood. He can go by this train and also come back by it.]

4. ap ka nam ys ryjysTər pər lykhū̃ga.

a. ap hi ka nam ys ryjysTər pər lykhū̃ga. [I'll only write your name and no one else's. Also /ap ka hi nam/.]

b. ap ka nam hi ys ryjysTər pər lykhū̃ga. [I'll only write your name, not your address, etc.]

c. ap ka nam ysi ryjysTər pər lykhū̃ga. [I'll write your name in this very register.]

d. ap ka nam ys ryjysTər pər hi lykhū̃ga. [I'll write your name only in this very register. Stronger than the last above. Also /ys ryjysTər hi pər/.]

e. ap ka nam bhi ys ryjysTər pər lykhū̃ga. [I'll write your name also. /ap ka bhi nam/ is also possible.]

f. ap ka nam ys ryjysTər pər bhi lykhū̃ga. [I'll write your name in this register, as well as in some other places.]

5. ys hoTəl mɛ̃ khana əccha dete hɔ̄y.

a. ysi hoTəl mɛ̃ khana əccha dete hɔ̄y. [In this very hotel]

b. ys hoTəl mɛ̃ hi khana əccha dete hɔ̄y. [Only in this very hotel -- nowhere else. Somewhat stronger than the last above. /ys hoTəl hi mɛ̃/ is also correct.]

c. ys hoTəl mɛ̃ khana hi əccha dete hɔ̄y. [Only the food is good; other things are not.]

d. ys hoTəl mɛ̃ khana əccha hi dete hɔ̄y. [The food is always good.]

e. ys hoTəl mɛ̃ khana əccha dete hi hɔ̄y. [They only serve good food in this hotel. Emphatic.]

f. ys hoTəl mɛ̃ bhi khana əccha dete hɔ̄y. [This hotel also serves good food.]

g. ys hoTəl mɛ̃ khana bhi əccha dete hɔ̄y. [The food is good as well as the service, etc.]

h. ys hoTəl mē khana əccha bhi dete hə̄y. [The food is good in this hotel too
    sometimes -- as well as occasionally bad.]
i. ys hoTəl mē khana əccha dete bhi hə̄y, ya nəhī̃. [Do they ever serve good
    food here or not?]

5. 506. Response.

1. aj šam ko ap kəhā̃ hõge.
2. kya, ap car bəje tək kylas mē hote hə̄y?
3. ap ki kylasē kys kys vəqt hoti hə̄y.
4. ap pakystan mē kəb tək rəh səkēge.
5. ravəlpynDi lahəwr se kytni dur həy.
6. kya, ap ke mwlk mē rel ke dərje hote hə̄y, ya nəhī̃.
7. kya, ap pakystan mē hoTəl mē Thəyrēge, ya kysi ke ghər mē.
8. ap log ys kyḷas ke bad kəhā̃ kəhā̃ jaēge.
9. ap ajkəl kəwn kəwnsi kytabē pəRh rəhe hə̄y.
10. kya, ap ko sygreT pina pəsənd həy?

5. 507. Conversation Practice.

Mr. Smith has just gotten out of a railway carriage.

S: qwli!
C: ji hā̃, sahəb!
S: mera saman ys Dybbe se wtaro, əwr kysi Təyksi mē rəkho!
C: bəhwt əccha, sahəb. mə̄y əbhi ap ke lie Təyksi bwla rəha hū̃. [He calls a taxi and
   speaks to the taxi driver:] sahəb ka saman wTha kər, əpni Təyksi mē rəkho!
T [to Mr. Smith]: ap kəhā̃ jana cahte hə̄y.
S: mə̄y hoTəl jana cahta hū̃. kya, ys šəhr mē koi əccha hoTəl həy?
T: ji hā̃, bəhwt hə̄y. kəysa hoTəl cahie. mə̄hge hoTəl hə̄y, əwr səste bhi hə̄y. səb əmrikən
   log yslamia hoTəl mē Thəyrte hə̄y. vw bəhwt mə̄hga həy.
S: nəhī̃. koi əwr hoTəl bətao!
T: ek əwr əccha əwr səsta hoTəl həy, məgər šəhr mē həy.
S: koi bat nəhī̃. vəhā̃ cəlo!

Mr. Smith arrives at the hotel. He addresses the hotel clerk.

S: jənab, ys hoTəl mē ek kəmra myl səkta həy?
C: ji hā̃. həmare pas do kəmre ys vəqt xali hə̄y. kəwnsa pəsənd hoga -- bəRa ya choTa.
   bəRe ka kyraya əTThays rupəe roz həy, əwr choTe ka kyraya teys rupəe roz həy.
S: kya, choTe kəmre ke sath γwslxana həy?
C: ji nəhī̃. syrf bəRe kəmre ke sath γwslxana həy, məgər γwslxane kysi kəmre se dur
   nəhī̃, əwr səb bəhwt saf hə̄y.
S: Thik həy. mwjhe bəRa kəmra dijie.
C: ap yəhā̃ kəb tək Thəyrēge.

159

S: mera xyal həy, ky mə̄y ek ya do həfte tək yəhā Thəyrūga.

C: ap kya kam kərte hə̄y.

S: mə̄y profesər hū. mə̄y səb pakystani yunyvərsyTiā dekhni cahta hū. kwch pakystani profesrō se bhi mylna həy.

C: bəhwt əccha. əpna nam əwr pəta ys ryjysTər pər lykhie. [To a coolie:] dekho, sahəb ka suTkes Təyksi se nykalo, əwr chəTe kəmre ke əndər rəkho!

S [to the clerk]: qwli ko kya dena cahie.

C: ws ko car ane ya aTh ane dijie. bəhwt kafi hə̄y.

   Mr. Smith enters his room and finds the bearer there.

S: twm kəwn ho. kya kər rəhe ho.

B: mə̄y hoTəl ka nəwkər hū, sahəb. mwjhe hamyd kəhte hə̄y. mə̄y cadər əwr təwlia bədəl rəha hū.

S: mwjhe ɣwsl kərna həy. kya, gərm pani həy?

B: pani həy, sahəb, məgər ThənDa hoga. swba gərm hota həy. mə̄y dəs mynəT mē̃ ap ke lie gərm pani la səkūga.

S: khana kys kys vəqt hota həy.

B: cae əbhi mylegi. swba ki cae chəy bəje se aTh bəje tək hoti həy. dyn ka khana ek bəje se səva tin bəje tək hota həy, əwr šam ka khana pəwne aTh bəje se nəw bəje tək hota həy. ys ke bad, ap ko əpne kəmre mē̃ khana myl səkta həy. khane ke kəmre mē̃ nəhī̃ myl səkta. ap kəwnsa khana khate hə̄y -- pakystani ya əmrikən?

S: ajkəl mə̄y syrf pakystani khana khata hū. vw mwjhe bəhwt pəsənd həy.

B: bəhwt əccha. kya, ap ko kysi əwr ciz ki zərurət həy?

S: hā. aj ka əxbar cahie. kwch phəl bhi cahta hū. mwjhe ənar, kele, səntre, əwr ə̄gur pəsənd hə̄y.

B: bəhwt əccha. mə̄y pəhle cadər lata hū. ws ke bad bazar se əxbar əwr phəl xərid ke laūga.

   Later Mr. Smith receives a telephone call. It is Mr. Hamyd.

S: mə̄y ysmyth hū. ap kəwn sahəb hə̄y.

H: mə̄y hamyd hū. adab ərz. myzaj šərif?

S: šwkria. ap ki bivi əwr ləRke kəyse hə̄y.

H: səb Thik hə̄y. kya, ap aj həmare sath khana kha səkte hə̄y?

S: ji hā. khana kys vəqt hoga.

H: aTh bəje šam ko. mə̄y gaRi ka yntyzam kərūga.

S: ap ki myhrbani! ap kyō̃ təklif fərma rəhe hə̄y. mə̄y yəhā se Təyksi pəkəR səkta hū.

H: mwjhe koi təklif nəhī̃ hogi. ap fykr nə kijie. əpni gaRi bhejūga. aTh bəjne mē̃ bis mynəT pər pəhw̄cegi. ap ke kəmre ka kya nəmbər həy.

S: mere kəmre ka nəmbər chəy həy. mə̄y ws vəqt kəmre mē̃ təyyar hūga. xwda hafyz.

H: xwda hafyz.

5.508. Conversation Stimulus.

The students should divide themselves into groups of two or three. Each group will prepare a brief dialogue about one of the following topics. When these have been corrected by the instructor, they may be memorised and presented to the rest of the class in the form of "plays."

1. A traveller at the railway station
2. Getting a room at the hotel
3. Giving instructions to a hotel servant
4. Talking to someone on the telephone
5. Making a purchase in the market

5.600. VOCABULARY

The vocabulary does not include the special object forms of the pronouns, demonstratives, etc. (e.g. /mwjhe/, /həmẽ/), the emphatic forms of the pronouns and demonstratives (e.g. /yyhi/, /ysi/, /mwjhi/), or the regular ordinal numerals ending in /vã/.

ənar M1	pomegranate
əTThays [or /əTThais/] A1	twenty-eight
əxbar M1	newspaper
ə̃gur M1	grape
bat F1	thing, matter, word, talk
bədəlna	to change, be changed, transform
bəjna	to ring, strike, play (intrans.)
bənd A1	closed, shut
bwlana	to call
byhtər A1	better
cabi F2	key
cadər F1	bedsheet
cəwtha A2	fourth
chəbbys [or /chəbbis/] A1	twenty-six
chəTa A2	sixth
ciz F1	thing, object, article
dərja M2	class, degree, level
dərvaza M2	door
dopəhr F1	early afternoon
Dybba M2	box, compartment, packet
fərmana	to command, grant, say, do
fykr F1	worry, concern
gaRi F2	car, cart, vehicle, automobile, train
gərm A1	hot
ɣwsl M1	bath
ɣwslxana M2	bathroom
həzar A1	thousand
hi Enclitic Particle	emphatic
hona	to be, become
hoTəl M1	hotel, restaurant
kəhna	to say, tell; call (something a name)
kər [or /ke/] Verbal Enclitic	having ... ed
kholna	to open
khyRki F2	window
koi A1 [OS: /kysi/]	anybody, somebody; any, some; approximately, about
kwrsi F2	chair
lykhna	to write

162

maf [literary: /mwaf/] PA1	forgiven
mil M1	mile
mwlk M1	country
mynəT M1	minute
nykalna	to take out
pəhw̃cna	to arrive
pəkəRna	to catch, seize, grab
pəta M2	address
qwli M1	coolie, porter, manual labourer
ravəlpynDi F2 [np]	Rawalpindi (a city in West Pakistan)
rel F1	railway, train
ryjysTər M1	register
sabwn [or /sabən/] M1	soap
saman M1	baggage, articles, things, raw materials, paraphernalia
səkna	to be able
səntra [literary: /sə̃gtəra/] M2	sp. of orange
səttays [or /səttais/] A1	twenty-seven
səw A1	hundred
suTkes M1	suitcase
sygreT M1	cigarette
šəhr M1	city
tək Post	up to, until
təklif F1	trouble, difficulty, pain, hurt
təwlia M2 [or F1]	towel
tis A1	thirty
Tɔyksi F2	taxi
Telifun M1	telephone
ThənDa A2	cold, cool
TykəT M1	ticket, stamp
vəhĩ Adv	right there
wnəttys [or /wnəttis/, or /wntis/ or /wntys/] A1	twenty-nine
wtarna	to take down, unload, cause to alight, take off (clothes)
wThana	to raise, lift, pick up
xansamã M1	cook
xərab A1	bad, spoiled, out of order, rotten, defective
yəhĩ Adv	right here
yntyzam M1	arrangement, management
ysTešən M1	station
zərurət F1	need, necessity

The tomb of Iltutmish, Delhi, built in 1235. Elegant calligraphy is seen here employed as wall ornamentation.

UNIT SIX

6.000. SCRIPT I

6.001. The Basic Structure of the Urdu Script.

Urdu is written in a modified form of the Arabic script. The direction of writing is from right to left (except for sequences of numeral figures, which read from left to right). There are thirty-five letters, representing consonants only. No special forms are employed for the capital letters.

Three varieties of this script are in common use: (1) /nəsx/ is employed for the Qwran ("Koran"), quotations from Arabic, etc. It is also the model upon which type fonts for Arabic, Persian, and Urdu are usually based. (2) /nəstaliq/ is the variety of greatest importance to the student, since roughly eighty percent of all published material is produced in this script. The use of the /nəsx/ movable type font has not gained much popularity, and most Urdu books, newspapers, and magazines are thus first handwritten by professional scribes in /nəstaliq/ and then lithographed. (3) /šykəsta/is an extremely cursive variety, used for personal letters, police and court documents, village records, etc.; its use is declining.

The original Arabic alphabet contained twenty-eight symbols. These represented consonants only. These are divisible into fifteen basic "shape groups." Various letters may have the same basic shape but are differentiated from other letters in their group by the addition of dots (etc.) above or below the symbol. Thus, "b", "t," "s" and also "n" and "y" to some extent share the same basic shape; they are distinguished, however, by one dot below, two dots above, three dots above, one dot above, and two dots below respectively. The maximum number of dots is three.

The Persians later added different dot combinations to various basic shapes to produce four more sounds not found in Arabic: /p, c, ž, g/. Similarly, those who adapted the alphabet to Urdu later added another diacritic to three basic shapes to produce /T, D, R/. Modified forms of one or another Arabic letter have also been set aside to represent special sound features: e.g. a form of "h" for aspiration (as in /ph, th, bh/), a form of "n" to indicate a nasalised vowel, etc.

As in English handwriting, there is a tendency to join the letters of a word together with ligatures. There are two basic kinds of letters: (1) "connectors," which may be joined both to a preceding and to a following letter; and (2) "nonconnectors," which may be joined only to a preceding letter. There are twenty-six of the former and nine of the latter.

The shape of a letter may also differ somewhat depending upon its position in the word and its joining or nonjoining to adjacent letters. A connector letter may have as many as four variant forms:

    (1) C- "initial": used at the beginning of a word or after a nonconnector. This form always connects with a following letter.

    (2) -C- "medial": used between two connectors and joined to both.

(3) -C "final": used after a connector at the end of a word.

(4) C "independent": used after a nonconnector at the end of a word.

Nonconnectors have only two forms:

(1) C "initial-independent": used at the beginning of a word, after another non-connector at the end of a word, or between two nonconnectors within a word.

(2) -C "medial-final": used after a connector either within or at the end of a word.

6.002. The Urdu Alphabet.

The following list presents the letters in their Urdu alphabetical order. Each letter is given in its independent (or initial-independent) form. To this the following information is added: (1) the letter's shape group (numbered from one to fifteen) and its status as a connector or nonconnector (symbolised as "C" and "N"); (2) its pronunciation (i.e. its equivalent in the author's phonemic script); wherever a letter cannot easily be equated with a single phonemic symbol, the pronunciation has been marked with an asterisk; and (3) the Urdu name of the letter.

LETTER	SHAPE GROUP AND CONNECTOR STATUS	PRONUNCIATION	URDU NAME
ا	1-N	a*	əlyf
ب	2-C	b	be
پ	2-C	p	pe
ت	2-C	t	te
ط	2-C	T	Te
ث	2-C	s	se
ج	3-C	j	jim
چ	3-C	c	ce

LETTER	SHAPE GROUP AND CONNECTOR STATUS	PRONUNCIATION	URDU NAME
ح	3-C	h	he [/bəRi he/]
خ	3-C	x	xe
د	4-N	d	dal
ڈ	4-N	D	Dal
ذ	4-N	z	zal
ر	5-N	r	re
ڑ	5-N	R	Re
ز	5-N	z	ze
ژ	5-N	ž	že
س	6-C	s	sin
ش	6-C	š	šin
ص	7-C	s	swad
ض	7-C	z	zwad
ط	8-C	t	to, toe
ظ	8-C	z	zo, zoe

LETTER	SHAPE GROUP AND CONNECTOR STATUS	PRONUNCIATION	URDU NAME
ع	9-C	*	əyn
غ	9-C	γ	γəyn
ف	10-C	f	fe
ق	10-C	q	qaf
ک	11-C	k	kaf
گ	11-C	g	gaf
ل	12-C	l	lam
م	13-C	m	mim
ن	2-C[1]	n	nun
و	14-N	v*	vao
ہ	15-C	h*	he [/choTi he/]
ی	2-C[1]	y*	ye

[1] "nun" and "ye" only partially belong to Group 2-C; their initial and medial shapes are the same, but their final independent shapes differ.

Urdu alphabetical order differs slightly from that of Arabic: the latter has "he" - "vao" - "ye" instead of "vao" - "he" - "ye." Some Urdu writers also list ء /həmza/ (Sec. 10.005) as a letter, placing it after ہ . Some also list ے /bəRi ye/ (Sec. 6.103) after /choTi ye/. Some dictionaries also give words beginning with آ /a/ (Sec. 6.101) separately from those beginning with ا alone.

6.003. Letters Representing the Same Sound.

In several cases more than one letter may stand for a single sound. Although these
letters represented different sounds in Arabic, they are not commonly distinguished in
Urdu. Many Arabic (and some Persian) words continue to be written with these letters,
however, and the student must learn the correct spelling. This is analogous to the problems
presented by English spelling, where one phonemic sequence may be written in many
different ways: e.g. /uw/ may be written "oe" as in "shoe," "ough" as in "through," "oo"
as in "coo," "o" as in "do," etc. In spite of these Arabic extra letters, however, Urdu
spelling is relatively phonemic. Out of each group of letters representing the same sound,
moreover, there is always one which is widely used in words of all historical origins,
whereas the others are limited to certain loanwords from Arabic and Persian. The "common
letter" is marked with an asterisk in the following lists:

LETTER	SHAPE GROUP AND CONNECTOR STATUS	PRONUNCIATION	URDU NAME
ت	2-C	t*	te
ط	8-C	t	to, toe
ث	2-C	s	se
س	6-C	s*	sin
ص	7-C	s	swad
ذ	4-N	z	zal
ز	5-N	z*	ze
ض	7-C	z	zwad
ظ	8-C	z	zo, zoe
ح	3-C	h	he [/bəRi he/]
ه	15-C	h*	he [/choTi he/]

6.004. The Vowels.

The earliest forms of the Arabic script contained no apparatus for writing vowels, since the structure of the language together with the context served to render any given passage clear. Later on, however, a set of diacritics was developed. These are written above or below the consonant symbol which they follow in speech. There are thus three diacritics for the Arabic short vowels /i/, /u/, and /a/ (Urdu /y/, /w/, /ə/). The three corresponding long vowels, /ii/, /uu/, /aa/, are represented by one of these diacritics followed on the main line of writing by one of the semi-vowel letters (called a "weak letter"): thus, /i/ followed by /y/ = /iy/ = /ii/ ("long ī"; Urdu /i/); the /u/ diacritic followed by /v/ = /uv/ = /uu/ ("long ū;" Urdu /u/); the /a/ diacritic followed by the special "carrier letter" /əlyf/ = /aa/ ("long ā"; Urdu /a/). Two diphthongs, /ay/ and /aw/ (Urdu /əy/ and /əw/) are symbolised by the /a/ diacritic followed by /y/ and /v/ respectively. In the following table, the position of the vowel diacritic relative to its consonant is shown by placing the vowel above or below the "C"; /əlyf/ is represented as"*."

SCRIPT	ARABIC	URDU	SCRIPT	ARABIC	URDU
C i	/Ci/	/Cy/	Cy i	/Cii/	/Ci/
u C	/Cu/	/Cw/	u Cv	/Cuu/	/Cu/
a C	/Ca/	/Cə/	a C*	/Caa/	/Ca/
a Cy	/Cay/	/Cəy/	a Cv	/Caw/	/Cəw/

As is clear from the above, this vowel-marking apparatus lacks sufficient symbols to represent all the Urdu vowels. /Ce/ and /Co/ must also be written /Cy/ and /Cv/. In a vowelled text, they may be distinguished from other vowels by having NO diacritic. Thus:

SCRIPT	URDU	SCRIPT	URDU
Cy i	/Ci/	u Cv	/Cu/
a Cy	/Cəy/	a Cv	/Cəw/
Cy	/Ce/[1]	Cv	/Co/

[1]There is indeed a special form of "ye" for /i/ and another for /e/, but these are differentiated only word-finally.

170

The above system may be somewhat cumbersome, but it is not inaccurate. The main obstacle faced by beginners, however, is the fact that the vowel diacritics are ALMOST NEVER written in materials intended for adult speakers of the language! In most cases, the consonantal skeleton of the word, plus its context, will be enough to prevent any ambiguity, and in cases where a native speaker would experience real difficulty, a vowel diacritic may optionally be added. Thus, the sequence "CC" may stand for /CC/, /CyC/, /CwC/, /CəC/; "Cy" for /Cy/, /Ci/, /Ce/, or /Cəy/; "Cv" for /Cw/, /Cu/, /Co/, /Cəw/; and only "C" + /əlyf/ stands unambiguously for /Ca/. In spite of this ambiguity, however, the system is not as formidable as it may seem at first glance. The student now knows enough Urdu to be able to employ context and basic grammar, as well as his purely lexical knowledge of the word.

6.100. LETTER GROUPS

6.101. The Vowel Diacritics.

Although the vowel diacritics are only rarely seen in an Urdu text meant for adult speakers, they are introduced here as an aid to the beginner. They are:

(a) The vowel /y/ is symbolised by ╱ placed under its consonant.

(b) The vowel /w/ is symbolised by 𝟡 placed over its consonant.

(c) The vowel /ə/ is symbolised by ╱ placed over its consonant.

The names of these diacritics are /zer/, /peš/, and /zəbər/ respectively.

6.102. Letter Group 1.

This group contains only ‍ا‍ /əlyf/. It is a nonconnector and has the following forms:

Independent-initial

Medial-final

Word initially, /əlyf/ indicates only that the word begins with a vowel. For /y/, /w/, and /ə/, a diacritic may be employed with /əlyf/: = initial /y/, = initial /w/, and = initial /ə/. Other vowels are written with /əlyf/ (+ a diacritic) followed by /y/ or /v/: = initial /i/, = initial /e/, = initial /əy/, = initial /u/, = initial /o/, = initial /əw/. Initial /a/ is written with /əlyf/ + a special symbol called /məd/ ("lengthener"): ⁓ . /məd/ is used only with /əlyf/. As stated above, the vowel diacritics are only sporadically written, and initial ‍ا‍ may thus stand for /y/, /w/, or /ə/; initial اِل for /i/, /e/, /əy/, etc.

After a consonant, /əlyf/ always denotes /a/. An exception (the Arabic definite article) will be discussed later.

6.103. Letter Group 2.

This group contains ب /b/, پ /p/, ت /t/, ٹ /T/, ش /s/ and partially ن /n/ and consonantal ی /y/. Letters of this shape group are connectors and have the following basic forms:

Initial	الب	الپ	الت	الٹ	الش
Medial	بب	پپ	تت	ٹٹ	شش
Final	الب الپ	الپ	الت	الٹ	الش
Independent	ب	پ	ت	ٹ	ش

Letters of this group are thus:

Initial	بـ	پـ	تـ	ٹـ	ثـ
Medial	ـبـ	ـپـ	ـتـ	ـٹـ	ـثـ
Final	ـب	ـپ	ـت	ـٹ	ـث
Independent	ب	پ	ت	ٹ	ث

The letter ث is an "uncommon Arabic consonant."

The letter ن /n/ differs somewhat from those above:

Initial   نـ

Medial   ـنـ

Final   ن

Independent   ن

The curve of the final and independent forms of   ن   is more rounded than that of

ب ، پ   , etc. and it also drops down below the main line of writing.

At the end of a word, the final and independent forms of   ن   may be written without

any dot to indicate the nasalisation of the preceding vowel: e.g.   یں   /ī/, /ē/, or /ay/;

ول   /ū/, /ō/, or /aw/;   ال   /ā/. Nasalisation within the word is commonly written

with   ن   /n/ (i.e. /nun/ WITH its dot): e.g.   تانٹا   /tanta/ or /tāta/. This occasionally

gives rise to ambiguity, and many Urdu speakers tend to close certain syllables containing

a nasalised vowel with the final or independent form of /nun/ without its dot and then begin

the next syllable as though it were a new word, thus avoiding ambiguity at the expense of

word unity. /nun/ without its dot (i.e. the nasalisation marker) is termed /nun γwnna/ in

Urdu.

The letter   ی   also has special forms:

Initial   یـ

Medial   ـیـ

Final   ی   ے

Independent   ی   ے

Initial   ی   stands only for consonantal /y/. As stated above, initial /i/, /e/, or

/əy/ is symbolised by /əlyf/ +   ی   .

Medial   ی   may represent consonantal /y/ or one of the vowels /i/, /e/, or /əy/

as described above.

There are two final and independent forms of   ی :   ی   is called /choTi ye/

"little ye" and is always pronounced as /i/. The second form,   ے   is called /bəRi ye/

"big ye" and is pronounced either as /e/ or as /əy/ (in which case it may occur with the diacritic ⟋ : ⟍). Except for the word /həy/ "is," the /e/ pronunciation is much more common.

After Letter Groups 2, 10, 11, and 12, the final shape of the /choTi ye/ looks like this ی . It is written almost below the preceding consonant. Letters of Groups 2, 11, and 12 have a slight modification of their initial shape before final /choTi ye/: ⟩ . E.g. بی /bi/, تی /ti/, etc. Further minor modifications of Group 2 shapes will be described later.

6.104. Letter Group 4.

This group contains د /d/, ڈ /D/, and ذ /z/. Letters of this group are non-connectors and have the following basic forms:

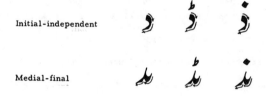

Initial-independent		
Medial-final		

Letters of this group are thus:

Initial-independent	د	ڈ	ذ
Medial-final	ـد	ـڈ	ـذ

The letter ذ is an "uncommon Arabic consonant."

Note that the initial-independent form of this shape group is written with a relatively closed angle. If the angle is too open, the letter may be confused with one of the ر group (see below).

6.105. Letter Group 5.

This group contains ‫ر‬ /r/, ‫ڑ‬ /R/, ‫ز‬ /z/, and ‫ژ‬ /ž/. Letters of this group are nonconnectors and have the following basic forms:

Initial-independent

Medial-final

Letters of this group are thus:

Initial-independent

Medial-final

The letter ‫ز‬ is the commonest representation of /z/. ‫ژ‬ /ž/ is very rare, occurring mostly in highly literary words borrowed from Persian.

The angle of letters of this group is comparatively wide; cf. Sec. 6.104 above.

Note that the diacritic ‫ط‬ is used to distinguish all of the retroflex consonants: ‫ٹ‬ /T/, ‫ڈ‬ /D/, and ‫ڑ‬ /R/. In some older books these retroflex sounds were symbolised by four dots above the same basic shapes or by a horizontal line: ‫ٿ‬ , and ‫ڋ‬ or ‫څ‬ , ‫ڌ‬ , and ‫ڗ‬ . These usages are now almost obsolete.

6.106. Letter Group 14.

This group contains only ‫و‬ /v/. It is a nonconnector and has the following forms:

Initial-independent

Medial-final

Initially, ‍ stands only for consonantal /v/. As stated above, an initial /u/, /o/, or /əw/ will be symbolised by /əlyf/ + ‍ .

Medially and finally, ‍ may represent /v/, /u/, /o/, or /əw/ as described above.

6.200. SCRIPT EXERCISES

6.201. Script Exercises.

Reading exercises should be drilled for fluency and for quick letter recognition. A copy of each exercise should then be submitted as homework; care should be taken to maintain the proper shapes and proportions of each letter.

The writing exercises should similarly be done as homework. They may then be drilled verbally or at the blackboard in class.

The word recognition sections will introduce the student to the written forms of words already known to him in phonemic transcription. Special notice will be taken of "irregular" spellings.

Urdu-English and English-Urdu sentences are also included. These contain only words previously introduced in phonemic transcription (or, in the case of the numerals, in the Script Units themselves). These sentences should also be written out as homework and then verbally drilled in class.

The vowel diacritics are introduced here as an aid to the beginner, but their use will be dispensed with as soon as is feasible. They will be employed in later texts only where real ambiguity might otherwise result.

6.202. Reading Drills.

1. Letters of all groups + /əlyf/:

Vowelled	ثَا	وَا	بَا	رَا	تَا	دَا	ڈَا	ڑَا
Unvowelled	ثا	وا	با	را	تا	دا	ڈا	ڑا
Vowelled	ذَا	زَا	پَا	ٹَا	یَا	ٹَا	نَا	آ
Unvowelled	ذا	زا	پا	ٹا	یا	ٹا	نا	آ

2. Letters of all groups + /ye/.

Vowelled	زِی	رِی	پِی	وِی	نے	ڑے	رَے	ڈی
Unvowelled	زی	ری	پی	وی	نے	ڑے	رے	ڈی

Vowelled	ثِی	دِی	ڈِی	رُکے	ذِی	بے	تَے	نِی
Unvowelled	ثی	دی	ڈی	رکے	ذی	بے	تے	نی

3. Letters of all groups + /vao/.

Vowelled	دو	ذُو	تُو	رُو	پُو	ثُو	ڈو	رُو
Unvowelled	دو	ذو	تو	رو	پو	ثو	ڈو	رو
Vowelled	ژُو	لُو	نُو	یُو	وُو	زُو	بو	تُو
Unvowelled	ژو	لو	نو	یو	وو	زو	بو	تو

4. Mixed sequences of the foregoing.

Vowelled	بُو	نَا	ثِی	وَا	رِی	دے	رِتی	پے
Unvowelled	بو	نا	ثی	وا	ری	دے	تی	پے
Vowelled	نے	ڈِی	تُو	یُو	ذَا	یَا	ژِی	بِی
Unvowelled	نے	ڈی	تو	یو	ذا	یا	ژی	بی

5. Sequences of two consonants.

Vowelled	بَد	نِب	رَد	ثَر	بَن	بُٹ	پَر	ڈُر
Unvowelled	بد	نب	رد	ثر	بن	بٹ	پر	ڈر

Vowelled	رِت	وَپ	تِب	دُز	تَر	مُڈ	دَپ	تَن

Unvowelled	رت	وپ	تب	دز	تر	مڈ	دپ	تن

6. Initial "short" vowels.

Vowelled	اِن	اِز	اُن	اُڈ	اِد	اُٹ	اُر	اَب

Unvowelled	ان	از	ان	اڈ	اد	اٹ	ار	اب

Vowelled	اَتَّا	اِتنا	اَنڈا	اَتڑی	اُردُو	اِزَار	اَندَر	اَنَار

Unvowelled	اتّا	اتنا	انڈا	اتڑی	اردو	ازار	اندر	انار

7. Initial "long" vowels.

Vowelled	اُود	اید	اَیب	اَور	آپ	ایڑی	ایر	اینٹ

Unvowelled	اود	اید	ایب	اور	آپ	ایڑی	ایر	اینٹ

Vowelled	آند	اُوب	آڈاب	اُوپَر	اِید	آنا	اور	آسْنا

Unvowelled	آند	اوب	آداب	اوپر	اید	آنا	اور	آسنا

8. Medial "long" vowels and diphthongs.

Vowelled	روز	دیر	بات	ڈار	پَیدا	ثَوب	تاپ	بید

Unvowelled	روز	دیر	بات	ڈار	پیدا	ثوب	تاپ	بید

Vowelled	بِیوی	تِین	روٹی	دیتَا	پُونَا	دُور	رَات	پِیر
Unvowelled	بیوی	تین	روٹی	دیتا	پونا	دور	رات	پیر

9. Final "long" vowels and diphthongs.

Vowelled	دَادَا	بَڑی	بَرتی	پَرتَّ	بَرتنے	پَانی	پِینی	بڑے
Unvowelled	دادا	بڑی	برتی	پرتا	برتنے	پانی	پینی	بڑے

Vowelled	آرزُو	آڑی	بیٹے	اَپنی	اِتوَارِی	بَازَِری	مِینے	پُرتَا
Unvowelled	آرزو	آڑی	بیٹے	اپنی	اتواری	بازاری	مینے	پرتا

10. Final nasalised vowels.

Vowelled	اَرزُوں	بَایَاں	تِیں	رَاتِیں	پُروں	تِینوں	اَنڈوں	اِینٹوں
Unvowelled	ارزوں	بایاں	تیں	راتیں	پروں	تینوں	انڈوں	اینٹوں

Vowelled	دَایاں	اِینٹِیں	بَاتوں	دِنوں	یُوں	بِینڈِیں	وُوں
Unvowelled	دایاں	اینٹیں	باتوں	روزوں	دنوں	یوں	ینڈیں	ووں

6.203. Writing Drills.

The student may use either ذ or ز for /z/, but ز is commoner. Here-after, unless instructions are given to the contrary, the "common" letter should be employed for /t/, /s/, /z/, and /h/.

All writing drills in this Unit should be done both with and without the vowel diacritics.

1. CV, CVy, and CVv sequences.

   sa   tu   sw   do   re   Ty   bi   va   ze   ni   ya

   zə   təw   nəy   Təw   rəy   nəw   že   Dəw   dəy   yəw

2. CVC sequences: "short" vowels only.

   bəd   dyp   rəd   pwr   dər   zər   nyb   Təp   bwR   bwz

3. CVC sequences: "long" vowels only.

   bap   rəyd   Dar   pəwd   der   dəyr   rud   zəyd   biR

   bit   sab   tap   top   baR   zad   var   nar   pir   rəwd

4. Initial vowels: both "long" and "short."

   əb   əwr   ap   or   əyb   is   uT   yn   wn   əwd   ad

5. Final vowels and diphthongs.

   doti   pota   bara   dada   bəRa   bəRe   bəRi   daru

   tano   boTi   bazu   baza   rozi   wrdu   roTi   əpne

6. Longer consonant sequences, etc.

   sabyt   pəRta   dena   wtarna   tez   əndər   upər

7. Final nasalised vowels.

   bã   donõ   dynõ   batẽ   dātõ   yadẽ   baRõ   yũ   dĩ

6.204. Word Recognition.

SCRIPT	PRONUNCIATION	SCRIPT	PRONUNCIATION
اب	əb	انار	ənar
اپنا	əpnə	اندر	əndər
اتارنا	wtarna	انڈا	ənDa
اِتنا	ytna	اور	əwr
اتوار	ytvar	آپ	ap
اردو	wrdu	آداب	adab
اِن	yn	آنا	ana
اَن	wn	بات	bat

182

SCRIPT	PRONUNCIATION	SCRIPT	PRONUNCIATION
بازار	bazar	تین	tin
بایاں	bāyā	دایاں	dāyā
بتانا	bətana	دو	do
برتن	bərtən	دور	dur
بڑا	bəRa	دن	dyn
بند	bənd	دینا	dena
بیوی	bivi	رات	rat
پانی	pani	روٹی	roTi
پر	pər	روز	roz
پونا	pəwna	نو	nəw
پیر	pir	یا	ya
پینا	pina		

6.205. Urdu-English Sentences.

1. بڑی روٹی دو

2. اندر آنا

3. تین بڑے برتن اتارو

4. اتنا پانی پینا

5. اپنی بات بتانا

6.206. English-Urdu Sentences.

1. Give [nonhonorific] [a] pomegranate and [an] egg!
2. Two or three days.
3. Come [inf.] [to] [the] big bazaar!

4. Give [nonhonorific] bread and water!
5. Now take down [nonhonorific or inf.] [a] vessel!

The Lahore Fort, begun by the Mughal Emperor Akbar in 1575. The Nawlakkha Pavilion and the Shish Mahal (shown here) were added by Shah Jahan.

UNIT SEVEN

7.000. CONVERSATION

The Smiths have planned to go with Dr. Rəhim and his family to see some of the city's historical monuments. Mr. and Mrs. Smith arrive at the Rəhims' home.

S: Can we come in? — kya, həm əndər a səkte hə̃y?

    may bring, might bring M/FP — laẽ

    outside Adv Comp Post — [se, ke] bahər

    season, weather M1 — məwsəm

R: Yes, please come [in]! How is the weather outside? — ji hã, təšrif laẽ! bahər məwsəm kəysa həy.

    heat, summer F2 — gərmi

    as much as, so much as [relative] A2 — jytna

    daily, every day Adv — rozana

    sky M1 — asman

    cloud M1 — badəl

    wind, breeze, air F1 — həva

    perhaps Conj — šayəd

    rain F1 — baryš

    may be, might be M/FS — ho

S: Today it's not as hot as it gets [lit. is] every day nowadays. There are a very few clouds in [lit. on] the sky. A cool breeze is blowing [lit. moving]. Perhaps there will be rain. — aj gərmi ytni nəhĩ həy, jytni ajkəl rozana hoti həy. asman pər thoRe thoRe badəl hə̃y. ThənDi həva cəl rəhi həy. šayəd baryš ho.

    if Conj — əgər

    then Conj — to

    ease F2 — asani

    whole, entire, complete A2 — sara

R: If it doesn't rain today, then we will easily [lit. with ease] be able to see the whole of Lahore by [lit. until] evening. — əgər aj baryš nə ho, to šam tək həm asani se sara lahəwr dekh səkẽge.

    sometime, ever, sometimes Adv — kəbhi

    such, like this A2 — əysa

    as, like, such as A2 — jəysa

S: There is never such heat in my country as there is in your country. — mere mwlk mẽ kəbhi əysi gərmi nəhĩ hoti, jəysi ap ke mwlk mẽ hoti həy.

    mountain M1 — pəhaR

    where [relative] Adv — jəhã

R: There are mountains in your country, and where there are mountains, there is less heat there. — ap ke mwlk mẽ pəhaR hə̃y, əwr jəhã pəhaR hote hə̃y, vəhã gərmi kəm hoti həy.

    reason, cause F1 — vəja [or /vəjəh/]

    child [girl] F2 — bəcci

    often, generally, most, the majority of A1 Adv — əksər

sick, ill, patient, sick person A1 M/F1	bimar
intention, desire M2	yrada
[I] may send, might send	bhejū

S: Because of the heat, my children are often sick. Therefore, it is my intention to send them to the mountain[s] in the summer. [Lit. It is my intention that I may send them ...]

gərmi ki vəja se, meri bəcciā əksər bimar rəhti hɔ̃y. ys lie, mera yrada həy, ky wnhɛ̃ gərmi mɛ̃ pəhaR bhejū.

Mrs. Rəhim enters the room.

son M2	beTa
to put on, wear	pəhnna
daughter F2	beTi

MR: Hello, Mrs. Smith! I'm ready to go. My sons are now putting on [their] clothes. --Aren't your daughters going along?

adab ərz mysəz ysmyth! mɛ̃y cəlne ko təyyar hū. mere beTe əbhi kəpRe pəhn rəhe hɔ̃y. --kya, ap ki beTiã nəhĩ cəlɛgi?

cinema M1	synima [or /sənema/, /səynma/, etc.]

MS: No, they're going to the cinema.

ji nəhĩ, vw aj synima jaɛ̃gi.

may go, might go M/FP	cəlɛ̃
Shalimar (a famous Mughal garden) M1 [np]	šalymar
may see, might see M/FP	dekhɛ̃
Mughal M1 A1	mwɣəl
old [of things], ancient A2	pwrana
famous A1	məšhur
garden M1	baɣ

MR: All right then, let us go. I think we should see Shalimar [Gardens] first. It is a very old and famous Mughal garden.

əccha, to həm cəlɛ̃. mera xyal həy, ky pəhle šalymar dekhɛ̃. yy mwɣlõ ka bəhwt pwrana əwr məšhur baɣ həy.

moon M1	cād
light F2	rəwšni
Kashmir M1 [np]	kəšmir
tree M1	dərəxt
kind, type, sort F1	qysm
flower M1	phul
able, worth A1 [/[ke] qabyl/ "worth ...ing"]	qabyl

R: It seems very beautiful in the light of the moon. Only in Kashmir is there a garden like this. In it there are two hundred year old trees. There is every kind of flower. It is worth seeing.

cād ki rəwšni mɛ̃ bəhwt xubsurət malum hota həy. syrf kəšmir mɛ̃ ys jəysa baɣ həy. ys mɛ̃ do do səw sal pwrane dərəxt hɔ̃y. hər qysm ke phul hɔ̃y. dekhne ke qabyl həy.

fort M2	qəla [or /qyla/]
wall F1	divar
stone, rock M1	pətthər
strong, stout A1	məzbut
time, period, era M2	zəmana
king M1	badšah

palace M1   məhl

to play   khelna

field, ground, plain M1   məydan

both A1   donõ

building, edifice F1   ymarət

under, underneath, below Comp Post   [ke] nice

jail, prison M2   qəydxana

when [relative] Conj   jəb

MR: [You] ought to see the Fort too. Its walls are of stone. It is three hundred years old, but yet [lit. up to now] it is very strong. It is also of the Mughal period. On one side of it is the king's palace, and in front there is a playing field. On both sides there are office buildings. Below the palace there is a prison also. When you go [lit. will go] to the Fort, then you will be able to see all these things.

qəla bhi dekhna cahie. ys ki divarē pətthər ki hɐy. yy tin səw sal pwrana həy, məgər əb tək bəhwt məzbut həy. yy bhi mwylõ ke zəmane ka həy. ys ke ek tərəf bədšah ka məhl həy, əwr samne khelne ka məydan həy. donõ tərəf dəftərõ ki ymartē hɐy. məhl ke nice ek qəydxana bhi həy. jəb ap qəle jaēge, to ap yy səb cizē dekh səkēge.

government F1   hwkumət

use, employment M1   ystemal

MS: Does the Pakistani Government use the Fort?

kya, pakystani hwkumət qəle ko ystemal kərti həy?

police F1   polis

possible PA1   mwmkyn

army F1   fəwj

may be doing, might be doing FS   kər rəhi ho

R: No, only some police live there. It's possible that the army may also be using it.

ji nəhĩ, syrf kwch polis vəhã rəhti həy. mwmkyn həy, ky fəwj bhi ws ko ystemal kər rəhi ho.

interesting, charming, fascinating A1   dylcəsp

royal A1   badšahi

mosque F1   məsjyd

MR: But perhaps for you the most interesting thing will be the Badshahi Mosque. [We] should go there first.

məgər šayəd ap ke lie səb se dylcəsp ciz badšahi məsjyd hogi. vəhã pəhle cəlna cahie.

Just outside the Badshahi Mosque:

[I] may take off, might take off, may remove, may unload, etc.   wtarũ

S: Should [I] take off [my] shoes here?   kya, yəhã jute wtarũ?

church M1   gyrja

hat, cap F2   Topi

watchman M1   cəwkidar

to leave, abandon, let go, release   choRna

R: Yes. You people take off [your] hat when you go [lit. having taken off the hat, go ...] into a church, and we take off [our] shoes when we go into a mosque. Please leave [your] shoes with this watchman!

ji hã. ap log gyrja mē Topi wtar kər jate hɐy, əwr həm məsjyd mē jute wtar kər jate hɐy. jute ys cəwkidar ke pas choRie.

high, tall A2	ūca
minaret M1	minar
to climb, ascend	cəRhna

S: What a high minaret! [Lit. How much high minaret it is!] Can [we] climb it? — kytna ūca minar həy! kya, ys pər cəRh səkte hə̃y?

upper, above, up, over Adv Comp Post	[ke] upər
sight, vision F1	nəzər
may climb, might climb M/FP	cəRhẽ

R: Yes. From up above the whole city can be seen [lit. comes to view]. Come on, let's climb! — ji hã. upər se sara šəhr nəzər ata həy. aie, cəRhẽ!

ground, earth, land F1	zəmin

MS: How high is it from the ground? — yy zəmin se kytna ūca həy.

foot, feet [measure] M1	fwT

R: [It] must be about a hundred and fifty feet. — koi DeRh səw fwT hoga.

waiting, expecting M1	yntyzar

MS: I won't climb [it]. I'll wait here. — mə̃y nəhĩ cəRhũgi. mə̃y yəhã yntyzar kərũgi.

At the top of the minaret:

house, bungalow F2	koThi
this way, hither Adv	ydhər
which way, whither [relative] Adv	jydhər
river M1	dərya

R: Your house is over this way, there where the river is visible [lit. whither the river is coming into view]. — ap ki koThi ydhər həy, jydhər dərya nəzər a rəha həy.

which way, whither?	kydhər

S: Which way is the University? — yunyvərsyTi kydhər həy.

roof F1	chət
picture [painting, photograph, etc.] F1	təsvir
to draw, pull	khẽcna [or /khə̃ycna/]
standing, upright, stationary PA2	khəRa
may get down, might get down [/wtərna/ "to get down, go down, alight, get off"]	wtrẽ

R: There in front -- the roof of the University is visible. Take a picture of the city from here! -- Look, those are our wives standing [down there]. All right, now let's go down. — vw samne -- yunyvərsyTi ki chət nəzər a rəhi həy. yəhã se šəhr ki təsvir khẽcie! -- dekhie, vw həmari biviã khəRi hə̃y. -- əccha, əb wtrẽ.

Down again, they inspect the mosque:

thousands A1	həzarõ
man, person M1	admi
prayer F1	nəmaz
woman F1	əwrət
man, male M1	mərd
separate, apart, distinct A1	ələg

R: Every Friday thousands of people offer [lit. read] [their] prayers here. Women also come, but [they] don't pray [lit. read] with the men. They pray separately.

hər jwme ko yəhã həzarõ admi nəmaz pəRhte hə̃y. əwrtẽ bhi ati hə̃y, məgər mərdõ ke sath nəhĩ pəRhtĩ. vw ələg pəRhti hə̃y.

   to hear, listen

   swnna

MS: Listen, [we] have to see the Fort too. Let's go soon.

swnie, qəla bhi dekhna həy. jəldi cəlẽ.

   sunshine F l

   dhup

   sharp, swift, clever, pungent A l

   tez

   then, again, even Conj

   phyr

   immediately, at once Adv

   fəwrən

MR: If the sunshine is too strong for you, then we can go home again at once.

əgər ap ke lie dhup zyada tez həy, to phyr həm fəwrən ghər cəl səkte hə̃y.

   so that, in order that Conj

   take

MS: No, but [we] should go to the Fort soon, so that it may not be closed.

nəhĩ, məgər qəle jəldi cəlna cahie, take bənd nə ho.

7.100. WORD STUDY

7.101.   /gərmi/ F2 is used both for "heat" and for "summer, the hot season." In the latter meaning it may also be treated as plural: e. g.

/gərmiõ mẽ həm log lahəwr jaẽge. /   We'll go to Lahore in the summer.

7.102.   /rozana/ Adv "every day, daily" is synonymous with /roz/ and /hər roz/. All of these expressions are common.

7.103.   When speaking of objects "in" the sky, the idiomatic Urdu usage is "<u>on</u>" the sky, using /pər/ "on."

7.104.   /həva/ F1 denotes both "wind" and "[still] air." There are also separate words for different types of wind, of course, just as there are in English (e. g. /lu/ F1 "scorching summer wind"). Note too that the wind does not "blow" in Urdu, but instead "moves" (using the verb /cəlna/ "to go, move along").

7.105.   /tək/ Comp Post "up to, until" is also used to indicate the boundary of a period of time by which an event takes place. In this usage it is best translated with English "by": e. g.

/vw swba tək aega. /   He'll come by morning. [I. e. morning is the
  further limit of the time period within which his coming is expected.]

/dopəhr tək ws ki dwkan pər pəhw̃cie! /   Please arrive at his shop by afternoon.

7.106.   /kəbhi/ Adv "sometime, ever, sometimes" has several important uses: (1) alone in an affirmative sentence meaning "sometime, ever"; (2) repeated as /kəbhi kəbhi/ denoting "sometimes, occasionally"; (3) alone in a negative sentence meaning "never"; (5) as /kəbhi nə kəbhi/ "sometime or other" (see Unit XV); and (6) with various other conjunctions and adverbs, giving the sense of "ever": e. g. /jəb kəbhi/ "whenever." E. g.

/kəbhi mere pas aie! /   Please come to [visit] me sometime!

/vw kəbhi kəbhi lahəwr ate hə̃y. /   He comes to Lahore occasionally.

/mə̃y wn ke pas kəbhi nəhĩ jaũga. /   I'll never go to [see] him.

/yəhã kəbhi nə aie! /   Please don't ever come here!

7.107.   /pəhnna/ "to put on, wear" is used both for the process of donning clothing and (usually with various stative auxiliaries) for the state of wearing a garment. /pəhnna/ is usually not employed for garments that must be wrapped, as a shawl, blanket, quilt, etc. (the verb used for these is /oRhna/ "to wrap"); nor is /pəhnna/ used for garments which are tucked or tied, as a sari (/saRi/ F2), a turban, a loincloth, etc. (/bãdhna/ "to tie, bind" is used for these).

/vw hər vəqt Topi pəhnta həy. /   He wears a hat all the time. [Here
  /pəhnna/ is used for the state of wearing the hat, rather than the
  process of donning it. Compare:]

/mə̃y Topi pəhnũga. /   I'll put on my hat.

/mə̃y šal oRhūga./   I'll put on [lit. wrap] a shawl.   [/šal/ F1 "shawl"]
/mə̃y saRi bādhūgi./   I'll put on [lit. tie] a sari.   [/saRi/ F2 "sari"]

7.108. The Shalimar Gardens are one of the beauty spots of Lahore. They were built
by the Mughal Emperor Shah Jahan, probably about 1638. There is also another beautiful
garden with the same name in the old Mughal summer resort of Srinagar, Kashmir.

7.109. /mwγəl/ M1 A1 "Mughal" or "Moghal" is the name of the Central Asian people
who invaded northern India in 1526 A.D. They founded a dynasty of kings which includes
such famous rulers as Humayun (/hwmayū/), Akbar (/əkbər/), Jahangir (/jəhāgir/), Shah
Jahan (/šah jəhan/), and Aurangzeb (/əwrə̄gzeb/).

7.110. /pwrana/ A2 denotes "old, ancient" of things only. "Old" of animate beings is
expressed by /buRha/ A2. /pwrana/ may be used with nouns denoting animates, however,
when one wishes to express "of olden times," "for a long time," etc. E.g.

> /yy həmari pwrani koThi həy./   This is our old house. [This may mean
> either "old" in the sense of "ancient, decrepit," or "old" in the sense
> of "possessed by us for a long time."]
>
> /həmara nəwkər buRha həy./   Our servant is old. [He is aged.]
>
> /yy həmara pwrana nəwkər həy./   This is our old servant. [He has been in
> our service for a long time, or perhaps he has since been replaced
> by a newer employee. In any case, he is not necessarily an old man.]

7.111. As an adjective, /qabyl/ A1 means "able, capable, competent." The compound
postpositional phrase / ... ke qabyl/, however, denotes "worth ... ing," "worthy of ...,"
etc. E.g.

> /vw bəhwt qabyl admi hə̃y./   He's a very capable man.
>
> /yy šəhr dekhne ke qabyl həy./   This city is worth seeing.
>
> /wn ki batē swnne ke qabyl hə̃y./   His words are worth hearing.
>
> /ys hoTəl ka khana khane ke qabyl nəhī./   This hotel's food is not worth
> eating.

7.112. /malum/ PA1 "known" is used idiomatically with /hona/ "to be, become":
/malum həy/ means "[it] is known," but /malum hota həy/ signifies "[it] seems." These
usages must be carefully distinguished. E.g.

> /mwjhe malum həy, ky vw əccha admi həy./   I know that he is a good
> man.
>
> /mwjhe malum hota həy, ky vw əccha admi həy./   It seems to me that he
> is a good man.
>
> /kya, ap ko yy ləRka hošyar malum hota həy?/   Does this boy seem
> intelligent to you?
>
> /vw admi rəhim sahəb malum hote hə̃y./   That man seems [to be] Mr.
> Rəhim.
>
> /yy kəpRa mwjhe əccha malum hota həy./   This cloth seems to me [to be]
> good.

7.113. /polis/ Fl "police" denotes the organisation rather than a single policeman. The latter will be expressed by /polisvala/ M2, introduced in Unit IX. Note that /polis/ is treated as a singular.

7.114. The Badshahi Mosque (/badšahi məsjyd/ "royal mosque") was built by the Mughal Emperor Aurangzeb in 1674. The four minarets are actually each about 143 feet, 6 inches high. It is one of the largest mosques in the world, and it is still in regular use.

7.115. "To appear, to be visible" is expressed by /nəzər ana/ "to come [into] view." Alone, /nəzər/ Fl means "vision, sight." E.g.

> /pəhaR se sara šəhr nəzər aega./ The whole city will be visible from the mountain.
> /age ja kər, ek bəRa bazar nəzər aega./ Going on ahead, a big market will be seen.
> /ws ki nəzər bəhwt xərab həy./ His vision is very poor.

7.116. /ghər/ Ml "house, home" and /məkan/ Ml "house, residential building" were discussed in Sec. 1.108. To these, /koThi/ F2 and /ymarət/ Fl may now be added. /koThi/ denotes a European style house of stone or brick. /ymarət/ may be used for any building, but its connotation will be that of "structure" (discussing some building from the point of view of its architecture or construction). /ymarət/ is also used of a nonresidential building (in contrast with /koThi/, /məkan/, and /ghər/), such as an office building, a bank, a school, etc.

7.117. /dərya/ Ml "river" is sometimes found in Urdu literature and poetry with the meaning "ocean, sea," but this is rare in speech.

7.118. The verb /khēcna/ "to pull, draw" is generally used with /təsvir/ Fl "picture" to signify "take a photograph." /təsvir khēcna/ also means "to sketch, draw a picture." In the case of photographs, /təsvir lena/ "to take a picture" and /təsvir wtarna/ "to take down a picture" are also found.

7.119. There is no single verbal root for "to stand" in Urdu. The predicate adjective /khəRa/ PA2 "standing, erect, upright, stationary" must be used with various verbalisers instead: /khəRa hona/ "to be standing, erect, upright"; /khəRa kərna/ "to stand [something] up, to erect"; /khəRa rəhna/ "to remain standing." "To stand up" is expressed by the complex-compound formation /khəRa ho jana/ (introduced in Unit XIII). E.g.

> /məy khəRa hū./ I am standing.
> /vw ləRki khəRi həy./ That girl is standing.
> /vw hər roz yəhã khəRa hota həy./ He [generally] stands here every day.
> /məy ys pətthər ko khəRa kərūga./ I'll stand this stone up [on end].
> /vw dəs ghənTe tək khəRa rəhega./ He'll remain standing for [lit. until] ten hours.

7.120. /admi/ M1 "man, person" has a broader meaning than /mərd/ M1 "man, male."
Compare:

> /kytne admi hõge./ How many people will there be? [The group may
> include both men and women.]
>
> /kytne mərd hõge./ How many MEN will there be? [In contrast to the
> number of women.]

/admi/ alone, however, always denotes a male:

> /ek admi šam tək aega./ One man will come by evening.

In various regional dialects and certain lower class urban dialects, /mərd/ is used for
"husband," and /əwrət/ is found for "wife."

7.121. /nəmaz/ F1 "prayer" is usually employed only for the ritual prayers performed
by Muslims: i.e. the five daily required prayers, the Friday congregational prayer, special
funeral prayers, etc. A spontaneous, non-ritual prayer is called /doa/ F1. The five daily
prayers have special names: /fəjr/ F1 is performed a little before sunrise; /zwhr/ F1
is prayed from about 1:00 P.M. to 3:00 P.M. ; /əsr/ F1 is offered in the late afternoon;
/məɣryb/ F1 is performed just after sunset; and /yša/ F1 is offered from about 8:00 P.M.
until midnight. Christian services are termed /ybadət/ F1 "worship," and Hindu prayers
are called /puja/ F1. Note that one "reads" /nəmaz/, employing /pəRhna/, but one "does"
/doa/, /ybadət/, and /puja/, using /kərna/.

7.122. The basic meaning of /tez/ A1 is "sharp (as a knife)." It also has a number
of useful subsidiary meanings: e.g.

> /myrcē bəhwt tez hɔ̃y./ The peppers are very strong [hot, sharp,
> pungent].
>
> /yy ləRka bəhwt tez həy./ This boy is very clever. [Compare American
> English, "This boy is very sharp."]
>
> /mɔ̃y bəhwt tez pəRh səkta hū̃./ I can read very rapidly. [Here /tez/
> is synonymous with /jəldi/.]

This word thus has a range of meanings which includes "sharp," "strong, pungent, hot,
piquant (as peppers, spices, liquor)," "clever, shrewd, smart," and "rapid, swift, fast."
Contrast this with /məzbut/ A1 which means "stout, strong, durable, lasting": e.g.

> /yy bəhwt məzbut kəpRa həy./ This is very strong [lasting, durable]
> cloth.
>
> /həmē ek məzbut mez cahie./ We need a strong [stout, sturdy] table.

Neither /tez/ nor /məzbut/ can be used to express "strong" of persons. Perhaps the
commonest word for this is /taqətvər/ A1: e.g.

> /vw bəhwt taqətvər admi həy./ He is a very strong man.

7.123. Complex Verbal Formations.

Hereafter a short list of useful complex verbal formations for new items in the
vocabulary will be given at the end of each Word Study section. For a discussion of the
various types of complex verbal formations, see Sec. 5.307. Each list will be divided into
the following sub-types:

A: Complex formations of this pattern are made with /hona/ "to be, become" and /kərna/ "to do, make." When /hona/ is employed, the formation is intransitive, and any agent is marked by /se/. The verb will agree with the subject. When /kərna/ is used, the formation is transitive, and the object is marked by /ko/ or its equivalent (or is unmarked; see Sec. 3.310). E.g.

/X Y se   saf hwa./ X was cleaned with Y. [/hwa/ will agree with X in number-gender.]

/X Y ko   saf kərta həy./ X cleans Y. [/kərta həy/ will agree with X in number-gender.]

B: This formation too is made with /hona/ and /kərna/. When /hona/ is used, the idea is intransitive, and any "object" of the verbal action possesses the noun of the complex formation. A "subject" may also be expressed, and this is marked with /ko/ or its equivalent: lit. "To X Y's --- is." When /kərna/ is employed, the formation is transitive, and the object again must possess the noun of the complex formation: lit. "X does Y's --- ." E.g.

/X ko Y ka yntyzar həy./ X is awaiting Y. [Lit. To X is Y's waiting.]

/X Y ka yntyzar kərta həy./ X waits for Y. [Lit. X does Y's waiting.]

/X Y ki tarif kərta həy./ X praises Y. [Note that the possessive postposition will agree with the gender of the noun of the complex formation.]

C: In the present and future tenses this formation is exactly like that of Type A described above. There are differences in the past tenses, however, and these will be discussed in Unit XI.

D: Transitive formations of this pattern are made with /dena/ "to give," /lena/ "to take," and /māgna/ "to ask for, request." Intransitive formations are often made with /mylna/ "to get." E.g.

/X Y ko yjazət deta həy./ X permits Y. [If the thing permitted is named, it will possess /yjazət/: /X Y ko   Z ki yjazət deta həy./ "X permits Y [to do] Z."]

/X Y se Z ki yjazət leta həy./ X takes permission for Z from Y.

/X Y se Z ki yjazət māgta həy./ X asks for permission for Z from Y.

/X ko Y se Z ki yjazət mylti həy./ X receives permission for Z from Y. [/mylti həy/ here agrees with /yjazət/.]

E: In the present and future tenses this type is like that described for D above. There are differences in the past tenses, however. Type E is rather rare.

F: All other complex formations, idioms, etc. will be listed under this heading.

A:

/ələg/

/[X se] ələg hona/ to separate [from X]

/[X ko Y se] ələg kərna/ to separate [X from Y]

/khəRa/

/khəRa hona/ to stand. [See Sec. 7.119.]

/[X ko] khəRa kərna/ to cause to stand, erect [X]

/məzbut/

/məzbut hona/ to be strong, sturdy, durable

/[X ko] məzbut kərna/ to strengthen [X]
/tez/
    /tez hona/ to be, become sharp
    /[X ko] tez kərna/ to sharpen [X]
/ūca/
    /ūca hona/ to be, become high, tall
    /[X ko] ūca kərna/ to make high, raise [X]
/ystemal/
    /[X ka] ystemal hona/ [X] to be used
    /[X ko] ystemal kərna/ to use, employ [X]

B:

/yntyzar/
    /[X ka] yntyzar hona/ [X] to be awaited
    /[X ka] yntyzar kərna/ to wait for [X]
/yrada/
    /[X ka] yrada hona/ to have a desire [to do] [X]
    /[X ka] yrada kərna/ to make a decision, express a desire [to do] [X]

F:

/baryš/
    /baryš hona/ to rain. [Not /gyrna/!]
/bəcca/
    /bəcca hona/ to give birth to a child, have a child
/dhup/
    /dhup hona/ to be sunny, sunshining
    /dhup pəRna/ sunshine to fall
/gərmi/
    /gərmi hona, pəRna/ to be hot, warm
/həva/
    /həva cəlna/ wind to blow
/hwkumət/
    /[X pər] hwkumət kərna/ to govern [X]
/nəmaz/
    /nəmaz pəRhna/ to perform [one's] prayers
/nəzər/
    /[X] nəzər ana/ [X] to be visible, appear
    /[X pər] nəzər Dalna/ to glance, look at [X]
/təsvir/
    /təsvir khẽcna/ to draw, sketch, take a picture
    /təsvir bənana/ to make, take a picture
    /təsvir lena/ to take a picture
    /təsvir wtarna/ to take a picture

7.201. Velar and Post-Velar Consonants.

In English there are two sounds produced by the back of the tongue raised to touch the velum: /g/ and /k/. Both of these are stops (i.e. no air is allowed to pass through the oral cavity during the period of contact between the tongue and the velum). /g/ is a voiced stop, and /k/ is unvoiced.

Urdu has both /k/ and /g/, and also their aspirated counterparts /kh/ and /gh/ (see Secs. 3.201 and 4.201). Urdu also has three other phonemes which are produced in this same articulatory area: /q/, /x/, and /ɣ/. These are "loan phonemes" in Urdu, having come into the language through Persian from Arabic. It should be noted that a knowledge of present-day Arabic or Persian cannot be relied upon to produce the correct Urdu pronunciation of these sounds, for although these languages continue to write /q/, /x/, and /ɣ/ as separate letters, there have been various phonetic modifications in their spoken forms. For example, /q/ has become modern Saudi Arabian /g/ and Egyptian /ʔ/ (a glottal stop). In Persian, /q/ and /ɣ/ have fallen together into one phoneme. All of the prestigeful dialects of Urdu, however, retain /q/, /x/, and /ɣ/ as distinct phonemes and pronounce them much as the classical Arabian grammarians described them centuries ago.

Speakers of German and various Scots dialects will find little difficulty with /x/: it is found in words like German doch, ach, etc. Scottish speakers will find a similar sound in loch. Speakers of Parisian French will find that the r in a word like Paris approximates /ɣ/, as does German g in some pronunciations of Wagen. The phoneme /q/, however, does not occur in any European language, to the author's knowledge.

Both /x/ and /ɣ/ are fricatives, the former voiceless and the latter voiced. By saying ak-ka, ak-ka, ak-ka and trying to relax the contact between the back of the tongue and the velum, letting a little air through and creating the /x/ friction, one may approach ax-xa, ax-xa, ax-xa. Once this has been mastered in medial position between two vowels, the student may then attempt to say just ax, ax, ax and xa, xa, xa. The same procedure should be followed for /ɣ/; starting with ag-ga, ag-ga, ag-ga, the student should attempt to relax the contact and fricativise the /g/ to /ɣ/.

The sound /q/ is a "hard k" as in kite, but pronounced farther back in the mouth. As an initial step, the student may try opening his mouth wide and saying ka, ka, ka "as far down in the throat as he can." All of these sounds should be thoroughly drilled with the instructor.

Since these sounds are "loan phonemes" in Urdu, many less prestigeful dialects and also many speakers of the more indigenous form of the language, Hindi, do not have them. Most such dialects render /q/ as /k/, /x/ as /kh/, and /ɣ/ as /g/ (or /gh/). In the Panjab, too, /q/ is pronounced as /k/ except by those well trained in Urdu. In Hyderabad, /q/ is often heard as /x/, and the contrast between /q/ and /x/ has thus disappeared.

In the contrasting examples which follow, words containing /kh/ and /gh/ are also included for practice in contrast and recognition.

198

/kal/ famine
/gal/ cheek
/xal/ mole, blemish

/xalyq/ Creator

/taka/ gazed at MS
/taga/ thread
/axa/ excellent! [Interjection]

/kəm/ little, less
/xəm/ twist, coil
/gwm/ lost, absent

/taki/ gazed at FS
/baɣi/ rebel
/taryk/ recluse ascetic
/faryɣ/ free, empty
/tarik/ dark
/tariki/ darkness
/səlax/ iron rod

/šax/ branch, bough

/ɣwrbət/ poverty
/yktysab/ gain
/yɣtynam/ seizing as plunder
/nwkta/ point [of a statement, etc.]
/ystykrah/ aversion
/ystyɣraq/ absorbtion, engrossment
/fəxr/ pride
/rəɣbət/ inclination
/məksur/ broken; marked with the vowel /y/
/məɣfur/ absolved, deceased
/həlki/ light in weight FS
/kəlɣi/ rooster's comb
/twrk/ Turk
/swrx/ red

/khal/ skin
/ghal/ mischief
/ɣal/ cave
/qal/ a saying
/ɣalyb/ dominant
/qalyb/ prototype
/bhakha/ language
/vagha/ Wagha [place name]
/aɣa/ master
/faqa/ fasting
/khəm/ pillar
/ɣəm/ grief, sorrow
/xwm/ wine pitcher
/qwm/ Qum [place name]
/jagi/ awoke FS
/baqi/ remainder
/fasyx/ one who annuls
/faryq/ one who distinguishes
/tarix/ history; date
/tarixi/ historical
/cəraɣ/ lamp
/təlaq/ divorce
/baɣ/ garden
/taq/ niche, shelf
/qwrbət/ nearness
/yxtysar/ brevity
/yqtybas/ extract, quotation
/nwqta/ dot
/ystyxraj/ expulsion
/ystyqrar/ settlement
/fəqr/ ascetic poverty
/rəqba/ area
/məxbut/ insane

/məqtul/ slain
/bəlxi/ belonging to Balkh [place name]
/həlqi/ gutteral, throaty
/gwrg/ wolf
/mwrɣ/ rooster
/qwrq/ seizure, sequestration

7.202. Phonetic Drill: Auditory Dictation.

1. khal kəm kal taki nwkta bhakha taryk tarik məksur həlki

2. yxtysar bəlxi swrx məxbut xəm fəxr ystyxraj fasyx xalyq xal

3. mwrɣ rəɣbət baɣi ɣəm aɣa ɣal ystyɣraq məɣfur ɣɣtynam faryɣ

4. həlqi fəqr yqtybas qal faryq qwm qwrq taq baqi faqa

5. gal gwm ghal jagi vagha gwrg rəɣbət kəlɣi baɣ baɣi ɣəm

6. səlax taryk šax məksur swrx taka tarix ystykrah xwm tariki
   axa

7. gal ɣalyb taga cəraɣ gwm aɣa ghal baɣi gwrg ɣal vagha

8. taka axa bhakha khal xwm xalyq kal taq həlqi twrk həlki

9. fəxr fəqr tarix tarik šax təlaq baɣi baqi rəqba rəɣbət

10. taki baqi taga aɣa khəm xəm gwm qwm nwkta nwqta ɣwrbət
    qwrbət

7.301. Substantive Composition: Various /i/ Suffixes.

Examples of three separate suffixes all having the form /i/ are to be found in the vocabulary given to date. These three do not include the Type II feminine suffix /i/ (see Sec. 7.302). Although not all of the following material will be of immediate use to the student, its inclusion here may prevent some otherwise justifiable confusion.

(1) Noun stem + /i/ = adjective: "belonging or pertaining to the noun." Constructions made with this suffix are grammatically Type I adjectives.

/əxbari/ journalistic, newspaper [adj.]
/ɔ̃grezi/ English
/badšahi/ royal
/bazari/ of the market: cheap, common
/dəftəri/ official, office [adj.]
/fəwji/ military, army [adj.]
/həvai/ aerial, air [adj.]
/kəšmiri/ Kashmiri
/lahəwri/ of Lahore, belonging to Lahore
/məwsmi/ seasonal, weather [adj.]
/məydani/ of the plains, flat
/mwlki/ of the country, national
/nami/ famous
/pakystani/ Pakistani
/pəhaRi/ mountainous, hilly, mountain [adj.]
/qimti/ valuable, high-priced
/šəhri/ urban
/ymarti/ architectural, building [adj.]
/yntyzami/ administrative

When this type of adjective refers to a country or area having an indigenous language, the adjective may also be employed as a Type II noun to denote that language; e.g.

/ɔ̃grezi/ F2 English
/kəšmiri/ F2 Kashmiri

Still further constructions can be made from the vocabulary given to date, but these are either considered weak by the informants or else are of very limited use.

(2) Noun stem + /i/ = noun of profession. Constructions made with this suffix are F2.

/cəwkidari/ post of watchman; watch; "watchmanship"
/DakTri/ the profession of doctor
/nəwkri/ service, employment, job; "servantship"
/profesri/ the post or profession of professor

(3) Adjective stem + /i/ = abstract noun. This is structurally the exact opposite of (1) above. All of these constructions are F2.

/asani/ ease
/bimari/ illness, sickness
/byhtəri/ betterment
/dosti/ friendship
/duri/ distance, "away-ness"
/dylcəspi/ interest, fascination, charm
/gərmi/ heat; summer
/hošyari/ cleverness, intelligence
/kəmi/ lack, scarcity, deficiency
/lali/ redness
/mafi/ forgiveness, pardon
/məzbuti/ strength, sturdiness, durability
/myhrbani/ kindness
/nəzdiki/ nearness
/rozi/ daily earnings. [Semantically rather different from the usual class-meaning of nouns made with /i/.]
/səfəydi/ whiteness
/təyyari/ preparation, readiness
/tezi/ sharpness, pungency, cleverness, swiftness
/xərabi/ badness, fault, defect
/xubsurti/ beauty
/xwdai/ divine rule; the universe

In the case of abstract nouns made from Type II adjectives by the addition of this suffix, /i/ occurs after what appears to be the MNS suffix /a/: e.g. /bəRai/ F2 "bigness, largeness." Although this formulation is perhaps useful for the beginner, it is probably historically inaccurate, since Urdu /ai/ here probably comes from the Sanskrit neuter suffix -yam. Examples possible from the vocabulary are:

/əcchai/ goodness
/bəRai/ bigness, largeness, greatness
/cəwthai/ one fourth. [Semantically somewhat different from the others.]
/choTai/ smallness
/mə̃hgai/ costliness, expensiveness
/ũcai/ height, tallness

7.302. Substantive Composition: the Type II Suffixes.

The Type II substantive suffixes occur with stems which themselves cannot stand alone as a word: e.g. /ləRka/ M2 "boy," /ləRki/ F2 "girl," but not */ləRk/. In the case of animate beings, the masculine form denotes a male and is grammatically masculine. The feminine form similarly denotes a female and is grammatically feminine.

These suffixes are also found with a great many stems denoting inanimate objects, and here the distinction is usually one of size: the masculine form denotes a larger object of the same general category, and the feminine form denotes a smaller object. Grammatically, of course, these are treated as "masculine" and "feminine," although such inanimate objects really have no sex gender. This is not a large class compared to the vast number of Urdu nouns which do not have such a size-gender distinction. There are also many nouns which occur in one form only: e.g. /kəmra/ M2 "room," but not */kəmri/ (logically "small room"). Animates given in the vocabulary so far include:

/bəcca/ male child
/bəcci/ female child
/bəkra/ male goat
/bəkri/ female goat
/beTa/ son
/beTi/ daughter
/ləRka/ boy
/ləRki/ girl
/mwrɣa/ rooster
/mwrɣi/ hen, chicken

All nouns made with /val/ + the Type II affixes belong to this group:

/phəlvala/ fruit seller [male]
/phəlvali/ fruit seller [female]

Inanimate nouns of this class include:

/cəmca/ big spoon, tablespoon
/cəmci/ little spoon, teaspoon
/chwra/ big knife
/chwri/ little knife, tableknife
/ghənTa/ big bell, big clock; hour
/ghənTi/ small bell
/juta/ shoe
/juti/ small shoe, slipper, local style of shoe
/pyala/ big cup
/pyali/ small cup, teacup

7.303. The Gender of Nouns Denoting Members of a Profession.

Nouns denoting the holder of a position, a rank, a title, or a member of a profession generally have a "usual gender," depending upon the sex of the usual incumbent of the post. Thus, /cəwkidar/ M1 "watchman" is almost always masculine, although in a special context it could conceivably be treated as feminine (e.g. referring to a female watchman in the women's ward of a hospital, etc.). Similarly, /nərs/ F1 "nurse" will almost always be feminine since the concept of a male nurse is uncommon in Pakistan. Some posts, however, may be held equally by members of either sex, and here context must indicate which gender is to be employed. E.g.

/ysmyth sahəb bəhwt əcche DakTər hɚy./ Mr. Smith is a very good doctor.

/mysəz ysmyth bəhwt əcchi DakTər hɚy./ Mrs. Smith is a very good doctor.

7.304. Type I Nouns Ending in /a/.

There are many nouns ending in /a/ in which the /a/ is not treated as the Type II MNS suffix but as a part of the stem. Such nouns may be either masculine or feminine, and their declension is exactly like that of any other Type I noun.

Masculine nouns of this type introduced so far include: /dərya/ M1 "river," /xwda/ M1 "God," and /gyrja/ M1 "church." Feminine nouns include only /həva/ F1 "wind, air." Some speakers also treat /gyrja/ as feminine. E.g.

MASCULINE			FEMININE		
MNS	∅	/dərya/	FNS	∅	/həva/
MOS	∅	/dərya/	FOS	∅	/həva/
MNP	∅	/dərya/	FNP	ē	/həvaē/
MOP	õ	/dəryaõ/	FOP	õ	/həvaõ/

In some cases indeed the final /a/ may be the Type II MNS suffix originally, but the word is treated as Type I "as a mark of respect." Such words include kinship terms referring to persons older than the speaker (and hence honorific): e.g. /cəca/ M1 "father's younger brother," /dada/ M1 "father's father," /nana/ M1 "mother's father," etc. This group also includes other words requiring an honorific context: e.g. /raja/ M1 "king." That the final /a/ in these words is historically the Type II MNS suffix can be seen from the fact that many of these stems combine with the Type II feminine suffix /i/ to form the feminine counterpart of the masculine noun: e.g. /cəci/ F2 "father's younger brother's wife," /nani/ F2 "mother's mother," etc. There are also a few cases of feminine kinship terms ending in /a/ and treated as Type I: e.g. /xala/ F1 "mother's sister" (the masculine counterpart of which is /xalu/ M1 "mother's sister's husband").

7.305. /õ/ - /iõ/ "Indefinitely Large Plurality."

The suffix /õ/ occurs with a few numeral adjectives denoting large units (e.g. /həzar/ A1 "thousand," /lakh/ A1 "hundred thousand," /kəroR/ A1 "ten million," /ərəb/ A1 "hundred million") and to various nouns denoting measures (e.g. /mil/ M1 "mile," /kos/ M1 "league," /mən/ M1 "maund (approximately 80 lbs.)").

This affix also occurs with a few of the numeral adjectives denoting decades, but its form is then /iõ/ rather than /õ/. Common are /dəsiõ/ "many tens," /bisiõ/ "many twenties," and /pəcasiõ/ "many fifties." Other constructions are possible but rare.

This suffix does not occur with /səw/ A1 "hundred"; for "many hundreds," a different stem is employed: /səykRa/ M2 "a hundred." Thus, /səykRõ/ "many hundreds." E.g.

/həzarõ admi vəhā kam kərte hõy./ Thousands of men work there.

/pakystani hwkumət ws ko lakhõ rupəe degi./ The Pakistan Government will give him lakhs [i.e. hundred thousands] of rupees.

/səykRõ ləRke ws kalyj mē pəRhte hõy./ Hundreds of boys study in that college.

/vw milõ dur jaēge./ They'll go miles and miles.

/vw hər roz mənõ am xəridte hõy./ They buy maunds and maunds of mangoes every day.

7.306. /õ/ "Total Plurality."

There is a second /õ/ suffix which must be carefully distinguished from that just
described above. This second suffix occurs with numeral adjectives up to ten, with some
decades, and with a few other quantitative adjectives. Note that the form of this suffix is
always /õ/, and thus a construction like /bisõ/ "all twenty" contrasts with /bisiõ/ "many
twenties."

The stem of the numeral "two" has a special form before this suffix: /don/. Thus,
/donõ/ A1 "both [i.e. all two]."

/chəy/ A1 "six" and /nəw/ A1 "nine" do not occur with this suffix.

Larger numerals, some quantitative adjectives, and the numbers "six" and "nine"
may indicate total plurality by another method: the adjective is repeated with an intervening
possessive postposition (/ke/ or /ki/ depending on the gender of the following noun): e.g.
/səw ke səw admi/ "the whole hundred men," /pəcas ke pəcas rupəe/ "the whole fifty
rupees," /həzar ki həzar kytabē/ "the whole thousand books," /chəy ki chəy kytabē/ "all
six books, the whole six books," etc. E.g.

/carõ tərəf pani həy./   There is water on all four sides.

/mãy tinõ dwkanõ mē dekhna cahta hū./   I want to look in all three shops.

/aThõ am xərab hãy./   All eight mangoes are bad.

/dəsõ admi kəl pəhw̃cēge./   All ten men will arrive tomorrow.

/mãy ap se səw ke səw rupəe lūga./   I'll take the whole hundred rupees
    from you.

/səb ke səb yəhã hãy./   Absolutely all are here.

/meri donõ bəhnē bimar hãy./   Both my sisters are ill.

7.307. Possessives as Predicate Adjectives.

A possessive adjective or phrase may also serve the purpose of a predicate adjective.

/yy admi lahəwr ka həy./   This man belongs to Lahore. [Lit. This man
    is Lahore's.]

/vw qəla mwylõ ke zəmane ka həy./   That fort is of the Mughal period.
    [Lit. That fort is of the period of the Mughals.]

/yy kam ek sal ka həy./   This is one year's work. [Lit. This work is
    of one year.]

/yy suTkes mere dost ka nəhĩ./   This suitcase is not my friend's. [Lit.
    This suitcase is not of my friend.]

/yy ciz kysi kam ki nəhĩ./   This thing is of no use. [Lit. This thing is
    not of any work. Note the idiomatic use of /kam/ here.]

/vw ryjysTər kys kam ka həy./   Of what use is that register? [Lit.
    That register is of which work?]

/mera yrada lahəwr jane ka həy./   It is my intention to go to Lahore.
    [Lit. My desire is of going [to] Lahore.]

/ys ki divarē pətthər ki hãy./   Its walls are [made] of stone.

/yy chwri meri həy./   This knife is mine. [Lit. This knife is my.
    English employs a special form of the possessive pronoun in such
    cases.]

7.308. Repetition of Substantives (Cont.).

The Conversation Section of this Unit contains an example of a repeated adjective which requires further discussion (see also Sec. 5.302):

> /ys mẽ do do səw sal pwrane dərəxt hɜ̃y./ In it there are two hundred year old trees.

The repetition of /do/ A1 "two" emphasises the distributiveness of various two hundred year old trees: there are many such trees scattered about the garden here and there. Note that in the case of compound numerals (e.g. /do səw/ "two hundred," /tin həzar/ "three thousand"), only the FIRST element is repeated. E.g.

> /mere pas pãc pãc səw mil dur se dost ate hɜ̃y./ [Various] friends come to [visit] me from five hundred miles away [each].

> /hər ymarət car car səw fwT ūci həy./ Each building is four hundred feet tall.

> /hər admi ko tin tin həzar rupəe dūga./ [I] will give each man three thousand rupees [apiece].

> /mwjhe chəy chəy pəyse əwr pãc pãc pəyse ke TykəT dijie./ Please give me stamps of six pəysa and five pəysa [each].

7.309. Adjective and Adverb Sets.

Several parellel sets of adjectives and adverbs denoting quantity, location, time, etc. are found in Urdu. These are based upon four roots: /y/ "near," /v/ (or /w/) "far," /j/ "relative," and /k/ "interrogative." Complete sets are:

NEAR		FAR		RELATIVE		INTERROGATIVE	
/yəhã/	here	/vəhã/	there	/jəhã/	where	/kəhã/	where?
/ydhər/	hither	/wdhər/	thither	/jydhər/	whither	/kydhər/	whither?
/ytna/	this much	/wtna/	that much	/jytna/	as much	/kytna/	how much?
/əysa/	like this	/vəysa/	like that	/jəysa/	as, such as	/kəysa/	how?

The /əysa/ and /ytna/ sets are grammatically Type II adjectives; the /yəhã/ and /ydhər/ sets are locative adverbs.

The /yəhã/ set differs semantically from the /ydhər/ set in that the former refers to place, the latter to direction. E.g.

> /ap kəhã ja rəhe hɜ̃y./ Where [i.e. to which place] are you going?

> /ap kydhər ja rəhe hɜ̃y./ Where [i.e. whither, in which direction] are you going?

A special construction, /ydhər wdhər/ "here and there, to and fro, hither and thither," may also be mentioned. E.g.

> /vw ydhər wdhər dekh rəhe hɜ̃y./ He is looking this way and that.

/jəysa/ A2 "as, such as" has several special uses: (1) preceded by a demonstrative and modifying a noun it means "like, resembling"; (2) in the MNS form and followed by /ky/ it is used as a clause-introducing conjunction meaning "just as, as"; (3) in the MOS form it is used as a clause-introducing adverb meaning "for example": e.g.

> /mwjhe ys jəysi ciz cahie./ I need this sort of thing. [Lit. To me this-as thing is needed.]

206

/ajkəl ws jəysa admi kəhā mylega./　These days where can a man such
　　as he [lit. he-as man] be found?

/ys jəysa kəpRa dijie./　Please give [me] this kind [lit. this-as] of cloth.

/yy bat Thik həy, jəysa ky ap bəta rəhe hə̄y./　This matter is correct,
　　just as you are telling [it].

/səb phəl, jəyse am, seb, əwr kele, ap ko pakystan mē myl səkte hə̄y./
　　You can get all the fruits, such as [or: for example] mangoes, apples,
　　and bananas, in Pakistan.

　Aside from the above, there are also various other incomplete or not-quite-parallel
sets:

NEAR	FAR	RELATIVE	INTERROGATIVE
/yy/ this	/vw/ that	/jo/ who, which	/kəwn/ who?
		/jəb/ when	/kəb/ when?
		/jəwnsa/ which	/kəwnsa/ which?
/yū/ this way, thus		/jū/ as	/kyō/ why?
			/kya/ what?

As mentioned in Sec. 5.303, /jo/ "who, which" has an OS form /jys/, an OP form
/jyn/, and special object forms /jyse/ and /jynhē/ paralleling /kəwn/ - /kys/ - /kyn/ -
/kyse/ - /kynhē/. Historically, there were once two other forms parallel to /kəwn/:
/jəwn/ "who [relative]," now used mainly with /sa/ as /jəwnsa/ A2 "which" (itself becoming
obsolete), and /təwn/ "he-she-it [correlative]," now totally out of use. The root /t/ is
found in older Urdu as the base of a fifth set, the "correlative" (i.e. the "answer" to the
relative set: Who follows my banner, he will be counted among the heroes.)

　The /yū/ "this way, thus" set similarly had a "far" form and a "correlative" form in
older Urdu: /vū/ or /vō/, and /tō/, /tū/, or /tyū/. These are now mainly obsolete.

　The /jəb/ "where" set has a correlative form, /təb/ "then," which is still much in use.
The correlative clause is more usually introduced by the conjunction particle /to/ in modern
Urdu, however.

　In normal sentence order, the relative clause should precede the correlative. Various
demands of style and emphasis, however, may require the reversal of this order. E.g.

/jəhā meri dwkan həy, vəhā vw rəhte hə̄y./　[There] where my shop is,
　　there he lives. [In English it might be more idiomatic to say: He
　　lives there where my shop is.]

/jydhər twmhē jana həy, wdhər mə̄y bhi jaūga./　Whichever way you have
　　to go, I'll go that way too.

/jytne pəyse vw ap ko dega, wtne mə̄y bhi de səkta hū./　As much money
　　as he will give you, I can give you that much too. [= I can give you
　　as much money as he will.]

/jəysa khana ap ko pəsənd həy, vəysā hi mylega./　You'll get just the
　　sort of food you like. [Lit. Just as [the sort of] food you like, just
　　that kind [you] will get.]

/yy ciz vəysi nəhī̆, jəysi ap ki dwkan pər myl səkti həy./　This thing is
　　not the same sort as can be obtained at your shop. [Lit. This thing
　　is not such, just as in your shop can be obtained.]

/jəysa kəpRa ap ko cahie, vəysa ap ko yəhā nəhī̆ mylega./　You will not
　　get the sort of cloth you need here. [Lit. As [the sort of] cloth you
　　need, such you will not get here.]

/jys ko cahie, wsi ko dūga./ Who[ever] needs [it], [I] will give [it] to
    him only.

/jəb ap jaēge, təb māy jaūga./ When you go, then I'll go.

/meri nəwkri ytni əcchi nəhī̃, jytni ap ki həy./ My job is not as good as
    yours. [Lit. My job is not this much good, as much as yours is.]

7.310. Nouns + Postpositions as Adverbs.

As has been previously noted, many Urdu adjectives may also function as adverbs: e. g.

/gaRi bəhwt tez ja rəhi həy./ The train is going very fast [rapidly,
    quickly]. [/gaRi/, of course, may refer to an automobile or other
    vehicle also.]

/vw bəhwt əccha lykhta həy./ He writes very well.

/vw ap ko byhtər bəta səkta həy./ He can tell you better.

Some nouns also function in this way: e.g.

/gaRi bəhwt jəldi pəhw̃cegi./ The train will arrive very quickly. [Note
    that /tez/ is usually employed for "rapidly, quickly" in the sense of
    speed, while /jəldi/ is used in a temporal sense: "soon, quickly."]

Various nouns followed by /se/ "with, by" also function as adverbs. Such formations
are idiomatic and nonpredictable. E. g.

/həm ws ke ghər asani se pəhw̃c səkte hɔ̄y./ We can reach his house
    easily [lit. with ease].

/myhrbani se ys ki cabi dijie!/ Please give [me] the key to this!
    [Equivalent to /myhrbani fərma kər/]

/vw vəqt se pəhw̃cega./ He will arrive on time.

/gaRi bəhwt tezi se ja rəhi həy./ The train is going very rapidly. [/tezi/
    F2 "speed, rapidity, strength, etc." This sentence has the same
    meaning as /... tez ja rəhi həy./; see above.]

/həm ws ke ghər mwškyl se pəhw̃c səkte hɔ̄y./ We can reach his house
    [only] with difficulty. [/mwškyl/ F1 A1 "difficulty, hardship;
    difficult, hard"]

/bədqysməti se, māy kəl ap se nəhī̃ myl səkūga./ Unfortunately, I won't
    be able to meet you tomorrow. [/bədqysməti/ F2 "ill fortune, bad
    luck"]

/vw der se aēge./ They will come late. [/der/ F1 "lateness, tardiness"]

/yy kam jəldi se kərē!/ Please do this work immediately! [This is some-
    what more emphatic than /yy kam jəldi kərē!/. /jəldi se/ idiomatically
    denotes "with all speed, hurriedly, immediately, at once," while
    /jəldi/ simply means "quickly, soon, early."]

Other postpositions besides /se/ are sometimes found in this type of construction, but
these are restricted and idiomatic. E. g.

/vw vəqt pər pəhw̃cega./ He'll arrive on time. [= /vəqt se/]

7.311. The Verb: the <S + /e/> Construction.

The "conditional" forms of the verb are made exactly like those of the future tense
paradigm, except that the suffix /g/ and the following /a/ - /e/ - /i/ suffixes are omitted.
The third person singular of the conditional form of /pəRhna/, for example, is thus /pəRhe/
(i. e. /pəRhega/ or /pəRhegi/ minus the final /ga/ or /gi/ -- the gender distinction is

obscured in the conditional form). Similarly, the conditional form corresponding to /dēge/ or /dēgi/ is /dē/, etc. A sample paradigm is:

PRONOUN	VERB:	MASCULINE OR FEMININE	
mə̄y		pəRhū	I may read, might read
[tu		pəRhe	thou mayest read, mightest read]
vw		pəRhe	he, she, it may read, might read
həm		pəRhē	we may read, might read
twm		pəRho	you [nonhonorific] may read, might read
ap		pəRhē	you [honorific] may read, might read
vw		pəRhē	they may read, might read

The negative employed with the conditional is usually /nə/.

Conditional forms of /hona/ "to be, become" may also be employed as auxiliaries with the present general tense, with the continuative, with the /səkna/ construction, etc. E. g.

/mwmkyn həy, ky fəwj bhi ws ko ystemal kər rəhi ho./ It is possible that the army may also be using it.

/šayəd vw bhi yy kam kərta ho./ Perhaps he may be doing this work too.

/mwmkyn həy, ky vw log ws kəmre mē pəRh rəhe hõ./ It is possible that those people are studying in that room.

/əgər mə̄y ws vəqt khana kha rəha hū, to ap nəwkər ko kytab de səkte hə̄y./ If I am eating at that time, you can give the book to the servant. [In older Urdu the first person singular conditional of /hona/ was /hoū/, and this form is still occasionally found. Other conditional forms are regular: /ho/, /hõ/.]

The name "conditional" is not strictly accurate, nor are such translations as "may ..." or "might ..." Conditional forms have several uses, and no one grammatical term seems thoroughly satisfactory (various earlier authors have called this form "subjunctive" or "aorist" also). Generally speaking, this form denotes a state or action which is considered doubtful, conditional, contingent, or desirable. Various functions are as follows:

(1) Asking permission or advice:

/kya, mə̄y jaū?/ Should [may, shall] I go?

/kya, həm yəhā bəyThē?/ Should [may, shall] we sit here?

/kya, mə̄y yy phəl kaTū?/ Should [may, shall] I cut this fruit?

(2) As a polite imperative, almost identical in meaning with the < S + /ie/ > formation introduced in Sec. 3.313. If there is any semantic distinction at all between these two forms, the < S + /ie/ > form may be said to be a trifle more emphatic. E. g.

/ap kəl təšrif laē!/ Please come tomorrow!

/ek pyali cae piē!/ Please drink a cup to tea!

/mere pas təšrif rəkhē!/ Please sit by me!

(3) In wishes, prayers, desires, and third person commands (the "hortatory": "let him ...," "let them ...," etc.). E. g.

/xwda ap ko lakhõ rupəe de!/ May God give you lakhs of rupees!

/nə koi khana khae, nə koi pani pie!/ Let no one eat food; let no one drink water!

(4) After various words and phrases indicating doubt, condition, contingency, possibility, desirability, etc. E. g.

    (a) /əysa nə ho, ky .../ "let it not be thus that ..., lest ..."

        /əysa nə ho, ky vw ws ke pas jae! / Let it not be that he should go to him!

    (b) /cahie ky .../ "it is necessary that ..."

        /ap ko cahie ky ap aj nə aē. / It is necessary that you do not come today.

    (c) /cahta həy, ky .../ "wants that ..."

        /mə̃y cahta hū, ky ap yy kytab pəRhē. / I want you to read this book.

    (d) /kaš/ "would that ...!" [Not yet introduced.]

        /kaš vw mere pas aē! / Would that he come to me!

    (e) /mwmkyn həy, ky .../ "it is possible that ..."

        /mwmkyn həy, ky mə̃y aj lahəwr jaū. / It is possible that I may go to Lahore today.

    (f) /mwnasyb həy, ky .../ "it is suitable that ..." [/mwnasyb/ Al "fitting, suitable" has not yet been introduced.]

        /mwnasyb həy, ky ap wse syrf ek rupəya dē. / It is proper that you give him only one rupee.

    (g) /take/ "in order that, so that"

        /mwjhe wn ka pəta dijie, take mə̃y wn ke ghər jaū. / Please give me their address, so that I may go to their house.

    (h) /xwda kəre [ky] .../ "May God will that ..."

        /xwda kəre, ky baryš nə ho. / May God will that it may not rain today.

        /xwda kəre mere dost yəhã aē. / God will [that] my friends may come here.

The following words and phrases are often followed by the conditional but may occur with other forms of the verb as well.

    (i) /šayəd/ "perhaps ..." [This is also colloquially found with the indicative, indicating a greater possibility of reality.]

        /šayəd mə̃y vəhã jaū. / Perhaps I may go there.

    (j) /yrada həy, ky .../ "it's [my, etc.] intention that ..." [And similarly, /xyal həy, ky .../ "it's [my, etc.] idea that ..." when followed by a clause denoting condition, desire, etc.]

        /mera yrada həy, ky mə̃y ap ke sath cəlū. / It is my desire that I go along with you.

    (k) / ... se kəho [kəhie, kəhē], ky .../ "tell ... that ..." [The conditional is only employed here when the person marked by /se/ and the subject of the following clause are the same.]

        /ws se kəho, ky vw vəhã nə bəyThe. / Tell him that he may not sit there.

        /ws ləRke se kəhie, ky vw meri kytab vapəs bheje. / Please tell that boy to send my book back.

    (l) With various adverbs, etc. denoting "where, " "when, " "how, " "how much, " etc. when the sense is "wherever, " "whenever, " "however, " "however much": e. g.

        /yy divar, kytni hi ūci ho, mə̃y ws pər cəRh səkta hū. / This wall, however high it may be, I can climb it.

/jəb bhi ap a səkē, mwjhe bətaē! /   Whenever you can come, please tell
me!

The above list is by no means exhaustive.

A fifth important use of the conditional will be discussed in the following Section.

7.312. Conditional Sentences.

The conditional clause (the "if" clause) is usually introduced by /əgər/ Conj "if. "
The resultative clause (the "then" clause) is commonly introduced by /to/ Conj "then. "
The conditional clause normally precedes the resultative clause, but, as was seen to be the
case with relative and correlative clauses, this order may occasionally be reversed. The
conditional clause may also be found with no introductory /əgər/ (or any other conditional
conjunction); the fact that the sentence is a conditional sentence will still be clear from
the presence of /to/ and the context. E. g.

/əgər ap jana cahte hə̄y, to həm aj cəl səkēge. /   If you want to go, then
we can go today. [Normal order]

/mə̄y bhi jaūga, əgər ap vəhā jaēge. /   I'll go too, if you go there.
[Reversed order]

/ap aēge, to mə̄y yy kam jəldi kərūga. /   [If] you will come, I'll do this
job quickly.

The verb form employed in either or both clauses may be either indicative or conditional.
An indicative verb implies a greater degree of reality in the mind of the speaker, and a
conditional verb indicates that the statement is more doubtful, more contingent, and less
likely of realisation.

Various tenses may be found in both clauses, the present, past, and future being the
commonest. The resultative clause may also consist of a question or an imperative.

(1) Conditional sentences with indicative verbs.

(a) Condition with the present; result with the present.

(b) Condition with the present; result with the future.

(c) Condition with the future; result with the future.

(d) Condition with the present or future; result with the imperative, etc.

Examples:

(1a) /əgər ap ke lie dhup zyada tez həy, to həm ghər cəlte hə̄y. /   If the
sunshine is too strong for you, then we will go [lit. go] home.

(1b) /əgər ap ke lie dhup zyada tez həy, to həm ghər cəlēge. /   If the sunshine is too strong for you, then we will go home.

(1c) /əgər ap ke lie dhup zyada tez hogi, to həm ghər cəlēge. /   If the sunshine will be too strong for you [at some future time], then we will
go home.

(1d) /əgər ap ke lie dhup zyada tez həy, to ghər jaie! /   If the sunshine is
too strong for you, then please go home!

Further examples:

(1a) /əgər vəqt həy, to həm əbhi pəhW̃cte hə̄y. /   If there is time, then we
will just arrive [lit. arrive].

(1b) /əgər yy ləRka hoš̌yar həy, to vw yy kytab səməjh səkega. /   If this
boy is clever, he'll be able to understand this book.

211

(1c) /əgər mə̄y jaūga, to mə̄y ap ke lie kəpRa laūga./ If I go [lit. will go], I'll bring you [some] cloth. [The likelihood of my going and my bringing the cloth is great.]

(1d) /əgər ap wn se mylna cahte hə̄y, to cəlie!/ If you want to meet them, then let's go!

(2) Conditional sentences with conditional verbs.

   (a) Condition with the conditional; result with the present.

   (b) Condition with the conditional; result with the future.

   (c) Condition with the conditional; result with the conditional.

   (d) Condition with the conditional; result with the imperative, etc.

Examples:

(2a) /əgər ap ke lie dhup zyada tez ho, to həm ghər cəl səkte hə̄y./ If the sunshine should be too strong for you, then we can go home.

(2b) /əgər ap ke lie dhup zyada tez ho, to həm ghər cəlēge./ If the sunshine should be too strong for you, then we will go home.

(2c) /əgər mə̄y lahəwr jaū, to mə̄y ap ke lie kəpRa laū./ If I should go to Lahore, then I would bring [some] cloth for you.

(2d) /əgər ap ke lie dhup zyada tez ho, to ghər jaie!/ If the sunshine should be too strong for you, then please go home!

In the first and second examples above, the condition is considered possible and the result factual, contingent upon the realisation of the condition. The time of the condition is present-future; the time of the result is present in the first example and future in the second. In the third example, the speaker considers both the condition and the result purely hypothetical: "going to Lahore" is just a distant possibility, but if that possibility were indeed to be realised, then the bringing of the cloth would also be realised.

Further examples:

(2a) /əgər ap yy kam kərē, to əccha həy./ If you should do this work, then it will be [lit. is] well.

(2b) /əgər mə̄y ys mwlk mē rəhū, to twm mere pas rəhoge./ If I should stay in this country, then you will stay with me.

(2b) /əgər ap ke lie myrcē zyada tez hō, to həm dusra salən dēge./ If the peppers should be too hot for you, then we will give you another [type of] curry.

(2b) /əgər ap yy kəpRa xəridē, to mə̄y pəyse dūga./ If you should buy this cloth, then I will give the money. [Here /mə̄y/ "I" receives a slightly stronger intonational stress.]

(2c) /mə̄y wn se mylū, to kəhū./ Should I meet him, I'd tell [him]. [Not much likelihood.]

(2c) /əgər baryš ho, to gərmi kəm ho./ If there should be rain, then the heat would be less. [Not much likelihood.]

(2d) /əgər ap cahē, to yəhā rəhē!/ If you wish, please stay here. [Here the conditional form is used as the polite imperative.]

The following further types of conditional sentences will not be of immediate use to the student, but a brief introduction to them may be included here for completeness' sake.

(3) A simple future condition and a simple future result:

   (3a) Condition with the past; result with the future.

Examples:

(3a) /əgər mə̄y lahəwr gəya, to mə̄y ap ke lie kəpRa laūga./ If I go to Lahore [in the future], I will bring [some] cloth for you. [/gəya/ MS

212

past of /jana/ "to go"]

(4) A past irrealis (condition contrary to fact) is made as follows:

    (4a) Condition with the present participle; result with the present participle.

    (4b) Condition with the present participle; result with the present, the perfect, the pluperfect, etc.

Examples:

    (4a) /əgər ap ke lie dhup zyada tez hoti, to həm kwch yntyzam kərte./ If the sunshine had been too strong for you, we would have made some arrangement. [Both the condition and the result are impossible of realisation or contrary to fact.]

    (4a) /əgər mə̃y lahəwr jata, to mə̃y ap ke lie kəpRa lata./ If I had gone to Lahore, I would have brought [some] cloth for you. [I did not go, however.]

    (4a) /əgər ap mwjhe bətate, to mə̃y yy kəbhi nə kərta./ If you had told me, I never would have done this.

    (4a) /əgər vw yy kəpRa car rupəe mẽ becte, to mə̃y xəridta./ If he had sold this cloth for [lit. in] four rupees, then I would have bought [it].

    (4b) /mə̃y cəla to jata, məgər bimar hũ./ I would have gone, but I am ill. [Here the concessive particle /to/ occurs within a compound verbal unit, /cəla jata/. This construction is described in Unit XIV.]

Still other less-common types of conditional sentences are found, and these will be described in later Units.

7.313. /to/ "Then, etc."

Apart from its uses in conditional and relative sentences, /to/ also occurs within a main clause as a particle. It is usually found just after the first "tactic block" in the sentence (i.e. if the subject comes first and consists of one word, /to/ will be the second; if the subject consists of three words, then /to/ will be the fourth, etc.). It is also found in various other positions in the sentence (see the last example in Sec. 7.312), and some of these usages are most complex.

When used as a particle, /to/ is as difficult to translate as German doch or English indeed. An idiomatic rendering of the connotations of /to/ in a given sentence may require as much a separate English phrase or even an auxiliary sentence. Uses of /to/ include: (a) the introduction of a new topic, (b) contrast, (c) concession, and (d) emphatic assertion. The student will be able to master the ramifications of this particle only through a careful comparison of the examples found in this and succeeding Units. Some examples are:

    /ap to aẽge. kya, ap ki beTiã nəhı̃ aẽgi?/ You will come. Won't your daughters come? [It is settled that you are coming. I now turn to the topic of your daughters: aren't they coming?]

    /ap nə jaie! mə̃y to lahəwr jaũga./ Please don't go! I will go to Lahore. [Here the emphasis is contrastive: even though you do not go, I must certainly go to Lahore.]

    /mə̃y to nəhı̃ jaũga./ I certainly won't go. [Contrastive and assertive emphasis.]

    /mə̃y to ws se kəhũga!/ I'll certainly tell him! [No fear that I won't!]

    /əccha, to həm cəlẽ!/ All right, then let us go! [Let us leave this other topic -- or these other people -- and go!]

/əccha, to khana khaē!/   All right, then, let's eat! [Enough conversation!]

/swno to!/   Now you listen! [All right, I have heard enough of your point of view. Now hear what I have to say.]

/ap wn ke ghər jaē ya nə jaē, mōy to jaūga./   [Whether] you go to his house or not, I will go anyway. [Contrastive and assertive emphasis.]

/ap bhi to wn ke ghər jaēge?/   You are going to his house too? [Here /to/ asks for confirmation, and an affirmative reply is expected.]

/ap to yy kam əcchi təra jante hōy./   You know this job very well. [Assertive emphasis.]

/ap to bəhwt dynõ se yəhā rəhte hōy. ap ko to yəhā ki səRkē malum hõgi./ You have lived [lit. live] here for a long time [lit. many days]. You must know the streets of this place [lit. here's streets]. [The first /to/ is assertive; the second is also assertive and anticipates that the statement will be proved to be true.]

/ -- to phyr kya yrada həy./   So then what is your desire? [Several courses of action have been suggested and discussed; the speaker now asks for a final decision.]

/yyhi to mōy kəh rəha hū!/   But this is exactly what I am saying! [The object, /yyhi/, is emphasised by placing it first.]

214

7.401. Supplementary Vocabulary.

The following numerals are all Type I adjectives. See Sec. 2.401.

ykəttys [or /yktys/]	thirty-one
bəttys	thirty-two
tētys [or /tetys/]	thirty-three
cə̄wtys	thirty-four
pə̄ytys	thirty-five
lakh	lakh, hundred thousand
kəroR	crore, ten million

The first five of the above have a "writing pronunciation" ending in /is/ instead of /ys/:
e.g. /tētis/. This is not common in speech.

Other items are:

bəcca M2	child [male]
wdhər Adv	thither, that way, that direction
wtna A2	that much, so much
vəysa A2	that sort, such, like that

7.402. Supplementary Exercise I: Substitution.

1. | tis | əwrtē əwr | cəwbys | mərd aēge. |
   |---|---|---|---|
   | thirty-one | | thirty-five | |
   | thirty-three | | thirty-two | |
   | twenty-seven | | thirty-four | |
   | thirty-one lakhs | | thirty-two thousand | |
   | crores | | lakhs | |

2. | əysa khana | khana cahie, jəysa | | yy həy. |
   |---|---|---|---|
   | this sort of grape | buy | as | this is |
   | that much money [sg.] | give | as much as | he needs |
   | thither | go | whither | that river is |
   | that sort of servant | be | as | Mr. Smith's servant is |
   | on this sort of field | play | as | this is |

3. ys mwlk mē bəhwt admi hə̄y.
   thirty-four thousand two hundred railway cars
   thirty-three Mughal forts
   thirty-two lakhs sixteen thousand children
   thirty-five crores [of] people
   thirty-one thousand mosques

7.501. Substitution.

1. <u>asman pər</u>   <u>thoRe thoRe badəl</u>   hə̄y.

   on the ground   my shoes

   on the roof   all the three men

   on the walls   very pretty pictures

   on the moon   very high mountains

   in the plain   very big trees

2. həm šam tək   <u>sara lahəwr</u>   <u>dekh səkē̃ge</u>.

   by tomorrow   the whole work   will be able to do

   by morning   on this mountain   will be able to climb

   in two weeks   all the books   will be able to read

   up to two days   his room   will be able to use

   by two years   all these bad men   will be able to remove

3. <u>yy bay</u>   <u>cād ki rəwšni mē</u>   bəhwt xubsurət   malum hota həy.

   this cloth   for me   very expensive

   the royal fort   from outside   very high

   this flower   in your hat   very pretty

   this river's water   here   very clean

   salt   in this curry   very strong

4. <u>ap ki koThi</u>   ydhər həy, jydhər   <u>dərya</u>   nəzər a rəha həy.

   thier place   the plain

   the king's garden   that tall tree

   their church   the prison

   the Mughals' fort   the old bazaar

   the moon   that black cloud

5. <u>vw jəga</u>   <u>dekhne</u>   ke qabyl həy.

   his house   seeing

   this kind of cigarette   smoking

   this matter   understanding

   this hotel   staying

   this pomegranate   eating

6. <u>syrf kəšmir mē</u>   ys jəysa <u>bay</u>   həy.

   in the Red Fort   palace

   in my garden   flower

   in my friend's shop   ghi

   only on those mountains   stone

   in the blue mosque   minaret

7. kytna <u>ūca minar</u> həy!
      bad mango
      strong vessel
      little money[1]
      old college
      beautiful river
    [1]For "little," use /kəm/.

8. kya, əbhi <u>jute</u>   <u>wtarū</u>?
      rice   should buy
      city   should go
      [my] own   should send
      address
      cinema   should see
      [my] own   should leave
      hat

9. <u>ap log</u>   <u>əksər</u>   <u>bimar</u>   hote hə̄y.
    American people every day busy
    mangoes   nowadays   bad
    this kind of   sometimes tall
    trees
    Pakistani [male] often   clever [= sharp]
    children
    fruit sellers   generally here

10. hər qysm <u>ke phul</u> hə̄y.
       of trees
       of mosques
       of prayers
       of buildings
       of stones

11. <u>pakystani fəwj</u>   <u>ws ko</u>   <u>ystemal</u>   kər rəhi həy.
    my wife   to him   telephone
    the police of Lahore for it   arrangement[s]
    my [girl] child   on it   work
    the government   this road use
    my sister   his   waiting[1]
      [1]i.e. "waiting for him"

12. əgər <u>baryš</u>   nə ho, to həm <u>ghər</u>   <u>cəl səkē̄ge</u>.
    too much light   picture   will be able to take
    sunshine   hat here will leave
    heat   [at] home will stay [lit. wait]
    meat   vegetable will eat
    light   how?   will read

13. <u>upər se</u>   <u>sara šəhr</u>   nəzər ata həy.
    from below   that church
    from inside   the playing ground

from outside	that tall minaret	
from the roof	the mountain	
from the palace	that old tree	

14. <u>vw</u>　　　　　　　bhi <u>mwylõ ke zəmane ka</u>　　həy.

this man	that country's	
this money	that watchman's	
this famous mosque	that king's	
this old hat	his daughter's	
this strong fort	the Pakistani army's	

15. <u>ws ki divarõ mẽ</u>　　　　<u>bəRe bəRe pətthər</u>　　hə̃y.

in the army	lakhs of men	
in this prison	all five men	
in his palace	thousands of pictures	
in my country	crores of people	
outside the garden	very small trees	

7.502.　Transformation.

1.　Change the verb forms underlined in the following sentences to their corresponding
　　conditional forms:　e.g.　/jata həy/ to /jae/.

　　a.　šayəd vw kəl <u>jaega.</u>

　　b.　əgər həm ys pəhaR pər <u>cəRhẽge</u>, to sara šəhr dekh səkẽge.

　　c.　əgər zyada həva <u>cəlegi,</u> to kya, həm yəhã Thəyr səkẽge?

　　d.　ys kwrsi pər təšrif <u>rəkhie!</u>

　　e.　əgər <u>jaũga,</u> to kyõ <u>jaũga.</u>

　　f.　əgər yy kəpRa ap ko pəsənd <u>həy</u>, to həm ysi ko <u>lẽge.</u>

　　g.　kya, mə̃y yəhã <u>bəyThũga</u>?

　　h.　thoRa pani <u>pijie!</u>

　　i.　kya, həm upər <u>cəRhẽge</u>?

　　j.　šayəd vw əndər <u>pəRh rəhe hə̃y.</u>

　　k.　kya, həm əb <u>wtrẽge</u>?

　　l.　əgər vw koThi xali <u>həy</u>, to ap ko <u>bətaũga.</u>

　　m.　šayəd upər se sara lahəwr nəzər <u>aega.</u>

　　n.　mera yrada həy, ky mə̃y pakystan mẽ kwch dyn <u>Thəyrũga.</u>

　　o.　jytne cavəl ap <u>de səkte hə̃y</u>, wtne <u>dijie!</u>

2.　Make the verbs underlined in the following sentences negative.

　　a.　mə̃y bahər <u>bəyThũ</u>?

　　b.　əgər ap ko pəsənd <u>ho,</u> to <u>khaie!</u>

　　c.　kya, jute yəhã <u>pəhnẽ</u>?

　　d.　əgər aj baryš <u>ho,</u> to həm əndər <u>rəhẽge.</u>

　　e.　šayəd vw yy qalin <u>xəridẽ.</u>

　　f.　wn ko cahie, ky vw səb kam <u>kərẽ.</u>

　　g.　mwmkyn həy, ky mə̃y aj <u>jaũ.</u>

h. kya, vw bahər khəRe h<u>ə̄y</u>?

i. meri beTi se kəho, ky vw aj synima <u>jae</u>.

j. mera yrada həy, ky ys pətthər ko zəmin se <u>nykalū</u>.

3. As described in Sec. 7.312, the sequence of verb forms in conditional sentences may follow several patterns, each having its own connotations of time and reality. Under each verb form underlined in the following sentences three alternate possibilities are listed; change each verb accordingly. Change /nəhī̆/ to /nə/ where necessary.

a. əgər pəyse kafi nəhī̆   <u>hə̄y</u>, to mə̄y kwch <u>de səkta hū</u>.

               future   future
               conditional   present
               conditional   future

b. əgər ap ys ciz ko ystemal <u>kər səkte hə̄y</u>, to le səkte hə̄y.

               conditional   future
               future   present
               conditional   present

c. əgər ap əbhi <u>jate hə̄y</u>, to ws ko pəkəR səkte hə̄y.

             conditional   future
             future   future
             present   future

d. əgər baryš   <u>ho rəhi ho</u>, to əbhi nə jaie!

             present   conditional
             conditional   conditional
             present   polite imperative

e. əgər mə̄y lahəwr <u>jata hū</u>, to vw mere sath <u>jate hə̄y</u>.

               future   future
               conditional   future
               conditional   conditional

f. əgər yy hoTəl saf <u>həy</u>, to həm yəhā Thəyr səkte hə̄y.

               conditional   future
               conditional   present
               future   future

g. əgər ap meri təsvir <u>khē̆cti hə̄y</u>, to əccha   <u>həy</u>.

               future   future
               conditional   present
               conditional   future

h. əgər twm yy kəmra saf   <u>kəroge</u>, to mə̄y bahər yntyzar <u>kərūga</u>.

               conditional   future
               conditional   conditional
               conditional   present

i. əgər fəwj ys səRək ko ystemal <u>kər rəhi ho</u>, to həm nəhī̆ <u>ja səkēge</u>.

               conditional   present
               present   future

present   present

j. əgər mə̃y wn se kəhũ, to šayəd vw a səkẽ.

                future   future

                conditional   future

                conditional   present

7.503. Fill the Blanks.

1. Fill the blanks in the following sentences with /õ/ "total plurality" or /õ/ - /iõ/ "indefinitely large plurality. " The proper suffix is indicated in brackets after each sentence by "a" for "total plurality" and "b" for "indefinitely large plurality. "

    a. kəl mere pas car __ admi aẽge. [a]

    b. hər roz vw bis __ TykəT xəridte hə̃y. [b]

    c. pakystan mẽ lakh __ ləRke pəRhte hə̃y. [b]

    d. pāc __ əwrtẽ ap ka yntyzar kər rəhi hə̃y. [a]

    e. kəl ysi gaRi se bis __ admi pəhw̃cẽge. [a, b]

    f. rəhim sahəb ser __ am kha səkte hə̃y. [b]

    g. vw məsjyd ko həzar __ rupəe dete hə̃y. [b]

    h. mə̃y kəl do __ admiõ se mylũga. [a]

    i. wn ke aTh __ bhai wn ke sath hə̃y. [a]

    j. mera šəhr yəhã se mil __ dur həy. [b]

7.504. Variation.

1. aj gərmi əbhi tək ytni nəhĩ həy, jytni rozana hoti həy.

    aj synima mẽ log əbhi tək ytne nəhĩ hə̃y, jytne hər roz hote hə̃y.

    ys sal ytni gərmi nəhĩ, jytni hər sal yəhã hoti həy.

    aj ytni həva nəhĩ cəl rəhi, jytni gərmiõ mẽ əksər cəlti həy.

    aj mə̃y ytna kam nəhĩ kər səkta, jytna mə̃y rozana kərta hũ.

    ajkəl pani dərya mẽ ytna nəhĩ, jytna əksər hota həy.

2. əgər baryš nə ho, to aj šam tək həm sara lahəwr dekh səkẽge.

    əgər baryš nə ho, to həm kəl swba tək səb yntyzam kər səkẽge.

    əgər kam nə ho, to ytvar tək ap ke pas Thəyr səkẽge.

    əgər kəl gərmi nə ho, to šam tək səb saman khol səkẽge.

    əgər kafi qwli nə hõ, to kəl rat tək həm səb pətthər nəhĩ nykal səkẽge.

    əgər dhup nə ho, to dopəhr tək pəhaR pər cəRh səkẽge.

3. mere mwlk mẽ əysi gərmi nəhĩ hoti, jəysi ap ke mwlk mẽ hoti həy.

    ap ke mwlk mẽ əyse pəhaR nəhĩ hote, jəyse kəšmir mẽ hote hə̃y,

    ys baγ mẽ əyse xubsurət phul nəhĩ hote, jəyse šalymar mẽ hote hə̃y.

    əmrika mẽ əysi ymartẽ nəhĩ hotĩ, jəysi ys šəhr mẽ hoti hə̃y.

    hoTəl mẽ əysa khana nəhĩ mylta, jəysa əpne ghər mẽ mylta həy.

    sare pakystan mẽ əysa cəwkidar nəhĩ mylega, jəysa həmara cəwkidar həy.

4. jəhã pəhaR hote hə̃y, vəhã gərmi kəm hoti həy.

220

jəhã baryš zyada hoti həy, vəhã dərəxt bəhwt ūce hote hə̄y.

jəhã həmara khelne ka məydan həy, vəhã həm səb dopəhr ko khana khaē̄ge.

jəhã log nəmaz pəRhte hə̄y, vəhã jute wtar kər jaie!

jəhã fəwj ki gaRiā jati hə̄y, vəhã ap ki gaRi nəhĩ ja səkegi.

jydhər se həva cəl rəhi həy, wdhər se baryš aegi.

5. jəb ap qəle jaē̄ge, to ap yy səb cizē̄ dekh səkēge.

jəb ap kəšmir jaē̄ge, to ap vw baɣ dekh səkē̄ge.

jəb ap chət se dekhē̄ge, to sara šəhr nəzər aega.

jəb mə̄y vapəs aūga, to asani se kwch səntre la səkūga.

jəb baryš ho rəhi ho, to koi bahər nəhĩ ja səkta.

jəb ap nice jaē̄, to ws nəwkər ko yy kəpRa bhi dhone ke lie dē̄.

6. šayəd ap ke lie səb se dylcəsp ciz badšahi məsjyd hogi.

šayəd ys divar ke lie yy pətthər səb se əccha hoga.

šayəd ap ke beTe ke lie yy kytab əcchi ho.

šayəd twmhare lie yy qalin bəhwt mə̄hga ho.

šayəd yn ke lie yy minar zyada ūca həy.

šayəd ap ke valyd sahəb ke lie həmari koThi zyada dur həy.

7. ys mē̄ do do səw sal pwrane dərəxt hə̄y.

ys šəhr mē̄ chəy chəy səw sal pwrani ymartē̄ hə̄y.

hər šəhr mē̄ car car lakh admi rəhte hə̄y.

ys mwlk mē̄ dəs dəs həzar fwT ūce pəhaR hote hə̄y.

ys məydan mē̄ ek vəqt mē̄ do do həzar ləRke khelte hə̄y.

ws qəle ki hər divar səw səw fwT ūci həy.

8. yy cād ki rəwšni mē̄ bəhwt xubsurət malum hota həy.

ap ki beTi pakystani kəpRõ mē̄ bəhwt xubsurət malum hoti həy.

ap ka nəwkər aj kwch bimar malum hota həy.

yy tinõ admi ys kam ke qabyl malum hote hə̄y.

yy Topi mere lie bəhwt choTi malum hoti həy.

həmare ghər ki divarē̄ ys təsvir mē̄ kwch kali malum hoti hə̄y.

9. vw ələg pəRhti hə̄y.

meri bivi nəmaz ələg pəRhti hə̄y.

ap ke valyd sahəb kyõ ələg rəhte hə̄y.

twm ys ko ələg rəkho!

həmara cəwkidar dusre nəwkrõ se kyõ ələg bəyThta həy.

mə̄y wn se ələg mylna cahta hū.

10. əccha, to həm cəlē̄!

əccha, to meri bat swno!

əccha, to yy Topi pəhnie!

əccha, to mə̄y wtrū?

əccha, to mə̄y jaū?

əccha, to mə̄y jata hū.

11. yy dekhne ke qabyl həy.

yy kəwfi pine ke qabyl həy.

yy kytabē pəRhne ke qabyl hə̃y.

yy xubsurət kəpRa pəhnne ke qabyl həy.

yy zəmin xəridne ke qabyl nəhĩ.

əysi batē swnne ke qabyl nəhĩ!

12. ap ki koThi ydhər həy, jydhər dərya nəzər a rəha həy.

vw pwrani ymarət ydhər həy, jydhər mwɣlõ ka qəla həy.

ap ke dost wdhər hə̃y, jydhər ap ki bivi khəRi hə̃y.

mə̃y wdhər wtərna cahta hũ, jydhər vw gaRi khəRi həy.

mə̃y ydhər yntyzar kərūga, jydhər yy bəRa pətthər həy.

həmara yrada həy, ky həm wdhər cəlē, jydhər səb log khana kha rəhe hə̃y.

13. qəle jəldi cəlna cahie, take bənd nə ho.

bazar se jəldi vapəs ana cahie, take səb yntyzam kər səkē.

wn ki sari batõ ko swnna cahie, take ap kwch lykh səkē.

ws divar pər cəRhie, take ap asani se təsvir khēc səkē.

hwkumət yy yskul jəldi kholegi, take ys šəhr ke bəcce bhi pəRh səkē.

chwri tez kijie, take gošt kaTē.

14. hər qysm ke phul hə̃y.

hər qysm ka khana asani se myl səkta həy.

polis mē səb qysm ke log mylte hə̃y.

ys pəhaR mē kytni qysm ke pətthər mylte hə̃y.

yəhã kysi qysm ka phəl nəhĩ mylta.

ys vəqt kysi qysm ki nəmaz nəhĩ pəRh səkte.

15. vw bhi mwɣlõ ke zəmane ka həy.

yy ymarət bhi mwɣlõ ke zəmane ki həy.

yy gyrja wn hi logõ ka həy.

pakystan ki hwkumət pakystaniõ hi ki həy.

yy divar ws badšah ke zəmane ki nəhĩ.

yy rəwšni cãd ki nəhĩ.

7.505. Translation.

Translate the English portions of the following into Urdu.

1. xwda kəre ky . . .

  he may be able to give up cigarette[s].

  today there may be some rain.

  he may listen to my word[s].

2. jəldi cəlie, take . . .

  we may arrive home by evening.

  my wife may not wait.

  we may meet [with] him.

3. wn ka yrada həy, ky . . .

  they may eat this kind of food.

  they may use my car.

they may do this work for their government.

4. šayəd . . .

this evening the moon may be visible.

he may get down from the car just now.

he may be working.

5. mwmkyn həy, ky . . .

your wife may be waiting.

my daughters may be arranging for the food. [1]

that woman may be putting on her clothes.

[1]"Arranging for the food" = "making the food's arrangement."

6. mɛ̃y cahta hũ, ky . . .

I may go to Kashmir after two days.

I may work in the police.

I may read this whole book today.

7. wn se kəho, ky . . .

they may wait.

they may please sit outside.

they should not come today.

8. mera xyal həy, ky . . .

we should go home after this.

we should wait for him. [1]

I may ask [from] him.

[1]"Wait for him" = "do his waiting."

9. əysa nə ho ky . . .

Mrs. Smith should hear this matter.

we may not reach there by that time.

he may be sick.

10. ap ko cahie, ky . . .

you should do this work quickly.

you should put on [your] own shoes here.

you should get down from the car.

7.506. Response.

1. jəhã ap rəhte hɛ̃y, kya, vəhã ɣwslxana həy?

2. kya, ap khana vəyse kha səkte hɛ̃y, jəyse pakystani khate hɛ̃y?

3. ap ki koThi kydhər həy.

4. kya, ap kəbhi təsvir khẽcte hɛ̃y?

5. əgər ap pakystan jaẽge, to ap kəwnsi pwrani ymartẽ dekhẽge.

6. kya, pwrane zəmane ki ymartẽ ap ke lie dylcəsp hɛ̃y?

7. jəb ap wrdu swnte hɛ̃y, to ap asani se səməjh səkte hɛ̃y, ya nəhĩ.

8. kya, ap ko pakystani əwrtõ ke kəpRe əcche malum hote hɛ̃y?

9. kya, ys šəhr mẽ koi məsjyd həy?

10. ap ke xyal mē, cād tək jana mwmkyn hǝy, ya nǝhī́.

11. jǝb ap pakystan jaēge, to ap kys qysm ke kǝpRe pǝhnēge.

12. kya, ap fǝwj mē jana cahte hǝy?

13. kya, ap ǝlǝg rǝhte hǝy, ya kysi ke sath rǝhte hǝy.

14. jǝb ap bimar hote hǝy, to ap khana choRte hǝy, ya nǝhī́.

15. ap ko kǝwnsa mǝwsǝm pǝsǝnd hǝy.

7.507. Conversation Practice.

Mr. Smith knocks on Dr. Rǝhim's door.

S: rǝhim sahǝb, adab ǝrz! kya, ap ys vǝqt mǝsruf hǝy?

R: ji nǝhī́. -- kya yrada hǝy.

S: aj ytvar hǝy, ǝwr mwjhe kwch kam nǝhī́. mera xyal hǝy, ky aj pwrane šǝhr cǝlē. log kǝhte hǝy, ky vw dekhne ke qabyl hǝy.

R: mǝy cǝlne ko tǝyyar hū́, mǝgǝr mwmkyn hǝy, ky aj sǝb dwkanē bǝnd hǒ.

S: to ǝwr kǝhā cǝlē? aj mǝwsǝm bǝhwt ǝccha hǝy, ǝwr yrada hǝy, ky bahǝr jaē.

R: aj ke ǝxbar mē hǝy, ky šayǝd šam tǝk baryš ho.

S: ǝccha? ys vǝqt asman saf hǝy, ǝwr badǝl nǝhī́ hǝy. hǝva cǝl rǝhi hǝy. jǝb mǝwsǝm ytna ǝccha hǝy, to kyǒ nǝ bahǝr cǝlē?

R: Thik hǝy. to kǝhā cǝlē? ys šǝhr mē pwrani ymartē bǝhwt hǝy, ǝwr bǝhwt ǝcche baɣ bhi hǝy. ajkǝl šalymar baɣ mē phul bǝhwt ǝcche hǒge. badšahi qǝla bhi dekhna cahie. vw bǝhwt dylcǝsp hǝy.

Mrs. Rǝhim enters the room.

MR: adab ǝrz!

R: hǝmara yrada bahǝr jane ka hǝy. ap ka kya xyal hǝy.

MR: Thik hǝy. ǝgǝr bahǝr cǝlna hǝy, to byhtǝr hǝy, ky mǝy kwch khane ka yntyzam kǝrū́.

S: bǝhwt ǝccha. meri bivi gaRi mē yntyzar kǝr rǝhi hǝy.

MR: wn ko ǝndǝr bwlaie! hǝm fǝwrǝn tǝyyar nǝhī́ ho sǝkte. mwjhe khane ka yntyzam kǝrna hǝy, ǝwr bǝcce bhi kǝpRe pǝhnēge.

S: Thik hǝy. mǝgǝr hǝmare sath khana nǝhī́ hǝy. ǝgǝr ap log ǝpne sath khana lēge, to hǝmǒ bhi kwch lana cahie.

MR: kyǒ? hǝmare pas bǝhwt hǝy. ap fykr nǝ kǝrē!

S: ji nǝhī́. mǝy ǝbhi pāc mynǝT mē lata hū́.

They make their preparations and go to the Shalimar Gardens.

S: ap log yǝhā wtrē! mǝy gaRi bǝnd kǝr ke ata hū́.

MS: yy ymarǝt kytni pwrani hǝy.

MR: koi tin sǝw sal pwrani hǝy.

MS: hǝmare mwlk mē ytni pwrani ymartē nǝhī́ hǝy, jytni yǝhā hǝy. syrf kwch koThiā ǝwr kwch gyrja hǝy. -- kya, yǝhā bhi jute wtarū́?

MR: ji nǝhī́. yy mǝsjyd nǝhī́ hǝy. yy to syrf baɣ hǝy.

R: ysmyth sahǝb kydhǝr hǝy. nǝzǝr nǝhī́ ate.

MR: vw samne kysi polis ke admi se bat kər rəhe hə̃y.

R: ap log Thəyrē! mə̃y ysmyth sahəb ke pas jata hū. vw mwjhe bwla rəhe hə̃y.

S: rəhim sahəb, yy sahəb kwch fərma rəhe hə̃y, məgər mə̃y nəhī̃ səməjh səkta.

R: kya bat həy, jənab.

P: sahəb ko bətaie, ky gaRi yəhã khəRi nəhī̃ kər səkte. dāī̃ tərəf, divar ke pas khəRi kərē.
-- vw samne, jəhã vw fəwj ki gaRi khəRi həy.

    Mr. Smith parks the car, and they all walk toward the gate.

MR: aie, pəhle kwch phəl xəridē!

MS: ap ke mwlk mē bəhwt qysm ke phəl hote hə̃y.

MR: yy gərmi ke məwsəm ke phəl hə̃y. mera xyal həy, ky jəyse phəl yəhã hote hə̃y, vəyse
hi phəl əmrika mē bhi hote hõge.

MS: ji nəhī̃. jəhã baryš əwr gərmi hoti həy, vəhã phəl əcche hote hə̃y.

    They stop at the gate.

MS: kya, yəhã TykəT xəridna həy?

R: ji nəhī̃. TykəT ki zərurət nəhī̃.

S: ys bəɣ ka yntyzam kəwn kərta həy.

R: ys ka yntyzam həmari hwkumət kərti həy.

MS: ytna pwrana bəɣ həy, məgər phyr bhi bəhwt xubsurət həy!

R: ji hã. həmare mwlk mē əwr bhi pwrani ymartē, qəle, əwr məsjydē hə̃y. pakystan mē
zəmin ke nice bhi kwch pwrane šəhr hə̃y. wnhē nykalne mē həmari hwkumət məsruf
həy, məgər ys ke lie vəqt cahie.

MR: ap log kəb tək batē kərēge! əndər cəlie!

R [pointing]: samne, chət ke nice, badšah ke bəyThne ki jəga həy. aie, ws məydan ki
tərəf cəlē! vəhã həmare bəcce khel səkēge.

MS: mə̃y yəhã ki təsvir khēcūgi, məgər koi əysa minar nəhī̃ həy, jəhã se səb kwch nəzər a
səke.

R: yy chət kafi ūci həy. yəhã se təsvir əcchi aegi.

MS: kya, yəhã badšah ka məhl bhi həy?

R: ji nəhī̃. məhl qəle mē həy. yy to syrf bəɣ həy.

MR: rəhim sahəb, nəmaz ka vəqt həy. ap nəmaz pəRhē!

R: maf kijie! mə̃y ap logõ se ələg ja kər nəmaz pəRhūga. nəmaz ke bad khana khaēge.

7.508. Conversation Stimulus.

Instructions for this type of exercise were given in Sec. 5.508. Topics may include:

1. Visiting an historical site.

2. An outing in the country.

3. Sightseeing in a Pakistani city.

4. Discussing the weather.

5. Comparing the weather, fruits, food, etc. of Pakistan to those of the student's own
country.

admi M1	man, person
asani F2	ease
asman M1	sky
əgər Conj	if
əksər A1 Adv	the majority of, most; often, generally
ələg A1	separate, apart, distinct
əwrət F1	woman
əysa A2	such, like this, thus, this kind
badəl M1	cloud
badšah M1	king
badšahi A1	royal
baɣ M1	garden
[ke] bahər Comp Post Adv	outside
baryš F1	rain
bəcca M2	(male) child, boy
bəcci F2	(female) child, girl
bəttys [or /bəttis/] A1	thirty-two
beTa M2	son
beTi F2	daughter
bimar A1 M/F1	sick, ill; sick person, patient
cãd M1	moon
cəRhna	to climb
cəwkidar M1	watchman
cõwtys [or /cõwtis/] A1	thirty-four
chət F1	roof
choRna	to leave, abandon, let go, release
dərəxt M1	tree
dərya M1	river
dhup F1	sunshine
divar F1	wall
donõ A1	both ("all two")
dylcəsp A1	interesting, fascinating, charming
fəwj F1	army
fəwrən Adv	at once, immediately
fwT M1	foot, feet (measurement)
gərmi F2	heat, warmth; summer, hot season
gyrja M1	church
həva F1	wind, breeze, air
hwkumət F1	government
jəb Conj	when [relative]
jəhã Adv	where [relative]

226

jəysa A2	just as, such as, as, like [relative]
jydhər Adv	whither, where [relative]
jytna A2	as much as, as many as [relative]
kəbhi Adv	sometime, ever, sometimes
kəroR Al	ten million
kəšmir Ml	Kashmir
khəRa PA2	standing, erect, upright, stationary
khelna	to play
khĕcna [or /khə̃ycna/]	to pull, draw
koThi F2	house of brick or stone
kydhər Adv	whither?
lakh Al	hundred thousand
məhl Ml	palace
mərd Ml	man, male
məsjyd Fl	mosque
məšhur Al	famous
məwsəm Ml	season, weather
məydan Ml	field, ground, plain
məzbut Al	strong, stout, durable, firm
minar Ml	minaret
mwγəl Ml Al	Mughal
mwmkyn PAl	possible
nəmaz Fl	prayer
ıəzər Fl	sight, vision
[ke] nice Comp Post Adv	beneath, below, under
pəhaR Ml	mountain
pəhnna	to put on, to wear
pətthər Ml	stone, rock
pə̃ytys [or /pə̃ytis/] Al	thirty-five
phul Ml	flower
phyr Conj	then, again, even [/phyr bhi/ "notwithstanding, even, even so"]
polis Fl	police
pwrana A2	old (of things), ancient, of olden times
qabyl Al	able, worth, capable, competent [/[ke] qabyl/ "worth . . . "]
qəla [also /qyla/] M2	fort
qəydxana M2	prison, jail
qysm Fl	kind, sort, type
rəwšni F2	light (luminescence)
rozana Adv	daily, every day
sara A2	whole, entire, the whole of, all
swnna	to hear, listen
synima [or /sənema/, /səynma/, etc.] Ml	cinema

šalymar M1 [np]	Shalimar (Gardens)
šayəd Conj	perhaps
take Conj	in order that, so that
təsvir F1	picture, portrait, photograph
tez A1	sharp, strong, pungent, piquant, clever, swift, rapid
tētys [or /tetys/, /tētis/, /tetis/] A1	thirty-three
to Conj Particle	then, so
Topi F2	hat, cap
[ke] upər Comp Post Adv	above, upper, up, over
ūca A2	high, tall
vəja [or /vəjəh/] F1	reason, cause
vəysa A2	such, like that, thus, that kind
wdhər Adv	thither, that way
wtərna	to get down, go down, get off, alight
wtna A2	that much, so much, that many, so many
ydhər Adv	hither, this way
ykəttys [or /ykəttis/, /yktys/, /yktis/] A1	thirty-one
ymarət F1	building
yntyzar M1	waiting, expecting
yrada M2	desire, wish, intention
ystemal M1	use, employment
zəmana M2	time, era, period
zəmin F1	ground, earth, land

Two pages from the "Tavalludnamah-i Muhammad," a manuscript written
in Deccani Urdu verse, dated 1724.

UNIT EIGHT

8.000.   SCRIPT II

Six letter groups will be introduced in this Unit:

8.001. Letter Group 3.

This group includes ﺞ /j/, ﭽ /c/, ﺡ /h/, and ﺥ /x/.

Letters of this shape group are connectors and have the following basic forms:

Initial	ﺟ	ﭼ	ﺣ	ﺧ
Medial	ﺠ	ﭽ	ﺤ	ﺨ
Final	ﺞ	ﭻ	ﺢ	ﺦ
Independent	ﺝ	ﭺ	ﺡ	ﺥ

Letters of this group are thus:

Initial	ﺟ	ﭼ	ﺣ	ﺧ
Medial	ﺠ	ﭽ	ﺤ	ﺨ
Final	ﺞ	ﭻ	ﺢ	ﺦ
Independent	ﺝ	ﭺ	ﺡ	ﺥ

The letter ﺡ occurs only in words of Arabic origin. A very few speakers --
mostly religious scholars -- attempt to give this letter its Arabic pronunciation: a voiceless pharyngealised /ḥ/. Most speakers, however, consider this an affectation.

Medial and final forms of this group join at the top, requiring preceding letters to be written on a slightly higher level. Letters of Group 2 have a special initial form before medial and final Group 3 letters: ⁄ . Similarly, a medial Group 2 letter has ⌐ before these forms:. e.g. بُچ /bəc/, بِنچ /bic/, نِچے /nice/, بجتا /bəjta/.

8.002. Letter Group 6.

This group includes س /s/ and ش /š/. Letters of this group are connectors and have two alternate sets of forms in free variation:

Initial		or			or
Medial		or			or
Final		or			or
Independent		or			or

Letters of this group are thus:

Initial				
Medial				
Final				
Independent				

The letter س is the commonest representation of /s/.

Letters of this group have a special shape before the two final forms of ى : ⌐ E.g. سی /si/, سے /se/, شے /šəy/. Before a medial or final letter of Group 3,

232

this group has ´ or ‿ , which joins at the top: e.g. چ /səc/, سخت /səxt/.

8.003. Letter Group 11.

This group includes ک /k/ and گ /g/. Letters of this group are connectors and have the following basic forms:

Initial	اگ	اگ
Medial	گ	گ
Final	گ	گ
Independent	گ	گ

Letters of this group are thus:

Initial	ک	گ
Medial	ک	گ
Final	ک	گ
Independent	ک	گ

Before /əlyf/ and /l/, special initial and medial forms are found: e.g. ک and ک

E. g. کا /ka/, تاگا /tāga/, لرکا /ləRka/, کل /kəl/.

The extra stroke distinguishing /g/ from /k/ is a relatively recent device: in older books both /k/ and /g/ are written ک .

8.004. Letter Group 12.

The only member of this group is ل /l/. It is a connector and has the following basic forms:

Initial   لٰ

Medial   لـ

Final   لٰ

Independent   ل

Before final forms of ى , this letter has a form rather similar to that of the Group 2 letters but without any dot: e.g. لى /li/, ل /le/. An initial /l/ + /əlyf/ is written لا /la/.

8.005. Letter Group 13.

The only member of this group is م /m/. It is a connector and has the following basic forms:

Initial   مـ

Medial   ـمـ

Final   مٌ

234

Independent م

The tiny loop of the initial and medial forms should be below the following stroke (مـ) rather than above it (ـمـ). مـ tends to be written almost below a preceding character, and letters of Group 2 have their ٮـ initial and ـٮـ medial forms before it.

8.006. Letter Group 15.

The only member of this group is ہ /h/, a connector. This letter has two separate sets of forms and functions: (1) as the consonant /h/, and (2) as the symbol for aspiration in sequence such as /ph/, /th/, /dh/, /Dh/, etc. The basic forms of consonantal /h/ are:

Initial ہـ

Medial ـہـ

Final ـہ

Independent ہ

Initial /h/ before /əlyf/ has a special form: ہـ . E.g. ہا /ha/.

Letter Group 2 has ٮـ as its initial form and ـٮـ as its medial form before /h/: e.g. نہیں /nəhĩ/, یہاں /yəhã/.

A few monosyllabic verb roots end in /h/. When this /h/ is word-final after a connector, it is written with a special form resembling /hh/: e.g. کہہ /kəh/ "say,"

بہہ /bəh/ "flow," سہہ /səh/ "endure." This is really nothing more than a writing convention serving to distinguish these words from که /ky[h]/ "that," بے /by[h]/ "with, by" (a Persian preposition), and سے /sy[h]/ "three" (Persian numeral occasionally employed in Urdu).

One of the curious phenomena of the Urdu writing system is that a great many words written with a final ه are pronounced as though they ended in ا /a/: e.g. کرایہ /kyraya/ M2 "fare, rent," پیسہ /pəysa/ M2 "money," درجہ /dərja/ M2 "class, level," etc. etc. Although this convention has its origins in Arabic and Persian, many Indic words have also come to have this spelling: e.g. راجہ /raja/ M2 "king," کمرہ /kəmra/ M2 "room," etc. In some cases both spellings are permitted, but the vast majority of words have a conventionally correct orthography and must be memorised. Among these, such common words as یہ /yy[h]/ "this," وہ /vw[h]/ "that," نہ /nə/ "not," کہ /ky[h]/ "that (conj.)" etc. are included.

Final ه may be pronounced in careful speech, however, whenever the speaker feels that it is an integral part of the stem rather than just an "ending." This letter is also usually pronounced after a "long" vowel (i.e. /i, e, u, o, a/). One may thus hear both /gwna/ and /gwnah/ for گناہ M1 "sin" (although the latter is more common); /jəga/, /jəgəh/, or /jəgha/ for جگہ F1 "place," etc. An /h/ will always be audibly present in the plural forms of such words: e.g. گناہوں /gwnahõ/ MOP "sins"; جگہیں /jəghē/ FNP "places," جگہوں /jəghõ/ FOP "places." Note that the Arabic pharyngealised /ḥ/ (/h/ in Urdu) ح is always felt to be an integral part of the stem. Although it too may be omitted in normal speed speech, one may hear /swbəh/ as well as /swba/ or /swbha/ for صبح F1 "morning."

Forms of the "aspiration h" are:

Initial   ﮪ

Medial   ﮬ

Final   ﮭ

Independent   ﮫ

This letter is traditionally called /do cəšmi he/ "two-eyed h."

Since this letter stands for the aspiration of a preceding consonant, the initial form cannot occur word-initially but only after a preceding nonconnector. In the /nəsx/ type font, however, this form is employed as the <u>only</u> initial form of /h/, whether it is used as a consonant or as an aspiration marker. It is also used as an abbreviation for /hyjri/, the Islamic Era, which began with the departure of the Prophet Muhammad in 622 A.D. from Mecca to Medina. See Sec. 12.003.

Letters of Group 2 have   /   as their initial form and   ◠   as their medial form before ﮪ : e.g.   پھل   /phəl/.

/do cəšmi he/ is also sometimes found after   ل ,   م ,   and   ن   in place of ه : e.g.   انہیں   or   انھیں   /ynhẽ/ "to these." This usage is becoming obsolete. Otherwise /choTi he/ and /do cəšmi he/ are almost never confused in writing in modern Urdu, and the student must learn to employ them correctly. For example, if one were to write   بھت   for   بہت , it might be read as /bhyt/, /bhwt/, or /bhət/, thus giving rise to confusion.

It may also be noted that, unlike   ه ,   /do cəšmi he/ is always pronounced word- and syllable-finally: e.g.   پڑھ   /pəRh/.

237

8.101. Reading Drill.

1. Letters of all new groups + /əlyf/.

Vowelled   خَا   اَ   هَا   حَا   سَ   گَ   جَا

Unvowelled   خا   ا   ها   حا   سا   گا   جا

Vowelled   ثَا   لاَ   چَا   گَا   سَا   خَا   اَ

Unvowelled   ثا   لا   چا   کا   سا   خا   ا

2. Letters of all new groups + /ye/.

Vowelled   سِی   حے   کے   شَے   جِی   ئَے   مِی

Unvowelled   سی   حے   کے   شے   جی   ے   می

Vowelled   شِنی   ئَے   ہِی   گِی   لِی   چَے   لے

Unvowelled   شنی   ہے   ہِی   گی   لی   چے   لے

3. Letters of all new groups + /vao/.

Vowelled   جو   ہُو   کو   لُو   خُو   مُو   شُو

Unvowelled   جو   ہو   کو   لو   خو   مو   شو

Vowelled   لُو   حَو   گُو   ہُو   سو   چو   مو

Unvowelled   لو   حو   گو   ہو   سو   چو   مو

238

4. Medial letters of all new groups.

Vowelled

بَجْنا مِلْنا چَلْنا سَکْنا مَہَکْنا مَنْگَل کَسَوٹی بَہُت

Unvowelled

بجنا ملنا چلنا سکنا مہکنا منگل کسوٹی بہت

Vowelled

مِسَز حَمد نمبَر چُچُ مَسجد شَہد سٹرکیں گوشت

Unvowelled

مسز حمد نمبر چچ مسجد شہد سٹرکیں گوشت

5. Final letters of all new groups.

Vowelled

کَل سٹرک بَس ہَم تَمام بارِش مِرچ خَیال

Unvowelled

کل سٹرک بس ہم تمام بارش مرچ خیال

Vowelled

گِلاس نمک پَھل بَج لوگ کالِج اِسم مُلک

Unvowelled

گلاس نمک پھل بج لوگ کالج اسم ملک

6. Medial aspirated consonants.

Vowelled

بَیٹھا دیکھی چڑھنا چھوڑا تھا بیٹھنا بھیجنا کَھرا

Unvowelled

بیٹھا دیکھی چڑھنا چھوڑا تھا بیٹھنا بھیجنا کھرا

Vowelled

لِکھو گھنٹا سیکھے تھوڑا پھُول رکھو گدھا اُنھوں

Unvowelled

لکھو گھنٹا سیکھے تھوڑا پھول رکھو گدھا انھوں

7. Final aspirated consonants.

Vowelled	لاکھ	ہاتھ	رکھ	بَیٹھ	ڈیڑھ	چکھ	دودھ	گڑھ
Unvowelled	لاکھ	ہاتھ	رکھ	بیٹھ	ڈیڑھ	چکھ	دودھ	گڑھ
Vowelled	سَاتھ	سَاٹھ	بَاندھ	لَٹھ	بَاگ	سَمجھ	دیکھ	آٹھ
Unvowelled	ساتھ	ساٹھ	باندھ	لٹھ	باگ	سمجھ	دیکھ	آٹھ

8. Final "h" = /a/.

Vowelled	یہِ،	گنَاہ	روزَہ	جگَہ	تیرَہ	سولَہ	زیَادَہ	زمَانَہ
Unvowelled	یہ	گناہ	روزہ	جگہ	تیرہ	سولہ	زیادہ	زمانہ
Vowelled	کمرَہ	سترَہ	شکریِہ	نَہ	وَالِدَہ	مُردَہ	شَرمِندَہ	اَنڈَازَہ
Unvowelled	کمرہ	سترہ	شکریہ	نہ	والدہ	مردہ	شرمندہ	انڈازہ

8.102. Writing Drills.

Writing drills in this Unit need not be done with the vowel diacritics.

1. Initial letters of all new groups.

    seb   gəz   hath   log   sal   mil   cini   cãd   hər   mə̃y

    kəm   xali   səw   car   mera   məgər   jəb   kəhã   mẽ

2. Medial letters of all new groups.

    bimar   ajkəl   əxroT   hošyar   pəhli   həmare   pəsənd

    əhkam[1]   rəkhna   kəhta   cəRhna   samne   tãga   cəmci

        [1]Write the Arabic /bəRi he/ for /h/ here.

3. Final letters of all new groups.

    ek   nam   kam   mə̃gəl   mwlk   pas   log   gərm   ələg

    kəl   dəs   gylas   begəm   šam   ysm   TykəT   baryš

4. Aspiration.

ghər	ghi	chwri	choTa	phəl	khyRki	hath	dudh
dekho	DeRh	kwch	mwjh	saRhe	ThənDa	khəRa	
lakh	bhi	dhup	kəbhi	ydhər	aTh	bwdh	choRo
pəRhna	dhona	jhĩga	bəyTho	piche	chət	koThi	

5. Consonantal /h/.

bəhn	šəhr	həy	hə̄y	dyhli	jəgəh	pəhli	badšah
həva	vəjəh	bəhwt	pəhnna	twmhari	byhtər	bahər	
məšhur	cahna	vəhā̃	nəhĩ	həm	hota	həzar	lahəwr

6. Final "h" = /a/.

All of the words in this drill are written with final /choTi he/ but are pronounced as though they were written with /əlyf/.

cəmca	kəmra	valyda	ana [the coin]	pəysa	rupəya	
dərja	dərvaza	yrada	zəmana	yslamia	bara	tera
cəwda	pəndra	gyara	sətra	sola	zyada	rozana

8.103. Word Recognition.

The student should now be able to write most of the words he has learned so far. He cannot yet write:

1. Words containing ص , ض , ظ , ط , ع , غ , ث ,

and ق . These letters will be introduced in Unit X.

2. Words containing various vowel sequences: e.g. /cae/, /jao/, /dijie/.

3. Words containing a doubled consonant: e.g. /əccha/, /Dybba/, /əTThara/.

The following can be written but require special notice:

1. The NS forms of the following words are written with ه , pronounced /a/.

Other number-case forms are regular: e.g. اراده /yrada/, اراوے /yrade/,

ارادوں /yradõ/. Words marked with an asterisk, however, retain the /h/ in

their plural forms: e.g. جگہ /jəga/, جگہیں /jəghē/, جگہوں /jəghõ/.

All other words ending in /a/ introduced so far are written with final ا .

SCRIPT	PRONUNCIATION	SCRIPT	PRONUNCIATION
ارادہ	yrada	زمانہ	zəmana
اسلامیہ	yslamia	زیادہ	zyada
بادشاہ	badšah*	سترہ	sətra*
بارہ	bara*	سولہ	sola*
پندرہ	pəndra*	شکریہ	šwkria
پیسہ	pəysa	کرایہ	kyraya
تاکہ	take*	کمرہ	kəmra
تیرہ	tera*	کہ	ky*
جگہ	jəga*	گیارہ	gyara*
چمچ	cəmca	نہ	nə*
چودہ	cəwda*	والدہ	valda
درجہ	dərja	وجہ	vəja*
دروازہ	dərvaza	وہ	vw*
روپیہ	rupəya	یہ	yy*
روزانہ	rozana*		

2. The following numeral adjectives are written with a final یس , pronounced /ys/:

پینتیس	pāytys	چوبیس	cəwbys
تیتیس	tētys	چونتیس	cāwtys

3. The following words are written with the "less-common" Arabic consonant symbols. Their spellings must be memorised.

اکثر	əksər	رحیم	rəhim

SCRIPT	PRONUNCIATION	SCRIPT	PRONUNCIATION
حکومت	hwkumət	محل	məhl

4. The suffix والا /val/ (+ the Type II endings) is usually written separately. In older works, however, it may also be found joined to the preceding word. E. g.

تانگے والا	tāgevala	جوتے والا	jutevala
پھل والا	phəlvala	کپڑے والا	kəpRevala

5. Irregular and "special notice" spellings:

پہنچنا pəhw̃cna. [Medial /w̃/ written as ن only. Archaic also پہونچنا.]

چھ chəy (or /che/). [Spelled as though "Ch-h."]

دکان dwkan. [Also spelled دوکان in older works.]

کہ kəh. [A monosyllabic word ending in /h/. See Sec. 8.006.]

مہنگا māhga. [ن written after ه to indicate nasalisation.]

یونیورسٹی yunyvərsyTi. [The second و functions as a consonant.]

6. Occasionally a phonologically indivisible word may be written as two words for orthographic reasons. This is often true of verbs in the future tense, in which the final /ga/ - /ge/ - /gi/ may be separated from the rest: e. g. لکھوں گا or لکھونگا /lykhūga/ "I will write"; بیٹھے گی or بیٹھیگی /bəyThegi/ "she will sit down"; etc. Conversely, two phonologically separate words may sometimes be written together as one word also: this is especially true of demonstratives, interrogatives, etc. + a postposition: e. g. اس کا or اسکا /ys ka/ "his, her, its"; اُس کو or اُسکو /ws ko/ "him, her, it"; کس کا or کسکا /kys ka/ "whose?"

If in doubt about a particular spelling, the student should consult the vocabulary at the back of the book.

8. 104. Urdu-English Sentences.

1. آج آپ کو کس جگہ جانا ہے ۔

2. میں اور کپڑا دیکھنا چاہتا ہوں ۔

3. وہ لاہور میں پانچ دن تک ٹھہر سکتی ہیں ۔

4. دیکھو میرا سامان ٹیکسی سے اتارنا ہے ۔

5. آسمان پر تھوڑے تھوڑے بادل ہیں ۔

6. اگر دھوپ نہ ہو تو ہم باہر چلیں گے ۔

7. جہاں بارش زیادہ ہوتی ہے وہاں درخت بہت ہوتے ہیں ۔

8. اِس ملک میں ایسے پہاڑ نہیں ہوتے ۔

9. میں آپ کی کتاب الگ رکھوں گا ۔

10. خدا کرے میں سگریٹ چھوڑ سکوں ۔

11. میرا خیال ہے کہ آج سینما دیکھوں ۔

12. ممکن ہے کہ آج سب دکانیں بند ہوں ۔

13. میں اِتنے خراب موسم میں باہر نہیں جا سکتا ۔

14. وہ پولیس کے آدمی سے بات کر رہے ہیں ۔

15. وہ کبھی کبھی لاہور آتے ہیں ۔

8.105. English-Urdu Sentences.

1.   Your sister is [generally] sick.
2.   Should we take off [our] shoes?
3.   He sits in front of the mosque every day.
4.   I can't read this book.
5.   The number of my room is six.
6.   How long [lit. until when?] will you be able to stay in Pakistan?
7.   His shop is behind the palace of the king.
8.   What is he saying?
9.   If you like this cloth [lit. if this cloth is pleasing to you], then we will take it.
10. When will the Rawalpindi train [lit. Rawalpindi's train] arrive?
11. It is possible that I may meet [lit. meet with] him today.
12. This is the oldest tree [lit. from all, old tree].
13. Perhaps there may be rain by evening.
14. It is about four hundred years old.
15. Today I will buy bananas, apples, and grapes.

The Shalimar Gardens, Lahore, built by the ·Mughal
Emperor Shah Jahan in 1637-8.

UNIT NINE

9.000. CONVERSATION

The two families have finished their picnic lunch and are sitting together under the trees in the Shalimar Gardens.

S: Rəhim Sahəb, do you come here often? | rəhim sahəb, kya, ap əksər yəhã ate hɔ̃y?

childhood M1	bəcpən
used to come MS	ata tha
period, time M2	ərsa
became MS	hwa
came MS	aya
marriage F2	šadi
remained, lived, stayed MS	rəha
occasion, opportunity M2	məwqa
met, got, mixed MS	myla

R: No. In [my] childhood [I] used to come a lot. But now it has been a long time that [I] have not come [lit. came]. After [my] marriage, [I] lived outside Lahore for four years. Therefore, [I] got no opportunity to come. | ji nəhĩ. bəcpən mẽ bəhwt ata tha. əb to bəhwt ərsa hwa, ky nəhĩ aya. šadi ke bad, car sal lahəwr se bahər rəha. ys lie ane ka məwqa nə myla.

Karachi (a city in West Pakistan) F2 [np]	kəraci
about, concerning Comp Post	[ke] bare [mẽ]
used to read, study FS	pəRhti thi
desire, enthusiasm, taste, predilection M1	šəwq
was MS	tha
really, actually Adv	vaqəi
praise F1	tarif
used to hear, listen FS	swnti thi
near about, round about, around Adv Comp Post	[ke] aspas
walk, promenade, stroll F1	səyr
was FS	thi

MR: I am from [lit. of] Karachi. [I] used to read about this in books. For this reason [I had] a great desire to see [it]. Really, it is even better than I had heard [lit. as much praise as I used to hear, it is even better than that]. Moreover [lit. second], around my house in Karachi there was no good place for a stroll. | mɜ̃y kəraci ki hũ. ys ke bare mẽ kytabõ mẽ pəRhti thi. ys vəja se, dekhne ka bəhwt šəwq tha. vaqəi, jytni tarif swnti thi, ws se bhi byhtər həy. dusre, kəraci mẽ mere ghər ke aspas koi əcchi səyr ki jəga nəhĩ thi.

memory, recollection F1	yad
time, occasion F1	dəfa
football M1 [also F1]	fwTbal
began to play MP	khelne ləge
noise, commotion M1	šor
began to make (noise) MP	məcane ləge

247

thoroughly, really, well Adv	xub
were playing MP	khel rəhe the
policeman M2	polisvala
spoke MS	bola
forbidden, prohibited PA1	məna
late, lateness F1	der
began to run away MP	bhagne ləge
ill fortune, bad luck F2 [np]	bədqysməti
fell MS	gyra
began to go MS	jane ləga
along behind Adv Comp Post	[ke] piche piche
ran away, fled, ran MP	bhage
wept, cried MP	roe
state, condition F1	halət
laughed MS	hə̃sa
future, in future A1 Adv	aynda
duty, obligation M1	fərz
law, rule M1	qanun
against, contrary Adv Comp Post	[ke] xylaf
punishment F1	səza
returned, came back MP	ləwTe
went MS	gəya
straight A2 Adv	sidha
arrived, reached MS	pəhw̃ca

R: About [lit. on] going for a stroll, I recall [lit. to me memory came] that I once came here with my four friends for a stroll. We also had a football. Having come inside, we started to play football and make noise. When we were playing hard [lit. thoroughly], a policeman came and said, "It is forbidden to play here! If [you] must play, then play outside the Garden!" Shortly after he went away [lit. a little late after his going], we again began to play. Hearing the noise, the policeman came back. On seeing him, we started to run off in all [lit. all four] directions, By bad luck the football fell from my hand[s]. The policeman at once picked it up and started off in the direction of his office. Now we ran along behind him, and, going into his room, wept a lot. Seeing our condition, the policeman laughed and said, "I forgive [you] this time. Don't ever do that [lit. thus] again! It is your duty not to disobey [lit. go against] the law! This time your punishment is this that you all go home! The football will remain with me until tomorrow morning. You can take it at that time." We cried a lot, but [we] didn't get the football back, and we returned to [our] homes. Early the next morning I

səyr kərne pər, mwjhe yad aya, ky ek dəfa mə̃y əpne car dostõ ke sath səyr kərne yəhã aya. həmare pas fwTbal bhi tha. əndər a kər, həm fwTbal khelne ləge, əwr šor məcane ləge. jəb həm xub khel rəhe the, to ek polisvala aya əwr bola, "yəhã khelna məna həy! əgər khelna həy, to baɣ se bahər khelo!" ws ke jane ke thoRi der bad, həm phyr khelne ləge. šor swn kər, vw polisvala vapəs aya. həm wse dekh kər, carõ tərəf bhagne ləge. bədqysməti se, mere hath se fwTbal gyra. polisvala fəwrən wse wTha kər, əpne dəftər ki tərəf jane ləga. əb to həm ws ke piche piche bhage, əwr ws ke kəmre mẽ ja kər bəhwt roe. polisvala həmari yy halət dekh kər, hə̃sa əwr bola, "əb to mə̃y maf kərta hū. aynda kəbhi əysa nə kərna! twmhara fərz həy, ky qanun ke xylaf nə cəlo! ys vəqt twmhari səza yy həy, ky əpne əpne ghər jao! fwTbal kəl swba tək mere pas rəhega. ws vəqt le səkte ho." həm bəhwt roe, məgər fwTbal vapəs nə myla, əwr ghər vapəs ləwTe. dusre roz swba, mə̃y gəya, əwr polisvale ke dəftər se fwTbal le kər sidha yskul pəhw̃ca.

248

went, and, taking the football from the policeman's office, went [lit. arrived] straight to school.

act, action, mischief F1	hərəkət [pl. usually /hərkətē/, /hərkətõ/]
used to do MP	kərte the

MR: Well! I didn't know you used to do such things in [your] childhood!

əccha! mwjhe malum nə tha, ky ap bəcpən mē yy hərkətē kərte the!

good, pure, virtuous A1	nek
were FP	thī
occurrence, event, happening M2	vaqea [or /vaqəya/]
holiday, vacation, leave F2	chwTTi
...'s place, chez Comp Post	[ke] hã
drama M2	Dyrama
alone, only A2	əkela
small garden M2	baɣica
darkness M2	ãdhera
-like, -ish Enclitic [follows a word and agrees with it in number-gender as though A2]	sa
came FS	ai
fear M1	Dər
attached, fastened, struck, hit MS	ləga
frightening, terrifying A2	Dəraona
voice, sound F1	avaz
čame FP	aī
screamed, yelled MS	cixa
ran away, fled, ran MS	bhaga
head M1	sər
struck, collided, ran into MS	Təkraya
blood M1	xun
began to come out MS	nykəlne ləga
were sleeping MP	so rəhe the
ran MP	dəwRe
sign, signal M2	yšara
scream, yell F1	cix
girlfriend (of a girl) F2	səheli
came out, emerged FP	nyklī
began to laugh FP	hãsne ləgī
ashamed, embarrassed PA1	šərmynda
although Conj	əgərce
had to go MS	jana pəRa
scolding, rebuke F1	DãT
fell, befell, happened FS	pəRi
wound, injury F1	coT

sign, scar, mark M1	nyšan
present, existing PA1	məwjud
souvenir, memento F2	nyšani

R: Oh yes, I know you from childhood! [Sarcastically:] You were really so very nice! Perhaps you don't recall that time [lit. event] when [lit. that] I came to your place with my mother during the summer vacations! One night I went to the school [to] see a play. When I returned home alone at eleven o'clock and arrived at the garden of the house, there was something whitish visible in the darkness under a tree. I felt a little afraid [lit. to me some fear attached]. Then from up on top of the tree there came some frightening noises [lit. voices, sounds]. I screamed with fear and ran off towards the house. As I was running [lit. in this fleeing], my head struck a wall, and blood began to flow [lit. come out]. Everyone was sleeping in the house. Because of [lit. from] my noise, they came out of their rooms and ran toward me. The servants ran toward the garden where I was pointing [lit. on my signal]. Hearing my screams, you and your girlfriends too came out from behind the tree, and came to me and really started to laugh. Seeing you [pl.], I was much ashamed. Although I had to go to the hospital, you all got a good scolding for this mischief [lit. act] too. The scar of that wound is still on my head. It is a memento of your childhood.

ji hã, mãy ap ko bəcpən se janta hũ! ap to bəhwt hi nek thĩ! šayəd ap ko vw vaqea yad nəhĩ, ky mãy əpni valda ke sath gərmiõ ki chwTTiõ mẽ ap ke hã aya! ek rat mãy yskul mẽ Dyrama dekhne gəya. jəb mãy gyara bəje əkela ghər vapəs aya, əwr koThi ke bayice mẽ pəhũca, to ãdhere mẽ ek dərəxt ke nice koi səfəyd si ciz nəzər ai. mwjhe kwch Dər ləga. phyr ws dərəxt ke upər se kwch Dəraoni avazẽ aĩ. mãy Dər se cixa, əwr ghər ki tərəf bhaga. ys bhagne mẽ, mera sər divar se Təkraya, əwr xun nykəlne ləga. ghər mẽ səb so rəhe the. mere šor se, vw əpne əpne kəmrõ se nykəl kər meri tərəf dəwRe. mere yšare pər, nəwkər bayice ki tərəf bhage. meri cixẽ swn kər, ap əwr ap ki səheliã bhi dərəxt ke piche se nyklĩ, əwr mere pas pəhũc kər xub hãsne ləgĩ. mãy ap logõ ko dekh kər šərmynda hwa. əgərce mwjhe həspətal jana pəRa, məgər ap səb pər bhi ys hərəkət pər xub DãT pəRi. ws coT ka nyšan əb tək mere sər pər məwjud həy. yy ap ke bəcpən ki nyšani həy.

heroism, bravery F2	bəhadri
answer, reply M1	jəvab

MR: There's nothing to match your heroism either! [Lit. There is also no answer to your heroism!]

ap ki bəhadri ka bhi jəvab nəhĩ!

courage F1	hymmət
village M1	gaõ
used to remain, live, stay MS	rəhta tha
who, which OS	jys
some, a few A1	cənd
used to play MP	khelte the
who, which NS NP	jo
used to frighten MP	Dərate the
ghost M1	bhut
traveller M/F1 A1	mwsafyr
stayed, waited MS	Thəyra
arrived, reached MP	pəhũce
was eating MS	kha rəha tha
finished eating MS	kha cwka
to sleep	sona

bedding, bedclothes M1	bystər
began to take out MP	nykalne ləge
worried, upset, troubled PA1	pərešan
time, term, period M1	dəwran
lamp M1	cyraɣ [or /cəraɣ/]
went out, became extinguished MS	bwjha
became FP	hwĩ
having become, having made oneself	bən kər
having feared	Dər kər
villager M2	gaðvala
mischief F1	šərarət
became FS	hwi
complaint F1	šykayət
arrived, reached FS	pəhw̌ci
therefore Conj	cwnãce
having scolded, rebuked	DãT kər
spoke MP	bole

S: Yes. In [one's] childhood everyone is like that [lit. just thus], and on such occasions courage does not stand by [us] [lit. give company]. I also recall an incident in [my] childhood. When I was ten years old, I used to live in a small village, outside of which there was an oldish house, where at night we few friends used to go and play. And whoever used to come [there], we used to frighten him [away]. It had the reputation [lit. was famous] among the people that there were [lit. are] ghosts in this house. Once a traveller came and stayed in this house. We arrived at that place. It was night time. That man was eating. When he finished eating, he went [lit. arrived] to his bedding to [go to] sleep. Just then [lit. in this much] we all together [lit. having met] began to make [lit. take out] frightening sounds. Hearing these, he became somewhat upset. Meanwhile the lamp went out, because of which [lit. from which] the room became dark [lit. darkness became in the room]. The frightening noises became louder [lit. more sharp]. After this one of us boys made himself up like a ghost [lit. having become a ghost], and came out in front of him, from which that traveller became afraid and fled outside leaving everything. The next day our mischief became known to the villagers, and a complaint reached our house. Thereupon my father scolded me and said, "If such a complaint about you arrives in the future, you will be punished!"

ji hã. bəcpən mẽ səb əyse hi hote hə̃y, əwr əyse məwqõ pər hymmət bhi sath nəhĩ deti. mwjhe bhi bəcpən ka ek vaqea yad həy. jəb mə̃y dəs sal ka tha, mə̃y ek choTe se gaõ me rəhta tha, jys ke bahər ek pwrana sa məkan tha, jəhã rat ko həm cənd dost ja kər khelte the. əwr jo bhi ata tha, wse həm Dərate the. logõ mẽ yy məšhur tha, ky ys məkan mẽ bhut hə̃y. ek dəfa, ek mwsafyr ys məkan mẽ a kər Thəyra. həm ws jəga pəhw̌ce. rat ka vəqt tha. vw admi khana kha rəha tha. jəb vw khana kha cwka, to sone ke lie bystər pər pəhw̌ca. ytne mẽ, həm səb myl kər Dəraoni avazẽ nykalne ləge. vw yy swn kər kwch pərešan hwa. ys dəwran mẽ cyraɣ bwjha, jys se kəmre mẽ ə̃dhera hwa. Dəraoni avazẽ əwr tez hwĩ. ys ke bad, həm mẽ se ek ləRka bhut bən kər ws ke samne aya, jys se Dər kər vw mwsafyr səb kwch choR kər bahər bhaga. dusre roz, gaðvalõ ko həmari šərarət malum hwi, to həmare ghər šykayət pəhw̌ci. cwnãce mere valyd sahəb mwjhe DãT kər bole, ky "əgər aynda twmhare bare mẽ əysi šykayət pəhw̌ci, to səza mylegi!"

9.101. Several terms roughly translatable as "time" have now been introduced: the common word is /vəqt/ M1. /zəmana/ M2 denotes "time, age, era, period": e.g.

/ws badšah ke zəmane mẽ/   in the time of that king

Three new items are: /ərsa/ M2 "time, period," /dəwran/ M1 "time, period," and /dəfa/ F1 "time(s)." The first two of these are semantically quite close and often overlap: e.g.

/ys ərse mẽ/   during this time, period

/ys dəwran mẽ/   during this time, period

/ərsa/, however, seems to have the connotation of a period seen from some point outside its duration: i.e. a period seen as a unit from the point of view of some earlier or later time: e.g.

/ek ərsa hwa, ky ap nəhĩ ae./   It's been a long time since [lit. that] you have not [lit. did not] come. [/ek ərsa hwa/ idiomatically means "it's been a long time."]

/kwch ərse ke bad, mə̃y yy kam kər səkta hũ./   I can do this job after some time.

/dəwran/, on the other hand, denotes a period seen from some indefinite point within its duration: "during the period, while the period was going on," etc. E.g.

/ys dəwran mẽ, ap se mylne ka məwqa nəhĩ myla./   During this period [I] had no opportunity to meet you.

/mə̃y ek ərse se lahəwr mẽ hũ, məgər ys dəwran mẽ yy kam nəhĩ kər səka./   I have been [lit. am] in Lahore for a long time, but during this period [I] have not been able to do this job. [Here again note the idiomatic translation of /ek ərse se/.]

/ys dəwran mẽ/ can also be translated "meanwhile." This may be contrasted with another construction: /ytne mẽ/ "meanwhile, just then, at that moment" (lit. "in this much"). E.g.

/mə̃y əpne kəmre mẽ kam kər rəha tha. ytne mẽ ap ae./   I was working in my room. Just then you came.

Either /ys ərse mẽ/ or /ys dəwran mẽ/ could have been substituted in the above example for /ytne mẽ/. They would denote a longer, more indefinite period during which the action occurred, and they would also lack the immediate, "punctilear" sense of /ytne mẽ/.

/dəfa/ is quite different from all of the above: it is used only in counting individual times or occasions: e.g.

/mə̃y syrf ek hi dəfa gəya./   I went only once.

/yy dusri dəfa həy, ky mə̃y myrcẽ kha rəha hũ./   This is the second time that I am eating peppers.

/ap kytni dəfa jaẽge./   How many times will you go?

/vw tin dəfa vapəs ae./   They came back three times.

9.102. /məwqa/ M2 "occasion, opportunity, time" must be distinguished from /vaqea/ M2 "event, incident, occurrence, happening, time." Compare the following:

/əysi batẽ kəhne ke lie, yy əccha məwqa nəhĩ!/   This is not a good time [occasion, opportunity] to say such things!

/kya, ap ko vw vaqea yad nəhĩ?/ Don't you recall that time [event, incident, happening]?

/vaqea/ is also pronounced as /vaqəya/. A less prestiged pronunciation is /vaqa/. The MOS MNP forms of /vaqea/ (or /vaqəya/) are /vaqəe/; the MOP form is /vaqəõ/. Speakers who say /vaqa/ give /vaqe/ for the MOS MNP form and /vaqõ/ for the MOP form, but these are not considered correct. Note also /vaqəi/ Adv "really, actually," which is derived from the same Arabic root.

9.103. /yad/ F1 "memory, recollection" occurs in various complex formations: (1) /yad ana/ means "to recall, remember, recollect, come to mind." The object remembered is the grammatical subject, and the person remembering is treated as an indirect object marked by /ko/ or its equivalent: e.g.

/ap mwjhe yad ate hə̄y./ I remember you. [Lit. You to me come to memory.]

/vw ləRki ynhē yad ati həy./ He remembers that girl.

(2) An alternate construction similar to complex verb formations of Type B (i.e. like /[X ki] tarif kərna/ "to praise [X]") is also found, still employing /ana/. The thing recollected possesses /yad/; the verb also agrees with /yad/; and the person remembering is marked by /ko/ or its equivalent: e.g.

/mwjhe ap ki yad ati həy./ I remember you. [This is exactly equivalent to /ap mwjhe yad ate hə̄y./ above.]

Both of these constructions denote lack of volition on the part of the person remembering: the memory comes to mind involuntarily. Remembering by conscious effort is expressed by /yad kərna/ (a Type A complex verbal formation). E.g.

/mə̄y ap ko yad kərta hũ./ I (deliberately, consciously) remember you.

9.104. /fwTbal/ M1 "football" is also treated as F1 by some speakers. Differences of opinion about the gender of recently introduced English words are frequent.

9.105. /bolna/ "to speak" denotes vocal articulation only. /kəhna/, on the other hand, is used for the transmission of a meaningful vocal message: "to say, tell, order." One may thus use /bolna/ for the noises made by some animals, but since the noise is not a meaningful message one cannot use /kəhna/.

/bolna/ is often used of languages: e.g.

/vw wrdu bol səkta həy./ He can speak Urdu.

/vw ə̄grezi mē bol rəhe the./ He was speaking in English.

/bolna/ may also take a few other nouns as objects (e.g. /jhuT/ M1 "lie, falsehood"), but it can never take a person as an indirect object. To say */vw mwjh ko bola/ "He said to me" is quite incorrect and would be considered "Sahib's Urdu." One may indeed hear servants in European households employing such a sentence, but the student should avoid this.

9.106. /[ke] thoRi der bad/ "a little later, shortly afterwards" is used either adverbially or as a sort of compound postpositional phrase. It seems to be a shortened form of

/[ki] thoRi der [ke] bad/, but the full form is not used.

> /vw thoRi der bad ae./ He came shortly afterwards.
>
> /ws ke thoRi der bad, vw vapəs ae./ Shortly after that he came back.

9.107. /carõ tərəf/ "in all directions, on all sides" is used adverbially or as a compound postposition. Note that although /tərəf/ is clearly feminine, the postpositional form is /ke carõ tərəf/ rather than /ki carõ tərəf/. Here one may compare /ke dãẽ tərəf/; see Sec. 4.108.

9.108. /gyrna/ "to fall down" and /pəRna/ "to fall, befall, happen" overlap in meaning: the former is used to denote the sharp or sudden falling of physical objects; the latter is also sometimes found with this meaning but also denotes the falling of intangibles and abstracts (e.g. "light," "a scolding," "heat," etc.). /pəRna/ is also employed for the slow falling of nonmeasurable or uncountably tiny objects (e.g. /ola/ M2 "hail" -- but not /baryš/ F1 "rain," which occurs only with /hona/). With various auxiliary verbs /pəRna/ also means "to lie, remain prostrate" (without conscious volition, as a corpse, a wet rag, an unconscious person, etc.). See Sec. 9.310. E.g.

> /dekho, vw admi gyr rəha həy!/ Look out, that man is falling! [One cannot say */vw admi pəR rəha həy./]
>
> /mwjh pər DãT pəRi./ I got a scolding. [Lit. On me a scolding fell.]
>
> /ws pər rəwšni pəR rəhi həy./ Light is falling on it.
>
> /bahər nə jaie! bəhwt tez dhup pəR rəhi həy./ Don't go outside! The sunlight is very strong. [Lit. Very strong sunlight is falling.]
>
> /bərf gyr rəhi həy./ Snow is falling. [One may also hear /bərf pəR rəhi həy./ /bərf/ F1 "snow, ice." Contrast:]
>
> /aj šayəd baryš hogi, məgər ole nəhĩ pəRẽge./ Today perhaps there'll be rain, but hail will not fall. [*/baryš pəRegi/ is not as idiomatic.]

/pəRna/ also means "to fall" in the sense of "falling geographically before or after something." E.g.

> /mera ghər wn ke ghər se pəhle pəRta həy./ My house comes before [i.e. is geographically situated before] their house.
>
> /ws ki dwkan meri dwkan ke bad pəRti həy./ His shop comes after [i.e. is geographically situated after] my shop.

9.109. /[ke] piche piche/ "along behind" has an idea of continuous action. This contrasts with /[ke] piche/, which just denotes location. E.g.

> /vw mere piche piche ae./ They came (following) along behind me.

9.110. "To obey the law" is /qanun ke sath cəlna/. Similarly "to disobey the law" is idiomatically /qanun ke xylaf cəlna/.

9.111. The compound postposition /[ke] hã/ may admit of many translations depending upon the context: "at ... place," "in ... country," "at ... house," etc. /hã/ occurs as the second element in the locative adverb set /yəhã/ "here," /vəhã/ "there," /jəhã/ "where," and /kəhã/ "where?" See Sec. 7.309.

/kya, ap ke hā am hote hɔ̄y?/ Are there mangoes in your country? [Or:
"in your area, " "at your place, " "in your region, " etc. etc.]

/rəhim sahəb mere hā Thəyrɛ̄ge./ Mr. Rəhim will stay at my place.

9.112. /baɣ/ M1 "garden" denotes a fairly large piece of land; /baɣica/ M2 denotes
a small house garden, orchard, plot, etc. The suffix /ica/ or /ca/ is historically from
Persian, where it functions as a diminutive. In Urdu, however, the final /a/ has become
identified with the Type II MNS suffix, and the other forms of /baɣica/ follow the Type II
pattern. For an analysis of Persian affixes in Urdu, see Unit XVIII.

9.113. /ləgna/ "to be attached, fastened, applied, fixed, stuck, struck, hit" occurs in
a wide variety of idiomatic formations. Some are:

(1) With nouns denoting bodily states or conditions. The one perceiving the condition
is treated as an object and marked by /ko/ or its equivalent. E.g.

/mwjhe kwch Dər ləga./ I felt somewhat afraid. [Lit. To me some
fear attached.]

/kya, ap ko gərmi ləg rəhi həy?/ Do you feel warm? [Lit. What, to
you does heat attach?]

(2) With nouns denoting wounds, arrows, bullets, etc. which strike and fix themselves
in the body. E.g.

/mwjhe coT ləgi./ I was wounded. [Lit. To me a wound attached.]

/meri goli ws ko nəhī̆ ləgi./ My bullet didn't hit him. [/goli/ F2 "pill,
bullet, small ball, pellet"]

(3) With adjectives, meaning "to feel, seem." This is analogous to (1) above. E.g.

/wn ki batē mwjhe əcchi nəhī̆ ləgtī̆./ I don't like his words. [I.e. What
he says is offensive to me.]

/yy jəga mwjhe saf nəhī̆ ləgti./ This place doesn't seem clean to me.

(4) With numerals, measures, and other quantifiers in the sense of "to cost, take,
require." E.g.

/ap ke məkan mē kytne pəyse ləgēge./ How much money will your house
cost?

/dəs rupəe ləgēge./ [It] will take ten rupees.

/vəhā jane ke lie kytne ghənTe ləgēge./ How many hours will it take to
go there?

9.114. /nyšan/ M1 "sign, mark, scar" and /nyšani/ F2 "memento, souvenir" are
both derived from the same historical source, but their meanings are quite different.
/nyšani/ is also used for "bookmark."

/yy ap ki nyšani həy./ This is a memento of you.

/yy ap ka nyšan həy./ This is your mark.

9.115. /bəhadri/ F2 and /hymmət/ F1 denote "heroism" and "courage" respectively,
with about the same semantic distinction as that found in English.

9.116. /ap ki bəhadri ka bhi jəvab nəhī̆!/ "There's nothing to match your heroism
either!" is used in a humorously sarcastic sense by Mrs. Rəhim. Just /jəvab nəhī̆!/ alone

255

may be heard as a sort of interjection denoting wonder, admiration, skeptical amazement, etc. Note that this idiom need not always be used sarcastically but may express real wonder and approbation. E.g.

/ys kytab ka jəvab nəhĩ́!/ This book is really wonderful! [Or, with sarcasm, "This book is really the limit!"]

/vaqəi, ap ka jəvab nəhĩ́!/ Really, you have no equal! [Or: "Really, you are impossible!"]

9.117. /[ka] sath dena/ denotes "to accompany, stand by" is a rather special idiom, since /sath/ is otherwise never treated as a real noun (i.e. it cannot be the subject of a sentence, be modified by an adjective, etc.).

/mɜ̃y ap ka sath dūga./ I'll accompany you.

/hymmət ap ka sath nəhĩ́ degi./ Courage will not stand by you.

9.118. /cənd/ Al "some, a few" indicates a number smaller than that denoted by /kwch/ Al "some." /cənd/ should also not be confused with /kəm/ Al, which means "few" as well, but in the sense of "too few, too little." E.g.

/vəhā̃ kwch log the./ There were some people there.

/vəhā̃ cənd log the./ There were some [a few, several] people there.

/vəhā̃ kəm log the./ There were too few people there.

9.119. Total joint effort or participation is expressed by /myl kər/, the conjunctive participle (see Sec. 5.308) of /mylna/ "to meet, get, mix." /myl kər/ normally follows the subject of its sentence. The subject usually includes a numeral adjective or an adjective denoting totality. E.g.

/həm səb myl kər Dəraoni avazē̃ nykalne ləge./ We all together started to make frightening noises.

/həm səb myl kər səyr ko jaēge./ We'll all go for a stroll together.

/byhtər yy hoga, ky həm səb myl kər khana khaē./ It will be better if [lit. that] we all eat together.

/dəs admi myl kər yy pətthər wTha səkte hɜ̃y./ Ten men [all] together can lift this stone.

/sare gaõvale myl kər yy kam kər səkte hɜ̃y./ All of the villagers together can do this job.

9.120. /cyraɣ/ [also pronounced /cəraɣ/] Ml denotes an oil lamp. An electric light is termed /bətti/ F2, which also means "candle" and "wick."

9.121. /bənna/ "to be made, built, constructed, turned into, made into" has many idiomatic usages. E.g.

/ap ka məkan kəb tək bənega./ When will your house be built [i.e. completed]?

/mera ləRka profesər bənna cahta həy./ My boy wants to become a professor. [One cannot say /hona cahta həy/ in the sense of "wants to make himself into."]

/pakystan mē̃ qalin əcche bənte hɜ̃y./ In Pakistan carpets are made well. [Usually translated by the impersonal "they" in English: "In

Pakistan they make carpets well."]

/ys se kya bənega./   What will come of this?

/vw bhut bən kər səb ko Dərate the./   He used to make himself up as a ghost and scare everyone.

/vw bəhwt bənta həy./   He gives himself airs. [This usage is quite idiomatic.]

9.122. /cwnāce/ Conj "therefore, thereupon, as a result of which" has a slightly more resultative emphasis than does /ys lie/. These forms are, however, almost interchangeable. Note /ys lie, ky ... / "for this reason that ... "

9.123. Complex Verbal Formations. See Sec. 7.123.

A:

/məna/

   /məna hona/ to be forbidden, prohibited

   /[X ko Y se] məna kərna/ to forbid [X from doing Y]

/pəreŠan/

   /[X se] pəreŠan hona/ to be worried, troubled [by X]

   /[X ko] pəreŠan kərna/ to worry, trouble [X]

/Šərmynda/

   /[X se] Šərmynda hona/ to be ashamed, embarrassed [because of X]

   /[X ko] Šərmynda kərna/ to embarrass [X]

B:

/səyr/

   /[X ki] səyr kərna/ to stroll around [X], take a pleasure trip around in [X]

/Šykayət/

   /[X ki] Šykayət hona/ to be a complaint against [X]

   /[X ki] Šykayət kərna/ to complain against [X]

/tarif/

   /[X ki] tarif hona/ [X] to be praised

   /[X ki] tarif kərna/ to praise [X]

D:

/jəvab/

   /[X ko] jəvab dena/ to answer [X], reply [to X]

   /[X se] jəvab māgna/ to seek an answer [from X]

   /[X ko] jəvab mylna/ [X] to get a reply. [Idiomatically also: "[X] to be dismissed from his post"]

/səza/

   /[X ko Y ki] səza dena/ to give a punishment [to X consisting of Y]

   /[X ko] səza hona/ [X] to be punished

   /[X ko] səza mylna/ [X] to receive punishment

F:

/avaz/

257

/avaz ana/ voice, sound to be audible, be heard

    /[X ko] avaz dena/ to call [to X]

    /[X ko] avaz nykalna/ to call out to, cry out [to X]

/bəhadri/

    /[X ko] bəhadri dykhana/ to act bravely [before X]

    /bəhadri kərna/ to act heroically

/chwTTi/

    /[X ko] chwTTi dena/ to give [X] a holiday. [Idiomatically also: "to dismiss [X] from his post"]

    /chwTTi kərna/ to take a holiday

/coT/

    /[X ko Y se] coT ləgna/ [X] to be wounded, receive an injury [from Y]

/der/

    /[X ko] der hona/ [X] to be late, tardy

    /der kərna/ to delay, be tardy

    /der ləgana/ to delay, take time

/hərəkət/

    /[X se, ke sath] hərəkət kərna/ to misbehave [with X], do some mischievous action [to X]

/hymmət/

    /[X ko] hymmət dykhana/ to act courageously [before X]

    /[X ki] hymmət kərna/ to take courage, have courage [to do X]

/nyšan/

    /[X pər] nyšan ləgana/ to put a mark [on X]

/sath/

    /[X ka] sath dena/ to accompany, stand by [X]

/šadi/

    /[X se, ke sath] šadi hona/ to be married [to X]

    /[X se, ke sath] šadi kərna/ to marry [X]

/šərarət/

    /[X se, ke sath] šərarət kərna/ to do mischief [to X]

/šəwq/

    /[X ko Y ka] šəwq hona/ [X] to enjoy, be interested in, have a taste [for Y]

    /[X se] šəwq fərmana, kərna/ to begin, taste [X]. [I.e. as food offered: /ys se šəwq fərmaie!/ "Please taste this!"]

/šor/

    /šor hona/ to be a noise, be noisy

    /šor kərna, məcana/ to make noise, raise a commotion

/yad/

    /[X ko Y] yad ana/ [X] to remember [Y]. [See Sec. 9.103.]

    /[X ko Y ki] yad ana/ [X] to remember [Y]

    /[X ko Y ki] yad hona/ [X] to remember [Y]

    /[X ko] yad kərna/ to deliberately recall [X], think about [X]

/yšara/

    /[X ko] yšara dena, kərna/ to give, make a signal [to X]

9.201. Flapped, Trilled, and Lateral Sounds.

There are three "r-like" sounds in Urdu and also a lateral "l." None of these are exactly identical with English "r" or "l," as pronounced either in standard southern British English or as in midwestern North American English.

The "r-like" sounds include: (1) /r/, a single dental flap, made as in Spanish or Italian by a quick tap of the tongue tip against the alveolar ridge just behind the upper front teeth. (2) /rr/, a dental trill, produced by repeated vibration of the tongue tip touching the alveolar ridge behind the upper front teeth (as for /r/). The contrast between these two sounds is found in Spanish, where, for example, pero "but" contrasts with perro "dog." (3) /R/, a retroflex flap, produced by the turning back of the tongue tip (as for /T/, /D/) and then flapping the tongue tip sharply forward and down against the back of the alveolar ridge. Although this sound does not occur in any dialect of English, a rapid American pronunciation of a word like hardy might be interpreted by a non-English-speaking Indian or Pakistani as /haRi/. (An Urdu speaker familiar with English spelling would render this as /harDi/, however.)

/r/ occurs at the beginning of words, medially between vowels, before and after consonants, and word-finally. /rr/ is found between vowels only. /R/ occurs between vowels, before and after consonants, and at the end of words. /R/ also occurs with /h/ as /Rh/: i.e. an aspirated retroflex flap.

Urdu /l/ is always a "light l": i.e. it is always dental with no raising of the back of the tongue. In American English, a final "l" is almost always a "dark l": i.e. it is produced by the tongue tip touching the alveolar ridge and with the back of the tongue raised. A "dark l" is incorrect for Urdu. The student should compare his pronunciation of a word like fail with the same word as pronounced by an Urdu speaker. One may also compare English null with Urdu /nəl/ Ml "tube, pipe, tap" or English sill with /syl/ Fl "lower grinding stone."

/bar/ time, turn	/baR/ edge, fence
/baRh/ flood	/bal/ hair
/kar/ car	/kal/ famine
/kər/ do!	/kəR/ sunflower seeds
/kəRh/ be embroidered [root]	/kəl/ yesterday, tomorrow
/bər/ engagement proposal for a girl	/bəR/ banyan tree
/bəRh/ grow, expand!	/bəl/ curve, twist, loop
/bwra/ bad	/bərra/ sheep
/bəRa/ big, large	/bəRha/ grew, expanded MS
/bəla/ calamity	/bəlla/ pole
/pərta/ reel for thread	/pəRta/ befalling MS
/pəRhta/ reading MS	/pəlta/ being brought up MS
/pəRna/ to happen, befall	/pəRhna/ to read, study
	/pəlna/ to be brought up

259

/gər/ if (poetic)

/gəRh/ citadel

/gara/ thick mud

/gaRha/ thick (as a fluid)

/kori/ unused, blank

/koRhi/ leper

/jərna/ to burn [alt. for /jəlna/]

/jhəRna/ to fall, drop

/sari/ whole, entire

/saRhi/ "sari," same as /saRi/

/mor/ peacock

/curi/ type of cake

/coli/ bodice

/khəra/ pure, genuine

/khəRa/ standing, erect

/bhərana/ to cause to fill

/zəra/ a little, a bit, just

/mədarys/ schools

/rakh/ ashes

/ru/ face

/rəb/ Lord, God

/gəR/ be dug in [root]

/gəl/ throat, neck

/gaRa/ dug, concealed MS

/gala/ flock of cotton

/kəwRi/ small shell, cowry

/koli/ weaver

/jəRna/ to be joined, fixed

/jəlna/ to burn

/saRi/ "sari," woman's costume

/sali/ younger sister-in-law

/moR/ turn, bend

/mol/ buying

/cuRi/ bangle

/cuhRi/ sweeper woman

/khərra/ rough draft

/khəla/ teased MS

/khəlla/ old shoe

/bhərrana/ to become hoarse

/zərra/ particle

/mwdərrys/ teacher

/lakh/ hundred thousand

/lu/ hot wind

/ləb/ lip

9.302. Phonetic Drill: Auditory Dictation.

1. ləb   lu   sali   gala   pəlta   jəlna   kəl   bal   mol   bəlla   khəla

2. ru   rakh   rəb   zəra   bwra   kori   pərta   bar   mor   kər

3. bəRa   kəwRi   saRi   gaRa   pəRta   jəRna   baR   moR   bəR   cuRi

4. saRhi   koRhi   pəRhta   pəRhna   kaRh   gəRh   baRh   gaRha

5. bwra   bərra   khərra   bhərana   mwdərrys   khəra   bhərrana   mədarys
   zərra   zəra

6. ləb   ru   sari   gəl   mor   rəb   gara   bal   sali   gər   pəlta   jəlna
   khəla

7. bəla   khəla   bəlla   khəlla

8. sari   gəR   bəRa   mor   kəR   zəra   saRi   gər   jəRna   jərna

9. pəRta   saRhi   kaRh   moR   cuRi   bəRha   gəRh   jəRna   koRhi

10. gəl   kər   bəlla   sari   sali   lu   bhərrana   coli   khəra   gaRha   pərta
    bəl   gara   gər

260

9.300. ANALYSIS

9.301. Substantive Composition: Verb Stems as Nouns.

Considering the number of verb stems available in Urdu, the occurrence of a verb stem as an independent noun is not really a frequent phenomenon. Nevertheless, many common examples exist. Those introduced so far include:

/cixna/ to scream, yell	/cix/ F1 scream, yell
/Dərna/ to fear, be afraid	/Dər/ M1 fear
/DāTna/ to scold, rebuke	/DāT/ F1 scolding, rebuke
/khelna/ to play	/khel/ M1 game, play

All of the above are Hindi in origin, but Persian examples are also found: e.g. /xərid/ F1 "purchase, purchase price." Questions of derivation will be dealt with in Units XVIII and XIX.

9.302. Substantive Composition: Compounds With /bəd/.

/bədqysməti/ F2 [np] "ill fortune, bad luck" is an example of the suffix /i/ "abstract noun formant" (see Sec. 7.301) affixed to an adjective which is itself a compound: /bəd/ "bad" + /qysmət/ F1 "fate, fortune" = /bədqysmət/ A1 "ill-fortuned." Aside from its use as an element in compounds, /bəd/ is also found as A1, meaning "bad, evil." Other compounds with /bəd/ possible with the vocabulary introduced so far include:

/nam/ M1 name	/bədnam/ A1 infamous
/nəzər/ F1 vision, sight	/bədnəzər/ A1 having the evil eye, having a wicked or lascivious glance
/surət/ F1 form, state, condition, case, face [not yet introduced.]	/bədsurət/ A1 ugly

All of the above occur with /i/ "abstract noun formant," although /bədnəzəri/ is rare.

9.303. The Relative Pronoun.

The relative pronoun /jo/ has already been mentioned in Unit VII (7.309). Its forms are:

/jo/	NS NP who, which
/jys/	OS whom, which
/jyn/	OP whom, which
/jyse/	OS whom, which. [Special object form]
/jynhẽ/	OP whom, which. [Special object form]

This pattern is similar to that of /kəwn/ "who?" discussed in Sec. 2.310.

All of the above except the special object forms may be used as "adjectives": i.e. modifying a following noun. This too is parallel to /kəwn/ and its forms. Compounds of /jo/ with other quantifiers and relative adjectives are also common: e.g. /jo kwch/ "whatever," /jo koi/ "whoever" (oblique: /jys kysi/). /jo/ also occurs with /ky/ as /jo ky/ or less commonly /ky jo/ with much the same meaning as /jo/ alone. No oblique forms of

/jo ky/ are found, however (i.e. */jys ky/, */jyn ky/ are not found, although informants stated that /jyse ky/ and /jynhẽ ky/ might rarely be heard).

/jo/ and its various forms are employed as follows:

(1) Correlational formations: Like /jəysa ... vəysa .../ "as ... so ...," /jytna ... wtna .../ "as much as ... that much ...," /jo/ may be used to introduce a relative clause. There is no special correlative pronoun, however, (like /vəysa/, /wtna/) although in old Urdu a pronoun /so/ fulfilled this function. In modern Urdu the correlative of /jo/ is mostly just /yy/ or /vw/; /so/ is rare.

(2) Appositional formations: the /jo/ clause has the same referent as some nearby noun or pronoun. Appositional clauses usually follow their referent, but they may also be found preceding it as well.

Examples of both usages:

/jo əccha admi hoga, vw əysi hərəkət nəhĩ kərega./ Who [i.e. he who] is a good man, he will not do such a thing [lit. action].

/mãy bhi wsi DakTər ke pas jaũga, jys ke pas ap jaẽge./ I will go to that same doctor, to whom you will go.

/vw admi, jo roz ata həy, mera dost həy./ That man, who comes every day, is my friend. [In this appositional usage, /jo ky/ or /ky jo/ could have also been employed.]

/jys jəga ap jate hãy, aj mãy bhi vəhã jaũga./ That place [to] which you go, I also will go there today.

/jyse ap pəsənd kərẽge, vwhi mwjhe pəsənd hoga./ Whichever one you will like, that same one will please me.

/vw ləRke, jynhẽ ap jante hãy, yəhĩ rəhte hãy./ Those boys, whom you know, live right here.

/jyn cizõ ki zərurət thi, vw məwjud hãy./ Those things which were necessary, they are present.

/jo kwch ap ko cahie, vw ap ko mylega./ Whatever you need, you will get it.

/jo koi bhi ana cahta həy, vw səkta həy./ Whoever wants to come, he can come. [/bhi/ has the force of "at all" here: "whosoever, whoever at all."]

/jo jo cizẽ ap ko cahiẽ, aj ja kər xəridie!/ Whatever things you need, please go today and buy [them]!

9.304. The Enclitic /sa/.

The enclitic /sa/ "-like, -ish" occurs after a preceding word (almost always an adjective). It renders the meaning of the adjective somewhat less definite. It may also be translated as "rather ..." or "quite ..." Note that /sa/ is treated like a Type II adjective, and /si/ or /se/ will occur depending upon the number-gender-case of the following noun.

/ek nili si ymarət nəzər ati həy./ There is a bluish building visible.

/ek bəRe se dərəxt ke nice khəRa həy./ [It] is standing beneath a rather large tree.

/mere pas car bəRe se suTkes hãy./ I have four largish suitcases.

/thoRa sa khana dijie!/ Please give [me] a little food!

In one or two cases the distinction between an adjective + /sa/ and the same adjective without it is somewhat more complex. /bəhwt/ Al "many, very, a lot, much" denotes an

indefinitely large quantity, while /bəhwt sa/ denotes a rather smaller quantity: "largish."
/bəhwt sa/ also enumerates the objects quantified, however, whereas /bəhwt/ simply refers
to an indefinite mass. In the case of /thoRa/ A2 "little, small" and /thoRa sa/, the latter
is generally more common since /sa/ tends to specify and diminish the quantity named.

/ws ke pas bəhwt pəyse hɛ̃y./   He has a lot of money. [/bəhwt/ here
denotes an indefinitely large quantity rather than an enumeration of
individual units. /bəhwt se pəyse/ is thus not idiomatic in the sense
of "a lot of money." /pəysa/ M2 may also denote a small coin,
however, and in this sense /bəhwt se pəyse/ could mean a lot of one
pəysa coins."]

/kəl bəhwt log aẽge./   Many people will come tomorrow. [/bəhwt se/
would denote a somewhat smaller number and would also tend to
individualise /log/: i.e. "many individuals, many separate persons."]

/mere pas bəhwt si kytabẽ hɛ̃y./   I have rather a lot of books. [Here
again the sense of specific, individual books is found. /bəhwt/ here
would simply denote a large and nonspecific aggregate of books.]

/mwjhe thoRa sa pani dijie!/   Please give me a little water! [/thoRa pani/
is not incorrect, but /thoRa sa pani/ is more frequently found.]

9.305. Sequences of Two or More Postpositions.

Two or even three postpositions may occur after a noun. The sense of these sequences
is usually self-evident. E.g.

/vw chət pər se gyra./   He fell off the roof. [Lit. from off. /pər se/
is idiomatically employed in Urdu where English might use just "off":
/se/ alone here would not be quite as idiomatic.]

/vw zəmin ke nice se nykla./   It came out of the ground. [Lit. from
below]

/dərəxt ke upər se avazẽ ane ləgĩ./   Voices started to come from up in
the tree.

/Dybbe mẽ se nykalo!/   Take [it] out of the box! [Here again /se/ alone
would not be quite as idiomatic.]

9.306. The Verb: Causal (Etc.) Stems.

The following discussion is presented at this point in its entirety primarily for ease of
reference. The student has not had forms of all of the types given below, but he will be
able to refer back to this Section as new items are introduced.

Urdu has two types of simplex stem: intransitive (which do not occur with a syntactic
object), and transitive (which may occur with an object, or with an object and an indirect
object, or even with two objects).

Two further stems may be formed from transitive or intransitive roots by means of
suffixes and sometimes by internal vowel alternation: the "causative" and the "double
causative." Vowel alternation (and sometimes various other devices) are also used to
produce an intransitive stem from a basically transitive stem. If a transitive stem exists,
then its causative, double, causative, and intransitive forms will all be predictable from it
(although not all of these need necessarily occur). If the root is basically intransitive, then
the causative and double causative stems are usually predictable from it. There are various

263

irregularities, of course, and the majority of verbs perhaps lack a complete "set" of stems.

Although examples of all of these stem types have not yet been introduced in this course, the student will have noted such pairs as the following:

/dekhna/ to see	/dykhana/ to show
/Dərna/ to fear, be afraid	/Dərana/ to frighten
/nykəlna/ to go out	/nykalna/ to take out
/wtərna/ to go down	/wtarna/ to take down

The four stem types may be characterised as follows:

(1) Intransitive: the verb takes no object, and the subject itself performs the action. E.g.

/mə̃y Dərta hū./ I fear.

/mə̃y wtərta hū./ I go down, descend, alight, get off.

(2) Transitive: the verb takes an object (or an object and an indirect object, or even two objects): e.g.

/mə̃y yy kam kərta hū./ I do this work.

/mə̃y wse swnta hū./ I hear it [or: him]; I listen to it [or: him].

(3) Causative: basically intransitive simplex stems are treated as transitive; transitive stems become causative: i.e. the subject causes some intermediate actor to perform the action on the object. If expressed, the intermediate actor will be marked by /se/ (or in some cases by other compound postpositions: e.g. /[ke] hath/ "by the hand of," /[ke] zərie/ "by, through, by means of"). E.g.

/mə̃y wse Dərata hū./ I frighten him. [I.e. I cause that he fears.]

/mə̃y wse cəlata hū./ I make it go, drive it. [I.e. I cause that it goes.]

/mə̃y ws se yy kam kəraūga./ I will get him to do this work. [Lit. I will cause this work to be done by him.]

/mə̃y wse swnata hū./ I tell it [or: him, to him]. [Lit. I cause that it be heard. Or: I cause him to hear.]

(4) Double Causative: basically intransitive simplex stems become causative; transitive stems become causative with meanings similar to those described under (3) above but with stronger connotations of intermediate causality. Again, the intermediary, if expressed, will be marked with /se/, /[ke] hath/, etc. Many causative and double causative stems of transitive verbs have almost identical meanings, but there are some which display semantic differences also. E.g.

/mə̃y yy saman qwli se wThvaūga./ I'll get the coolie to pick up the luggage. [Lit. I will cause the luggage to be picked up by the coolie.]

/mə̃y ws se yy kam kərvaūga./ I'll get him to do this work. [This carries more causal connotations than the third example under (3) above.]

/mə̃y ap ko ws se yy bat swnva səkta hū./ I can have him tell you this matter. [Lit. I can cause you to hear this matter by means of him.]

/mə̃y əpne lie əysi hi ciz bənvaūga./ I'll get just such a thing made for myself.

The formation of these various stem forms from a basically transitive simplex verb is as follows:

(1) The causative suffix /a/ occurs after roots consisting of a monosyllable ending in a consonant (or a consonant + /h/): e.g.

/kərna/ to do	/kərana/ to cause to do
/lykhna/ to write	/lykhana/ to cause to write

Internal vowel alternation occurs when the simplex stem contains one of the long vowels (/i, e, a, u, o/: stems containing /i/ or /e/ have /y/ in their causative form; those with /u/ or /o/ have /w/; and those with /a/ have /ə/. Simplex stems having a nasalised long vowel (/ĩ, ẽ, ã, ũ, õ/) generally have /y/, /w/ or /ə/ without nasalisation in their causative forms. There are, however, various exceptions to this (see the fifth example below). Stems having /əy/ generally have /y/ in their causative forms, but those having /əw/ retain the /əw/ diphthong intact. E. g.

/dekhna/ to see	/dykhana/ to show
/kaTna/ to cut	/kəTana/ to cause to be cut
/kholna/ to open	/khwlana/ to cause to be opened
/khẽcna/ to pull, draw	/khycana/ to cause to be pulled, drawn
/mãgna/ to ask for, request	/məgana/ to cause to be asked for, requested

Simplex stems ending in a vowel (only /i, e, a, u, o/ occur) have the same pattern of alternation as that just described, but the causative suffix is /la/ rather than /a/. E. g.

/dena/ to give	/dylana/ to cause to be given
/dhona/ to wash	/dhwlana/ to cause to be washed
/pina/ to drink	/pylana/ to cause to be drunk

Some items are irregular:

/khana/ to eat	/khylana/ to feed, cause to eat. [*/khəlana/ might have been expected.]
/lena/ to take	/lyvana/ to cause to be taken. [This form is almost obsolete in modern Urdu. */lylana/ might have been expected.]

As might be expected from Sec. 4.315, stems ending in /əCəC(h)/ have /əCC(h)/ instead before the causative suffix /a/. E. g.

/pəkəRna/ to catch, grab	/pəkRana/ to cause to be caught
/səməjhna/ to understand	/səmjhana/ to cause to be understood, to explain

Occasional changes also occur in the final root consonants of causative stems: e. g. simplex transitive stems ending in /R/ may have a root-final /T/ instead in their causative form. E. g.

/choRna/ to leave, abandon	/chwTana/ to cause to be left, abandoned. [Also /chwRana/ in modern Urdu.]

Some stems ending in /əh/ have the alternate /la/ as the form of the causative suffix. Various stems ending in /kh/, /Th/, and rarely in other aspirates also have optional forms with /la/, although these are not generally considered elegant in standard Urdu. E. g.

/kəhna/ to say, tell	/kəhlana/ to cause to say; to be called, named. [/kəhana/ exists but is rare; /kəhlana/ is standard.]
/sikhna/ to learn	/sykhlana/ to cause to be learned. [/sykhana/ is standard.]
/dekhna/ to see	/dykhlana/ to show, cause to be seen. [/dykhana/ is considered better.]

(2) The formation of the double causative stem of transitive verbs is almost identical with the above; the suffix, however, is /va/ instead of /a/ (and /lva/ instead of /la/).

Internal vowel alternations, consonant modifications, etc. are as described above, except that, under the provisions of Sec. 4.315, /əCəC(h)/ cannot become */əCC(h)/ when /va/ is employed. E.g.

/kərna/ to do	/kərvana/ to cause to be done
/dekhna/ to see	/dykhvana/ to cause to be seen, cause to see, cause to be shown
/kaTna/ to cut	/kəTvana/ to cause to be cut
/dhona/ to wash	/dhwlvana/ to cause to be washed
/pina/ to drink	/pylvana/ to cause to be drunk, to give to drink
/khana/ to eat	/khylvana/ to cause to be eaten, to cause to be fed
/pəkəRna/ to catch, grab	/pəkəRvana/ to cause to be caught
/choRna/ to leave, abandon	/chwTvana/ to cause to be left, abandoned. [Also /chwRvana/.]
/kəhna/ to say, tell	/kəhlvana/ to cause to be told

Many transitive verbs have a double causative stem but no causative. E.g.

/nykalna/ to take out	/nykəlvana/ to cause to be taken out. [But no */nyklana/.]
/bhejna/ to send	/bhyjvana/ to cause to be sent. [But no */bhyjana/.]
/wtarna/ to take down	/wtərvana/ to cause to be taken down. [But no */wtrana/.]

One of this group has an unusual alternation of /c/ with /k/:

/becna/ to sell	/bykvana/ to cause to be sold

(3) Some transitive verbs also have an intransitive stem. Such verbs are taken as basically transitive rather than as basically intransitive because it is possible to predict the intransitive form from the transitive but not vice versa. In every case the intransitive stem consists of the causative or double causative stem form but without /a/ or /va/. E.g.

/wtarna/ to take down	/wtərna/ to go down, alight, get off. [I.e. the same stem form as /wtərvana/, except that the double causative suffix /va/ does not occur.]
/nykalna/ to take out	/nykəlna/ to go out
/khēcna/ to pull, draw	/khycna/ to be pulled, drawn
/kaTna/ to cut	/kəTna/ to be cut, get cut
/becna/ to sell	/bykna/ to be sold, get sold
/choRna/ to leave, abandon	/chwTna/ to escape, get free
/kholna/ to open	/khwlna/ to come open
/dekhna/ to see	/dykhna/ to be seen, be visible
/dhona/ to wash	/dhwlna/ to be washed, get washed

The formation of various stem forms from a basically intransitive simplex verb is as follows:

(1) The causative stem is formed by the addition of the suffix /a/. The rules given above for vowel alternation also apply here, and the suffix alternant /la/ occurs after stems which would otherwise end in a vowel. As stated above, the meaning of the causative stem of an intransitive verb is really transitive rather than causative. Examples of all types:

/bəjna/ to ring, strike, play [intrans.]	/bəjana/ to ring, strike, play [trans.]
/bənna/ to be made	/bənana/ to make, build, construct
/cəlna/ to go, move	/cəlana/ to cause to go, move, drive
/məcna/ to be raised (voice, noise, commotion)	/məcana/ to raise (noise, commotion)
/wThna/ to rise, get up	/wThana/ to raise, lift
/bhagna/ to flee, run away	/bhəgana/ to chase away, cause to flee
/cixna/ to scream	/cyxana/ to cause to scream
/bəyThna/ to sit	/byThana/ to seat, cause to sit
/bolna/ to speak	/bwlana/ to call. [Note the semantic change.]
/rona/ to weep, cry	/rwlana/ to make cry
/sona/ to sleep	/swlana/ to put to sleep
/pyghəlna/ to melt [intrans.]	/pyghlana/ to melt [trans.]

Occasional irregularities, both of form and meaning, are also found. E.g.

/Thəyrna/ to wait	/Thəyrana/ or /Thəhrana/ to make wait, hold back, delay. [The alternate stem form /Thəhr/ is rather archaic in the intransitive form (/Thəhrna/), but the causative form /Thəhrana/ is sometimes found.]
/cwkna/ to be finished [only after verb stems.]	/cwkana/ to finish, settle (a bill). [Used only as an independent stem.]

(2) The double causative form is identical to that just described, except that the suffix is /va/ (or /lva/) instead of /a/. E.g.

/bənna/ to be made	/bənvana/ to cause to be made
/bwjhna/ to be extinguished, go out (light)	/bwjhvana/ to cause to be extinguished
/pəhw̌cna/ to arrive	/pəhw̌cvana/ to cause to arrive, to have something brought
/hə̃sna/ to laugh	/hə̃svana/ to cause to laugh
/rona/ to weep, cry	/rwlvana/ to cause to weep [through some intermediary]
/wThna/ to rise, get up	/wThvana/ to cause to be lifted, raised

As has just been seen, Urdu verb stems may be divided into two major classes: transitive and intransitive. Transitive verbs may be modified to produce causative, double causative, or intransitive stem forms; intransitives occur with similar modifications to produce causative and double causative stems. Although this pattern of stem formation holds good generally throughout the language, there are nevertheless a great many defective sets; i.e. simplex stems from which a complete set of derived forms cannot be made. It will be useful to add a list of all verbs introduced so far at this point, divided into classes of permitted occurrence of derived stems. The student is not expected to learn these forms at this time -- indeed, some stems are quite rare (e.g. /lyvana/ from /lena/ "to take") -- but it is important that the basic structure of this system be learned in order that verbs introduced in later Units will not be just "new words" with no apparent system, but will fit into an established pattern.

I.   Basically Transitive Simplex Stems.

Ia. Transitive only: i.e. no intransitive, causative, or double causative forms are found: /bətana/, /fərmana/, /janna/.

Ib. Transitive and Causative only: /lena/.

Ic. Transitive, Causative, and Double Causative: /dena/, /kəhna/, /kərna/, /khana/, /khelna/, /lykhna/, /pəhnna/, /pəkəRna/, /pəRhna/, /pina/, /rəkhna/, /swnna/.

Id. Transitive and Double Causative only: /bhejna/, /DāTna/, /puchna/, /xəridna/.

Ie. Transitive, Causative, Double Causative, and Intransitive: /choRna/, /dekhna/, /dhona/, /kaTna/, /khēcna/, /kholna/.

If. Transitive, Double Causative, and Intransitive: /becna/, /nykalna/, /wtarna/.

II. Basically Intransitive Simplex Stems.

IIa. Intransitive only: /ana/, /cahna/, /hona/, /jana/, /lana/, /rəhna/, /səkna/.

IIb. Intransitive and Causative only: /ləwTna/, /Thəyrna/.

IIc. Intransitive, Causative, and Double Causative: /bəjna/, /bənna/, /bəyThna/, /bhagna/, /bolna/, /bwjhna/, /cəlna/, /cəRhna/, /cixna/, /cwkna/, /dəwRna/, /Dərna/, /gyrna/, /hə̃sna/, /ləgna/, /məcna/, /mylna/, /pəhw̄cna/, /pəRna/, /rona/, /sona/, /wThna/.

III. Intransitive-Transitive Simplex Stems.

IIIa. Intransitive-Transitive, Causative, and Double Causative: /bədəlna/, /səməjhna/

IIIb. Intransitive-Transitive only: /Təkrana/.

No examples of other possible types have as yet been introduced:

I. Basically Transitive Simplex Stems.

Ig. Transitive and Intransitive only.

Ih. Transitive, Causative, and Intransitive.

II. Basically Intransitive Simplex Stems.

IId. Intransitive and Double Causative.

III. Intransitive-Transitive Simplex Stems.

IIIc. Intransitive-Transitive and Causative.

IIId. Intransitive-Transitive and Double Causative.

9.307. The Verb: The Past Participle.

The past participle consists of a verb stem + a set of endings identical with those described for the present participle (Secs. 2.312 and 3.312). A sample paradigm is:

MS	/pəRha/
MP	/pəRhe/
FS	/pəRhi/
FP	/pəRhī/

This participle is employed alone with no auxiliary as the simple past tense. It denotes a single action or state occurring at a unitary point of past time. When the verb stem is intransitive, the participle agrees with its subject in number and gender so far as possible (for transitive stems, however, see Sec. 11.303). A complete intransitive paradigm is:

PRONOUN	VERB: MASCULINE	FEMININE	
mə̃y	dəwRa	dəwRi	_I ran
[tu	dəwRa	dəwRi	thou ranst]

PRONOUN	VERB: MASCULINE	FEMININE	
vw	dəwRa	dəwRi	he, she, it ran
həm	dəwRe	dəwRĭ	we ran
twm	dəwRe	dəwRĭ	you [nonhonorific] ran
ap	dəwRe	dəwRĭ	you [honorific] ran
vw	dəwRe	dəwRĭ	they ran

The first person plural feminine is commonly expressed by the MP verb rather than the expected FP form: i.e. /həm dəwRe/ instead of /həm dəwRĭ/.

Stems ending in /a/, /ə/, or /o/ have stem alternants ending in /y/ before the MS suffix /a/. E.g.

/aya/ came [MS]	/roya/ wept, cried [MS]
/gəya/ went [MS]	/soya/ slept [MS]

No /y/ occurs, however, before the other affixes:

/ae/ came [MP]	/roe/ wept, cried [MP]
/ai/ came [FS]	/roi/ wept, cried [FS]
/aĭ/ came [FP]	/roĭ/ wept, cried [FP]
/gəe/ went [MP]	/soe/ slept [MP]
/gəi/ went [FS]	/soi/ slept [FS]
/gəĭ/ went [FP]	/soĭ/ slept [FP]

Note that no /y/ is found in the MS form of the past participles of stems ending in other vowels:

/pia/ drank [MS]	/hwa/ became [MS]

Six verbs have irregular past stem alternants. In most dialects one of these six is also rapidly becoming obsolete. Two of these introduced in this Unit are:

(1) /gə-/ is the past stem of /ja-/ "go." Its forms have been given above.

(2) /hw-/ is the past stem of /ho-/ "be, become."

The past forms of /ho-/ just mentioned are employed in the sense of "became": i.e. a progression from one state to another state in the past. The simple static past ("was," "were") is rendered by another set of quite irregular forms, which are the past tense counterparts of /həy/, /hə̃y/, etc. Both sets of forms are as follows:

/hwa/ became [MS]	/tha/ was [MS]
/hwe/ became [MP]	/the/ were [MP]
/hwi/ became [FS]	/thi/ was [FS]
/hwĭ/ became [FP]	/thĭ/ were [FP]

The negative for the simple past tense is either /nə/ or /nəhĭ/. Both are correct, but the latter carries slightly stronger connotations of emphasis and negation. /nə/ is often found in connected narratives where no special emphasis is desired, while /nəhĭ/ is found in isolated (and hence slightly more emphatic) statements. Compare:

/fwTbal vapəs nə myla./ [I] didn't get the football back. [The negative follows naturally and unemphatically from the context; see Sec. 9.000]

/fwTbal vapəs nəhĭ myla./ [I] didn't get the football back. [The statement is an independent element in the discourse: perhaps the answer to a question like, "What happened to the football?"]

9.308. The Verb: /tha/ as an Auxiliary.

The past tense copula /tha/ (and other forms of its paradigm) functions exactly like the present tense auxiliary /həy/ (etc.) in a variety of auxiliary verb formations. Some of these are:

(1) The < PreP + /tha/ > construction: the "imperfect": "used to do." The present participle agrees with the auxiliary in number-gender, except in the feminine plural, where no nasalisation occurs to match the nasalisation of the auxiliary (Cf. Sec. 3.312). A sample paradigm is:

/kərta tha/ used to do [MS]
/kərte the/ used to do [MP]
/kərti thĩ/ used to do [FS]
/kərti thĩ/ used to do [FP]. [Never */kərtĩ thĩ/.]

As previously stated, the MP form is most frequently employed for the first person feminine plural: i.e. /həm khate the/ "we used to eat" instead of /həm khati thĩ/.

The negative for this construction is /nəhĩ/.

(2) The < S + /rəha/ > construction provides a "past continuative": "was doing," etc. Again the MS form is employed for the first person feminine plural. The negative used with this formation is /nəhĩ/. A sample paradigm is:

/kər rəha tha/ was doing [MS]
/kər rəhe the/ were doing [MP]
/kər rəhi thi/ was doing [FS]
/kər rəhi thĩ/ were doing [FP]

(3) The < S + /səkta tha/ > construction: "used to be able to ..." Other remarks made for nos. 1 and 2 above apply here also. A sample paradigm is:

/kər səkta tha/ was able to do [MS]
/kər səkte the/ were able to do [MP]
/kər səkti thi/ was able to do [FS]
/kər səkti thĩ/ were able to do [FP]

(4) The < /cahie/ + /tha/ > construction: "must have ..., ought to have ..." A sample paradigm is:

/cahie tha/ was needed, must have, ought to have [MS]
/cahiẽ the/ were needed, must have, ought to have [MP]
/cahie thi/ was needed, must have, ought to have [FS]
/cahiẽ thĩ/ were needed, must have, ought to have [FP]

Some speakers do not employ the nasalised form /cahiẽ/ before the auxiliary, using /cahie/ instead. The negative for this formation is /nəhĩ/.

Some examples:

/ap ko vəhã jana cahie tha./ You ought to have gone there.
/kya, ap ko yy cizẽ cahiẽ thĩ?/ Did you need these things? [See Sec. 3.314.]
/yy pyali dhoni cahie thi./ [You] should have washed this cup.

9.309. The Verb: the < S + /cwkna/ > Construction.

The second member auxiliary /cwkna/ means "to be completed, finished, ended" or, since the connotation of termination which it bears is rather weak, just "already." Like /səkna/ "to be able," it never occurs as an independent verb but must always follow the stem of some other verb. The < S + /cwkna/ > formation is most commonly employed in the past tenses, less frequently in the future, rarely in the present, and not at all in the various continuative formations. /cwkna/ agrees, so far as possible, with the person-number-gender of the subject of its clause. Some examples are:

/mə̃y kam kər cwka./ I finished this work.

/mə̃y yy təsvir dekh cwka./ I've already seen this picture. [Lit. finished seeing.]

/jəb həm yy kam kər cwkẽge, to səyr kərne jaẽge./ When we finish [lit. will finish] this work, we'll go far a stroll.

/jəb ap khana kha cwkẽ, to mwjhe Telifun kərẽ. phyr həm donõ bazar cəlẽge./ When you finish eating dinner, please telephone me. Then we both will go to the market.

Although negative forms of this construction are indeed occasionally found, they are not considered to be good Urdu.

9.310. The Verb: the < I + /pəRna/ > Construction.

The infinitive occurs with forms of /pəRna/ "to fall, befall, happen" meaning "must do ..., be forced to do ..., cannot help but do ..." The person compelled to perform the action is marked by /ko/ or its equivalent. One thus says: "To X going befell," etc. This construction is closely comparable to the < I + /həy/ > construction (see Sec. 2.313), which also means "must do ..., have to ..." There is an important semantic difference, however. Compare:

/mwjhe jana həy./ I have to go. [I.e. I have the duty, obligation, necessity, etc. to go.]

/mwjhe jana pəRta həy./ I have to go. [I.e. I am forced, compelled to go. I cannot do otherwise.]

If the verb is transitive and has an object, both the infinitive and the occurring form of /pəRna/ will agree with the object in number-gender so far as possible. There are dialects, however, in which the infinitive does not agree with the object but remains invariably masculine nominative singular -- exactly parallel with formations like < I + /həy/ > and < I + /cahie/ >. If the infinitive is intransitive, or if no object occurs, then the infinitive and the occurring form of /pəRna/ will both be masculine singular. E.g.

/mwjhe ek əwr kytab xəridni pəRi./ I was compelled to buy one more book. [Cf. /mwjhe ek əwr kytab xəridni həy./ "I have to buy one more book." and /mwjhe ek əwr kytab xəridni cahie./ "I ought to buy one more book." The infinitive (/xəridni/) and the occurring form of /pəRna/ both agree with /kytab/ F1 "book."]

/ap ko dena pəRega./ You'll have to give [it]. [No object is expressed, and the infinitive and the occurring form of /pəRna/ are both MS.]

/ap ko vw chwri deni pəRegi./ You'll have to give that knife. [The object is expressed. It governs the number-gender of both /deni/ and /pəRegi/.]

/aj mwjhe do suTkes xəridne pəRēge./   Today I'll have to buy two suitcases.

9.311. The Verb: The < OI + /ləgna/ > Construction.

A form of the infinitive is also found before forms of /ləgna/ "to attach, be fastened,
applied, struck." This construction means "to begin to ..." It is important to note that,
unlike the preceding construction, here the infinitive invariably occurs in the oblique form
(i.e. ends in /e/) before the occurring form of /ləgna/. This infinitive never changes to
agree with the person-number-gender of either the subject or the object. The occurring
form of /ləgna/, however, does agree with the subject in person-number-gender so far as
possible.

This construction signifies the beginning of some act or process which may continue
over an indefinite period of time: e.g. playing, weeping, going, etc. The beginning of a
single unitary act is not usually signified by the < OI + /ləgna/ > construction but by a
complex verb formation involving /šwru/ M1 "beginning": /[X ko] šwru kərna/ "to begin
[X]."

The negative is almost never employed with the < OI + /ləgna/ > construction. "Not to
begin" is normally expressed by /nəhī/ and some form of /šwru kərna/ (or, intransitively,
/šwru hona/).

Past tense examples of this construction are commonest, while future tense forms
also occur. Present tense occurrences are somewhat more rare. E.g.

/mə̃y khelne ləga./   I started to play.
/vw ləRke dəwRne ləge./   Those boys started to run.
/vw ləRkiã rone ləgī./   Those girls started to cry.
/vw ws vəqt khelne ləgēge./   At that time they'll start to play.
/wn ke valyd jane ləge./   Their father started to go.

Note the agreement of the verb in the following sentences:

/vw pani pine ləga./   He began to drink the water.
/vw cae pine ləga./   He began to drink the tea.
/wse pani pina pəRa./   He had to drink the water.
/wse cae pini pəRi./   He had to drink the tea.

9.312. The Verb: The OI + Verbs of Motion.

The oblique infinitive ending in /e/ also occurs directly before various verbs of motion.
The commonest of these are, of course, /jana/ "to go" and /ana/ "to come." Although one
might expect a postposition between the OI and the verb, this is not idiomatic: i.e. /kərne
gəya/ "went to do" and not /kərne ko gəya/ or /kərne ke lie gəya/.

The negative /nəhī/ (and less commonly /nə/) occasionally occurs between the OI and
the verb. See the last example below.

/vw əpna kam kərne gəya./   He went to do his work.
/vw ws ko Thik kərne aya./   He came to fix it.
/vw ap se mylne ae./   He came to meet you.

/meri beTi khana khane gəi. /　My daughter went to eat dinner.

/mə̃y pani pine jaũga. /　I'll go to drink water.

/vw əpna kam kərne nəhĩ gəya. /　He did not go to do his work.

9.313. Conditional Clauses With the Past Tense.

A very common type of conditional sentence is that in which the conditional clause contains a past tense verb, and the resultative clause contains a verb in the future tense (etc.). This denotes a simple future condition and a simple future result, both with a high degree of likelihood. This formation was mentioned in Sec. 7.312 (3), and it has now been introduced in this Unit. E. g.

/əgər aynda twmhare bare mẽ əysi šykayət pəhw̃ci, to səza mylegi. /　If such a complaint about you reaches me [lit. arrives] in the future, [you] will be punished.

/əgər məsjyd ka dərvaza bənd hwa, to həm kəl dekhne aẽge. /　If the door of the mosque is shut [in the future], then we will come [to] see [it] tomorrow.

/əgər mə̃y ytvar ko lahəwr nə gəya, to ap ke sath jaũga. /　If I don't go to Lahore on Sunday, then I'll go with you.

9.401. Supplementary Vocabulary.

The following numerals are all Type I adjectives. See Sec. 2.401.

chəttys	thirty-six
sə̃ytys	thirty-seven
əRtys	thirty-eight
wntalys [or /wncalys/ in some Eastern dialects]	thirty-nine
calys	forty

As with other numerals ending in /ys/, there is a "spelling pronunciation" ending in /is/ for all of the above.

Other items are:

bərf F1 [Some speakers treat this as F1 when referring to "snow" and as M1 when speaking of "a piece of ice".]	snow, ice
masTər M1	teacher, master
sərdi F2	cold [noun]

9.402. Supplementary Exercise I: Substitution.

1. masTər sahəb ki kylas mẽ <u>pəccys</u>   ləRke hə̃y.

   thirty-nine
   forty
   twenty-two
   only thirty-six
   thirty-eight

2. <u>gərmi</u> ke məwsəm mẽ, <u>dhup</u> bəhwt <u>hoti hə̃y</u>.

heat	grapes	are
cold	snow	is
heat	fruits	are
heat	rain	is
cold	wind	is

9.500. VOCABULARY AND GRAMMAR DRILL

9.501. Substitution.

1. <u>bəcpən mɛ̃</u>   mɛ̃y bəhwt   <u>ata tha.</u>
   in the field   used to run
   on Saturday   used to do work
   in that time[1]   used to eat
   at his place   used to laugh
   on such an occasion   used to fear
       [1]Here "time" should be translated /zəmana/.

2. bəhwt ərsa hwa, ky   <u>vw</u>   <u>nəhɪ̃ aya.</u>
                we   did not laugh
                we   did not meet with you
                rain   did not fall
                you   were not seen[1]
                I   did not go there
       [1]Lit. "did not come [to] view."

3. <u>mere ghər ke aspas</u>   <u>koi səyr ki jəga</u>   nəhɪ̃ <u>thi.</u>
   in the house of your   any servant   was
   girlfriend
   in that big mosque   any person   was
   in this building   any window   was
   in that time   any good king   was
   with [/se/] the   to me any complaint   was
   villagers

4. <u>əndər a kər,</u>   həm <u>fwTbal</u>   <u>khelne ləge.</u>
   having gone outside   noise   started to make
   having gone home   complaint started to make
   having gone into the   prayer   started to read
   mosque
   having arrived there   voices   started to give
   having eaten food   tea   started to drink

5. jəb həm <u>khel rəhe the,</u> to <u>ek polisvala</u>   <u>aya.</u>
        were doing mischief   the villagers   arrived
        were sleeping   the boys   started to make noise
        were taking   the children   started to laugh
        pictures
        were climbing on   our mother   started to fear
        the tree
        were going   rain   started to fall[1]
       [1]Lit. "become."

6. <u>wse</u>   <u>fəwrən wTha kər,</u> vw <u>əpne dəftər mɛ̃</u>   <u>gəya.</u>
   clothes   having changed   mosque   arrived
   food   having eaten   school   arrived

275

ghost	having seen	from fear	fled
hat	having put on	from the house	went out
blood	having seen	hospital	went

7. kya, ap <u>bəcpən mẽ</u>   <u>yy hərkətẽ kərte the?</u>
in school	used to do this mischief
on the roof	used to sleep
against the law	used to go
in this garden	used to play
in this condition	used to stay

8. mẽy <u>əpni valda ke sath</u>   <u>ap ke hã</u>   <u>aya.</u>
with my brother	their place	went
with the traveller	my place	arrived
with my friend	in the city	went to see the cinema
with my servant	the market	went to buy fruit
with my friends	prayer	went to read

9. <u>ek dərəxt ke nice</u>   <u>koi səfəyd si ciz</u>   <u>nəzər ati həy.</u>
on your hand	a blackish mark	is seen
under that wall	a biggish stone	is seen
in the mosque	a tallish minaret	is seen
near the fort	a smallish palace	is seen
in this vessel	a little bit of sugar	is seen

10. <u>ek rat,</u>   mẽy <u>Dyrama</u>   <u>dekhne</u>   gəya.
yesterday	stroll	do
many times	football	play
at that time	his condition	see
that day	arrangement of the marriage	do
after a little while	with [/se/] my friend	meet

11. <u>ws coT ka nyšan</u>   <u>mere sər pər</u>   məwjud həy.
that palace	in the old fort
this law	in the book
the sign of blood	on the road
the coolie	outside the carriage
your girlfriend	in the garden

12. <u>ap ki bəhadri</u>   ka jəvab nəhĩ!
| this book |
| your courage |
| this mischief |
| this drama |
| this season |

13. <u>vw admi</u>   <u>khana</u>   <u>kha rəha tha.</u>
| that boy | on the tree | was climbing |
| your girlfriend | from the roof | was going down |

our watchman	fruit	was buying
my father	us	was scolding
the policeman	signal	was giving

14. jəb vw <u>khana</u>   <u>kha cwka</u>,   to mə̃y <u>khane ləga.</u>

	complaint	finished making	started to cry
	--	finished speaking	started to write
	mischief	finished making	started to laugh
	book	finished reading	started to read
	this work	finished doing	started to scold

15. vw <u>yy</u>   <u>swn kər</u>   kwch pərešan   hwa.

	this matter	having said	somewhat ashamed
	baggage	having taken	ready
	oranges	having eaten	sick
	this book	having written	famous
	home	having come	ready

9.502. Transformation.

1. Change the underlined verb forms in the following sentences to:
   a. the simple past: e.g. /ata həy/ to /aya/.
   b. the imperfect: e.g. /ata həy/ to /ata tha/.
   c. the past continuative: e.g. /ata həy/ to /a rəha tha/.

a. vw ləRkiā̃ bayice mẽ dəwRti hə̃y.
b. ys dəftər mẽ bəhwt kam hota həy.
c. bazar mẽ dudh <u>mylta həy</u>.
d. vw gaõ se <u>ata həy</u>.
e. gaRi Thik vəqt pər nəhĩ̄ pəh̆wcti.
f. vw car bəje əpne dəftər se <u>ləwTta həy</u>.
g. vw bhut se nəhĩ̄ <u>Dərte</u>.
h. vw Dər se <u>cixti həy</u>.
i. ap xub <u>sote hə̃y</u>.
j. twm ws kəpRevale ki dwkan pər <u>jate ho</u>.

2. Change the underlined verbs in the following sentences to:
   a. The inflected (oblique) infinitive + the past tense of /ləgna/: e.g. /khata həy/ to /khane ləga/.
   b. The stem + the past tense of /cwkna/: e.g. /khata həy/ to /kha cwka/.

a. vw səyr <u>kərta həy</u>.
b. cyray <u>bwjhta həy</u>.
c. vw bat <u>kərta həy</u>.
d. ləRka kytab <u>pəRhta həy</u>.
e. vw kəpRe <u>bədəlti həy</u>.
f. ə̃grez hwkumət <u>kərte hə̃y</u>.
g. qwli saman <u>wtarta həy</u>.

h. phəlvala dwkan <u>kholta</u> həy.

i. vw dwkan se phəl <u>xəridta</u> həy.

j. vw šadi ka yntyzam <u>kərta</u> həy.

3. Change the underlined verb forms in the following sentences to the corresponding simple past tense forms. See Sec. 9.313.

a. əgər mə̃y ləhəwr <u>jaũga</u>, to ap ke lie ek kytab laũga.

b. əgər mə̃y yəhã kwch ərsa əwr <u>rəhũ</u>, to yy səb cizẽ təyyar kər səkũga.

c. əgər twm yskul se <u>bhagoge</u>, to twmhẽ səza mylegi.

d. əgər kəl swba bərf <u>gyrti həy</u>, to mə̃y dəftər nəhĩ jaũga.

e. əgər vw vəqt pər <u>ləwTta həy</u>, to həm səb sath cəlẽge.

f. əgər vw kəmre se bahər nəhĩ <u>nykəlta həy</u>, to həm polis ko bwlaẽge.

g. əgər vw vəqt pər nəhĩ <u>pəhw̃cta həy</u>, to həm ws ka yntyzar nəhĩ kərẽge.

h. əgər ap se yy kam ek dyn mẽ nəhĩ <u>hota həy</u>, to kysi əwr ko bwlana pəRega.

i. əgər mə̃y ap ke lie fwTbal <u>laũ</u>, to kya, ap ko pəsənd aega?

j. əgər aj qəla bənd <u>hoga</u>, to həm kəl dekhne jaẽge.

9.503. Variation.

1. mə̃y šərmynda hwa.

mə̃y əpne valyd ke samne šərmynda hwa.

mə̃y ys bat pər əpne valyd ke samne šərmynda hwa.

mə̃y əpni ys hərəkət pər šərmynda nəhĩ hwa.

vw əpni šərarət pər gaõvalõ ke samne šərmynda hwe.

vw kalyj mẽ əpne profesər ke samne šərmynda hwi.

2. vw ap ki bəhwt tarif kərti həy.

vw pakystan ki bəhwt tarif kərta həy.

vw kylas ke bad profesər ki bəhwt tarif kərne ləga.

ws ki səheli ws ki hymmət ki tarif kərne ləgi.

badšah əpni fəwj ki tarif kər rəha tha.

vw ys kytab ki tarif nəhĩ kərta.

3. ap ki nyšani əb tək mere pas həy.

mere bəcpən ke dost ki nyšani mere pas məwjud həy.

ap ki koi nyšani ys vəqt mere pas nəhĩ.

ap ki yy nyšani mə̃y əpne pas rəkh rəha hũ.

mə̃y ap ko əpne dost ki nyšani dykha səkta hũ.

kya, ap əpni koi nyšani mwjhe de səkẽge?

4. ləRkõ ko zyada khelne se məna kərna cahie.

əpne bəccõ ko šərarət kərne se məna kijie!

mere valyd sahəb mwjhe synima jane se məna kərte the.

polis ys səRək pər jane se məna kərti həy.

DakTər mwjhe zyada kəwfi pine se məna kərte həy.

DakTər kəwfi ke zyada ystemal ko məna kərte hə̃y.

5. ys məsjyd ke aspas bəhwt si ymartẽ hə̃y.

ys məhl ke aspas bəhwt si pwrani divarẽ hãy.

ys pwrane qəle ke aspas bəhwt se baγ the.

gaõ ke aspas kwch bəRe məydan hãy.

mere ghər ke aspas cənd dwkanẽ thĩ.

ap ke aspas kys qysm ke log rəhte hãy.

6. mwjhe vəhã jana pəRa.

ysmyth sahəb ko kəraci jana pəRega.

chwTTi ke bad, mwjhe ghər jana pəRa.

ytvar ko bhi, mwjhe kalyj jana pəRta həy.

synima ke bad, ap ko fəwrən ghər jana pəRega.

aj mwjhe yskul nəhĩ jana pəRa.

7. jəb mãy kam kər cwka, to mãy ws ke hã gəya.

jəb mãy khana kha cwka, to həm səb myl kər ws ke hã gəe.

jəb mãy saman wtar cwka, to ytne mẽ ek qwli aya.

jəb mãy γwsl kər cwka, to mãy kəpRe bədəlne ləga.

jəb mãy gaRi se wtər cwka, to mwjhe suTkes yad aya.

jəb vw ja cwka, to mwjhe ws ki yad ai.

8. ws dyn, mwjhe bolne ka məwqa nəhĩ myla.

ys dəwran mẽ, mwjhe cae pine ka məwqa nəhĩ myla.

ws vəqt, həmẽ khana khane ka məwqa nəhĩ myla.

ys ərse mẽ, həmẽ qəla dekhne ka məwqa nəhĩ myla.

āynda, ap ko yy kam kərne ka məwqa nəhĩ mylega.

pəhaR pər ja kər, ap ko xub səyr kərne ka məwqa mylega.

9. ap nəhĩ ae, cwnãce mwjhe vəhã əkela jana pəRa.

ap nəhĩ ae, cwnãce mwjhe sara kam kərna pəRa.

dwkan bənd thi, cwnãce mãy cini nə xərid səka.

mere pas vw kytab nə thi, cwnãce mwjhe ghər vapəs jana pəRa.

do dyn se baryš ho rəhi thi, cwnãce mãy yskul nə ja səka.

mere sər mẽ coT ləgi, cwnãce mwjhe həspətal jana pəRa.

10. vw ek choTe se gaõ mẽ rəhte the.

mãy ek choTe se šəhr mẽ rəhti thi.

meri səheli ws səfəyd si ymarət mẽ rəhti həy.

bəhwt se log ys gaõ mẽ rəhte hãy.

ys təsvir mẽ, ek bəRa sa qəla nəzər ata həy.

ws ke pas ek əcchi si gae thi.

11. jo ləRka yəhã rəhta tha, vw kəhã gəya.

jo jo phul əcche hãy, mãy səb xəridũga.

jyn ləRkõ se həm myle, vw kəl həmare pas aẽge.

jys kam se ap məna kərẽge, mãy vw nəhĩ kərũga.

jys se aj həmẽ mylna tha, vw həspətal mẽ həy.

ap, jys məwqe ka yntyzar kər rəhe hãy, vw kəbhi nəhĩ aega.

12. ap ka fərz həy, ky hwkumət ke qanun pər cəlẽ.

ap ka fərz həy, ky əpni valda ko pərešan nə kərẽ.

ap ka fərz həy, ky kylas ka kam roz kərē.

ap ka fərz həy, ky ap ys ke bare mē kwch malum kərē.

həmara fərz həy, ky həm hər roz pāc vəqt nəmaz pəRhē.

həmara fərz həy, ky həm dusrõ ko təklif nə dē.

13. bədqysməti se, mə̃y gaRi nəhī pəkəR səka.

bədqysməti se, mə̃y Thik vəqt pər nəhī pəhw̃c səka.

bədqysməti se, mə̃y wn se nə myl səka.

bədqysməti se, mə̃y kəl bimar tha.

bədqysməti se, mə̃y ws vəqt vəhā məwjud nəhī tha.

bədqysməti se, mə̃y aj əpni kytab nəhī laya.

14. vw qanun ke xylaf batē kərne ləge.

vw polisvale ke xylaf šykayət kərne ləge.

vw qanun ke xylaf təsvirē khēcne ləgī.

vw kylas mē mere xylaf bolne ləge.

vw logõ se mere xylaf kwch batē kəh rəhe the.

twmhē bəRõ ke xylaf əysi batē nəhī kərni cahiē.

15. səb əpne əpne ghər vapəs ləwTe.

swba, mere ləRke əpne əpne yskul jate hə̃y.

yəhā səb əpne əpne kam mē məsruf rəhte hə̃y.

meri ləRkiã əpni əpni səheliõ ke sath khelti hə̃y.

həm səb əpna əpna khana əpne sath late hə̃y.

ws məwqe pər, hər admi əpna əpna vaqea bətane ləga.

9.504. Translation.

Translate the following sentences into English. Then, laying aside the original, translate the English translation back into Urdu. The instructor should discuss problems of
idiom and usage.

1. Examples of /pəRna/.

a. ws qwli ko gaRi se mera saman wtarna pəRa.

b. səb ko nəmaz pəRhni pəRti həy.

c. ap ko Dyrame ke lie car TykəT xəridne pəRēge.

d. ap ki ys hərəkət pər mwjhe šərmynda hona pəRa.

e. ws ləRke ki šərarət pər, mwjhe ws ko DāTna pəRa.

f. baryš nə hone ki vəja se, bəhwt gərmi pəRi.

g. cād ki rəwšni zəmin pər pəR rəhi thi.

h. ws gaõ se pəhle, ek dərya pəRta həy.

i. ys šərarət ki vəja se, həm pər xub DāT pəRi.

j. aj bəhwt tez dhup pəR rəhi həy.

2. Examples of /ləgna/.

a. mere ləRke baγice mē khelna ləge.

b. vw mwjhe əmrikən ləgte hə̃y.

c. dhup ki vəja se, mwjhe gərmi ləg rəhi həy.

d. cavəl mwjhe əcche ləgte h̃əy.

e. ws məkan mẽ, mwjhe Dər ləgne ləga.

f. ys kam mẽ kytne dyn ləgẽge.

g. wn ko coT ləgi.

h. vw admi mwjhe əccha nəhĩ ləgta.

i. ys ymarət ke bənane mẽ kytne rupəe ləgẽge.

j. yəh̃ə se kəraci jane ke lie, kytne ghənTe ləgte h̃əy.

3. Examples of /bənna/.

a. ws dwkan mẽ suTkes əcche bənte h̃əy.

b. yy məkan kytne dyn̄ə mẽ bənega.

c. yy kəpRa kəh̃ə bənta həy.

d. cini pakyṣtan mẽ, bhi bənti həy.

e. m̃əy bəRa ho kər profesər bən̄uga.

f. aj kwch pəyse nəhĩ bəne.

g. ws ki bivi bəhwt bənti həy.

h. ap ke ys kam se kwch nəhĩ bəna.

i. ys Dyrame mẽ ap tāgevala bən̄ege, əwr m̃əy phəlvala bən̄uga.

j. ys qysm ki Topi syrf pakystan mẽ bənti həy.

9.505. Response.

1. kya, ap bəcpən mẽ fwTbal khelte the?

2. ap yəh̃ə kytne bəje ae.

3. ap əmrika mẽ kəwnse šəhr mẽ rəhte the.

4. kəl rat ap kəh̃ə the.

5. kya, ap bəcpən mẽ šərarət kərte the?

6. ys se pəhle, ap kəwnse yskul mẽ pəRhte the.

7. kya, ap pər bhi kəbhi DāT pəRi?

8. kya, ap ko əpne bəcpən ka koi vaqea yad həy?

9. kya, bəcpən mẽ ap bhi mwsafyr̃ə ko Dərate the?

10. kya, ap Thik vəqt pər yskul pəh̃w̆cte the, ya der se.

11. ap ki šadi kəb hwi.

12. kya, ap ko pwrane šəhr dekhne ka šəwq həy?

13. kya, ap ke dəftər ke aspas koi b̃əyk həy?

14. pakystan ke bare mẽ ap ka kya xyal həy.

15. ap kytni dəfa əpne mwlk se bahər gəe.

9.506. Conversation Practice.

After finishing their picnic lunch, the two families are still sitting in Shalimar Gardens.

MS: šərarət to həm bhi kərte the, məgər həmari šərarət kysi əwr qysm ki hoti thi. šayəd ap ko malum həy, ky šəhr ke log gaõvalõ se zyada tez hote h̃əy, əwr bhut ke bare mẽ səməjhte h̃əy, ky vw koi ciz nəhĩ, əwr wn se nəhĩ Dərte.

281

mɛ̃y jəb niw yark mɛ̃ thi, to satvĭ kylas mɛ̃ pəRhti thi. yskul ka vəqt swba nəw
bəje se šam car bəje tək tha. dopəhr ko, bara bəje se ek bəje tək khane ke lie ek ghənTe
ki chwTTi hoti thi. həm səb əpna əpna khana əpne sath late the. həmare masTər bhi
əpna khana əpne sath late the, əwr əpne əpne kəmrõ mɛ̃ rəkhte the.

ek dyn, mɛ̃y əwr meri ek səheli masTər sahəb ke kəmre mɛ̃ kysi kam ke lie gəe,[1]
masTər sahəb vəhā̃ məwjud nəhĭ the. wn ka khana wn ki mez pər tha. yy dekh kər,
həmẽ ek šərarət ka xyal aya. həm vw khana wTha kər bahər nykle, əwr dusre kəmre
mɛ̃ ja kər khane ləge.

thoRi der bad, masTər sahəb əpne kəmre mɛ̃ pəhw̃ce. khane ka vəqt tha, məgər
jəb khana nəhĭ myla, to pərešan hwe, əwr sidhe həmare kəmre mɛ̃ ae, jəhā̃ həm khana
kha rəhe the, əwr əpni ys šərarət pər xub hɛ̃s rəhe the. masTər sahəb ko dekh kər,
həm fəwrən bahər ki tərəf bhage. vw həmẽ pəkəR kər bole, ky "twm kəhā̃ jati ho!"

həm pəhle hi Dər rəhe the. yy swn kər, əwr bhi pərešan hwe. jəb masTər sahəb
ki nəzər khane pər pəRi, to vw puchne ləge, ky "mera khana kəhā̃ həy!" mɛ̃y boli,
"mwjhe to malum nəhĭ." vw mez ki tərəf yšara kər ke bole, ky "yy kys ki hərəkat həy!
yy mera khana yəhā̃ kəwn laya!" yy dekh kər, həm rone ləge. masTər sahəb DāT kər
bole, ky "əcchi ləRkiā̃ əysi hərkətẽ nəhĭ kərtĭ." həm bəhwt šərmynda hwe, əwr kylas
ki tərəf bhage.

MR: yy bhi əccha hwa, ky syrf DāT hi pəRi. malum hota həy, ky masTər sahəb bəhwt
šərif admi the.

MS: ji hā̃. vw vaqəi bəhwt nek admi the, əwr həmẽ bəhwt əcchi əcchi batẽ bətate the. həm
səb bhi wnhẽ bəhwt pəsənd kərte the. vw əksər həm se kəhte the, ky "mere bad, meri
batẽ yad aẽgi." əwr vaqəi Thik həy. əgərce əb ərsa hwa, ky mɛ̃y masTər sahəb se
nəhĭ myl səki, əwr mwjhe malum nəhĭ, ky vw əb kəhā̃ hɛ̃y, məgər wn ki batẽ aj bhi
mwjhe yad hɛ̃y.

R: mera xyal həy, ky əb həmẽ ghər cəlna cahie. ys lie ky baɣ bənd ho rəha həy.

S: ji hā̃. mera bhi yyhi xyal həy. aj ka dyn bəhwt dylcəsp rəha. səyr bhi hwi, əwr xub
batẽ bhi hwĭ.

MS: əysa məwqa hər roz nəhĭ ata. aj ka dyn vaqəi bəhwt əccha tha.

R: aie, gaRi mɛ̃ təšrif rəkhie. əb ghər cəlte hɛ̃y.

MS [getting into the car]: šwkria.

MR: mwjhe larəns roD pər wtərna həy. ys lie ky mwjhe əpni səheli ke hā̃ jana həy. wn se
kwch zəruri kam həy.

R: bəhwt əccha, məgər jəldi vapəs aie!

MR: kyɔ̃? əgər der se ati hū̃, to kya, ap bhi mwjhe bhut bən kər Dəraẽge?

R: ji nəhĭ, yy to ap hi ka kam tha. mɛ̃y to ys lie kəhta hū̃, ky aj šam ko khane ka bhi
yntyzam kərna həy.

MR: bəhwt əccha. jəldi ləwTũgi. ap fykr nə kərẽ!

---

[1]Note that Mrs. Smith employs the masculine plural everywhere for the first person
plural feminine: i.e. /həm gəe/ instead of /həm gəĭ/. The latter would also be
quite correct.

9.507. Conversation Stimulus.

If the student wishes to employ past tense verbs in constructing dialogues for this exercise, he must take care to use only those which are <u>intransitive</u>. He may also use /lana/ "to bring," /bədəlna/ "to change," and perhaps /səməjhna/ "to understand." Both transitive and intransitive verbs may be employed in the past imperfect, past continuous, < S + /cwkna/ >, or < OI + /ləgna/ > formations, however. The past tense of transitive verbs will be introduced in Unit XI. It may be easier for the student at this stage to construct dialogues employing only present or future verb forms.

Topics may include the following:

1.   A bit of childhood mischief.
2.   A ghost story.
3.   A policeman and some children.
4.   One's childhood neighbourhood.
5.   A visit to Shalimar Gardens.

9.600. VOCABULARY

Hereafter, the stem class of each new verb will be listed in the Vocabulary section of each Unit according to the classification given in Sec. 9.306. This will be followed by the stem vowel of the derived forms. E. g.

> /bwjhna/ [IIc: /w/]. [IIc denotes an intransitive simplex stem which may have both a causative and a double causative form. The vowel of these forms is /w/. Thus: /bwjhana/ "to extinguish, put out" and /bwjhvana/ "to cause to be extinguished, have put out."]

If the new verb is itself a derived form, its stem type (i. e. causative, double causative, or intransitive), its simplex form, and its stem class will be listed. Abbreviations are: "C" = "causative"; "DC" = "double causative"; and "I" = "intransitive." E. g.

> /Dərana/ [C: /Dərna/: IIc]. [This denotes that /Dərana/ is the causative form of the simplex /Dərna/, which is a IIc stem (see above).]

Irregular past stems are listed in the Vocabulary preceded by an asterisk. They are not counted as "new words." New verbs with regular past stems are given as usual in their infinitive forms.

[ke] aspas Comp Post Adv	around, in the vicinity of, near about, surrounding, in the environs of
avaz F1	voice, sound
aynda A1 Adv	future; in future
əgərce Conj	although
əkela A2	alone, only, single
ərsa M2	period, term, time
əRtys [or /əRtis/] A1	thirty-eight
ə̃dhera M2 A2	darkness; dark
baγica M2	garden, orchard
[ke] bare [mẽ] Comp Post	about, concerning
bəcpən M1	childhood
bədqysməti F2 [np]	ill fortune, bad luck, misfortune
bəhadri F2	heroism
bənna [IIc: /ə/]	to be made, built, constructed; to result; to be transformed into, become, be turned into
bərf F1 [or M1]	snow, ice
bhagna [IIc: /ə/]	to flee, run away, run
bhut M1	ghost
bolna [IIc: /w/]	to speak, say, utter
bwjhna [IIc: /w/]	to go out (light), become extinguished
bystər M1	bedding
calys [or /calis/] A1	forty
cənd A1	few, a few, some few
chəttys [or /chəttis/] A1	thirty-six
chwTTi F2	vacation, holiday, leave
cix F1	scream, cry, yell

284

cixna [IIc: /y/]	to scream, cry, yell
coT Fl	wound, injury
cwkna [IIc: /w/ -- in other meanings]	to be finished, completed, already ...
cwnãce Conj	therefore, thereupon
cyraɣ [or /cəraɣ/] Ml	lamp
dəfa Fl [np]	time, occasion
dəwran Ml [np]	time, term, period
dəwRna [IIc: /əw/]	to run
der Fl	lateness, tardiness
DāT F˙	scolding, reprimand
DāTna [Id: /ə/]	to scold, reprimand
Dər Ml	fear, fright
Dərana [C: /Dərna/: IIc]	to frighten, terrify
Dəraona A2	frightening, terrifying
Dərna [IIc: /ə/]	to fear, be afraid
Dyrama M2	drama, play
fərz Ml	duty, obligation
fwTbal Ml [or Fl]	football
gaõ Ml	village
gaõvala M2 A2	villager
*gəya / gəe / gəi / gəĩ	went [irreg. past of /jana/ "to go"]
gyrna [IIc: /y/]	to fall
halət Fl	state, condition
[ke] hã Comp Post	[at ...] place, at, chez
hərəkət Fl	act, action, motion; mischief, mischievous act
hõsna [IIc: /õ/]	to laugh
*hwa / hwe / hwi / hwĩ	became [irreg. past of /hona/ "to be, become"]
hymmət Fl	courage
jəvab Ml	answer, reply
jo NS NP	who, which, what [sg. or pl.]
jyn OP	whom, which [pl.]
jynhẽ Pl. Sp. Obj. Form	whom [pl.]
jys OS	whom, which [sg.]
jyse Sg. Sp. Obj. Form	whom [sg.]
kəraci F2 [np]	Karachi (a city in West Pakistan)
ləgna [IIc: /ə/]	to be attached, fixed, applied, stuck, struck; to begin
ləwTna [IIb: /əw/]	to return, go back
masTər Ml	teacher, master
məcana [C: /məcna/: IIc]	to raise (noise, commotion)
məna PA1	forbidden, prohibited
məwjud PA1 [rarely A1]	present, existing
məwqa M2	occasion, opportunity, time
mwsafyr Ml	traveller

nek A1	good, virtuous, pure
nykəlna [I: /nykalna/: If]	to go out, emerge
nyšan M1	mark, sign, scar
nyšani F2	memento, souvenir
pərešan PA1	worried, upset, troubled
pəRna [IIc: /ə/]	to fall, befall, happen; to be compelled to, have to ...
polisvala M2	policeman
qanun M1	law, regulation, statute
rona [IIc: /w/ + /l/]	to cry, weep
sa Enclitic [follows a word and agrees with it in number-gender like A2]	-ish, -like, rather, quite
səheli F2	girlfriend (of a girl only)
sər M1	head
sərdi F2	cold; cold season, winter
səyr F1	walk, stroll, promenade, pleasure or sight-seeing trip
səza F1	punishment
sə̃ytys [or /sə̃yʌis/] A1	thirty-seven
sidha A2 Adv	straight, direct
sona [IIc: /w/ + /l/]	to sleep
šadi F2	marriage
šərarət F1	mischief
šərmynda PA1	ashamed, embarrassed
šəwq M1	desire, enthusiasm, taste, predilection
šor M1	noise, uproar, commotion
šykayət F1	complaint
tarif F1	praise [also "definition" and "introduction"]
*tha / the / thi / thĩ	was, were [irreg. past of /hona/ "to be, become"]
Təkrana [IIIb]	to collide, strike together, run into, strike, hit
vaqəi Adv	really, truly
vaqea [or /vaqəya/] M2	occurrence, event, happening, incident
wntalys [or /wntalis/ or /wncalys/ or /wncalis/] A1	thirty-nine
xub Adv	thoroughly, well, really
xun M1	blood
[ke] xylaf Comp Post Adv	against, contrary to, in opposition to
yad F1	memory, recollection
yšara M2	sign, signal

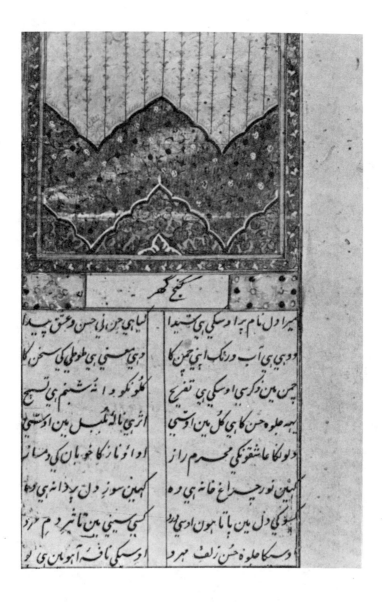

The title page of a manuscript of the works of
Mirza Muhammad Rafi Sawda, written during the
poet's lifetime (i.e. before 1781).

UNIT TEN

10.000. SCRIPT III

Items to be introduced in this Unit include: (1) the four remaining letter groups, (2) the /həmza/, a special symbol used to mark the beginning of a vowel initial syllable within the word, (3) a diacritic used to indicate a doubled consonant, and (4) various less common symbols and conventions employed in Arabic and Persian loanwords.

10.001. Letter Group 7.

This group includes ص /s/ and ض /z/. Letters of this shape group are connectors and have the following basic forms.

Initial	صـ صـ	ضـ ضـ
Medial	ـصـ ـصـ	ـضـ ـضـ
Final	ـص ـص	ـض ـض
Independent	ص ص	ض ض

Letters of this group are thus:

Initial	صـ صـ	ضـ ضـ
Medial	ـصـ ـصـ	ـضـ ـضـ
Final	ـص ـص	ـض ـض
Independent	ص ص	ض ض

These letters are found only in loanwords of Arabic origin.

289

Letters of Group 2 have a slightly taller initial form before members of this group (and also before Groups 8, 9, and 10, below): ل e.g. نصیحت /nəsihət/, بصارت /bəsarət/.

10.002. Letter Group 8.

This group includes ط /t/ and ظ /z/. Letters of this shape group are connectors and have the following basic forms:

Initial	ط	ظ
Medial	ط	ظ
Final	ط	ظ
Independent	ط	ظ

Letters of this group are thus:

Initial	ط	ظ
Medial	ط	ظ
Final	ط	ظ
Independent	ط	ظ

These letters are found only in loanwords of Arabic origin.

10.003. Letter Group 9.

This group contains ع (see below for pronunciation) and غ /γ/. Letters of this shape group are connectors and have the following basic forms:

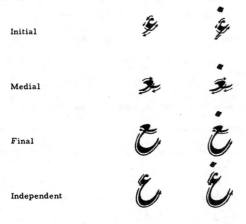

Initial		
Medial		
Final		
Independent		

Letters of this group are thus:

Initial		
Medial		
Final		
Independent		

Note that final shapes of this group are joined to a preceding letter at the side, whereas final forms of Group 3 were seen to join at the top: e.g. نصیح /fəsih/, بلیغ /bəliy/.

The letter ع has no easily assignable phonemic value in Urdu. A few careful scholars attempt to give this letter the voiced pharyngeal fricative pronunciation that it has in Arabic, but most speakers would consider this an affectation. Various values of are:

1.   Initially, ع is equivalent to initial ا : i.e. it has no effect on the following vowel and serves only as a "carrier": e.g. عورت /əwrət/, عمر /wmr/,

291

عرصه /ərsa/. عام /am/.

2. ع between vowels functions as a syllable boundary marker only: e.g. تقارف /təarwf/, جماعت /jəmaət/, معلّم /mwəllym/, تعقّب /təəsswb/. In less careful speech, these vowel clusters (/əa/, /aə/, /əə/, and occasionally even /wa/ and /wə/) tend to become /a/: i.e. /tarwf/, /jəmat/, /tasswb/ -- but never */mallym/ for /mwəllym/. Note, however, /maf/ for معاف /mwaf/.

3. ع after a consonant has no discernible phonemic representation as pronounced by most speakers: e.g. متعه /mwta/, مشعل /məšəl/, النعام /ynam/, منتقد /mwnəqəd/.

4. ع after a vowel and before a consonant has the effect of modifying the quality of the vowel: ع + /y/ = /e/; ع + /w/ = /o/; ع + /ə/ = /a/. In very careful literary speech these may sound something like /yə/ or /eə/, /wə/ or /oə/, and /aə/. E.g. تعليم /talim/ or literary /taəlim/, اعتبار /etybar/ or /eətybar/, معجزه /mojyza/ or /mwəjyza/, تعريف /tarif/ or /taərif/, etc. Many words have only one pronunciation, however: e.g. بعد /bad/, شعر /šer/, شعبه /šoba/, شعله /šola/.

5. Word-finally after a consonant, ع is pronounced /a/: e.g. جمع /jəma/, دفع /dəfa/, موقع /məwqa/. When /y/, /w/, or /ə/ are followed by ع at the end of the word, the phonemic representation may be /e/, /o/ and /a/; it may be /y/, /w/, and /ə/; or, in very literary pronunciation, it may be /yʔ/ (or even /eʔ/), /wʔ/, or /əʔ/. Final /ə/ + ع , however, is almost always pronounced /a/. E.g. تصنّع /təsənno/, /təsənnw/, or /təsənnwʔ/, مواقع /məvaqe/, /məvaqy/, /məvaqyʔ/ or even /məvaqeʔ/, etc. Word-final ع after other vowels has no effect on their pronunciation: e.g. دفاع /dyfa/, ممنوع /məmnu/, توزيع /təwzi/. A very literary speaker, however, might pronounce these words something like /dyfaə/, /məmnuə/, and /təwziə/.

10.004. Letter Group 10.

This group contains ف /f/ and ق /q/. Letters of this shape group are
connectors and have the following basic forms:

Initial

Medial

Final

Independent

Letters of this group are thus:

Initial

Medial

Final

Independent

Medial ف may sometimes be confused with medial غ . The loop of the former
should be a rounded oval, however, while the latter is written with sharp corners and a·
flattened top: e.g. نفل /nəfl/, بغل /bəɣəl/.

Final and independent forms of ف differ slightly from those of ق . The final
flourish of ف should be longer and flatter, whereas that of ق should be a deeper,
rounder curve. Initial and medial forms of these two letters differ only in the number of
their dots, however.

293

10.005. /həmza/.

The writing system of Classical Arabic makes provision only for two basic syllable patterns: CV(V) and CV(V)C. There is thus no way to write a syllable beginning with a vowel (i. e. V(V)C), especially medially within a word. Since vowel-initial syllables are a common feature of Urdu phonology, some Arabic consonantal letter had to be chosen as the "carrier" for the initial vowel of such a syllable.

As was seen in Sec. 6.102, the letter ا is used to write a word-initial syllable beginning with a vowel: e. g. اب /əb/. This letter cannot be so used word-medially, however, and thus the glottal stop, termed /həmza/, was selected for this function: ء . Although this letter represents the glottal stop (/ʔ/) in Arabic, it has no phonemic value in Urdu and is thus easily adapted to serve as a syllable boundary marker. Wherever a vowel-initial syllable follows a vowel-final syllable, /həmza/ serves to mark the boundary: e. g. /bəta-o/, /di-e/, /ga-õ/, etc. (Certain exceptions will be noticed below.)

If /həmza/ were an ordinary consonantal letter written on the line like other characters, all would have been simple. Unfortunately for the student, however, /həmza/ is written above the main line of writing as a sort of diacritic, and in most cases it must be written upon a "chair," a silent consonantal letter which "carries" the /həmza/. This "chair" may be either ی , و , or ا , depending upon preceding and following vowels, etc.

Rules for the writing of the /həmza/ and its "chair" are quite complex. This, together with the intricacies of Urdu syllable structure, has led to a certain amount of inconsistency and difference of opinion. The most important rules for the writing of /həmza/ are as follows:

1. According to the rules of Arabic orthography, /həmza/ should be written on every initial ا , since ا is only a carrier letter. One should thus write اِس /ys/, اُس /ws/, and اَب /əb/, etc., but this practice is never followed in

294

Urdu. If the short vowels are written at all, they are written directly above or below ‏ا‎ , and /həmza/ is omitted.

2. Word-medially, /həmza/ is written as follows:

a. When followed by a front vowel (/i, e, y, ī, ē, ȳ/), /həmza/ has a special "chair": a letter ‏ی‎ without its dots: ‏ئـ‎ , ‏ـئـ‎ . E.g. ‏بَتائی‎ /bətai/, ‏بَتائے‎ /bətae/, ‏بَتائِیں‎ /bətaī/, ‏بَتائیں‎ /bətaē/, ‏ہوئی‎ /hwi/, ‏ہوئے‎ /hwe/, ‏ہوئیں‎ /hwī/, ‏روئی‎ /roi/, ‏روئے‎ /roe/, ‏روئِیں‎ /roī/, ‏گئی‎ /gəi/, ‏کئی‎ /kəi/, ‏آئنده‎ /aynda/, ‏فرمائش‎ /fərmayš/, ‏قائم‎ /qaym/, etc. Logically, words like /kie/, /die/ and /lie/ should be written ‏کِئے‎ , ‏دِئے‎ , and ‏لِئے‎ , but they are traditionally written without the medial ‏یـ‎ : ‏کِے‎ , ‏دِے‎ , and ‏لِے‎ . Some modern authors have taken to writing these only with the medial ‏یـ‎ and no /həmza/: ‏کِیے‎ , etc. General usage favours the ‏کِے‎ spelling, however.

b. The /ie/ ending of the polite imperative is also variously written, the most complete way being ‏سُنِئیے‎ /swnie/, ‏آئیے‎ /aie/, ‏بَتائِیے‎ /bətaie/, ‏چاہِئیے‎ /cahie/, ‏دھوئیے‎ /dhoie/. These forms may also be found written only with a /həmza/ or only with a ‏یـ‎ : e.g. ‏سُنِے‎ or ‏سُنِیے‎ /swnie/. Verb stems ending in /a/ must always have both /həmza/ and ‏یـ‎ in the polite imperative in order to distinguish it from the MP past participle: e.g. ‏بَتائِیے‎ /bətaie/ but ‏بَتائے‎ /bətae/, ‏آئِیے‎ /aie/ but ‏آئے‎ /ae/.

c. When a back vowel (/u, o, w, ū, ō, w̄/) follows a syllable ending with a vowel, the /həmza/ is written directly upon the ‏و‎ representing the vowel. E.g. ‏جاؤ‎ /jao/ (here /həmza/ is written directly upon the ‏و‎ which represents the /o/ vowel), ‏جاؤں‎ /jaū/, ‏چلاؤ‎ /cəlau/, ‏چھوؤ‎ /chuo/, ‏چھوؤں‎ /chuū/, ‏تَفاؤل‎ /təfawl/, ‏آنسوؤں‎ /āsuō/, ‏پاؤں‎ /paō/, ‏پِیؤ‎ /pio/, ‏پِیؤں‎ /piū/, ‏دھوؤ‎ /dhoo/, etc. Sequences of /iu/, /io/, and /iū/ tend

295

to omit the /həmza/ in modern usage. Sequences of /eu/, /eo/, and /eū/ are

rare but usually seem to have the /həmza/: e.g. پیوَّ or پیوَ /pio/, پیوَّں

or پیوں /piū/, کھیوَ /kheo/, کھیوَّں /kheū/.

d. Sequences of a front vowel (/i, e, y/) + /a, ə, ā, ə̄/ do not require a /həmza/:

e.g. لڑکیاں /ləRkiā/, but note لڑکیوں /ləRkiə̄/, نیت /niət/, زیادہ

/zyada/, کیا /kia/ -- or /kya/.

e. Sequences of a back vowel (/u, o, w/) + /a, ə, ā, ə̄/ are normally written with

a /həmza/ upon a و but may optionally omit it, especially in common words.

E.g. ہوا /hwa/, مؤثر /mwəssər/, مواخذہ /mwaxəza/ سوا /soa/,

مؤلف /mwəllyf/.

f. Sequences of /əə/ are written with /həmza/ upon an /əlyf/: e.g. تأسف

/təəsswf/.

g. Sequences of /aə/ are written with /əlyf/ followed by /həmza/ with no chair

(i.e. written on the main line of writing): e.g. قرأت /qyraət/ (often

written قرأت and pronounced /qyrət/), برأت /bəraət/ (often pronounced

/bərət/ or even /bərrət/).

h. The sequence /əa/ is written with /əlyf/ + /məd/ (i.e. /həmza/ + /əlyf/ = آ).

See Sec. 6.101. E.g. مآثر /məasyr/, مآب /məab/.

i. After a consonant before a vowel, /həmza/ has no effect upon the pronunciation.

If the vowel is a front vowel (see above), /həmza/ is written upon ـﺋ ; if it

is a back vowel, /həmza/ is written upon و ; and if it is /ə/, /həmza/ is

written upon /əlyf/. E.g. جرأت /jwrət/, مسئلہ /məsyla/. In Arabic

/həmza/ here represents the glottal stop: /jwrʔət/, /məsʔyla/, etc.

Although they are thus only "silent letters" in Urdu, spelling tradition never-

theless requires that they continue to be written.

j. After a consonant, /həmza/ + /əlyf/ is written آ and pronounced /a/. E.g.

قرآن /qwran/, مرآة /myrat/ (see Sec. 10.007 for ة /t/). Again, these /həmza/ letters are simply traditional spellings, although they represented phonemic glottal stops in Arabic: /qwrʔan/, /myrʔat/, etc. In modern usage one may occasionally find these words with the /məd/ omitted:

قران , etc.

k. /w/ followed by /həmza/ before a consonant is usually pronounced /o/ (or occasionally /u/). Although the /həmza/ should be written upon و , it is commonly omitted. E.g. مؤمن /momyn/, or more commonly مومن (Arabic /mwʔmyn/).

l. /ə/ followed by /həmza/ before a consonant is written upon /əlyf/ and is pronounced /a/. E.g. تأنيث /tanis/, مأمور /mamur/, تأليف /talif/, تأريخ /tarix/ (Arabic /təʔniθ/, /məʔmur/, /təʔlif/, and /təʔrix/). /həmza/ is written only rarely in these words (and almost never in تاريخ).

3. A word-final /həmza/ is written in some Arabic loanwords. It is a "silent letter" with no phonemic representation whatsoever. In most cases it is written on the main line of writing without a "chair," and it is often omitted. E.g. ادباء /wdəba/, شعراء /šwəra/, ابتداء /ybtyda/ (also commonly written ابتدا), جزء /jwz/ (more commonly written جز), اشیاء /əšya/ (commonly اشیا), etc.

4. The Persian enclitic /e/ "of" (called the /yzafət/ "addition") is written as a /həmza/ over word-final ه or ى . The /yzafət/ is written as ◌ِ under other word-final letters (and is often omitted entirely). This construction is very frequently found in literature and poetry. It will be described in detail in Sec. 18.302. E.g. دیدهٔ دل /didəe dyl/ "vision of the heart," خانهٔ خدا /xanəe xwda/ "house of God."

10.006. The /təšdid/.

297

A doubled consonant (e.g. /bb/, /nn/, etc.) is written only once, and a diacritic ﺳ ,

called /təšdid/ or /šəd/, is placed over it to indicate the doubling. E.g. بچّہ /bəcca/,

ڈبّہ /Dybba/, چھٹّی /chwTTi/, سکّہ /sykka/, اچّھا /əccha/, پتّھر /pətthər/,

مؤنّث /mwənnəs/, اطّلاع /yttyla/.

There is one important exception, however: ن is written twice when a verb stem

ending in /n/ occurs before the infinitive suffix /n/. E.g. پہننا /pəhnna/, جاننے /janne/,

بننی /bənni/. Compare سننا /swnna/ "to hear" with سنّت /swnnət/ F1 "traditional

practice of the Prophet Muhammad."

10.007. The /ta mərbuta/.

The letter ة with two dots over it is occasionally employed for /t/. This symbol is

found only in a very few Arabic loanwords. In Arabic this convention is called /ta mərbuta/,

and it represents the FS noun and adjective ending /ət/. Although many Arabic loanwords

borrowed into Urdu originally had this suffix, in most of them it has been replaced either by

ة /a/ (as in اشارہ /yšara/, ارادہ /yrada/, etc.), or else by ت (as in حرکت

/hərəkət/, شرارت /šərarət/, etc.). A few words, mostly connected with religious matters

or else highly literary in style, retain ة however: e.g. زکوٰة /zəkat/, صلوٰة /səlat/,

مرآة /myrat/, etc. For the و in /zəkat/ and /səlat/, see Sec. 10.011.

10.008. The /tənvin/.

In Arabic, adverbs are grammatically treated as substantives (i.e. noun-like words)

in the accusative case. These may either be "definite" (with a suffix /a/, written ´), or

"indefinite" (with a suffix /ən/, written ˝ upon ة and ء , and ا after other

letters). Urdu has borrowed a great many Arabic indefinite adverbs (but not the definite

forms), and these are written with their case ending intact, pronounced /ən/. E.g. فوراً

/fəwrən/, تقریباً /təqribən/, مثلاً /məslən/, حقیقتاً /həqiqətən/, دفعتاً /dəfətən/.

The other Arabic indefinite case endings (nominative ٌ /wn/ and genitive ٍ /yn/) are only rarely seen in Urdu.

10.009. The /jəzm/ or /swkun/.

The diacritic ˒ or ˆ or ۰ placed over a consonant specifies that the consonant is not followed by any vowel: i.e. "C̊ C" can only be pronounced /CC/ and never /CyC/, /CwC/, or /CəC/. The /jəzm/ is employed only where real ambiguity might otherwise arise: e.g. in foreign proper names, in very rare words, in quotations from Arabic (especially in quotations from the Holy Qwran), etc. E.g. مِنْسْک /mynsk/, خرُشْچوْت /xruščəwf/ "Khrushchev," etc.

10.010. The /əlyf məqsura/.

Final /a/ in certain Arabic loanwords is written یٰ (i.e. a small /əlyf/ written on /ye/). This convention, called the /əlyf məqsura/, is relatively rare in Urdu. If a further suffix is added to the word, یٰ becomes ا E.g. دعویٰ /dava/ "claim," موسیٰ /musa/ "Moses," عیسیٰ /isa/ "Jesus," but note عیسائیٰ /isai/ "Christian."

10.011. The "Dagger /əlyf/."

Still another way of writing /a/ in Arabic loanwords is the "dagger /əlyf/": a small /əlyf/ used as a diacritic above the consonant which it follows in pronunciation. This usage is confined to certain words and is not frequent in Urdu. E.g. رحمٰن /rəhman/, ابرٰهیم /ybrahim/ (also spelled ابراہیم), اعلیٰ /ala/, صلوٰة /səlat/, زکوٰة /zəkat/ (see Sec. 10.007 above). In the latter two examples the "dagger /əlyf/" is written over a silent و . This reflects the original Arabic root: ṣ-l-w and z-k-w.

10.012. The Arabic Definite Article.

Many "set phrases," Muslim proper names, etc. contain the Arabic definite article, always written ال . At the beginning of such a phrase, it is pronounced /əl/: E.g. البتّہ /əlbətta/ "otherwise, in fact," الغرض /əlɣərəz/ "in short," الحق /əlhəq/ "certainly." Within a phrase the /əlyf/ continues to be written, but the /ə/ is replaced by the final vowel of the preceding word. (Note that all words obligatorily end in a vowel before

ال according to the rules of Arabic grammar.) If the preceding vowel is a long vowel

(/i, u, a/), it will be read /y/, /w/, or /ə/. If the following word begins with a vowel,

this vowel is retained after the article. E.g. فى الفور /fylfəwɾ/ "at once" (not */fi əlfəwr/),

فى الحقيقت /fylhəqiqət/ "in truth," بالكل /bylkwl/ "entirely" (not */by əlkwl/), عبدالحق

/əbdwlhəq/ "Abd-ul-Haqq" (lit. "Slave of the Truth (God)," a proper name), حتّى الامكان

/həttəlymkan/ "so far as possible" (not */həttə əlymkan/), الوالاعلى /əbwlala/ "Abu-l-Ala"

(lit. "Father of the Highest," a proper name; note the final و read as /w/, the retention

of the initial /əlyf/ of اعلى , and the final /əlyf məqsura/).

The /l/ of the definite article is not pronounced as such, however, when it occurs

before a consonant produced at the alveolar-dental point of articulation: i.e. ت /t/,

ث /s/, د /d/, ذ /z/, ر /r/, ز /z/, س /s/, ش /š/,

ص /s/, ض /z/, ط /t/, ظ /z/, ل /l/, and ن /n/. Before these con-

sonants the /l/ of the article is omitted in pronunciation (though never in writing!), and

the consonant is doubled. Thus, instead of */əbdwlrəhman/ عبدالرحمن "Abdur Rahman,"

(lit. "Slave of the Compassionate," a proper name), one finds /əbdwrrəhman/. In the

case of words beginning with /l/, the /l/ of the article coalesces with the initial /l/ of the

word to produce /ll/; e.g. الواللّيث /əbwlləys/ "Abu-l-Lays" (lit. "Father of the Lion,"

a proper name). In colloquial speech this doubling may be omitted, and one will hear

/əbdwrəhman/, /əbwləys/, etc. The ل of the article continues to be written, even

though it is not pronounced as /l/, and a ّ is written over the following consonant to

indicate the doubling. This practice tends to be ignored in printing and writing, however.

Further examples: اعتمادوالدّولة /etymadwddəwla/ "Reliance of the State" (a title; not

*/etymadwldəwla/), شمس الدّين /šəmswddin/ "Shams-ud-Din" (lit. "Sun of the Faith," a

proper name; not */šəmswldin/), عبدالرّب /əbdwrrəb/ "Abdur Rabb" (lit. "Slave of

the Lord," a proper name; not */əbdwlrəb/), اللّه /əllah/ "God" (a contraction of

/əlylah/ "the God"; note the /tənvin/ and the "dagger /əlyf/").

10.013. The /vəsl/.

A sign ‏ٵ‎ called /vəsl/ should be placed over the /əlyf/ of the definite article to indicate the ellision of the vowel /ə/, but this practice is rarely followed. It does occur, however, in Arabic passages quoted in Urdu scholarly texts; e.g. the full vowelling of ‏شَمْسُ ٱلدِّين‎ should be ‏شمس الدّين‎ ; ‏عَبْدُٱلرَّبِّ‎ should be ‏عبدالرّب‎ , etc.

10.014. The Silent /vao/.

Certain Persian words are written with an initial ‏خو‎ pronounced only as /x/: e.g. ‏درخواست‎ /dərxast/, ‏نخواب‎ /xab/, ‏خوامِش‎ /xahyš/, ‏خواجه‎ /xaja/ (not */xvaja/), (/dər/ here was originally a preposition). Note also the spellings of ‏خود‎ /xwd/ "self" (not */xud/) and ‏خوش‎ /xwš/ "happy" (not */xuš/), in which ‏و‎ is pronounced only as /w/. Compare ‏خوب‎ /xub/ "thoroughly" and ‏خون‎ /xun/ "blood," however. These spellings are irregular and must be individually learned.

301

10.100. SCRIPT EXERCISES

10.101. Reading Drills.

1. Letters of all new groups + /əlyf/.

Vowelled	غَا	ضَا	طَا	نَا	صَا
Unvowelled	عا	صا	ط	نا	صا
Vowelled	ضَا	ظَا	فَا	تَا	طَا
Unvowelled	ضا	ظا	فا	تا	طا

2. Letters of all new groups + /ye/.

Vowelled	تَے	طِی	نِی	صَے	عِی
Unvowelled	تے	طی	نی	صے	عی
Vowelled	ضِی	ظے	غے	طے	غِی
Unvowelled	ضی	ظے	غے	طے	غی

3. Letters of all new groups + /vao/.

Vowelled	طو	صُو	فُو	غو	طُو
Unvowelled	طو	صو	فو	غو	طو
Vowelled	فُو	عُو	ضُو	قُو	صو
Unvowelled	فو	عو	ضو	قو	صو

4. Medial letters of all new groups.

Vowelled   نَقَل   مَصرُوف   بَعد   تَصویر   مُغَل

Unvowelled   نقل   مصروف   بعد   تصویر   مغل

Vowelled   وَقت   نَظَر   اِنتِظار   بایَغیچہ   بَغَل

Unvowelled   وقت   نظر   انتظار   بایغیچہ   بغل

5. Final letters of all new groups.

Vowelled   صِرف   فَرض   شَوق   حافِظ   باغ

Unvowelled   صرف   فرض   شوق   حافظ   باغ

Vowelled   مَوقَع   مَنَع   تَشریف   عَرض   چِراغ

Unvowelled   موقع   منع   تشریف   عرض   چراغ

6. Medial /həmza/.

Vowelled   گَئے   لِئے   جاؤ   روئی   چائے   سَتّائیس   قائِم

Unvowelled   گئے   لئے   جاؤ   روئی   چائے   ستائیس   قائم

Vowelled   ہُوا   چاہِیے   بائیں   لِکھِیے   ہُوئیں   آئے   آزمائش

Unvowelled   ہوا   چاہیے   بائیں   لکھیے   ہوئیں   آئے   آزمائش

7. Final /həmza/.

Vowelled	اُدَبا،	شُعَرا،	اِرْتِقاء	اِبْتِدا،
Unvowelled	ادبا،	شعرا،	ارتقاء	ابتدا،
Vowelled	رُؤَسا،	أَشیا،	اِقْتِدا،	اُمَرا،
Unvowelled	روَسا،	اشیا،	اقتدا،	امرا،

8. /təšdid/.

Vowelled	بِچّہ	مُؤَنَّث	اَچّھی	ڈِبَّہ	اُنِّیس	اِکِّیس	
Unvowelled	بچہ	مَوَنَّث	اچھی	ڈبَہ	انیس	اکیس	
Vowelled	تَیّار	بُنّا	پَتّھر	سِلّہ	ہِمَّت	سُنَّت	
Unvowelled	تیّار	بنّا	پتّھر	سلّہ	ہمّت	سنّت	

9. /tənvin/.

Vowelled	حقیقۃً	فوْرًا	مَثَلًا	تَقریباً	دَفعۃً
Unvowelled	حقیقۃً	فوْرًا	مثلًا	تقریباً	دفعۃً
Vowelled	خُصوصًا	اِتِّفاقاً	قانُوناً	یَقیناً	مَجبُوراً
Unvowelled	خصوصًا	اتفاقاً	قانوناً	یقیناً	مجبوراً

10. Other Writing Conventions.

Vowelled	خَواب	عَبْدُالرَّحْمٰن	صَلوٰۃ	تَأَلُّف	کُبْریٰ

Unvowelled	خواب	عبدالرّحمن	صلوة	تأمّت	كبرٰى
Vowelled	مُؤَيَّد	أَلْغَرُض	بِأُلْكُل	مُتَأَثِّر	وُسطٰى
Unvowelled	مؤيّد	الغرض	باكل	متأثر	وسطٰى

10.102. Writing Drills.

Writing drills need no longer be done with the vowel diacritics. For the correct spelling of Arabic loanwords, the student should consult either the Word Recognition section of this and preceding script Units or the vocabulary at the end of this book.

1. Initial letters of all new groups.

   swbəh   tərəf   sabwn   zərurət   saf   əwrət   zəruri

   wmr   ɣwsl   qimət   fəwj   ymarət   ɣwslxana   fwTbal

   qalin   sahəb   ərsa   fykr   qysm   syrf   ərz   qabyl

2. Medial letters of all new groups.

   profesər   vəqt   məsruf   yntyzam   bayica   yntyzar   bad

   məzbut   xubsurət   təsvir   nəzər   bədqysməti   mwɣəl

3. Final letters of all new groups.

   baɣ   təšrif   fərz   hafyz   tərəf   cyraɣ   məwqa

   šəwq   məna   bərf   ərz   saf   təklif   saf   syrf

4. Medial /həmza/.

   gəe   lie   gae   bətae   cae   gəi   kəi   die   jaoge   hwi

   aūga   dhooge   piūga   dijie   aie   swnie   jaẽge   hwe

   hwa   aynda   gaõ   ləRkiā   soe   gəĩ   dia   roega   ai

5. /təšdid/.

   chwTTi   əTThara   wnnis   əccha   Dybba   pətthər

   təyyar   hymmət   swnna   bənna   ykkis   chəbbis   bəcca

6. Other writing conventions. All items used in this exercise have been given as examples in this Unit.

   əbdwrrəb   xahyš   xwd   bylkwl   fəwrən   təqribən   isa

   zəkat   təəsswf   wdəba   xab   rəhman   fylfəwr   səlat

   isai   mwənnəs   talif   məasyr   jwrət   məsyla   jwz

305

10.103. Word Recognition.

1. The following items contain a final **θ**. Note the pronunciation of اگرچہ and چنانچہ

SCRIPT	PRONUNCIATION	SCRIPT	PRONUNCIATION
اشاره	yšara	چنانچہ	cwnāce
اگرچہ	əgərce	ہفتہ	həfta
باغیچہ	baγica		

2. The following words are written with /həmza/, /təšdid/, or with both /həmza/ and /təšdid/.

SCRIPT	PRONUNCIATION	SCRIPT	PRONUNCIATION
اٹھارہ	əTThara	پچیس	pəccis
اٹھائیس	əTThays	تیار	təyyar
اچھا	əccha	تیئیس	teis
اکتیس	ykəttis	چاہئے	cahie [or چاہیئے]
اکیس	ykkis	چائے	cae
انتیس	wnəttis (or /wntis/)	چھبیس	chəbbis
اتیس	wnnis	چتیس	chəttis
آئندہ	aynda	چھٹی	chwTTi
بائیس	bais	ڈبہ	Dybba
بتیس	bəttis	ڈراؤنا	Dəraona
بچہ	bəcca	ڈھائی	Dhai
بچی	bəcci	ستائیس	səttais
بھائی	bhai	گاؤں	gaõ
پتھر	pətthər	گاؤں والا	gaõvala

306

SCRIPT	PRONUNCIATION	SCRIPT	PRONUNCIATION
گائَے	gae	ہِمّت	hymmət
لِئَے	lie		

3. The following words are written with "less common" Arabic consonant or with other special writing conventions.

SCRIPT	PRONUNCIATION	SCRIPT	PRONUNCIATION
استعمال	ystemal	صرف	syrf
انتظار	yntyzar	ضرورت	zərurət
انتظام	yntyzam	ضروری	zəruri
بعد	bad	طرف	tərəf
تصویر	təsvir	عرصہ	ərsa
تعریف	tarif	عرض	ərz
جمعرات	jwmerat	عمارت	ymarət
جمعہ	jwma	عمر	wmr
حافظ	hafyz	عورت	əwrət
حالت	halət	فرض	fərz
حرکت	hərəkət	فوراً	fəwrən
خوبصورت	xubsurət	قلعہ	qəla
دفعہ	dəfa	مصروف	məsruf
صابن	sabwn	مضبوط	məzbut
صاحب	sahəb	معاف	maf [or /mwaf/]
صاف	saf	معلوم	malum
صبح	swbəh [or /swba/]	منع	məna

307

SCRIPT	PRONUNCIATION	SCRIPT	PRONUNCIATION
موقع or موقعہ	ˌməwqa	واقعہ	vaqea
نظر	nəzər	واقعی	vaqəi

10.104. Urdu-English Paragraph.

ہمیں قلعہ بھی دیکھنا چاہئے ۔ اس کی دیواروں میں بڑے بڑے مضبوط پتھر ہیں ۔ یہ قلعہ مغلوں کے
زمانے کا ہے ۔ اس میں ایک طرف بادشاہ کا محل اور سامنے کھیلنے کا میدان ہے جس کے دونوں طرف
دفتروں کی عمارتیں ہیں ۔ محل کے نیچے تہہ خانہ ہے ۔ جب ہم قلعے جائیں گے تو یہ سب چیزیں دیکھ
سکیں گے ۔ قلعہ دیکھنے کے بعد میرا خیال ہے کہ ہم بادشاہی مسجد چلیں گے ۔ وہ بھی بہت دلچسپ
جگہ ہے ۔ اگر ہم ابھی چلیں تو شام تک آسانی سے یہ سب چیزیں دیکھ سکیں گے ۔

10.105. Urdu-English Sentences.

1. آداب عرض اسمتھ صاحب، مزاج شریف ؟

2. مسٹر رحیم کو مرچ مت دو ۔ یہ مرچ نہیں کھاتیں ۔

3. میں چھبیس دن کے بعد واپس آؤں گا ۔

4. مجھے ساڑھے تین سیر چاول اور ایک سیر چینی دیجئے ۔

5. یہاں سے راولپنڈی کوئی دو سو میل دور ہے ۔

6. دوپہر کو ایک گھنٹے کی چھٹی ہوتی ہے یا نہیں ؟

7. جناب، یہ ڈرامہ واقعی بہت اچھا تھا ۔

8. مجھے جمعرات کو بھی کالج جانا پڑتا ہے ۔

308

9. جب میں گاڑی سے اُتر چکا تو مجھے سوٹ کیس یاد آیا۔

10. ہم اپنی شرارت پر بہت شرمندہ ہوئے۔

11. ہمیں واپس جانے کا موقع نہیں ملا۔

12. ہر آدمی کا فرض ہے کہ وہ قانون پر چلے۔

13. بہت عرصے سے آپ نظر نہیں آئے۔

14. اپنے چھوٹے بھائی کو شرارت کرنے سے منع کیجیے۔

15. میں پھر اس قسم کا صابن کبھی نہیں استعمال کروں گا۔

10.106. English-Urdu Sentences.

1. I used to come here a lot in [my] childhood.
2. Yesterday we went to see a play.
3. The girl was screaming from fear.
4. My father praises you a lot.
5. When she finished eating, she went to his place.
6. I feel hot. [Lit. To me heat is attaching.]
7. How old is this building?
8. In its walls there are very sturdy stones.
9. Please call him inside!
10. I went only once.
11. This place does not seem clean to him.
12. He displayed much courage.
13. You ought to have gone to their place.
14. That big building will be visible from here.
15. During this time, the girls did not come to Karachi.

A commercial building in Karachi.

UNIT ELEVEN

11.000. CONVERSATION

marker of the subject of a past tense transitive verb Postposition	ne
several, a good many Al	kəi
did, made MS [irreg. PasP of /kərna/]	kia
but Conj	lekyn

MR: Where were you all day today? I called your office several times but didn't get you.

aj ap sare dyn kəhã rəhe. mə̃y ne ap ke dəftər kəi dəfa Telifun kia, lekyn ap nə myle.

had sat down MS	bəyTha tha
officer, executive M/Fl	əfsər
lawyer, pleader M/Fl	vəkil
conversation, chat Fl [np]	batcit
court Fl	ədalət

R: I was very busy today. I had only just sat down in the office, when an officer of our head office came. A famous lawyer also was with him. [We] had a conversation with the lawyer for awhile, and then all three of us went [lit. arrived] to court.

aj mə̃y bəhwt məsruf rəha. dəftər mẽ thoRi si der bəyTha tha, ky həmare bəRe dəftər ke ek əfsər tə̃rif lae. wn ke sath ek məšhur vəkil bhi the. kwch der vəkil sahəb se batcit hwi, əwr phyr həm tinõ ədalət pəhw̃ce.

MR: What did you have to do at the court?

ədalət mẽ kya kam tha.

medicine F2	dəvai
company F2	kəmpni
lawsuit M2	mwqədma [or /mwqəddyma/]
date; history Fl	tarix
case Ml	kcs
presented, offered PA1	peš
difficulty, difficult Fl Al	mwškyl
because Conj	kyõke
easy Al	asan

R: These days there is a lawsuit going on between our hospital and a pharmaceutical company [lit. company of medicines]. Its date was today. On going to the court, [we] came to know that our case would be presented after an hour. It was very difficult [lit. a big difficulty], because sitting for an hour was not very [lit. some] easy.

ajkəl dəvaiõ ki ek kəmpni se həmare həspətal ka mwqədma cəl rəha həy. aj ws ki tarix thi. ədalət ja kər, malum hwa, ky həmara kes ek ghənTe ke bad peš hoga. bəRi mwškyl thi, kyõke ek ghənTe tək bəyThna kwch asan nə tha.

rest, ease, comfort Ml [np]	aram
would have done MP	kərte

MR: Why didn't you come home? It would have been better if you had come home and rested.

ap ghər kyõ nə ae. byhtər tha, ky yəhã a kər aram kərte.

beginning, start Ml [np]	šwru

R: At first [I] had just this idea, but in the

pəhle yrada to yyhi tha, lekyn ys dəwran

311

meantime a very interesting case began. We started to listen to it.

MR: What was the case?

theft	F2	cori
last, former	A2	pychla
thief	M/F1	cor
rich, wealthy, rich man	M1 A1	əmir
road, way	M2	rasta
person	M1	šəxs
certainty, assurance, confidence	M1 [np]	yəqin
pocket	F1	jeb
gave	MS [irreg. PasP of /dena/]	dia
unconscious	A1	behoš
took	MS [irreg. PasP of /lena/]	lia

R: It was a case of theft. It's an incident of the past week, that a thief went [lit. arrived] to the house of a rich man at twelve o'clock at night. At the main gate of the house was a watchman. The thief said to the watchman "I am a traveller. I had to go to the house of a friend of mine, but I don't know the way. I'll be very grateful [lit. it will be your great kindness], if you give me permission to sleep the night with you." The watchman believed this person's words and said, "No matter! You can sleep here on my bedding!" A little later this person took a cigarette out of his pocket and started to smoke. He gave a cigarette to the watchman also, in which there was a drug [lit. unconscious making medicine]. The watchman took the cigarette and began to smoke.

MR: He was a very clever fellow!

to get up, arise	[IIc: /w/]	wThna
dog	M2	kwtta
to throw	[Id: /y/]	phēkna
poison	M1	zəhr
finished, ended	[also "dead"] PA1	xətm

R: Then this person got up from the bedding and went [lit. arrived] to the door of the house, where there was a dog. This person took a little meat out of his pocket and threw it toward the dog. There was poison in the meat. Thus he finished off the dog also.

tricky, deceitful, clever	A1	calak

MR: What a tricky fellow he was! Was there poison also in the cigarette?

R: No, there was only a drug [lit. unconscious making medicine].

---

mẽ ek bəhwt dylcəsp kes šwru hwa. həm wse swnne ləge.

vw kya kes tha.

cori

pychla

cor

əmir

rasta

šəxs

yəqin

jeb

dia

behoš

lia

ek cori ka mwqədma tha. yy pychle həfte ka vaqea həy, ky cor rat ke bara bəje ek əmir admi ke ghər pəhw̃ca. koThi ke bəRe dərvaze pər cəwkidar məwjud tha. cor ne cəwkidar se kəha, ky "mə̃y mwsafyr hũ. mwjhe əpne dost ke ghər jana tha, lekyn mwjhe raste ka pəta nəhĩ. ap ki bəRi myhrbani hogi, əgər ap mwjhe rat ko əpne pas sone ki yjazət dẽ." cəwkidar ne ys šəxs ki batõ pər yəqin kia, əwr kəha, ky "koi bat nəhĩ! twm yəhã mere bystər pər so səkte ho." thoRi der bad, ys šəxs ne əpni jeb se sygreT nykala, əwr pine ləga. ys ne sygreT cəwkidar ko bhi dia, jys mẽ behoš kərne ki dəvai thi. cəwkidar ne yy sygreT lia, əwr pine ləga.

bəhwt hošyar admi tha!

wThna

kwtta

phēkna

zəhr

xətm

phyr yy šəxs bystər se wTha. əwr koThi ke dərvaze pər pəhw̃ca, jəhã ek kwtta məwjud tha. ys šəxs ne əpni jeb se thoRa sa gošt nykala, əwr kwtte ki tərəf phẽka. gošt mẽ zəhr tha. əyse ws ne kwtte ko bhi xətm kia.

calak

kytna calak šəxs tha! kya, sygreT mẽ bhi zəhr tha?

nəhĩ, ws mẽ syrf behoš kərne ki dəvai thi.

312

MR: What happened after this?

	ys ke bad kya hwa.
would have been, become MS	hota
entirely, completely Adv	bylkwl
almost, approximately Adv	təqribən
forty-five Al	pə̃ytalys
property, goods Ml	mal
to steal [Ia]	cwrana

R: Then what else would have happened? Now the way was entirely clear. This person went into the house and stole 45,000 Rs. [worth] of property and came out of the house [again].

phyr kya hota? əb to rasta bylkwl saf tha. yy šəxs ghər ke əndər gəya, əwr təqribən pə̃ytalys həzar rupəe ka mal cwra kər, koThi se bahər nykla.

consciousness Ml [np]	hoš

MR: Didn't the watchman regain consciousness during this time?

kya, cəwkidar ko ys dəwran mẽ hoš nəhĩ aya?

to find, obtain, acquire [Ia]	pana
certainly, necessarily Adv	zərur
dead, corpse M2 Al	mwrda
people of the house, family members Mp2	ghərvale
to awaken [C: /jagna/; IIc]	jəgana
all, entire, complete Al	təmam
they, he (honorific) [Special form of /vw/ used with /ne/]	wnhõ
cupboard F2	əlmari
criminal, culprit Ml Al	mwjrym
search Fl	təlaš
did, made FS [irreg. PasP of /kərna/]	ki
attempt, try Fl	košyš
caught, apprehended PAl	gyryftar

R: A little while later the watchman returned to consciousness. When he did not find the traveller there, he understood that there was something wrong [lit. that there is some matter]. He ran toward the house, where he found the dog dead at the door. He awakened the family members at once. The family members ran toward the main room, where their goods were. They saw that the money cabinet was empty, [and] thereupon [they] telephoned the police at once. The police started a search for the criminal, and after a week of effort they apprehended him.

thoRi der bad, cəwkidar ko hoš aya. jəb ws ne mwsafyr ko vəhã nə paya, to vw səmjha, ky zərur koi bat həy. vw ghər ki tərəf bhaga, jəhã dərvaze pər kwtte ko mwrda paya. ws ne fəwrən ghərvalõ ko jəgaya. ghərvale bəRe kəmre ki tərəf bhage, jəhã wn ka saman tha. wnhõ ne dekha, ky rupõ ki əlmari xali həy, cwnãce fəwrən polis ko Telifun kia. polis ne mwjrym ki təlaš šwru ki, əwr ek həfte ki košyš ke bad wse gyryftar kia.

MR: Really, it was very interesting case. -- Wasn't your suit presented?

vaqəi, bəhwt dylcəsp kes tha. kya, ap ka mwqədma peš nəhĩ hwa?

argument, debate, discussion Fl	bəhs
judge M/Fl	jəj
question Ml	səval
did, made MP [irreg. PasP of /kərna/]	kie

evidence, giving witness F2 — gəvahi

witness M/F1 — gəvah

continuing, current, in force, issuing PA1 — jari

R: After this our suit was presented. Our lawyer gave a very good argument. The judge asked me some questions also. After my evidence two more witnesses were presented as well. Our suit continued for about an hour and a half. — ys ke bad, həmara mwqədma peš hwa. həmare vəkil sahəb ne bəhwt əcchi bəhs ki. jəj sahəb ne mwjh se bhi kwch səval kie. meri gəvahi ke bad, do əwr gəvah bhi peš hwe. koi DeRh ghənTe tək həmara mwqədma jari rəha.

decision M2 — fəysla

MR: Wasn't the suit decided? — kya, mwqədme ka fəysla nəhĩ hwa?

hope, anticipation F1 — wmmid

next, forthcoming, first A2 — əgla

R: Not yet, but there is hope that it will be [decided] by [lit. until] next week. — əbhi to nəhĩ hwa, lekyn wmmid həy, ky əgle həfte tək hoga.

mail, post F1 — Dak

had said MS — kəha tha

have brought MP — lae hõy

MR: In the morning I had told you to bring some postage stamps. Have you brought them? — swba, mõy ne ap se Dak ke kwch TykəT lane ke lie kəha tha. kya, vw lae hõy?

order, command M1 — hwkm

would have believed, obeyed MS [inf. /manna/] — manta

would have allowed to come FP — ane detĩ

R: If I hadn't obeyed your order, would you have let me come into the house? — əgər mõy ap ka hwkm nə manta, to kya, ap mwjhe ghər mẽ ane detĩ?

always Adv — həmeša

MR: Oh yes, just as you always follow only my orders! Come on [lit. please bring], where are my stamps? — ji hã, jəyse ap həmeša mere hi hwkm pər cəlte hõy! laie, mere TykəT kəhã hõy!

postoffice M2 — Dakxana

had gone MS — gəya tha

letter M1 — xət

registry, registration F2 — ryjysTri

money order M1 — məni arDər

to cause to be done [C: /kərna/; Ic] — kərana

receipt F1 — rəsid

[I] have brought MS — laya hũ

card, postcard M1 — karD

envelope M2 — lyfafa

R: After eating lunch I went at once to the postoffice. [I] registered your letters and got the money order made, the receipts for which are these. I've brought the six pəysa and thirteen pəysa stamps, but [I] forgot to bring the postcards and the envelopes. — mõy khana kha kər, fəwrən Dakxane gəya tha. ap ke xət ryjysTri kie, əwr məni arDər bhi kəraya, jyn ki rəsidẽ yy hõy. chəy chəy pəyse əwr tera tera pəyse ke TykəT to laya hũ, lekyn karD əwr lyfafe lana yad nə rəha.

well, anyway, good; wellbeing, good luck F1 Adv. — xəyr

day after tomorrow, day before yesterday M1 Adv	pərsõ
self Adv	xwd

MR: Oh well, no matter. Tomorrow is Sunday. Day after tomorrow I'll bring [them] myself.

xəyr, koi bat nəhĩ. kəl ytʋar həy. pərsõ. mɛ̃y xwd laũgi.

A servant enters and announces the arrival of Mr. əxtər to see Dr. Rəhim. Mrs. Rəhim leaves the room.

service F1	xydmət

R: Come in, Mr. əxtər, come in! Tell [me] what I can do for you [lit. what service can I do]?

aie, əxtər sahəb, təšrif laie! fərmaie, kya xydmət kər səkta hū.

new A2	nəya
Multan (a city of West Pakistan) M1 [np]	mwltan
to cause to be sent [DC: /bhejna/: Id]	bhyjvana
since Conj	cũke
air, aerial A1	həvai
ship, vessel M1	jəhaz
file (of documents, etc.) M1 [also F1]	fayl
paper M1	kaɣəz

ə: Today some new goods for our hospital are coming by the evening train. We have to send these goods to the Multan hospital. Since I'm going to Karachi on the six o'clock plane, therefore you will have to make all these arrangements. Keep this file with you. In it are some necessary papers and receipts concerning these goods.

aj həmare həspətal ka kwch nəya mal šam ki gaRi se a rəha həy. həmɛ̃ yy mal mwltan ke həspətal ko bhyjvana həy. cũke mɛ̃y chəy bəje ke həvai jəhaz se kəraci ja rəha hū, ys lie ap ko yy səb yntyzam kərṇa hoga. yy fayl əpne pas rəkhẽ. ys mẽ saman ke bare mẽ kwch zəruri kaɣəz əwr rəsidẽ hɛ̃y.

to make, build, construct [C: /bənna/: IIc]	bənana

R: All right. [To the servant:] Make tea for Mr. əxtər!

bəhwt əccha. -- əxtər sahəb ke lie cae bənao!

otherwise Conj	vərna
would have drunk MS	pita

ə: No thanks. Time is short, otherwise I would certainly have drunk [some tea]. Now I'll take my leave [lit. please give permission].

ji nəhĩ, šwkria, jənab. vəqt bəhwt kəm həy, vərna mɛ̃y zərur pita. əb yjazət dijie.

R: Very well. Goodbye!

əccha. xwda hafyz.

ə: Goodbye.

xwda hafyz.

11.100. WORD STUDY

11.101. /lekyn/ Conj "but" is almost entirely synonymous with /məgər/ Conj "but". The former is commoner in written Urdu, and the latter is frequent in speech.

11.102. As a technical term, /vəkil/ M/F1 "lawyer" denotes a pleader, a junior member of the legal profession. A senior lawyer is termed /əyDvokeT/ M/F1 "advocate." /vəkil/, however, is the common term for "lawyer."

11.103. /batcit/ F1 "conversation, chat" is an example of an "echo compound": a meaningful (/bat/ F1 "word, matter") joined with a meaningless second element (/cit/). This phenomenon is discussed in Sec. 19.305. Note the difference between /batcit/ and /bəhs/ F1 "discussion, debate, argument."

/wn se bat hwi./   It has been discussed with him. [Lit. with him a word became.]

/wn se batcit hwi./   [There] was a conversation with him.

/wn se bəhs hwi./   There was a discussion [argument, debate] with him.

11.104. /dəvai/ F2 "medicine, remedy, drug" has an alternate form /dəva/. Both are interchangeable.

11.105. /tarix/ F1 has two meanings: (a) "date (of the month, year, etc.)" and (b) "history." E.g.

/kəl pəhli tarix thi./   Yesterday was the first [lit. first date].

/pakystan ki tarix pəRhni cahie./   [You] ought to study the history of Pakistan.

11.106. /mwškyl/ occurs as an F1 noun meaning "difficulty, hardship, problem" and also as a Type I adjective denoting "hard, difficult," etc. E.g.

/yy bhi ek mwškyl thi./   This also was a problem [difficulty, hardship].

/yy ek mwškyl kam tha./   This was a hard task.

11.107. /šwru/ M1 "beginning, start" is frequently found in complex verbal constructions with /kərna/ and /hona/. These denote "to begin (trans.)" and "to begin (intrans.)" respectively. Complex verbal formations with /šwru/ may be compared with the <OI + /ləgna/ > construction discussed in Sec. 9.311. The former denote the beginning of a single act or event, and the focus is upon the beginning. The <OI + /ləgna/ > formation, however, denotes the gradual inception of an action, the beginning of an act or event which may continue indefinitely, etc., and the focus is upon the event itself. There is considerable semantic overlap between these formations, however.

Formations with /šwru/ fall into the Type A pattern of complex verbal constructions: i.e. in the past tenses the object (the thing begun) governs the number-gender of the occurring form of /kərna/. If the object is an infinitive, the occurring form of /kərna/ will be MS (see the third example below). If the infinitive itself has an object, the number-

316

gender of the object governs the number-gender of the infinitive, as well as that of the form of /kərna/. This is exactly like the <I + /cahie/> construction, described in Sec. 3.314. E.g.

> /mə̃y ne nəmaz šwru ki./ I began the prayer. [/nəmaz/ is F1 and the verb must thus agree.]
>
> /nəmaz šwru hwi./ The prayer began. [*/nəmaz hone ləgi./ is not idiomatic, since a prayer is not an act which gradually starts up.]
>
> /mə̃y ne lykhna šwru kia./ I began to write.
>
> /mə̃y ne kytab lykhni šwru ki./ I began to write the book. [/kytab/ F1 "book" governs the gender of /lykhni/ and the number-gender of /ki/.]
>
> /mə̃y ne kytab ko lykhna šwru kia./ I began to write the book. [As usual, /ko/ "cuts off" the object from the verb, and the latter is then treated as MS.]
>
> /mə̃y ne vw kwrsi bənani šwru ki thi./ I had begun to make that chair. [/kwrsi/ F2 "chair" governs /bənani/ and /ki thi/.]
>
> /mə̃y ne ws kwrsi ko bənana šwru kia tha./ I had begun to make that chair.
>
> /mə̃y ne hə̃sna šwru kia./ I started to laugh. [/mə̃y hə̃sne ləga./ is also correct. If there is any difference at all, it may be that /hə̃sna šwru kia/ focusses attention upon the beginning of the act as a single unitary event, while /hə̃sne ləga/ indicates the inception and increase of the action as well as indefinite continuity.]

11.108. /cor/ M1 "thief" and /cori/ F2 "theft" are another illustration of the /i/ "abstract noun formant" suffix (see Sec. 7.301). /cwrana/ Ia "to steal" is from the same root and seems to be the causative of */cwrna/ or */corna/, but no such simplex verb is in use. /cori kərna/ "to steal, commit theft" is synonymous with /cwrana/. /cori kərna/ only occasionally occurs with an object (i.e. the thing stolen), while /cwrana/ almost always has an object. E.g.

> /ws ne vəhã cori ki./ He committed theft there.
>
> /ws ne vəhã se yy phəl cwrae./ He stole these fruits from there.

11.109. /pychla/ A2 "previous, former, preceding, rear, behind" contains the same root as /piche/ Adv Comp Post "behind." /əgla/ A2 "next, subsequent, approaching, front, forthcoming" is similarly formed from the same root as /age/ Adv Comp Post "in front, ahead." Some Eastern dialects employ these two terms with exactly opposite meanings: /əgla/ for "previous" and /pychla/ for "latter, next." The former usage is perhaps more widespread, however, and will be that adopted in this book.

11.110. /səRək/ F1 denotes a relatively large street, highway, or thoroughfare, and usually one which is metalled or paved. /rasta/ M2, on the other hand, denotes an unpaved road or less permanent thoroughfare. /rasta/ is also employed in the metaphorical senses of "way (to an address)" and "way, manner, course of action." /səRək/ does not have these metaphorical meanings. E.g.

> /baryš ki vəja se, rasta bəhwt xərab həy./ Because of the rain, the road is very bad.

317

/myhrbani fərma kər, mwjhe lahəwr ka rasta bətaie!/ Please tell me
the way to Lahore.

/mera əpna rasta həy./ I have my own way [course of action]. [i.e.
I don't necessarily do as others do.]

11.111. /pəta/ M2 means "address" and also "clue, trace, information, knowledge."
E. g.

/mwjhe kya pəta./ What do I know? [What information do I have about
it?]

/mwjhe pəta həy, ky vw cor həy./ I know that he is a thief. [Synonymous
with /mwjhe malum həy, ky .../ and, in this sentence, with /mə̃y
janta hũ, ky .../.]

/mwjhe pəta nəhĩ tha, ky ap bimar hə̃y./ I did not know that you were
[lit. are] sick.

/ys kytab ka pəta nəhĩ cəla./ There's no trace of this book. [/pəta cəlna/
"to have information, be traced, have knowledge of."]

/cor ka pəta əb tək nə ləga./ There's no trace [information] about the
thief as yet. [/pəta ləgna/ "to have information, be traced, found."
/pəta cəlana/ and /pəta ləgana/ mean "to search out, trace (as a
thief, lost article)."]

/polis ne cor ka pəta ləgaya./ The police traced the thief. [Also /pəta
cəlaya/. Compare:]

/mə̃y ne hər dwkan se pəta kia, məgər yy kytab nə myl səki./ I sought
information from every shop, but this book could not be obtained.
[/pəta kərna/ means "to seek information, ask about."]

11.112. /xətm/ PA1 "finished, completed, terminated, ended" occurs in complex
verbal formations with /kərna/ and /hona/. These constructions are often found with a
noun object (e.g. "I finished the book"), but they are less frequent with an infinitive object
(e.g. "I finished writing") and still less frequent with an infinitive + a noun object (e.g.
"I finished writing the letter"). In place of the latter two, one finds the <S + /cwkna/ >
formation (see Sec. 9.309).

/mə̃y ne yy kam xətm kia./ I finished this work.

/mə̃y ne cae xətm ki./ I finished the tea. ["Drinking" is here understood.]

/mə̃y ne lykhna xətm kia./ I finished writing. [/mə̃y lykh cwka./ is
rather more idiomatic.]

/mə̃y ne xət lykhna xətm kia./ I finished writing the letter. [If the
context is known -- whether the letter is being written, read, etc.
-- the preferred form would be /mə̃y ne xət xətm kia./. If the action
must be specified, then the <S + /cwkna/ form might be employed
instead: /mə̃y xət lykh cwka./. In many cases formations with /xətm/
are grammatically correct but quite unidiomatic: e.g. */mə̃y ne
cae pini xətm ki./. This would normally be expressed as in the
second example above or as /mə̃y cae pi cwka./]

11.113. /calak/ A1 means "clever" in a pejorative sense: "tricky, deceitful, cunning."
It occasionally overlaps with /hošyar/ A1 "clever, intelligent" and with /tez/ A1 "sharp,
smart, clever."

11.114. /təqribən/ Adv "about, approximately" is equivalent to /koi/ A1 "anybody, somebody; approximately" in the special meaning given in Sec. 5.304.

11.115. /mal/ M1 "property, goods, merchandise, stock" occasionally overlaps with /saman/ M1 "baggage, personal effects, goods."

11.116. /ghərvala/ M2 denotes "family member" and also "husband" among certain segments of middle class Indo-Pakistani culture. The feminine form, /ghərvali/ F2 is similarly used in middle class society for "wife." The educated classes prefer /bivi/ or a more literary work like /əhlia/ F1 for "wife." The MP form, /ghərvale/, denotes "family members, people of the household."

11.117. /əlmari/ F2 cupboard, chest of drawers, cabinet, clothes-press, wardrobe" is from Portuguese almario. This word is also found in English as almirah.

11.118. /[X] ko wmmid həy, ky .../ and /[X] wmmid kərta həy, ky .../ can both be roughly translated "[X] hopes that ..." Clauses following these phrases are indicative rather than conditional: i.e. one says, "I hope that he will come" rather than "I hope that he may come." /wmmid kərna/ is rare in the past tenses, and "[X] hoped that ..." is idiomatically expressed by /[X] ko wmmid thi, ky .../. E.g.

/mɜ̃y wmmid kərta hū̃, ky vw kəl aẽge./ I hope that they will come tomorrow. [Also /mwjhe/wmmid həy, ky .../]

/mwjhe wmmid həy, ky ap əmrika bhi dekhẽge./ I hope that you will see America too.

/mwjhe wmmid həy, ky vw aẽge./ I hoped that he would [lit. will] come. [/mɜ̃y ne wmmid ki thi, ky .../ would also be correct but would be less frequent.]

11.119. /TykəT/ M1 "ticket" is also used for "stamp (postal, tax, etc.)."

11.120. /Dakxana/ M2 "postoffice" is a compound like /qəydxana/ M2 "jail." See Sec. 5.301.

11.121. /xəyr/ is used as an adverb to mean "oh well, ...," "Anyway, ...," etc. It also occurs as a F1 noun denoting "good luck, wellbeing" and, in beggar's language, "alms." E.g.

/xəyr, həm nəhĩ ja səkte./ Oh well, we cannot go.

/yy to xəyr hwi, ky mɜ̃y vəhã məwjud nəhĩ tha./ This was good luck that I wasn't present there.

/xwda ke nam pər, kwch xəyr do!/ In the name of God, give some alms!

11.122. /xwd/ Adv "self" refers only to the subject of its clause and never to an object or to any other noun in the sentence. It usually occurs either just after the subject (or the subject + /ne/) or else just before the verb of the clause. /xwd/ may refer to a singular or a plural subject. E.g.

/mɜ̃y xwd jaūga./ I'll go myself.

319

/vw log xwd jante hɚy./   Those people know [it] themselves.

/ws ne xwd masTər sahəb ko dekha./   He himself saw the teacher.
[This is identical in meaning with:]

/ws ne masTər sahəb ko xwd dekha./   He himself saw the teacher.
[/xwd/ cannot refer to /masTər/.]

/mɚy ne xwd ws ko kyraya dia./   I myself gave him the fare.

11.123.   Both /bənana/ and /kərna/ can be translated as "to make" in some contexts.
The former means "construct, build, prepare, manufacture, " however, while the latter
denotes "to perform (an action), do. " One must thus say /cae bənana/ "to make tea"
rather than */cae kərna/ since tea is "prepared" rather than "performed. " Both of these
verbs have idiomatic usages, however, which will require the student's close attention.

11.124.   Complex Verbal Formations.

A:

/asan/
        /[X ke lie] asan hona/ to be easy [for X]
        /[X ko] asan kərna/ to make [X] easy
/əmir/
        /[X se] əmir hona/ to become wealthy [from X]
        /[X ko] əmir kərna, bənana/ to make [X] rich
/behoš/
        /[X se] behoš hona/ to become unconscious [from X]
        /[X ko Y se] behoš kərna/ to make [X] unconscious [with Y]
/cori/. [See also under B.]
        /[X ko] cori kərna/ to steal [X]
/fayl/
        /fayl hona/ to be filed
        /[X ko] fayl kərna/ to file [X]
/gəvah/
        /[X ka] gəvah hona/ to become a witness [for X]
        /[X ko] gəvah kərna/ to make [X] a witness
/gyryftar/
        /gyryftar hona/ to be caught, apprehended
        /[X ko] gyryftar kərna/ to apprehend, catch [X]
/jari/
        /jari hona/ to continue, be in force
        /[X se] jari hona/ to issue [from X]
        /[X ko] jari kərna/ to issue, establish, enforce [X]
        /jari rəhna/ to remain in force, in effect, continue
        /[X ko] jari rəkhna/ to issue, establish [X]
/mwškyl/
        /mwškyl hona/ to be, become difficult

320

/[X ko] mwškyl kərna/ to make [X] difficult
/peš/
    /peš ana/ to come forward, to present oneself
    /peš hona/ to be presented, come forward, present oneself
    /[X ko Y] peš kərna/ to present [X to Y]
/ryjysTri/
    /ryjysTri hona/ to be registered
    /[X ko] ryjysTri kərna/ to register [X]
/šwru/
    /šwru hona/ to begin, start
    /[X ko] šwru kərna/ to begin, start [X]
/təlaš/. [See also under B.]
    /[X ko] təlaš kərna/ to search [for X]
/təmam/
    /təmam hona/ to be, become complete
    /[X ko] təmam kərna/ to complete [X]
/vəkil/
    /[X ko] vəkil kərna/ to appoint [X] as one's lawyer
/xətm/
    /xətm hona/ to be finished, completed
    /[X ko] xətm kərna/ to finish, complete [X]

B:

/cori/. [See also under A.]
    /[X ki] cori hona/ [X] to be stolen
    /[X ki] cori kərna/ to steal [X]
/dəvai/. [See also under D.]
    /[X ki] dəvai kərna/ to cure [X]
/fəysla/. [See also under D.]
    /[X ka] fəysla hona/ [X] to be decided
    /[X ka] fəysla kərna/ to decide [X]
/košyš/
    /[X ki] košyš hona/ [X] to be tried, attempted
    /[X ki] košyš kərna/ to try, attempt [X]
    /[X ke lie] košyš kərna/ to try, attempt [X], try [for X]
/təlaš/. [See also under A.]
    /[X ki] təlaš hona/ [X] to be sought, looked for
    /[X ki] təlaš kərna/ to search, look for [X]
/wmmid/. [See also under F.]
    /[X ki] wmmid kərna/ to hope for [X]
/xydmət/
    /[X ki] xydmət kərna/ to serve [X]

D:

/dəvai/. [See also under B.]

/[X ko] dəvai dena/ to give medicine [to X]

/[X se] dəvai mylna/ to receive medicine [from X]

/fəysla/. [See also under B.]

/[X ka] fəysla dena/ to give a decision [about X]

/gəvahi/

/[X ki] gəvahi dena/ to give evidence [about X]

/[X se Y ki] gəvahi lena/ to take evidence [from X about Y]

/[X ki] gəvahi rəkhna/ to accept (enter) the evidence [of X]

/hwkm/

/[X ko Y ka] hwkm dena/ to order [X] [to do Y]

/[X se Y ka] hwkm mylna/ to receive an order [to do Y] [from X]

F:

/aram/

/[X se] aram hona, mylna/ to get rest [from X]

/aram kərna/ to rest, relax

/aram pana/ to find rest, relaxation, relief

/batcit/

/[X ki Y se] batcit hona/ [X] to converse [with Y]

/[X se] batcit kərna/ to converse [with X]

/bəhs/

/[X ki Y se] bəhs hona/ [X] to dispute, argue, debate [with Y]

/[X se Y pər] bəhs kərna/ to dispute [with X] [about Y]

/hoš/

/[X ko] hoš ana/ [X] to become conscious

/[X ko] hoš mē lana/ to bring [X] to consciousness

/kes/

/[X ke xylaf] kes hona/ to be a case [against X]

/[X ke xylaf] kes kərna/ to pursue a (court) case [against X]

/məni arDər/

/məni arDər kərna, kərana/ to make out a money order

/mwqədma/

/[X ke xylaf] mwqədma hona/ to be a suit [against X]

/[X ke xylaf] mwqədma kərna/ to pursue a suit [against X]

/səval/

/[X se Y pər] səval kərna/ to ask [X] [about Y]

/[X se Y ka] səval kərna/ to ask [X] [for Y]

/yəqin/

/[X ko Y pər] yəqin ana/ [X] to become certain [of Y]

/[X ko Y ka (or Y pər)] yəqin hona/ [X] to become certain [of Y]

/[X pər] yəqin kərna/ to believe, be confident [of Y]

11.201. Doubled Consonants.

Almost all Urdu consonants may occur "doubled" (or "long", or "geminated", etc., according to one's choice of terminology). In effect, this means that the consonant is held for a period roughly twice as long as the same consonant "undoubled" (or "plain", or "short", or "ungeminated", etc.). In a word like /bəcca/ "child", the first syllable (/bəc/) ends in an unreleased /c/; the second syllable begins with /c/, which is released upon the /a/. The /cc/ of /bəcca/ "takes about twice as long to say" as the /c/ of /bəca/ "msc. sg. escaped".

English makes very little use of "doubled" consonants. Except for a very few pairs (such as "wholly" versus "holy" in the author's dialect), the only phenomena analogous to Urdu "doubled" consonants are such compounds as "mop-pail", "flat-top", "bookcase", etc. The student should practice with these: e.g., holding the "k" of "bookcase" for an exaggerated length of time without releasing it; then releasing it as part of the following syllable: "book--case". Each Urdu consonant should then be "doubled" in nonsense syllables and thoroughly practiced: e.g., /əp-pə/, /ət-tə/, /əb-bə/, /ən-nə/, /əh-hə/, etc. Finally, a list of all Urdu words containing this phenomenon should be made, and each item should be drilled. All consonants except /R/, the rare /ž/, and the even rarer /ʔ/ occur "doubled".

"Doubled" consonants also occur with an aspirated release. Consonants which can be followed by aspiration include /p, t, T, c, k, b, d, D, j, g/ and /R/ (which never occurs doubled). There are thus four possibilities for each consonant: /C/, /CC/, /Ch/, and /CCh/.

"Doubled" and "doubled"-aspirated consonants occur only between vowels. The Urdu writing system recognises "doubled" and "doubled"-aspirated consonants at the ends of words also, but there is no phonetic difference in normal speech.

/r/ versus /rr/ and /l/ versus /ll/ have already been treated in the preceding Unit but are repeated here for completeness' sake.

/səba/ breeze

/bəca/ escaped, saved MS
/bycha/ spread out MS
/gəda/ beggar
/gədha/ donkey
/soDa/ soda

/šyfa/ healing, recovery
/ləga/ attached, hit MS
/bəghar/ hot ghi, spices, etc. put as a sort of sauce or basting upon cooking food
/dəya/ deceit, treachery
/kəha/ said MS

/jwbba/ cloak
/səbha/ society, meeting
/bəcca/ child
/bycchu/ scorpion
/gədda/ quilt
/bwddha/ Buddha
/əDDa/ stand, depot
/gəDDha/ pit, cavity
/šəffaf/ crystal clear, neat
/ləgga/ compatibility
/bəgghi/ buggy

/mwrəyyən/ greasy, oily
/tərəhhwm/ pity, compassion

/bəja/ struck, played MS	/chəjja/ eaves
/bwjha/ went out, extinguished MS	/gəjjha/ abundance, store of wealth
/təka/ gazed at MS	/tykka/ a small piece of roasted meat
/lykha/ wrote MS	/lykkha/ wrote (alternate pron.) MS
/bəla/ calamity	/bəlla/ pole
/əma/ Oh!	/əmmã/ mother
/əna/ ego, self	/ənna/ nurse, nanny
/jəpa/ recited MS	/kwppa/ a large earthen vessel for oil
/jəpha/ recited (alternate pron.) MS	/gwppha/ tassel, braid
/vəqar/ dignity, prestige	/bəqqal/ grain merchant
/bwra/ bad	/bərra/ sheep
/məsa/ evening	/məssa/ wart
/dəša/ condition, plight	/pəšša/ gnat
/kəta/ was spun	/kwtta/ dog
/kətha/ narrative, recital	/kəttha/ catechu bark
/pəTa/ double-edged sword	/pəTTa/ dog collar
/məTha/ buttermilk	/pəTTha/ nerve, sinew
/həva/ air, wind	/həvva/ Eve
/səxa/ generosity, liberality	/mwrəxxəs/ permitted (to leave)
/bəya/ weaver bird	/bhəyya/ Brother!
/məza/ taste, enjoyment, pleasure	/ləzzət/ sweetness, relish, delight

11.202. Phonetic Drill: Auditory Dictation.

1. bəja təka səba gəda tykka jwbba kəta chəjja kwtta gədda

2. bycha lykha bəghar lykkha gədha bycchu bəgghi məTha bwddha
   pəTTha

3. šyfa kəha məza əmmã šəffaf ənna məsa tərəhhwm ləzzət əma
   əna məssa

4. səxa jəpa bərra ləgga bəlla mwrəxxəs kwppa bəya bwra ləga
   bhəyya bəla

5. lykkha kəttha gwppha bycchu pəTTha bwddha gəDDha gəjjha bəgghi

6. səbha gədha bwjha gəDDha bəgghi bwddha gəjjha bəghar

7. kəha dəša vəqar dəɣa tərəhhwm bəqqal pəšša mwrəɣɣən həva
   həvva

8. chəjja bəca əma məza kəta pəTTa šyfa bəja lykha ləggi

11.300. ANALYSIS

11.301. Substantive Composition: the Prefix /be/.

/hoš/ M1 "consciousness" and /behoš/ A1 "unconscious" are an illustration of the
prefix /be/ "un-, -less." This prefix is of Persian origin but has a wide distribution in
Urdu. It occurs with a great many nouns (including many of Hindi origin), and the resulting
constructions are adjectives, adverbs, or both. In an informal joking style, /be/ may be
found with almost any noun, and some authors employ it in unusual formations to lend
novelty to their style. Most of the /be/ constructions possible with nouns introduced so
far will be of little use to the student at present, however, and only a few common examples
will suffice:

/bəs/ M1 ability, capability	/bebəs/ A1 Adv helpless
/fykr/ F1 worry, thought	/befykr/ PA1 Adv carefree, without worry
/ghər/ M1 house, home	/beghər/ A1 Adv homeless
/məwqa/ M2 opportunity, occasion	/beməwqa/ A1 Adv out of place, inappropriate
/vəqt/ M1 time	/bevəqt/ A1 Adv at the wrong time, out of place

Examples:

/vw bylkwl bebəs admi həy./   He's a completely helpless person.

/ap befykr rəhie!/   Please don't worry! [Lit. Please remain without-
care!]

/vw ləRki beghər həy./   That girl is homeless.

/wnhõ ne beməwqa yy bat kəhi./   He said this thing at the wrong time.

/vw bevəqt aya./   He came at an inappropriate time. [/bevəqt/ and
/beməwqa/ are almost synonymous.]

11.302. Transitive Subjects Marked by /ne/.

The subject of a transitive verb in the past tenses must be marked by /ne/ (see Sec.
11.303). In some cases, the form of the subject before /ne/ differs from the form employed
before other postpositions, and it is necessary thus to detail the entire system.

(1) As with other postpositions, the oblique form of a noun occurs before /ne/. If the
subject contains more than one noun, usually only the last noun will be followed by /ne/,
although all will be oblique. Each noun may be followed by /ne/, however, if each is to be
individually particularised. E.g.

/ws ləRke ne mwjhe bwlaya./   That boy called me.

/ws ləRki ne mwjhe bwlaya./   That girl called me.

/wn ləRkõ ne mwjhe bwlaya./   Those boys called me.

/wn ləRkiõ ne mwjhe bwlaya./   Those girls called me.

/ləRkõ, ləRkiõ, əwr əwrtõ ne dekha, ky masTər saheb a rəhe hǣy./
The boys, girls, and women saw that the teacher was [lit. is] coming.
[/ne/ occurs only once, after the last noun of the series. All are
oblique, however.]

/ləRkõ ne, ləRkiõ ne, əwr əwrtõ ne -- səb ne dekha, ky masTər sahəb a
rəhe hõy. /   The boys, the girls, and the women -- all saw that the
teacher was [lit. is] coming. [Each group is individually particularised,
and a comma juncture sets off each phrase from the others. A dash
juncture separates the series from /səb ne/, which sums them all up.]

(2) The personal pronouns occur in their <u>nominative</u> forms before /ne/. If the subject
contains more than one pronoun (a noun and a pronoun, a pronoun and a demonstrative, etc.)
then each item must be followed by /ne/. The following pronouns occur in their nominative
forms:

/mõy ne dekha. /   I saw.

[/tu ne dekha. /   Thou sawest]

/həm ne dekha. /   We saw.

/twm ne dekha. /   You [non-honorific] saw.

/ap ne dekha. /   You [honorific] saw.

(3) The singular demonstratives, the relative pronoun /jo/ "who, which, " and the
interrogative /kəwn/ "who?" occur in their normal oblique forms before /ne/:

/ys ne dekha. /   He [she, it, this one] saw.

/ws ne dekha. /   He [she, it, that one] saw.

/jys ne dekha. /   who saw. [Incomplete sentence.]

/kys ne dekha. /   Who saw?

(4) The plural demonstratives, the plural of the relative pronoun /jo/ "who, which, "
and the plural of the interrogative /kəwn/ "who?" <u>have</u> <u>special</u> <u>forms</u> <u>found</u> <u>only</u> <u>before</u> /ne/.
These forms consist of the usual oblique plural demonstrative (etc.) + /hõ/.

/ynhõ ne dekha. /   They [these, he, she] saw.

/wnhõ ne dekha. /   They [those, he, she] saw.

/jynhõ ne dekha. /   who [pl.] saw. [Incomplete sentence.]

/kynhõ ne dekha. /   Who [pl.] saw? [Modern usage tends to avoid /kynhõ/,
employing /kyn logõ ne/ "which people?" instead.]

/mõy ne, ap ne, əwr wnhõ ne dekha, ky masTər sahəb a rəhe hõy. /   I,
you, and they saw that the teacher was [lit. is] coming. [/ne/ is
obligatory after each member of a series of pronouns or demonstratives.
Note that one starts with "I" in Urdu, whereas the first person pronoun comes last in such a sequence in English.]

11. 303.   The Verb: the Past Tense of Transitive Verbs.

As was seen in Sec. 9. 307, the simple past tense of an intransitive verb consists of
just the past participle. This participle was seen to agree with its subject (so far as
possible) in number-gender with the subject of its clause. The past participle consists of
the Stem + the Type II affixes.

The past participle of transitive verbs is constructed in exactly the same way, and it
too occurs with no auxiliaries as the simple past tense. There is an important difference
in agreement, however: <u>the subject of a past tense transitive verb is followed by</u> /ne/, <u>and</u>
<u>the verb then no longer agrees with its semantic subject in number-gender!</u> /ne/ thus "cuts
off" the semantic subject from its verb. So far as the number-gender of the verb are
concerned, three cases arise:

(1) [Subj. + /ne/] [MS verb]. If there is no expressed object, then the verb is treated as masculine singular irregardless of the number-gender of the semantic subject. E.g.

/ws ləRke ne dekha./ That boy saw.

/ws ləRki ne dekha./ That girl saw. [Although /ləRki/ is F2, it is "cut off" from its verb by /ne/, and the verb is then treated as MS.]

(2) [Subj. + /ne/] [obj. + /ko/ (etc.)] [MS verb]. If the object is a pronoun it is obligatorily marked by /ko/ (or one of the special object forms discussed in Sec. 5.303 is employed). If the object is a demonstrative, it is usually marked by /ko/, but instances of a nominative demonstrative object are found. If the object is marked by /ko/, or is a special object form, then the verb must be masculine singular. Similarly, if a noun object is marked by /ko/, then the verb must be masculine singular. In the case of nouns, however, there is a real option: definite animate objects tend to be marked by /ko/, while definite inanimate objects may be marked by /ko/ or may be nominative; indefinite objects are always nominative and cannot be marked by /ko/. Examples of objects marked by /ko/ and special object forms:

/mə̃y ne wse bwlaya./ I invited him. [/bwlaya/ does not necessarily agree with the number-gender either of /mə̃y/ or of /wse/. /ne/ "cuts off" /bwlaya/ from the subject, and the special object form "cuts it off" from agreement with the number-gender of /wse/]

/mə̃y ne ap ko bwlaya./ I invited you. [When /ap/ is an object, it is obligatorily marked by /ko/. /bwlaya/ must thus be MS.]

/mə̃y ne ws ləRke ko dekha./ I saw that boy. [Again, /ne/ and /ko/ effectively "cut off" the verb from both its subject and object.]

/mə̃y ne ws ləRki ko dekha./ I saw that girl.

/meri valda ne ws ləRki ko dekha./ My mother saw that girl.

/mə̃y ne wn ləRkõ ko dekha./ I saw those boys.

/mə̃y ne wn ləRkiõ ko dekha./ I saw those girls.

/profesərõ ne wn ləRkõ ko dekha./ The professors saw those boys.

/ws nəwkər ne ap ke valyd sahəb ko bwlaya./ That servant called your father.

/ws ne mere hath ko pəkRa./ He grasped my hand.

(3) [Subj. + /ne/] [nominative obj.] [verb agreeing with the object in number-gender]. If the object is not marked by /ko/ or its equivalent, then the verb agrees with the object in number-gender.

/mə̃y ne vw ləRka dekha./ I saw that boy. [When no /ko/ occurs, the object must be nominative. The verb agrees with /ləRka/ here. This is identical in meaning with the third example above.]

/mə̃y ne vw ləRke dekhe./ I saw those boys. [/dekhe/ is MP, agreeing with /ləRke/.]

/mə̃y ne vw ləRki dekhi./ I saw that girl.

/mə̃y ne vw ləRkiã dekhĩ./ I saw those girls.

/ws ləRki ne bəhwt se ləRke dekhe./ That girl saw many boys.

/ws ne kayəz xərida./ He bought paper. [/kayəz/ is an indefinite object and thus cannot be followed by /ko/. /dekha/ agrees with /kayəz/.]

/ws ne cavəl xəride./ He bought rice. [/cavəl/ is indefinite. It is idiomatically treated as a plural.]

/ws ne ek kwrsi xəridi./ He bought a chair.

/mə̃y ne bəhwt si kytabẽ xəridĩ. / I bought many books. [/bəhwt si kytabẽ/ is an indefinite object, and /ko/ thus cannot occur.]

/mə̃y ne əpna saman wThaya. / I picked up my baggage. [Note that in spite of /ne/ /əpna/ A2 "[one's] own" is still used when the semantic subject and the possessor of some other noun in the sentence are the same.]

/ws əfsər ne əlmari se əpni faylẽ nykalĩ. / The officer took his files out of the cabinet.

Aside from the simple past, there are other formations made with the past participle: the perfect, the past perfect, the future perfect, etc. Whenever the verb of these tenses is transitive, then the subject will be marked by /ne/, and there will be no subject-verb agreement, as described above. These formations will be discussed in following sections.

There are also a number of constructions which do NOT mark the subject with /ne/ in the past tenses. Agreement between the subject and the verb thus remain obligatory, and there is no distinction between transitive and intransitive in these formations. They include:

(1) <S + /rəha tha/> "the past continuous": e.g.

/mə̃y khana kha rəha tha. / I was eating.

/meri bivi khana kha rəhi thĩ. / My wife was eating.

(2) <PreP + /tha/> "the past imperfect": e.g.

/mə̃y khana khata tha. / I used to eat.

/meri bivi khana khati thĩ. / My wife used to eat.

(3) <I + /cahie tha/> "should have ...": e.g.

/ap ko kaɣəz xəridna cahie tha. / You should have bought paper.

/ap ko yy kwrsi xəridni cahie thi. / You should have bought this chair.

(4) <I + /pəRna/> "have to ...": e.g.

/ap ko yy kam kərna pəRa. / You had to do this work.

/mwjhe yy ciz xəridni pəRi. / I had to buy this thing.

(5) <I + /tha/> "have to ...": e.g.

/ap ko yy kam kərna tha. / You had to do this work.

/mwjhe ek kwrsi xəridni thi. / I had to buy a chair. [Note that in nos. 3, 4, and 5, the "logical subject" is marked by /ko/, and /kwrsi/, /kam/, etc. are the "grammatical subjects" of these sentences.]

(6) <OI + /ləgna/> "to begin to ...": e.g.

/mə̃y khana khane ləga. / I started to eat.

/meri bivi khana khane ləgi. / My wife started to eat.

(7) <S + /cwkna/> "to finish ...": e.g.

/mə̃y khana kha cwka. / I finished eating.

/meri bivi khana kha cwki. / My wife finished eating.

(8) <S + /səkna/> "to be able to ...": e.g.

/mə̃y khana kha səka. / I could eat.

/meri bivi khana kha səki. / My wife could eat.

There is also a small class of verb stems which may occur with an object but whose subjects are not marked by /ne/ in the past tenses. These are thus syntactically transitive and grammatically intransitive, and there is the usual agreement between the subject and its verb form. These include: [Verbs not introduced as yet are marked with an asterisk and are included for completeness' sake only.]

328

*/bhulna/ to forget

/lana/ to bring. [Historically this is a compound of /lena/ "to take" and /ana/ "to come": /le ana/ becomes /lana/ (although /le ana/ also occurs). Since /ana/ is intransitive, /lana/ is treated as intransitive. E.g.]

>   /mɜ̃y ap ke lie ek kytab laya./   I brought a book for you. [/laya/ is MS, agreeing with /mɜ̃y/ "I".]

There is a somewhat larger group of verb stems which are both transitive and intransitive. They are more often transitive when an object is expressed, and more often intransitive when there is no object. Furthermore, several verbs which are normally transitive occur in one or two formations in which they are treated as intransitive, and vice versa. This group includes:

>   /bədəlna/ to change. [Both transitive and intransitive.]

>   /ws ki halət bədli./ His condition changed.

>   /mɜ̃y ne ws ko bədla./ I changed it.

*/bəkna/ to talk nonsense. [This verb is usually transitive when an object occurs and sometimes even when no object is expressed.]

*/bhərna/ to fill, be filled. [Like /bədəlna/.]

/bolna/ to speak, say, utter. [Although this verb is generally intransitive even when an object is expressed, there are a few idiomatic transitive usages.]

>   /ws ne jhuT bola./   He told a lie. [/jhuT/   M1 "lie, falsehood."]

>   /mɜ̃y ne səc bola./   I spoke the truth. [/səc/ M1 A1 "truth, true."]

/cahna/ to wish, want, desire. [Usually transitive, but treated as intransitive when the subject is /dyl/ M1 "heart," /ji/ M1 "heart, life," /mən/ M1 "mind, heart," etc.]

>   /mera dyl caha, ky mɜ̃y lahəwr jaū./   My heart wished [i.e. I desired very much] that I go to Lahore.

*/harna/ to lose (a game, battle, etc.). [Intransitive with no object; generally transitive with an object.]

>   /mɜ̃y ne mwqədma hara./   I lost the lawsuit.

*/jitna/ to win. [Like /harna/.]

*/pələTna/ "to turn over, overturn, return. [Like /bədəlna/.]

/səməjhna/ to understand. [Both transitive and intransitive. No apparent rule.]

/Təkrana/ to collide, strike, run into. [Like /bədəlna/.]

*/wləTna/ to turn over, turn upside down. [Like /bədəlna/.]

There are also number of verbs which are intransitive in Urdu but whose English equivalents are transitive. E.g.

>   /Dərna/ to fear. [E.g.]

>   /mɜ̃y ws se Dəra./   I feared him. [Lit. I was afraid from him.]

>   */ləRna/ to fight. [E.g.]

>   /mɜ̃y ws se ləRa./   I fought him. [Lit. I fought with him.]

The converse is also true: there are several stems which are transitive but whose English equivalents are treated as intransitive. E.g.

*/chĩkna/ to sneeze. [Also occasionally intransitive.]

*/həgna/ to defecate.

*/jhãkna/ to peep, peer. [Also rarely intransitive.]

*/mutna/ to urinate

*/thukna/ to spit

The negative of a past transitive verb is either /nə/ or /nəhī́/, exactly as described in Sec. 9.307.

Every new formation will require a separate discussion of its transitive-intransitive status as it is introduced.

11.304. The Verb: Irregular Past Participles.

As was stated in Sec. 9.307, there are only six "irregular" past participles in Urdu, and of these, one is almost obsolete. Two of these were introduced in Sec. 9.307; the other three common irregular past participles are:

	/dena/ to give	/kərna/ to make, do	/lena/ to take
MS	/dia/	/kia/	/lia/
MP	/die/	/kie/	/lie/
FS	/di/	/ki/[1]	/li/
FP	/dī́/	/kī́/	/lī́/

[1]Although /ki/ "made, did (FS)" is homophonous with /ki/ "of (F)," the context almost completely prevents any chance of ambiguity.

Examples:

/ghər ja kər, ws ne aram kia./ He went home and rested.

/ws ne meri bəhwt tarif ki./ He praised me [lit. did my praise] a lot.

/mə̃y ne wse dəs rupəe die./ I gave him ten rupees.

/mə̃y ne ws se əpni kytabẽ vapəs lī́./ I took my books back from him.

The sixth irregular past participle is /mwa/ (like /hwa/, see Sec. 9.307) "died, dead" from /mərna/ "to die." /mwa/ is dialectal and is totally unknown in some regions. The regular past participle, /məra/ (etc.), is now almost universal.

There is still one more minor irregularity which deserves mention: verb stems consisting of a single syllable containing a short vowel and ending in /Th/, /ch/, or /kh/ -- i.e. stems of the patterns CVTh, CVch, or CVkh -- tend to double the final aspirated stop before the number-gender affixes of the past participle. Thus, from the stem /lykh/ "write," one may get /lykkh/ + /a/, /e/, etc. This usage is generally optional and varies from dialect to dialect. No examples have been found for stems ending in /ph/, /th/, or other consonants.

This phenomenon is frequently found for the following two stems:

*/cəkhna/ to taste. PasP: /cəkkha/, /cəkkhe/, etc. Less commonly /cəkha/.

/rəkhna/ to put, place. PasP: /rəkkha/, /rəkkhe/, etc. Less commonly /rəkha/.

With other verbs this modification is optional and dialectal.

*/bychna/ to be spread. PasP: /bycha/ or /byccha/.

*/dwkhna/ to hurt, pain. PasP: /dwkha/ or /dwkkha/.

/lykhna/ to write. PasP: /lykha/ or /lykkha/.

/wThna/ to get up. PasP: /wTha/ or /wTTha/.

Of the above, only /rəkkha/ and /cəkkha/ are widely accepted as standard.

11.305. The Verb: the <PasP + /həy/> and the <PasP + /tha/> Constructions.

The "perfect tense" (i.e. "I have done," etc.) consists of the past participle + the
present tense of the auxiliary verb. Similarly, the "past perfect" (i.e. "I had done," etc.)
is composed of the past participle + the past tense of the auxiliary. The transitive-intransitive division, the use of /ne/, the agreement of the verb with a "/ko/-less" object -- all
are exactly as described for the simple past tense. A sample intransitive paradigm is as
follows:

PRONOUN	PERFECT		PAST PERFECT	
	MASCULINE	FEMININE	MASCULINE	FEMININE
mə̃y	gəya hũ	gəi hũ	gəya tha	gəi thi
[tu	gəya həy	gəi həy	gəya tha	gəi thi]
vw	gəya həy	gəi həy	gəya tha	gəi thi
həm	gəe hə̃y	gəi hə̃y	gəe the	gəi thĩ
twm	gəe ho	gəi ho	gəe the	gəi thĩ
ap	gəe hə̃y	gəi hə̃y	gəe the	gəi thĩ
vw	gəe hə̃y	gəi hə̃y	gəe the	gəi thĩ

As with other tenses, women often employ the first person masculine plural instead of
the expected feminine form.

As in the present tense, the nasalisation of the participle is omitted before an auxiliary
verb. When the participle is used alone as the simple past tense, on the other hand, a
feminine plural form will always be nasalised.

The transitive paradigm is identical with that given above, except that /ne/ "cuts off"
the subject from the verb, and the verb either agrees with a nominative object or else
reverts to a "neutral" masculine singular, as discussed above in Sec. 11.303. Since a
pronominal object cannot be nominative (i.e. a personal pronoun object must either be a
special object form or must be marked with /ko/), forms like */dekha hũ/ do not occur.
An example will make this clear:

/ws ne mwjhe dekha həy./ He has seen me. [Since a pronominal object
cannot be nominative, "me" must be expressed either by /mwjhe/ or
by /mwjh ko/. Only if a nominative pronominal object were possible
could one expect to find sentences like */ws ne mə̃y dekha hũ./ "He
has seen me." In this case, /mə̃y/ would govern the number-gender
of the verb. This is not possible in Urdu, however.]

The negative of the perfect is usually /nəhĩ/ but may sometimes be /nə/; conversely,
the negative of the past perfect is usually /nə/ but may occasionally be /nəhĩ/.

Examples of the perfect and past perfect:

/mə̃y ne vw admi dekha həy./ I have seen that man. [Past perfect:
/dekha tha/.]

/mə̃y ne vw admi dekhe hə̃y./ I have seen those men. [Past perfect:
/dekhe the/.]

/mə̃y ne ws admi ko dekha həy./ I have seen that man. [Past perfect:
/dekha tha/.]

/mə̃y ne wn admiõ ko dekha həy./ I have seen those men. [Past perfect:
/dekha tha/.]

/mə̃y ne vw ləRki dekhi həy./ I have seen that girl. [Past perfect:
/dekhi thi/.]

/mə̃y ne vw ləRkiã dekhi hə̃y./ I have seen those girls. [Past perfect:
/dekhi thĩ/.]

/mə̃y ne ws ləRki ko dekha həy./ I have seen that girl. [Past perfect:
/dekha tha/.]

/mə̃y ne wn ləRkiõ ko dekha həy./ I have seen those girls. [Past
perfect: /dekha tha/.]

11.306. Complex Verbal Formations in the Past Tenses.

Complex verbal formations have already been discussed in Secs. 5.307 and 7.123.
In the past tenses they occur as follows:

(1) Type A formations:

    (a) A Type I adjective or predicate adjective undergoes no change for number-
    gender, of course. The verb agrees with any expressed nominative object
    of the construction. E. g.

      /mə̃y ne Telifun Thik kia./ I fixed the telephone. [/Thik/ is Al and
      does not show number-gender. /kia/ agrees with /Telifun/ Al
      "telephone. "]

      /mə̃y ne yy ciz Thik ki./ I fixed this thing. [/ki/ agrees with /ciz/ F1
      "thing. "]

    (b) If the object of the construction is nominative, a Type II adjective agrees with
    the object in number-gender. The verb must also agree. E. g.

      /mə̃y ne yy kam əccha kia./ I did this work well. [Both /əccha/ M2
      "good, well" and /kia/ agree with /kam/ M1 "work. "]

      /mə̃y ne yy ciz əcchi bənai./ I made this thing well. [/əcchi/ and /bənai/
      agree in number-gender with /ciz/.]

      /mə̃y ne yy təsvir bəRi ki./ I enlarged this picture. [/bəRi/ A2 "big"
      and /ki/ agree with /təsvir/ F1 "picture. "]

    (c) If the object is marked by /ko/ or is a special object form, the adjective and
    the verb must both be MS. E. g.

      /mə̃y ne wse šərmynda kia./ I made him ashamed. [/šərmynda/ PA1
      "ashamed" does not show number-gender. /kia/ is MS.]

      /mə̃y ne ys təsvir ko bəRa kia./ I enlarged this picture. [/təsvir/ is
      "cut off" from the verb by /ko/, and both the verb and the predicate
      adjective must thus be MS in form.]

    (d) A noun occurring in a complex verbal formation does not affect the number-
    gender of the verb. Instead, the verb agrees with a nominative object (and not
    with the number-gender of the noun of the complex verbal formation). Again,
    if the object is marked by /ko/, the verb must be MS in form. E. g.

      /ws ne kãTa ystemal kia./ He used a fork. [/kia/ agrees with the
      number-gender of /kãTa/ M2 "fork, thorn. "]

      /ws ne chwri ystemal ki./ He used a knife. [/chwri/ F2 "knife"
      governs the number-gender of /ki/.]

      /ws ne chwri ko ystemal kia./ He used the knife. [/ko/ "cuts off" /chwri/
      from its verb, and the latter must thus be MS.]

      /mə̃y ne yy nəmbər yad kia./ I memorised this number. [/yad/ "memory"
      is F1, but /kia/ is MS, agreeing with the number-gender of the
      object, /nəmbər/ M1 "number. " Compare:]

      /mə̃y ne wn ke nam yad kie./ I memorised their names. [/nam/ M1
      "name" is MP here, and /kie/ must agree.]

332

/məy ne wn ki batē yad kī. /   I memorised their words. [/batē/ "words" is FP, and the verb must thus be /kī/.]

(2) Type B formations:

(a) When the substantive part of the complex verbal formation is an adjective or predicate adjective, two cases arise: (a) When the construction is intransitive, using /hona/, the subject <u>possesses</u> the adjective or predicate adjective (employing /ka/ if the subject is MS, /ke/ if MP, and /ki/ if FS or FP), and the verb agrees with the subject. (b) If the construction is transitive, employing /kərna/, the subject is marked by /ne/, the logical object by /ko/, and some third element may possess the adjective or predicate adjective, using /ka/. The verb is then treated as MS. E. g.

/məy ys ka pabənd hū. /   I adhere to this. [/pabənd/ PA1 "restricted, bound to, following, adhering, observing." /məy/ thus governs both /ka/ and /hū/.]

/meri valda ys ki pabənd həy. /   My mother adheres to this. [/valda/ F1 "mother" governs both /ki/ and /həy/.]

/mere valyd sahəb ys ke pabənd həy. /   My father adheres to this.

/ws ne mwjhe ys ka pabənd kia. /   It restricted me to this. [The subject is marked by /ne/; the logical object is the special object form /mwjhe/; and the thing to which the object is restricted possesses the predicate adjective. The verb is MS since it cannot agree with either the subject or the object. /ka/ is similarly MS.]

(b) When the substantive portion of the complex verbal formation is a noun, the logical object possesses this noun. If the noun is masculine, /ka/ is used, and if the noun is feminine, the object possesses the noun with /ki/. Note that the verb also agrees with the noun in number-gender.

/məy ne ws ka yntyzar kia. /   I waited for him. [Lit. I did his waiting. /yntyzar/ "waiting" is M1, and thus /ka/ and /kia/ must be used.]

/məy ne ws ki tarif ki. /   I praised him. [Lit. I did his praise. /tarif/ "praise" is F1, and thus /ki/ and /ki/ must be employed.]

/jəj sahəb ne ys kes ka fəysla kia. /   The judge decided this case. [/fəysla/ "decision" is M2.]

/polis ne ws ki tələš ki. /   The police searched for him. [Lit. The police made his search. /tələš/ "search" is F1.]

(3) Type C formations:

(a) This formation is quite similar to Type A discussed above. An occurring object is marked by /ko/ (or a special object form may be employed), but, unlike Type A constructions, the number-gender of the verb is governed <u>not</u> by the number-gender of the object but by that of the noun of the complex verbal formation. No constructions of Type C have been introduced as yet. E. g.

/ws ne mwjhe nəsihət ki. /   He advised me. [/nəsihət/ "advice" is F1. /ki/ here agrees with the number-gender of /nəsihət/. If this formation had been Type A, the verb would have been MS: */nəsihət <u>kia</u>/.]

/ws ne əpne ləRke ko hydayət ki. /   He guided his boy. [/hydayət/ "guidance, instruction" is F1, and /ki/ agrees with it.]

(4) Type D formations:

(a) Transitive formations of this type are made with /dena/ "to give," /lena/

333

"to take, " /māgna/ "to ask for, request. " Intransitive forms are made with /mylna/ "to get, meet" or with /hona/ "to be, become. " In the past tenses this pattern resembles the Type C formation: the object is marked by /ko/ (or is a special object form); the noun of the complex verbal formation is never marked by /ko/, and the verb always agrees with this noun in number-gender. E. g.

/ws ne mwjhe jəvab dia. / He answered me. [Lit. He gave me an answer. /jəvab/ "answer" is M1, and the verb must thus be MS.]

/ws ne mwjrym ko səza di. / He punished the culprit. [Lit. He gave punishment to the culprit. /səza/ "punishment" is F1, and /di/ is thus required.]

/badšah ne fəwj ko hwkm dia. / The king gave an order to the army. [/hwkm/ "command, order" is M1.]

/badšah ne fəwj ko do nəe hwkm die. / The king gave two new orders to the army. [/hwkm/ "commands, orders" is here MP.]

/mwjrym ko səza myli. / The culprit received punishment.

/māy ne ws se yjazət li. / I took permission from him. [/yjazət/ "permission" is F1, and /li/ is thus required.]

/ws ko jəvab myla. / He got an answer.

(5) Type E formations:

(a) A very small group of complex verbal formations are made with /dena/, /mylna/, etc. but are otherwise similar to Type A formations: i. e. the verb agrees in number-gender with a nominative object; if the object is marked by /ko/ or is a special object form, the verb is treated as masculine singular. No constructions of Type E have been introduced as yet. E. g.

/ws ne əpni kytabõ ko tərtib dia. / He put his books in order. [/tərtib/ "order, arrangement" is F1, and had this construction been Type D, the verb would have had to be /di/. The verb does not agree with the noun of the complex verbal formation, however, and must thus be a "neutral" MS.]

There are also various substantives which may be found in more than one of the above categories. Usage differs from dialect to dialect and from speaker to speaker. E. g.

/māy ne vw kytab təlaš ki. / I searched for that book. [Type A: /ki/ agrees with the nominative object /kytab/ F1 "book. "]

/māy ne ws kytab ki təlaš ki. / I searched for that book. [Type B: the object possesses the noun of the complex verbal formation. These two examples are synonymous.]

/cor ne ws ko cori kia. / The thief stole that. [Type A: although /cori/ "theft" is F2, the verb is MS.]

/cor ne ws ki cori ki. / The thief stole that. [Type B.]

A great many complex verbal formations cannot be fitted easily into any of the above categories, nor are they numerous enough to warrant the establishment of further basic types, at least so far as the needs of the beginner are concerned. These will thus be grouped all together under the heading "Type F. "

11.307. The Verb: The Past Conditional.

As was stated in Sec. 7.312 (4), in its simplest form the "past conditional" consists of just the present participle. This agrees in number-gender with the subject of the clause (which does not take /ne/). This form denotes a "past irrealis": an act or state which is unrealiseable or contrary to fact. The negative for this form is always /nə/. E.g.

> /əgər mə̃y lahəwr jata, to ap ke lie yy ciz lata./ If I had gone to Lahore, I would have brought this thing for you.

> /yy to əccha hota!/ This would have been good! [This implies that the condition is now unrealiseable.]

> /əgər mə̃y vəhã nə hota, to vw šərarət zərur kərta./ If I had not been there, he would certainly have done [some] mischief. [Note that /vəhã nəhî hota/ means "is not generally there," while /vəhã nə hota/ means "would not have been there."]

The past conditional is also employed after past tense forms of various expressions denoting doubt, condition, obligation, etc. Present tense forms of these phrases are followed by the conditional. See Sec. 7.312. E.g.

> /ap ko cahie tha, ky ap vw kytab xəridte./ You should have bought that book.

> /ap ke lie zəruri tha, ky ap vəhã zərur pəhw̃cte./ It was necessary for you that you certainly should have arrived there. [But you didn't.]

> /ap ka fərz tha, ky ap qanun ke xylaf nə cəlte./ It was your duty not to have disobeyed the law. [But you did!]

> /kaš ky vw ata!/ Would that he had come! [/kaš/ "would that ..." has not yet been introduced.]

> /byhtər tha, ky ap jəvab dete./ It would have been better if you had answered.

The indicative may also be employed for the verb of the result clause. This usage is somewhat uncommon, however. E.g.

> /əgər mə̃y jata, to əccha tha./ If I had gone, it would have been well. [/hota/ would be commoner here instead of /tha/.]

The "past perfect conditional" seems to be identical in meaning with the past conditional, so far as the author could determine. This formation consists of the past participle of the main verb + the present participle of /hona/: e.g. /kia hota/, /dia hota/, /li hoti/, etc. If the main verb is transitive, then the subject must be marked by /ne/, and, like other past tense transitive formations, the verb agrees in number-gender with a nominative object, etc. (see Sec. 11.303). E.g.

> /əgər ap ne yy kam kia hota, to əccha hota./ If you had done this work, then it would have been well. [/kia hota/ agrees in number-gender with /kam/ M1 "work, job."]

As was seen for the present conditional, the past conditional can be employed with many tense-aspect constructions besides the indicative: e.g. the continuative, the <S + /səkna/>, the <S + /cwkna/>, the <OI + /ləgna/>, the <OI + /dena/>, etc. etc. Most of these will be of little use to the student at present. A few examples may be added, however, for completeness' sake:

> /əgər vw so rəha hota, to cəwkidar ki avaz nə swnta./ If he had been sleeping, [he] would not have heard the watchman's voice.

> /əgər bəcca nə rone ləgta, to polisvale wse nə dekhte./ If the child had not begun to cry, the policemen would not have seen him.

> /ap ko cahie tha, ky ap pəhle yy kam kər cwkte./ You should have finished this work first. [Rather archaic usage.]

/əgər ap yy kam kər səkte, to mɜ̃y ap ko zərur deta./   If you could have
   done this work, I would certainly have given [it] to you. [Or:]

/əgər ap yy kam kər səkte, to mɜ̃y ne ap ko zərur dia hota./   If you could
   have done this work, I would certainly have given [it] to you.
   [Synonymous with the preceding example.]

11.308. The Verb: the <OI + /dena/> Construction.

"To allow, let, permit to do ..." is expressed by the oblique infinitive + an inflected
form of /dena/ "to give." In the past tenses the subject of this construction is marked by
/ne/, and the occurring form of /dena/ agrees with a nominative object, if one is present.
If the object is a special object form or is marked by /ko/, then the form of /dena/ will
be masculine singular. Note that while the form of /dena/ may agree with the object in
number-gender, the infinitive always ends in /e/ and does not change. E.g.

/mɜ̃y ne əpne beTe ko syrf ek əxbar xəridne dia./   I let my son buy only
   one newspaper. [/dia/ agrees with /əxbar/ M1 "newspaper."]

/mɜ̃y ne əpne beTe ko syrf do əxbar xəridne die./   I let my son buy only
   two newspapers. [/die/ agrees with /əxbar/.]

/mɜ̃y ne əpne beTe ko syrf ek kytab xəridne di./   I let my son buy only
   one book. [/di/ agrees with /kytab/ F1 "book." Note that the
   infinitive remains /xəridne/ and does not change to /xəridni/.]

/mɜ̃y ne əpne beTe ko syrf do kytabē xəridne dĩ./   I let my son buy only
   two books.

/mere valyd sahəb ne mwjhe kəbhi sygreT nəhĩ pine dia./   My father
   never let me smoke a cigarette. [/dia/ agrees with /sygreT/ M1
   "cigarette."]

/jəj sahəb ne vəkil ko bəhs nə kərne di./   The judge didn't let the lawyer
   argue. [/di/ agrees with /bəhs/ F1 "argument, debate, discussion."]

/mɜ̃y ap ko kəbhi nəhĩ jane dũga./   I will never let you go.

/jane do!/   Let it go! [I.e. No matter, nevermind!]

/wse bəyThne dijie!/   Please let him sit down!

/mwjhe sone do!/   Let me sleep!

/ap ko cahie tha, ky ap wse jane dete./   You ought to have let him go.

11.309. The Verb: The Sequence of Tenses.

The simple past tense is employed in narratives in which each event follows the
preceding one without particular emphasis upon relative times or relative completion of
each act. E.g.

/ys šəxs ne əpni jeb se ek sygreT nykala, əwr pine ləga. ys ne ek sygreT
   cəwkidar ko bhi dia, jys mē behoš kərne ki dəvai thi. cəwkidar ne yy
   sygreT lia, əwr pine ləga./   This person took a cigarette out of his
   pocket and started to smoke. He gave a cigarette to the watchman
   too, in which there was a drug [lit. unconscious making medicine].
   The watchman took the cigarette and started to smoke.

In this narrative, /nykala/, /dia/, /lia/ and /thi/ are simple past tense verbs. By
their grammatical form they indicate nothing about the relationship of these events to one
another in time or in relative completion. Only their linear order in the sentence suggests
that these actions occurred in just this sequence in time. /pine ləga/, which occurs twice,

is also simple past in time, but displays an aspect (inceptive action) as well as simple tense.

If the speaker wishes to relate the events described in the narrative to one another in terms of relative time, relative completion, or affective reference of a previous event upon a later one, then the perfect and past perfect tenses may be used.

(1) The perfect tense expresses a past action whose results, effects, or reference are still present. E. g.

/ws ne šadi ki./ He married. [Simple past. There is no necessary connection between this event and the present context.]

/ws ne šadi ki həy./ He has married. [The marriage took place in the past but may still continue in the present.]

/mə̃y ne lahəwr dekha./ I saw Lahore. [Simple past.]

/mə̃y ne lahəwr dekha həy./ I have seen Lahore. [This utterance is related to a present context: perhaps someone has mentioned the city, and the speaker wishes to relate his own experience to the present context.]

/mə̃y ap ke lie TykəT laya./ I brought stamp[s] for you. [No necessary connection with the speaker's present.]

/mə̃y ap ke lie TykəT laya hū./ I have brought stamp[s] for you. [-- And here they are! The past action is related to the present context by using the perfect.]

/sahəb, ek admi aya./ Sir, a man came. [Simple past: no necessary relation to the present.]

/sahəb, ek admi aya həy./ Sir, a man has come. [--And he is still present.]

/kəl, mə̃y ne ek xət lykha, əwr aj wse bheja həy./ Yesterday I wrote a letter, and today I have sent it. [The writing of the letter is expressed by the simple past tense and is thus not specifically related in time, effect, etc. to the subsequent action. The sending, however, is related to some present context by using the perfect.]

(2) The past perfect expresses an action or event whose results, effects or reference were completed in the past and have no present reference. The past perfect event is usually related to some later past event (expressed or implied), and the results, effects, or reference of the past perfect event cease at the time of the second event. The past perfect may also be employed to indicate only remote past time (i. e. with no reference to some later past event). E. g.

/ws ne šadi ki thi./ He had married. [The marriage took place in the past but has no present reference. It may mean that he is no longer married, or that some later past event took place, and the speaker wishes to relate these to one another in relative time.]

/ws dəwran mə̃, mə̃y ne lahəwr dekha tha./ During that period I saw [lit. had seen] Lahore. [The action was completed during the period specified by /dəwran/, and there are no present effects or reference.]

/mə̃y wn ke ghər gəya tha, məgər vw nə myla./ I went [lit. had gone] to his home but didn't find him. [The act of going to his home was completed before the subsequent past event of not finding him.]

/kəl, mə̃y ne ek xət lykha tha, əwr aj wse bheja həy./ Yesterday I wrote [lit. had written] a letter, and today [I] have sent it. [The temporal relationship between the two events is clarified by the use of the past perfect, and the relationship of the second event to the present context is specified by the perfect.]

337

/mə̃y ne yy xəbər swni thi, əwr wsi vəqt nəwkər ko bazar bheja tha. /
I heard [lit. had heard] this news, and at that very time [I] sent [lit.
had sent] the servant to the market. [Both actions were completed in
the past, and both lack present reference. Some subsequent past
event is implied.]

/mə̃y ws vəqt tək gaRi Thik nə kər səka tha. ys lie mə̃y ap ke hã der se
pəhw̃ca. / I could not fix [lit. had not been able to fix] the car by
that time. Therefore I arrived at your place late. [Again, the
relative temporal relationship of the first event to the second is
specified by the past perfect.]

/jəb mə̃y əmrika mẽ tha, mə̃y ne pakystan ke bare mẽ bəhwt si kytabẽ
pəRhi thĩ. / When I was in America, I read [lit. had read] many
books about Pakistan. [Some further past event is implied.]

/jəb ap pəhw̃ce, to mə̃y khana kha cwka tha. / When you arrived, I had
[already] finished eating supper. [The eating was completed by the
time of your arrival.]

The sequence of tenses after verbs (or expressions) of seeing, hearing, knowing,
guessing, understanding, and other verbs of sense perception is quite different from that
found in English. In Urdu, after expressions denoting sense perception, the verb of the
subordinate clause is treated like "direct speech": i.e. it will be present tense if it refers
to the present at the time of the narrative, future if referring to the future tense at the time
of the narrative, etc. This is totally unlike English, which has a complex set of rules for
the sequence of tenses. For example, in English one says, "He saw that the house was
empty." The English speaker says, "I hoped that he would come. " In Urdu one says,
"I hoped that he will come. " E. g.

/jəb mə̃y ne swna, ky vw ghər xali həy, to mə̃y wse dekhne gəya. / When
I heard that the house was [lit. is] empty, I went to look at it.

/mə̃y ne swna, ky vw ghər xali tha. / I heard that the house was empty.
[It was empty at some time before that of the past narrative.]

/mwjhe wmmid thi, ky ap təšrif laẽge. / I hoped [lit. to me was hope],
that you would come [lit. will come].

/cəwkidar səmjha, ky zərur koi bat həy. / The watchman felt [lit. under-
stood] that there was [lit. is] something the matter.

/mwjhe malum tha, ky ap a rəhe hə̃y. / I knew [lit. to me was known]
that you were coming [lit. are coming].

/həm ne swna, ky ap kəl yəhã Thəyrẽge. / We heard that you would stay
[lit. will stay] here tomorrow.

Clauses containing relative and subordinative elements (e. g. /jəb/ "when, " /jəhã/
"where, " /jo/ "who, which, " etc.) are not treated as direct speech. If such a clause refers
to the same time as the main clause, then it must contain a verb of the same tense. E. g.

/vw koThi ke dərvaze pər pəhw̃ca, jəhã ek kwtta məwjud tha. / He
arrived at the door of the house, where there was a dog.

/vw ghər ki tərəf bhaga, jəhã ws ne kwtte ko mwrda paya. / He ran
towards the house, where he found the dog dead.

11.310. The Conjunction /ky/.

The conjunction /ky/ was introduced in Unit IV in the meaning of "that. " This word
may sometimes also be translated as "when. " In such cases, it denotes immediate,
sequential action: e. g. "I had just come in when he saw me. " /jəb/ Conj "when, " on the

338

other hand, has temporal reference only. A clause beginning with /ky/, of course, can never precede the main clause, as do clauses containing /jǝb/ and other relative and subordinate elements. E.g.

/dǝftǝr mē thoRi si der bǝyTha tha, ky hǝmare bǝRe dǝftǝr ke ek ǝfsǝr tǝ̃rif lae. / [I] had only just sat down in the office for a little while, when an officer of our head office came. [The first event had only just occurred when the second took place.]

/ǝbhi mǝ̃y yskul pǝhw̃ca hi tha, ky malum hwa, ky masTǝr sahǝb nǝhĩ ae. / I had only just arrived at school, when it became known that the teacher had not come. [/pǝhw̃ca hi tha/ stresses the immediate quality of the action. Compare:]

/jǝb mǝ̃y yskul pǝhw̃ca, to malum hwa, ky masTǝr sahǝb nǝhĩ ae. / When I arrived at school, it became known that the teacher had not come. [/jǝb/ denotes general temporal reference only.]

/mǝ̃y ǝbhi khana kha rǝha tha, ky kysi ne avaz di. / I was just eating supper, when someone called. [Compare:]

/jǝb mǝ̃y khana kha rǝha tha, to kysi ne avaz di. / When I was eating dinner, someone called.

339

11.401. Supplementary Vocabulary.

The following numerals are all Type I adjectives. See Sec. 2.401.

yktalys	forty-one
bəyalys [or /bealys/ or /byalys/]	forty-two
tetalys [Eastern /tētalys/]	forty-three
cəvalys [Also /cə̄valys/]	forty-four

As with other numerals ending in /ys/, there is a spelling pronunciation ending in /is/ for all of the above.

Other items are:

jagna [IIc: /ə/]	to wake up (intrans.)
jynhǒ OP [used only before /ne/]	whom, which [pl. relative]
kynhǒ OP [used only before /ne/]	who, which [pl.]?
ynhǒ OP [used only before /ne/]	these, they, he, she (honorific)

11.402. Supplementary Exercise I: Substitution.

1. aj ki Dak mē pǎytalys xət əwr sǎytys kaṟd hǎy.

forty-two	forty-four
twenty-two	forty-three
thirty-three	forty-one
forty-five	sixteen
forty-two	thirty-eight

2. jəb mǎy vapəs aya, to ys ne mwjhe dekha.

arose	they, those
awoke	he, this one
arrived	he, that one
got down	somebody
came in	they, these

11.403. Supplementary Exercise II: Variation.

1. ap mē se, syrf pǎytalys ləRkǒ ne pakystan dekha həy.
    ap mē se, syrf ynhǒ ne pakystan dekha həy.
    ap mē se, kytnǒ ne pakystan dekha həy.
    ap mē se, kynhǒ ne pakystan dekha həy.
    kya, ap mē se, kysi ne pakystan dekha həy?
    ap mē se, jynhǒ ne pakystan dekha həy, hath wThaē.
2. ynhǒ ne əmrika ki tarix pəRhi həy.
    kys ne əmrika ki tarix pəRhi həy.
    kynhǒ ne əmrika ki tarix pəRhi həy. [1]

bəyalys ləRkõ ne əmrika ki tarix pəRhi həy.

jys ne əmrika ki tarix pəRhi həy, mwjhe bətaie!

jynhõ ne əmrika ki tarix pəRhi həy, mwjhe bətaẽ.

[1]/kynhõ/ is becoming obsolete. Modern speakers generally prefer /kyn logõ
[ne]/.

11.501. Substitution.

1.

mə̃y	ne ədalət mẽ gəvah	peš kia.
the lawyer	his case	did[1]
the officer	all the papers	did
the police	the culprit	did
the policeman	the register	did
they	his picture	did

[1]Unless /ko/ is used, "did" here must agree with the number-gender of the object. See Sec. 11.303.

2.

ysmyth sahəb ne	mere lyfafe	ystemal kie.
the judge	to the culprit	gave punishment
the doctor	to the sick boy	gave medicine
the lawyer	his case	began
the teacher	from the boys	questioned
the watchman	to them	answered

3.

yy dəvai	həspətal	ke lie	ai həy.
this letter	you		has come[1]
this envelope	that person		has come
this mail	the woman		has come
this lawyer	his file		has come
these receipts	Mr. əxtər		have come

[1]"has come" and "have come" must agree with the subject.

4.

ws ne	ədalət mẽ	yy təsvir	dekhi thi.
	in front of the dog	the meat	had thrown
	from the postoffice	the money order	had gotten done
	about Pakistan	many books	had read
	from the rich man's house	45,000 Rs. of property	had stolen
	in front of me	a receipt	had made

5.

vəqt bəhwt kəm	tha,	vərna mə̃y zərur jata.
	is	would have written
	is	would have eaten
	is	would have sat down
	is	would have slept
	was	would have arrived

6.

həm	wsi vəqt	Dakxane	gəe the.
	at once	the court	had arrived
	on that very day	Multan	had come back
	for a little while	on the minaret	had climbed
	in the evening	from the roof	had come down

	after about five minutes	from the office	had gone out

7. byhtər tha, ky ap **šor nə məcate,**

    had not praised him

    had not taken the money

    had not awakened him

    had not searched for it

    had not argued with him

8. **koi DeRh ghənTe** tək **həmara mwqədma** jari **rəha.**

about five minutes	our conversation	remained[1]
half an hour	our argument	remained
seven years	this order	remained
two hours	this class	remained
last year	this law	remained

> [1]"Remained" must, of course, agree with the subject.

9. **wə šəxs** ne **cəwkidar** se kwch nəhĭ kəha.

the thief	the judge
the officer	that person
the king	his son
they	the lawyer
the traveller	the policeman

10. **ys əwrət** ne **səRək pər** | **dəs rupəe** | **pae.**

I [MS]	here	much rest	found[1]
the watchman	at the door	this letter	found
the thieves	in my cupboard	nothing	found
the dogs	on the ground	meat	found
the police	in the curry	poison	found

> [1]Unless /ko/ is used, "found" must agree with the number-gender of the object. See Sec. 11.303.

11.502. Transformation.

1. Change the underlined verb forms in the following sentences to the simple past tense. Insert /ne/ where necessary. In transitive sentences be sure to make the verb agree in number-gender with a nominative object; see Sec. 11.303.

   a. mšy bylkwl nəhĭ **səməjhta hŭ.**

   b. vw təqribən calys həzar rupəe **cwraĕge.**

   c. mšy wse təlaš **kərta hŭ.**

   d. mšy wə ki təlaš **kərta hŭ.**

   e. mwjrym bhagne ki košyš **kərta həy.**

   f. vəkil sahəb ko bəhs kərne ka məwqa **mylega.**

   g. jəj sahəb pərsŏ ys kes ka fəysla **dĕge.**

   h. pakystan ki hwkumət ek nəya hwkm jari **kəregi.**

343

i. vw əpne karD ryjysTri kərēge.

j. mə̃y ws ko yy xət nəhī́ pəRhne dū̃ga.

2. Change the underlined verb forms in the following sentences to the perfect tense. Other instructions are as for (1) above.

    a. kya, koi cae lane ke lie jaega?

    b. mə̃y bhi mwltan dekhū̃ga.

    c. mə̃y aj ek məni arDər bhyjvaū̃ga.

    d. ys šəhr ki polis wse pəkRegi.

    e. meri bivi khana kha cwki.

    f. cəwkidar mwjh se sygreT leta həy.

    g. səb log həvai jəhaz se jaēge.

    h. mə̃y ap ke lie yy fayl bənata hū̃.

    i. vw yy Dyrama zərur dekhēge.

    j. meri beTi bhi pakystan ki tarix pəRhti həy.

3. Change the underlined verb forms in the following sentences to the past perfect. Other instructions are as for (1) above.

    a. mə̃y pychle sal kəraci gəya.

    b. həmara kes bhi wsi dyn peš hoga.

    c. kəl həm xub aram kərēge.

    d. mə̃y ws pər yəqin nəhī́ kərūga.

    e. ap ws ke lie bəhwt košyš kərte hə̃y.

    f. mə̃y əpne Dybbe ko təlaš kərta hū̃.

    g. cəwkidar ghərvalõ ko jəgaega.

    h. ys ke bad, mwjhe jana pəRega.

    i. vw mwjhe əndər jane dēge.

    j. vəkil sahəb ys məwqe pər bəhs kərēge.

4. Change the underlined verb forms in the following sentences to the simple past. Insert /ne/ where necessary. Make two versions of each sentence: one employing /ko/ with the object, and the other with a nominative object. Make any other necessary changes.

    a. mə̃y əwr ap yy Dyrama dekhēge.

    b. vw dərvaza kholega.

    c. mere beTe əwr beTiã əpne kəpRe pəhnēge.

    d. meri bivi əpne xət xwd ryjysTri kərati hə̃y.

    e. mə̃y yy kytabē̃ pəRhū̃gi.

    f. qwli mera saman wThaega.

    g. vəkil sahəb əpne gəvah peš kərēge.

    h. badšah yy qanun jari rəkhega.

    i. meri beTiã rupõ ki əlmari bənd nəhī́ kərtī́.

    j. mə̃y aj vw cadər bədlū̃gi.

5. Change the underlined verbs in the following sentences to the past conditional. Change the negative from /nəhī́/ to /nə/, where necessary.

344

a. əgər vw bimar həy, to ghər <u>jaega</u>.

b. əgər vw mwjhe nəhĩ <u>bwlaēge</u>, to mə̃y nəhĩ <u>jaūga</u>.

c. əgər ap cəwkidar ko nə <u>DāTē</u>, to vw sari rat <u>soega</u>.

d. əgər mə̃y TykəT nə <u>xəridū</u>, to mwjhe əndər ane nəhĩ <u>dēge</u>.

e. əgər ap ke pas koi kaɣəz <u>ho</u>, to mə̃y ys xət ka jəvab əbhi <u>lykhūga</u>.

f. əgər yy kam ap ke lie zyada mwškyl <u>həy</u>, to ap ki kəmpni ap se nəhĩ <u>kəraegi</u>.

g. əgər həmē mwltan jana pəRta <u>həy</u>, to ap ke hā nəhĩ <u>aēge</u>.

h. əgər twm šor <u>məcaoge</u>, to polis twmhē fəwrən gyryftar <u>kəregi</u>.

i. əgər ap log məsruf nə <u>hõ</u>, to mere sath Dyrama <u>dekh</u> səkte <u>hə̃y</u>.

j. əgər vw fəwrən cabi ki təlaš nə <u>kərē</u>, to əlmari bənd <u>rəhegi</u>.

11.503. Fill the Blanks.

1. Fill the blanks with the correct adjectival and verbal suffixes. See Sec. 11.303.

a. badšah ne ys məsjyd ka minar ūc __ kəra __.

b. badšah ne ys ymarət ko ūc __ kəra ___.

c. phəlvale ne phəl səst __ k __.

d. kəpRevale ne kəpRa səst __ k __.

e. bəccõ ne yy cadər kal __ k __.

f. bəccõ ne ys cadər ko kal __ k __.

g. phəlvale ne əpni qimət adh __ k __.

h. polis ne do əwrtē gyryftar k __.

i. ws ne əpni səheli ko šərmynd __ k __.

j. nəwkər ne dudh ko ThənD __ k __.

11.504. Variation.

1. wnhõ ne mwjhe jane nəhĩ dia.

wnhõ ne mwjhe bəhs kərne nəhĩ di.

ynhõ ne əpne ləRkõ ko sygreT nəhĩ pine dia.

cəwkidar ne mwsafyr ko əndər nəhĩ ane dia.

polisvale ne wnhē šor nəhĩ kərne dia.

jəj sahəb ne həmē bolne nəhĩ dia.

2. mə̃y ne khyRki kholni šwru ki.

wnhõ ne lyfafa kholna šwru kia.

həmare dost ne wse wThana šwru kia.

DakTər sahəb ne dəvai deni šwru ki.

vəkil sahəb ne tarix ke bare mē puchna šwru kia.

polis ne cor ko təlaš kərna šwru kia.

3 ap jəldi jaie, vərna ap nəhĩ pəhw̃c səkēge.

ap ko jəldi jana cahie, vərna ap vəqt pər nəhĩ pəhw̃cēge.

ap ko jəldi jana pəRega, vərna ap Dakxana bənd paēge.

ap ko jəldi jana tha, vərna mə̃y bhi sath cəlta.

ap ne yy kam bəhwt tez kia tha, vərna ytni jəldi təyyar nə hota.

ap ne yy kam xwd kia, vərna kəbhi nə hota.

4. cũke mɐ̃y ap ka xət ryjysTri nə kər səka, ys lie šayəd nəhĭ pəhw̌cega.

cũke ap məni arDər nə kəra səke, ys lie ap ke dost ko bəhwt mwškyl hogi.

cũke mwjhe mwltan ke raste ka pəta nəhĭ həy, ys lie mɐ̃y ap se puchta hũ.

cũke aj jəj sahəb ədalət mɛ̃ nəhĭ hɐ̃y, ys lie həmara kes peš nəhĭ hoga.

cũke rupõ ki əlmari xali thi, ys lie vw fəwrən səmjha, ky cori hwi həy.

cũke vw log, jynhõ ne yy hərəkət thi, aj məwjud nəhĭ hɐ̃y, ys lie mɐ̃y kwch nəhĭ
kər səkta.

5. ajkəl ys ədalət mɛ̃ mera mwqədma jari həy.

tin həfte tək, ysi ədalət mɛ̃ mera mwqədma jari rəha.

jəj sahəb əwr vəkil sahəb ki bəhs bəhwt der tək jari rəhi.

pakystan ki hwkumət ne tin sal tək yy qanun jari rəkkha.

həmari kəmpni ke əfsər ne ek nəya hwkm jari kia.

ws mwsafyr ke sər se xun jari tha.

6. mɐ̃y pərsõ ap ke lie ek xət laya tha.

mɐ̃y kəl ap ke lie do pyali cini laya tha.

meri səheli xwd ap ke lie yy kytab lai thi.

cor vəhã se cori kər ke, bəhwt sa saman laya tha.

wn ke valyd sahəb dəftər ja kər, əpni fayl vapəs lae the.

mɐ̃y xət bhyjva kər, ws ki rəsid vapəs laya tha.

7. mwsafyr ne əpne suTkes ki təlaš ki.

mwsafyr ne əpna suTkes təlaš kia.

polis ne zəhr ki bəhwt təlaš ki.

mɐ̃y ne pərsõ ws lyfafe ki bəhwt təlaš ki, məgər vw nə myla.

ws kəmpni ne polis se ws šəxs ki təlaš kərai.

mɐ̃y ne əpne nəwkər se ys fayl ki təlaš kərai.

8. vw əfsər, jyse ap jante hɐ̃y, aj məwjud nəhĭ.

vw məni arDər, jo ap ne kəl bheja tha, aj vapəs aya həy.

vw tarix ki kytab, jo masTər sahəb ne kəl bətai thi, bəhwt hi asan həy.

vw šəxs, jyse ap ne kəl behoš paya tha, aj swba hoš mɛ̃ aya həy.

vw ləRke, jynhõ ne yy šərarət ki thi, aj ae hɐ̃y.

vw bat, jo ap ne kəl kəhi thi, mɐ̃y nəhĭ manta.

9. swba, jo sabwn mɐ̃y ne lane ke lie kəha tha, kya, vw lae hɐ̃y?

pərsõ, jo təwlia mɐ̃y ne xəridne ke lie kəha tha, kya, vw lae ho?

kəl, jo kam mɐ̃y ne kərne ke lie kəha tha, kya, ap ne vw kia həy?

pərsõ, jo rəsidẽ wnhõ ne bənane ke lie kəha tha, kya, vw təyyar hɐ̃y?

kəl, mɐ̃y ne jo gošt phẽkne ke lie kəha tha, vw twm ne phẽka, ya nəhĭ.

pərsõ, həm ne jo mal bhyjvane ke lie kəha tha, twm ne wse bheja, ya nəhĭ.

10. mɐ̃y syrf do mynəT bəyTha tha, ky vw bəhs kərne ləge.

əbhi cor məkan se bahər nyk̇la hi tha, ky polis ne wse gyryftar kia.

həm sone ke kəmre mɛ̃ gəe hi the, ky ytne mɛ̃ ap ae.

mwqədma əbhi šwru nəhĭ hwa tha, ky pəta cəla, ky jəj sahəb aj bimar hɐ̃y.

mẽy thoRi si der soya tha, ky wnhõ ne mwjhe jəgaya.

vw baɣice mẽ thoRi si der bəyThe'the, ky bhut dərəxt ke piche se nykla.

11.505. Translation.

Translate the second portions of the following sentences into Urdu. Be careful of the tense sequence. See Sec. 11.309.

1. cəwkidar ne dekha, ky ...

the boy was coming from home.

the dog was present there.

the man had finished smoking a cigarette.

a person was standing at the door.

the money cabinet was empty.

2. mẽy ne swna həy, ky ...

tomorrow you would go to Lahore.

he was coming in the evening.

the food was good in this hotel. [Lit. the food is gotten well ...]

today there was a holiday in school.

he doesn't see movies. [Treat "movie" as singular.]

3. mwjhe wmmid thi, ky ...

he would not come.

the teacher would be in school.

I would be able to sleep all day.

our case would be presented today.

she would certainly arrive by that date.

4. mẽy səmjha, ky ...

Mr. əxtər was an officer in this bank.

he mostly stayed [at] home.

there would be an interesting case presented today.

you were going to the court.

he would give evidence today.

5. wn ka xyal tha, ky ...

he was an American.

we were going to Karachi.

he was coming straight from the office.

I always obey [lit. believe] my wife's command.

the mail would not come today.

11.506. Response.

1. ap pərsõ kəhã gəe the.
2. kya, ap ne xwd kəbhi bhut dekha həy?
3. kya, ap ko ədalət jane ka šəwq həy?

4. pakystani bõykõ ke vəqt kya kya hõy.

5. kya, ap wrdu ko asan səməjhte hõy?

6. kya, ap ne kysi kəmpni mẽ nəwkri ki həy?

7. kya, ap həmeša əpne xət ryjysTri kər ke bhejte hõy?

8. swba, ap kys vəqt wThte hõy.

9. aj kəwnsi tarix həy.

10. kya, ap kəbhi həvai jəhaz se kəraci gəe hõy?

11. ys vəqt, ap ki jeb mẽ kytne pəyse hõy.

12. kya, ap təmam pakystan dekhna cahte hõy, ya syrf cənd jəghẽ?

13. kya, ap ko bəhs kərne ka šəwq həy?

14. kya, ap ke ghər se məni arDər ate hõy?

15. kya, ap ne kəbhi qəydxana dekha həy?

11.507. Conversation Practice.

Mr. Smith and Dr. Rəhim visit the postoffice.

R: kya, ap ko TykəT lene hõy?

S: ji hã, kwch TykəT lene hõy, əwr kwch karD əwr lyfafe bhi cahiẽ. ek xət ryjysTri
kərana həy, əwr do məni arDər bhi bhyjvane hõy.

R: aie, pəhle yəhã se TykəT əwr lyfafe xəridẽ.

They go to the stamp window. Mr. Smith addresses the clerk.

S: mwjhe bis bis pəyse ke dəs TykəT cahiẽ, əwr pəccys pəccys pəyse ke bhi dəs TykəT
cahiẽ. bara karD əwr aTh lyfafe bhi dijie. səb kytne ke hõge.

Cl: chəy rupəe chəbbys pəyse ke. yy lijie.

S: əmrika xət bhejne ke lie, kytne pəyse ləgte hõy.

Cl: həvai xət bhejne ke lie dəs ane, əwr həvai lyfafe ka səva rupəya.

S: əgli Dak kəb nyklegi.

Cl: šam ko, tin bəje.

S: šwkria. [To Dr. Rəhim:] ryjysTri kəhã hoti həy.

R: vw samne həy. aie, wdhər cəlẽ.

S [at the registry window]: mwjhe yy xət ryjysTri kərana həy.

Cl: laie, mwjhe dijie, ys pər pəccys pəyse ke TykəT əwr cahiẽ.

S: kya, məni arDər bhi ap hi kərte hõy?

Cl: ji nəhĩ. məni arDər ki khyRki age həy.

S [at the money order window]: mwjhe yy məni arDər əmrika bhyjvana həy, əwr ek məni
arDər kəraci bhejna həy.

Cl: kəraci to məni arDər ja səkta həy, lekyn əmrika həm nəhĩ bhejte.

S: to mẽy yy pəyse əmrika kəyse bhejũ.

Cl: ap bãyk se bhyjva səkte hõy. pakystan mẽ Dakxana dusre mwlk mẽ pəyse nəhĩ bhejta.
yy kam həmare bãyk kərte hõy.

S: kəwnsa bãyk yy kam kərta həy.

Cl: ap kysi bãyk mẽ jaẽ. vw yy pəyse əmrika bhej səkte hõy. laie, kəraci ke məni arDər ke pəyse mwjhe dijie.

S: yy səw rupəe ka məni arDər həy. ys pər kytne pəyse ləgẽge.

Cl: ek rupəya pəccys pəyse. yy ys ki rəsid həy.

Mr. Smith thanks the clerk and turns to Dr. Rəhim.

S: mera xyal həy, ky mə̃y carTərD bə̃yk jaũ. vəhã əziz sahəb se bhi mylna cahta hũ.
dusre, yy məni arDər wn ke bə̃yk se niw yark bhyjvaũga. kya, ap bhi mere sath cəlẽge?

R: ji nəhĩ. mwjhe aj əpne bəRe dəftər jana həy, jəhã əpne əfsər se kwch nəi dəvaiõ ke bare
mẽ batcit kərni həy.

S: bəhwt əccha. mə̃y bə̃yk jata hũ. phyr šam ko khane pər mylẽge. xwda hafyz!

Mr. Smith arrives at the Chartered Bank and goes to Mr. əziz' office.

ə: aie, ysmyth sahəb! təšrif laie! kya xydmət kər səkta hũ.

S: mwjhe kwch pəyse niw yark əpne bhai ko bhyjvane həy. mə̃y pəhle Dakxane gəya tha,
əwr wnhõ ne bətaya, ky yy pəyse syrf bə̃yk bhej səkta həy.

ə: əgərce yy bəhwt asan nəhĩ, lekyn koi bat nəhĩ. ap əpne bhai ka pəta ys kaγəz pər lykhie.
mə̃y košyš kərũga.

S: yy pəyse kytne dynõ mẽ pəhwc səkte həy.

ə: wmmid həy, ky tin həfte mẽ. -- ap kəwfi piẽge, ya cae.

S: əgər kəwfi ho, to byhtər həy.

When the coffee arrives, Mr. Smith begins to ask some general questions about the
bank.

S: ap ke dəftər ke vəqt kya hə̃y.

ə: gərmiõ mẽ swba sat bəje se, dopəhr ke ek bəje tək, əwr sərdiõ mẽ, swba nəw bəje se
šam ke car bəje tək.

S: kya, həfte əwr ytvar ko chwTTi hoti həy?

ə: ji nəhĩ. syrf ytvar ko chwTTi kərte hə̃y, əwr jwme ke roz bara bəje chwTTi hoti həy.

S: ap ke bə̃yk ki ymarət bəhwt xubsurət həy. bylkwl nəi malum hoti həy.

ə: ji hã, yy ymarət əbhi pychle sal bəni həy.

S: carTərD bə̃yk pakystan mẽ kys kys jəga həy.

ə: təqribən təmam bəRe šəhrõ mẽ həy. əwr dusre mwlkõ mẽ bhi hər bəRe šəhr mẽ məwjud
həy.

S: ji hã, mwjhe yad aya -- niw yark mẽ bhi həy.

ə: kya, kəwfi əwr piẽge?

S: ji nəhĩ, šwkria. əb mə̃y yjazət cahta hũ. mera yrada həy, ky aj ədalət jaũ.

ə: kya, koi kam həy?

S: ji nəhĩ. syrf vəhã ja kər koi mwqədma swnũga. ədalət bhi bəhwt dylcəsp jəga həy.
əgər ap ke pas kwch vəqt həy, to ap bhi mere sath cəlẽ.

ə: bəhwt əccha, mə̃y bhi cəlta hũ.

Mr. Smith and Mr. əziz arrive at the court, where they find a case in progress.

ə: yy vəkil sahəb, jo dãẽ tərəf khəRe hə̃y, bəhwt məšhur vəkil hə̃y. yn ka nam əxtər həy.

S: jəj sahəb kəhã hə̃y. nəzər nəhĩ ate.

ə: šayəd əpne kəmre mẽ hə̃y. dekhie, vw a rəhe hə̃y.

S: mera xyal həy, ky age cəl kər bəyThẽ. vəhã se byhtər swn səkẽge.
ə: Thik həy. aie, vw samne do kwrsiã xali hẽy.

The case begins.

S: vaqəi, yy vəkil sahəb bəhwt qabyl malum hote hẽy. kytni əcchi bəhs kər rəhe hẽy!
ə: ji hã.
S: ws mwjrym ki tərəf dekhẽ. bylkwl pəresan nəhĩ həy. əgərce thoRi der bad wse qəydxane jana həy.
ə: ys mẽ pəresan hone ki kya bat həy! qəydxana ws ke lie koi nəi jəga nəhĩ. šayəd ws ne pəhle bhi kəi dəfa dekha həy. pwrana cor malum hota həy.
S: vw samne kəwn sahəb hẽy.
ə: yy polis əfsər hẽy, əwr mwqədme mẽ gəvah hẽy. ys ke bad yn ki gəvahi hogi.
S: ys kes ka fəysla kəb hoga.
ə: do həfte ke bad. mera xyal həy, ky mwjrym ko do ya tin sal ki səza hogi.
S: mwqədma to xətm ho rəha həy. əb cəlna cahie.
ə: ji hã. koi dusra kes to kafi der ke bad šwru hoga. -- kya, ap bhi mere sath bãyk cəlẽge?
S: ji nəhĩ. kya, ap ko yad həy, ky aj həfta həy. šam ko mere hã khane pər ana həy.
ə: ji hã. xub yad həy. koi saRhe chəy bəje aũga.
S: bəhwt əccha. xwda hafyz!

11.508. Conversation Stimulus.

Topics may include the following:
1. A court case.
2. A visit to the postoffice: buying stamps.
3. A visit to the postoffice: sending a money order.
4. A trip to the bank.
5. A chat with a lawyer.

aram M1	rest, ease, comfort
asan A1	easy
ədalət F1	court (of law)
əfsər M/F1	officer
əgla A2	next, forthcoming, first, ahead
əlmari F2	cupboard, cabinet
əmir M1 A1	rich, wealthy, rich man
batcit F1	conversation, chat
bəhs F1	argument, debate, discussion
bənana [C: /bənna/: IIc]	to make, build, construct
bəyalys [or /bəyalis/, /bealys/ or /bealis/, /byalys/ or /byalis/] A1	forty-two
behoš A1	unconscious
bhyjvana [DC: /bhejna/: Id]	to cause to be sent
bylkwl Adv	entirely, completely
calak A1	tricky, deceitful, clever
cəvalys [or /cəvalis/, or /cə̄valys/ or /cə̄valis/] A1	forty-four
cor M/F1	thief
cori F2	theft
cwrana [Ia]	to steal
cūke Conj	since
dəvai F2	medicine, remedy, drug
*dia / die / di / dī	gave [irreg. past of /dena/ "to give"]
Dak F1	mail, post
Dakxana M2	postoffice
fayl F1 [or M1]	file (of document, etc.)
fəysla M2	decision
gəvah M/F1	witness
gəvahi F2	evidence, giving witness
ghərvala M2	member of the family, husband
gyryftar PA1	caught, apprehended, arrested
həmeša Adv	always, forever
həvai A1	air, aerial
hoš M1 [np]	consciousness
hwkm M1	order, command
jagna [IIc: /ə/]	to awaken, wake up (intrans.)
jari PA1	continuing, current, in force, issuing
jəgana [C: /jagna/: IIc]	to awaken (trans.)
jəhaz M1	ship, vessel
jəj M/F1	judge

351

jeb F1	pocket
jynhõ OP [used only before /ne/]	whom, which [pl. relative]
kaɣəz M1	paper
karD M1	card, postcard
kəi A1	several, a good many
kəmpni [or /kəmpəni/] F2	company
kərana [C: /kərna/: Ic]	to cause to be done
kes M1	case
*kia / kie / ki / kī	did, made [irreg. past of /kərna/ "to do, make"]
košyš F1	try, attempt
kwtta M2	(male) dog
kynhõ OP [used only before /ne/]	whom, which? [pl. interrog.]
kyõke Conj	because
lekyn Conj	but
*lia / lie / li / lī	took [irreg. past of /lena/ "to take"]
lyfafa M2	envelope
mal M1	property, goods, stock
manna [Ic: /ə/]	to believe, obey
məni arDər M1	money order
mwjrym M1 A1	culprit, criminal
mwltan M1 [np]	Multan (a city in West Pakistan)
mwqədma M2	lawsuit
mwrda M2 A1	dead, corpse
mwškyl F1 A1	difficulty, difficult
nəya A2	new
ne Post	marker of the subject of a past tense transitive verb
pana [Ia]	to find, obtain, acquire, get
pərsõ Adv M1	day before yesterday; day after tomorrow
pãytalys [or /pãytalis/] A1	forty-five
peš PA1	presented, offered
phẽkna [Id: /y/]	to throw, toss
pychla A2	last, former
rasta M2	road, way
rəsid F1	receipt
ryjysTri F2	registry, registration
səval M1	question
šəxs M1	person
šwru M1 [np]	beginning, start
tarix F1	date; history
təlaš F1	search
təmam A1	complete, all, entire
təqribən Adv	almost, approximately, about

tetalys [or /tetalis/, /tḗtalys/ or forty-three
    /tḗtalis/] A1
vəkil M/F1 lawyer, pleader
vərna Conj otherwise
wmmid F1 hope, anticipation
wnhõ OP [used only before /ne/] they, those
wThna [IIc: /w/] to get up, arise, rise
xət M1 letter
xətm PA1 finished, ended, dead
xəyr F1 Adv well, anyway, good; wellbeing, good luck
xwd Adv self
xydmət F1 service
yəqin M1 [np] certainty, assurance, confidence
yktalys [or /yktalis/] A1 forty-one
ynhõ OP [used only before /ne/] they, these
zəhr M1 poison
zərur Adv certainly, necessarily

An Arabic quatrain written in elegant calligraphy.

UNIT TWELVE

12.000.   SCRIPT IV

The presentation of the Urdu writing system will be completed in this Unit with the description of (1) numerals, (2) systems of writing amounts of money and prices, (3) dates, (4) punctuation, and (5) certain special signs.

12.001.   Numerals.

Sequences of numerals are written from left to right. Recent practice also tends to insert commas into longer sequences, either after thousands, millions, etc., according to the British system, or else after the /lakh/, /kəroR/, etc.

SYMBOL	WRITTEN FORM	PRONUNCIATION	MEANING
۱	ایک	ek	one
۲	دو	do	two
۳	تین	tin	three
۴	چار	car	four
۵	پانچ	pāc	five
۶	چھ	chəy	six
۷	سات	sat	seven
۸	آٹھ	aTh	eight
۹	نو	nəw	nine
۰	صفر	syfr	zero

E.g., ۷۳۰ /sat səw tis/ "730", ۱٬۵۰۶ /ek həzar, pāc səw chəy/ "1,506", ۲۲ /bays/ "22", ۱۳۹ /ek səw wntalys/ "139", ۱٬۳۶٬۲۵٬۴۳۰ /ek kəroR, sə̄ytys lakh, pəccys həzar, chəy səw tis/ (also written ۱۳٬۶۲۵٬۴۳۰) "13,725,630".

12.002.   Amounts of Money and Prices.

The decimal system has been recently introduced both in India and Pakistan, and thus the old system (a /rupəya/ = 16 /ana/, each of which = 4 /pəysa/, each of which = 3 /pai/) is rapidly becoming obsolete. In the older notation, the /rupəya/, /ana/, and /pai/ (the /pəysa/ was not indicated) were written from left to right in three columns separated by diagonal slashes; an empty column was marked by a dash, except when the amount was less than a /rupəya/, in which case the /rupəya/ column was not written at all. E. g., ‎ /do rupəe, bara ane, tin pai/ "Rs. 2/12/3", ‎ /sat rupəe, chəy pai/ "Rs. 7/-/6", ‎ /pə̃ytalys rupəe, do ane/ "Rs. 45/2/-", ‎ /tera ane/ "Rs. -/13/-".

The diagonal slash is now employed in Pakistan as a decimal point: ‎ /pã̄c rupəe, pəccys nəe pəyse/ "Rs. 5. 25". In India, the English decimal point, the diagonal slash, and occasionally a ‎ written on the line are all used (in roughly this order of preference): ‎ or ‎ or ‎ /tin rupəe, calys pəyse/ "Rs. 3. 40".

An even more archaic system, called /rəqəm/ "amount, numeral notation" contains special characters for each digit from one through nine and also for each decade ("ten", "twenty", "thirty", etc.). Modified forms of each digit may be written below the decade symbol to indicate the numbers within the decade ("twenty-eight", "thirty-two", etc.). The number of /ane/ may be added to the left of the /rupəya/ symbol, using ordinary Urdu numerals followed by the sign ‎ . A quarter, a half, and three quarters of an /ana/ can be shown by further symbols. Although this notation contains symbols for numerals up to the /lakh/ and the /kəroR/, all but the lower figures are now quite obsolete. One may' occasionally find prices written in this notation in smaller cities and towns, however, and also in small shops in such places as Lahore's Old City. The system will be of little use to the student at this stage and is given here merely for reference.

SYMBOL	VALUE	SYMBOL	VALUE	SYMBOL	VALUE
‎	-/-/3	‎	-/-/9	‎	-/1/3
‎	-/-/6	‎	-/1/-	‎	-/1/6

SYMBOL	VALUE	SYMBOL	VALUE	SYMBOL	VALUE
لَن�	-/1/9	عسم	12/-/-	معم	70/-/-
ڔ	-/2/-	بسم	13/-/-	لسم	80/-/-
صم	1/-/-	لعسم	14/-/-	لعم	90/-/-
غار	2/-/-	هسم	15/-/-	مار	100/-
سے	3/-/-	عسم	16/-/-	مار	200/-
لعم	4/-/-	معسم	17/-/-	سار	300/-
صم	5/-/-	مسم	18/-/-	لعمار	400/-
سے	6/-/-	لوعم	19/-/-	صمار	500/-
معم	7/-/-	عسم	20/-/-	سمار	600/-
سے	8/-/-	سم	30/-/-	معمار	700/-
لعم	9/-/-	لعم	40/-/-	سار	800/-
عم	10/-/-	صم	50/-/-	نعمار	900/-
لعم	11/-/-	سم	60/-/-	الفم	1,000/-
				لاكھ	lakh/-

E.g., مائے "Rs. 155", لنٌ صرُ "Rs. 5/1/9", للعسم "Rs. 24/9/6", مالِمسلِر
"Rs. 221/1/3".

12.003. Dates.

Reading from right to left, the day of the month is written first (followed by the /
sign), then the month, and finally the year. A special sign is usually written under the
numerals denoting the year: ‿ (derived from Arabic سنة "year"). Dates
according to the Christian era are indicated by a small ؏ (derived from the ع of
عيسوی /isvi/ "Christian") following the ‿ sign. A small ھ is written after dates

357

according to the Muslim calendar (for بجری /hyjri/, the date of the departure of the Prophet Muhammad for Madina in 622 A.D.). "B.C." is shown by ق م (for تبل مسیح /qəble məsih/ "before Christ"). E.g. ۱۲اگست سنه۱۹۶۴ "August 12, 1964 A.D.", "7 Mwhərrəm, 1384 A.H." ۵۱رجولالی سنه۵۷قم "July 15, 57 B.C.".

12.004. Punctuation.

SYMBOL	VALUE
۔	Period
،	Comma
:	Colon
؛	Semicolon
؟	Question mark
!	Exclamation mark
" "	Quotation marks
( )	Brackets
ــؔ	No. (E.g., ۱ؔ "no. 1")
ـہؔ	Footnote (E.g., ۲ؔ "footnote 2")

12.005. Special Signs.

SYMBOL   VALUE

ؐ   Sign placed over the name of the Prophet Muhammad. It stands for the Arabic phrase صَلَّی اللّٰهُ عَلَیْهِ وَسَلَّم /səlləllaho ələyhe və səlləm/ "may God's peace and blessings be upon him! Pious Muslims never utter the name of the Holy Prophet without adding this phrase. It is also . abbreviated صلعم . E.g. مُحَمَّد /mwhəmməd, səlləllaho ələyhe və səlləm/ "Muhammad, God's peace and blessings be upon him!"

358

SYMBOL	VALUE

عليه ، ع   Sign placed over the name of other Prophets; it stands for عَلَيْهِ ٱلسَّلَام

/ələyhyssəlam/ "upon him be peace!" E.g., عِيسَى /isa,

ələyhyssəlam/ "Christ, upon him be peace!"

رض   Sign placed over the names of the Companions of the Prophet; it stands

for رَضِيَ ٱللَّهُ عَنْهُ /rəziəllaho ənho/ "may God be pleased with him!"

(For a woman عَنْهَا /ənha/, for msc. pl., عَنْهُمْ /ənhwm/, for

dual عَنْهُمَا /ənhwma/). E.g., أَبُو بَكْرٍ /əbu bəkr, rəziəllaho ənho/

"əbu bəkr, may God be pleased with him!"

ر٦   Sign placed over the names of saints, great religious authorities, and

other deceased pious persons. It stands for رَحْمَةُ ٱللَّهِ عَلَيْهِ /rəhmət wlla

ələyh/ "may God have mercy upon him!" It is, of course, used

only with the names of Muslims. E.g., شَاه وَلِيِّ ٱللَّهِ /šah vəliwllah,

rəhmət wlla ələyh/ "šah vəliwllah, may God have mercy upon him!"

‒   Sign placed over proper names, especially upon the nom-de-plume of a

poet. E.g., مِير تَقِي مِير /mir təqi mir/ "mir təqi (whose nom-de-plume

is) mir" أَسَدُ ٱللَّهِ خَان غَالِب /əsədwllah xā γalyb/ "əsədwllah xā (whose

nom-de-plume is) γalyb".

ـع   Sign used to introduce a couplet (شِعْر /šer/).

ع   Sign used to introduce a half-couplet (a مِصْرَع /mysra/).

12.006. The /əbjəd/ System.

The material presented below is for reference only. It will be of use only to an
advanced student.

Each of the twenty-eight consonantal letters of the original Arabic alphabet has an
assigned numerical value. The letters comprising a book title, a name, a hemistich of
poetry, etc. may thus be chosen so that their total will give the date of writing, the person's
date of birth, the date of some historical event, etc. The order of the letters in the /əbjəd/
system differs from the usual alphabetical order and is best expressed in eight mnemonic
"words":

359

$$\text{اَبْجَد هَوَّز حُطّی کَلَمَن سَعْفَص قَرَشَت ثَخَّذ ضَظَغ}$$

Ignoring the vowel diacritics and the /təšdid/, which have no value at all in the /əbjəd/ reckoning, it is seen that the first nine letters above represent digits, the next nine decimals, the next nine hundreds, and the last letter stands for one thousand. Letter values are thus as follows:

ا = 1	ح = 8	س = 60	ت = 400
ب = 2	ط = 9	ع = 70	ش = 500
ج = 3	ى = 10	ف = 80	خ = 600
د = 4	ک = 20	ص = 90	ذ = 700
ه = 5	ل = 30	ق = 100	ض = 800
و = 6	م = 40	ر = 200	ظ = 900
ز = .7	ن = 50	ش = 300	غ = 1000

Some special points are:

1. As stated above, such diacritics as those representing the short vowels, the /təšdid/, the /swkun/, etc. have no value in the /əbjəd/ system.

2. Doubled letters -- i. e. those having a /təšdid/ written upon them -- are counted as single letters: e.g. مُحَمَّد /mwhəmməd/, where /m/ = 40, /ḥ/ = 6, /m/ = 40, and /d/ = 4 -- a total of 90.

3. Later additions to the original twenty-eight letters of the alphabet have the same numerical values as those of the Arabic letters phonetically and graphemically similar to them. Thus, the value of پ is the same as that of ب (2), ت = ت (400), چ = ج (3), ڈ = د (4), ڑ = ر (200), ژ = ز (7), and گ = ک (20).

4. آ (/əlyf/ + /məd/; Sec. 6.102) is counted as 1 by some writers and as 2 (i. e. /əlyf/ + /əlyf/) by others: e.g. آخِر /axyr/, where /əlyf/ + /məd/ = 1 or 2, /x/ = 600, and /r/ = 200 -- a total of either 801 or 802.

5.   ئ /əlyf məqsura/ (Sec. 10.010) is taken as ی (10): e.g. عيسىٰ /isa/,

where /'/ = 70, /y/ = 10, /s/ = 60, and /əlyf məqsura/ = 10, a total of 150.

6.   The "dagger /əlyf/" (Sec. 10.011) is not counted.

7.   The   ء /həmza/ (Sec. 10.005) is problematical: some writers take it as 1

(i.e. as /əlyf/), while others do not count it at all. Some count it as /əlyf/ when
it represents a root letter, but not when it stands for the /yzafət/ (Secs. 10.005
and 18.302). Some authorities state that when /həmza/ is written on a "chair"
(i.e. /əlyf/, /vaw/, or /ye/), the value of the "chair" should be taken and /həmza/
should be ignored.

8.   Some writers count   ة /ta mərbuta/ (Sec. 10.007) as 5, following the Arabic

tradition; others count it as   ت (400).

Some examples of the /əbjəd/ system are as follows:

انتخاب يادگار

> /yntyxabe yadgar/ The Selection of Memorable[s]. [The title of a book
> of biographical notices of Urdu poets by /əmir əhməd əmir minai/.
> The title gives the date of writing: 1290 A.H. /yntyxab/ M1
> "election, selection, choice"; /yadgar/ M1 "memorial, memento,
> souvenir, something memorable."]

مذہبِ عشق

> /məzhəbe yšq/ The Religion of Love. [The title of a book by /nyhal cənd
> lahəwri/. The title gives the date of writing: 1217 A.H. /məzhəb/
> M1 "religion"; /yšq/ M1 [np] "love, romantic affection."]

غلام حليم

> /ɣwlam həlim/ ɣwlam həlim. [The chronogrammatic name of the great
> religious scholar /šah əbdwləziz/. The name gives his birthdate:
> 1159 A.H. /ɣwlam/ M1 "slave"; /həlim/ PA1 "forbearing (one of
> the names of God)."]

کہی اس کی تاريخ يوں برمحل يہ تخانۂ چين ہے بے بدل

> /kəhi ys ki tarix yū bərməhəl -- yy bwtxanəe cin həy bebədəl./ [I] stated
> the date of this appropriately thus: this temple of China is without
> peer. [The letters of the second hemistich of this verse by /ɣwlam
> həmdani mwshəfi/ give the date of composition of the long narrative
> poem /syhrwlbəyan/ by /mir həsən/: 1199 A.H. It was customary
> for an author to obtain chronogrammatic verses of this sort from his
> friends and colleagues. /yū/ Adv "thus"; /bərməhəl/ A1 Adv
> "appropriate, proper"; /bwtxana/ M2 "pagan temple"; /cin/ M1
> [np] "China" (the "temple of China" is a symbol for something
> beautifully and elaborately decorated); /bebədəl/ A1 Adv "without
> peer, matchless." Poetic word order differs from normal prose

order for considerations of metre: the prose equivalent would be:
/ys ki tarix yū bərməhəl kəhi -- yy bwtxanəe cin bebədəl həy. /.]

لکھی ہے اے قمر میں نے یہ تاریخ   یہ اچھا باغ ہے اردو زباں کا

/lykhi həy, əy qəmər, mɛ̃y ne yy tarix -- yy əccha baɣ həy wrdu zəbā ka. /
O Qəmər, I wrote this date: this is an excellent garden of the Urdu
language. [The second hemistich of this verse by /mwhəmməd nəqi
jan qəmər gəyavi/ gives the date of writing of the great Urdu dictionary /fərhãge asəfia/ by /səyyəd əhməd dyhləvi/: 1335 A. H. /əy/
Interj "O!"; /qəmər/ M1 "moon" (here used as the poet's pen-name;
see Sec. 24. 207); /zəban/ F1 "language, tongue" (the final /n/ becomes a nasalised vowel for reasons of metre). Normal prose order
would be: /əy qəmər, mɛ̃y ne yy tarix lykhi həy -- yy wrdu zəban ka
əccha baɣ həy. /.]

دیکھا جو مجھے فکر میں تاریخ کی مجروح   ہاتف نے کہا گنجِ معانی ہے تہِ خاک

/dekha jo mwjhe fykr mɛ̃ tarix ki, məjruh -- hatyf ne kəha, gənje məani
həy təhe xak. / When [he] saw me in contemplation [lit. worry,
thought] of the date, Məjruh, the angel said, "The treasure of tran-
scendant thoughts lies [lit. is] beneath the dust. " [This verse by
/mir məhdi hwsəyn məjruh dyhləvi/ commemorates the death of the
famous poet /myrza əsədwllah xã ɣalyb/: the words after /kəha/ give
the date 1285 A. H. /jo/ Rel Pron "who, which" sometimes means
"if" or "when, " especially in poetry; /məjruh/ PA1 "wounded,
smitten" (here used as the poet's pen-name; see above); /hatyf/ M1
"angel, voice from heaven"; /gənj/ M1 "treasure, hoard"; /məani/
Fp1 "meanings, thoughts, flights of imagination"; /təh/ F1
"bottom, underneath, fold"; /xak/ F1 [np] "earth, dirt, soil,
dust. " Normal prose order: /jo mwjhe tarix ki fykr mɛ̃ dekha,
hatyf ne kəha, gənje məani təhe xak həy. /.]

تاریخِ وفات اُس کی جو پوچھے کوئی حالی   کہہ دو کہ ہوا خاتمہ اردو کے ادب کا

/tarixe vəfat ws ki jo puche koi, hali -- kəh do, ky hwa xatyma wrdu ke
ədəb ka. / If anyone asks the date of his death, Hali -- say that Urdu
literature has ended. [This verse by /əltaf hwsəyn hali/ commemorates
the death of /mwhəmməd hwsəyn azad/, one of the great prose stylists
of Urdu, in 1327 A. H. : only the words after /ky/ are counted. /vəfat/
F1 "death (honorific)"; /hali/ PA1 "contemporary, timely, one in a
state of mystic experience" (used as the poet's pen-name -- the word
is otherwise rare in Urdu); /kəh do/ "say! " (see Sec. 13. 303);
/xatyma/ M2 "end, conclusion, termination"; /ədəb/ M1 "literature. " Prose order would be: /jo koi ws ki tarixe vəfat puche, hali,
kəh do, ky wrdu ke ədəb ka xatyma hwa. /.]

Urdu writers on the subject of the /əbjəd/ go on to list a number of variations --
special conventions by which an author may indicate that certain letter values are to be
added to or subtracted from the total in order that the correct date may be obtained. These
are complex and will concern only those who wish to make an exhaustive study of classical
Urdu literature. In modern Urdu, the entire /əbjəd/ system has largely fallen into disuse,
but it is still a useful tool for those who wish to study older works in the language.

12.101. Reading Drills.

1. Numerals.

۲۷۵	۱۴	۱,۸۹۰	۱۰,۷۵ ,۶۲۳	۹ ۶۳	۱۰۵
۸,۴۱۰	۹۳۵	۱ ۱۸	۱۴,۶۳۱	۳۹,۱۲۱	۱۹
۱,۳۲,۲۰۱	۷۲۹	۱۳۸	۲,۲۹,۳۶,۲۱۴	۱۲۹	۱۳۵

2. /rəqəm/. [Optional].

3. Other Notations for Money.

۳/۶۱	۶/۱۲/۹	۱۹/ـ	۵.۲۸	۱۶۱۲	۵۶۹/۱۰/۳
۱.۳۶	۹/ـ/۳	۱۶/۳۵	۱۱.۲۱	۹/۸/۹	۱۸,۹۰۳/۴/۹

4. Dates

(Muslim months are vowelled for reading purposes. Read the year figures as "X hundred, Y ... " rather than "one thousand, X hundred, Y ...": e.g., "1945" = "nineteen hundred, forty-five" rather than "one thousand, nine hundred, forty-five.")

5. Other Symbols.

6. Text.

The following is part of the Conversation of Unit VIII. The student should read it aloud several times, striving for speed and accuracy. It should also be drilled in class.

مسٹر رحیم۔ آج آپ سارے دن کہاں رہے ؟ میں نے آپ کے دفتر کئی دفعہ ٹیلی فون کیا لیکن آپ نہ ملے ۔

مسٹر رحیم۔ آج میں بہت مصروف رہا ۔ دفتر میں تھوڑی سی دیر بیٹھا تھا کہ ہمارے بڑے دفتر کے ایک افسر تشریف لائے ۔ اُن کے ساتھ ایک مشہور وکیل بھی تھے۔ کچھ دیر وکیل صاحب سے بات چیت ہوئی اور پھر ہم تینوں عدالت پہنچے۔

مسٹر رحیم۔ عدالت میں کیا کام تھا ؟

مسٹر رحیم۔ آج کل دواییوں کی ایک کمپنی سے ہمارے ہسپتال کا مقدمہ چل رہا ہے ۔ آج اُس کی تاریخ تھی ۔ عدالت جا کر معلوم ہوا کہ ہمارا کیس ایک گھنٹے کے بعد پیش ہوگا ۔ بڑی مشکل تھی ۔ کیونکہ ایک گھنٹے تک بیٹھنا کچھ آسان نہ تھا۔

مسٹر رحیم۔ آپ گھر کیوں نہ آئے ؟ بہتر تھا کہ یہاں آکر آرام کرتے ۔

مسٹر رحیم۔ پہلے ارادہ تو یہی تھا۔ لیکن اِس دوران میں ایک بہت دلچسپ کیس شروع ہوا۔ ہم اُسے سننے لگے ۔

مسٹر رحیم۔ وہ کیا کیس تھا ؟

مسٹر رحیم۔ ایک چوری کا مقدمہ تھا ۔ یہ پچھلے ہفتے کا واقعہ ہے کہ چور رات کے بارہ بجے ایک امیر کے گھر پہنچا ۔ کوٹھی کے بڑے دروازے پر چوکیدار موجود تھا۔

364

12.102. Writing Drills.

1. Numerals.

178   29,710,534   96   5,702   612   187   3,27,465

2. /rəqəm/. [Optional].

5/-/-   18/1/6   57/-/3   151/8/-   7/8/-   6/3/9

3. Other Notations for Money.

14/10/9   2.12   99/8/-   175.34   15/2/6   2,305.17

4. Dates.

22 Mwhərrəm, 1110 A.H.   17 November, 1923 A.D.

16 Səfər, 1345 A.H.   25 March, 1845 A.D.   1 June, 54 B.C.

5. Other Symbols.

(Copy the following, adding the proper special sign)

اَبُوحَنِیفَہْ   (deceased religious authority)   مُحَمَّد   (Prophet)   آدَم   (Prophet)

رمیر سوز   (poet)   شَاہ حَاتِم   (poet)   اِبْن عَبَّاس   (Companion of the Prophet)

12.103. Word Recognition.

Only words written with "uncommon" Arabic consonants, with final ۃ = /a/, or with other special conventions will be listed in this section.

SCRIPT	PRONUNCIATION	SCRIPT	PRONUNCIATION
اکتالیس	yktalys	شخص	šəxs
بالکل	bylkwl	شروع	šwru
بحث	bəhs	ضرور	zərur
بیالیس	bealys	عدالت	ədalət
پینتالیس	pə̄ytalys	تیتالیس	tetalys
تقریباً	təqribən	چوالیس	cəvalys
ڈاک خانہ	Dakxana	چونکہ	cūke
راستہ	rasta	حکم	hwkm

365

SCRIPT	PRONUNCIATION	SCRIPT	PRONUNCIATION
خط	xət	لفافہ	lyfafa
خود	xwd	مردہ	mwrda
فیصلہ	fəysla	مقدمہ	mwqədma
کاغذ	kaɣəz	ورنہ	vərna
		ہمیشہ	həmeša

12.104. Urdu-English Sentences.

1. میں نے یہ گاڑی ۱۵,۶۲۷ روپیّے میں خریدی۔

2. میں یہاں بارہ تاریخ کو پہنچا تھا۔

3. میرے والد صاحب سنہ ۱۹۱۲ء میں امریکہ میں تھے۔

4. پاکستان کی حکومت نے ایک نیا حکم جاری کیا۔

5. شاید میری والدہ مجھے جانے نہیں دیں گی۔

6. مغل بادشاہ کی فوج ۷ار صفر سنہ ۱۱ء کو دہلی پہنچی۔

7. اُنہوں نے دو گھنٹے تک اُس کی تلاش کی۔

8. اُنہوں نے یہ کام سنہ ۱۹۱۴ء میں شروع کیا۔

9. اگر آپ شور مچائیں گے۔ تو باہر جانا پڑے لگا۔

10. اُنہوں نے یہ قانون ۱۹ اگست سنہ ۱۹۳۵ء میں جاری کیا۔

11. جج صاحب نے وکیل صاحب سے بحث کی۔

اِس خط پر ۲/۱۳/۹ کے ٹکٹ لگیں گے۔

13.

کیا، آپ میرے لئے منی آرڈر بھجوا سکتے ہیں ؟

14.

اِس کا کرایہ ایک گھنٹے کے لئے ۲.۲۵ ہے ۔

15.

آپ کا مکان بالکل نیا لگتا ہے ۔

12.105. English-Urdu Sentences.

1. She had married in 1945.
2. Yesterday my son wrote ("had written") a letter, and today he has sent it.
3. I arrived (in) Lahəwr in 1938.
4. This even took place ("became") on (/ko/) August 12th.
5. On (/ko/) the 20th of Rəmzan, 1123 A.H., the king gave this order to his army.
6. They bought this book for (/mē/) Rs. 3/10/-.
7. I sold my car for (/mē/) Rs. 8,000.
8. These medicines have come for the hospital.
9. The judge made the decision on (/ko/) the 17th of November.
10. I searched for my suitcase.
11. He opened this shop on (/ko/) 18 Səfər, 1341 A.H.
12. On this letter 13/8/6 in postage (13/8/6 of stamps) will be required ("will attach").
13. The price of this carpet is Rs. 430/12/-.
14. I'll wait for you until evening. After that, I'll go home.
15. He bought the picture for (/mē/) about Rs. 5000.

The High Court of Pakistan, Lahore.

13.000. CONVERSATION

Mr. Smith has brought his youngest daughter to the hospital. She has become slightly ill overnight, and he wishes to have Dr. Rəhim examine her.

bed M1

pələ̃g

to lay down [C: /leTna/: IIc]

lyTana

R: Come [in], Mr. Smith. Please have your daughter lie down on this bed!

aie, ysmyth sahəb, bəcci ko ys pələ̃g pər lyTaie!

nature, disposition, temperament, health F1

təbiət

pain M1

dərd

fever M1

bwxar

became MS

ho gəya

cough F2

khãsi

manages to do FS

kər pati

S: Her health has been bad since yesterday evening. First there was some pain in [her] head. Fever developed [lit. became] in the evening, and since morning she can't even manage to talk because of [her] cough.

kəl šam se ys ki təbiət xərab həy. pəhle, sər mẽ kwch dərd tha. šam ko bwxar ho gəya, əwr swba se khãsi ki vəja se bat nəhĩ kər pati.

R: What did she eat yesterday?

kəl ys ne kya khaya tha.

feast, party; invitation F1

davət

fish F2

məchli

S: Yesterday we went to a party. There [we] ate fish and rice.

kəl həm log ek davət mẽ gəe the. vəhã məchli əwr cavəl khae the.

stomach, belly M1

peT

R: Is there pain in [her] stomach also?

kya, peT mẽ bhi dərd həy?

S: No, there's no pain in [her] stomach, but at night [her] fever was very high [lit. sharp]. Mrs. Smith was very worried.

ji nəhĩ, peT mẽ to dərd nəhĩ həy, lekyn rat ko bwxar bəhwt tez tha. mysəz ysmyth to bəhwt pərešan thĩ.

worry, upset, anxiety, disturbance F2

pərešani

way, manner F1

təra [or /tərəh/]

has seen MS

dekh lia həy

minor, ordinary, common A1

mamuli

R: There's no reason to worry [lit. in this is no matter of worry]. I've had a good look at her [lit. I have seen [her] in a good way]. There is only fever and a common cough.

ys mẽ pərešani ki koi bat nəhĩ. mẽy ne əcchi təra dekh lia həy. syrf bwxar əwr mamuli khãsi həy.

S: What is the reason for it?

ys ki kya vəja həy.

care, caution F1

yhtiat

influenza M2 [np]

nəzla

cold, catarrh M1 [np]

zwkam

becomes MS

ho jata həy

common, general A1

am

R: These days the weather is not good. If
[you] don't take care, [you] get the flu
and a cold [lit. the flu and cold become].
This thing is extremely [lit. entirely]
common.

ajkəl məwsəm əccha nəhĩ. əgər yhtiat nə
rəkhẽ, to nəzla əwr zwkam ho jata həy. yy
ciz bylkwl am həy.

equal, even, level, straight, uniform,
alike, equivalent, adjoining; continually
A1 Adv

bərabər

to cough [IIc: /ə/]

khãsna

S: Just see how she is continually coughing.

yy dekhie, kys təra bərabər khãs rəhi həy.

dose; foodstuffs F1

xwrak

has caused to drink FS [/pylana/: C:
/pina/: Ic]

pyla di həy

prescription; copy (of a book) M2

nwsxa

may cause to be requested, may order,
may send for P [/mãgvana/: DC:
/mãgna/: Ic]

mãgva lẽ

pill, small ball (as a marble), bullet F2

goli

may cause to eat, may feed P [/khylana/:
C: /khana/: Ic]

khyla dẽ

vial, small bottle F2

šiši

may cause to drink P [see /pyla di həy/
above]

pyla dẽ

method, manner, way M2

təriqa

to pour, put in, throw in [If: /ə/]

Dalna

fresh A1 [also A2]

taza

to mix, cause to meet, introduce, join
(two objects together) [C: /mylna/: IIc]

mylana

R: Don't worry! I've given [her] a dose of
medicine to drink. Send for this prescription from the market. After three hours
give [her] these two pills, and give [her]
another dose from this bottle. The method
of [doing] this is; that you pour a dose
of medicine in a glass, and, having mixed
[it] with a little fresh water, give [it to
her] to drink.

ap fykr nə kərẽ! mẽy ne dəvai ki ek xwrak
pyla di həy. yy nwsxa bazar se mãgva lẽ.
tin ghənTe ke bad yy do goliã khyla dẽ, əwr
ys šiši mẽ se ek xwrak əwr pyla dẽ. ys
ka təriqa yy həy, ky gylas mẽ ek xwrak
dəvai Dalẽ, əwr thoRa taza pani myla kər
pyla dẽ.

S: What should [we] give [her] to eat?

khane ko kya ciz dẽ.

R: Only milk and rice.

syrf dudh əwr cavəl

dysentery F1

pecyš

diarrhea M1

dəst

S: Very well. Furthermore [lit. second],
since yesterday I have also been suffering
with dysentery [lit. to me also from
yesterday dysentery's complaint is]. This
morning I had diarrhea accompanied by
pain [lit. with pain diarrhea came].

bəhwt əccha. -- dusre, mwjhe bhi kəl se
pecyš ki šykayət həy. aj swba dərd ke sath
dəst aya.

excrement, stool, toilet, excrementation
M2

paxana

examination, inspection M2

mwayna

R: You ought to have your stool examined.

S: Yes, for this reason I've brought [a sample] with me. Here it is.

    by, to, by means of, by the hand of Comp Post

    [I M] will cause to be sent

    suitable, fitting, proper A1

    may see P

R: Please wait a little while. I'll just have it sent out by the servant for examination. Meanwhile, if you'd like to [lit. understand suitable], you may have a look at our hospital.

    nurse F1 [rarely M1]

    leaves, abandons MP

S: Very well. [We will] leave the little girl with the nurse.

    They set out to inspect the hospital.

    operation M1

    long, tall A2

    X-ray M1

R: This is our operating room. Adjoining it, this long room is for X-ray [work].

    machine F1

S: Are these machines made in Pakistan?

    England M1 [np]

R: No, we send for most of [our] apparatus from America and England.

    radio M1

S: Where is this radio playing [lit. going]?

    tuberculosis F1 [np]

    patient, ill person M1

    ward M1

    world F1

    sadness, grief, sorrow M1

    happy, glad PA1

    sickness F2

    forgets MS [/bhulna/: IIc: /w/]

R: This is the T.B. patients' ward. We keep the patients far from the cares of the world. Thus, the sick [person] remains happy and forgets his illness.

    true A1

    way, manner M1

    person, human being M1

S: Very good. Really, you truly [lit. on a true way] perform a service for mankind.

---

ap ko əpne paxane ka mwayna kərana cahie.

ji hã, ysi lie mǝy əpne sath laya hũ. yy lijie.

[ke] hath

bhyjva dũga.

mwnasyb

dekh lẽ

ap kwch der yntyzar kərẽ. mǝy əbhi yse nəwkər ke hath mwayne ke lie bhyjva dũga. ys dəwran mẽ, əgər ap mwnasyb səmjhẽ, to həmara həspətal dekh lẽ.

nərs

choR dete hǝy

bəhwt əccha. bəcci ko nərs ke pas choR dete hǝy.

apre\u0161ən [or /əpre\u0161ən/]

ləmba

eksre

yy həmara apre\u0161ən ka kəmra hǝy. ys ke bərabər, yy ləmba kəmra eksre ke lie hǝy.

mə\u0161in

kya, yy mə\u0161inẽ pakystan mẽ bənti hǝy?

ỹglystan

ji nəhĩ, həm əksər saman əmrika əwr ỹglystan se mǝgvate hǝy.

reDyo

yy reDyo kəhã cəl rəha hǝy.

Ti bi

məriz

varD

dwnya

ɣəm

xw\u0161

bimari

bhul jata hǝy

yy Ti bi ke mərizõ ka varD hǝy. həm mərizõ ko dwnya ke ɣəmõ se dur rəkhte hǝy. ys təra, bimar xw\u0161 rəhta hǝy, əwr əpni bimari bhul jata hǝy.

səhih [common: /səhi/]

təwr

ynsan

bəhwt xub. vaqəi, ap səhih təwr pər ynsan ki xydmət kərte hǝy.

part, portion, section M2	hyssa
eye F1	ākh
ear M1	kan
nose F1	nak
et cetera Adv	vəɣəyra
remedy, cure, healing, treatment M1	ylaj
cholera M2 [np]	həyza

R: In that section of the hospital the eye, ear, nose, etc. are treated, and here are the patients suffering from [lit. of] cholera.

həspətal ke ws hysse mē, ākh, kan, əwr nak vəɣəyra ka ylaj hota həy, əwr yəhā həyze ke məriz hēy.

number, amount F1 [np]	tadad [literary: /taədad/]
comparison, contest, confrontation, competition M2. [/[ke] mwqable mē/ Comp Post "compared with"]	mwqabla [literary: /mwqabəla/]

S: Here the number of patients is large compared to other wards.

yəhā mərizō ki tadad dusre varDō ke mwqable mē zyada həy.

month M2	məhina
had spread MS [/phəylna/: IIc: /əy/]	phəyl gəya tha
special A1	xas
have opened (intrans.) MP [/khwlna/: I: /kholna/: Id]	khwl gəe
to stop, check [If: /w/]	rokna
innoculation, spot, beauty mark M2	Tika
to attach, hit, strike, fix [C: /ləgna/: IIc]	ləgana
arrangement, management M1 [np]	bəndobəst
to cause to be attached, hit, struck, fixed [DC: /ləgna/: IIc]	ləgvana

R: Yes, perhaps you know that cholera has [lit. had] spread in our city last month. Therefore special wards for cholera have been opened in every hospital. There are arrangements in various places [lit. place place] for innoculations to stop cholera. Haven't you had [yourself] innoculated?

ji hā, šayəd ap ko malum hoga, ky pychle məhine həmare šəhr mē həyza phəyl gəya tha. ys lie, hər həspətal mē həyze ke lie xas varD khwl gəe hēy. jəga jəga həyze ko rokne ke lie Tike ləgane ka bəndobəst həy. kya, ap ne Tika nəhī ləgvaya?

dirt, filth F2	gəndəgi
to spread (trans.) [C: /phəylna/: IIc]	phəylana

S: Yes, [we] had [it] done last week. -- I think that dirt spreads cholera.

ji hā, pychle həfte ləgvaya tha. -- mera xyal həy, ky gəndəgi həyze ko phəylati həy.

germs Mpl	jərasim
born, produced, procured, found PA1	pəyda
cleanliness F2 [np]	səfai
best A1	byhtərin
method, way, medium, means, resource M2	zəria

R: Cholera germs are produced in filth. Cleanliness is the best way of stopping cholera. Therefore a special arrangement for cleanliness has to be set up in the city.

gəndəgi mē həyze ke jərasim pəyda hote hēy. səfai həyze ko rokne ka byhtərin zəria həy. ys lie, šəhr mē səfai ka xas yntyzam rəkhna pəRta həy.

S: What's going on in This room?

urine M1 [np]

R: Here the urine, stools, and blood, etc. of the patients is tested.

S: Your hospital is very large. Is this a government [run] hospital?

help, aid, assistance F1 [np]

sorrow, regret, grief, concern M1 [np]

leisure, free time, leave F1

remaining, rest A1

R: This is the city's biggest hospital. It operates [lit. goes] with the help of the government and of rich people. I'm sorry that I don't have time, otherwise I would show you the remaining sections of the hospital.

short A1

profitable, useful, beneficial A1

obtained, acquired PA1

S: Never mind. I also have to go home now. I have gotten a great many new and useful things from this short tour.

ys kəmre mẽ kya ho rəha həy.

pešab

yəhã mərizõ ke pešab, paxane, əwr xun vəɣəyra ka mwayna hota həy.

ap ka həspətal bəhwt bəRa həy. kya, yy gəwrnmənT ka həspətal həy?

mədəd

əfsos

fwrsət

baqi

yy šəhr ka səb se bəRa həspətal həy. yy hwkumət əwr əmir logõ ki mədəd se cəlta həy. mwjhe əfsos həy, ky mwjhe fwrsət nəhĩ, vərna həspətal ke baqi hysse bhi ap ko dykhata.

mwxtəsər

mwfid

hasyl

koi bat nəhĩ. mwjhe bhi əb ghər cəlna cahie. ys mwxtəsər si səyr se bəhwt si nəi əwr mwfid batẽ hasyl hwĩ.

13.100. WORD STUDY

13.101. /təbiət/ F1 means "nature, temperament, disposition, " but it is also often employed for "health." E.g.

/ap ki təbiət kəysi həy. / How is your health?

/ajkəl meri təbiət əcchi nəhĩ. / These days my health is not good.

13.102. /dərd/ M1 "pain" may refer either to actual physical pain or metaphorically to mental anguish. /ɣəm/ M1 denotes "sorrow, grief, sadness," and /əfsos/ M1 is used mostly for "regret, sorrow." E.g.

/mere sər mẽ dərd həy. / I have a pain in my head.

/mwjhe ys ciz ka ɣəm həy. / I am sad about this thing.

/mwjhe əfsos həy, ky mə̃y nəhĩ ja səka. / I am sorry that I couldn't go.

13.103. /davət/ F1 means both "party, feast" and "invitation." "To go to a party" is usually expressed by /davət mẽ jana/ "to go in a party," and one sometimes hears /davət pər jana/. E.g.

/wnhõ ne meri davət ki. / They gave a party for me. [Lit. they made my party. /davət kərna/ is a Type B complex verbal formation.]

/wnhõ ne mwjhe davət di. / He gave me an invitation.

/kəl mə̃y davət mẽ gəya tha. / Yesterday I went to a party.

13.104. The student has now seen four words which may be translated "manner, way." Each has its own semantic range and usage:

(1) /təriqa/ M2 means "method (of doing something), plan of action, way, manner": e.g.

/ap yy kam kys təriqe se kərẽge. / By what method will you do this task?

(2) /təra/ F1 means "manner, way." It is used with various oblique demonstratives and interrogatives (/ys/, /ws/, /jys/, and /kys/) and with a few common adjectives. In these formations /təra/ is not followed by a postposition. Like various time words and phrases previously introduced, /təra/ is thus an unmarked oblique adverbial. E.g.

/ap ys təra kijie! / Please do it this way!

/mə̃y kys təra jaũ. / How [by what means] shall I go?

/mə̃y wse əcchi təra janta hũ. / I know him well. [Lit. good way.]

/mə̃y ne hər təra košyš ki, lekyn kysi təra bat nəhĩ bəni. / I tried in every way, but the matter could not be done in any way.

/jys təra ap ko cahie, wsi təra bəna dũga. / Just as you require, I'll make [it] in just that way.

/[ki] təra/ also functions as a compound postposition, meaning "like, as, in the manner of": e.g.

/yy kəpRe pakystani kəpRõ ki təra malum hote hə̃y. / These clothes look like [lit. seem to be like] Pakistani clothes.

/ynsanõ ki təra bat kəro! / Talk like a man!

/pəhli kytab ki təra, yy kytab bhi mwškyl həy. / Just like the first book, this book also is difficult.

374

/təra təra/ means "various kinds, many varieties." /təra təra/ always possesses the noun it modifies. E. g.

/mɛ̃y ne pakystan mɛ̃ təra təra ke phəl dekhe hɛ̃y./ I saw various types of fruits in Pakistan.

(3) /təwr/ M1 has much the same meaning as /təra/, but it is employed primarily with more literary adjectives of Persian and Arabic origin. It is followed by the postposition /pər/ "on," and /X təwr pər/ may often be translated as an adverb: "X-ly." /[ke] təwr pər/ is also employed as a compound postposition meaning "as, by way of, for." E. g.

/səhih təwr pər, ap ynsan ki xydmət kərte hɛ̃y./ Truly [lit. on a true way] you serve mankind.

/am təwr pər, yy ciz pakystan mɛ̃ nəhĩ bənti./ Generally [lit. on a common way] this thing is not made in Pakistan.

/yy mwjhe xas təwr pər pəsənd həy./ This is especially pleasing [lit. on a special way] to me.

/log yy səbzi dəvai ke təwr pər ystemal kərte hɛ̃y./ People use this vegetable as [lit. on the way of] a medicine.

/yy kytab meri nyšani ke təwr pər rəkh lẽ./ Keep this book as [lit. on the way of] a souvenir of me.

/vw gəvah ke təwr pər ədalət mɛ̃ peš hwa./ He was presented as [lit. on the way of] a witness in court.

(4) /zəria/ M2 denotes "means, medium, source, resource, agency, way, manner." E. g.

/ap kys zərie se yəhã ae./ How [by which means] did you come here?

/ap kys ke zərie se yəhã ae./ By whose agency did you come here. [Who sent you?]

/mɛ̃y yunyvərsyTi ke zərie se yəhã aya hũ./ I have come here through [by means of, sent by, supported by] the university.

/mɛ̃y ne yy kytab wn ke zərie se bheji./ I sent this book through [by means of, by the agency of] him.

/mera koi zəria nəhĩ./ I have no resource[s]

13.105. /bərabər/ A1 Adv has several meanings: "even, equal, level, straight, uniform, alike, equivalent, adjoining," and, as an adverb, "continually." E. g.

/bəcca bərabər ro rəha həy./ The child is continually crying.

/yy zəmin bylkwl bərabər həy./ This land is completely level.

/meri əwr ap ki wmrẽ təqribən bərabər hɛ̃y./ Our ages [lit. my and your ages] are approximately equal.

/pakystan əwr hyndostan ka rupəya təqribən bərabər həy./ The Pakistani rupee is about equivalent to the Indian rupee. [/hyndostan/ M1 [np] "India."]

/ws ka kəmra mere kəmre ke bərabər həy./ His room adjoins my room. [Here /[ke] bərabər/ functions as a compound postposition.]

/donõ əlmariã bərabər ki hɛ̃y./ Both cupboards are of equal [size]. [/ki/ refers to "size," which is understood here.]

13.106. /xwrak/ F1 denotes "dose (of medicine)" and also "foodstuffs." In the latter meaning, it differs from /khana/ M2 "food, dinner, meal," in that /khana/ refers to a specific food or meal, while /xwrak/ is employed for "foodstuffs" in general. E. g.

/ajkəl əcchi xwrak nəhĩ mylti. /　These days good foodstuffs are not available.

/DakTər sahəb ne mwjhe ek xwrak pyla di. /　The doctor gave me a dose [of liquid medicine] to drink.

/mə̃y ne dəvai ki ek xwrak kha li. /　I ate a dose of [solid] medicine.

13. 107.　/mylana/, the causative of /mylna/ "to meet, get, " denotes "to cause to meet, introduce, join (two objects together), mix, mingle, "　E. g.

/mə̃y ap ko ysmyth sahəb se mylana cahta hũ. /　I want to have you meet Mr. Smith.

/pani mẽ thoRi si cini mylani cahie. /　[You] ought to mix a little sugar in the water.

/mwjhe do səw nəmbər se mylaie! /　Please get me number 200. [When requesting a telephone number from an operator.]

13. 108.　/pecyš/ F1 "dysentery" has symptoms which include diarrhea, stomach cramps, nausea, blood in the stools, etc.　/dəst/ M1 "diarrhea" may thus denote one of the symptoms of /pecyš/, or it may signify diarrhea due to some other cause.

13. 109.　/paxana/ M2 "excrement, stool, toilet, defecation" is from Persian /pa/ "foot" + /xana/ "house of, room for": "foot room, " so named because in older houses the toilet was built at the foot (i. e. lowest part) of the house.　/paxana/ has now become generalised to include human excrement and the act of defecation.　It must be noted that, except among the very anglicised, the Indian or Pakistani attitude towards this necessary human function is considerably more free than that found among northern Europeans and Americans.　One may thus hear sentences like the following in polite society:

/maf kijie, paxana kəhã həy. /　Excuse me, where is the toilet?

/vw əbhi paxane mẽ həy. /　He's now in the toilet.

/mwjhe paxane jana həy. /　I have to go to the toilet.

13. 110.　/mwayna/ M2 denotes "examination (of an object, of a person), inspection (of a school, factory, etc.), testing (of some substance in the laboratory). "　It cannot be used for "(school) examination, test": in this meaning /ymtyhan/ M1 "examination, test" is employed.

13. 111.　/hath/ M1 "hand, arm" also occurs as a compound postposition: /[ke] hath/ "by. "　This form is generally used only with a few verbs, the commonest being /bhejna/ "to send" (and /bhyjvana/ "to cause to be sent").　It also occurs with /becna/ "to sell" (and /bykvana/ "to cause to be sold"), but /ko/ also be employed here as well as /[ke] hath/.　E. g.

/mə̃y ne nəwkər ke hath ek xət bhyjvaya. /　I sent a letter by [lit. the hand of] the servant. [/se/ cannot be substituted here for /[ke] hath/.]

/mə̃y ne yy ciz ws ke hath bec di. /　I sold this thing to him. [/ws ko/ or /wse/ are also correct, though less idiomatic.]

13.112. /ləmba/ A2 "long" also means "tall." Note that /ūca/ A2 "high" cannot be used for persons. E.g.

/vw bəhwt ləmba admi həy./ He is a very tall man. [Never */ūca admi/.]

13.113. /Ti bi/ F1 [np] "tuberculosis" is a term well known even in remote villages. There is also an Urdu term: /təp dyq/ (literary /təpe dyq/) F1 [np], from /təp/ F1 "fever" + /dyq/ F1 A1 "trouble, worry, vexing, harassing."

13.114. /məriz/ M1 "patient" may denote either a bedridden person or simply one suffering from some disease. /bimar/ M1 A1 "sick, sick [person]" usually carries the connotation of an illness serious enough to keep the sufferer in bed or at least inactive. /bimari/ F2 "sickness, illness" is made with the /i/ suffix discussed in Sec. 7.301 (3). An abstract noun also exists for /məriz/, but this is made on an Arabic pattern (see Unit XVII): /mərz/ (or /mərəz/) M1 "sickness, illness." There is no discernible difference of meaning between /mərz/ and /bimari/. E.g.

/aj vw bimar həy./ He's sick today. [One cannot say */aj vw məriz həy/.]

/vw Ti bi ka məriz həy./ He is suffering from [lit. a patient of] T.B. [One cannot say */Ti bi ka bimar həy/.]

13.115. /admi/ M1 "man, person" and /mərd/ M1 "man, male" were discussed in Sec. 7.120. /ynsan/ M1 "man, person, human being" may now be added. /ynsan/ carries connotations of the higher qualities of man: nobility, generosity, humanitarianism, etc. The following is the last line of a couplet by Qasim Rizvi (/qasym ryzvi/), a modern poet:

/admi myl gəe, lekyn həmẽ ynsã nə myle./ [We] found men, but we did not find Men. [Here /ynsan/ becomes /ynsã/ for reasons of metre.]

13.116. /mwqabla/ M2 means "confrontation, comparison, competition, match, contest." As a compound postposition, /X ke mwqable mẽ/ means "in comparison with X." E.g.

/ys ka mwqabla nəhĩ./ This is incomparable!

/ys ke mwqable mẽ, vw əccha həy./ In comparison with this, that is good.

/yn donõ kytabõ ka mwqabla kəro!/ Compare both of these books!

/mera əwr ws ka mwqabla hwa./ He and I had a confrontation. [In American slang, "a showdown face to face."]

/ws ne mera mwqabla kia./ He confronted me. [I.e. defied me face to face.]

13.117. /Tika/ M2 "innoculation, vaccination" originally meant "spot, blemish." It is also used for the spot of red which Hindu girls (and now ladies of other communities as well) wear on their foreheads between their eyebrows. /Tika/ also denotes a type of jewelled pendant which is worn between the brows.

13.118. /bəndobəst/ M1 [np] and /yntyzam/ M1 both mean "arrangement." The former originally meant something minor (e.g. /cae ka bəndobəst/ "arrangements for tea"), while the latter denoted something on a larger scale. This difference in meaning is now disappearing.

13.119. /jərasim/ Mpl "germs" is actually the Arabic broken plural of /jərsuma/ M2 "germ, microbe." The singular form is very rarely found in Urdu, however. For broken plurals, see Sec. 17.304.

13.120. /pešab/ M1 "urine" is originally a Persian compound of /peš/ "front, before" + /ab/ "water." See Sec. 13.109.

13.121. /fwrsət/ F1 denotes "leisure, free time, leave" while /chwTTi/ F2 denotes "vacation, time taken as leave." E.g.

> /əfsos həy, ky kəl mwjhe fwrsət nə myl səki, vərna mɚy ap ki davət mɛ̃ zərur ata./ It is too bad that I could not get time yesterday, otherwise I would have certainly come to your party. [/chwTTi/ could be substituted here but would mean "leave of absence (from a job, etc.)."]

13.122. /mwxtəsər/ A1 "short" is employed mainly with abstract nouns: e.g. a short speech, a short tour, a short story, etc. "Short" of material objects (e.g. clothing, a piece of wood, a person's stature) is expressed by /choTa/ A2 "small." "Short (of time)" is expressed by /kəm/ A1 "too little" or by /thoRa/ A2 "little (in quantity)," although /mwxtəsər/ may also occasionally be found. In joking language, /mwxtəsər/ may also be employed for "short (of stature)." E.g.

> /ys mwxtəsər si səyr ke bad, mwjhe lahəwr vapəs jana pəRa./ After this short excursion, I had to go back to Lahore.
>
> /wnhõ ne bəhwt mwxtəsər sa jəvab dia./ They gave a very short reply.
>
> /vw to bəhwt mwxtəsər sa admi həy!/ He's just a little fellow! [Joking style.]
>
> /yy kəpRe mere lie choTe hɚy./ These clothes are too short [lit. small] for me. [/mwxtəsər/ cannot occur here.]
>
> /davət ke lie, vəqt bəhwt kəm həy./ For a party, there's too little time. [/mwxtəsər/ may also occur here, but is less common.]

13.123. /hasyl/ PA1 "obtained, acquired" is generally used to refer to the acquisition of something beneficial and good. One does not ordinarily say */mwjhe ɣəm hasyl hwa./ "I got grief." On the other hand, one can say, /ws se mwjhe xwši hasyl hwi./ "I received happiness from that." /hasyl hona/ "to be obtained, acquired" is used mainly with abstracts: happiness, knowledge, etc. /hasyl kərna/ "to obtain, acquire" may, however, be employed both with abstracts and with material objects. It is also more common than /hasyl hona/. E.g.

> /mɚy ne ws ke dəftər se yy fayl hasyl ki./ I got this file from his office.
>
> /wnhõ ne Dyrame ke lie do TykəT hasyl kie./ He got two tickets for the play.
>
> /bəRi mwškyl se yy kytab hasyl hwi./ This book was obtained with great difficulty.

378

13.124. Some Complex Verbal Formations.

A:

/am/

   /am hona/ to become common, general

   /[X ko] am kərna/ to make [X] common

/bərabər/

   /bərabər hona/ to become equal, equivalent, level

   /[X ko] bərabər kərna/ to make [X] equal, equivalent level

/gənda/

   /gənda hona/ to be, become dirty, filthy

   /[X ko] gənda kərna/ to dirty [X]

/hasyl/

   /[X ko Z se Y] hasyl hona/ [Y] to be obtained [by X from Z]

   /[X ko Y se] hasyl kərna/ to obtain [X from Y]

/ləmba/

   /ləmba hona/ to be, become long, tall

   /[X ko] ləmba kərna/ to make [X] long, tall

/mwxtəsər/

   /mwxtəsər hona/ to be, become short

   /[X ko] mwxtəsər kərna/ to make [X] short

/pəyda/

   /pəyda hona/ to be produced, born, found

   /[X ko] pəyda kərna/ to produce, bear, find [X]

/taza/

   /taza hona/ to be fresh

   /[X ko] taza kərna/ to freshen [X]

/xwš/

   /xwš hona/ to be, become happy

   /[X ko] xwš kərna/ to make [X] happy, please [X]

B:

/aprešən/

   /[X ka] aprešən hona/ [X] to be operated upon

   /[X ka] aprešən kərna/ to operate upon [X]

/bəndobəst/

   /[X ka] bəndobəst hona/ [X] to be arranged

   /[X ka] bəndobəst kərna/ to arrange [X]

/davət/. [See also under D and F.]

   /[X ki] davət hona/ a party to be given [for X]

   /[X ki] davət kərna/ to give a party [for X]

/eksre/

   /[X ka] eksre hona/ [X] to have an X-ray taken

   /[X ka] eksre kərna/ to take an X-ray [of X]

/yəm/

    /[X ko Y ka] yəm hona/ [X] to be sad [about Y]

    /[X ka] yəm kərna/ to grieve [about X]

/hyssa/

    /[X ke] hysse kərna/ to divide [X] up into pieces

/mədəd/. [See also D.]

    /[X ki] mədəd hona/ [X] to be aided, helped

    /[X ki] mədəd kərna/ to help [X]

/mwayna/

    /[X ka] mwayna hona/ [X] to be examined, inspected

    /[X ka] mwayna kərna/ to examine, inspect [X]

/mwqabla/

    /[X ka] mwqabla hona/ [X] to be confronted. [Or: to be a contest of X (a game, competition).]

    /[X ka] mwqabla kərna/ to confront [X]. [Or:]

    /[X se Y ka] mwqabla kərna/ to compare [Y with X]

/səfai/

    /[X ki] səfai hona/ [X] to be cleaned

    /[X ki] səfai kərna/ to clean [X]

/yhtiat/

    /[X ki] yhtiat kərna/ to take care of, look after [X]

    /[X mē] yhtiat kərna/ to be careful, cautious [about X]

    /yhtiat se/ carefully, cautiously

/ylaj/

    /[X ka] ylaj hona/ [X] to be cured

    /[X ka] ylaj kərna/ to cure, treat [X]

    /[X ka] ylaj rəhna/ to be a patient of [X (a doctor)]

D:

/davət/. [See also B and F.]

    /[X ko] davət dena/ to invite [X]

    /[X ko] davət mylna/ [X] to receive an invitation

/mədəd/. [See also B.]

    /[X ko] mədəd dena/ to help [X]

    /[X se] mədəd lena/ to take help [from X]

    /[X ko] mədəd mylna/ [X] to receive help

F:

/əfsos/

    /[X ko Y pər] əfsos hona/ [X] to be sorry, feel regret [about Y]

    /[X pər] əfsos kərna/ to regret [X]

/bimari/

    /[X ko] bimariləgna/ [X] to fall ill, be struck down by an illness

/bwxar/

    /[X ko] bwxar ana, hona/ [X] to get a fever

/davət/. [See also B and D.]

    /davət mẽ [pər] jana/ to go to a party

/dərd/

    /[X ko Y mẽ] dərd hona/ [X] to have a pain [in Y]

    /dərd kərna/ to hurt (a part of the body)

/dəst/

    /[X ko] dəst ana/ [X] to have diarrhea

/fwrsət/

    /[X ko] fwrsət mylna, pana/ [X] to get free time

/həyza/

    /[X ko] həyza hona/ [X] to get cholera

/məchli/

    /məchli pəkəRna/ to catch fish

/nəzla/

    /[X ko] nəzla hona/ [X] to catch a cold

/paxana/

    /[X ko] paxana ana/ [X] to feel a call of nature

    /paxana jana/ to go to the toilet

    /paxana kərna/ to have a bowel motion

/pərešani/

    /[X ko] pərešani hona/ [X] to be distressed, have worry, be anxious

/pecyš/

    /[X ko] pecyš hona/ [X] to have dysentery

/pešab/

    /[X ko] pešab ləgna/ [X] to feel a call of nature

    /pešab kərna/ to urinate

/reDyo/

    /reDyo bənd kərna/ to shut off a radio

    /reDyo cəlna/ to play (radio)

    /reDyo ləgana/ to turn on a radio

/Ti bi/

    /[X ko] Ti bi hona/ [X] to get tuberculosis

/Tika/

    /[X ke] Tika ləgana/ to innoculate, vaccinate [X]. [Here /ke/ is used since some part of X's body is understood: e.g. /X ke hath mẽ/.]

/xwši/

    /[X ko Y se] xwši hona/ [X] to be made happy [by Y]

/zwkam/

    /[X ko] zwkam hona/ [X] to get the flu

13.201. Word Recognition.

1. The Persian comparative and superlative suffixes, /tər/ and /tərin/, are written separately (except for بهتر /byhtər/ "better" and بهترین /byhtərin/ "best"). E.g.

SCRIPT	PRONUNCIATION	SCRIPT	PRONUNCIATION
زیاده تر	zyadətər	خاص ترین	xastərin
عام تر	amtər	خوبصورت ترین	xubsurəttərin

2. The following words are written with "uncommon" Arabic consonants, with final

ه = /a/, or with other special spelling conventions:

SCRIPT	PRON.	SCRIPT	PRON.
احتیاط	yhtiat	خوش	xwš
ارٹالیس	əRtalys	خوشی	xwši
پاخانہ	paxana	دعوت	davət
تازہ	taza	ذریعہ	zəria
تعداد	tadad	سینتالیس	sə̄ytalys
ٹیکہ	Tika	شیشہ	šiša
جراثیم	jərasim	صحیح	səhih
چھیالیس	chealys	صفائی	səfai
حاصل	hasyl	طبیعت	təbiət
حصہ	hyssa	طرح	təra
خاص	xas	طریقہ	təriqa
خوراک	xwrak	طور	təwr

SCRIPT	PRONUNCIATION	SCRIPT	PRONUNCIATION
عام	am	معائنہ	mwayna [or: معاینہ]
علاج	ylaj	معمولی	mamuli
فرصت	fwrsət	مقابلہ	mwqabla
گندا	gənda (orig. گندہ)	مہینہ	məhina
گندگی	gəndəgi	نزلہ	nəzla
مختصر	mwxtəsər	نسخہ	nwsxa
مریض	məriz	وغیرہ	vəyəyra
مرض	mərz	ہیضہ	həyza

13.202. Reading Drill I: Text.

The following is part of Sec. 13.000. Read it aloud several times, striving for speed and accuracy.

مسٹر رحیم ۔ آئیے اسمتھ صاحب ۔ بچّی کو اِس پلنگ پر لٹائیے ۔

مسٹر اسمتھ۔ کل شام سے اِس کی طبیعت خراب ہے ۔ پہلے سر میں کچھ درد تھا ۔ شام کو بخار ہو گیا اور صبح سے کھانسی کی وجہ سے بات نہیں کر پاتی ۔

مسٹر رحیم ۔ کل اِس نے کیا کھایا تھا ؟

مسٹر اسمتھ کل ہم لوگ ایک دعوت میں گئے تھے ۔ وہاں مچھلی اور چاول کھاتے تھے ۔

مسٹر رحیم ۔ کیا، پیٹ میں بھی درد ہے ؟

مسٹر اسمتھ جی نہیں ۔ پیٹ میں تو درد نہیں ہے ۔ لیکن رات کو بخار بہت تیز تھا ۔ مسز اسمتھ تو بہت پریشان تھیں ۔

مسٹر رحیم۔   اس میں پریشانی کی کوئی بات نہیں ۔ میں نے اچھی طرح دیکھ لیا ہے ۔ صرف بخار اور
معمولی کھانسی ہے۔

مسٹر اسمتھ۔   اس کی کیا وجہ ہے ؟

مسٹر رحیم۔   آج کل موسم اچھا نہیں ۔ اگر احتیاط نہ رکھیں تو نزلہ اور زکام ہو جاتا ہے۔ یہ چیز
بالکل عام ہے۔

مسٹر اسمتھ۔   یہ دیکھئے کس طرح برابر کھانس رہی ہے ۔

مسٹر رحیم۔   آپ فکر نہ کریں ۔ میں نے دوائی کی ایک خوراک پلا دی ہے ۔ یہ نسخہ بازار سے
منگوالیں ۔ تین گھنٹے کے بعد یہ دو گولیاں کھلا دیں۔ اور اس شیشی میں سے
ایک خوراک اور پلا دیں۔ اس کا طریقہ یہ ہے کہ گلاس میں ایک خوراک دوائی
ڈالیں اور تھوڑا تازہ پانی ملا کر پلا دیں ۔

13. 203.   Reading Drill II: Sentences.

Read the following sentences aloud and translate them into English.

۱۔   ہمارے گھر کے نزدیک ایک اور کھانے کی دکان کھل گئی ہے ۔ جس میں بہترین کھانا
ملتا ہے ۔

۲۔   میں نے اُن کو برابر کا حصہ دیا۔ پھر بھی اُنہوں نے شکایت کی۔

۳۔   میرے افسر کو کام سے فرصت نہیں ملتی ورنہ میں اُنہیں ضرور دعوت دیتا۔

۴۔   کل مجھے بخار ہو گیا تھا لیکن اس کی دو گولیاں کھانے کے بعد شام تک میری طبیعت کچھ بہتر
ہو گئی۔

۵۔ آج اُن کے ہاں بچّہ پیدا ہوا ۔ یہ بڑی خوشی کی بات ہے ۔ کیونکہ اُن کی بیوی کا خیال
تھا کہ اُن کے بچّہ نہیں ہوگا۔

۶۔ اِس بات چیت سے بہت سی نئی اور مفید باتیں معلوم ہوئیں ۔

۷۔ بیٹھنے کے مریض نے ایک گلاس پانی مانگا مگر مسافر ڈر سے اُس کے نزدیک نہیں گیا۔

۸۔ یہاں کے ڈاکٹر اُس کا علاج نہ کر پائے ۔ اِس لئے اُس کو انگلستان جانا پڑا۔

۹۔ آج میں اِتنا مصروف رہا کہ ریڈیو سننے کا موقع نہیں ملا۔

۱۰۔ ٹیکہ لگانے کا طریقہ بہت آسان ہے ۔ اِس طرح لگائیے تو بچّے کو تکلیف نہیں ہوگی۔

۱۱۔ وہ لوگ بہت گندے ہیں ۔ عام طور پر وہ دریا میں پیشاب اور پاخانہ کرتے ہیں ۔ اور
پھر اُسی جگہ کا پانی پی لیتے ہیں ۔

۱۲۔ وکیل صاحب بہت نیک انسان ہیں ۔ جب کوئی اُن سے مدد مانگتا ہے تو وہ اُس کی
مدد ضرور کرتے ہیں ۔

۱۳۔ ہیضہ روکنے کے بہت سے طریقے ہیں ۔ اِن میں صفائی کا بندوبست کرنا ، ٹیکہ لگوانا
اور گندگی سے دُور رہنا سب سے ضروری ہیں۔

۱۴۔ اِن کو چچ صاحب کے ذریعے یہ نوکری ملی ہے۔

۱۵۔ اِس وارڈ میں عام بیماریوں کا علاج ہوتا ہے ۔ خاص طور پر کان ، ناک اور آنکھ
وغیرہ ۔ مگر پیٹ کی بیماریوں کا علاج یہاں نہیں ہوتا ۔ آپ کو دوسرے وارڈ میں جانا
پڑے گا ۔

13.204. Writing Drill I: Text.

Counting each speaker's part as one paragraph, write out the first twenty paragraphs
of Sec. 13.505 (Conversation Practice) in the Urdu script (i.e. down through /šwkria. məy
xwd le leta hū. /).

385

13.205. Spelling Review.

Write out the following words in the Urdu script. Check your spelling and handwriting against the correct forms of these words.

(1) nəzər		(11) fəwrən	
(2) yntyzam		(12) phəlvala	
(3) bəhs		(13) hymmət	
(4) fəysla		(14) Dybba	
(5) əksər		(15) məzbut	
(6) cəwkidar		(16) Dəraona	
(7) məhl		(17) səttays	
(8) mõhga		(18) təqribən	
(9) hərəkət		(19) qəla	
(10) ərsa		(20) ərz	

13.206. Writing Drill III: Response Drill.

Answer the following questions in writing.

۱۔ آپ کو کونسا کھانا خاص طور پر پسند ہے ؟

۲۔ کیا آپ برت کو پسند کرتے ہیں ؟ کیوں ؟

۳۔ کیا آپ کل مچھلی پکڑنے گئے تھے ؟

۴۔ ایک سال میں کتنے مہینے ہوتے ہیں ۔ اور ایک مہینے میں کتنے ہفتے ہوتے ہیں ؟

۵۔ کیا آپ کے ملک کے مقابلے میں پاکستان زیادہ گرم ملک ہے ؟

۶۔ اس شہر میں پاکستانیوں کی تعداد تقریباً کتنی ہو گی؟

۷۔ کیا آپ چائے میں دودھ اور چینی ڈالتے ہیں ؟

۸۔ ٹی بی کے مریض کو شادی کرنی چاہئے یا نہیں ؟

۹۔ آپ شام کو عام طور پر کیا کرتے ہیں ۔ کام کرتے ہیں یا آرام کرتے ہیں ؟

۱۰۔ کیا آپ کو ریڈیو سننے کا شوق ہے ؟

13. 207.   **English to Urdu Sentences.**

1.   Day before yesterday Mr. Rəhim gave a party for us.
2.   Give the patient a dose to drink from that vial.
3.   She can go to school today. She has only a minor cough.
4.   My son wants to become a doctor. He hopes that he'll be able to serve mankind.
     [Lit. to him is hope that he'll be able to do men's service.]
5.   In England they generally make good machines.
6.   Truly, in this world there are only sorrow and regret.
7.   I have heard that filth spreads germs.
8.   What is the number of T. B. patients in this ward?
9.   He cures [diseases of] the eye, ear, nose, etc.
10. The lawyer was sorry that he gave the judge trouble again.
11. If you don't take care, you'll get the flu.
12. I want to introduce you to my mother.
13. I'll order the second part of this book for you.
14. It would have been suitable, that you should have had [lit. would have had applied]
     a vaccination.
15. How many times have you had an X-ray taken [lit. caused to be done] this year?

13.300. ANALYSIS

13.301. Substantive Composition: the Suffix /gi/.

Another suffix which is used to form abstract nouns is /gi/. It is of Persian origin, and it is thus added only to Persian (or Perso-Arabic) adjectives. /gi/ is really only another form of /i/ (7.301 (3)), since /gi/ occurs only after stems ending in an original /ə/, while /i/ is found after other consonants and vowels. Word-final /ə/ and /a/ have fallen together in Urdu and are both pronounced /a/. In script, however, an original final /ə/ is often written with ٥ , and final /a/ is written with ١ . The orthography for a given word, however, most often depends upon its language of origin, and there are thus many anomalies.

Note that adjectives which may occur with /gi/ have two stem forms: one ending in /a/ when the word is an adjective, and one ending in /ə/ before /gi/. Only three items have occurred thus far which may have the suffix /gi/:

/gənda/ A1 dirty, filthy	/gəndəgi/ F2 dirt, filth
/šərmynda/ PA1 ashamed, embarrassed	/šərmyndəgi/ F2 embarrassment, shame
/taza/ A1 fresh	/tazgi/ F2 freshness [Orig. /tazəgi/.]

In modern Urdu, /gənda/ is A2, and its MNS form is written with ١ . /šərmynda/, however, is PA1 (composed of /šərm/ F1 "shame" + /ynd/, an adjective-forming suffix + /a/), and the final /a/ of /šərmynda/ is always written as ٥ . This ٥ is dropped, however, before /gi/: شرمندگی . /taza/ is a Type I adjective, although many poeple treat it as Type II (saying, e.g. /tazi roTi/ "fresh bread," /taze phəl/ "fresh fruit," etc. for /taza roTi/, /taza phəl/). Those who treat /taza/ as A1 thus write all of its forms with ٥ , while those who treat it as A2 write the MNS form with ٥ and the remaining forms with ے or ی as the situation requires.

13.302. Substantive Composition: The Persian Comparative and Superlative Affixes.

388

Unlike Urdu, Persian expresses the comparative and superlative degrees of an adjective by means of suffixes. These formations are of common occurrence in Urdu.

(1) The comparative suffix is /tər/. This is added to an adjective stem of Persian (or Perso-Arabic) derivation.

(2) The superlative degree is made by suffixing /in/ to the comparative form.

Note that adjectives ending in original /ə/ (usually written *ø*) end in /a/ in Urdu, but comparative and superlative forms of these adjectives have /ə/ instead before /tər/ and /tərin/: e.g. /zyada/ Al "much, more, too much" but /zyadətər/ Al Adv "more, most often" and /zyadətərin/ Al "most." Similarly, /taza/ Al "fresh," /tazətər/ Al "fresher," and /tazətərin/ Al "freshest."

The comparative form may occur as an adjective in Urdu, or as an adverb, or as a real comparative (e.g. /X Y se Z-tər həy./ "X is Z-er than Y."). The superlative generally occurs as an adjective, and the latter is somewhat more common than the comparative form. About thirty of the adjectives introduced thus far can occur with /tər/ or /tər/ + /in/, but only a few of these will be of immediate use to the student, and many of these forms are very rare. The list includes:

/am/ Al common	/amtər/	/amtərin/
/asan/ Al easy	/asantər/	/asantərin/
/əmir/ Al rich	/əmirtər/	/əmirtərin/
[positive not used]	/byhtər/	/byhtərin/
/calak/ Al clever	/calaktər/	/calaktərin/
/dur/ Al Fl far	/durtər/	/durtərin/
/dylcəsp/ Al interesting	/dylcəsptər/	/dylcəsptərin/
/gərm/ Al hot	/gərmtər/	/gərmtərin/
/hošyar/ Al intelligent	/hošyartər/	/hošyartərin/
/kəm/ Al little, less	/kəmtər/	/kəmtərin/
/məsruf/ Al busy	/məsruftər/	/məsruftərin/
/məšhur/ Al famous	/məšhurtər/	/məšhurtərin/
/məzbut/ Al strong	/məzbuttər/	/məzbuttərin/
/mwfid/ Al profitable	/mwfidtər/	/mwfidtərin/
/mwnasyb/ Al fitting	/mwnasybtər/	/mwnasybtərin/
/mwškyl/ Al difficult	/mwškyltər/	/mwškyltərin/
/mwxtəsər/ Al short	[not used]	/mwxtəsərtərin/
/nəzdik/ Al near	/nəzdiktər/	/nəzdiktərin/
/nek/ Al good, pure	/nektər/	/nektərin/
/peš/ PAl front, offered	/peštər/	[not used]
/qabyl/ Al able	/qabyltər/	/qabyltərin/
/saf/ Al clean	/saftər/	/saftərin/
/səhih/ Al true	/səhihtər/	/səhihtərin/
/šərif/ Al noble	/šəriftər/	/šəriftərin/
/taza/ Al fresh	/tazətər/	/tazətərin/
/təmam/ Al complete	/təmamtər/	/təmamtərin/

/tez/ A1 sharp	/teztər/	/teztərin/
/xas/ A1 special	/xastər/	/xastərin/
/xərab/ A1 bad	/xərabtər/	/xərabtərin/
/xubsurət/ A1 beautiful	/xubsurəttər/	/xubsurəttərin/
/xwš/ PA1 happy	/xwštər/	/xwštərin/
/zyada/ A1 many, more	/zyadətər/	/zyadətərin/

Examples:

/vəhā ka nəzdiktərin rasta yy samne həy./ The nearest road to go [lit. of] there is this [one] in front [of you].

/vw kylas ka hošyartərin ləRka həy./ He is the most intelligent boy in the class. [The Urdu construction is much commoner, of course: /vw kylas ka səb se hošyar ləRka həy./]

/lahəwr kəraci se gərmtər həy./ Lahore is hotter than Karachi. [/ . . . se gərm . . ./ is more common.]

/ys kylas ke zyadətər ləRke hošyar hȳy./ Most of the boys in this class are intelligent. [As an adjective, /zyadətər/ means "most of, the majority of."]

/vw zyadətər šam ko yəhā ate hȳy./ He generally comes here in the evening. [As an adverb, /zyadətər/ means "most often, usually, generally."]

/ys se peštər, mȳy ne yy ciz dekhi həy./ I have seen this thing before this. [/peštər/ here can be replaced by /pəhle/.]

/halət xərabtər ho gəi./ The state [of affairs] has become worse.

/vw badšah ka xastərin admi həy./ He's the king's special man. [I.e. one of his intimate subordinates.]

/ys təriqe ne yy kam asantər kər dia./ This method made this job easier. [Commoner: / . . . əwr asan kər dia./.]

13.303. The Verb: Compound Verbal Formations.

One of the most striking and characteristic features of the Urdu verbal system is the phenomenon of "compound verbs." These consist of the stem of a "main verb" followed by an inflected form of one of several "auxiliary verbs." The main verb has its usual meaning, but the auxiliary verb loses its original meaning to a large extent and functions only as a sort of "aspect indicator," adding various connotations to the meaning of the main verb (e.g. the way the action occurs, the direction of the action in relation to the speaker, etc.). Some common auxiliaries are:

(a) /dena/ "to give" as an auxiliary denotes "the completion of a single action done for someone else's benefit, action done away from the subject."

(b) /lena/ "to take" denotes "the completion of a single action done for the subject's own benefit, action upon the subject, or action towards the subject."

(c) /jana/ "to go" denotes "a single action expressing a completed transition from one state to another."

(d) /bəyThna/ "to sit" expresses "intensity, force, or violent action done for no good reason."

(e) /wThna/ "to rise, get up" denotes "sudden action."

(f) /pəRna/ "to fall, befall" expresses "sudden action with connotations of abrupt-

390

ness and violence."

(g) /Dalna/ "to pour" denotes "completed violent action."

(h) /rəkhna/ "to put, place" denotes "action performed deliberately and with lasting effects."

There are other compound verb auxiliaries also, but these are of less importance. The student has already encountered /rəhna/ "to live, stay" used as a sort of compound verb in the continuative formation (i. e. S + /rəha həy/; Sec. 5.311).

Compound verbs must be distinguished from "complex verbal formations" (Sec. 5.307) and also from "conjunct verbal formations." The latter are similar in form to the compound verb: both consist of a stem + a following inflected verb. In the conjunct verb formation, however, both the stem and the following inflected verb retain their original meanings, and the first stem may be treated as only a "short form" of the conjunctive participle (Sec. 5.308). Thus, /kər gəya/ "did and went" is a conjunct verb, being really nothing more than a "short form" for /kər ke gəya/ "having done, went." On the other hand, /kər dia/ "did (for someone else)" is considered a compound verb since /dena/ has lost most of its original meaning and functions here only as an aspect satellite of /kərna/. If /kər dia/ meant "did and gave," it would then be classed as a conjunct verb, but this is never the case: "did and gave" must always be expressed by /kər ke dia/ (i. e. "having done, gave"). The number of aspect auxiliaries functioning in compound verbal formations is limited, and the student will therefore experience little difficulty in distinguishing compound from conjunct verbal formations.

It must also be noted that compound verbal formations carry a slight degree of emphasis and are thus commonest in affirmative declarative or interrogative sentences. If an utterance contains several clauses, each of which has a verb, the compound verbal formation tends to occur only in the last clause. E. g.

/mɛ̃y swba dəs bəje ghər se nykla, gyara bəje kalyj pəhw̃ca, tin bəje tək kalyj mɛ̃ rəha, phyr bazar gəya, vəhã khana khaya, əwr ws ke bad ghər vapəs a gəya./ I left home at ten in the morning, reached college at eleven o'clock, remained at the college until three o'clock, then went to the market, ate there, and after that came back home.

In the preceding utterance only the last clause contains a compound verb: /a gəya/ "came." If used as independent sentences (and if the singleness and completeness of the action were to be emphasised), then some of the other clauses of the above utterance could also have compound verbs. E. g.

/mɛ̃y swba dəs bəje ghər se nykəl gəya./ I went out of the house at ten o'clock in the morning.

/mɛ̃y gyara bəje kalyj pəhw̃c gəya./ I arrived at the college at eleven o'clock.

/mɛ̃y ne vəhã khana kha lia./ I ate there.

Compound verbal formations are NEVER used with the following:

(a) the continuative (i. e. S + /rəha həy/; Sec. 5.311), which is itself a type of compound verbal formation. Thus, /kər rəha həy/ "is doing" and never */kər de rəha həy/, etc.

(b) S + /cwkna/ "to finish" (Sec. 9.309). Thus, /kər cwka/ "finished doing" and never */kər de cwka/, etc.

(c) OI + /ləgna/ "to begin" (Sec. 9.311). Thus, /kərne ləga/ "began to do" and never */kər dene ləga/, etc.

(d) S + /səkna/ "to be able" (Sec. 5.310). Thus, /kər səka/ "could do" and never */kər de səka/, etc.

(e) S + /kər/ "having done ..." (Sec. 5.308). Thus, /kər ke/ "having done" and never */kər de kər/, etc.

Compound verbs are rarely used in negative utterances. If one asks, /kya, ap ne yy kam kər lia həy?/ Have you done this work [for yourself]?" an **affirmative** answer might indeed include a compound verb:

/ji hã, mə̃y ne kər lia./ Yes, I have done [it].

A negative response, however, cannot contain a compound verb:

/ji nəhĩ, mə̃y ne nəhĩ kia./ No, I haven't done [it].

The use of a compound verbal formation in a negative sentence carries special connotations, usually of negation contrary to all expectations. In such cases the verb is often split into two parts, and the negative (sometimes accompanied by the particle /to/) is placed between them. E.g.

/mə̃y ap ke pəyse cwra nəhĩ lũga!/ I won't steal your money! [Although you seem to think I will!]

/mə̃y ne de to nəhĩ dia!/ I haven't given it! [Although you seem to think that I have!]

Negative compound verbal formations may also be found in one further case: in clause beginning with /jəb tək/ "until" (lit. until when). E.g.

/jəb tək vw hwkm nə de dẽ, mwjrym qəydxane mẽ rəhega./ Until he gives the order, the culprit will remain in jail. [Note that the Urdu here is literally: "until he may not give the order ..."]

/jəb tək mə̃y vapəs nə a jaũ, twm yəhĩ bəyTho!/ Until I return, you sit right here! [Again the Urdu clause is literally negative: until I may not return ..."]

Older grammars also list examples of compound verbal formations in negative clauses which begin with /əgər/ "if" (i.e. conditional clauses), but the author's informants felt that these were incorrect in modern Urdu.

Further shades of emphasis may be obtained by inserting /to/, /bhi/ or /hi/ between the two stems of a compound verbal formation. As was seen above, /to/ also occurs in these formations in negative sentences, but /bhi/ and /hi/ do not seem to share this distribution. E.g.

/mə̃y de hi dũga!/ I will indeed give [it]! [Even though you think I won't.]

/mə̃y vəqt pər yskul pəhw̃c hi gəya./ I got to school on time [after all].

/mə̃y ne wnhẽ yy kytab de hi di./ I [finally] gave him this book [after all]. [I was finally compelled to give it to him.]

/mə̃y ne wnhẽ yy kytab de bhi di./ I've [already] given him this book. [Didn't you know?]

/mə̃y ne wnhẽ yy kytab de to di./ I've [already] given him this book. [Are you doubting my word?]

Of the compound verbal formations listed above, three have been introduced in this Unit, and the others will be added later. Those given so far include:

(1) /jana/ "to go" occurs as an auxiliary after intransitive verb stems. It denotes a

single, completed transition from one state to another. If the action cannot be a single act, then /jana/ cannot be used: i.e. verbs which cannot denote a single, completable transition by their semantic nature cannot occur with /jana/: e.g. /khelna/ "to play," /rona/ "to cry," /hə̄sna/ "to laugh," etc. /jana/ cannot occur as an auxiliary with itself: i.e. one cannot say */ja jata həy/. E.g.

> /aj vw bimar ho gəya./ Today he fell ill. [/ho gəya/ denotes a single completed transition from one state to another. /aj vw bimar hwa./ is indeed grammatically correct, but it would only rarely be found as an independent utterance, since it does not carry strong enough connotations of completed transition. It would, however, occur as an initial or medial clause in a multi-clause utterance:]

> /apke jane ke bad, vw bimar hwa, əwr əbhi tək həspətal mē̃ həy./ After your departure, he fell ill and is still in the hospital.

> /mə̄y ghər a kər so gəya./ I came home and went to sleep. [Compare:]

> /mə̄y ghər a kər soya./ I came home and slept. [Here there is no emphasis on the completion of the transition from waking to sleeping.]

> /yy kam tin dyn mē̃ ho gəya./ This work was done [lit. became] in three days. [A single completed act. Compare:]

> /yy kam tin dyn mē̃ hwa./ This work was done in three days. [Here there is no emphasis on the transition to a completed state.]

> /thoRi der ke bad mə̄y vəhā̃ pəhw̃c gəya./ After a little while I arrived there. [Emphasis on the completion of the action. Compare:]

> /thoRi der ke bad mə̄y vəhā̃ pəhw̃ca./ After a little while I arrived there. [No special emphasis.]

/jana/ is also employed with transitive verbs denoting the "taking in" of sense perceptions: eating, drinking, understanding, etc. This has connotations quite similar to those of the S + /lena/ formation discussed below. E.g.

> /mə̄y səməjh gəya./ I understood. [The emphasis is on the completion of the action. Note that the subject is not marked by /ne/ when /jana/ is the auxiliary, even though the main verb stem is transitive!]

> /vw səb pani pi gəya./ He drank up all the water. [The emphasis here is upon the completeness of the action and the exhaustion of the available amount of water.]

> /vw səb khana kha gəya./ He ate up all the food. [Again the emphasis is on the exhaustion of the amount of food.]

With some intransitive verbs and with most transitive verbs, /jana/ retains its indepedent meaning and thus functions as a part of a conjunct (rather than a compound) verbal formation. Some example are also ambiguous. E.g.

> /vw wTh gəya./ He got up. [/wTh jana/ may be considered a compound verbal formation here. The same sentence, however, may be translated "he got up and went," and this is then an example of a conjunct verbal formation (standing for /wTh kər gəya/. Context must be employed to resolve the ambiguity.]

> /vw səb kam kər gəya./ He did all the work and went. [With /kərna/, a transitive verb, /jana/ must act as the second main stem in a conjunct verbal formation.]

> /vw səb pani pi gəya./ He drank up all the water. [Or: He drank all the water and went. This sentence is ambiguous: it may stand for a compound verbal formation or for /pi kər gəya/.]

(2) /dena/ "to give" occurs as an aspect auxiliary with transitive verbs. It expresses a single action directed away from the subject of the main verb, or an action done to or for

someone else by the subject. As with other transitive constructions, the subject is marked by /ne/ in the past tenses. /dena/ may also occur as an auxiliary after itself. E.g.

/mə̃y ne ws ko de dia./ I gave [it] to him. [The emphasis is on the completion of a single act done for someone else than the subject. Here /dena/ occurs as an auxiliary after itself.]

/mə̃y ne tin dəfa wse kwch pəyse die./ I gave him some money three times. [Since the action is not a single act (but rather one repeated three times), a compound verbal formation cannot be employed here.]

/mə̃y ne ap ki kytab rəkh di./ I put down your book. [Action away from the subject or for someone else's benefit.]

/myhrbani fərma kər, əpna ysme šərif yəhã lykh dijie./ Please write down your name here. [For me, not for your own benefit.]

/ws ne mere lie bəhwt əcche jute bəna die./ He made very good shoes for me.

/Dybba khol do!/ Open the box! [For someone else --- not for your benefit.]

/mə̃y ne ek məni arDər bhej dia./ I sent a money order. [Action away from the subject or for someone else's benefit.]

(3) /lena/ "to take" similarly occurs as an aspect auxiliary mainly with transitive verbs (a few instances of both /lena/ and /dena/ with intransitive stems will be discussed in Sec. 19.308). It denotes a single action done for the subject's benefit, to the subject, or upon the subject's person (whether beneficial or not), or action toward the subject. The subject of a S + /lena/ compound in the past tenses is marked by /ne/. /lena/ may also occur as an auxiliary after itself. E.g.

/mə̃y ne ws se le lia./ I took [it] from him. [The emphasis is upon a single completed action performed in the direction of the subject or for the subject's own benefit.]

/ws ne kəpRe pəhn lie./ He put on [his own] clothes.

/mə̃y ne əpni kytab rəkh li./ I put down my book. [Action for my own benefit. This is also translatable as "I put away my book" (i.e. kept it for myself).]

/yy nwsxa lykh lijie!/ Please write down this prescription! [For your own use.]

/ws ne əpne lie bəhwt əcche jute bəna lie./ He made very good shoes for himself.

/Dybba khol lo!/ Open the box! [For your own benefit.]

/mə̃y ne səməjh lia./ I understood. [A complete act performed for the subject's own benefit. Almost synonymous with /səməjh gəya/, above.]

/mə̃y ne səb khana kha lia./ I ate all the food. [Completed single action for one's own benefit. This is almost synonymous with /kha gəya/, above.]

/wnhõ ne bəhwt pani pi lia./ They drank a lot of water. [For their own benefit.]

13.304. The Verb: the <S [or OI] + /pana/> Construction.

A compound verbal formation differing from those just described in various ways is the <S + /pana/> (or its alternate form <OI + /pana/> formation. This construction means "to manage to...," "get a chance to...," or "to be allowed to...": e.g. /kər paya/ or

394

/kərne paya/ "managed to do, got a chance to do, was allowed to do." There seems to be
no real difference between the <S + /pana/> and the <OI + /pana/> forms; informants stated
that one or the other "felt better" in various contexts. Usually, however, when the negative
/nə/ or /nəhɨ́/ occurred before the main verb stem, the <S + /pana/> form was preferred
(i.e. /nə kər paya/). When the negative was inserted between the main verb stem and /pana/,
then the <OI + /pana/> form was considered best (i.e. /kərne nəhɨ́ paya/). In affirmative
sentences the <S + /pana/> form was most common.

This construction differs from the compound verbal formations discussed in Sec. 13.303
as follows: (1) it often occurs in the negative; (2) all three emphatic particles (/to/, /hi/,
and /bhi/) may occur between the stem or inflected infinitive and the form of /pana/; (3)
the subject of this construction in the past tenses is NOT marked by /ne/, even though /pana/
"to find" is a transitive verb when occurring independently. E.g.

> /mə̃y hi yy kam kər paya./ I was the only one who [lit. I-emphatic]
> could manage to do this task.

> /mə̃y yy kam nə kər paya./ I couldn't manage to do this task. [Or: I
> couldn't get a chance to do this task.]

> /mwjhe wmmid həy, ky vw vəhā pəhw̃cne nəhɨ́ paega./ I hope that he will
> not manage to reach there. [Also: /pəhw̃c nə paega/.]

> /mə̃y mwš̌kyl se ws ka xət pəRh paya./ With difficulty I managed to read
> his letter.

> /mə̃y əbhi khana nə kha paya tha, ky vw a gəe./ I had not yet managed to
> eat dinner when he came. [Also: /khane nə paya tha/.]

> /bimari ki vəja se, vw cəl nəhɨ́ pata./ Because of sickness, he can't
> manage to walk.

> /vw jane nə pae!/ Don't let him go! [Here /pae/ is the conditional form
> of the verb (Sec. 7.311). With a different intonation, this sentence
> might mean "they did not manage to go" -- i.e. /pae/ being the MP
> form of the past tense.]

13.400. SUPPLEMENTARY VOCABULARY

13.401. Supplementary Vocabulary.

The following numerals are all Type I adjectives. See Sec. 2.401.

chealys [or /chəyalys/ or /chyalys/]	forty-six
sə̄ytalys	forty-seven
əRtalys	forty-eight
wncas [or /wnəncas/]	forty-nine
pəcas	fifty

As with other numerals ending in /ys/, the first three above also have a spelling pronunciation ending in /is/. See Sec. 4.401.

Other items are:

gənda A2	dirty, filthy
leTna [IIc: /y/]	to lie down
māgna [Ic: /ə̄/]	to ask for, request
mərz M1 [or /mərəz/]	sickness, illness
šiša M2	glass, windowpane, mirror
xwši F2	happiness

13.402. Supplementary Exercise I: Substitution.

1. ys həspətal mē <u>sə̄ytalys</u>   varD hə̄y.
   fifty
   forty-eight
   twenty-nine
   forty-six
   forty-nine

2. yəhā ys mərz ke <u>calys</u> məriz hə̄y.
   fifty
   thirty-two
   forty-seven
   forty-six
   forty-one

13.403. Supplementary Exercise II: Translation.

Translate the following sentences into Urdu:
1. This city has become very dirty.
2. There is no glass in this window.
3. She asked for a glass of milk.
4. Please lie down on the bed.
5. I became very happy about this. [Lit. To me from this much happiness became.]

13.501. Substitution.

1. mɛ̃y ne wse <u>dəvai ki ek xwrak</u>   <u>pyla di həy</u>.
                fresh water   have given to drink
                fish and milk   have given to eat
                fever medicine [= fever's   have given
                medicine]
                a new prescription   have had sent
                one part   have given

2. yəhã <u>mərizõ</u> ki tadad <u>dusre varDõ</u> ke mwqable mẽ <u>zyada</u>   həy.
      books   other shops   less
      women   men   much more
      doctors   other countries   more
      nurses   our hospital   much less
      machines   England   more

3. <u>bimar</u>   <u>ys təra</u>   <u>xwš</u>   rəhta həy.
    a man   this way   busy
    he   this very way happy
    sorrow   this way   far
    water   which way   fresh
    the curry   this way   hot

4. yəhã   <u>ys bimari</u>   ka ylaj hota həy.
        eye
        ear, nose, etc.
        cholera
        dysentery
        stomach illnesses
        [= stomach's illnesses]

5. həmare <u>šəhr mẽ</u>   <u>həyza</u>   <u>phəyl gəya</u>.
    in this village   cholera germs   has spread[1]
                   [= cholera's
                   germs]

    in my room   rain water [=   has spread
                   rain's water]

    in this country   influenza   has spread
    on the table   papers   have spread
    in our house   filth   has spread

    [1]The verb of each of these sentences must agree with the subject in number-gender.

6. həmẽ əpne šəhr mẽ <u>həyza rokne</u>   ka bəndobəst kərna həy.
                     vaccination
                     keeping cleanliness
                     making blood tests [= blood's

```
                              test doing]
                              stopping tuberculosis
                              a new X-ray machine
```

7. vw <u>səhih</u> təwr pər <u>ynsanõ ki xydmət</u>   kərta həy.
   special   caution
   general   waiting for me [= my waiting]
   general   a comparison of both [= both's
                      comparison]
   special   for me, try
   true   its examination

8. <u>mere sər</u> mẽ <u>bəhwt dərd</u> <u>tha.</u>
   his stomach   minor trouble   was[1]
   this ward   many patients   were
   his urine   blood   was
   the vial   only one dose   was
   the city   much filth   was

   [1]The verb of each of these sentences must agree with the subject in number-
   gender.

9. <u>aram</u>   <u>Ti bi ke mərizõ</u> ke lie <u>zəruri</u>   həy.
   this operation   that doctor   easy
   this method   stopping fever   best
   this pill   the cough   beneficial
   this bed   that patient   too long
   time   this party   little

10. mẽy   <u>əpni bimari</u>   bhul gəya.
    the rest of the luggage
    this event
    my grief
    this method
    their number

13.502. Transformation.

1. Change the underlined verbs in the following sentences (a) to a compound verbal
   formation with /dena/ (e.g. /kia/ to /kər dia/), and (b) to a compound verbal
   formation with /lena/ (e.g. /kia/ to /kər lia/). Retain the same tense.
   a. mẽy ne salən mẽ nəmək <u>Dala.</u>
   b. nərs ne nwsxe pər nyšan <u>ləgaya.</u>
   c. ws ne fəwj ko qəle ke samne <u>roka.</u>
   d. vw xun ka mwayna <u>kəraega.</u>
   e. wnhõ ne yy məšin aprešən ke kəmre mẽ <u>rəkkhi həy.</u>
   f. mẽy ne xət <u>pəRha.</u>
   g. mẽy ne məchli ka ek hyssa <u>kaTa.</u>
   h. nəwkər ne pəlãg ki cadər <u>bədli.</u>

                              398

i. meri nərs yy sare kaɣəz fayl se <u>nykalegi</u>.

j. ws ne kəpRe <u>dhoe</u>.

k. mə̃y gaRi se saman <u>wtarūga</u>.

l. DakTər sahəb kəl tək dəvai ki goliã <u>bənaẽge</u>.

m. nəwkər se kəhẽ, ky vw mwjhe sat bəje <u>jəgae</u>.

n. vw saRhe chəy bəje tək dəvai ki xwrak təyyar <u>kərega</u>.

o. jəb tək vw dərvaza nə <u>khole</u>, ap əndər nə jaẽ.

2. Change the underlined verbs in the following sentences to a compound verbal formation with /dena/ (e.g. /dia/ to /de dia/). Retain the same tense.

   a. ws ko sygreT <u>choRna</u> cahie.

   b. əgər ap wse yy kytab <u>dẽ</u>, to vw xwš ho jaega.

   c. badšah ne əpni fəwj ko kwch mədəd <u>bheji</u>.

   d. cor ne sara vaqea polis ko <u>bətaya</u>.

   e. jəb šiši xali ho jae, to wse <u>phẽko</u>!

   f. gaõvalõ ne wse ys <u>šərarət</u> pər DāTa tha.

   g. bhut ne õdhere mẽ wse <u>Dəraya</u>.

   h. kya, DakTər ne məriz ko dəvai <u>pylai həy</u>.

   i. bəcce ko dusri goli tin bəje <u>khylaẽ</u>.

   j. wnhõ ne əpne jəvab mẽ yy bat <u>kəhi</u>.

3. Change the underlined verbs in the following sentences to a compound verbal formation with /lena/ (e.g. /lia/ to /le lia/). Retain the same tense.

   a. mə̃y ne bəRi mwškyl se yy səval <u>səmjha</u>.

   b. mə̃y ne səb dwnya <u>dekhi</u>.

   c. bwxar ki vəja se, ws ne dəftər se chwTTi <u>li</u>.

   d. ws ne šiši mẽ se ek xwrak <u>pi thi</u>.

   e. wnhõ ne mera pəta ws dwkan se <u>pucha tha</u>.

   f. kafi təlaš ke bad, mə̃y ne əpne dost ko <u>paya</u>.

   g. bəhwt košyš ke bad, polis ne mwjrym ko <u>pəkRa</u>.

   h. ws ne šadi ke məwqe pər mere kəpRe <u>pəhne</u>.

   i. mwsafyr ne bhi mwjh se ek gylas pani <u>māga</u>.

   j. wnhõ ne sare am əwr õgur <u>khae</u>.

4. Change the underlined verb forms in the following sentences to a compound verbal formation with /jana/ (e.g. /hwa/ to /ho gəya/). Retain the same tense.

   a. vw cori ke mal se əmir <u>bəna</u>.

   b. kwtte ko dekh kər, bəcca <u>bhagega</u>.

   c. əgər vw dərəxt se <u>gyrega</u>, to coT ləgegi.

   d. məriz əpne pəlõg pər <u>leTa</u>.

   e. əmrika ki tərəf se, həmare mwlk ko mədəd <u>pəhw̃ci</u>.

   f. sare dyn kam kərne ke bad, šam ko kwch fwrsət <u>myli thi</u>.

   g. əgle məhine se ys həspətal mẽ ek nəya varD <u>khwlega</u>.

   h. rat ko bəcca Dər kər <u>jaga</u>.

   i. aj mə̃y swba sat bəje so kər <u>wTha</u>.

j. mwrɣi pəkəRne ke lie, vw divar pər cəRha.

k. vw vəhã kwch der ke lie Thəyra.

1. əgər vw jəldi aẽ, to həm səb sath synima jaẽge.

m. vw məsjyd mẽ nəmaz pəRhne ke lie bəyTha tha.

n. jəb mãy kalyj se nykla, to dəs bəje the.

o. tez həva ki vəja se, cyraɣ bwjha.

5. Change the following sentences from affirmative to negative, replacing the compound verbal formation with a noncompound form. Retain the same tense.

a. mãy ne əpna əxbar vapəs mãg lia.

b. ws ne dhup mẽ kəpRe phəyla die.

c. həmari hwkumət ne ys həspətal ko mədəd de di həy.

d. twm yəhã bəyTh jao!

e. wnhõ ne mwjhe dəvai ki ek xwrak pyla di thi.

f. ws əfsər ne Təyksi rok li.

g. mwjrym ne ws ke gylas mẽ zəhr myla dia.

h. vw məriz pəlõg pər leT gəya.

i. meri bəhn ne yy kytab ỹglystan se mãgva li.

j. yy mwlk əmrika se mədəd le lega.

6. Change the underlined verb forms in the following sentences to the <S + /pana/> formation (e.g. /kia/ to /kər paya/, /bəyTh səka/ to /bəyTh paya/). Retain the same tense.

a. əbhi mãy təyyar nə hwa tha, ky vw a gəya.

b. zyada məsruf hone ki vəja se, mãy vəhã nə ja səka.

c. bimari ki vəja se, vw nəhĩ wTh səke.

d. cor ka xyal rəkhẽ, ky vw bhag nə jae!

e. šor ki vəja se, mãy kwch bhi nəhĩ swn səka.

f. bəRi košyš ke bad mãy so səka.

g. mãy thoRi hi der bəyTha tha, ky mere əfsər ka Telifun aya.

h. mãy əbhi kəpRe nə dho səka tha, ky pani bənd ho gəya.

i. jəldi mẽ mãy khana nə kha səka.

j. nəwkər se kəhẽ, ky kwtta bahər nə nykle!

13. 503. Variation.

1. vw bərabər khã̃s rəhi həy.

meri choTi bəcci bərabər cix rəhi həy.

Ti bi ke məriz bərabər khã̃ste hãy.

pecyš ke məriz bərabər bimar rəhte hãy.

ws ki təbiət bərabər xərab rəhti həy.

swba se mwjhe bərabər dəst a rəhe hãy.

2. mwjhe ap se myl kər xwši hasyl hwi.

mwjhe ys se kwch mwfid batẽ hasyl hwĩ.

wnhẽ pychle sal ws ki mədəd hasyl thi.

mɞ̃y ne pakystan se kwch kytabē hasyl kī̃.

həm log ap se ys ki rəsid hasyl kərni cahte hɞ̃y.

vəkil sahəb ədalət se ys mwqədme ki fayl hasyl nəhī̃ kər səkēge.

3. khā̃si ki vəja se, vw bat bhi nəhī̃ kər pati.

dərd ki vəja se, vw cəl nəhī̃ pata.

pecyš ki vəja se, vw pəlɞ̃g se wTh nəhī̃ pate.

ys bimari ki vəja se, mɞ̃y vəhā̃ nə ja paya tha.

ws ke šor ki vəja se, mɞ̃y jəvab bhi nə de paya.

həyza phəylne ki vəja se, mɞ̃y vəhā̃ nə ja paya.

4. mɞ̃y ne rəhim sahəb ko ysmyth sahəb se mylaya.

mɞ̃y ap ko əpne dostõ se mylana cahta hū̃.

mɞ̃y ne salən mē kwch pani myla dia.

mɞ̃y ne ysmyth sahəb se hath mylaya.

dəvai ki ek xwrak pani mē myla kər pi lijie!

ap ne mwjhe səhih nəmbər se nəhī̃ mylaya. [1]

[1]Speaking to a telephone operator.

5. nərs am təwr pər bimarõ ko khana khylati hɞ̃y.

ap səhih təwr pər mərizõ ki xydmət kərte hɞ̃y.

yyhi DakTər am təwr pər Tika ləgata hɞ̃y.

mɞ̃y xas təwr pər sygreT choRna cahta hū̃.

həm xas təwr pər ys qysm ki məšinē ÿglystan se mɞ̃gvate hɞ̃y.

əbhi tək yy bat saf təwr pər malum nə ho səki hɞ̃y.

6. mɞ̃y ap ko əcchi təra janta hū̃.

vw yy kam kys təra kəre.

mɞ̃y ys təra kam nəhī̃ kərna cahta.

mɞ̃y ysi təra dusre dərvazõ ko bhi bənd kər lūga.

ap ysi təra do ghənTe ke bad ek əwr xwrak pi lijie!

jys təra bhi ho səke, yy kam kər lijie!

7. mwnasyb hoga, ky ap ws DakTər se bat kərē̃.

mwnasyb hoga, ky ap əpne paxane ka mwayna kəraē̃.

mwnasyb tha, ky vw səb kaɣəz wsi vəqt bhej deta.

mwnasyb tha, ky vw yy mwqədma choR dete.

zyada mwnasyb hɞ̃y, ky ap ws ki bat man lē̃.

mwnasyb nəhī̃, ky ap hər həfte chwTTi kərē̃.

8. mwjhe əfsos hɞ̃y, ky mwjhe fwrsət nəhī̃.

mwjhe əfsos hɞ̃y, ky ws ko həspətal jana pəRa.

mwjhe əfsos hɞ̃y, ky ap ko meri vəja se pərešani hɞ̃y.

mwjhe əfsɵs hɞ̃y, ky mɞ̃y ap ki davət mē nəhī̃ a səkũga.

mwjhe əfsos to hoga, lekyn kya kərū̃ -- mɞ̃y ap ke hā̃ nəhī̃ a səkũga.

mwjhe ys bat ka əfsos tha, ky mɞ̃y ap se nə myl səka.

9. ys dəvai ki vəja se, dərd bylkwl bənd ho gəya.

zwkam ki vəja se, meri nak bylkwl bənd ho gəi.

ys mərz ki vəja se, ws ke kan bənd ho gəe.

401

yy dəvai khane ki vəja se, meri pecyš bənd ho gəi.

goli nə khane ki vəja se, dəst əwr bhi tez ho gəe.

šor ki vəja se, ws ki ākh khwl gəi.

10. həmē əksər məšinē əmrika se māgvani pəRti hāy.

wnhē yy šišiā ỹglystan se māgvani pəRti hāy.

ap ko yy kytab Dak ke zərie se māgvani pəRegi.

ap ko yy nwsxa bazar se māgva lena cahie.

kya, māy ys fayl ka baqi hyssa māgva lū?

mera xyal həy, ky ap kwch taza goliā māgva lē.

11. māy əpna ɣəm bhul gəya.

ap ko əpna ɣəm bhul jana cahie.

māy ws ka mwayna kərne ka təriqa bhul gəya.

reDyo swnne se, məriz əpni təklif bhul səkta həy.

ws bərtən mē taza pani Dalna nə bhulie!

əpna nam zərur lykh dijie, vərna māy bhul jaūga.

12. ap ko yy aprešən kəra lena cahie.

ap ko əpne bəcce ka aprešən kəra dena cahie.

wnhõ ne kan ka aprešən kəra lia həy.

wnhõ ne ws ka ylaj kəra dia həy.

māy ne əpna eksre kəra lia həy.

wnhõ ne nəwkər se məkan ki səfai kəra li.

13. ws varD ke mwqable mē, yy varD əccha həy.

yy šəhr, ws šəhr ke mwqable mē, gənda həy.

yəhā pakystaniõ ki tadad, dusrõ ke mwqable mē zyada həy.

māy yn donõ məšinõ ka mwqabla kər ke bəta dūga.

badšah ka mwqabla kərne ke lie, bəhwt hymmət cahie.

ws ne səb logõ ke samne mera mwqabla kia.

14. vəkil sahəb ki bəhs bəhwt mwxtəsər thi.

meri kytab bəhwt hi mwxtəsər həy.

ws ne ys dəwran mē mwxtəsər si bat ki.

gəvah ne jəj ko bəhwt mwxtəsər jəvab die.

DakTər ne mwxtəsər sa mwayna kia.

nərs ne ek mwxtəsər sa nwsxa lykha, əwr mwjhe de dia.

15. əgər yhtiat nə rəkhē, to nəzla ho jata həy.

əgər ghər mē yhtiat nə rəkhē, to gəndəgi phəyl jati həy.

əgər yəhā yhtiat nə rəkhē, to jərasim pəyda ho jaēge.

əgər yhtiat nə rəkhē, to eksre saf nəhī̃ aega.

əgər yhtiat rəkhte, to ap ko khāsi nə hoti.

əgər twm yy əlmari yhtiat se bənaoge, to əcchi bənegi.

13.504. Response.

1. kya, ap ne kəbhi eksre ki məšin dekhi həy?

2. kya, ys šəhr ke həspətal hwkumət ki mədəd se cəlte hāy, ya əmir logõ ki mədəd se.

3. kya, ap ko kəbhi pecyš̌ hwi·həy?
4. kya, ap ko kəbhi həspətal jana pəRa? kya š̌ykayət thi.
5. kytne dyn həspətal mē̃ rəhe the.
6. kya, ap ko kəbhi apreš̌ən kərana pəRa?
7. am təwr pər, ap ki təbiət kəysi rəhti həy.
8. jəb ap ko zwkam əwr nəzla hota həy, to kya ylaj kərte hə̃y.
9. ap ne ys sal həyze ka Tika ləgvaya həy, ya nəhĩ.
10. kya, ys š̌əhr mē̃ səfai ka bəndobəst əccha həy?
11. həyze ko rokne ke lie, kəwn kəwnse təriqe mwfid hə̃y.
12. jərasim kəhã pəyda hote hə̃y.
13. kya, ap ko swba əxbar pəRhne ki fwrsət mylti həy?
14. kya, ap hwkumət ki tərəf se pakystan jaẽge?[1]
15. kya, ap ynsan ki xydmət kərni cahte hə̃y?

[1]Lit. "from the direction of the government": i.e. "supported by, on behalf of, sent by the government."

13.505. Conversation Practice.

Mr. Smith has called Dr. Rəhim to his house.

S: mwjhe əfsos həy, ky ap ko phyr təklif di, lekyn vəja yy həy, ky bəcci ki təbiət xərab ho gəi həy. aie, vw dusre kəmre mē̃ leTi həy.

R: əb wse kya š̌ykayət həy.

S: jo dəvaiã ap ne di thĩ, vw bərabər de rəhe hə̃y. bwxar to wsi dyn wtər gəya tha, lekyn khãsi əwr zwkam baqi həy. kəl swba se dəst a rəhe hə̃y, əwr peT mē̃ bhi kwch dərd həy.

R: khane ko kya ciz di thi.

S: dudh əwr cavəl.

R: xəyr, koi bat nəhĩ. mə̃y ne yy nwsxa lykh dia həy. nəwkər ko mere sath bhejē̃. mə̃y kwch dəvaiã əpne ghər se bhyjva dũga. baqi ap bazar se mə̃gva lē̃.

S: mə̃y nəwkər ko əbhi ap ke sath bhejta hũ.

R: əccha. əb yjazət dijie.

S: cae təyyar həy. cae pi kər jaie.

R: bəhwt əccha. -- ap ki təbiət kəysi həy.

S: əb to kwch Thik həy. mə̃y ap ki dəvaiã ystemal kər rəha hũ.

R: əb paxana kəysa ata həy.

S: aj swba mamuli sa dəst aya tha, əwr peT mē̃ dərd bhi nəhĩ hwa.

R: bəs, khane mē̃ thoRi si yhtiat rəkhē̃.

S: ji hã. ysi lie kəl mə̃y əxtər sahəb ke hã nəhĩ gəya. wnhõ ne meri davət ki thi.

R: ap ne bəhwt əccha kia.

S: dusre, dəvai ki syrf ek xwrak baqi həy. əgər mwmkyn ho, to nəwkər ke hath kwch dəvai mere lie bhi bhej dē̃.

R: bəhwt əccha.

S: lijie, cae təyyar həy. cini əwr dudh mə̃y ne nəhĩ Dala.

R: š̌wkria. mə̃y xwd le leta hũ.

S: šəhr mẽ əb həyze ki kya halət həy.

R: pəhle se byhtər həy. hwkumət ki košyš se, ys ko rokne mẽ bəhwt mədəd myli həy, jys ki vəja se šəhr mẽ səfai ka bəhwt əccha bəndobəst ho gəya həy. kyõke yy əysa mərz həy, jys ke lie səfai ka rəkhna bəhwt zəruri həy.

S: ajkəl ap ke pas kam bəhwt hoga.

R: ji hã. bylkwl fwrsət nəhĩ mylti. əksər rat ko bhi der se ghər ata hũ.

S: lekyn ys təra ap mwlk ki bəhwt xydmət kər rəhe hɛ̃y. -- cae əwr lijie.

R: ji nəhĩ, šwkria. mwjhe əb cəlna cahie, kyõke aj šəhr jana həy. həspətal mẽ bhi kwch log mera yntyzar kər rəhe hɛ̃y.

S: əccha, xwda hafyz.

R: xwda hafyz.

        The next day Mr. Smith calls on Dr. Rəhim at the hospital.

R: aj swba se mɛ̃y ytna məsruf hũ, ky bəRi mwškyl se khana khane ki fwrsət myl səki.

S: kya, aj bəhwt zyada məriz ae?

R: məriz bhi zyada ae. dusre, həmare həspətal ke kwch DakTər həyze ke mərizõ ko dekhne ke lie šəhr gəe hɛ̃y.

S: vaqəi, aj ap ke kəmre mẽ bhi mərizõ ki tadad pəhle se zyada həy. kya, yy kysi xas bimari ke məriz hɛ̃y?

R: ji nəhĩ, kəi qysm ki bimariõ ke məriz hɛ̃y. -- jəyse ãkh, kan, nak, vəɣəyra. kysi ke pešab əwr xun ka mwayna kərna həy, əwr kysi ka əksre hona həy.

S: kya, səb məriz pəhle ys varD mẽ ate hɛ̃y?

R: syrf am bimariõ ke səb məriz pəhle yəhã ate hɛ̃y, kyõke yy am mərizõ ka varD həy. yəhã ke DakTər hər məriz ka mwxtəsər sa mwayna kərte hɛ̃y. phyr jys təra mwnasyb səməjhte hɛ̃y, ylaj šwru kər dete hɛ̃y. lekyn xas bimariõ ke məriz sidhe dusre varDõ mẽ jate hɛ̃y.

S: yy təriqa əccha həy. yy mərizõ ke lie bhi mwfid həy, əwr DakTərõ ko bhi ys mẽ asani həy.

R: hã ! mɛ̃y bhul gəya. bəcci ki təbiət əb kəysi həy.

S: pəhle se byhtər həy. aj swba to xwš malum hoti thi.

R: kya, aj koi dəst aya həy?

S: ji nəhĩ, lekyn peT mẽ dərd əbhi baqi həy.

R: koi bat nəhĩ. vw bhi šam tək xətm ho jaega.

S: kya, mere lie dəvai təyyar həy?

R: ji hã, mɛ̃y ne nərs ko lane ke lie bheja həy. ap ko thoRi der yntyzar kərna pəRega. mwjhe əfsos həy, ky mwjhe car bəje ek aprešən ke lie jana həy. ys lie əb yjazət cahta hũ.

S: əccha. kya, mɛ̃y phyr kəl a jaũ?

R: koi zərurət nəhĩ. pərsõ aie.

S: bəhwt əccha. xwda hafyz.

R: xwda hafyz.

        13. 506. Conversation Stimulus.

        Topics may include the following:

1. A doctor examines a patient.
2. A visit to a hospital.
3. A cholera outbreak.
4. Prescribing for a sick person.
5. The treatment of T. B. patients.

am A1	common, ordinary, general, public
aprešən [or /əprešən/] M1	operation
ā́kh F1	eye
əfsos M1 [np]	sorrow, regret, grief, concern
əRtalys [or /əRtalis/] A1	forty-eight
baqi A1	rest, remaining
bəndobəst M1 [np]	arrangement, management
bərabər A1 Adv	equal, even, level, straight, uniform, alike, equivalent, adjoining; continually, constantly
bhulna [IIc: /w/]	to forget
bimari F2	sickness, illness
bwxar M1	fever
byhtərin A1	best
chealys [or /chəyalys/, /chyalys/, /chealis/, /chəyalis/, or /chyalis/] A1	forty-six
davət F1	party, feast, invitation
dərd M1	pain
dəst M1	diarrhea
dwnya F1	world
Dalna [If: /ə/]	to pour, put in, throw in
eksre M1	X-ray
fwrsət F1	leisure, free time, leave
gənda A2	dirty, filthy
gəndəgi F2	filth, dirt, uncleanliness
goli F2	pill, pellet, marble, small ball, bullet
γəm M1	sadness, grief, sorrow
hasyl PA1	obtained, acquired
həyza M2 [np]	cholera
hyssa M2	part, portion, section, piece
jərasim Mp1	germs, microbes, bacteria
kan M1	ear
khā́si F2	cough
khā́sna [IIc: /ə/. C and DC rare]	to cough
khwlna [I: /kholna/: Ie]	to open (intrans.), be opened
khylana [C: /khana/: Ic]	to feed, give to eat, cause to eat
ləgana [C: /ləgna/: IIc]	to attach, hit, strike, fix
ləgvana [DC: /ləgna/: IIc]	to cause to be attached, hit, struck, fixed
ləmba A2	long, tall
leTna [IIc: /y/]	to lie down, lie
lyTana [C: /leTna/: IIc]	to cause to lie down, lay down
mamuli A1	minor, ordinary, common

mãgna [Ic: /ə̃/]	to ask for, request
məchli F2	fish
mədəd F1 [np]	help, aid, assistance
məhina M2	month
məriz M1	patient, sick person
mərz M1	sickness, illness
məšin F1	machine
mãgvana [DC: /mãgna/: Ic]	to cause to be requested, to order, send for
mwayna M2	examination, inspection
mwfid A1	profitable, useful, beneficial
mwnasyb A1	suitable, fitting
mwqabla [literary: /mwqabəla/] M2	comparison, contest, competition, confrontation, match [/[ke] mwqable mẽ/ Comp Post "compared with"]
mwxtəsər A1	short
mylana [C: /mylna/: IIc]	to mix, cause to meet, introduce, join (two objects together)
nak F1	nose
nərs F1 [rarely M1]	nurse
nəzla M2 [np]	influenza
nwsxa M2	prescription; copy (of a book)
paxana M2	excrement, stool, toilet, excrementation
pəcas A1	fifty
pəlãg M1	bed
pərešani F2	worry, upset, anxiety, disturbance
pəyda PA1	born, produced, procured, found
pecyš F1	dysentery
pešab M1 [np]	urine
peT M1	stomach, belly
phəylana [C: /phəylna/: IIc]	to cause to spread, spread (trans.)
phəylna [IIc: /əy/]	to spread (intrans.)
pylana [C: /pina/: Ic]	to cause to drink, give to drink
reDyo M1	radio
rokna [If: /w/]	to stop, check, prevent
səfai F2 [np]	cleanliness
səhih [common: /səhi/] A1	true
sãytalys [or /sãytalis/] A1	forty-seven
šiša M2	glass, windowpane, mirror
šiši F2	small bottle, vial
tadad [literary: /taədad/] F1 [np]	number, amount
taza A1 [or A2]	fresh
təbiət F1	nature, disposition, temperament, health
təra [or /tərəh/] F1	way, manner, kind
təriqa M2	method, manner, way, plan of action

təwr M1	way, manner
Ti bi F2 [np]	tuberculosis
Tika M2	vaccination, innoculation, spot, blemish, red spot worn on the forehead
varD M1	ward
vəɣəyra Adv	et cetera
wncas [or /wnəncas/] A1	forty-nine
xas A1	special, private
xwrak F1	dose; foodstuffs
xwš PA1	happy, glad
xwši F2	happiness, joy, pleasure
yhtiat F1	care, caution
ylaj M1	remedy, cure, healing, treatment
ynsan M1	man, human being
ȳglystan M1 [np]	England
zəria M2	method, means, way, medium, resource
zwkam M1 [np]	cold, catarrh

A villager using oxen to thresh the harvest, India.

UNIT FOURTEEN

14.000. CONVERSATION

Mr. əziz has taken Mr. Smith to visit his village, where they plan to stay for a few days.

dirt, soil, earth, clay F2 | myTTi [or /məTTi/]
are built MP | bəne hwe hɔ̄y
lane, alley F2 | gəli
narrow, tight, distressed Al | tɔ̄g
wide, broad A2 | cəwRa

S: Your village is very beautiful. Although the houses are made of clay, the lanes are narrow, and the markets also are not very wide, still every place appears very clean.

ap ka gaɔ̃ bəhwt xubsurət həy. əgərce məkan myTTi ke bəne hwe hɔ̄y, gəliã tɔ̄g hɔ̄y, əwr bazar bhi zyada cəwRẽ nəhĩ̃, lekyn hər jəga bəhwt saf nəzər ati həy.

animal Ml | janvər
health Fl | syhət
crop, harvest Fl | fəsl
manure, fertiliser Fl | khad
is used for FS [lit. gives work [as]] | kam deti həy
(agricultural) field Ml | khet
throw (away and) come (back) MP [conjunct verb: = /phēk kər ate hɔ̄y/] | phēk ate hɔ̄y

ə: Cleanliness is very necessary for the health of the people of the village and their animals. Moreover, filth is useful as fertiliser in the fields. Therefore, the villagers throw away all the filth outside in the fields [lit. having thrown, come].

səfai gaɔ̃ ke logɔ̃ əwr wn ke janvərɔ̃ ki syhət ke lie bəhwt zəruri həy. dusre, gəndəgi fəslɔ̃ mē̃ khad ka kam deti həy. ys lie, gaɔ̃vale təmam gəndəgi bahər khetɔ̃ mē̃ phēk ate hɔ̄y.

collection, sum, plural; gathered, collected Fl PAl | jəma

S: Why are the people gathered here? Don't they go to the fields?

yy log yəhã̄ kyɔ̃ jəma hɔ̄y. kya, yy khetɔ̃ pər nəhĩ̃ jate?

young, youth Ml Al | jəvan
go off MP | cəle jate hɔ̄y
old (of persons) A2 M2 | buRha
in connection with, about, concerning Comp Post PA1 | [ke] mwtəəllyq [common: /mwtallyq/]
one another, each other Adv | apəs
keep on doing MP | kərte rəhte hɔ̄y

ə: The young men of the village always go off to the fields early in the morning and return home in the evening. The old men generally remain in the village and take care of cleanliness in the village, manage the homes, or, in [their] leisure time, keep chatting among themselves about the village.

gaɔ̃ ke jəvan admi həmeša swba swba khetɔ̃ pər cəle jate hɔ̄y, əwr šam ko ghər vapəs ləwTte hɔ̄y. buRhe admi am təwr pər gaɔ̃ mē̃ rəhte hɔ̄y, əwr gaɔ̃ mē̃ səfai ka xyal rəkhte hɔ̄y, ghərɔ̃ ka yntyzam kərte hɔ̄y, ya fwrsət ke vəqt, gaɔ̃ ke mwtəəllyq apəs mē̃ batē̃ kərte rəhte hɔ̄y.

411

S: Do the women also work in the fields?

    hardworking, industrious A1

    along with Comp Post

    wood, stick F2

    to break, pick, pluck [Ie: /w/]

    to cook, make ripe, ripen [C: /pəkna/: IIc]

ə: Like the men, village women also are very industrious. They work right along with the men. They cut wood from the trees, pick fruit, and come home and cook dinner.

    front [one] A2

    cooked, ripe, ready, matured, solid, substantial, permanent (as a brick or stone house, a paved road, etc.) A2

S: What is this permanent [i.e. brick or stone] building in front [lit. front-one permanent building]?

    education F1

    agriculture F1 [np]

    to teach [C: /sikhna/: Ic]

    entered, inserted PA1

ə: This is the school of this place [lit. of here]. Compared to the city, in the village there is very little education because most of the people teach their children agricultural work and don't get them entered in school.

    farmer M1

    to learn [Ic: /y/]

S: In this day and age [lit. in these days' time] education is very necessary, because through education the farmer can learn various [lit. new new] methods of agriculture.

    canal F1

    bank, shore, side M2 [/[ke] kynare/ Comp Post "on the bank, along the bank, on the side of"]

    is spread out FS

    wheat F1 [or M1]

    to ripen, get cooked, become mature [IIc: /ə/]

ə: My land begins from here and extends up to the left bank of that canal. These days the wheat crop is almost ready. It will only take a little while to ripen [lit. only in ripening some lateness will attach].

S: In this season is there only the wheat crop?

    besides, in addition to, moreover Comp Post

---

kya, əwrtẽ bhi khetõ pər kam kərti hẽy?

myhnəti [common: /myhnti/]

[ke] sath sath

ləkRi

toR'na

pəkana

gaõ ki əwrtẽ bhi, mərdõ ki təra, bəhwt myhnəti hoti hẽy. vw mərdõ ke sath sath kam kərti hẽy. dərəxtõ se ləkRiã kaTti hẽy, phəl toRti hẽy, əwr ghər a kər khana pəkati hẽy.

samnevala

pəkka

yy samnevali pəkki ymarət kya həy.

talim

zəraət

sykhana

daxyl

yy yəhã ka yskul həy. gaõ mẽ šəhr ke mwqable mẽ talim bəhwt kəm hoti həy, kyõke əksər log əpne bəccõ ko zəraət ka kam sykhate hẽy, əwr yskul mẽ daxyl nəhĩ kərate.

kysan

sikhna

ajkəl ke zəmane mẽ, talim bəhwt zəruri həy, kyõke talim ke zərie se kysan zəraət ke nəe nəe təriqe sikh səkta həy.

nəhr

kynara [literary: /kənara/]

phəyli hwi həy

gəndwm

pəkna

yəhã se meri zəmin šwru hoti həy, əwr ws nəhr ke baẽ kynare tək phəyli hwi həy. ajkəl gəndwm ki fəsl təqribən təyyar həy. syrf pəkne mẽ kwch der ləgegi.

kya, ys məwsəm mẽ syrf gəndwm ki fəsl hoti həy?

[ke] ylava [or /əlava/]

barley M1 [np]	jəw
pea[s] M1	məTər
oil M1	tel
seed M1	bij
raw, unripe, immature, nonpermanent (as a building of mud or unbaked brick, a dirt road, etc.), crude A2	kəcca
October M1 [np]	əktubər
November M1 [np]	nəwmbər [or /nəvəmbər/]
March M1 [np]	marc
April M1 [np]	əprəyl
near, nearby, almost Comp Post Adv	[ke] qərib

ə: Oh no, besides wheat, the crops of barley, peas, and oil seed are planted [lit. are standing], which are still somewhat unripe. This crop we plant [lit. attach] in the month[s] of October and November, and [we] cut [it] about March or April.

ji nəhĩ, gəndwm ke ylava, jəw, məTər, əwr tel ke bijõ ki fəslẽ bhi khəRi həy, jo əbhi kwch kəcci hə̃y. yy fəsl həm əktubər əwr nəwmbər ke məhine mẽ ləgate hə̃y, əwr marc ya əprəyl ke qərib kaT lete hə̃y.

S: When is the rice crop?

cavəl ki fəsl kəb hoti həy.

rainy season F1	bərsat
to sow [Ia]	bona
to be cut, get cut [I: /kaTna/: Ie]	kəTna
muskmelon M2	xərbuza
watermelon M1	tərbuz

ə: They sow rice in the months of the rainy season and cut [it] at the start of the winter. When any crop is through being cut, then at once [they] plant some vegetable or fruit, etc. -- like muskmelons or watermelons -- and they don't let the land lie fallow [lit. remain empty].

cavəl bərsat ke məhinõ mẽ bote hə̃y, əwr sərdiõ ke šwru mẽ kaTte hə̃y. jəb koi fəsl kəT cwkti həy, to fəwrən koi səbzi ya phəl vəɣəyra -- jəyse xərbuze ya tərbuz -- ləga dete hə̃y, əwr zəmin ko xali nəhĩ rəhne dete.

difference M1	fərq

S: What difference does this make? [Lit. from this what difference befalls?]

ys se kya fərq pəRta həy.

profit, benefit, advantage M2	fayda
different, various A1	mwxtəlyf
keep on growing FP [/wgna/: IIc "to grow"; /w/]	wgti rəhti hə̃y
time, turn, occasion F1 [/bar bar/ Adv "time after time, repeatedly, again and again"]	bar
to cause to grow, plant [C: /wgna/: IIc]	wgana
weak, debilitated A1	kəmzor

ə: Its advantage is that various crops keep growing in the land, because of which the land does not go bad, because from growing the same crop repeatedly the land becomes weak.

ys ka fayda yy həy, ky zəmin mẽ mwxtəlyf fəslẽ wgti rəhti hə̃y, jys se zəmin xərab nəhĩ hoti, kyõke bar bar ek hi fəsl wgane se zəmin kəmzor ho jati həy.

S: There are also many trees visible in the fields.

khetõ mẽ bəhwt se dərəxt bhi nəzər a rəhe hə̃y.

sweet A2

(habitually) send for MP [/mə̃gana/ "to request, send for, order"; C: /mãgna/: Ic]

ə: These are mango trees. Mangoes from here are very sweet. We always get mangoes for ourselves from here.

grain M1

S: All of the grain and vegetables, etc., for your place must also come from here.

although, on the other hand, certainly, but Conj

fifty-five A1

distance, space M2

ə: Yes, we get grain from here, although [on the other hand] vegetable[s] do not come from here because the city is at a distance of fifty-five miles from here.

plow M1

to cause to go, drive, run (a machine, etc.) [C: /cəlna/: Ic]

S: Why are these farmers plowing now? These days it is time to cut the crop.

preparation, readiness F2

labour, hard work, effort F1

hunger F1 [np]

thirst F1 [np]

keeps on doing MS

to become tired [IIc: /ə/]

ə: This is the preparation for the next crop. Our farmer works very hard because he has to do all the work himself. Whether there be cold or heat, hunger or thirst, he keeps on working and never gets tired.

to escape, be saved, be left over [IIc: /ə/]

S: In our country machines do most of the work, by which the farmer's time is saved.

littleness, scarcity, lack, deficiency F2

ox M1

(female) water buffalo F1

ə: In our country there is a great scarcity of machines. Therefore, the farmer does [his] work with the help of the ox, the cow, and the water buffalo, etc.

(male) horse M2

make use of MP [lit. take work [from]]

S: In our country in a few [lit. certain certain] place[s] [they] make use of horses in the fields.

miTha

mə̃gaya kərte hə̃y

yy am ke dərəxt hə̃y. yəhã ke am bəhwt miThe hote hə̃y. həm əpne lie yəhĩ se am mə̃gaya kərte hə̃y.

ənaj

ap ke hã to səb ənaj əwr səbzi vəyəyra bhi yəhĩ se ati hogi.

əlbətta

pəcpən

fasyla

ji hã, ənaj to yəhĩ se mə̃gvate hə̃y, əlbətta səbzi yəhã se nəhĩ ati, kyõke šəhr yəhã se pəcpən mil ke fasyle pər hə̃y.

həl

cəlana

yy kysan əb kyõ həl cəla rəhe hə̃y. ajkəl to fəsl kaTne ka vəqt hə̃y.

təyyari

myhnət

bhuk

pyas

kərta rəhta həy

thəkna

yy əgli fəsl ki təyyari həy. həmara kysan bəhwt myhnət kərta həy, kyõke səb kam wse xwd kərna pəRta həy. sərdi ho ya gərmi, bhuk ho ya pyas, kam kərta rəhta həy, əwr kəbhi nəhĩ thəkta.

bəcna

həmare mwlk mẽ əksər kam məšinẽ kərti hə̃y, jys se kysan ka vəqt bəc jata həy.

kəmi

bəyl

bhə̃ys

həmare mwlk mẽ məšinõ ki bəhwt kəmi həy. ys lie kysan bəyl, gae, əwr bhə̃ys vəyəyra ki mədəd se kam kərta həy.

ghoRa

[se] kam lete hə̃y

həmare mwlk mẽ kysi kysi jəga khetõ mẽ ghoRõ se kam lete hə̃y.

414

mustard seed F1 [np]   sərsõ

plant, shrub M2   pəwda

ə: Look at this, this is a field of mustard   yy dekhie, yy sərsõ ka khet həy. ys ka
plants. [We] cook its greens [lit. plant]   pəwda səbzi ke təwr pər pəkate hãy, əwr
as a vegetable and extract oil from its   ys ke bijõ se tel nykalte hãy.
seeds.

green A2   həra

colour, tint, paint, dye, appearance,   rãg
aspect M1

yellow A2   pila

S: How beautiful the yellow flower [lit. flower   həre rãg ke pəwde mẽ, pile rãg ka phul
of yellow colour] appears on [lit. in] the   kytna xubsurət malum hota həy!
green plant [lit. plant of green colour]!

(water) well M2   kũã

keeps on going, moving MS   cəlta rəhta həy

to cause to arrive, make reach, bring   pəhw̃cana
[C: /pəhw̃cna/: IIc]

to fill, be filled [IIId: /ə/]   bhərna

washerman, laundryman M1   dhobi

ə: This is the well, which goes almost all   yy kũã həy, jo təqribən hər vəqt cəlta rəhta
the time and delivers water to [lit. in]   həy, əwr fəslõ mẽ pani pəhw̃cata həy. ys
the crops. Aside from this, people get   ke ylava, log yəhã se pani bhərte hãy, əwr
[lit. fill] water from here, and the village   gaõ ke dhobi yəhã a kər kəpRe dhote hãy.
washermen come here and wash clothes.

cattle dung M1   gobər

to dry [IIc: /w/]   sukhna

S: Why is this cow dung drying in the sun?   yy gobər dhup mẽ kyõ sukh rəha həy.

poor A1 M1   yərib

to dry, cause to dry [C: /sukhna/: IIc]   swkhana

to cause to burn, set fire to, light, burn   jəlana
[C: /jəlna/: IIc]

fire F1   ag

ə: The village people are poor. They cannot   gaõ ke log yərib hote hãy. vw ləkRi nəhĩ
buy wood. Therefore, they dry cattle dung   xərid səkte. ys lie gobər ko swkha kər
and burn it and use it for the fire.   jəlate hãy, əwr ys se ag ka kam lete hãy.

S: Come on, let's sit for awhile on the bank   aie, thoRi der ys nəhr ke kynare bəyThẽ!
of this canal!

must have become MS   ho gəya hoga

ə: I think that now we ought to go back to the   mera xyal həy, ky əb gaõ vapəs cəlna cahie,
village because it is 1:30 [lit. one and a   kyõke DeRh bəj rəha həy. dusre, khana
half is striking]. Moreover, food must be   bhi təyyar ho gəya hoga, əwr vw log həmara
ready, and those people must be waiting   yntyzar kər rəhe hõge.
for us.

please go [polite imperative]   cəliega

pleasure, choice, desire, will F2 [np]   mərzi

S: Let's go. Just as you wish.   cəliega. jəysi ap ki mərzi həy.

14.101. /kam/ M1 "work, job, task" is employed in the following useful idioms:

(1) /[X Y ka] kam deta həy. / [X] is used as [Y]. [I.e. the main purpose of X may be something other than Y, but here X is made to serve as Y.]

(2) /[X Y se Z ka] kam leta həy. / [X] makes use [of Y as Z]. [I.e. the original purpose of Y may not be Z, but here X makes use of Y for the purpose of Z.]

(3) /[X Y ko Z ke] kam mẽ lata həy. / [X] makes use [of Y as Z]. [I.e. X uses Y as Z, as a part of Z, as something useful to Z, as an aid to Z, etc.]

(4) /[X Y ke] kam [mẽ] ata həy. / [X] is useful [as Y]. [I.e. X can serve as Y, as an aid to Y, as a part of Y, etc. Y here will usually be a verbal infinitive + the object of the infinitive, but it may also be a simple noun or noun phrase: see examples 7 and 8.]

Examples:

/yy Dybba suTkes ka kam deta həy. / This box is used [or: is useful] as a suitcase.

/mẽy ne ys Dybbe se suTkes ka kam lia. / I used this box as a suitcase.

/jəb mere pas koi pyali nə thi, to meri Topi ne pyali ka kam dia. / When I had no cup, then my hat was useful as a cup.

/həm ys məkan se məsjyd ka kam lete hẽy. / We use this house as a mosque.

/gaõvale gəndəgi se khad ka kam lete hẽy. / The villagers use filth as fertiliser.

/yəhã ke log yn bijõ ko dəvai ke kam mẽ late hẽy. / People here [lit. of here] use these seeds for medicine.

/yy ciz khane ke kam [mẽ] ati həy. / This thing is used [or: useful] as food. [I.e. It is included in the list of foodstuffs. /ke/ remains /ke/ whether /mẽ/ follows /kam/ or not. The use of /mẽ/ depends upon one's dialect and individual preferences.]

/yy bərtən khana pəkane ke kam ata həy. / This vessel is used for the cooking of food. [Note that this construction contains a verbal infinitive, /pəkana/; this is perhaps the most common usage.]

14.102. /khet/ M1 denotes a field used for agricultural purposes; /məydan/ M1 means "open field, plaza, parade ground." Note that "to go [to work in] the fields" may be expressed either by /khetõ pər jana/ -- lit. "to go on the fields" -- or by /khetõ mẽ jana/ "to go in the fields."

14.103. /apəs mẽ/ "among [our, your, them]selves" is used to indicate reciprocal action within a group. It always refers to the subject of the main verb. A possessive reciprocal is also possible: /apəs ka [or: /ki/, /ke/]/" "[our, your, their] own ..." or "among [our, your, them]selves." E.g.

/gaõvale apəs mẽ batẽ kər rəhe the. / The villagers were talking among themselves.

/vw ləRke syrf apəs mẽ fwTbal khelte hẽy. dusre ləRkõ ke sath nəhĩ khelte. / Those boys play football only among themselves. They do not play with other boys.

/yy həmari apəs ki bat həy. / This is a matter among ourselves.

14.104. /swba swba/ may denote (a) "very early in the morning on one specific day" or (b) "early in the morning on various days." In the first usage the repetition is intensive, in the second distributive. It is noteworthy that most other time words cannot occur in this construction: i.e. one cannot say */dopəhr dopəhr/, */šam šam/, etc. /roz roz/ "daily" has, however, been previously noted above.

/mə̃y aj swba swba səyr ke lie bahər cəla gəya./ I went out for a walk very early this morning.

/həm log swba swba wThte hə̃y./ We [generally] get up very early.

14.105. /[X ka] xyal rəkhna/ means "to take care of [someone or something]" and also "to consider, think of, watch out for, be watchful of." E.g.

/vw mere bəcce ka xyal rəkhti həy./ She takes care of my child.

/ap ka fərz həy, ky buRhõ ka xyal rəkhē./ It is your duty to take care of [consider, look out for] the old.

14.106. /[ke] sath sath/ "right along with, accompanying, alongside" is another instance of repetition with intensive meaning. Compare /[ke] piche piche/ "along behind," introduced in Unit IX. E.g.

/ys ke sath sath, yy bhi xyal rəkhna cahie./ Along with this, [you] ought to consider this too.

/mera kwtta mere sath sath yskul cəla aya./ My dog came right along with me to school.

14.107. /toRna/ "to break (trans.)" is a Class Ie verb: its causative is /twRana/ and its double causative /twRvana/. It has an irregular intransitive form, however: /TuTna/ "to break (intrans.)." Note that /toRna/ (etc.) are also used for "to pick, pluck (fruit, flowers, etc.)." E.g.

/yy ləkRi TuT gəi./ This stick broke.

/mə̃y ne yy ləkRi toRi./ I broke this stick.

/mə̃y yy phəl ws se twRva lũga./ I'll get him to pick this fruit.

/yy rupəya bazar se twRa kər lao!/ Go and get this rupee changed in the market. [Lit. this rupee from the market having had broken bring!]

/meri ləRki baɣ mē phul toR rəhi thi./ My daughter [lit. girl] was picking flowers in the garden.

14.108. /pəkka/ A2 has many meanings: "ripe, cooked, ready, matured, solid," etc. It is used to denote "paved, metalled, asphalted, macadamized" of roads and "stone, brick, or other permanent construction" of buildings. It also means "fast" of colours and dyes. In all of these meanings /pəkka/ is the opposite of /kəcca/ A2 "unripe, raw, green, immature, nonpermanent (i.e. unpaved or dirt roads, clay or unbaked brick buildings, non-fast dyes)." /pəkka/ is, of course, related to /pəkna/ IIc "to be cooked, ripe." E.g.

/kya, vəhã jane ke lie pəkki səRək həy?/ Is there a paved road to go there?

/yy phəl pəkka nəhĩ./ This fruit is not ripe.

/vw mera pəkka dost həy./ He's my real friend.

417

/həmara məkan to pəkka həy, lekyn chəte̅ kəcci he̅y. /   Although our
nouse is permanent [i.e. of stone or baked brick], the roofs are nonpermanent [i.e. of unbaked clay, etc.].

/yy kəcca rasta ws gao̅ ko jata həy. /   This unpaved road goes to that
village.

/yy am bylkwl kəcca həy. /   This mango is completely unripe.

14.109.   Almost all educated Urdu speakers now employ the English months in reckoning
time. Muslims of the old culture, however, still employ the Islamic lunar calendar (dating
from the departure of the Prophet Muhammad from Mecca for Madina in 622 A.D.), and
this is universally employed to determine the dates of Islamic religious festivals, the month
of fasting (/rəmzan/), etc. The Christian year 1966 is equivalent to 1385-86 A.H. ("After
Hijra"). The Islamic months are all M1. They are:

/mwhərrəm/	محرم	/rəjəb/	رجب
/səfər/	صفر	/šaban/	شعبان
/rəbiwləvvəl/	ربیع الاوّل	/rəmzan/	رمضان
/rəbiwssani/	ربیع الثّانی	/šəvval/	شوّال
/jəmadiwləvvəl/	جمادی الاوّل	/ziqad/	ذی قعده (ذوالقعده)
/jəmadiwssani/	جمادی الثّانی	/zwlhyj/ [or /zylhyj/]	ذی الحج

Near the cities the villagers may use either the English or the Islamic calendar (or
both, for various purposes), but the further one goes from the urban areas, the more
likely one is to encounter the old Hindu twelve month semi-solar calendar. This is called
/səmbət/ F1 [np] or /bykrəmi/ A1, and it dates from the accession of King Vikramaditya
to the throne in 57 B.C. The Christian year 1966, thus, corresponds to 2022-23 Səmbət.
The Hindu months are all M1. They are:

/cəyt/	چیت	/kwar̄/ [or /asyn/ or /əsvəj/]	کنوار
/bəysakh/	بیساکھ	/katyk/	کاتک
/jeTh/	جیٹھ	/əghən/	اگہن
/əsaRh/	اساڑھ	/pus/	پوس
/savən/	ساون	/magh/	ماگھ
/bhado̅/	بھادوں	/phagwn/	پھاگن

418

Perhaps on the analogy of the Hindu and Islamic months, all English months are usually treated as M1. Some speakers, however, treat those ending in /i/ (i. e. /jənvəri/, /fərvəri/, /məi/, and /julai/) as F2 [np]. Since the beginner is likely to encounter only the English calendar (in its Urduised form), this alone will be used throughout this book. Those month names not given in Sec. 14. 000 will be found in Sec. 14. 400.

14. 110. /[ke] qərib/ Comp Post "near, nearby" is generally interchangeable with /[ke] nəzdik/. /[ke] qərib/, however, may also mean "approximately, about, nearly. " E. g.

/vw dəs bəje ke qərib pəhw̃c gəya. / He arrived about ten o'clock. [One cannot say */dəs bəje ke nəzdik/.]

/vw mere qərib rəhte hə̃y. / They live near me. [/mere nəzdik/ may be substituted here.]

14. 111. /fəsl bona/ "to plant a crop" and /fəsl ləgana/ "to plant [lit. attach] a crop" are generally synonymous, except that /bona/ necessarily refers to crops which are grown from seeds that are sown, while /ləgana/ may also refer to those which are transplanted (as rice shoots).

14. 112. Northern India and Pakistan really have only three major seasons: summer, winter, and the rains (/bərsat/ F1). The rainy season begins about the 15th of June and lasts roughly until the middle of September; winter lasts until March, the chilliest months being late December and January; and the hottest summer months are May and June.

14. 113. /fərq/ M1 "difference" is idiomatically used with /pəRna/ "to fall, befall" meaning "to make a difference. " E. g.

/ys se koi fərq nəhɨ̃ pəRega. / This won't make any difference. [Lit. from this no difference will befall.]

/fərq/ is also common in other constructions. E. g.

/yn mẽ kya fərq həy. / What is the difference between [lit. in] these?

/koi fərq nəhɨ̃. / No difference at all.

14. 114. /wgna/ IIc "to grow" is used only of plants, crops, etc. "To grow (of a person)" is expressed by /bəRa hona/ or /bəRa ho jana/, lit. "to become big. " E. g.

/ys sal cavəl ki fəsl nəhɨ̃ wgi. / This year the rice crop did not grow.

/mera ləRka bəRa ho gəya. / My son has grown [up].

14. 115. /bar/ F1 "time, turn, occasion" occurs in almost the same constructions as /dəfa/ F1, except that while /bar bar/ "repeatedly, again and again" is found, */dəfa dəfa/ does not occur. E. g.

/aj mə̃y ne wse do dəfa dekha. / Today I saw him twice. [Or: /do bar/.]

/yy dusri bar mə̃y ne am khae hə̃y. / This [is] the second time I have eaten mangoes. [Or: /dusri dəfa/.]

/vw mwjhe bar bar təklif deta həy. / He gives me trouble again and again.

14.116. /mə̃gana/ "to order, send for, cause to be requested," the causative of
/mã́gna/ Ic "to ask, request," is almost identical in meaning with /mə̃gvana/ (the double
causative form), except that the latter may have slightly stronger connotations of intermediate action. This phenomenon was discussed in Sec. 9.306. E.g.

> /həm vəhã̃ se məšinẽ mə̃gate hə̃y./   We send for [order, get] machines
> from there. [Or: /mə̃gvate hə̃y/.]

14.117. /cəlana/ "to cause to go," the causative of /cəlna/ IIc "to go, move," has
many uses: "to drive (a car, machine, boat, train, etc.)," "to run (a machine, a business),"
"to fire (a gun, bullet)," "to stir (with a spoon)," "to pursue, prosecute, transact, run,"
etc. etc. Some examples are:

> /kya, ap gaRi cəla səkte hə̃y?/   Can you drive a car?

> /yy nərs eksre məšin cəlana janti həy./   This nurse knows how to run
> an X-ray machine. [/eksre məšin cəlana/ is the object of /janti həy/,
> just as /eksre məšin/ is the object of /cəlana/.]

> /vw dwkan cəlana nəhĩ́ janta./   He doesn't know how to run a shop.

> /əpna kam cəlate rəho!/   Keep on with your own work!

> /ws ne mwjh pər goli cəla di./   He shot a bullet at [lit. on] me.

> /salən ko bar bar cəmce se cəlana cahie./   [You] ought to stir the curry
> from time to time with a spoon.

14.118. /bəcna/ "to escape, be saved, be left over" occurs in two major contexts:
(a) "to escape a danger, punishment," etc., and (b) "to be left over (as food)." "To
escape from prison" is not /bəcna/ but /bhagna/ "to flee." E.g.

> /vw ys mwqədme mẽ səza se bəc gəya./   In this lawsuit he escaped
> punishment. [I.e. he may have been fined, but he was not sent to
> jail.]

> /twm ws ki DãT se nəhĩ́ bəc səkoge./   You won't be able to escape his
> scolding.

> /kytabẽ jəlne se bəc gəĩ́./   The books were saved from burning.

> /bəhwt khana bəc gəya./   A lot of food is left over.

14.119. /sərsõ/ F1 [np] denotes a species of the mustard plant (Sinapis dichotoma)
from which oil is extracted. This oil is used for many things: cooking, lubrication, etc.
What Europeans know as mustard comes from another plant (Sinapis vacemosa or S. chinensis),
and this is called /rai/ F2 [np] in Urdu.

14.120. /kũã̃/ M2 "well" denotes either the traditional type of well known in the West
or the Persian wheel variety. In this Unit Mr. əziz is referring to the latter.

14.121. /gobər/ M1 "cattle dung" refers only to the excrement of oxen, cows, or the
water buffalo. There are other words for the dung of horses, sheep, etc.

14.122. /jəysi ap ki mərzi həy./ "[It] is just as your pleasure." -- or just /ap ki
mərzi./ -- are the commonest polite ways of expressing "Just as you please" or "It's up
to you."

14.123. Some Complex Verbal Formations.

A:

/cəwRa/

   /cəwRa hona/ to be, become wide

   /[X ko] cəwRa kərna/ to widen [X]

/daxyl/

   /[X mē] daxyl hona/ to enter [into X]

   /[X ko Y mē] daxyl kərna/ to enter [X in Y], insert [X in Y]

/jəma/

   /[X əwr Y] jəma hona/ [X and Y] to gather, assemble

   /[X ko] jəma kərna/ to gather, collect, assemble [X]

/kəmzor/

   /kəmzor hona/ to be, become weak

   /[X ko] kəmzor kərna/ to weaken [X]

/pəkka/

   /pəkka hona/ to become ripe, mature

   /[X ko] pəkka kərna/ to make [X] ripe, mature, solid, substantial, permanent (as a road)

/pila/

   /[X ka rə̄g] pila hona/ [X's colour] to become yellow

   /[X ko] pila kərna/ to make [X] yellow

/tə̄g/. [See also under F.]

   /tə̄g hona/ to become tight, straitened

   /[X ka hath] tə̄g hona/ [X] to become pressed for money

   /[X ko] tə̄g kərna/ to tighten [X], to distress, tease, press [X]

B:

/təyyari/

   /[X ki] təyyari hona/ preparation [for X] to be made

   /[X ki] təyyari kərna/ to prepare [for X]

D:

/talim/

   /[X ko] talim dena/ to educate [X]

   /[X se] talim lena/ to receive an education [from X]

   /[X ko] talim mylna/ [X] to get an education

   /[X se] talim pana/ to receive an education [from X]

F:

/ag/

   /[X ko] ag dykhana/ to set a match [to X]

   /ag jəlana/ to start, light a fire

   /[X mē] ag ləgana/ to set a fire [in X]

/bhuk/

/[X ko] bhuk ləgna/ [X] to be hungry

/fayda/

/[X ko Y se (or mẽ)] fayda hona/ [X] to receive a profit [from (or in) Y]

/[X se] fayda wThana/ to get a profit [from X]

/fərq/

/[X əwr Y mẽ] fərq kərna/ to distinguish [between X and Y]

/[X se Y mẽ] fərq pəRna, hona/ to be a difference [in Y because of X]

/həl/

/həl cəlana/ to plow

/kəmi/

/[X mẽ] kəmi ana/ a deficiency to appear [in X]

/[X mẽ] kəmi kərna/ to create a scarcity, deficiency [in X]

/mwtəəllyq/

/[X Y se] mwtəəllyq hona/ [X] to become related, connected [with Y]

/[X se Y ko] mwtəəllyq kərna/ to connect, relate [Y with X]

/myhnət/

/myhnət kərna/ to work hard

/pyas/

/[X ki] pyas bwjhna/ [X's] thirst to be quenched

/[X ko] pyas ləgna/ [X] to be thirsty

/qərib/

/[X ke] qərib ana/ to draw near [to X]

/[X ko əpne] qərib lana/ to bring [X] close [to oneself]

/rə̃g/

/[X mẽ] rə̃g dena/ to colour [X]

/[X ko ek nəya] rə̃g dena/ to give [a new] aspect [to X]

/tə̃g/. [See also under A above.]

/[X Y se] tə̃g ana/ [X] to be fed up [with Y]

/tel/

/[X ko] tel dena, ləgana/ to oil [X]

/zəraət/

/zəraət kərna/ to practice agriculture

14.201. Word Recognition.

The following words are written with "uncommon" Arabic consonants, with final ة = /a/, or with other special spelling conventions.

SCRIPT	PRONUNCIATION	SCRIPT	PRONUNCIATION
البتّہ	əlbətta	فائدہ	fayda
پودہ	pəwda	فصل	fəsl
تعلیم	talim	کنارہ	kynara
جمع	jəma	کنواں	kūã
خربوزہ	xərbuza	متعلق	mwtəəllyq
زراعت	zərəət	محنت	myhnət
صحت	syhət	محنتی	myhnəti
علاوہ	ylava	مرضی	mərzi
فاصلہ	fasyla		

14.202. Reading Drill I: Text.

The following is a portion of the Conversation Section of this Unit. Read it aloud, striving for speed and accuracy.

مسٹر اسمتھ۔ آپ کا گاؤں بہت خوبصورت ہے ۔ اگرچہ مکان متّی کے بنے ہوئے ہیں۔ گلیاں تنگ ہیں اور بازار بھی زیادہ چوڑے نہیں ۔ لیکن ہر جگہ بہت صاف نظر آتی ہے۔

مسٹر عزیز۔ صفائی گاؤں کے لوگوں اور اُن کے جانوروں کی صحت کے لئے بہت ضروری ہے ۔ دوسرے گندگی فصلوں میں کھاد کا کام دیتی ہے ۔ اس لئے گاؤں

والے تمام گندگی باہر کھیتوں میں پھینک آتے ہیں۔

مسٹراسمتھ۔ یہ لوگ یہاں کیوں جمع ہیں ؟ کیا یہ کھیتوں پر نہیں جاتے ؟

مسٹرعزیز۔ گاؤں کے جوان آدمی ہمیشہ صبح سویرے کھیتوں پر چلے جاتے ہیں اور شام کو گھر واپس لوٹتے ہیں ۔ بوڑھے آدمی عام طور پر گاؤں میں رہتے ہیں ۔اور گاؤں میں صفائی کا خیال رکھتے ہیں ۔گھروں کا انتظام کرتے ہیں یا فرصت کے وقت گاؤں کے متعلق آپس میں باتیں کرتے رہتے ہیں۔

مسٹراسمتھ۔ کیا عورتیں بھی کھیتوں پر کام کرتی ہیں ؟

مسٹرعزیز۔ گاؤں کی عورتیں بھی مردوں کی طرح بہت محنتی ہوتی ہیں۔ وہ مردوں کے ساتھ ساتھ کام کرتی ہیں۔ درختوں سے لکڑیاں کاٹتی ہیں ۔ پھل توڑتی ہیں اور گھر آکر کھانا پکاتی ہیں ۔

مسٹراسمتھ۔ یہ سامنے والی پکی عمارت کیا ہے؟

مسٹرعزیز۔ یہ یہاں کا اسکول ہے ۔ گاؤں میں شہر کے مقابلے میں تعلیم بہت کم ہوتی ہے ۔ کیونکہ اکثر لوگ اپنے بچوں کو زراعت کا کام سکھاتے ہیں اور اسکول میں داخل نہیں کراتے ۔

مسٹراسمتھ۔ آج کل کے زمانے میں تعلیم بہت ضروری ہے ۔ کیونکہ تعلیم کے ذریعے سے کسان زراعت کے نئے نئے طریقے سیکھ سکتا ہے۔

مسٹرعزیز۔ یہاں سے میری زمین شروع ہوتی ہے اور اُس نہر کے بائیں کنارے تک پھیلی ہوئی ہے ۔ آج کل گندم کی فصل تقریباً تیار ہے ۔ صرف پکنے میں کچھ دیر لگے گی ۔

مسٹراسمتھ۔   کیا اس موسم میں صرف گندم کی فصل ہوتی ہے؟

مسٹرعزیز۔   جی نہیں۔ گندم کے علاوہ جَو، مٹر اور تیل کے بیجوں کی فصلیں بھی کھڑی
ہیں جو ابھی کچھ پکی ہیں۔ یہ فصل ہم اکتوبر اور نومبر کے مہینے میں لگاتے ہیں اور
مارچ یا اپریل کے قریب کاٹ لیتے ہیں۔

مسٹراسمتھ۔   چاول کی فصل کب ہوتی ہے؟

مسٹرعزیز   چاول برسات کے مہینوں میں بوتے ہیں اور سردیوں کے شروع میں کاٹتے
ہیں۔ جب کوئی فصل کٹ چکتی ہے تو فوراً کوئی سبزی یا پھل وغیرہ جیسے
خربوزے یا تربوز لگا دیتے ہیں اور زمین کو خالی نہیں رہنے دیتے۔

14. 203. Sentences.

Read the following sentences aloud and translate them into English.

۱۔ ہم لوگ اس پودے کا پھل دوائی کے طور پر استعمال کرتے ہیں۔ یہ زکام کے لئے بہت
مفید ہے۔

۲۔ ہمارے کسان زمین میں مختلف فصلیں اگاتے رہتے ہیں۔ اس طرح زمین کمزور نہیں ہوتی۔

۳۔ میں گھر اگر روزانہ اخبار پڑھا کرتا ہوں۔ مگر آج مجھے فرصت نہیں ملی۔

۴۔ اگر آپ اس کچے راستے پر گاڑی چلانی چاہتے ہیں تو پولیس سے اجازت لینی پڑے گی۔

۵۔ میری چھوٹی بہن پاکستانی عورتوں کے متعلق بار بار پوچھتی رہتی ہے۔ وہ پاکستان کے
بارے میں کچھ نہیں جانتی۔

۶۔ اس دوران میں پیسے نہ ہونے کی وجہ سے میں تنگ ہو گیا تھا۔ اس لئے مکان بیچنا پڑا۔

۷۔ اُس نے اپنے بیٹے کو ہسپتال میں داخل کرانے کی بہت کوشش کی۔ مگر وارڈ میں

425

جگہ نہ ملی ۔

۸۔ آپ کے ہاں تو مشینوں سے کام لیتے ہوں گے مگر ہمارے ملک میں جانوروں سے کام لیتے ہیں ۔

۹۔ گاؤں والوں کے لئے تعلیم بہت ضروری ہے ۔ اِس طرح وہ زراعت کے نئے طریقے سیکھ سکتے ہیں ۔

۱۰۔ امریکہ کی مدد کے علاوہ اُس ملک کو اور حکومتوں سے بھی مدد مل رہی ہے ۔

۱۱ جولائی اور اگست میں اِتنی گرمی نہیں ہوتی کیونکہ یہ برسات کا موسم ہوتا ہے ۔

۱۲۔ مجھے بھوک بالکل نہیں لگ رہی ہے ۔ البتہ تھوڑی سی پیاس ہے ۔

۱۳۔ سرسوں کے بیجوں سے ہم لوگ تیل نکالتے ہیں مگر بارش کی کمی کی وجہ سے اِس سال سرسوں کی فصل اچھی نہیں ہو سکی ۔

۱۴۔ کھیت میں محنت کرنے سے وہ غریب آدمی بہت تھک گیا ہے ۔ آرام کرکے پھر اپنا ہل اُٹھائے گا ۔

۱۵۔ جب عورتیں کنویں سے پانی بھر رہی ہوں تو وہاں دھوبیوں کے لئے کپڑے دھونا منع ہے ۔

14. 204. Writing Drill I: Text.

Counting each speaker's part as one paragraph, write out the first ten paragraphs of Sec. 14.505 (Conversation Practice) in Urdu script (i. e. down through /lekyn phyr bhi kysi kysi jəga ghoRe khetõ pər kam kərte hə̄y. /).

14. 205. Spelling Review and Dictionary Drill.

Write out the following words in Urdu script and place them in Urdu alphabetical order.

(1) bhə̄ys
(2) nəzla

(3) kwtta
(4) cəvvən

(5) gyrja	(13) rozana
(6) mwxtəlyf	(14) cūke
(7) saf	(15) əlbətta
(8) mə̃gana	(16) aynda
(9) wgna	(17) zəria
(10) wgana	(18) daxyl
(11) mwtəəllyq	(19) kūā̃
(12) bad	(20) zəraət

14. 206. Response Drill.

Answer the following questions in writing.

۱۔ کیا آپ نے کبھی جَو کی روٹی کھائی ہے ؟

۲۔ کیا اِس شہر میں غریبوں کی تعلیم کا بندوبست ہے ؟

۳۔ کیا امریکہ میں سرسوں اُگاتے ہیں ؟

۴۔ آپ کے والد کے پاس کتنے بَیل اور گائیں ہیں ؟

۵۔ آپ کا گھر یونیورسٹی سے کتنے فاصلے پر ہے؟

۶۔ جب کچھ کھاتا پچ جاتا ہے تو کیا آپ غریبوں کو دے دیتے ہیں؟

۷۔ آپ نے کس یونیورسٹی سے تعلیم حاصل کی ہے ؟

۸۔ کیا سَیر کرنے سے یا پہاڑ پر چڑھنے سے آپ جلدی تھک جاتے ہیں؟

۹۔ چاول کی فصل کاٹنے کا موسم کب ہوتا ہے ؟

۱۰۔ گوبر کس کس کام میں آتا ہے ؟

14. 207. English to Urdu Sentences.

1. I [habitually] go to the cinema on Saturday.
2. That farmer must be planting his crop [at] this time.
3. The biggest market of this city is very broad, but around it are very narrow lanes.

4. A good deal of [lit. enough] my time will be saved by [lit. from] this new method.
5. My dog comes along with me to [lit. on] the fields.
6. There is no special difference between this green book and that yellow book. [Lit. In this book of green colour and that book of yellow colour special difference is not.]
7. This well goes all the time and delivers water to [lit. in] the fields.
8. You people also must [habitually] use such machines.
9. What is the advantage in going [to] Multan? Your friend will not be present there now [lit. up to now].
10. Go into the mosque and gather all the people. [One] must prepare for the prayer [lit. do the prayer's preparation] at once.
11. Please come to [lit. in] this party. We will wait for you [lit. do your waiting] there.
12. We dry cattle dung and burn [it]. It burns very well.
13. My plow has broken. I will have to go to the city today.
14. England is about five thousand mile[s] distant [lit. on a distance of] from Pakistan.
15. I don't know anything about agriculture, but I want to learn.

14.301. Adverbs + /val/ + the Type II Affixes.

In Sec. 4.308 it was shown that a noun + /val/ + one of the Type II affixes may occur as a noun of profession, etc.: e.g. /phəlvala/ M2 "(male) fruitseller," /phəlvali/ F2 "(female) fruitseller." Many locatives and temporals may occur with /val/ (+ a Type II affix), and these may be either M/F2 or A2. E.g.

/əndər/ inside	/əndərvala/ [one] inside
/bahər/ outside	/bahərvala/ [one] outside
/bərabər/ adjoining, equal	/bərabərvala/ [one] adjoining, [one] equal
/nəzdik/ near, nearby	/nəzdikvala/ [one] near
/nice/ under, beneath	/nicevala/ [one] under, beneath
/samne/ in front, opposite	/samnevala/ [one] in front, opposite
/sath/ with, accompanying	/sathvala/ [one] with, accompanying
/upər/ above, up	/upərvala/ [one] above, upper [one]
/vəhã/ there	/vəhãvala/ [one] there
/yəhã/ here	/yəhãvala/ [one] here

Examples of temporals with /val/ + a Type II affix:

/aj/ today	/ajvala/ [one from] today
/kəl/ tomorrow, yesterday	/kəlvala/ [one from] tomorrow, yesterday
/pərsõ/ day after tomorrow, day before yesterday	/pərsõvala/ [one from] the day after tomorrow, [one from] the day before yesterday

Examples:

/əndərvali kwrsi bahər nykal do!/ Take out the chair that is inside! [Lit. The inside-one chair outside take out!]

/vw upərvale kəmre mẽ rəhte hãy./ He lives in the room above. [Lit. the above-one room.]

/bahərvale ko əndər bwlao!/ Call in the person outside! [Lit. outside-one.]

/yəhãvalõ ka yyhi təriqa həy./ This is the very way [method, custom] of the people here. [Lit. [It] is the here-ones' this-very way.]

/vw kəlvali bat mwjhe yad nəhf./ I don't remember that matter from yesterday. [Lit. that yesterday-one matter.]

14.302. The Verb: the <PasP + /hwa həy/> Construction.

A _stative_ form of an intransitive verb is made with the past participle of the verb + the past participle of /hona/ ± an inflected form of the auxiliary /həy/, /tha/, etc. This construction denotes a past action which results in a state continuing up to the time of some later action. Compare:

/vw bəyTha həy./ He has sat. [Simple perfect tense.]

/vw bəyTh gəya həy./ He has sat down. [The compound verb form denotes the completion of a single, unitary action.]

/vw bəyTha hwa həy./ He is [in a state of] sitting. [The act of sitting resulted in a state which continues up to the present.]

This construction is really an example of the use of the past participle + /hwa/, discussed further in Sec. 16.302. It must be remembered that only intransitive verbs are normally found in this formation (i.e. one cannot say */māy ne khana khaya hwa həy./). In modern Pakistan, however, one may sometimes hear sentences like /māy ne yy kam kia hwa həy./ which means (a) "I had already completed this job [before you asked]," or (b) "I have already had experience with this [type of] work." The author's informants, however, considered such constructions to be only marginally "correct."

The <PasP + /hwa həy/> construction does not occur with compound stems (i.e. one cannot say */phəyl gəya hwa həy/), nor does it occur in the negative. The negative form of /bəyTha hwa həy/ is simply /nəhī bəyTha həy/ "is not sitting." E.g.

/vw əbhi a kər soya həy./ He has just come [home] and has gone to sleep. [No particular emphasis on the action.]

/vw so gəya həy./ He has gone to sleep. [The completion of the transition from waking to sleeping is emphasised.]

/vw soya hwa həy./ He is [in a state of] sleeping.

/vw leTa hwa həy./ He is [in a state of] lying down.

/ap ki kytab zəmin pər pəRi hwi həy./ Your book is lying on the ground.

/cyraγ bwjhe hwe the./ The lamps were [in a state of being] extinguished.

/dərvaza khwla hwa hoga./ The door must be [lit. will be] [in a state of standing] open.

14.303. The Verb: Another Conjunct Verb.

Sec. 14.000 contains another example of a conjunct verb, discussed in Sec. 13.303: /phēk ate hāy/ "throw [and] come [back]." The criterion is, of course, that both /phēkna/ "to throw" and /ana/ "to come" retain their independent meanings, and the full conjunctive form /phēk kər ate hāy/ "having thrown, come" can be substituted. As an aid to the student, further examples of conjunct verbs will be briefly analysed in the Word Study Section or the Analysis Section of the Unit in which they occur.

14.304. The Verb: /cəla jana/ and /cəla ana/.

The past participle of /cəlna/ "to go, move" is found with inflected forms of /jana/ "to go" and /ana/ "to come" in a special sort of compound: /cəla jana/ means "to go away," and /cəla ana/ means "to come, come along." Although these two formations do not normally occur in the negative, an emphatic negative is possible: e.g. /cəla to nəhī gəya/ "[he] really has not gone away [although you may think so]."

Note that although /cəl jana/, the expected completive form of /cəlna/, does occur, it has quite different meanings: "to start off, begin." "To go away" is expressed only by /cəla jana/. Since /cəla jana/ and /cəla ana/ have quite different meanings from the past participles of other verbs + /jana/ and /ana/, the student must treat these two formations as unique. E.g.

430

/vw cəla gəya. /　He went away.

/mɛ̄y vapəs cəla aya. /　I came along back.

/kəl meri beTi cəli jaegi. /　Tomorrow my daughter will leave. [Note that both /cəli/ and /jaegi/ are inflected for number-gender.]

/əb to gaRi cəli gəi. /　Now the train has left. [Compare:]

/ws ki dwkan cəl gəi. /　His shop has started [to flourish].

14. 305.　The Verb:　the <PreP + /rəhna/> Construction.

The _iterative_ form of the verb is composed of the present participle of the main verb + an inflected form of /rəhna/ "to live, stay" + an auxiliary /həy/, /tha/, etc. This construction denotes the constant or intermittent repetition of a series of individual actions. It is often translatable as "keeps . . . ing. " This construction should not be confused with the <S + /rəha həy/> "continuative" construction (Sec. 5. 311): /lykh rəha həy/ means "[he] is [in the act of] writing, " while /lykhta rəhta həy/ denotes "[he] keeps on [repetitively, intermittently] writing. "

Negative forms of this construction are not found (i. e. */nəhˇ kərta rəhta həy/ is not possible), nor are compound verb stems employed with it (i. e. one cannot say */kər deta rəhta həy/). Furthermore, /rəhna/ itself cannot occur as the main verb in this formation (i. e. one cannot say */rəhta rəhta həy/).

Special notice must be taken of /jata/ "going" + /rəhna/: this may have two meanings: (a) "to keep on going" (the expected meaning), and (b) "to disappear, pass away, die. " E. g.

/vw meri dwkan pər bərabər ate rəhte hɛ̄y. /　He keeps on coming to my shop.

/vw mwjhe DāTta rəhta həy. /　He keeps scolding me.

/mwjhe bətate rəhie! /　Please keep telling me! [I. e. at intervals, from time to time.]

/mɛ̄y košyš kərta rəhūga. /　I'll keep on trying.

/vw rat ko der tək kam kərta rəha. /　He kept on working until late at night.

/mɛ̄y wn ke hā jata rəhta hū. /　I keep going to their place.

/nek log ys dwnya se jate rəhe. /　Virtuous people have disappeared from this world.

14. 306.　The Verb:　the <PasP + /kərna/> Construction.

An _habitual_ aspect is expressed by the past participle of a main verb + an inflected form of /kərna/ "to do, make" (+ an auxiliary, etc.). This formation indicates that the action of the main verb is performed habitually or customarily. In the past tenses, how-ever, it may denote only simple repetition of the action with no particular habitual reference.

There are several important peculiarities: (1) the past participle of the main verb is _always_ MS in form and does not necessarily agree with its subject in number-gender (i. e. /aya kərti həy/ "[she] habitually comes" and not */ai kərti həy/); (2) in the past tenses this formation is treated as though it were always intransitive (i. e. the subject is always nominative and is not marked by /ne/, and the verb agrees with the subject in number-

431

gender); (3) the past participle of /jana/ "to go" in this construction is not /gəya/ but /jaya/ (i.e. /jaya kərta hū/ "[I] habitually go" and not */gəya kərta hū/); (4) unlike other constructions just described, the "habitual" may occur with compound verbal formations (e.g. /kər dia kərta həy/ "[he] habitually does [for someone else]") and also in negative sentences (e.g. /nəhĩ kia kərta/ "[he] does not habitually do"). E.g.

/mə̃y ap ke hã aya kərūga./ I'll [habitually] come to your.place.

/mə̃y ws ki dwkan pər jaya kərta hū./ I [habitually] go to his shop.

/əgər ap ki yyhi mərzi həy, to mə̃y ap ke hã nəhĩ aya kərūga./ If this [lit. this-emphatic] is your pleasure, then I will not [habitually] come to your place.

/vw həmeša mera kam kər dia kərta tha./ He always used to [habitually] do my work [for me].

/vw əksər həmare hã a jaya kərte hə̃y./ They generally come to our place. [An instance of the compound verb /a jana/ "to come (completive)."]

/vw chət se pətthər phēka kia./ He kept on throwing stones from the roof. [An instance of the past tense of this formation used for simple repetition. Compare, however:]

/vw həmeša ysi bat pər roya kie, məgər wn ke beTe ne kəbhi wn ki bat nəhĩ swni./ He always used to weep over this matter, but his son never listened to his word[s].

14.307. The Verb: The Future of /hona/ as an Auxiliary Verb.

The use of the future tense of /hona/ "to be, become" to denote likelihood or assumption was discussed in Sec. 5.309. There it was seen that this usage is possible for various tenses and aspects. E.g.

/vw γərib hoga./ He must be [lit. will be] poor.

/əmrika mē bhi yyhi cizē bote hõge./ In America too [they] must sow [lit. will generally sow] these very same things.

/əb vw kam kər rəha hoga./ Now he must be working [lit. will be working].

Similarly, any verbal form may be made "assumptive" by adding the proper future form of /hona/. Note that this has no effect upon the treatment of transitive verbs in the past tenses: even with the future of /hona/ added as an auxiliary, a transitive verb still requires the subject to be marked by /ne/, and the verbal form agrees with any nominative object. Note also that this "assumptive" formation may occur with compound verbal formations, in negative sentences, etc. E.g.

/vw bimar nəhĩ hwa hoga./ He must not have become sick. [Compare: /vw bimar nəhĩ hwa./ "He did not become sick." Here /hoga/ agrees with the number-gender of the subject of the intransitive verb.]

/vw γərib ho gəya hoga./ He must have become poor. [Here /hoga/ is added to the completive compound verb /ho jana/ "to become."]

/ap ne yy kam kər dia hoga./ You must have finished this work. [/hoga/ agrees in number-gender with /kam/ Ml "work."]

/ws ne yy kytab pəRh li hogi./ He must have read this book. [Similarly, /hogi/ agrees in number-gender with the object of the transitive compound verb /pəRh lena/ "to read (for oneself)."]

/vw ləRki yy məšin to cəla səkti hogi./ That girl must be able to run

432

this machine. [Here /hogi/ occurs with the <S + /səkna/> construction.]

/yy fəsl kəT cwki hogi./   This crop must have already been cut. [Here
/hogi/ occurs with the <S + /cwkna/> formation.]

/vw bəcci cixne ləgi hogi./   That girl must have started to cry. [Here
/hogi/ occurs with the <OI + /ləgna/> formation.]

/ap ke bəcce synima jate rəhte hõge./   Your children must keep going
to the cinema. [Here /hõge/ is used with the <PreP + /rəhna/>
construction.]

/vw log yəhã aya kərte hõge./   Those people must [habitually] come here.
[Here /hõge/ occurs with the <PasP + /kərna/> construction.]

14.308.   The Verb: The <S + /iega/> Construction.

The polite imperative was seen to consist of the stem of a main verb + the suffix /ie/
(see Sec. 3.313).   When the suffix /ga/ is added to the polite imperative form, the latter is
rendered still more polite and ceremonious.   It is also somewhat more forceful: "you will
please do ..." Note that /ga/ remains the same for all number-gender combinations: i.e.
/bəyThiega/ "please sit down!" may be employed for any number or gender, and */bəyThiegi/
or */bəyThiege/ do not occur. E.g.

/təšrif rəkhiega!/   Please sit down!

/šəwq fərmaiega!/   Please begin [to eat]! [Lit. please do [your]
pleasure!]

/yy ciz nyšani ke təwr pər rəkh lijiega!/   Please keep this as a memento!

/mere lie ek nwsxa lykh dijiega!/   Please write out a prescription for
me!

/kəl se nə aiega!/   Please don't come from [i.e. starting with] tomorrow!

14.400. SUPPLEMENTARY VOCABULARY

14.401. Supplementary Vocabulary.

The following numerals are all Type I adjectives. See Sec. 2.401.

ykavən [or /ykyavən/ or /ykkyavən/ or /ykkavən/	fifty-one
bavən	fifty-two
tyrpən [or /tyrepən/]	fifty-three
cəvvən	fifty-four

The remaining months are: [Plurals, though possible, are rare. All months are M1, although some speakers treat those ending in /i/ as F2. See Sec. 14.109.]

jənvəri	January
fərvəri	February
məi	May
jun	June
julai	July
əgəst	August
sytəmbər	September
dysəmbər	December

Other items are:

jəlna [IIc: /ə/]	to burn (intrans.)
TuTna [I: /toRna/: Ie]	to break (intrans.)

14.402. Supplementary Exercise I: Substitution.

1. ys kysan ke pas p̄əytalys   bəyl əwr calys   bh̄əysē h̄əy.

fifty-five	fifty-four
fifty-three	forty-four
thirty-seven	fifty-one
fifty-two	fifty-three
forty-nine	fifty

2. sytəmbər mē tis dyn hote h̄əy, ya ykəttys.

June

December

October

July

January

May

August

April

November

March

February

3. kya, səb ləkRiã <u>bwjh gəf?</u>

      have burned
      have broken
      have fallen
      have arrived
      have been cut

435

14.500. VOCABULARY AND GRAMMAR DRILL

14.501. Substitution.

1. <u>ap ka məkan</u>   <u>myTTi</u>   ka bəna hwa həy. [1]
   this table   wood
   that old wall   stone
   this glass   America
   this sheet   good cloth
   this carpet   Pakistan

   [1]Make /ka_ bəna_ hwa_ həy/ agree in number-gender with the subject of each
   sentence.

2. <u>gəndəgi</u>   <u>khad</u>   ka kam deti həy. [1]
   this cupboard   suitcase
   this thing   medicine
   cattle dung   fertiliser
   this carpet   bedding
   ghi   oil

   [1]Make /deti_ həy/ agree in number-gender with the subject of each sentence.

3. mɔ̃y hər sal ap ko   <u>yy səb cizɛ̃</u>   pəhw̃caya kərūga.
                     sweet mangoes
                     various types of fruits
                     watermelons and muskmelons
                     peas, barley, etc.
                     wheat and oil

4. həm <u>gae</u>   se bəhwt se kam lete hɔ̃y.
       ox
       water buffalo
       horse
       this well
       goats

5. <u>həm logõ</u>   ne bar bar   <u>yy fəsl</u>   <u>ləgai.</u> [1]
   the farmers   vegetable   sowed
   the youths   plow   made go
   the women   water   filled
   the washermen   clothes   washed
   that old man   fire   lighted

   [1]Make the verb agree with the number-gender of the object.

6. əb <u>khana</u>   <u>təyyar</u>   ho gəya hoga.
      that farmer   old
      that plant   green
      this banana   sweet

436

          its colour   yellow
          his ox   weak

7. mwjhe   <u>sərdi</u>   ləg rəhi həy.
          hunger
          thirst
          heat
          wind
          sunshine

8. vw <u>samnevali</u>   ciz dykhao!
          upper
          inside
          accompanying
          adjoining
          outside

9. <u>khana</u>   <u>pəkne</u>   mē kwch der ləgegi.
    education   getting
    agriculture   learning
    new methods   teaching
    fruit   picking
    wheat   cutting

10. vw <u>gaõ</u>   ke mwtəəllyq apəs mē batē kərte rəhte hõy.
          crops
          canal
          animals
          the unpaved roads
          his health

11. <u>bəhwt sa khana</u>   bəc gəya hoga.[1]
    some green colour
    much grain
    many seeds
    some mustard plants [lit.
    mustard's plants]
    much manure

    [1]Make /bəc gəya hoga/ agree in number-gender with the subject of the
    sentence.

12. <u>səb gaõvale</u>   <u>məsjyd ke samne</u>   jəma ho gəe.
    all the farmers   on the bank of the canal
    some young boys   in the market
    the old men   in that narrow lane
    the washermen   at the well [/ke pas/ "at"]
    all the animals   by the permanent wall

13. <u>šadi ka yntyzam kərne</u>   ki vəja se, vw bəhwt thək gəya.
    plowing [lit. making go the plow]
    doing labour

                              437

cooking much food

cutting sticks

planting the crop

14. ys ke ylava, <u>ws ki syhət</u>   ko bhi dekhna cahie.

                    its profit

                    this difference

                    the distance

                    his labour

                    its scarcity

15. <u>yy məšin</u>   <u>tel nykalne</u>   ke kam ati həy. [1]

    this medicine   stopping cholera

    this car   bringing manure

    this vessel   filling water

    this cupboard   keeping clothes

    this oil   cooking food

[1] Make /ati həy/ agree in number-gender with the subject.

14. 502. Transformation.

1. Change the underlined verb forms in the following sentences to "stative" forms
(e.g. /gyra həy/ to /gyra hwa həy/). Retain the same tense but remember to
change completive compound verb forms to noncompound forms (e.g. /a gəya həy/
to /aya hwa həy/).

    a.   pakystan mẽ həyza <u>phəyl gəya həy</u>.

    b.   kysan khet ke qərib <u>bəyTha həy</u>.

    c.   ek həl nəhr ke kynare <u>pəRa həy</u>.

    d.   ajkəl ek buRha admi <u>aya həy</u>.

    e.   vw ləRka ys dərəxt pər <u>cəRha tha</u>.

    f.   kəl ki davət mẽ se, kwch khana <u>bəca həy</u>.

    g.   ws ka rõg pəhle se <u>bədəl gəya həy</u>.

    h.   vw aTh bəje <u>jaga tha</u>.

    i.   mera xyal həy, ky vw ys vəqt <u>soya hoga</u>.

    j.   vw bhut se <u>Dəra həy</u>.

    k.   ys dəvai mẽ pani <u>myl gəya həy</u>.

    l.   vw bazar <u>gəya həy</u>.

    m.   mwjhe bhuk <u>ləgi həy</u>.

    n.   vw mwsafyr mere gaõ mẽ <u>Thəyra həy</u>.

    o.   vw kam ki vəja se bəhwt <u>thək gəe hãy</u>.

2. Change the underlined verb forms in the following sentences to the "iterative"
form (e.g. /kərta həy/ to /kərta rəhta həy/). Retain the same tense. Remember
that the subject of the <PreP + /rəhna/> formation is always nominative, and thus
the subject of a past tense sentence containing a transitive verb must be made
nominative, dropping /ne/, and the verb must agree in number-gender with the

438

subject.

a. vw hər roz wn ki batē <u>swnta həy</u>.

b. vw əksər səbzi əwr goŝt <u>pəkati hə̄y</u>.

c. kysan hər roz khet mē həl <u>cəlata həy</u>.

d. yy məŝin ysi təra <u>cəlegi</u>.

e. mere xyal mē, vw mwjhe təklif <u>dega</u>.

f. bəcce məydan mē sare dyn <u>khelte hə̄y</u>.

g. vw mere ghər taza xərbuze <u>pəhw̄cate hə̄y</u>.

h. həm ghər ka saman ws dwkan se <u>mə̄gate the</u>.

i. dhobiŏ ne ys kūē pər kəpRe <u>swkhae</u>.

j. wnhŏ ne mere xylaf yy batē <u>kəhī̆</u>.

k. həspətal mē hər roz nəe məriz daxyl <u>hote hə̄y</u>.

l. vw əksər kylas mē <u>bolta tha</u>.

m. əyse mwjrym həmeŝa polis ko tə̄g <u>kərte hə̄y</u>.

n. mə̄y əpni fəsl ke cavəl əksər wn ke hā <u>bhejta tha</u>.

o. ws ne əpni buRhi valda ki xydmət <u>ki</u>.

3. Change the underlined verb forms in the following sentences to the "habitual" form (e.g. /kərta həy/ to /kia kərta həy/). Retain the same tense.

a. vw hər roz nəw bəje yskul jane ki təyyari <u>kərta həy</u>.

b. dhobi dhup mē nəhr ke kynare kəpRe <u>swkhata həy</u>.

c. kysan əktubər ke məhine mē fəsl <u>kaTega</u>.

d. Tika ləgvane se, bimari mē fayda <u>hota həy</u>.

e. vw log apəs mē mere mwtəəllyq batē <u>kərte the</u>.

f. vw lahəwr mē tə̄ga <u>cəlata həy</u>.

g. əwrtē dərəxtŏ se phul <u>toRti hə̄y</u>.

h. ləRkiã kūē se pani <u>nəhī̆ bhərtī̆</u>.

i. kysan bərsat ke məwsəm mē yy fəsl <u>nəhī̆ bote</u>.

j. mə̄y hər roz dəs bəje ke qərib dəftər <u>pəhw̄cū̆gi</u>.

k. vw hər roz swba swba khet se səbzi <u>lati həy</u> əwr <u>pəkati həy</u>.

l. gərmi ki vəja se, dopəhr ko kysan kam <u>nəhī̆ kərte</u>.

m. əksər ysi vəqt mwjhe bhuk <u>ləgti həy</u>.

n. həm səb ənaj gaŏ se <u>mə̄gate the</u>.

o. kysan sal mē kəi bar khetŏ mē khad <u>Dalte hə̄y</u>.

p. vw həmare gaŏ se pəndra mil ke fasyle pər <u>rəhte the</u>.

4. Change the underlined verb forms in the following sentences to the "assumptive" form (e.g. /kia həy/ to /kia hoga/). Retain the same tense and aspect.

a. ys dəfa ki fəsl se, təqribən kytna fayda <u>hwa</u>.

b. baryŝ nə hone ki vəja se, fəslŏ ka rə̄g pila <u>ho gəya</u>.

c. roTi <u>jəl gəi</u>.

d. ap ne yy kam əpne valyd ki mərzi ke xylaf <u>kia həy</u>.

e. ap ke mwlk mē bəhwt bərf <u>pəRti həy</u>.

f. bimari ki vəja se, vw kəmzor <u>ho gəya</u>, əwr cəl <u>nəhī̆ pata</u>.

g. ys dəvai ke ystemal se, kwch fərq zərur hwa həy.

h. mwsafyr ko pyas ke sath bhuk bhi ləg rəhi həy.

i. gaõ ke үərib log gobər swkhate hə̃y, əwr ws se ag jəlate hə̃y.

j. bərsat ke məwsəm mē cavəl ki fəsl wga kərti həy.

k. vw mere əfsər se meri šykayət kərte rəhte həy.

l. vw yy kytab xətm kər cwka həy.

m. əb to ap bhi wrdu səməjhne ləge hə̃y.

n. yəhã ke kysanõ ne bhi fəsl wgane ke nəe nəe təriqe sikh lie hə̃y.

o. ys dəwran mē, ap ne to bəhwt pəyse jəma kər lie.

5. Change the underlined verb forms in the following sentences (a) to the polite imperative ending in /iega/ (e.g. /kəhie/ to /kəhiega/), and (b) to the conditional (also used as a polite imperative) ending in /ē/ (e.g. /kəhie/ to /kəhē/).

a. gaõ ke mwtəəllyq kwch fərmaie.

b. ap yəhã mera yntyzar kijie.

c. myhrbani fərma kər, mwjhe ghər pəhw̃ca dijie.

d. həmare hã davət mē zərur təšrif laie.

e. mere lie bhi kwch gəndwm gaõ se mə̃gva lijie.

14.503. Variation.

1. gaõvale khetõ mē təmam gəndəgi phēk ate hə̃y.
   DakTər sahəb mərizõ ke lie nwsxe lykh gəe.
   ləRke dwkan ke səb šišiã toR gəe.
   mə̃y ws dwkan se tarix ki səb kytabē xərid laya.
   vw səb nəwkərõ se yy bat kəh gəya.
   qwli səb saman vəhã se wTha laya.

2. yy Dybba mez ka kam nəhĩ de səkta.
   ys məkan se həm məsjyd ka kam bhi lete hə̃y.
   həm log bəylõ se həl cəlane ka kam lete hə̃y.
   gaõvale gobər ko jəlane ke kam mē late hə̃y.
   yy mez kytabē rəkhne ke kam ati hə̃y.
   yy myTTi məkan bənane ke kam aegi.

3. ys kũē ke ylava, baqi səb kũē bənd ho gəe hə̃y.
   yn do ləRkõ ke ylava, baqi səb ləRke yskul mē daxyl ho gəe hə̃y.
   gəndwm ke ylava, əwr bəhwt si qysm ke ənaj hote hə̃y.
   ap ke ylava, vəhã əwr koi nəhĩ jata.
   meri bivi ke ylava, baqi səb əwrtē xwd khana pəkati hə̃y.
   ys kysan ke ylava, baqi səb log talim hasyl kərni cahte hə̃y.

4. yy bəyl bəhwt əccha həy, əlbətta ajkəl kwch kəmzor malum hota həy.
   ys kəpRe ka rə̃g həra həy, əlbətta dhup mē pila malum hota həy.
   yy gaRi bəhwt pwrani həy, əlbətta cəlne mē bəhwt tez həy.
   mera nəwkər bəhwt myhnəti həy, əlbətta calak həy.
   yəhã əksər məkan myTTi ke bəne hwe hə̃y, əlbətta wn ki chətē pəkki hə̃y.

vw bəhwt əccha ləRka həy, əlbətta kəbhi kəbhi vw bhi šərarət kərta həy.

5. əgər ap ki mərzi yyhi həy, to həm əbhi cəle jate h̃əy.

əgər ap ki mərzi yy hoti, to həm cəle jate.

əgər ws ki mərzi yy nə thi, to kyõ cəli gəi.

əgər ap ki mərzi yyhi thi, to yəh̃a kyõ ae.

əgər ap ki syhət yəh̃a əcchi nəh̃i ho səkti, to ap ko cəla jana cahie.

əgər ap ki syhət yəh̃a əcchi nəh̃i ho səki, to ap ko yəh̃a se cəla jana pəRega.

6. ys gaõ ke mwtəəllyq, ap ka kya xyal həy.

gaõ ki talim ke mwtəəllyq, ap ka xyal kya həy.

ys dəvai ke mwtəəllyq, kys se puchna cahie.

pakystan ki tarix ke mwtəəllyq, ap wn se pucha kijie.

pakystan ke mwtəəllyq, tarix ki bəhwt si kytabẽ məwjud h̃əy.

kya, ap zəraət ke mwtəəllyq kwch jante h̃əy?

7. kysan dhup mẽ bhi həl cəlate rəhte h̃əy.

ap əpne bhai ki gaRi əksər cəlate rəhte hõge.

həm log hər sal ek hi fəsl wgate rəhte h̃əy.

əcche kysan həmeša zəraət ke nəe nəe təriqe sikhte rəhte h̃əy.

m̃əy hər məhine nəi nəi məšinẽ m̃əgata rəhta h̃u.

vw hər ghənTe ke bad dəvai ki ek xwrak pita rəha.

8. əktubər mẽ, ws ki šadi ki təyyari šwru hwi thi.

əprəyl mẽ, fəsl ləgane ki təyyari šwru hwi thi.

jun əwr julai mẽ, həmare mwlk mẽ, bərsat ka məwsəm šwru ho jata həy.

bərsat mẽ, kysan cavəl ki fəsl boni šwru kərte h̃əy.

əktubər mẽ, həm jəw ki fəsl boni šwru kərte h̃əy.

jun tək, həmari səb fəslẽ kəT cwkti h̃əy.

9. mera dost dusre mwlkõ ke TykəT jəma kia kərta tha.

kysan ys dərəxt ke nice jəma hwa kərte h̃əy.

mera beTa janvərõ ko pani pylaya kərta həy.

ap swba swba do gylas dudh pia kərẽ.

vw ek sal tək γəribõ ko bərabər khana khylaya kia.

m̃əy hər roz wrdu pər kam kia kərũga.

10. ys ka pəwda səbzi ke təwr pər pəkate h̃əy.

həm ys ka phəl dəvai ke təwr pər ystemal kərte h̃əy.

gae ka gobər khetõ mẽ khad ke təwr pər Dalte h̃əy.

yy təsvir mwjhe nyšani ke təwr pər de dijiega.

yy qalin bystər ke təwr pər kam mẽ laiega.

yy admi gəvah ke təwr pər ədalət mẽ peš hwa tha.

11. kysan fəsl ləga rəhe hõge.

kysan fəsl ləga cwke hõge.

kysan hər sal yyhi fəsl ləgaya kərte hõge.

kysanõ ne fəsl ləga li hogi.

əb to kysan fəsl ləgane ləge hõge.

ap šayəd zəraət ke pwrane t−əriqe ystemal kərte rəhe hõge.

12. ek kəcci səRək nəhr ke sath sath jati həy.

mera beTa hər jəga mere sath sath jaya kərta həy.

həmari əwrtẽ mərdõ ke sath sath myhnət kərti hə̃y.

mwsafyr cəwkidar ke sath sath vapəs cəla aya.

həmẽ dwnya ke sath sath bədəlna pəRta həy.

pecyš ke sath sath, mwjhe bwxar bhi ho gəya.

13. həmare əfsər kəmre mẽ daxyl hwe.

do nəe məriz ys varD mẽ daxyl ho gəe hə̃y.

vw buRha kysan məsjyd mẽ daxyl hwa.

mə̃y ne əpne beTe ko yskul mẽ daxyl kia.

wnhõ ne wn ka nam ryjysTər mẽ daxyl kia.

mə̃y ne əpni valda ko həspətal mẽ daxyl kəraya.

14. vw ləRkiã bylkwl mərdõ ki təra nəzər ati hə̃y.

yy məriz bylkwl buRhõ ki təra cəlta həy.

vw bylkwl janvərõ ki təra rəhta həy.

yy phəl bylkwl tərbuz ki təra wgta həy.

həm sərsõ ka pəwda bylkwl səbzi ki təra pəkate hə̃y.

ws mwjrym ne bylkwl bəccõ ki təra rona šwru kia.

15. vw əpne bəccõ ka xyal rəkhta həy.

həm logõ ko əpni syhət ka xyal rəkhna cahie.

həm logõ ko gaõvalõ ki talim ka xyal rəkhna cahie.

ws calak admi ka xyal rəkhna cahie.

kysanõ ko hər vəqt əpni fəslõ ka xyal rəkhna pəRta həy.

nərs ko cahie, ky vw məriz ka xyal rəkhe.

16. yy juta mere lie tə̃g hoga.

yy kəpRe mere lie bəhwt tə̃g hə̃y.

pəyse nə hone ki vəja se, mə̃y bəhwt tə̃g ho gəya hũ.

mə̃y ws ki hərkətõ se tə̃g a gəya hũ.

wnhõ ne mwjhe bəhwt tə̃g kia.

dəftər mẽ mere əfsər mwjhe tə̃g kərte rəhte hə̃y.

14.504. Response.

1. kya, ap kəbhi gaõ mẽ rəhe hə̃y?
2. kya, ap hər šəxs ke lie talim zəruri səməjhte hə̃y?
3. kya, ap swba swba səyr ke lie jaya kərte hə̃y?
4. šəhr ke məkanõ əwr gaõ ke məkanõ mẽ kya fərq həy.
5. khetõ mẽ gəndəgi jəma kərne se kya fayda hota həy.
6. gaõvale gobər ko swkha kər, ws se kya kam lete hə̃y.
7. bərsat ke məwsəm mẽ, kəwn kəwnsi fəslẽ bote hə̃y.
8. kya, əmrika ke khetõ mẽ bəylõ se kam lete hə̃y?
9. gaõ mẽ kũẽ se kya kam lete hə̃y.
10. ap ke mwlk mẽ, kysan fəslẽ kəb ləgate hə̃y, əwr kəb kaTte hə̃y.

442

11. ap ko kəwnsa rə̃g zyada pəsənd həy.

12. ap ne talim kəhã se hasyl ki.

13. kya, ap əpne lie khana xwd pəkate hə̃y?

14. ap həfte mẽ kytni bar synima dekhte hə̃y.

15. sərsõ kya kya kam deti həy.

14.505. Conversation Practice.

After supper, Mr. Smith chats with some of the villagers.

V: həm log ap ke mwlk ke mwtəəllyq kwch batẽ puchni cahte hə̃y.

S: bəRi xwši se puch səkte hə̃y.

V: ap ka mwlk yəhã se kytni dur həy.

S: mera mwlk yəhã se koi dəs həzar mil ke fasyle pər həy.

V: kya, ap ke mwlk mẽ bhi log zəraət kərte hə̃y?

S: kyõ nəhĩ! əgər həm zəraət nə kərẽ, to kəhã se khaẽ!

V: həm ne to yy swna tha, ky vəhã log gaRiã bənate hə̃y, əwr məšinẽ cəlate hə̃y.

S: bylkwl Thik həy. yy kam bhi kərte hə̃y. lekyn zəraət səb se zyada zəruri həy. həmare
mwlk mẽ bhi ysi təra kysan hə̃y, kũẽ hə̃y, nəhrẽ hə̃y, fəslẽ wgti hə̃y, kəTti hə̃y, khetõ
pər kam hota həy, vəɣəyra.

V: kya, ap bhi ysi təra fəslẽ bote hə̃y, əwr kaTte hə̃y, əwr ysi təra janvərõ se kam lete hə̃y?

S: ji hã. həmára kysan bhi yyhi fəslẽ wgata həy. ysi təra myhnət kərta həy, lekyn həmare
hã fəsl wgane əwr kaTne ka təriqa mwxtəlyf həy. həmare mwlk mẽ janvərõ se bəhwt kəm
kam lete hə̃y, kyõke hər qysm ki məšinẽ məwjud hə̃y. fəsl bone ki məšin həy, fəsl kaTne
ki məšin həy, phəl toRne ki məšin həy. həm həl bhi məšinõ ke zərie se cəlate hə̃y.
lekyn phyr bhi kysi kysi jəga ghoRe khetõ pər kam kərte hə̃y.

V: kya, ap ke hã gae, bhãys, əwr bəyl nəhĩ hote?

S: həmare mwlk mẽ təqribən səb janvər məwjud hə̃y, lekyn həm yn sc khetõ pər kam nəhĩ
lete. əlbətta wn ka dudh pite hə̃y, əwr gošt khate hə̃y.

V: kya, ap bhi khetõ mẽ khad Dalte hə̃y?

S: ji hã. khad fəslõ ke lie bəhwt zəruri həy. gobər ke ylava, həm kəi dusri cizõ se bhi
khad bənate hə̃y, əwr wse jəma kərte rəhte hə̃y, əwr fəsl bone ke vəqt khetõ mẽ ystemal
kərte hə̃y. həm gobər nəhĩ jəlate, kyõke yy fəslõ ke lie bəhwt mwfid həy, əwr byhtərin
qysm ki khad həy.

V: yy həm bhi jante hə̃y, lekyn həm log ɣərib hə̃y, əwr ləkRi nəhĩ xərid səkte. dusre, yəhã
dərəxt bəhwt kəm hote hə̃y.

S: ap ko cahie, ky ap khetõ ke kynare əwr dusri xali jəghõ pər dərəxt ləgaẽ. yn dərəxtõ se
ap ko ləkRi bhi mylegi, əwr dusre bəhwt se fayde bhi hõge.

V: ap ke mwlk mẽ kəwn kəwnsi fəslẽ hoti hə̃y.

S: təqribən yyhi fəslẽ vəhã bhi hoti hə̃y. jəyse gəndwm, cavəl, jəw, məTər, tel ke bij,
əwr ys ke ylava phəlõ əwr səbziõ ki fəslẽ bhi hoti hə̃y.

V: kya, ap ke hã əwrtẽ bhi khetõ pər kam kərti hə̃y?

S: həmare mwlk mẽ əwrtẽ bhi mərdõ ke sath sath kam kərti hə̃y. šəhrõ mẽ əwrtẽ hoTlõ,
bə̃ykõ, əwr dəftərõ mẽ kam kərti hə̃y, əwr gaõ ki əwrtẽ khetõ pər kam kərti hə̃y.

lekyn wnhē zyada myhnət nəhī̃ kərni pəRti, kyõke həmare mwlk mē təqribən hər qysm ki məšinē məwjud hə̃y, jyn se wn ka kafi vəqt bəc jata həy.

V: kya, ap ke gaõ mē ysi təra ke məkan, bazar, əwr gəliā̃ hoti hə̃y?

S: həmare gaõ mē myTTi ke, ya kəcce məkan bəhwt kəm hote hə̃y. təqribən təmam məkan pəkke nəzər aēge, jyn ki chət ləkRi ki hoti həy. ap ke gaõ ki gəliā̃ əwr bazar bəhwt tə̃g hə̃y. yy syhət ke lie əcchi ciz nəhī̃. ysi lie, həmare mwlk mē gaõ ki gəliā̃ əwr bazar kafi cəwRe hote hə̃y.

V: kya, ap ke gaõ mē bhi məsjydē əwr yskul hote hə̃y?

S: həmare gaõ mē məsjydē nəhī̃ hotī̃. gyrja hote hə̃y. lekyn kəi bəRe šəhrõ mē məsjydē hə̃y, əlbətta yskul hər jəga məwjud hə̃y. talim gaõvalõ ke lie xas təwr pər bəhwt zəruri həy, kyõke kytabõ mē fəsl wgane əwr zyada ənaj pəyda kərne ke nəe nəe təriqe məwjud hə̃y. ysi lie, gaõ ke hər bəcce, jəvan, əwr buRhe ko talim hasyl kərni cahie.

V: həm log əpne bəccõ ko bəcpən se hi zəraət sykhate hə̃y.

S: yy bəhwt əcchi bat həy, lekyn zəraət sikhne ke sath sath vw talim bhi hasyl kər səkte hə̃y. ap ki hwkumət ne ysi lie hər jəga yskul khole hə̃y, take ap log əpne bəccõ ko yskul mē daxyl kəraē̃.

V: maf kijie, həm ne ap ko bəhwt təklif di, lekyn ys batcit se həmē bəhwt si mwfid əwr nəi batē malum hwī̃.

S: ys mē təklif ki kya bat həy! mə̃y əbhi kəl tək yəhī̃ hū̃. kəl šam ko phyr mylēge, əwr gaõ ke bare mē kwch əwr batē kərēge. mwjhe to ap logõ se myl kər bəhwt xwši hwi.

14. 506. Conversation Stimulus.

Topics may include the following:
1. North American agricultural methods.
2. A visit to a village.
3. Crops and seasons.
4. A comparison between village and city life.
5. Village health education.

444

ag F1	fire
apəs Adv	one another, each other
əgəst M1 [np]	August
əktubər M1 [np]	October
əlbətta Conj	although, on the other hand, certainly, but
ənaj M1	grain
əprəyl M1 [np]	April
bar F1	time, turn, occasion [/bar bar/ Adv "repeatedly, time after time, again and again"]
bavən A1	fifty-two
bəcna [IIc: /ə/]	to escape, be saved, be left over
bərsat F1	rainy season
bəyl M1	ox
bhərna [IIId: /ə/]	to fill, be filled
bhə̃ys F1	(female) water buffalo
bhuk F1 [np]	hunger
bij M1	seed
bona [Ia]	to sow
buRha A2 M2	old (of persons)
cəlana [C: /cəlna/: IIc]	to cause to go, run (a machine, business, etc.), drive, stir
cəwRa A2	wide, broad
cəvvən A1	fifty-four
daxyl PA1	entered, inserted
dhobi M1	washerman
dysəmbər M1 [np]	December
fasyla M2	distance, space
fayda M2	profit, benefit, advantage
fərq M1	difference
fərvəri M1 [or F2] [np]	February
fəsl F1	crop, harvest
gəli F2	lane, alley, narrow street
gəndwm F1 [or M1]	wheat
ghoRa M2	(male) horse
gobər M1	cattle dung
ɣərib A1 M1	poor
həl M1	plow
həra A2	green
janvər M1	animal
jəlana [C: /jəlna/: IIc]	to cause to burn, set fire to, light, burn
jəlna [IIc: /ə/]	to burn (intrans.)

jəma F1 PA1	collection, sum, plural; gathered, collected
jənvəri M1 [or F2] [np]	January
jəvan M1 A1	young, youth (young person)
jəw M1 [np]	barley
julai M1 [or F2] [np]	July
jun M1 [np]	June
kəcca A2	raw, unripe, immature, nonpermanent (as an unpaved road or a building of clay or unbaked bricks), crude
kəmi F2	littleness, scarcity, lack, deficiency
kəmzor A1	weak, debilitated
kəTna [I: /kaTna/: Ie]	to be cut, get cut
khad F1	manure, fertiliser
khet M1	(agricultural) field
kũã M2	(water) well
kynara [literary: /kənara/] M2	bank, shore, side [/[ke] kynare/ Comp Post "on the bank, along the bank, on the side of"]
kysan M1	farmer, peasant
ləkRi F2	wood, stick
marc M1 [np]	March
məi M1 [or F2] [np]	May
mərzi F2 [np]	choice, pleasure, desire
məTər M1	pea[s]
mə̄gana [C: /mā̄gna/: Ic]	to request, send for, order
miTha A2	sweet
[ke] mwtəəllyq [common: /mwtallyq/] Comp Post	in connection with, about, concerning
mwxtəlyf A1	different, various
myhnət F1	hard work, labour
myhnəti [common: /myhnti/] A1	hardworking, industrious
myTTi [or /məTTi/] F2	dirt, earth, soil, clay
nəhr F1	canal
nəwmbər [or /nəvəmbər/] M1 [np]	November
pəcpən A1	fifty-five
pəhw̃cana [C: /pəhw̃cna/: IIc]	to cause to arrive, make reach, bring, send
pəkana [C: /pəkńa/: IIc]	to cook, make ripe, ripen
pəkka A2	cooked, ripe, ready, matured, solid, substantial, permanent (as a brick or stone house, a paved road, etc.)
pəkna [IIc: /ə/]	to ripen, get cooked, become mature
pila A2	yellow
pəwda M2	plant, shrub
pyas F1 [np]	thirst
[ke] qərib Comp Post Adv	near, nearby, almost
rə̃g M1	colour, tint, paint, dye, aspect, appearance

sərsō F1 [np]	mustard seed plant
sikhna [Ic: /y/]	to learn
sukhna [IIc: /w/]	to become dry
swkhana [C: /sukhna/: IIc]	to dry (trans.), cause to dry
syhət F1	health
sykhana [C: /sikhna/: Ic]	to teach, cause to learn
sytəmbər M1 [np]	September
talim F1	education
tərbuz M1	watermelon
təyyari F2	preparation, readiness
tɔ̄g A1	narrow, tight, distressed, straightened, harassed
tel M1	oil
thəkna [IIc: /ə/]	to become tired, fatigued
toRna [Ie: /w/]	to break, pick, pluck
tyrpən [or /tyrepən/] A1	fifty-three
TuTna [I: /toRna/: Ie]	to break (intrans.)
wgana [C: /wgna/: IIc]	to plant, cause to grow
wgna [IIc: /w/]	to grow (intrans.)
xərbuza M2	muskmelon
ykavən [or /ykyavən/ or /ykkyavən/ or /ykkavən/] A1	fifty-one
[ke] ylava [or /əlava/] Comp Post	besides, in addition to, moreover
zəraət F1 [np]	agriculture

Winnowing the grain, Pakistan.

15.000. CONVERSATION

Mr. əziz and Mr. Smith have stayed overnight with their village hosts. Early the next morning Mr. əziz comes to get Mr. Smith.

ə: Have you read this morning's paper?

kya, ap ne aj swba ka əxbar pəRha həy?

news F1

xəbər

S: No, is there some special news?

ji nəhī̃ -- kya, koi xas xəbər həy?

sad, sorrowful Ai

əfsosnak

east M1 [np]

məšryq

sixty A1

saTh

situated, located PA1

vaqe

sudden, unexpected; suddenly, unexpectedly A1 Adv

əcanək

flood M1

səylab

dike, embankment M1

bənd

fifty-six A1

chəppən

to die [I: /marna/: Ie]

mərna

ruined, destroyed, spoiled PA1

təbah

bridge M1

pwl

loss, damage, harm, wastage, injury M1

nwqsan

ə: Yes, there is very sad news. To the east of our village about sixty miles away there is another village. This village is situated upon the bank of a river. Yesterday evening all of a sudden there was [lit. came] a flood in the river, because of which the dyke of the river broke, and water spread throughout the village, due to which about fifty-six houses fell down, many [lit. enough] of the villagers' animals died, most of the crops were destroyed, and, besides this, the bridge of the river was also damaged [lit. to the bridge also damage has arrived].

ji hā̃, bəhwt əfsosnak xəbər həy. həmare gaõ ke məšryq ki tərəf təqribən saTh mil dur, ek əwr gaõ həy. yy gaõ dərya ke kynare pər vaqe həy. kəl rat, əcanək, dərya mē səylab a gəya, jys se dərya ka bənd TuT gəya, əwr sare gaõ mē pani phəyl gəya, jys ki vəja se koi chəppən məkan gyr gəe, gaõvalõ ke kafi janvər mər gəe, əksər fəslē təbah ho gəĩ, əwr ys ke ylava, dərya ke pwl ko bhi nwqsan pəhw̃ca həy.

wealth, riches F1 [np]

dəwlət

life F2

zyndəgi

spoiled, ruined, laid waste, destroyed PA1

bərbad

S: Really, this is very sad news. Crops and animals are the villagers' wealth. If these things are destroyed, then the villagers' life is ruined.

vaqəi, bəhwt əfsosnak xəbər həy! fəslē əwr janvər gaõvalõ ki dəwlət hə̄y. əgər yyhi cizē təbah ho jaē, to gaõvalõ ki zyndəgi bərbad ho jati həy.

communication, transportation F1 [np]

amədorəft

connection, succession, chain, series, link M2

sylsyla

ə: Very correct, but the biggest loss is the breaking of the dike and the damage to the

bylkwl Thik həy, lekyn səb se bəRa nwqsan bənd TuTne əwr pwl ko nwqsan pəhw̃cne ka

449

bridge. From this, the government
has lost lakhs of rupees, and moreover
[lit. second], the chain of communication
has been completely cut off.

    state, condition M1

S: What is the condition of the water in the
river now?

    control, custody, grasp, hold M1 [np]

    has been found MS

ə: Just now news has come that the water has
been brought under control [lit. control
has been found upon the water].

S: Have some people gone from here to help
the villagers [lit. for the villagers' help]?

    has been sent MS

    flour M2

    lentils, pulses F1

    has been caused to be sent MS

ə: Yes, some men were sent from here this
very morning to that village, and plenty of
[lit. enough] supplies of food [and] drink
were sent with them, such as flour, lentils,
meat, etc.

    form, state, condition, case, face F1

    one another, each other

S: Well done. This way the poor people will
be helped because it is the duty of every
person to help one another.

ə: Where do you desire to go today?

    forest, jungle M1

    village elder M1

S: I think [we] should go to the forest today.
We'll stroll around for awhile. Then we
will come back quickly because today we
have to go to a party at the village elder's
place.

ə: Come! This road leads directly to the
forest.

    environment, surroundings M1 [np]

    climate F1 [np]

    simple, plain A1 [or A2]

    wonderful, marvellous, strange A1

    pleasure, enjoyment, delight, taste M1
    [np]

S: I like village life very much. The
surroundings here, the climate, the green
green fields, the busy and simple life of
the people, possess a wonderful charm.

    merit, goodness, good quality F2

    some, a number of A1

    evil, badness, bad quality, vice F2

həy. ys se hwkumət ko lakhõ rupəe ka
nwqsan hwa həy, əwr dusre, amədorəft ka
sylsyla bylkwl bənd ho gəya həy.

    hal

əb dərya mẽ pani ka kya hal həy.

    qabu

    pa lia gəya həy

əbhi əbhi xəbər ai həy, ky pani pər qabu
pa lia gəya həy.

kya, yəhã se kwch log gaõvalõ ki mədəd
ke lie gəe hõy?

    bhej dia gəya həy

    aTa

    dal

    bhyjvaya gəya həy

ji hã, yəhã se swba hi kwch admiõ ko ws
gaõ bhej dia gəya həy, əwr wn ke sath
khane pine ka kafi saman, jəyse aTa, dal,
əwr gošt vəyəyra bhi bhyjvaya gəya həy.

    surət

    ek dusra

yy bəhwt əccha kia. ys surət se yərib logõ
ki kwch mədəd ho jaegi, kyõke ek dusre ki
mədəd kərna hər ynsan ka fərz həy.

aj kydhər cəlne ka yrada həy.

    jõgəl

    nəmbərdar

mera xyal həy, ky jõgəl ki tərəf cəlẽ. kwch
der səyr kərẽge. phyr jəldi vapəs ləwT
aẽge, kyõke nəmbərdar sahəb ke hã davət
pər jana həy.

aie! yy rasta sidha jõgəl ko jata həy.

    mahəwl

    abohəva

    sada

    əjəb

    lwtf

mwjhe gaõ ki zyndʊgi bəhwt pəsənd həy.
yəhã ka mahəwl, abohəva, həre həre khet,
logõ ki məsruf əwr sada zyndəgi, ek əjəb
lwtf rəkhti həy.

    xubi

    baz

    bwrai

are found FP

mind Ml

effect, trace, impression, influence Ml

ə: I myself like village life very much,
although along with many good points, some
bad points are found more here than in the
city, which sometimes have an [unpleasant]
effect upon the mind.

meaning, concern Ml

S: What do you mean by bad points?

    example, illustration F1

    fight, war, battle F2

    quarrel, squabble M2

    but Conj

    extended family, household, lineage,
    dynasty Ml

ə: For example, quarrels [lit. fight-quarrel]
in the village start over a rather minor
matter. This quarreling does not stay
[limited] only to one or two men, but whole
families [lit. family of family] are
destroyed in it.

S: Is there any special reason for this type
of fighting?

    basically, in reality, in the first place
    Adv

    landowner, landlord Ml

    enmity F2

    to fight [IIc: /ə/]

    thought, reflection, idea, concern Ml
    [np]

    some ... or the other OS

    enemy M/F1 A1

    revenge, exchange, retaliation M2

ə: The basic reason [lit. in reality the
reason] is this that in the village besides
farmers and poor people, wealthy landlords
live there too. Because of some ancient
enmity these landlords keep fighting among
themselves and constantly keep thinking
[lit. every time remain in this very
thought] that [they] should take revenge
from their enemy [lit. enemy landlord] in
some way or other.

S: Does this type of quarrel occur here often?

    story, tale, matter M2

    information F1

    opponent, opposing M/F1 A1

    party F2

    to force one's way in, enter, creep in,
    sneak in [IIc: /w/]

---

pai jati hə̄y

dymaɣ [or /dəmaɣ/]

əsər

mwjhe xwd gaõ ki zyndəgi bəhwt pəsənd
həy, əgərce bəhwt si xubiõ ke sath sath,
baz bwraiā̃ šəhr ke mwqable mē̃ yəhā̃
zyada pai jati hə̄y, jo kəbhi kəbhi to dymaɣ
pər bəhwt əsər kərti hə̄y.

mətləb

bwraiõ se ap ka kya mətləb həy.

mysal

ləRai

jhəgRa

bəlke

xandan

mysal ke təwr pər, gaõ mē̃ mamuli si bat
pər ləRai jhəgRa šwru ho jata həy. yy
ləRai jhəgRa syrf ek ya do admiõ tək hi
nəhī̃ rəhta, bəlke ys mē̃ xandan ke xandan
təbah ho jate hə̄y.

kya, ys qysm ki ləRai ki koi xas vəja həy?

dərəsl

zəmindar

dwšməni

ləRna

soc

kysi nə kysi

dwšmən

bədla

dərəsl vəja yy həy, ky gaõ mē̃ kysanõ əwr
ɣərib logõ ke ylava, əmir zəmindar bhi
rəhte həy. yy zəmindar kysi pwrani
dwšməni ki vəja se apəs mē̃ ləRte rəhte
hə̄y, əwr hər vəqt ysi soc mē̃ rəhte hə̄y,
ky kysi nə kysi təra əpne dwšmən zəmindar
se bədla lē̃.

kya, ys qysm ke jhəgRe yəhā̃ əksər hote
rəhte hə̄y?

qyssa

yttyla

mwxalyf

parTi

ghwsna

451

angry, annoyed A1

anger, rage M2

kill [nonhonorific]! [/marna/ "to beat, hit, kill"; Ie: /ə/]

killed MS [/marna/; see above]

ə: There is a story of just last month: that a landlord's servant informed him that two water buffaloes of the opposing party had gotten into [lit. have entered] his field and were spoiling [lit. are spoiling] the crops. Hearing this, the landlord became very angry and in a rage gave an order to the servant to kill both the buffaloes [lit. that you [nonhonorific] kill both buffaloes!]. Thereupon this servant took two other men with him and arrived there and killed both buffaloes.

stupid M/F1 A1

to kill [/marna/; see above]

instead of Comp Post

S: They are very stupid men! Instead of killing the buffaloes, [they] ought to have taken [them] out of the field. -- What happened after this?

have been killed FP

leader, chief M1

message M1

endurance, toleration, bearing, putting up with F1 [np]

will be done FS

end, conclusion, result, consequence M1

bad, evil A2

figure, number, amount F1

paid, accomplished, fulfilled PA1

ə: When this became known to the opposing party that their two buffaloes had been killed, their chief sent this message by the hand of one person, that "We will not stand for this action. [Lit. With us this action will not be tolerated.] Either [you, nonhonorific] return our buffaloes, or else the consequence[s] will be very bad." The other landowner replied, that "Your [non-honorific] buffaloes have done much damage to our crops. Either pay the amount of this damage or else get ready for a fight!"

strange, extraordinary A1

result, effect, issue, outcome M2

S: [It] is a very strange thing! What result is gained from fighting over such a minor matter? Was there a fight about this thing?

staff, stick, cudgel F2

naraz

γwssa

mar Dalo

mar Dala

əbhi pychle məhine ka qyssa həy, ky ek zəmindar ke nəwkər ne wse yy yttyla di, ky ws ke khet mẽ mwxalyf parTi ki do bhɔ̃ysẽ ghws ai hɔ̃y, əwr fəslõ ko xərab kər rəhi hɔ̃y. zəmindar yy swn kər bəhwt naraz hwa, əwr γwsse mẽ nəwkər ko hwkm dia, ky "donõ bhɔ̃ysõ ko mar Dalo!" cwnãce yy nəwkər do əwr admiõ ko sath le kər vəhã pəhw̃ca, əwr donõ bhɔ̃ysõ ko mar Dala.

bevwquf

mar Dalna

[ki] bəjae [or /[ke] bəjae/]

bəhwt bevwquf admi the! bhɔ̃ysõ ko mar Dalne ki bəjae, khet se nykal dena cahie tha. -- ys ke bad kya hwa.

mar di gəi hɔ̃y

sərdar

pəyγam

bərdaš̌t

ki jaegi

ənjam

bwra

rəqəm

əda

jəb mwxalyf parTi ko yy malum hwa, ky wn ki do bhɔ̃ysẽ mar di gəi hɔ̃y, to wn ke sərdar ne ek š̌əxs ke hath yy pəyγam bheja, ky "həm se yy hərəkət bərdaš̌t nəhĩ ki jaegi. ya t̉o həmari bhɔ̃ysẽ vapəs kəro, vərna ys ka ənjam bəhwt bwra hoga!" dusre zəmindar ne yy jəvab dia, ky "twm̃hari bhɔ̃ysõ ne həmari fəslõ ka bəhwt nwqsan kia həy, ya to ys nwqsan ki rəqəm əda kəro, vərna ləRai ke lie təyyar ho jao!"

əjib

nətija

bəhwt əjib bat həy! ytni mamuli si bat pər ləRne se kya nətija hasyl hota həy. kya, ysi bat pər ləRai ho gəi?

laThi

452

gun F1	bənduq
pistol M1	pystəwl
to cause to understand, to explain, convince, reason with, expostulate, remonstrate with [C: /səməjhna/: IIIa]	səmjhana
fell to fighting FP	ləR pəRĭ
were killed MP	mare gəe
wounded, injured M/F1 A1	zəxmi

ə: In the evening the two parties gathered outside the village. Besides sticks, these people had gun[s] and pistols too. People reasoned with them a great deal, but [it] had no effect upon them, and both parties fell to fighting with one another. In this fight three men were killed, twenty men were injured, and all the rest were arrested.

šam ko donõ parTiã gaõ ke bahər jəma ho gəĭ. yn logõ ke pas, laThiõ ke ylava, bənduq əwr pystəwl bhi the. logõ ne donõ ko bəhwt səmjhaya, lekyn yn pər koi əsər nə hwa, əwr donõ parTiã apəs mẽ ləR pəRĭ. ys ləRai mẽ tin admi mare gəe, bis admi zəxmi hwe, əwr baqi səb gyryftar ho gəe.

certainly Adv	yəqinən

S: Certainly there must be a court case going on now!

yəqinən əb mwqədma cəl rəha hoga!

fine (penalty) M2	jwrmana
story, tale F2	kəhani
estimate, conjecture, guess M2	əndaza
error, mistake F2	yələti

ə: Yes. After the decision of the case, some will be punished [with jail], and some will be fined. From this story you yourself can estimate how many people were harmed by one small mistake.

ji hã. mwqədme ke fəysle ke bad, kwch logõ ko səza hogi, əwr kwch logõ ko jwrmana hoga. ys kəhani se ap xwd əndaza ləgaẽ, ky ek choTi si yələti se kytne admiõ ko nwqsan pəhw̃ca.

important, urgent A1	əhəm
knowledge, science, learning M1	ylm
intellect, wisdom, sense, mind, reason F1 [np]	əql
understanding, comprehension, perception F1 [np]	səməjh
to think, consider, meditate, imagine, ponder [Ia]	socna
step, pace, footstep, foot M1	qədəm
wrong, mistaken A1	yələt
principle, basis, rule M1	wsul

S: Really, this is a very bad thing. I think that an important reason for such evils is the lack of education. Because education teaches reason right along with knowledge, and the man who has intellect and understanding takes [lit. raises] a step after thinking and never operates [lit. goes] upon such erroneous principles.

vaqəi, yy bəhwt bwri ciz həy. mera xyal həy, ky əysi bwraiõ ki əhəm vəja talim ki kəmi həy. kyõke talim ylm ke sath sath əql bhi sykhati həy, əwr jo ynsan kwch əql əwr səməjh rəkhta həy, vw socne ke bad qədəm wThata həy, əwr əyse yələt wsulõ pər nəhĭ cəlta.

God M1 [np]	əllah
thanks, gratitude M1 [np]	šwkr
gradually, by and by Adv	rəfta rəfta
are [gradually] becoming FP	hoti ja·rəhi hə̃y

ə: Yes. Thank God that through the effort of our government these things are gradually becoming less; otherwise thirty [or] forty years ago [lit. before thirty forty years from today] such evils were much more [prevalent].

ji hã. əllah ka šwkr həy, ky həmari hwkumət ki košyš se, yy cizē rəfta rəfta kəm hoti ja rəhi hə̄y, vərna aj se tis calys sal pəhle, to əysi bwraiã bəhwt zyada thī.

just as, at the same time as Adv

jū jū

will keep on increasing FS [/bəRhna/ "to extend, increase, grow, expand, thrive, proceed"; IIc: /ə/]

bəRhti jaegi

if God wills Inter

ynšaəlla[h]

will keep on lessening FP [/ghəTna/ "to lessen, decrease, abate, become deficient"; IIc: /ə/]

ghəTti jaēgi

S: Just as education goes on increasing, if God wills, these evils will keep decreasing.

jū jū talim bəRhti jaegi, ynšaəlla[h] yy bwraiã ghəTti jaēgi.

must be about to come MP

ane vale hõge

ə: I think that now we ought to go back because those people must also be coming, and they will be waiting for us.

mera xyal həy, ky əb həmē vapəs cəlna cahie, kyõke vw log bhi ane vale hõge, əwr həmara yntyzar kər rəhe hõge.

15.101. /əxbar/ Ml "newspaper" is originally the Arabic "broken plural" (see Sec. 17.304) of /xəbər/ F1 "news." These words must be treated as entirely separate items in Urdu, however.

15.102. /vaqe/ PA1 "situated, located," /vaqəya/ M2 "event, occurrence," and /vaqəi/ Adv "really" are all derivatives from the same Arabic root: v-q-' "to fall, happen, be situated." Arabic root patterns employed in Urdu will be described in Unit XVII. Even if -- or perhaps **especially** if -- the student knows Arabic, he must be careful to learn the Urdu meaning and usage of each borrowed Arabic word.

15.103. /bənd/ was introduced as a predicate adjective meaning "tied, shut, closed" in Unit V. As a masculine noun, /bənd/ has many meanings: "dike, embankment," "strings or laces of a garment," "a stanza of verse," "a trick in wrestling," etc. Only the first of these meanings has been introduced here.

15.104. /mərna/ "to die" is the intransitive form of a Type Ie verb, /marna/ "to hit, beat, strike" (see Sec. 9.306). With the intensive auxiliaries /dena/ or /Dalna/, /marna/ also means "to kill." The double causative form /mərvana/ is usually employed for "to cause to be killed." The causative form /mərana/ also occurs but is less common in this meaning. E.g.

> /vw mər gəya./ He died. [The completive auxiliary /jana/ is almost always added to /mərna/ in an independent clause.]
>
> /wnhõ ne wse mara./ They beat him.
>
> /wnhõ ne wse mar Dala./ They killed him. [Or: /... mar dia./; /marna/ + either /dena/ or /Dalna/ can only mean "to kill."]
>
> /ws ləRai mẽ dəs admi mare gəe./ Ten men were killed in that battle. [/mara jana/ always means "to be killed"; "to be beaten" is expressed by another verb stem entirely: /pyTna/ "to be beaten," not yet introduced.]
>
> /wn ke dwšmənõ ne wse mərva dia./ His enemies had him killed.

It is important to note that /mərna/ "to die" is nonhonorific. If one is speaking of the death of a respected person, one does not say */vw mər gəe./. Instead, there are various honorific expressions. Although not introduced in this Unit, two of the commonest of these may be mentioned here:

> /wn ka yntyqal ho gəya./ He died. [/yntyqal/ Ml [np] is used for "death, demise" but originally denotes "transfer."]
>
> /wnhõ ne vəfat pai./ He died. [/vəfat/ F1 [np] "death, demise."]

15.105. /təbah/ PA1 denotes "destroyed, ruined" in a physical sense, while /bərbad/ PA1 means "ruined, spoiled" in an abstract or nonphysical context. /təbah/ is often employed metaphorically, however, and thus the meanings of these two words overlap considerably in usage. E.g.

/meri zyndəgi bərbad ho gəi./   My life has been ruined.   [Or metaphorically: / ... təbah ho gəi./.]

/meri myhnət bərbad ho gəi./   My labour has been spoiled.   [/təbah/ is
perhaps less idiomatic here since the sense of "physically destroyed"
cannot easily be extended to "labour" in the abstract sense.]

15.106. /hal/ M1 "condition, state" is used for a general, abstract, or nonspecific
condition: e.g. the condition of a country, the total state of a person's wellbeing, etc.
/halət/ F1 "state, condition" refers to an immediate, specific condition which is open to
change: e.g. the state of a person's health (especially that of a sick person), one's
financial condition, the condition of an unstable country, etc. E.g.

/ap ka kya hal həy./   How are you? [A general and nonspecific state:
i.e. "How is life treating you?"]

/ap ki halət kəysi həy./   How is your condition? [This implies that the
"state" is a specific condition open to change: e.g. the recent state
of a sick person's health, etc.]

/meri halət xərab ho gəi./   My condition has become bad. [I.e. health,
finances, etc.]

15.107. /dal/ F1 denotes the whole range of lentils and pulses -- i.e. legumes rather
like the "split pea." There are many varieties of /dal/: e.g. /mūg ki dal/, /maš ki dal/,
/ərhər ki dal/, /cəne ki dal/, /wRəd ki dal/, /məsur ki dal/, etc., the differences
between which can only be known by a trip to an Indian or Pakistani market.

/dal/ is kept in a dried form much like the "split pea" in Western cooking. It is cooked
as a sort of thick soup and is eaten as a side dish along with bread or rice and a meat dish.
A sample meal in a Muslim home in North India or Pakistan might thus consist of rice or
bread (i.e. /cəpati/ F2 "thin patty of unleavened wheat bread") or both, plus a meat dish
(/salən/, etc.), plus /dal/, and possibly some other vegetable dish. A little pickle (/əcar/
M1) or chutney (/cəTni/ F2) may be provided to give greater variation. To these dishes,
of course, a wide selection of further dishes may be added.

15.108. /ek dusra/ "one another, each other" expresses reciprocal action by two
parties. If there are more than two actors, /apəs mē/ "among ... selves" is employed.
E.g.

/həm ne vəhā pəhli dəfa ek dusre ko dekha./   We saw each other for the
first time there.

/donō ne ek dusre mē yyhi bwrai pai./   Both found this very same fault
in one another. [I.e. Each found this very fault in the other.]

/donō bhai ek dusre se ləR pəRe./   Both brothers fell to fighting with each
other. [In English, perhaps, "with each other" is somewhat super-
fluous, but it is idiomatic in Urdu.]

/səb bhai apəs mē ləR pəRe./   All the brother fell to fighting among
themselves.

/donō ko ek dusre pər yəqin tha./   Both had confidence in [lit. on] each
other.

/vw donō ek dusre ke dwšmən the./   Each was the other's enemy. [Lit.
Both were each other's enemy.]

456

15.109. /nəmbərdar/ M1 "village elder" contains the English word "number" + the Persian present verbal stem /dar/ "having" (see Sec. 18.307). The /nəmbərdar/ is sometimes appointed by the government, but in some areas the post is also hereditary. His functions are primarily the recording, checking, etc. of village land revenues. He may also function as the head of the village council (/pə̄cayət/ F1), see to guests of the village, etc., and he may also have some minor police powers over local disputes and misdemeanours. There is also an alternate form, /ləmbərdar/, with /l/ dissimilated from /n/.

15.110. /əjəb/ A1 and /əjib/ A1 both mean "strange." The former has a greater connotation of "wonderful, marvellous," while the latter connotes "strange, unusual, extraordinary."

15.111. /baz/ A1 denotes "some individual ... s"; /kwch/ A1 is used for "some aggregate of ... s." E.g.

/baz log/   some [individual] people
/kwch log/   some [group, aggregate of] people
/kwch cavəl/   some rice. ["Rice" is almost always an aggregate, and one cannot thus say */baz cavəl/ unless one means "some individual types of species of rice."]

15.112. /dymaɣ/ M1 "mind, brain" must be distinguished from /əql/ F1 [np], which is also sometimes translatable as "mind." /əql/ has, however, a connotation of "reason, sense, intellect." /soc/ M1 [np] "thinking, pondering, cogitation" is rather uncommon, although the verbal form /socna/ "to think" is frequent. Still another word in the same semantic area is /səməjh/ F1 [np] "understanding, comprehension, perception."

15.113. /ləRai/ F2 "fight, war, battle" usually denotes a physical struggle; /jhəgRa/ M2 "quarrel" is almost always verbal.

15.114. /bəlke/ Conj "but, but in addition to, but moreover, but on the other hand" contrasts with /lekyn/ Conj and /məgər/ Conj, both of which mean "but." E.g.

/səylab se, syrf fəslō ko hi nwqsan nəhī̃ pəhw̃ca, bəlke dərya ka bənd bhi TuT gəya./ Because of [lit. from] the flood, not only were the crops damaged, but [in addition] the bridge over [lit. of] the river was broken. [/ ... hi ... nəhī̃ ... bəlke ... bhi .../ is usually translatable as "not only ... but also .../.]

/vw ek qabyl profesər hi nəhī̃, bəlke ek bəhwt əccha dost bhi həy./ He is not only an able professor, but [he] is also a very good friend.

/mə̄y kam nəhī̃ kərūga, bəlke syrf dekhūga./ I will not work, but [on the other hand] will only look [on].

/yy koi xubi nəhī̃, bəlke bwrai həy./ This is no virtue at all, but [it instead] is a vice.

15.115. /xandan/ M1 "extended family" includes the totality of one's relations, sometimes equivalent to "tribe" or "clan." Neither of these latter terms -- nor the term "family" -- fits exactly.

15.116. /dərəsl/ Adv "in fact, basically, in the first place" consists of the Persian preposition /dər/ "in" + /əsl/ F1 A1 "root, source, origin, foundation; originally." /əsl/ occurs as a separate word in Urdu, but /dər/ occurs only in "frozen phrases" borrowed directly from Persian. The Urdu equivalent of /dərəsl/ is /əsl mẽ/, and this is also common. E.g.

/dərəsl ys sal fəslõ ko pani nəhĩ myl səka, ys lie vw sukh gəĩ./ In fact, the crops could not get water this year; therefore they dried up. [/əsl mẽ/ can be substituted.]

/dərəsl mᵊy vəhã məwjud nəhĩ tha. ys lie jhəgRa ho gəya./ In fact, I was not present there. Therefore there was a quarrel. [Again /əsl mẽ/ is substitutable.]

/ws ki əsl hi xərab həy./ His origin is bad. [I.e. He comes of bad stock.]

/əsl bat to yy həy, ky vw mwjh se naraz hᵊy./ The real matter is this, that he is angry with me.

/əsl mẽ ys bat pər jhəgRa ho gəya, ky ws ne meri rəqəm əda nə ki thi./ In the first place [i.e. in fact] the quarrel was over this matter, that he had not paid my sum [of money: i.e. loan].

15.117. /zəmindar/ M1 "landlord, landowner" consists of /zəmin/ F1 "land" + the Persian present verbal stem /dar/ "having" (see Sec. 18.307). /zəmindar/ denotes the owner of any piece of agricultural land, but it is most often employed for the owner of an estate farmed by tenant farmers -- traditionally a semi-feudal, peasant-overlord relationship. The /zəmindari/ system has been officially abolished both in India and in Pakistan, but it still continues to flourish in some parts of the Subcontinent.

15.118. /qyssa/ M2 "story, tale" may also be used for "event, matter." /kəhani/ F2 "story, tale" is more often employed for a fictional narrative, however, although it is also occasionally found in the meaning of "event, matter." E.g.

/yy kya qyssa həy./ What is this matter? [This is like the American colloquial expression, "What's the story here?"]

/yy kya kəhani həy./ What is this story? [The speaker implies that the tale is likely to be fictional.]

/mera qyssa swnie!/ Please hear my story! [I.e. Please hear what has happened to me! This could also refer to a fictional story, of course.]

/meri kəhani swnie!/ Please hear my tale! [This will probably be a fictional narrative.]

15.119. /ghwsna/ denotes "to enter by force, thrust oneself into, enter a narrow place (as an animal does its burrow), creep into (as a thief into a house)." E.g.

/vw mere ghər mẽ ghws gəya./ He got into my house. [I.e. thrust his way in, crept in, etc., as the context demands.]

Compare this with other expressions denoting "to enter." E.g.

/vw mere ghər mẽ aya./ He came into my house. [This sentence does not specify the method or duration of his entering.]

/vw mere ghər ke əndər aya./ He came inside my house. [Here the location is more precisely specified.]

/vw mere ghər mḗ daxyl hwa. /   He entered my house. [This sentence
is a trifle more literary than the preceding examples.]

/vw mere ghər ke əndər daxyl hwa. /   He entered into my house. [Again
the location is more elaborately specified.]

15. 120.   /naraz/ A1 "angry, annoyed" denotes a milder degree of displeasure than
/ɣwssa/ M2 "anger, rage. "

15. 121.   /sərdar/ M1 "leader" is used for the leader of a village group, the chief of
a Frontier tribe (e. g.   a Pathan (/pəThan/) or Balochi (/bəloci/) tribal leader), or a male
member of the Sikh religion (always with the honorific /ji/ added: /sərdar ji/).   "Leader"
in the political sense is not usually expressed by /sərdar/ but by some term like /qayd/ M1,
/sərbərah/ M1, or the English loanword /liDər/ M/F1.

15. 122.   /ənjam/ M1 "end, conclusion" overlaps the semantic range of /nətija/ M2
"result, outcome" to some extent. E. g.

/ws ka ənjam kya hwa. /   What was his end? [I. e.   What was his fate?]

/ws ke beTe ka ənjam bəhwt bwra hwa. /   His son came to a bad end.
[Lit.   His son's end was very bad.]

/ws ki hərkətṍ ka bəhwt bwra nətija nykla. /   His actions brought about
a very bad result. [Lit.   His action's very bad result came out.]

15. 123.   /bwra/ A2 is used for moral, abstract, or intangible badness: e. g.   "a bad
action, " "a bad boy, " etc.   /xərab/ A1 more often refers to badness in the physical,
tangible sense: e. g.   "a bad (spoiled) mango, " "a bad road, " "a bad (out of order) machine, "
etc.   /xərab/ is also employed metaphorically for "immoral" and "evil, " but /bwra/ is not
generally used for "bad" in the physical sense.

15. 124.   /əda/ PA1 "paid, accomplished, fulfilled, performed" has various uses. E. g.

/mə̃y ne vw dəs rupəe əda kie. /   I paid that ten rupees.

/mə̃y ne əpna fərz əda kia. /   I performed my duty.

/mə̃y ne pā̃cṍ vəqt ki nəmaz əda ki. /   I performed all five daily prayers.

/ws ne Dyrame mḗ bəhwt əccha rol əda kia. /   He performed very well
[lit.   performed a very good role] in the play. [/rol/ M1 "role. "]

/əda/ also occurs as a F1 noun meaning "grace, manner, blandishment, act of coquetry. "
In the meaning of "paid (etc.), " /əda/ is derived from Arabic, while /əda/ in the sense of
"blandishment (etc.)" is historically from Persian.   These two items must be treated as
separate words.

15. 125.   /ya to ... vərna ... / "either ... or otherwise ... " introduces a new use of
/ya/ Conj "or. " Much more common (but with less contrastive force) is /ya [to] ... ya
... / "either ... or ... " E. g.

/ya to wn ke hã̄ əbhi cəlie, vərna phyr ytvar ko cələ̄ge. /   Either [let us]
go to his place now, or otherwise [we] will go on Sunday.

/ya to šor məcana bənd kəro, ya yəhã̄ se cəle jao! /   Either stop making
noise, or else go away!

/ya to mere sath cəlie, ya yəhĩ so jaie./ Either come [lit. go] with me, or sleep right here!

/ya vw yəhã rəhega, ya mɛ̃y yəhã rəhũga./ Either he will stay here, or I will stay here.

/donõ cizɛ̃ ap ke samne hɛ̃y. ya yse pəsənd kər lɛ̃, ya wse pəsənd kər lɛ̃./ Both things are in front of you. Either choose this one or that one. [Lit. Either like this, or like that.]

/ya vw yələt kəhta həy, ya mɛ̃y yələt kəhta hũ. ys lie ky donõ səhih nəhĩ ho səkte./ Either he is wrong [lit. says wrong] or I am wrong [lit. say wrong]. Because both cannot be correct.

15.126. /zəxm/ M1 "wound" denotes an open wound. /coT/ F1 means "injury, wound" but does not specify whether the skin is broken or not.

15.127. /qədəm/ M1 is not the usual word for "foot"; more common are /pəyr/ M1 or /paδ/ M1. /qədəm/ is common, however, in the meanings of "footstep, pace, step." E.g.

/ap yy qədəm nə wThaie!/ Please don't take this step!

/vw syrf cənd qədəm age rəhta həy./ He lives only a few steps ahead.

/hər qədəm pər ap əysi bwraiã paɛ̃ge./ At every step you will find such evils. [Also /qədəm qədəm pər/.]

15.128. /əllah/ M1 [np] "God" is usually employed only for the Islamic concept of the Deity, although the Jewish and Christian conceptions of the Supreme Being are sometimes called by this term also. More common for the Judaeo-Christian Deity is /xwda/ M1 "God," a term which Muslims also use for /əllah/. In Hindi the Supreme Being is termed /bhəgvan/ M1 or /iʃvər/ M1; deities of the Hindu pantheon are called /deota/ M1 and /devi/ F2.

15.129. /rəfta rəfta/ Adv "gradually, by and by" is only used in this repeated form. /rəfta/ cannot occur as an adverb alone.

15.130. Various set phrases expressing pious sentiments have been borrowed directly from Arabic and Persian, or have been translated into Urdu from an Arabic or Persian source. These phrases are very frequent in conversation, and in some cases, to omit them is to give an impression of impoliteness or even hostility. A few of the commonest are:

(1) /əlhəmdwlyllah[h]/ "praise be to God!" is usually added to almost any statement which describes something that has turned out well. E.g.

/əlhəmdwlylla[h] ws ki təbiət pəhle se byhtər həy./ Thank God [that] his health [lit. disposition] is better than before.

(2) The Urdu form of the preceding phrase is /əllah ka ʃwkr həy, ky .../ "thank God that ..." E.g.

/əllah ka ʃwkr həy, ky vw vapəs a gəya./ Thank God that he has returned.

(3) /ynʃaəlla[h]/ "if God wills" is almost obligatory whenever one speaks of a desirable future possibility. E.g.

460

/ynšaəlla[h] mǟy əgle sal əmrika jaūga./ If God wills, I'll go to America
next year. [A /,/ is optional after /ynšaəlla[h]/.]

(4) /mašaəlla[h]/ "what God wills" is used whenever one speaks of something worthy
of praise or something which one wishes to protect from harm: e.g. someone's good
health, a friend's children, the excellence of a piece of work, etc. E.g.

/ap ke bəcce, mašaəlla[h], bəhwt xubsurət hǟy./ Your children, as God
wills, are very handsome. [Among traditional Muslims, to omit this
phrase is to leave the children open to evil influences and hence an
act of hostility.]

(5) /xwda nəxasta/ "may God forbid" is the opposite of /ynšaəlla[h]/; this phrase is
used whenever one speaks of some undesirable future possibility which one hopes will be
avoided. E.g.

/xwda nəxasta, əgər vw mər gəya, to sare xandan ka kya hal hoga./ God
forbid, if he dies, then what will be the condition of the whole family?

As can be seen from the foregoing, the idea of "attracting evil" is very strong in
traditional Muslim society. As a further illustration, /dwšmən/ M/Fl Al "enemy" is
used as a euphemistic substitute for the name of a loved one whenever one must speak of
something unpleasant happening to that person. In this usage, /dwšmən/ is always
idiomatically plural: thus, instead of saying "X is ill," one says "X's enemies are ill."
E.g.

/mere valyd sahəb ke dwšmənõ ki təbiət xərab ho gəi həy./ My father's
health [lit. disposition] has become bad. [I.e. My father's enemies'
disposition ...]

15.131. Some Complex Verbal Formations:

A:
/əda/
/əda hona/ to be paid, accomplished, fulfilled
/[X ko] əda kərna/ to pay, accomplish, fulfill, perform [X]
/[X ko Y] əda kərna/ to pay [Y to X]
/bərbad/
/bərbad hona/ to be spoiled, ruined, destroyed
/[X ko] bərbad kərna/ to spoil, ruin, destroy [X]
/bərdašt/. [See also B.]
/bərdašt hona/ to be borne, tolerated
/[X ko] bərdašt kərna/ to bear, tolerate [X]
/γələt/
/γələt hona/ to be, become wrong, mistaken
/jwrmana/
/[X ko] jwrmana kərna/ to fine [X]
/naraz/
/naraz hona/ to be, become annoyed, angry
/[X ko] naraz kərna/ to annoy, anger [X]
/qabu/. [See also F.]

/[X ko] qabu kərna/   to overpower, get control of [X]
/təbah/
   /təbah hona/   to be destroyed, ruined, laid waste
   /[X ko] təbah kərna/   to destroy, ruin [X]
/xəbər/. [See also D.]
   /[X ko Y ki] xəbər kərna/   to inform [X of Y]

B:

/əndaza/. [See also F.]
   /[X ka] əndaza hona/   [X] to be estimated, guessed, conjectured
   /[X ka] əndaza kərna/   to estimate, guess, conjecture [X]
/ənjam/. [See also D.]
   /[X ka] ənjam hona/   [X] to be completed, brought to an end
/nwqsan/. [See also D and F.]
   /[X ka] nwqsan hona/   [X] to be harmed, suffer loss
   /[X ka] nwqsan kərna/   to harm, damage [X]
/šwkr/
   /[X pər Y ka] šwkr kərna/   to thank [Y for X]. [Y is always God. If one
   thanks a person then /šwkr kərna/ cannot be used; /šwkria kərna/ will
   be employed instead.]

D:

/ənjam/. [See also B.]
   /[X ko] ənjam dena/   to complete [X]
/əql/
   /[X ko] əql dena/   to set [X] straight
/bədla/
   /[X ko Y ka] bədla dena/   to give [X] the exchange [for Y], to pay [X for Y]
   /[X se] bədla lena/   to take revenge [from X]
   /[X ko Y ka] bədla mylna/   [X] to receive the exchange [for Y], [X] to be
   repaid [for Y]
/bwrai/
   /[X ko] bwrai dena/   to give a bad name [to X]
/mysal/
   /[X ko Y ki] mysal dena/   to give [X] an example [of Y]
   /[X ko Y ki] mysal mylna/   [X] to get an example [of Y]
/nwqsan/. [See also B and F.]
   /[X ko] nwqsan dena/   to cause loss, damage [to X]
   /[X se] nwqsan mylna/   to be damaged [through, because of, by X]
/xəbər/. [See also A.]
   /[X ko Y ki] xəbər dena/   to give [X] news [of Y]
   /[X ko Y ki] xəbər mylna/   [X] to be given news [of Y]
/yttyla/
   /[X ko Y ki] yttyla dena/   to give [X] information [about Y]
   /[X ko Y ki] yttyla mylna/   [X] to be informed, get information [about Y]

F:

/əndaza/. [See also B.]

/[X ka] əndaza ləgana/ to make an estimate [about X], guess [X]

/əsər/

/[X mẽ Y ka] əsər ana/ the influence [of Y] to become apparent [in X]; [X] to inherit the qualities [of Y]

/[X pər] əsər Dalna/ to influence [X]

/[X pər Y ka] əsər hona/ [Y] to have an influence [upon X]

/[X pər] əsər kərna/ to influence [X]

/[X ka] əsər lena/ to be influenced [by X]

/bənd/

/[X pər] bənd bādhna, ləgana/ to build a dike, dam [on X]. [/bādhna/ "to tie, bind."]

/bənduq/

/bənduq bhərna/ to load a gun

/[X pər] bənduq cəlana/ to fire a gun [at X]

/bevwquf/

/[X ko] bevwquf bənana/ to make a fool [of X]

/bevwquf bənna/ to play the fool, act stupidly

/bwra/

/[X mẽ] bwra bənna/ to be wrongly involved [in the matter of X], to be blamed [in the matter of X]

/dwšmən/

/[X ko] dwšmən bənana/ to make an enemy [of X]

/[X ka] dwšmən bənna, hona/ to become an enemy [of X]

/dwšməni/

/[X əwr Y mẽ] dwšməni Dalna/ to create enmity [between X and Y]

/[X se Y ki] dwšməni hona/ [Y] to remain an enemy [of X]

/[X se] dwšməni kərna, nykalna/ to be an enemy of, have enmity [with X]

/yələti/

/[X se] yələti hona/ [X] committed a mistake (with no conscious will whatsoever)

/[X mẽ] yələti kərna/ to make a mistake [in X]

/ywssa/

/[X ko Y pər] ywssa ana/ [X] to become angry [on Y]

/[X pər] ywsse hona/ to become angry [with X]. [Note that the correct form is always /ywsse̱/.]

/[X pər] ywssa wtarna/ to expend rage [upon X]

/jhəgRa/

/[X se Y ka] jhəgRa cəlna/ [Y] to have a quarrel [with X]

/[X əwr Y mẽ] jhəgRa Dalna/ to cause a quarrel [between X and Y]

/[X se Y ka] jhəgRa hona/ [Y] to have a quarrel [with X]

/[X se] jhəgRa kərna/ to quarrel [with X]

/[X se Y ka] jhəgRa pəRna/ [Y] to have a quarrel [with X]

/jwrmana/. [See also A.]

/jwrmana bhərna/   to pay a fine
   /[X ko, pər] jwrmana hona/   [X] to be fined
/laThi/
   /[X pər] laThi cəlana/   to attack [X] with a stave
   /[X ke, pər] laThi marna/   to strike [X] with a stave
/ləRai/
   /[X se] ləRai hona/   to be a fight, battle [with X]
   /[X se] ləRai kərna/   to fight [with X]
/lwtf/
   /[X ko Y mẽ] lwtf ana/   [X] to get pleasure [in Y]
   /[X se] lwtf wThana/   to take pleasure [in X]
/mar/
   /[X ko Y pər] mar pəRna/   [X] to be beaten [because of Y]
/mətləb/
   /[X ka] kya mətləb həy. /   What does [X] mean?
   /[X se Y ka] kya mətləb həy. /   What concern does [Y] have [with X]?
   /[X se] əpna mətləb nykalna/   to utilise [X] for one's own purposes
/nətija/
   /[X ka] yy nətija hona/   [X] to have this result
   /[X ko Y ka] nətija mylna/   [X] to receive the result [of Y]
   /[X se] yy nətija nykalna/   to obtain this result [from X]
   /[X ka] yy nətija nykəlna/   [X] to have this result
/nwqsan/. [See also B and D.]
   /[X ko] nwqsan pəhw̃cana/   to harm, cause loss, damage [X]
   /[X ko] nwqsan pəhw̃cna/   [X] to be harmed, caused loss, damaged
   /[X mẽ] nwqsan wThana/   to suffer a loss [in X]
/pystəwl/
   /pystəwl bhərna/   to load a pistol
   /[X pər] pystəwl cəlana/   to fire a pistol [at X]
/qabu/. [See also A.]
   /[X ke] qabu mẽ ana/   to fall under [X's] control, come into the custody,
        grasp [of X]
   /[X ko] qabu mẽ kərna, lena/   to overpower [X], get control [of X], take [X]
        into custody
   /[X pər] qabu pana/   to gain control [over X], make [X] manageable
/qədəm/
   /[X mẽ] qədəm wThana/   to take a step [in the matter of X]
/səməjh/
   /[X Y ki] səməjh mẽ ana/   [Y] to come to understand [X]
/səylab/
   /səylab ana/   to be a flood
/surət/
   /[X ki] surət nykalna/   to find a way [for X], to find a method by which [X]
        can be done, etc.

/zəxm/

/[X ka] zəxm bhərna/ [X's] wound to heal

/[X ko Y mɛ̃] zəxm ana, pəRna/ [X to be wounded [in Y (a limb)]]

15.200. SCRIPT

15.201. Word Recognition.

(1) Compounds containing the Persian connective /o/ "and" are usually written as separate words:

SCRIPT	PRONUNCIATION	SCRIPT	PRONUNCIATION
آب و ہوا	abohəva	بندوبست	bəndobəst
آمدورفت	amədorəft		

(2) The following words are written with "uncommon" Arabic consonants, with final
ه = /a/, or with other special spelling conventions:

SCRIPT	PRONUNCIATION	SCRIPT	PRONUNCIATION
اثر	əsər	زنده	zynda
اصول	wsul	ساده	sada
اطّلاع	yttyla	سلسله	sylsyla
الله	əllah	صورت	surət
اندازه	əndaza	عجب	əjəb
انشاءالله	ynšaəlla[h]	عجیب	əjib
بدله	bədla	عقل	əql
بعض	baz	علم	ylm
بلکه	bəlke	غصّه	ɣwssa
جرمانه	jwrmana	غلط	ɣələt
حال	hal	غلطی	ɣələti
دراصل	dərəsl	قصّه	qyssa
رفته رفته	rəfta rəfta	لطف	lwtf

466

SCRIPT	PRONUNCIATION	SCRIPT	PRONUNCIATION
ماحول	mahəwl	نتیجہ	nətija
مثال	mysal	نقصان	nwqsan
مطلب	mətləb	واقع	vaqe
ناراض	naraz	یقیناً	yəqinən

15.202. Reading Drill I: Text.

The following is part of Sec. 15.000. Read it aloud several times, striving for speed and accuracy.

مسٹر عزیز۔ کیا آپ نے آج صبح کا اخبار پڑھا ہے ؟

مسٹر اسمتھ۔ جی نہیں ۔ کیا کوئی خاص خبر ہے ؟

مسٹر عزیز۔ جی ہاں۔ بہت افسوس ناک خبر ہے ۔ ہمارے گاؤں کے مشرق کی طرف تقریباً ساٹھ میل دور ایک اور گاؤں ہے ۔ یہ گاؤں دریا کے کنارے پر واقع ہے ۔ کل رات اچانک دریا میں سیلاب آگیا جس سے دریا کا بند ٹوٹ گیا اور سارے گاؤں میں پانی پھیل گیا جس کی وجہ سے کوئی چھپن مکان گر گئے ۔ گاؤں والوں کے کافی جانور مر گئے ۔ اکثر فصلیں تباہ ہوگئیں اور اس کے علاوہ دریا کے پُل کو بھی نقصان پہنچا ہے۔

مسٹر اسمتھ۔ واقعی بہت افسوس ناک خبر ہے ۔ فصلیں اور جانور گاؤں والوں کی دولت ہیں ۔ اگر یہی چیزیں تباہ ہو جائیں تو گاؤں والوں کی زندگی برباد ہو جاتی ہے ۔

مسٹر عزیز۔ بالکل ٹھیک ہے لیکن سب سے بڑا نقصان بند ٹوٹنے اور پُل کو نقصان پہنچنے کا ہے ۔ اس سے حکومت کو لاکھوں روپے کا نقصان ہوا ہے ۔ اور دوسرے آمدو رفت کا سلسلہ بالکل بند ہو گیا ہے ۔

مسٹراسمتھ۔ اب دریا میں پانی کا کیا حال ہے؟

مسٹرعزیز۔ ابھی ابھی خبر آئی ہے کہ پانی پر قابو پا لیا گیا ہے۔

مسٹراسمتھ۔ کیا یہاں سے کچھ لوگ گاؤں والوں کی مدد کے لئے گئے ہیں؟

مسٹرعزیز۔ جی ہاں۔ یہاں سے صبح ہی کچھ آدمیوں کو اس گاؤں بھیج دیا گیا ہے۔ اور اُن
کے ساتھ کھانے پینے کا کافی سامان جیسے آٹا۔ دال اور گوشت وغیرہ بھی
بھجوایا گیا ہے۔

مسٹراسمتھ۔ یہ بہت اچھا کیا۔ اس صورت سے غریب لوگوں کی کچھ مدد ہو جائے گی۔ کیونکہ
ایک دوسرے کی مدد کرنا ہر انسان کا فرض ہے۔

مسٹرعزیز۔ آج کدھر چلنے کا ارادہ ہے؟

مسٹراسمتھ۔ میرا خیال ہے کہ جنگل کی طرف چلیں۔ کچھ دیر سیر کریں گے۔ پھر جلدی واپس لوٹ
آئیں گے کیونکہ آج نمبردار صاحب کے ہاں دعوت پر جانا ہے۔

مسٹرعزیز۔ آئیئے۔ یہ راستہ سیدھا جنگل کو جاتا ہے۔

مسٹراسمتھ۔ مجھے گاؤں کی زندگی بہت پسند ہے۔ یہاں کا ماحول آب و ہوا۔ ہرے
ہرے کھیت۔ لوگوں کی مصروف اور سادہ زندگی ایک عجب لطف رکھتی ہے۔

مسٹرعزیز۔ مجھے خود گاؤں کی زندگی بہت پسند ہے۔ اگرچہ بہت سی خوبیوں کے
ساتھ ساتھ بعض برائیاں شہر کے مقابلے میں یہاں زیادہ پائی جاتی ہیں
جو کبھی کبھی تو دماغ پر بہت اثر کرتی ہیں۔

مسٹراسمتھ۔ برائیوں سے آپ کا کیا مطلب ہے؟

مسٹرعزیز۔ مثال کے طور پر گاؤں میں معمولی سی بات پر لڑائی جھگڑا شروع ہو جاتا ہے۔
یہ لڑائی جھگڑا صرف ایک یا دو آدمیوں تک ہی نہیں رہتا بلکہ اس میں

خاندان کے خاندان تباہ ہو جاتے ہیں۔

مسٹر اسمتھ۔ کیا اس قسم کی لڑائی کی کوئی خاص وجہ ہے؟

مسٹر عزیز۔ دراصل وجہ یہ ہے کہ گاؤں میں کسانوں اور غریب لوگوں کے علاوہ امیر زمیندار بھی رہتے ہیں۔ یہ زمیندار کسی پرانی دشمنی کی وجہ سے آپس میں لڑتے رہتے ہیں اور ہر وقت اس سوچ میں رہتے ہیں کہ کسی نہ کسی طرح اپنے دشمن زمیندار سے بدلہ لیں۔

مسٹر اسمتھ۔ کیا اس قسم کے جھگڑے یہاں اکثر ہوتے رہتے ہیں؟

مسٹر عزیز۔ ابھی پچھلے مہینے کا قصہ ہے کہ ایک زمیندار کے نوکر نے اُسے یہ اطلاع دی کہ اُس کے کھیت میں مخالف پارٹی کی دو بھینسیں گھس آئی ہیں اور فصلوں کو خراب کر رہی ہیں۔ زمیندار یہ سن کر بہت ناراض ہوا اور غصہ میں نوکر کو حکم دیا کہ دونوں بھینسوں کو مار ڈالو۔ چنانچہ یہ نوکر دو اور آدمیوں کو ساتھ لے کر وہاں پہنچا اور دونوں بھینسوں کو مار ڈالا۔

مسٹر اسمتھ۔ بہت بے وقوف آدمی تھے۔ بھینسوں کو مار ڈالنے کی بجائے کھیت سے نکال دینا چاہتے تھا۔ اس کے بعد کیا ہوا؟

مسٹر عزیز۔ جب مخالف پارٹی کو یہ معلوم ہوا کہ اُن کی دو بھینسیں مار دی گئی ہیں تو اُن کے سردار نے ایک شخص کے ہاتھ یہ پیغام بھیجا کہ "ہم سے یہ حرکت برداشت نہیں کی جائے گی۔ یا تو ہماری بھینسیں واپس کرو ورنہ اس کا انجام بہت برا ہوگا۔" دوسرے زمیندار نے یہ جواب دیا کہ "تمہاری بھینسوں نے ہماری فصلوں کا بہت نقصان کیا ہے یا تو اس نقصان کی رقم ادا کرو ورنہ لڑائی کے لئے تیار ہو جاؤ۔"

15. 203. Reading Drill II: Sentences.

Read the following sentences aloud and translate them into English.

۱۔ جب لوگوں کو آمد و رفت بند ہونے کا پتہ چلا تو وہ پریشان ہو گئے۔

۲۔ یہ غلط ہے۔اس کا مطلب یہ نہیں ہے بلکہ کچھ اور ہے۔

۳۔ پاکستان میں عام لوگوں کا کھانا صرف آٹے کی روٹی کچھ دال اور گوشت کا سالن ہے۔

۴۔ جوں جوں پودوں میں یہ جراثیم پھیلتے گئے فصلیں برباد ہوتی گئیں۔

۵۔ دعوت میں آنے والوں کو پاکستانی کھانا کھلایا جائے گا۔

۶۔ اُسے اکثر سمجھایا جاتا ہے لیکن وہ اپنی شرارتیں نہیں چھوڑتا۔

۷۔ لوگ صرف اُس کی برائیوں کو دیکھتے ہیں لیکن مجھے معلوم ہے کہ اُس میں کچھ خوبیاں بھی ہیں۔

۸۔ اِس موقع پر بالکل سادہ کپڑے پہنے جاتے ہیں۔

۹۔ بعض ڈاکٹروں کا خیال ہے کہ اِس سال ٹی بی پر قابو پا لیا جائے گا۔

۱۰۔ جنگل میں ایک پرانا قلعہ ہے جو اب بالکل تباہ ہو گیا ہے اگر آپ دیکھنے کا ارادہ رکھتے ہیں تو چوکیدار آنے والا ہے۔وہ آپ کو دکھا دے گا۔

۱۱۔ یہ عمارت سنہ ۱۹۴۱ء میں بنائی گئی تھی سنہ ۱۹۵۰ء کے سیلاب میں تباہ ہو گئی اور اب صرف کچھ پتھر اور دیواریں باقی ہیں۔

۱۲۔ مجھے یہ اندازہ نہ تھا کہ یہ کام اِتنا مشکل ہو گا۔

۱۳۔ دراصل اِس لڑائی کی وجہ یہ تھی کہ اُس نے زمیندار صاحب کی گائے کو مار ڈالا تھا۔ اِس طرح دشمنی پیدا ہو گئی اور رفتہ رفتہ بڑھتی گئی۔

۱۴۔ صبح صبح سیر کرنے میں عجب لطف آتا ہے۔

۱۵۔ اِس دروازے کی چابی ابھی نمبردار صاحب لائیں گے۔پھر ہم اِس کمرے کو دیکھ سکیں گے۔

470

اِس سال بارش نہ ہونے سے کسان بہت پریشان ہیں ۔ اگر ایک ہینہ کے اندر بارش نہ
ہوئی تو فصلیں تباہ ہو جائیں گی ۔

۱۷۔ زمیندار صاحب کو یہ معلوم نہ تھا کہ ایسی مشینیں کرایہ پر بھی ملتی ہیں ورنہ وہ اُنہیں انگلستان
سے نہ منگواتے ۔

15. 204. Writing Drill I; Text.

Counting each speaker's part as one paragraph, write out the first ten paragraphs of
Sec. 15. 506 (Conversation Practice) in Urdu script (i. e. down through /... kwch nə kwch
bəndobəst kərna cahie. /).

15. 205. Spelling Review and Dictionary Drill.

Write out the following words in Urdu script and place them in Urdu alphabetical order.

(1) zynda	(20) təsvir
(2) ag	(21) məzbut
(3) zəraət	(22) pəhw̃cna
(4) mwxalyf	(23) bənna
(5) ylm	(24) məwqa
(6) nwqsan	(25) vaqe
(7) jəw	(26) jo
(8) həl	(27) qanun
(9) mərzi	(28) mwxtəsər
(10) jū	(29) pɛ̃ytalis
(11) dyhli	(30) səhih
(12) hal	(31) pəwna
(13) hymmət	(32) gyara
(14) həva	(33) mwtəəllyq
(15) yntyzam	(34) əndaza
(16) xansamā	(35) upər
(17) ɣwsl	(36) kəi
(18) ərsa	(37) šərmynda
(19) fərz	(38) yəqinən

15. 206. Response Drill.

Answer the following questions in writing; (Answers to these questions should be based
upon Secs. 15. 000 and 15. 506.)

۱۔ اسمتھ صاحب کے قصّے میں زمیندار کیوں مارا گیا ؟

۲۔ اسمتھ صاحب کے قصّے میں زمیندار صاحب اُس آدمی کو کیوں نکالنا چاہتے تھے ؟

۳۔ پاکستان میں گاؤں والوں کی لڑائیوں کی سب سے اہم وجہ کیا ہے؟

۴۔ کیا آپ کے خیال میں دشمنی رکھنا اور بدلہ لینا صحیح اصول ہیں؟

۵۔ نمبردار صاحب کے گاؤں میں اسکول جانے والے لڑکوں کی تعداد بڑھ گئی ہے یا گھٹ گئی ہے؟

۶۔ کیا اسمتھ صاحب ایک غریب خاندان میں پیدا ہوئے تھے ؟

۷۔ عزیز صاحب کے خیال میں سیلاب کا سب سے بڑا نقصان کیا تھا؟

۸۔ عزیز صاحب کی کہانی میں لڑائی کا کیا نتیجہ نکلا؟

۹۔ کیا یہ بات صحیح ہے کہ اسمتھ صاحب کا گاؤں امریکہ کے شمال میں واقع ہے ؟

۱۰۔ کیا اسمتھ صاحب کے والد صاحب کی اپنی زمین تھی ؟

15. 207. **English to Urdu Sentences.**

1. I have heard that the dike of the river is about to break.
2. When he suddenly burst out crying, I asked him, [that] "Why are you crying?"
3. So long as [lit. until when] you are alive, your wealth will be useful [lit. will come into work].
4. When you die [lit. died], then your wealth will be of no use at all [lit. will not come into any work].
5. My crops have suffered a loss worth ten thousand rupees. [Lit. To my crops ten thousand rupees of loss has happened.]
6. I'll pay your amount [in] some way or other.
7. Not only have the crops been ruined, but [in addition] the whole village has been destroyed.
8. The landlord and the village elder fell to fighting with one another.
9. In that fight two hundred men were killed, and about a hundred and fifty were wounded.
10. You yourself can estimate what the result of this will be.
11. Either go with me to Lahore, or else you'll have to wait here.
12. Because of this medicine, my stomach pain [lit. my stomach's pain] is growing less.

13. This sad event affected his life most unfortunately. [Lit. This sad event poured [a] very bad effect upon his life.]

14. In Pakistan education is gradually expanding. For example, in our village three new schools have been opened.

15. Somebody or other must have given him this message.

15.300. ANALYSIS

15.301. Substantive Composition: Persian Copulative Compounds.

Many Persian loanwords are in fact compounds of two elements joined by /o/ "and."
Stems employed in such compounds may be nouns, adjectives, participles, verb stems, etc.
(see Sec. 18.307) in Persian, but in Urdu some of these constructions are better treated as
single words. In compounds like /bəndobəst/ M1 [np] "arrangement, management," for
example, no word juncture occurs between /bənd/ and /o/ or between /o/ and /bəst/, and
this construction behaves as a unitary word in the intonation pattern. Other such compounds,
however, must be treated as two separate words joined by /o/: these usually consist of
two words which have independent status in Urdu: e.g. /dərd o ɣəm/ "pain and grief"
(/dərd/ M1 "pain" and /ɣəm/ M1 "grief, sorrow"); word juncture is common, though not
obligatory, between the elements of this compound. These Persian loan formations
become more and more frequent as one progresses through various types of prose into the
realm of Urdu poetry.

Items introduced thus far include:

> /abohəva/ F1 [np] climate. [Two nouns: /ab/ "water" (which does not
> occur independently in Urdu with this meaning) + /həva/ F1 "air,
> wind," which does occur as a separate Urdu word.]
>
> /amədorəft/ F1 [np] communication, transportation. [Two past stems:
> /aməd/ from the root /amə/ "come" and /rəft/ from /rəf/ "go."]
>
> /bəndobəst/ M1 [np] arrangement, management. [Present and past
> stem of the same verb root: /bəs/ "tie, bind." See Sec. 18.307.]

These Persian loan constructions are analogous to those Urdu formations discussed in
Sec. 3.110: i.e. two nouns, infinitives, etc. employed as a single unit with no intervening
conjunction. Like the Persian compounds, these Urdu formations consist of two items which
are almost synonymous, or which share some common semantic feature (and which are
often alliterative or metrically similar as well). E.g.

> /chwri kāTa/   knife [and] fork
>
> /dyn rat/   day [and] night
>
> /khana pina/   food [and] drink
>
> /ləRai jhəgRa/   fighting [and] quarreling
>
> /do tin/   two [or] three: [Such numerical compounds are common: they
> differ from the preceding examples, however, in that they mean
> "two or three," "four or five," rather than "two and three," etc.]

15.302. Substantive Composition: the Prefix /na/.

Another negative prefix occurring mostly with Persian loanwords is /na/ "un-, non-."
This element is found with nouns, adjectives, and predicate adjectives, and the resulting
construction is usually an adjective (and occasionally a predicate adjective). This prefix is
seen in this Unit in /naraz/ A1 "angry, annoyed." This word is somewhat unusual since
*/raz/ does not occur as an independent word; the positive form is /razi/ PA1 "pleased,
satisfied, agreed." The abstract noun form of /naraz/ is also unexpected: /narazgi/ F2

"annoyance, displeasure." (As was seen in Sec. 13.301, /gi/ normally occurs only after Perso-Arabic adjectives ending in an original /ə/; one might thus have expected /narazi/, a form which is indeed given as a rare variant in some dictionaries.) Other examples possible with the vocabulary given so far include:

/ciz/ F1 thing	/naciz/ M/F1 A1 most humble. [A self-deprecatory term used when speaking of oneself in highly polite letters, etc.]
/kafi/ A1 enough	/nakafi/ PA1 insufficient
/mwmkyn/ PA1 possible	/namwmkyn/ PA1 impossible
/mwnasyb/ A1 suitable, fitting	/namwnasyb/ A1 unsuitable
/pəsənd/ PA1 pleasing	/napəsənd/ PA1 displeasing
/qabyl/ A1 able, capable	/naqabyl/ A1 incapable, unfit
/təmam/ A1 all, complete	/natəmam/ A1 incomplete, imperfect
/wmmid/ F1 hope	/nawmmid/ PA1 hopeless, despairing
/xwš/ PA1 happy	/naxwš/ A1 unhappy

Two of the above are found with the abstract noun formant suffix /i/:

/nawmmid/ PA1 hopeless, despairing	/nawmmidi/ F2 hopelessness, despair
/naxwš/ A1 unhappy	/naxwši/ F2 unhappiness

15.303. Substantive Composition: the Suffix /nak/.

Still another adjective formant suffix found in Persian loanwords is /nak/ "-full." This affix occurs with nouns denoting something unpleasant, painful, terrible, etc., and the resultant formation is an adjective. Of the vocabulary given thus far, the following constructions are found:

/əfsos/ M1 sorrow, regret	/əfsosnak/ A1 sad, sorrowful
/dərd/ M1 pain	/dərdnak/ A1 painful, anguished

15.304. Emphatic Totality: the <X ka X> Construction.

Emphatic totality or plurality is sometimes expressed by the repetition of a noun or adjective, with the repetitions separated by /ka/, /ke/, or /ki/. In the singular, this construction expresses the totality of the noun: e.g. /xandan ka xandan/ "the whole family," /fəsl ki fəsl/ "the whole crop." In the plural, this formation denotes emphatic plurality: whole quantities of the noun: e.g. /xandan ke xandan/ "whole families," /šəhr ke šəhr/ "city after city," /fəslẽ ki fəslẽ/ "whole crops," etc. Note that the noun preceding /ke/ or /ki/ does not usually take the expected MOP or FOP ending /õ/. Some speakers, however, do use the oblique plural forms, saying /fəslõ ki fəslẽ/ instead of /fəslẽ ki fəslẽ/. This construction is rather limited, and the student would be wise to check with an Urdu speaker about the idiomaticity of any given construction. E.g.

/šəhr ka šəhr təbah ho gəya./ The whole city was destroyed.

/ghər ke ghər təbah ho gəe./ Whole houses [house after house] were destroyed.

/fəsl ki fəsl bərbad ho gəi. /   The whole crop was destroyed.

/səb ke səb yəhā se cəle gəe. /   Absolutely everyone [lit. all of all]
went away from here.

/həyze ki vəja se, sare ke sare gaõvale bimar ho gəe. /   Because of
cholera, absolutely all of the villagers became sick.

/təmam ki təmam fəsl təbah ho gəi. /   The entire crop was destroyed.

15.305.   The <X nə X> Construction: " ... or Other. "

Another construction, limited only to a few indefinites and adverbs, expresses "...
or other. " Examples are:

/koi nə koi/   somebody or other

/kysi nə kysi/   somebody or other. [The oblique form of /koi nə koi/.]

/kwch nə kwch/   something or other

/kəbhi nə kəbhi/   some time or other

/kəhī̃ nə kəhī̃/   somewhere or other. [/kəhā̃/ "where?" + /hi/: note
that /kəhī̃/ is used only to mean "somewhere" and never "where-
emphatic?"]

This construction should not be confused with the "distributive" formation, in which
the word is repeated without /nə/:

/koi koi/   various persons

/kwch kwch/   various things, somewhat

/kəbhi kəbhi/   now and then

/kəhī̃ kəhī̃/   here and there

Examples of the <X nə X> construction:

/vəhā̃ koi nə koi zərur hoga. /   Somebody or other will certainly be there.

/yəhā̃ koi nə koi to wse zərur janta hoga. /   Somebody or other must
surely know him here. [Note that /to/ often accompanies the /X nə
X/ construction;   /to/ adds a connotation of emphatic assertion or
insistance.]

/yy jəga kysi nə kysi ko zərur malum hogi. /   This place must certainly
be known to someone or other.

/yy kam kysi nə kysi təriqe se ho səkta həy. /   This job can be done by
some method or other.

/ys sylsyle mē̃, kwch nə kwch ho səkta həy. /   In this connection something or other can be done [lit. can become].

/mere khane ke lie, kwch nə kwch to bəc gəya hoga. /   Something or other
must have been left over for my dinner.

/vw šəxs kəbhi nə kəbhi to yəhā̃ aega. /   That person will come here at
some time or other.

/tələš kərne ke bad, mwjrym kəhī̃ nə kəhī̃ zərur myl jaega. /   After
searching, the culprit will certainly be found somewhere or other.

/dwnya mē̃ həmešа kəhī̃ nə kəhī̃ ləRai hoti rəhti həy. /   In the world there
is always a fight going on somewhere or other.

15.306.   The Relative Adverb /jū̃/ "As, Like. "

/jū̃ jū̃/ "just as, at the same time as" is the repeated form of the now nearly obsolete

476

adverb /jū/ "as, how, in the manner of, like," mentioned in Sec. 7.309. In old Urdu, a relative clause beginning with /jū jū/ was followed by a correlative clause that began with /tū tū/ (or /tyū tyū/) "thus, in that way." This is no longer so in modern Urdu; the correlative clause now requires no introductory element.

Although /jū/ no longer occurs alone, it may occur with /hi/ "emphatic particle" meaning "at the time that, at the moment that ..." E.g.

/jū jū vw buRha hota jaega, ws ki nəzər kəmzor hoti jaegi./ As he grows [lit. keeps becoming] old[er], his sight will become weak[er].

/jū jū mɛ̄y age gəya, mera Dər bəRhta gəya./ As I went on ahead, my fear kept increasing.

/jū jū ap bəRhte jaẽge, gaõ nəzdik ata jaega./ As you keep moving ahead, the village will keep coming closer.

/jū hi mɛ̄y əndər aya, ws ne mwjhe pəkəR lia./ The moment I entered, he caught me.

15.307. The Verb: Two More Conjunct Verbs.

Sec. 15.000 contains two further examples of conjunct verbal formations (see Secs. 13.303 and 14.303): /ləwT aẽge/ "will return [MP]" and /ghws ai hɛ̄y/ "have entered [FP]."

15.308. The Verb: the <S + /Dalna/> Construction.

A transitive verb stem + an inflected form of /Dalna/ "to pour" denotes violent completive action. This construction has the same restrictions as those listed for other intensive auxiliaries in Sec. 13.303. E.g.

/ws ne wse mar Dala./ He killed him. [Lit. hit-poured. /mar Dalna/ appears to mean "to hit intensively" but is always used for "to kill."]

/ws ne fəwrən dərəxt kaT Dala./ He cut the tree down [violently] at once.

/vw wse khol Dalega./ He'll open it [forcefully, violently].

/mɛ̄y ne ek ghənTe mẽ sari kytab pəRh Dali./ I finished reading the whole book in one hour. [I.e. I read the whole book completely and intensively: "finished it off."]

/mɛ̄y ne yy kam kər Dala./ I finished this job. [I.e. I did this work intensively and completely.]

/vw to mwjhe mar Dalne ləge the, ky polis a gəi./ They had started to kill me when [lit. that] the police arrived. [The <S + /Dalna/> construction is sometimes found as the stem nucleus of other tense-aspect constructions also; here it occurs in the <OI + /ləgna/> formation; see Sec. 9.311. Another example:]

/vw to sare ke sare dərəxt kaT Dalne ləge the, ky nəmbərdar a gəya./ They were about to cut down all the trees when the village elder came.

15.309. The Verb: the <S + /pəRna/> Construction.

An intransitive verb stem + an inflected form of /pəRna/ "to fall, befall, happen" denotes violent, sudden, and possibly unexpected action. This construction also has the same restrictions as were given for other intensive auxiliaries in Sec. 13.303. The distribution of this formation is limited, of course, to occurrences with verb stems denoting actions which can take place suddenly. The <S + /pəRna/> construction must be carefully distinguished from the <I + /pəRna/> form, which means "to be compelled to ..., must ..." (see Sec. 9.310). E.g.

/vw ləRka ro pəRa./   That boy burst out crying. [Lit. cry-fell.]

/vw chət pər se gyr pəRa./   He fell off the roof. [The connotation is that he fell suddenly and violently.]

/əjəb pərešani a pəRi həy./   A strange distress has come. [I.e. has come all of a sudden -- has come suddenly and overwhelmed [us].]

/məy swba sat bəje əpne ghər se cəl pəRa tha./   I had started off from my house at seven o'clock in the morning. [/cəl pəRna/ idiomatically means "to start off."]

/əpna ghər choR kər, vw dusrõ ke ghər ja pəRa./   Having left his own house, he went [and planted himself as a burden] to the house of others. [/ja pəRna/ idiomatically means "to go and force oneself upon."]

/bəcce ko nə marẽ! vw ro pəRega./   Don't hit the child! He'll burst out crying.

/meri yy bat swn kər, vw hõs pəRa./   On hearing these words [lit. this word] of mine, he burst out laughing.

15.310. The Verb: the <PreP + /jana/> Construction.

The present participle is found with an inflected form of /jana/ "to go." This construction has four important uses:

(1) With an animate subject (i.e. a subject which has the power of willing), the <PreP + /jana/> construction may mean "to keep on ... ing." This often has the sense of "persevering in spite of some obstacle." Although this construction may occur in any tense form, it does not occur with the aspect and intensive auxiliaries (except the continuative). It is also not found in negative sentences. E.g.

/vw kam kərta jata həy./   He keeps on [determinedly, perseveringly] at his work.

/məy bolta jaũga, əwr ap lykhte jaẽge./   I'll keep on speaking, and you keep on writing. [I.e. I will go on dictating, and you will keep writing down what I say.]

/məy əpna kam kərta gəya./   I kept right on doing my work. [Perhaps in spite of some obstacle.]

/jəhã tək ho səkega, məy əpna kam kərta jaũga./   So far as possible [lit. up to where [it] will be able to become], I'll keep on doing my work.

(2) With an inanimate subject (i.e. a subject which has no will of its own), this construction denotes the gradual modification of a state: "to go on ... ing." E.g.

/yy bwraiã kəm hoti ja rəhi hõy./   These evils are gradually decreasing. [I.e. They are slowly becoming less over a period of time.]

/gəndwm mõhgi hoti ja rəhi həy./   Wheat is continuing to be become [more and more] expensive.

/əgər ap log bərabər yyhi fəsl wgate jaẽge, to zəmin kəmzor hoti jaegi./ If you people go on [i.e. insist, persevere] sowing only this crop, the soil will keep getting weaker. [Other examples were given above in Sec. 15. 306.]

478

(3) The <PreP + /jana/> construction may also have the sense of "concomitant action";
i. e. the performance of an action while some other action is also in progress. In such
cases the connotation of determination or perseverance against obstacles may be lost to
some extent. E. g.

/kam kərte jao, jəb tək ky həm səb yəhā məwjud hɜ̃y./ Keep on working,
so long as [lit. until when that] we are all here.

/jo kwch mɜ̃y kəh rəha hū, əcchi təra swnte jao!/ Whatever I am saying,
you go on listening [to it] well!

/meri bivi khana pəkati jati həy, əwr batē bhi kərti jati həy./ My wife
keeps on cooking and also keeps on talking. [Here the connotation of
determination or perseverance is still maintained; see also the
second example under (1) above.]

/əbhi to kwch nəhī̃ hwa. dekhte jao, kya hota həy!/ As yet nothing has
happened. Just keep watching what happens!

(4) This construction has still another usage: in some cases the inflected form of
/jana/ retains its original meaning of "to go, " and the present participle has the force of
the <S + /kər/> formation (i. e. the "conjunctive participle"; see Sec. 5.308). E. g.

/yy cizē wn ke hā dete jaie!/ Please give these things to him [lit. at
his place] on your way! [Lit. These things ... giving, please go!]

/əbhi kafi vəqt həy. cae pite jaie!/ There is still enough time. Please
have some tea before you go! [Lit. Drinking tea, please go!
Roughly equivalent to /cae pi kər jaie!/]

/bəcca ro rəha həy. yse dudh pylati jaie!/ The child is crying. Please
give him milk before you [F] go! [Lit. To him milk giving, please
go!]

15. 311. The Verb: the <PasP + /jana/> Construction.

It was shown in Sec. 9.306 that Urdu contains two basic types of verbal stems: (1)
basically intransitive stems, which may be made transitive or causative by the addition of
affixes, stem vowel alternation, etc. and (2) basically transitive stems, which may be made
causative, double causative, or intransitive by much the same methods. An intransitive
stem thus produced from a transitive base stem is often best translated by an English
passive construction. E. g.

/kaTna/ to cut   /kəTna/ to be cut
/kholna/ to open   /khwlna/ to be opened, to come open
/toRna/ to break   /TuTna/ to be broken, to break (of oneself)

There is also a true passive construction. This consists of the past participle + an
inflected form of /jana/ "to go." The difference between this passive formation and an
intransitive verb stem derived from a transitive base stem must be noted: the former is
employed when the action is intentionally performed, but the actor is unknown (or un-
revealed); the latter is used when the action occurs of itself, and no willing of the action
is implied. Compare:

/gylas TuT gəya./ The glass broke. [No actor is implied; the focus is
upon the breaking of the glass alone. Compare:]

/gylas toRa gəya./ The glass was broken. [This implies that the breakage
was intentional, but the actor is either unknown or not revealed.]

/dərəxt kəT gəya./   The tree was cut [down].   [The focus is upon the
action of cutting, and, although the action must have been performed
by some actor, none is implied in this sentence. Compare:]

/dərəxt kaTa gəya./   The tree was cut [down].   [The cutting was
deliberately and intentionally done by some actor not expressed or
not known.]

A sample paradigm of the passive construction is:

PRONOUN	VERB: MASCULINE	FEMININE	
mə̃y	mara jata hū̃	mari jati hū̃	I am hit
[tu	mara jata həy	mari jati həy	thou art hit]
vw	mara jata həy	mari jati həy	he, she, it is hit
həm	mare jate hə̃y	mari jati hə̃y	we are hit
twm	mare jate ho	mari jati ho	you [nonhonorific] are hit
ap	mare jate hə̃y	mari jati hə̃y	you [honorific] are hit
vw	mare jate hə̃y	mari jati hə̃y	they are hit

As previously noted, women usually employ the masculine plural form for "we": /həm
mare jate hə̃y/ instead of /həm mari jati hə̃y/.

The past participle and the inflected form of /jana/ both agree with the subject (so far
as possible) in number, gender, and person. The passive is found with all aspect and
intensive auxiliaries (i. e. /cwkna/, /səkna/, /dena/, /lena/, etc. etc.). It occurs in all
tenses and is common in negative sentences.

It is noteworthy that the actor is never expressed in an Urdu passive sentence: "The
man was hit by me. " is simply not possible; if the actor is to be expressed, then the
active form of the sentence must be employed instead: "I hit the man. "

The instrument by which an action is performed can be expressed in a passive sentence,
however, usually with /se/ "with. " If the verb is causative or double causative, this
instrument may be a person (e. g. "This tree was caused to be cut by the servant. "), but
this person is still only the instrument -- the real subject (i. e. the one who caused the
servant to act) is never expressed. Similarly, the source or origin of a passive action may
be expressed by such postpositions as /[ke] hath/ "by, by the hand of, " /[ke] zərie [se]/
"through, by means of, " /[ki] tərəf se/ "from, from the direction of, " etc. E. g.

/xət lykha gəya. /   The letter was written.

/xət ws se lykhvaya gəya. /   The letter was caused to be written by him.
[/ws se/ "by him" here refers to the person employed as an instrument by the unknown actor.]

/xət qələm se lykha gəya. /   The letter was written by a pen. [/qələm/
Ml [or Fl] "pen" is the instrument.]

/səb pəyse de die jaẽge. /   All of the money will be given away.

/səb fəsl kaT li gəi həy. /   All of the crop has been cut. [By an unknown
actor for the benefit of the speaker.]

/mwjrym nəhī̃ pəkRa ja səka. /   The culprit could not be caught.

/kytab mə̃gvai ja cwki həy. əb to ap ko xəridni pəRegi. /   The book has
already been ordered [lit. has finished being caused to be requested].
Now you will have to buy [it].

/aj sərsõ kaTi ja rəhi həy./   Today the mustard seed [crop] is being cut.

/səb saman pəhw̃caya jaega./   All of the baggage will be delivered [lit. will be caused to arrive.]

/yy pəyyam nəwkər ke hath bhyjvaya gəya./   This message was sent by the hand of the servant.

/yy saman həvai jəhaz ke zərie [se] mãgvaya gəya./   These goods were ordered by [lit. by means of] airplane.

/yy kytabẽ yskul ki tərəf se masTər sahəb ko pes̆ ki gəĩ./   These books were presented to the teacher on behalf of the school.

Examples of less frequent constructions:

/əb to ys qysm ke kəpRe hər jəga pəhne jane ləge hãy./   Now this sort of clothing has begun to be worn everywhere.

/ws ke bad ek nəya pwl bənaya jana tha, lekyn nəhĩ bən səka./   After that a new bridge was to be built, but it could not be constructed. [/bənaya jana tha/ is also stylistically archaic; better would be /... ek nəya pwl bənna tha .../.]

/ek xət əwr lykha jana cahie./   One more letter ought to be written. [Also old-fashioned: this is now better expressed with an active construction: /ek xət əwr lykhna cahie./]

The student may sometimes see examples of the "habitual" construction (i.e. <PasP + /kərna/>; see Sec. 14.306) or the "iterative" construction (i.e. <PreP + /rəhna/>; see Sec. 14.305) in passive sentences quoted in older grammars (e.g. /pəkaya kia jata həy/ "is habitually being cooked" or /pəkaya jata rəhega/ "will repeatedly be cooked"), but these are now so rare as to be practically non-existent.

Another important "irregularity" must yet be noted: viz. where the <u>subject</u> of the passive sentence would be the <u>object</u> of the corresponding active sentence, the transitive object-marker /ko/ may be optionally carried over into the passive sentence! The logical subject of the passive verb, then, appears to be an object marked by /ko/, and the sentence is grammatically "subject-less." In such sentences the passive verb must then be treated as impersonal: it is always masculine singular in form. E.g.

/kwch admiõ ko ws gaõ bhej dia gəya həy./   Some men have been sent to that village. [The logical subject /kwch admi/ "some men" is here marked by /ko/, and the verb is then made MS. The same sentence without /ko/ is equally correct and is also perhaps somewhat more common:]

/kwch admi ws gaõ bhej die gəe hãy./   Some men have been sent to that village. [Here the MP verb agrees with the MP subject, as one might expect. The active form of this sentence would be:]

/[ws ne] kwch admiõ ko ws gaõ bhej dia həy./   [He] has sent some men to that village. [Informants felt that the /ko/ of this sentence "carried over" into the first example above.]

/ws ləRki ko bwlaya gəya həy./   That girl has been called. [Or:]

/vw ləRki bwlai gəi həy./   That girl has been called. [This is the expected form. The active sentence would be:]

/[ws ne] ws ləRki ko bwlaya həy./   [He] has called that girl.

One more construction based on the passive formation is worthy of the student's attention: this is the "passive of incapability." In this formation, the actor is always expressed (marked by /se/ "with, by"), and the sentence is always negative. Some examples will clarify its use:

481

/bimari ki vəja se, ws əwrət se pəkaya nəhĩ jata. /   Because of illness,
that woman cannot [i. e. is physically unable to] cook. [Here the
logical subject, /əwrət/ "woman, " is marked by /se/, and the verb
thus cannot agree with the subject in number-gender-person. Since
there is no object (which would otherwise govern the number-gender
of the verb), the verb is treated as impersonal and is MS.]

/dərd ki vəja se, meri bivi se cəla nəhĩ jata. /   Because of pain, my wife
cannot walk. [Note that in these examples the negative /nəhĩ/ "not"
stylistically occurs between the PasP and the form of /jana/.]

/kəl rat, pəresani ki vəja se, mwjh se soya nəhĩ gəya. /   Last night
because of anxiety I could not sleep. [Here, as in all of these examples,
the sense of physical incapability is emphasised., /məy nəhĩ so səka/
is also correct but is less emphatic.]

/yy kytab mwjh se pəRhi nəhĩ jati. /   I just can't read this book. [Here
the object, /kytab/ F1 "book, " governs the number-gender of the
verb.]

/mwjh se vəhā jaya nəhĩ jata. /   I am just not able to go there. [Note
that in this construction not only are intransitive verbs found in
apparently "passive" formations, but the past participle of /jana/
"to go" is /jaya/ rather than /gəya/ as was seen for the "habitual"
construction in Sec. 14.306!]

/mwjh se yy dəvai pi nəhĩ jati. /   I just can't drink this medicine. [Again,
note that the number-gender of the expressed object governs that of
the verb. Compare:]

/mwjh se əwr khana khaya nəhĩ jaega. /   I just will not be able to eat any
more food.

15.312. The Verb: the <OI + /vala/> Construction.

Various uses of /val/ + the Type II affixes have been previously discussed in Secs.
4.308 and 14.301. The inflected infinitive + /val/ + the Type II affixes is employed as
follows:

(1) As an adjective:

/vw vaqəi kam kərnevala ləRka həy. /   He is really a hardworking boy.
[Lit. work-doing-one boy.]

/vw bəhwt pəRhnevala ləRka həy. /   He is a boy who reads a lot. [Lit.
much reading-one boy.]

/aj vw fwTbal khelnevale ləRke nəhĩ aẽge. /   Today those boys who play
football will not come. [Lit. football playing-one boys.]

/yy nwqsan denevali ciz həy. /   This is a harmful thing. [Lit. loss
giving-one thing.]

(2) As a Type II noun:

/səb khelnevalõ ko jəma kijie! /   Please gather all the players! [Lit.
playing-ones.]

/pakystan mẽ kəpRe dhonevale səb mərd hote hə̃y. /   In Pakistan all the
clothes washers are men. [Lit. clothes washing-ones.]

/ys xəbər se, swnnevalõ ko bəhwt əfsos hwa. /   By this news, all the
hearers were made very sad. [Lit. To all hearing-ones much
sorrow became.]

(3) Followed by an inflected form of the verb /hona/ "to be, become, " <OI + /vala/>
construction gives an inceptive meaning: i.e. "about to ..., " "on the point of ...ing. "
Here, however, the inflected infinitive must be treated as a separate word unit since the

482

emphatic particle /hi/ can occur between it and /val/. This construction is extremely common. E. g.

> /mɛ̃y əbhi ane vala hū. / I am on the point of coming. [I. e. I have not left yet, but I am on the point of departure.]

> /yy divar gyrne vali həy. / This wall is about to fall down.

> /vw log əb nykəlne vale hõge. / Those people must be about to go out.

> /yy ləRka cori kərne hi vala tha, ky polis pəhw̃c gəi. / This boy was on the very point of committing theft, when [lit. that] the police arrived.

> /mɛ̃y ap ko bətane hi vala tha, ky ws ne mwjhe rok dia. / I was just on the point of telling you, when [lit. that] he stopped me.

15.400. SUPPLEMENTARY VOCABULARY

15.401. Supplementary Vocabulary.

The following numerals are all Type I adjectives. See Sec. 2.401.

səttavən	fifty-seven
əTThavən	fifty-eight
wnsəTh	fifty-nine

Other items are:

jwnub M1 [np]	south
mar F1 [np]	beating
məγryb M1 [np]	west
šymal [or /šwmal/] M1 [np]	north
zəxm M1	wound
zynda A1	alive, living

15.402. Supplementary Exercise I: Substitution.

1.
səttays	əwr tis	kytne hote hə̃y.	səttavən.
twenty-five	thirty-three		fifty-eight
forty	nineteen		fifty-nine
twelve	forty-four		fifty-six
seventeen	forty-three		sixty
twenty-two	thirty-two		fifty-four

2.
kya, ap ka mwlk pakystan ke	jwnub mẽ	vaqe həy?
	in the east	
	in the north	
	in the west	
	near	
	in the south	

15.501. Substitution.

1. <u>sygreT</u>   <u>twmhari syhət</u>   pər bwra əsər Dalega.[1]
    these quarrels   the life of the villagers
    this story   the mind of children
    such an   the young [pl.]
    environment
    this error   your future life
    this news   the patient

[1]Make /Dalega/ agree in number-gender with the subject of each sentence.

2. ws ne ys sylsyle mẽ   <u>səməjh</u>   se kam nəhĩ lia.
                          reason
                          mind
                          his knowledge
                          his principle
                          his wealth

3. mera xyal həy, ky   <u>jə̃gəl</u>   ki tərəf cəlẽ.
                        west
                        east
                        the landlord's
                        field
                        north
                        south

4. ws ne wse   <u>laThi</u>   se mara.
                pistol
                gun
                bullet
                stone
                knife

5. mə̃y   <u>əpne dwšmən</u>   se   <u>bədla</u>   le lũga.
          that lawyer   [a] fine
          that landlord   this amount
          the village elder   some flour and lentils
          the opposing party   revenge
          the chief   the pistol

6. <u>ws ka dost</u>   <u>əcanək</u>   <u>mər gəya hoga.</u>[1]
    the water of the   gradually   must have decreased
    flood
    the chain of   surely   must have been cut
    communication
    the door   by [lit. with]   must have opened
                          mistake

this news	easily [lit. with ease]	must have spread
he	with difficulty	must have escaped

[1]Make the verb of each sentence agree with its subject in number-gender.

7. <u>məyryb</u>   se, ap ka kya mətləb həy.
revenge
family
a bad environment
virtues
caution

8. <u>fəsl təbah hone</u>   se, həmē bəhwt nwqsan pəhw̄ca həy.
communication becoming closed
the dam breaking
the flood
these quarrels
his error

9. wnhõ ne <u>wn bimariõ</u>   pər qabu pa lia.
         enemies
         flood
         cholera
         opposing party
         tuberculosis

10. <u>gaõvalõ ki zyndəgi</u>   <u>bərbad</u>   ho jaegi. [1]
the pleasure of a simple life | finished
the fighters [lit. fighting-ones] | wounded
the villagers' fields | destroyed
his friends | opposed
the leader | angry

[1]Make /ho jaegi/ agree in number-gender with the subject of each sentence.

11. <u>ws ki yy šərarət</u>   bərdašt nəhĩ ki ja səkti.
the heat of this country
this strange climate
the filth of this city
this act of his
this hunger and thirst

12. ws ko   <u>mar Dalne</u>   ki bəjae,   <u>nykal dena</u>   cahie tha.
         beating   explaining
         fighting   thinking
         throwing [away]   cooking
         playing   studying
         selling   keeping

13. **əysi bwraiŏ**   ki əhəm vəja,   <u>talim ki kəmi</u>   həy.

     his virtues   his good environment

     his enmity   my wealth

     this action   his lack of intellect

     his anger   this mischief of mine

     his sorrow   his son's illness

14. jū jū   <u>talim</u>   bəRhti jaegi,[1]   mwlk ko fayda hota jaega.

       these evils   will keep on decreasing

       knowledge   will keep on spreading

       our crops   will keep on growing

       machines   will keep on increasing

       agriculture   will keep on expanding

[1]Make the verb of each sentence agree with its subject in number-gender.

15. <u>ys surət se</u>   <u>ws ki kwch mədəd</u>   <u>ho gəi həy.</u> [1]

     in fact   these vices   have increased

     in this connec-   the estimate   had become wrong
     tion

     instead of that   a new man   has come

     for example   the prices of flour and   have decreased
                       lentils

     certainly   a wonderful pleasure   is obtained

[1]Make the verb of each sentence agree with its subject in number-gender.

15.502. Transformation.

1. Change the underlined verb forms in the following sentences to the <S + /pəRna/> formation (e.g. /hŏsa/ to /hŏs pəRa/). Retain the same tense.

     a.   donŏ ləRkiã apəs mẽ <u>ləRĩ.</u>

     b.   ləRai ke dəwran, dwšmən ki fəwj həmare mwlk mẽ <u>a gəi.</u>

     c.   yy pəyyam swn kər, mwxalyf parTi həmare khetŏ ki tərəf <u>cəli.</u>

     d.   vw meri surət dekh kər <u>hŏse.</u>

     e.   yy əfsosnak qyssa swn kər, vw <u>roya.</u>

     f.   vw minar pər se <u>gyr gəya.</u>

     g.   vw swba sat bəje ghər se <u>nykla.</u>

     h.   šor ki vəja se, vw <u>jag gəya.</u>

     i.   beTe ke mərne ki yttyla pa kər, badšah ghoRe se <u>wtər gəya.</u>

     j.   kylas ke dəwran, vw əcanək <u>bola.</u>

2. Change the underlined verb forms in the following sentences to the <S + /Dalna/> formation (omitting, of course, any other intensive auxiliaries). Retain the same tense (e.g. /mar die/ to /mar Dale/).

     a.   mwxalyf parTi ne həmare sərdar ko <u>mar dia.</u>

     b.   zəmindar ne əpni səb bhŏysẽ <u>bec dĩ.</u>

     c.   ws ne ləRai mẽ laThi se tin admi zəxmi <u>kər die.</u>

d. bəcce ne yəqinən šiša toR dia hoga.

e. ws ne jə̃gəl ke əksər dərəxt kaT die.

f. syrf do ghənTe mẽ ws əwrət ne səb khana pəka lia.

g. ɣwsse mẽ a kər, ws ne dhobi ke səb kəpRe jəla die.

h. ws ne ek rat mẽ puri kytab pəRh li.

i. ws ne əpni sari rəqəm ɣəribõ ko de di.

j. əgər polis vəhã vəqt pər nə pəhw̃cti, to vw wse mar dete.

3. Change the underlined verb forms in the following sentences to the <OI + /vala/>
formation (e.g. /a rəha tha/ to /ane vala tha/). Retain the tense of the auxiliary.

a. gaRi əbhi əbhi a rəhi hogi.

b. vw log səyr ko ja rəhe hə̃y.

c. cor dərvaza toR rəha tha, ky mə̃y a gəya.

d. mə̃y so rəha tha, ky rəhim sahəb ne avaz di.

e. mə̃y synima ka TykəT xərid rəha tha, ky mere dost ne mwjhe məna kər dia.

f. Ti bi ke jərasim šəhr mẽ phəyl rəhe the, ky wn pər qabu pa lia gəya.

g. zəxmi pyas se mər rəha tha, ky mədəd pəhw̃c gəi.

h. ləRke mwsafyr ko pərešan kər rəhe the, ky masTər ne a kər pəkəR lia.

i. vw kəpRe bədəl rəha tha.

j. bhə̃ysẽ khet mẽ ghws rəhi thĩ, ky kysan ne rok dia.

4. Change the underlined verb forms in the following sentences to the <PreP + /jana/>
formation (e.g. /bəRhti hə̃y/ to /bəRhti jati hə̃y/). Retain the tense of the original,
including any continuative formations, but omit any intensive formations.

a. talim ki vəja se, yy bwraiã rəfta rəfta ghəT rəhi hə̃y.

b. ys dəvai ke ystemal se, ap ki təklif kəm ho jaegi.

c. pani nə mylne ki vəja se, fəslẽ sukh gəĩ.

d. həmari fəwj dwšmən ke mwlk ki tərəf bəRh rəhi thi.

e. vw həmara saman kəraci se bhyjvaẽge.

f. gəndəgi ki vəja se, bimari phəyl rəhi həy.

g. əgərce vəhã bəhwt šor tha, phyr bhi vw əpna kam kərta rəha.

h. əgər ap ys vəqt gəndwm nəhĩ xəridẽge, to aynda əwr bhi mə̃hgi ho jaegi.

i. sərdi ki vəja se, pəhaR pər rəhna mwškyl ho gəya.

j. ysi raste pər sidhe cəle jao!

5. (a) Change the underlined verb forms in the following sentences to the "passive"
formation (e.g. /kərta həy/ to /kia jata həy/); (b) omit the subject, and (c)
whenever an object occurs in the present active sentence, the verb of the passive
sentence must be made to agree with it in number-gender. E.g.

/mə̃y yy kytab kəl xərid lũga. / I will buy this book tomorrow. [This
becomes:]

/yy kytab kəl xərid li jaegi. / This book will be bought tomorrow.

a. ws ne mwjhe yy xəbər pəhw̃cai.

b. məriz ne sari dəvai pi li.

c. mə̃y ys ki ek mysal peš kər səkta hũ.

d. həm ap ka sara saman ap ke ghər pəhw̃ca dẽge.

e. hwkumət ne ws pwl pər amədorəft bənd kər di həy.

f. mwjrym ne ədalət mē jwrmana əda kər dia.

g. baz log sada zyndəgi bəhwt pəsənd kərte hēy.

h. vw həmeša ysi soc mē rəhta həy, ky əpne dwšmən se bədla le.

i. mēy yy səb rəqəm rəfta rəfta əda kər dūga.

j. həmari hwkumət talim phəylane ke lie qədəm wTha rəhi həy.

k. əbhi əbhi xəbər ai həy, ky gaõvalõ ne səylab pər qabu pa lia həy.

l. pychli ləRai mē, dwšmən ne ə̄grezõ ke bəhwt se šəhr təbah kər die.

m. nəmbərdar ne nəwkər ke hath yy pəyɣam bhyjvaya.

n. jo cizē həmare mwlk mē nəhĭ bəntĭ, həm wnhē bahər se mēgva lēge.

o. wnhõ ne əndaza ləgaya həy, ky ys ymarət pər dəs həzar rupəe ləgēge.

p. əmir logõ ne fəysla kia həy, ky vw ɣərib logõ ki mədəd kərēge.

q. həm kysi nə kysi surət se wnhē yy yttyla pəhw̄ca dēge.

r. pwl TuTne ki vəja se, polis ne amədorəft ka sylsyla bənd kər dia həy.

s. masTər ne ləRke ko səza di.

t. həm yəhā̃ ke mahəwl ko byhtər bənane ka koi nə koi təriqa nykalēge.

6. Change the underlined verb forms in the following sentences from intransitive to transitive-passive (e.g. from /wgti həy/ to /wgai jati həy/). Some verbs belong to that class having transitive and intransitive stems (i.e. the transformation will be from /khwlta həy/ to /khola jata həy/, for example); others require the causative to express a transitive passive (e.g. /pəkta həy/ to /pəkaya jata həy/). Retain the same tense and aspect.

a. Dybba khwl gəya.

b. kwtta ghər se nykəl gəya.

c. kəl səb ləkRiã kəT jaēgi.

d. ləRka dərəxt se wtər gəya.

e. məkan bəhwt jəldi bən jaega.

f. khyRki ka šiša TuT gəya.

g. nəmbərdar sahəb mər gəe.

h. dal pək gəi.

i. koThi jəl gəi.

j. kəpRe dhup mē sukh gəe.

15.503. Variation.

1. həm ne ys sylsyle mē səb kwch malum kər lia həy.

həm ne ys sylsyle mē səb kwch pəta cəla lia həy.

həm ne talim ke sylsyle mē bəhwt kwch malum kər lia həy.

həm ne ys sylsyle mē yttyla de di həy.

ap se ys sylsyle mē pucha jaega.

ap kys sylsyle mē pakystan gəe the.

2. həm ne mwxalyf parTi pər qabu pa lia.

ynšaəlla[h], həm həyze pər qabu pa lēge.

polis ne mwjrym ko əpne qabu mē le lia.

polis ne mwjrym ko qabu kər lia.

ws ne ghoRe ko qabu mē kər lia.

cor mwškyl se həmare qabu mē aya.

3. vw ys sylsyle mē koi qədəm nəhī̃ wThaega.

əmrika kəšmir ke jhəgRe mē koi qədəm nəhī̃ wTha səkta.

vw həyze ko rokne ke sylsyle mē koi qədəm nəhī̃ wTha səkte.

hwkumət yn bwraiõ ko rokne ke sylsyle mē qədəm wThane vali həy.

vw ədalət ke fəysle ke xylaf zərur qədəm wThaega.

ws ne yy qədəm əpne wsul ke xylaf wThaya həy.

4. dwnya ka səb se bəRa šəhr əmrika mē vaqe həy.

zəmindar sahəb ka məkan pəhaR ke nice vaqe həy.

kəšmir pakystan ke šymal mē vaqe həy.

ws badšah ka məhl jə̄gəl mē vaqe tha.

yy šəhr lahəwr ke jwnub mē vaqe həy.

kya, badšahi məsjyd lahəwr ke məšryq mē vaqe həy?

5. ləRai kərne mē, mwjhe ek əjəb lwtf ata həy.

əysi kəhaniõ mē, həmē lwtf ata həy.

əyse mahəwl mē, mwjhe ek əjəb lwtf ata həy.

bədla lene mē, ap ko kya lwtf ata həy.

əxbar pəRhne mē, mwjhe kwch lwtf nəhī̃ ata.

mə̄y ne zyndəgi mē bəhwt lwtf wThaya.

6. rat ke bara bəje, cor ghər mē ghws aya.

šam ko do bəkriã ghər ke əndər ghws aī̃.

ap ke ghoRe əksər mere khetõ mē ghws ate hə̄y.

do admi pystəwl le kər wn ke kəmre mē ghws ae.

vw meri mərzi ke xylaf dəftər mē ghws aya.

fəwj dwšmən ke qəle mē ghws gəi.

7. ys təra bwraiã nəhī̃ ghəTēgi, bəlke əwr bəRh jaēgi.

dwšmən ne mwqabla nəhī̃ kia, bəlke Dər kər bhag gəya.

nəmbərdar ws ki hərəkət pər naraz nəhī̃ hwa, bəlke bəhwt xwš hwa.

həmē ys šərarət pər syrf DāT hi nəhī̃ pəRi, bəlke mar bhi pəRi.

vw syrf pəRhta hi nəhī̃, bəlke kam bhi kərta həy.

vw kəmzor hi nəhī̃, bəlke bimar bhi hə̄y.

8. jū̃ jū̃ vw cixta gəya, ws ki avaz kəmzor hoti gəi.

jū̃ jū̃ səfai bəRhti jaegi, bimariã kəm hoti jaēgi.

jū̃ jū̃ vw ɣwsse mē ata gəya, ws pər log əwr bhi zyada hə̄ste gəe.

jū̃ jū̃ ənaj mə̄hga hota jaega, ɣəribõ ki zyndəgi mwškyl hoti jaegi.

jū̃ jū̃ məɣryb kəmzor hota jata həy, məšryq ki halət byhtər hoti jati həy.

jū̃ hi həmē yy xəbər myli, həm səb ro pəRe.

9. yəhã həmeša koi nə koi jhəgRa hota rəhta həy.

vw ləRka həmeša kysi nə kysi kam mē məsruf rəhta həy.

mwjhe kəhī̃ nə kəhī̃ ys ki mysal myl jaegi.

490

ap ko kəbhi nə kəbhi ys sylsyle mẽ socna pəRega.

kwch nə kwch zərur bəc gəya hoga.

ys se kwch nə kwch fayda zərur hwa həy.

10. mwjh se hər roz yəhã aya nəhĩ jata.

mwjh se ys vəqt khana pəkaya nəhĩ jata.

mwjh se ys se zyada khana khaya nəhĩ jata.

mwjh se əysi gəRi cəlai nəhĩ jati.

mwjh se ws ki yy halət dekhi nəhĩ jati.

11. ya to həmari rəqəm əda kəro, vərna ləRai ke lie təyyar ho jao!

ya to yəhĩ khana kha lo, vərna əgle ysTešən pər kha lena.

ya to koi surət nykalie, ya ys ka xyal choR dijie!

ya to meri kytab vapəs kəro, ya ys ke pəyse do!

ya to mere sath yskul cəlo, vərna ghər jao!

ya to yunyvərsyTi jao, vərna mere sath bazar cəlo!

12. yn jhəgRõ ki vəja se, xandan ke xandan təbah ho gəe hẽy.

səylab ki vəja se, fəslõ ki fəslẽ bərbad ho gəi hẽy.

pychli ləRai mẽ, šəhr ke šəhr jəla die gəe the.

yy yttyla pa kər, ghər ka ghər mwjh se naraz ho gəya.

ag ləgne se, gaõ ka gaõ jəl gəya tha.

yy xəbər swn kər, səb ke səb ɣwsse mẽ a gəe.

13. mwxalyf parTi ko marne ki bəjae, səmjha dena cahie tha.

fayde ki bəjae, ap ko nwqsan wThana pəRega.

pəRhne ki bəjae, ws ne əpna sara vəqt khelne mẽ bərbad kia.

əpne wsulõ pər cəlne ki bəjae, vw wn ke xylaf cəlne ləga.

pychli rəqəm əda kərne ki bəjae, ws ne kwch pəyse əwr mãg lie.

pəyyam pəhw̃cane ki bəjae, vw həmare dwšmənõ ke pas cəla gəya.

14. ws bəcce ka yy hal dekh kər, mwjhe bəhwt ɣwssa aya.

nəwkər se yy xəbər swn kər, zəmindar sahəb ws pər ɣwsse hwe.

dwšmən se bədla lene ki bəjae, ws ne əpna ɣwssa mwjh pər wtara.

mera pəyyam pa kər, vw naraz hone ləga.

ws ka nətija dekh kər, mere valyd sahəb bəhwt naraz hwe.

twmhari šərarət ka yy ənjam hoga, ky vw həmeša twm se naraz rəhega.

15. mera xyal həy, ky baryš hone vali həy.

mera xyal həy, ky vw lahəwr jane vala həy.

mera xyal həy, ky polis cor ko gyryftar kərne vali həy.

mere xyal mẽ, vw apəs mẽ ləRne vale the.

mere xyal mẽ, gəRi ane vali hogi.

mẽy səməjhta hũ, ky hwkumət ys sylsyle mẽ qədəm wThane vali həy.

15.504. Translation.

The following two sets of sentences illustrate the /X X/ versus the /X nə X/ construction (see Sec. 15.305). Translate the following sentences into English and discuss the

semantic ramifications of each with the instructor. Then, with the book closed, retranslate your translations into Urdu.

1. yy ciz kəhĩ kəhĩ mylti həy.
   kysi kysi ko ws jəga ka pəta həy.
   ys kytab ko koi koi pəRh səkta həy.
   mwjhe dyhli kwch kwch yad həy.
   vw həmare hã kəbhi kəbhi ata həy.

2. yy ciz kəhĩ nə kəhĩ zərur mylegi.
   kysi nə kysi ko ws jəga ka zərur pəta hoga.
   ys kytab ko koi nə koi zərur pəRh səkta hoga.
   ap ko dyhli kwch nə kwch to yad hogi.
   vw həmare hã kəbhi nə kəbhi zərur aega.

15.505. Response.

1. kya, ap zəmindar xandan se hõy?
2. kya, ap ke hã ləRai jhəgRe hote rəhte hõy?
3. wn ki vəja kya həy.
4. kya, ap ko ləRai jhəgRe mẽ lwtf ata həy?
5. kya, ap ne kəbhi əpne dwšmən se bədla lia həy?
6. kya, ap ne kəbhi ədalət mẽ jwrmana əda kia həy?
7. kya, ap bənduq cəlana jante hõy?
8. kya, ap bəccõ ki šərarət bərdašt kər səkte hõy?
9. gaõ ki zyndəgi mẽ kəwn kəwnsi bwraiã hõy.
10. gaõ ke sada mahəwl mẽ rəhne ki kya kya xubiã hõy.
11. kya, ap ke mwlk mẽ bhi səylab ate hõy?
12. ap ke mwlk ki abohəva kəysi həy.
13. ap ka ghər kys šəhr mẽ vaqe həy.
14. aj ke əxbar mẽ koi xas xəbər həy? vw kya həy.
15. kya, ap pakystan jane ke bare mẽ soc rəhe hõy?

15.506. Conversation Practice.

Mr. Smith is a guest at the home of the village /nəmbərdar/. They have just finished dinner.

N: kya, ap ke mwlk mẽ bhi əysa khana pəkaya jata həy?

S: həmare mwlk mẽ yy təmam cizẽ -- jəyse aTa, dal, gošt vəɣəyra -- myl jati hõy, lekyn ynhẽ mwxtəlyf təriqõ se pəkaya jata həy. mysal ke təwr pər, khane mẽ myrcẽ zyada nəhĩ Dali jatĩ. ap log həmare mwqable mẽ myrcẽ bəhwt zyada ystemal kərte hõy.

N: kya, ap ko gaõ ki zyndəgi əwr yəhã ka mahəwl pəsənd həy?

S: ji hã, bəhwt pəsənd həy. dərəsl mãy bhi ek zəmindar xandan mẽ pəyda hwa tha. mera gaõ əmrika ke jwnub mẽ vaqe həy. vəhã mere vəlyd sahəb ki kwch zəmin həy. ys lie mwjhe khet, fəslẽ, jõgəl, nəhr, əwr gaõ ki abohəva bəhwt pəsənd hõy.

492

N: kya, ap ko həmara gaõ pəsənd aya?

S: bəhwt pəsənd aya. əgərce bəhwt si cizē mere gaõ se mwxtəlyf hɛ̄y -- jəyse həm həl vəɣəyra ki bəjae, məšinõ se zəraət kərte hɛ̄y. ys ke ylava, həmare gaõ mē talim kafi am həy, jo ap ke hã bəhwt kəm həy.

N: yy bylkwl Thik həy. yəhã talim ki bəhwt kəmi həy. logõ ko bəhwt səmjhaya jata həy, ky əcchi fəsl wgane ke lie bhi talim bəhwt əhəm ciz həy. lekyn phyr bhi bəhwt se əyse log hɛ̄y, jo əpne bəccõ ko yskul nəhĩ bhejte.

S: ap ki hwkumət ne jəga jəga yskul ysi lie khole hɛ̄y, ky ap əpne bəccõ ko yskul mē daxyl kəraē, take vw talim hasyl kərē. ys təra ylm ke sath sath vw zəraət ke nəe nəe təriqe bhi sikh səkēge. šwru mē həmare mwlk mē bhi talim ki kəmi thi, lekyn əb rəfta rəfta phəyl gəi həy.

N: vaqəi, talim bəhwt zəruri ciz həy. həmari hwkumət ys sylsyle mē bəhwt košyš kər rəhi həy. aj se tin car sal pəhle, yskul mē ləRkõ ki tadad syrf səttavən ya əTThavən thi, lekyn ys vəqt DeRh səw ke qərib həy. wmmid həy, ky ynšaəlla[h] ysi təra talim bəRhti jaegi.

S: ys ke ylava, ek dusri ciz jo ap ke gaõ mē bəhwt pai jati həy, vw apəs ke ləRai jhəgRe hɛ̄y. əziz sahəb ne aj swba mwjhe ek jhəgRe ka qyssa bətaya, ky gaõ ki do parTiã mamuli si bat pər apəs mē ləR pəRĩ, jys mē kwch admi mare gəe, əwr bəhwt se admi zəxmi hwe. yy bəhwt əfsosnak bat həy. əyse ləRai jhəgRõ ko rokne ka kwch nə kwch bəndobəst kərna cahie.

N: ys qysm ki ləRaiõ ki ek əhəm vəja talim ki kəmi həy. yyhi vəja həy, ky yy log choTi si bat bhi bərdašt nəhĩ kər pate, əwr fəwrən ləRne ke lie təyyar ho jate hɛ̄y.

S: gaõ ke əmir zəmindarõ ko cahie, ky vw əyse məwqõ pər ɣwsse ki bəjae, bərdašt se kam lē, ɣərib logõ ki mədəd kərē, əwr gaõ ki halət byhtər bənane ki košyš kərē. mera mətləb yy həy, ky əgər logõ ko zyndəgi əcche əwr sada wsul bətae jaē, to pwrani dwšməniã xətm ho səkti hɛ̄y, əwr zyndəgi yəqinən byhtər bən səkti həy.

N: əb to halət pəhle se bəhwt byhtər ho gəi həy, vərna aj se kafi ərsa pəhle to yy bwraiã bəhwt pai jati thĩ. bylkwl mamuli si bat pər ləRai ho jati thi, jys mē bəhwt nwqsan hota tha. ek zəmindar əpne mwxalyf zəmindar se hər vəqt bədla lene ki fykr mē rəhta tha, ky kysi təra ləRai ki koi surət nykəl ae.

S: yy cizē syrf am zyndəgi pər hi bwra əsər nəhĩ Daltĩ, bəlke ys təra ghər ke ghər təbah ho jate hɛ̄y.

N: kya, ap ke hã bhi ys qysm ke ləRai jhəgRe hote rəhte hɛ̄y?

S: həmare mwlk mē bhi əyse ləRai jhəgRe hote rəhte hɛ̄y, lekyn ajkəl bəhwt kəm ho gəe hɛ̄y. mwjhe yad həy, ky ek dəfa mere gaõ mē ek bevwquf admi ne mamuli si bat pər ek šəxs ko mar Dala.

N: kya, ws šəxs se ys ki pwrani dwšməni thi?

S: ji nəhĩ. vaqea yy tha, ky ek zəmindar ke bəhwt se məkan the, jyn mē mwxtəlyf log kyrae pər rəhte the. ek šəxs, jo ws ke məkan mē rəhta tha, kysi vəja se kyrae ki rəqəm əda nəhĩ kər səka. ek dyn šam ke vəqt zəmindar ys šəxs ke ghər gəya, əwr tin həfte ka kyraya mãga. ys šəxs ne kəha, ky "əbhi mere pas pəyse nəhĩ hɛ̄y, lekyn jəb myl jaēge, fəwrən rəqəm əda kər di jaegi." zəmindar ne kəha, ky "mɛ̄y ys se zyada yntyzar nəhĩ kər səkta. ys lie twm mere məkan se nykəl jao!" yy swn kər, ys šəxs ko bəRa ɣwssa

493

aya, əwr jəvab dia, ky "mə̃y əbhi bə̀tata hū!"[1] yy kəh kər, əpne məkan mē̃ fəwrən ghws gəya, əwr əndər se ek bənduq wTha laya. bahər a kər, ws ne zəmindar pər bənduq cəla di. zəmindar wsi vəqt mər gəya. ys sari kəhani se ap xwd əndaza ləgaē, ky əgər ys šəxs mē̃ thoRi si əql hoti, to əysi hərəkət nə kərta.

N: yy to vaqəi bəhwt əfsosnak vaqea həy. həmare hā̃ əysa nəhī̃ hota. yəhā̃ ləRai jhəgRõ ki vəja to pwrani dwšməni həy, jys ka nətija yy nykəlta həy, ky choTi si yələti xandan ke xandan bərbad kər Dalti həy. dərəsl əyse log, qədəm wThane se pəhle, bylkwl nəhī̃ socte, əwr əql əwr səməjh se kam nəhī̃ lete.

S: yy ciz bylkwl səhih həy. əysi yələtiõ ka ənjam həmešᵃ bwra hi hoⱡa həy. yn bwraiõ ko dur kərne ke lie talim bəhwt zəruri həy.

N: mera xyal həy, ky əb bahər cəlē. aj məwsəm bəhwt əccha həy. thoRi der səyr kərte hə̃y.

S: bylkwl Thik həy. aie, cəlē.

[1]An idiomatic way of saying, "All right, now I'm going to fix you!" or "Now I'll teach you a good lesson!"

15.507. Conversation Stimulus.

Topics may include the following:

1. A comparison of life in a North American, English, etc. village with that of a village in Pakistan.
2. A quarrel.
3. A flood.
4. A fictional narrative.
5. The evils of quarreling.

abohəva F1 [np]	climate
amədorəft F1 [np]	communication, transportation
aTa M2	flour
əcanək A1 Adv	sudden, unexpected; suddenly, unexpectedly
əda PA1	paid, accomplished, fulfilled, performed
əfsosnak A1	sad, sorrowful
əhəm A1	important, urgent
əjəb A1	wonderful, marvellous, strange
əjib A1	strange, extraordinary
əlla[h] M1 [np]	God
əndaza M2	estimate, conjecture, guess
ənjam M1	end, conclusion, result, consequence
əql F1 [np]	intellect, wisdom, sense, mind, reason
əsər M1	effect, trace, impression, influence
əTThavən A1	fifty-eight
baz A1	some, a number of
bədla M2	revenge, exchange, retaliation
[ki] bəjae [or /[ke] bəjae/] Comp Post	instead of
bəlke Conj	but, but in addition to, but moreover, but on the other hand
bənd M1	dike, embankment
bənduq F1	gun
bərbad PA1	spoiled, ruined, laid waste, destroyed
bərdašt F1 [np]	endurance, toleration, bearing, putting up with
bəRhna [IIc: /ə/]	to extend, increase, grow, expand, thrive, proceed
bevwquf M/F1 A1	stupid
bwra A2	bad, evil
bwrai F2	evil, badness, bad quality, vice
chəppən A1	fifty-six
dal F1	lentils, pulses
dərəsl Adv	in the first place, in fact
dəwlət F1 [np]	wealth, riches
dwšmən M/F1 A1	enemy
dwšməni F2	enmity
dymaγ [or /dəmaγ/] M1	mind
ghəTna [IIc: /ə/]	to lessen, decrease, abate, become deficient
ghwsna [IIc: /w/]	to force one's way in, enter, creep in, sneak in
γələt A1	wrong, mistaken
γələti F2	error, mistake
γwssa M2	anger, rage

hal M1	state, condition
jə̃gəl M1	forest, jungle
jhəgRa M2	quarrel, squabble
jū jū Adv	just as, at the same time as
jwnub M1 [np]	south
jwrmana M2	fine (penalty)
kəhani F2	story, tale
laThi F2	staff, stick, cudgel, stave
ləRai F2	fight, war, battle
ləRna [IIc: /ə/]	to fight
lwtf M1 [np]	pleasure, enjoyment, delight, taste
mahəwl M1 [np]	environment, surroundings
mar F1 [np]	beating
marna [Ie: /ə/]	to beat, strike, hit, kill
məɤryb M1 [np]	west
mərna [I: /marna/: Ie]	to die
məšryq M1 [np]	east
mətləb M1	meaning, concern
mwxalyf M/F1 A1	opponent, opposing
mysal F1	example, illustration
naraz A1	angry, annoyed
nəmbərdar M1	village elder, a minor administrative (etc.) post (see Sec. 15.109)
nətija M2	result, effect, issue, outcome
nwqsan M1	loss, damage, harm, wastage, injury
parTi F2	party
pəɤɤam M1	message
pwl M1	bridge
pystəwl M1	pistol
qabu M1	control, custody, grasp, hold
qədəm M1	step, pace, footstep, foot
qyssa M2	story, tale, event, matter
rəfta rəfta Adv	gradually, by and by
rəqəm F1	figure, number, amount
sada A1 [or A2]	simple, plain
saTh A1	sixty
səməjh F1 [np]	understanding, comprehension, perception
səmjhana [C: /səməjhna/: IIIa]	to cause to understand, to explain, convince, reason with, expostulate, remonstrate with
sərdar M1	leader, chief
səttavən A1	fifty-seven
səylab M1	flood
soc M1 [np]	thought, reflection, idea, concern
socna [Ia]	to think, consider, meditate, imagine, **ponder**

surət F1	form, state, condition, case, face
sylsyla M2	connection, succession, chain, series, link
šwkr M1 [np]	thanks, gratitude
šymal [or /šwmal/] M1 [np]	north
təbah PA1	ruined, destroyed, spoiled
vaqe PA1	situated, located
wnsəTh A1	fifty-nine
wsul M1	principle, basis, rule
xandan M1	extended family, household, lineage, dynasty
xəbər F1	news
xubi F2	merit, goodness, good quality
yəqinən Adv	certainly, surely
ylm M1	knowledge, science, learning
ynšaəlla[h] Inter	if God wills
yttyla F1	information
zəmindar M1	landowner, landlord
zəxm M1	wound
zəxmi M/F1 A1	wounded
zynda A1	alive, living
zyndəgi F2	life